I0319268

John M. Evans

Baptist Hymn and Tune Book

for public worship

John M. Evans

Baptist Hymn and Tune Book
for public worship

ISBN/EAN: 9783337286309

Printed in Europe, USA, Canada, Australia, Japan

Cover: Foto ©Lupo / pixelio.de

More available books at **www.hansebooks.com**

THE BAPTIST HYMN AND TUNE BOOK,

FOR

PUBLIC WORSHIP

MUSIC ADAPTED AND ARRANGED

BY

JOHN M. EVANS.

PHILADELPHIA:
THE BIBLE AND PUBLICATION SOCIETY,
No. 1420 CHESTNUT STREET.
2 TREMONT TEMPLE, BOSTON; 76 EAST NINTH ST., NEW YORK; 408 WABASH AVENUE, CHICAGO, ILL.; 209 NORTH SIXTH STREET, ST. LOUIS, MO.

COMPLETE—UNABRIDGED.

THIS Edition of the Baptist Hymn and Tune Book is not an abridgment; it contains all the hymns, all the tunes, all the chants, all the useful indices, of the first and larger edition.

The hymns are all arranged consecutively, as in the various editions of the Baptist Hymn Book without music. The number in brackets at the right hand of each hymn gives the page of the larger *Hymn and Tune Book* on which it will be found. .

WESTCOTT & THOMSON
Stereotypers, Philada.

JAS. B. RODGERS CO.,
Printers, Philada.

TABLE OF CONTENTS.

	HYMN
WORSHIP.	
In General	1-39
Lord's Day	40-56
Sanctuary	57-85
Morning	86-92
Evening	93-99
GOD.	
Perfections	100-143
Creating	144-147
Governing	148-165
Redeeming	166-172
THE LORD JESUS CHRIST	173-184
Born	185-196
Living	197-215
Dying	216-241
Rising	242-257
Ascending	258-262
Interceding	263-270
Reigning	271-286
THE HOLY SPIRIT	287-305
THE TRINITY	306-314
MAN.	
Lost	315-322
Warned and Entreated	323-348
Convicted of Sin	349-363
Invited to Christ	364-389
Coming to Christ	390-409
Trusting in Christ	410-461
Loving Christ	462-487
Happy in Christ	488-521
Praising Christ	522-556
Consecrated to Christ	557-576
Communing with Christ	577-595
Aspiring after Conformity to Christ	596-636
Loving Others for Christ's Sake	637-654

MAN (*Continued*).

	HYMN
Finding Refuge in Christ from Sorrow	655–683
Acquiescing in Christ's Will	684–694
Working for Christ	695–702
Warring for Christ	703–720

THE HOLY SCRIPTURE 721–735

THE CHURCH.

Founded and Preserved	736–751
ORDINANCES.	
Baptism	752–778
Communion	779–799
OFFICERS.	
Ministers	800–809
Deacons	810, 811
WORK.	
Revivals	812–842
Sunday-Schools	843–859
Opening Houses of Worship	860–869
Missions	870–889

TIME AND ETERNITY.

Our Country	890–893
Fast	894–897
Thanksgiving	898–903
Old and New Year	904–911
Meeting and Parting	912–915
Mortality of Man	916–928
Death	929–939
Burial	940–951
Resurrection	952–957
Judgment	958–965
Heaven	966–988
Prayer for Christ's Coming	989–1000

DOXOLOGIES.

SELECTIONS FOR CHANTING.

Baptist Hymn and Tune Book.

WORSHIP.

OLD HUNDRED. L. M. W. Franc.

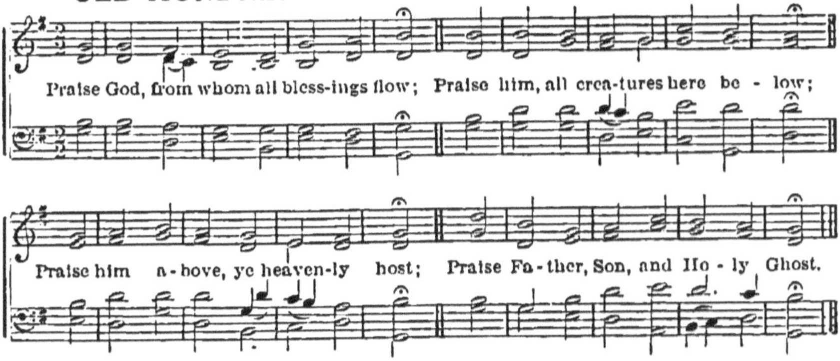
Praise God, from whom all bless-ings flow; Praise him, all crea-tures here be - low;
Praise him a-bove, ye heaven-ly host; Praise Fa-ther, Son, and Ho - ly Ghost.

BROWN. C. M. Wm. B. Bradbury.

2 *Let us draw near.* C. M. (12)

1 Come, let us lift our joyful eyes
Up to the courts above,
And smile to see our Father there,
Upon a throne of love.

2 Come, let us bow before his feet,
And venture near the Lord;
No fiery cherub guards his seat,
Nor double flaming sword.

3 The peaceful gates of heavenly bliss
Are opened by the Son;
High let us raise our notes of praise,
And reach th' almighty throne.

4 To thee ten thousand thanks we bring,
Great Advocate on high;
And glory to th' eternal King,
Who lays his anger by.

3 *Joyful Worship.* L. M. (9)

Tune—Old Hundred.

1 Ye nations round the earth rejoice
Before the Lord, your sovereign King;
Serve him with cheerful heart and voice,
With all your tongues his glory sing.

2 The Lord is God; 'tis he alone
Doth life and breath and being give:
We are his work, and not our own,
The sheep that on his pastures live.

3 Enter his gates with songs of joy;
With praises to his courts repair;
And make it your divine employ
To pay your thanks and honors there.

4 The Lord is good, the Lord is kind,
Great is his grace, his mercy sure;
And the whole race of man shall find
His truth from age to age endure.

MIGDOL. L. M. Dr. L. Mason.

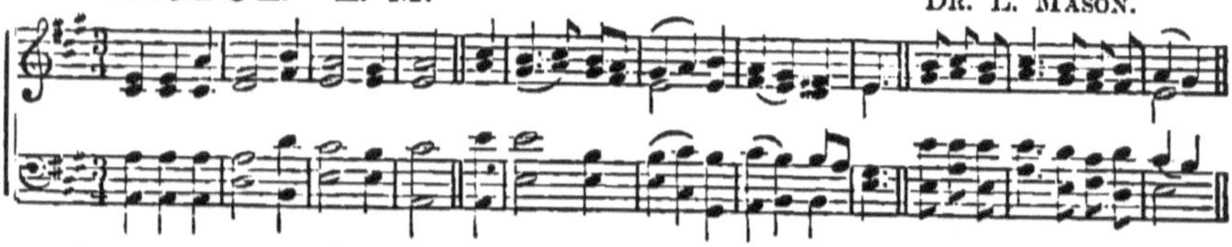

4 *The King of Glory.* L. M. (10)

1 Oh, hallow'd is the land and bless'd,
Where Christ the Ruler is confess'd!
Oh, happy hearts and happy homes,
To whom the great Redeemer comes!

2 Lift up your heads, ye mighty gates,
Behold the King of glory waits!
The King of kings is drawing near;
The Saviour of the world is here.

3 Fling wide the portals of your heart:
Make it a temple set apart
From earthly use for heaven's employ,
Adorned with prayer and love and joy.

4 Redeemer, come! I open wide
My soul to thee; here, Lord, abide!
Thankful and glad my song I raise,
And give to thee a life of praise.

5 L. M. (9)

Before Jehovah's awful Throne.

Tune—Old Hundred, No. I.

1 Before Jehovah's awful throne,
Ye nations, bow with sacred joy:
Know that the Lord is God alone;
He can create and he destroy.

2 His sovereign power, without our aid,
Made us of clay, and formed us men;
And when, like wand'ring sheep, we strayed
He brought us to his fold again.

3 We are his people, we his care,
Our souls, and all our mortal frame:
What lasting honors shall we rear,
Almighty Maker, to thy name?

4 We'll crowd thy gates with thankful songs,
High as the heavens our voices raise;
And earth, with her ten thousand tongues,
Shall fill thy courts with sounding praise.

5 Wide as the world is thy command,
Vast as eternity thy love:
Firm as a rock thy truth shall stand,
When rolling years shall cease to move.

LYONS. 10s & 11s. Haydn.

6 10s & 11s. (13)

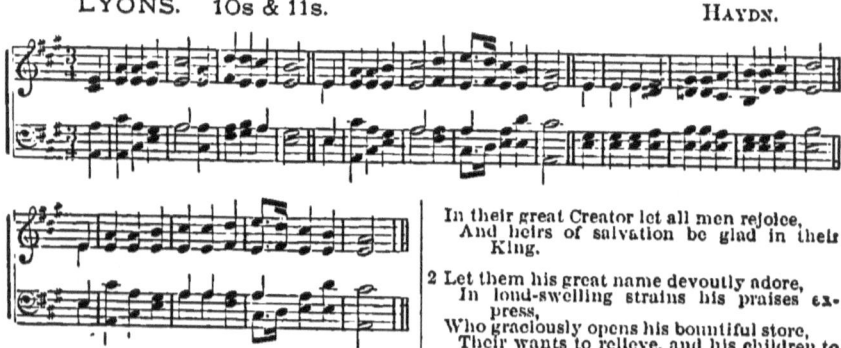

God praised in the Congregation.

1 Oh, praise ye the Lord! prepare your glad voice
His praise in the great assembly to sing;
In their great Creator let all men rejoice,
And heirs of salvation be glad in their King.

2 Let them his great name devoutly adore,
In loud-swelling strains his praises express,
Who graciously opens his bountiful store,
Their wants to relieve, and his children to bless.

3 With glory adorned, his people shall sing
To God, who defence and plenty supplies;
Their loud acclamations to him, their great King,
Through earth shall be sounded and reach to the skies.

BROWN. C. M. Wm. B. Bradbury.

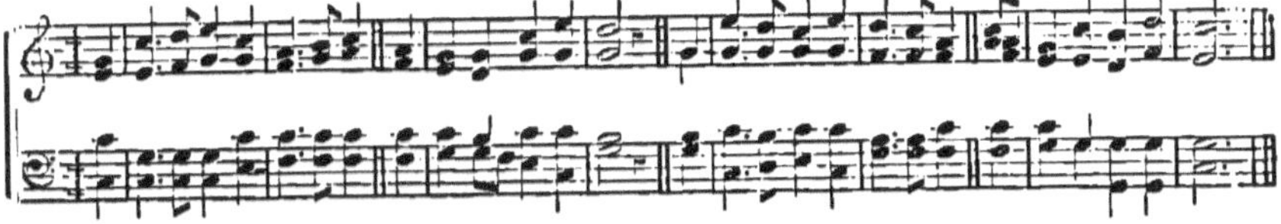

7 *Praise God, all ye his Servants.* C. M. (121

1 Praise God, ye gladdening smiles of morn;
Praise him, O silent night;
Tell forth his glory, all the earth;
Praise him, ye stars of light.

2 Praise him, ye stormy winds, that rise
Obedient to his word;
Mountains and hills and fruitful trees,
Join ye and praise the Lord.

3 Praise him, ye heavenly hosts, for ye
With purer lips can sing:
Glory and honor, praise and power,
To him, the eternal King.

4 Praise him, ye saints, who here rejoice
To do his heavenly will;
The incense of whose prayers ascends
Upon his altar still.

5 Praise him, all works of his that own
His Spirit's blest control.
O Lord my God, how great art thou!
Bless thou the Lord, my soul!

HENSON. 11s & 8s. Carmina Sacra.

8 *The Greatness of God.* 11s & 8s. (19)

1 The Lord is great! ye hosts of heaven adore him;
And ye, who tread this earthly ball,
In holy songs rejoice aloud before him,
And shout his praise, who made you all.

2 The Lord is great! his majesty, how glorious!
Resound his praise from shore to shore;
O'er sin and death and hell, now made victorious,
He rules and reigns for evermore.

3 The Lord is great! his mercy, how abounding!
Ye angels, strike your golden chords;
Oh, praise our God, with voice and harp resounding,
The King of kings, and Lord of lords!

SUTTON. 8s & 7s.

1st time.
D. C.
2d time.

9

Praise from all Creatures. 8s & 7s. (18)

1 PRAISE the Lord; ye heavens, adore him;
Praise him, angels, in the height;
Sun and moon, rejoice before him;
Praise him, all ye stars of light.

2 Praise the Lord, for he hath spoken;
Worlds his mighty voice obeyed;
Laws which never can be broken,
For their guidance he hath made.

3 Praise the Lord, for he is glorious;
Never shall his promise fail;
God hath made his saints victorious;
Sin and death shall not prevail.

4 Praise the God of our salvation;
Hosts on high, his power proclaim;
Heaven and earth, and all creation,
Praise and magnify his name.

LYONS. 10s & 11s. HAYDN.

10

10s & 11s. (13)

Salvation to God and the Lamb.

1 YE servants of God, your Master proclaim,
And publish abroad his wonderful name;
The name all-victorious of Jesus extol;
His kingdom is glorious, and rules over all.

2 God ruleth on high, almighty to save,
And still he is nigh, his presence we have;
The great congregation his triumph shall sing,
Ascribing salvation to Jesus our King.

3 Salvation to God, who sits on the throne,
Let all cry aloud, and honor the Son;
The praises of Jesus the angels proclaim,
Fall down on their faces, and worship the Lamb.

4 Then let us adore and give him his right,
All glory and power and wisdom and might;
All honor and blessing, with angels above,
And thanks never ceasing for infinite love.

11

Universal Praise. H. M. (20)

Tune—SUTHERLAND, next page.

1 Let every creature join
To bless Jehovah's name,
And every power unite
To swell th' exalted theme;
Let nature raise, | A general song
From every tongue | Of grateful praise.

2 But oh, from human tongues
Should nobler praises flow,
And every thankful heart
With warm devotion glow,
Your voices raise, | Above the rest
Ye highly blest; | Declare his praise.

3 Assist me, gracious God;
My heart, my voice, inspire,
Then shall I humbly join
The universal choir;
Thy grace can raise | And tune my song
My heart and tongue, | To lively praise.

SUTHERLAND. H. M.

W. B. BRADBURY.

12 L. M. (10)

The Creation invited to praise God.

Tune—MIGDOL, No. 4.

1 FROM all that dwell below the skies,
Let the Creator's praise arise;
Let the Redeemer's name be sung,
Through every land, by every tongue.

2 Eternal are thy mercies, Lord;
Eternal truth attends thy word:
Thy praise shall sound from shore to shore,
Till suns shall rise and set no more.

13 *God praised by all.* L. M. (10)

Tune—MIGDOL, No. 4.

1 PRAISE ye the Lord—let praise employ,
In his own courts your songs of joy;
The spacious firmament around
Shall echo back the joyful sound.

2 Recount his works in strains divine,
His wondrous works, how bright they shine!
Praise him for all his mighty deeds,
Whose greatness all your praise exceeds.

3 Let all whom life and breath inspire
Attend, and join the blissful choir;
But chiefly, ye who know his word,
Adore and love and praise the Lord!

SILVER STREET. S. M.

L. SMITH.

14 S M. (27)

Bless the Lord for ever and ever.

1 STAND up, and bless the Lord,
Ye people of his choice;
Stand up, and bless the Lord your God
With heart and soul and voice.

2 Though high above all praise,
Above all blessing high,
Who would not fear his holy name,
And laud, and magnify?

3 Oh, for the living flame
From his own altar brought,
To touch our lips, our souls inspire,
And wing to heaven our thought!

4 God is our strength and song,
And his salvation ours;
Then be his love in Christ proclaimed
With all our ransomed powers.

5 Stand up, and bless the Lord;
The Lord your God adore;
Stand up, and bless his glorious name,
Henceforth, for evermore!

SUTHERLAND. H. M.

W. B. BRADBURY.

15 *All should join in Praise.* H. M. (20)

1 YE tribes of Adam join,
With heaven and earth and seas,
And offer notes divine
To your Creator's praise.
Ye holy throng | In worlds of light
Of angels bright | Begin the song.

2 Thou sun, with dazzling rays,
And moon that rul'st the night,
Shine to your Maker's praise,
With stars of twinkling light:
His power declare, | And clouds that fly,
Ye floods on high, | In empty air

3 The shining worlds above
In glorious order stand;
Or in swift courses move,
By his supreme command;
He spake the word, | From nothing came,
And all their frame | To praise the Lord.

4 Let all the nations fear
The God that rules above;
He brings his people near,
And makes them taste his love:
While earth and sky | His saints shall raise
Attempt his praise, | His honors high.

MORETON. 11s & 8s.

16 11s & 8s. (26)

God praised in the Sanctuary.

1 BE joyful in God, all ye lands of the earth;
Oh, serve him with gladness and fear;
Exult in his presence with music and mirth;
With love and devotion draw near.

2 Jehovah is God, and Jehovah alone,
Creator and Ruler o'er all;
And we are his people; his sceptre we own·
His sheep, and we follow his call.

3 Oh, enter his gates with thanksgiving and song,
Your vows in his temple proclaim:
His praise in melodious accordance prolong,
And bless his adorable name.

4 For good is the Lord, inexpressibly good,
And we are the work of his hand;
His mercy and truth from eternity stood,
And shall to eternity stand.

RELIANCE. 11s.

FINE.
D.C.

17 (26)

The Lord's Prayer. 11s.

1 Our Father in heaven, we hallow thy name,
May thy kingdom holy on earth be the same;
Oh, give to us daily our portion of bread:
It is from thy bounty that all must be fed.

2 Forgive our transgressions, and teach us to know
That humble compassion which pardons each foe;
Keep us from temptation, from evil and sin,
And thine be the glory for ever! Amen!

HEBER. C. M. GEO. KINGSLEY.

18 *The Lord's Prayer.* C. M. (22)

1 Our Father, God, who art in heaven,
All hallowed be thy name;
Thy kingdom come; thy will be done
In heaven and earth the same.

2 Give us this day our daily bread;
And as we those forgive
Who sin against us, so may we
Forgiving grace receive.

3 Into temptation lead us not;
From evil set us free;
And thine the kingdom, thine the power,
And glory, ever be.

MIGDOL. L. M. DR. L. MASON.

19 *Universal Praise.* L. M. (10)

1 Loud hallelujahs to the Lord,
From distant worlds, where creatures dwell;
Let heaven begin the solemn word,
And sound it dreadful down to hell.

2 Wide as his vast dominion lies,
Make the Creator's name be known;
Loud as his thunder shout his praise,
And sound it lofty as his throne.

3 Jehovah!—'tis a glorious word;
Oh, may it dwell on every tongue;
But saints, who best have known the Lord,
Are bound to raise the noblest song.

4 Speak of the wonders of that love
Which Gabriel plays on every chord;
From all below, and all above,
Loud hallelujahs to the Lord.

20 L. M. (9)

Praise to the Great Jehovah.

Tune—OLD HUNDRED, No. 1.

1 Be thou, O God, exalted high;
And as thy glory fills the sky,
So let it be on earth displayed,
Till thou art here, as there, obeyed.

2 O God, my heart is fixed; 'tis bent
Its thankful tribute to present;
And, with my heart, my voice I'll raise
To thee, my God, in songs of praise.

3 Thy praises, Lord, I will resound
To all the listening nations round;
Thy mercy highest heaven transcends;
Thy truth beyond the clouds extends.

4 Be thou, O God, exalted high;
And as thy glory fills the sky,
So let it be on earth displayed,
Till thou art here, as there, obeyed.

LYONS. 10s & 11s. HAYDN.

21 10s & 11s. (13)

God Glorious.

1 OH, worship the King, all glorious above,
And gratefully sing his wonderful love,
Our Shield and Defender, the Ancient of days,
Pavilioned in splendor, and girded with praise.

2 Oh, tell of his might, and sing of his grace,
Whose robe is the light, whose canopy space;
His chariots of wrath the deep thunder-clouds form,
And dark is his path on the wings of the storm.

3 Thy bountiful care, what tongue can recite?
It breathes in the air, it shines in the light,
It streams from the hills, it descends to the plain,
And sweetly distils in the dew and the rain.

4 Frail children of dust, and feeble as frail,
In thee do we trust, nor find thee to fail;
Thy mercies how tender! how firm to the end!
Our Maker, Defender, Redeemer, and Friend.

5 Father Almighty, how faithful thy love!
While angels delight to hymn thee above,
The humbler creation, though feeble their lays,
With true adoration shall lisp to thy praise.

SILVER STREET. S. M. L. SMITH.

22 S. M. (27)

Exhortation to Praise.

1 COME, sound his praise abroad,
And hymns of glory sing;
Jehovah is the sovereign God,
The universal King.

2 Come, worship at his throne;
Come, bow before the Lord:
We are his work, and not our own;
He formed us by his word.

3 To-day attend his voice,
Nor dare provoke his rod,
Come, like the people of his choice,
And own your gracious God.

23 *Praise and Holy Fear.* L. M. (11)

Tune—MIGDOL, No. 25.

1 COME, let our voices join to raise
A sacred song of solemn praise:
God is a sovereign King: rehearse
His honor in exalted verse.

2 Come, let us turn, with holy fear,
To him who now invites us near;
Accept the offered grace to-day,
Nor lose the blessing by delay.

3 Come, seize the promise while it waits,
And march to Zion's heavenly gates;
Believe, and take the promised rest:
Obey, and be for ever blest.

SUTHERLAND. H. M. W. B. BRADBURY.

24 H. M. (20)

Earth's Response to Heaven.

1 SHALL hymns of grateful love
Through heaven's high arches ring,
And all the hosts above
Their songs of triumph sing?
And shall not we take up the strain,
And send the echo back again?

2 Shall they adore the Lord,
Who bought them with his blood,
And all the love record
That led them home to God?
And shall not we take up the strain,
And send the echo back again?

3 Oh, spread the joyful sound!
The Saviour's love proclaim;
And publish all around
Salvation through his name:
Till all the world take up the strain,
And send the echo back again.

MIGDOL. L. M. DR. L. MASON.

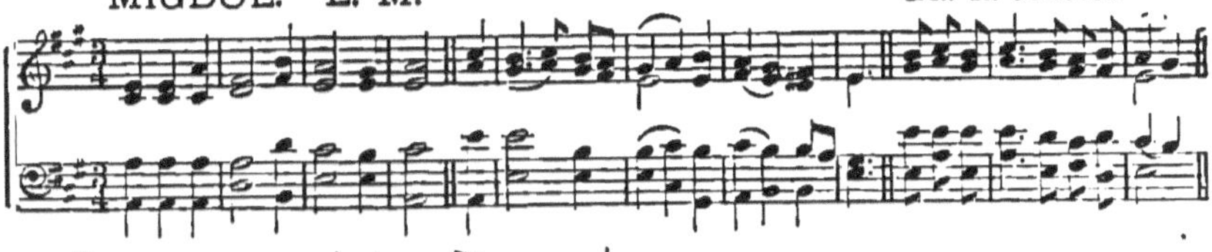

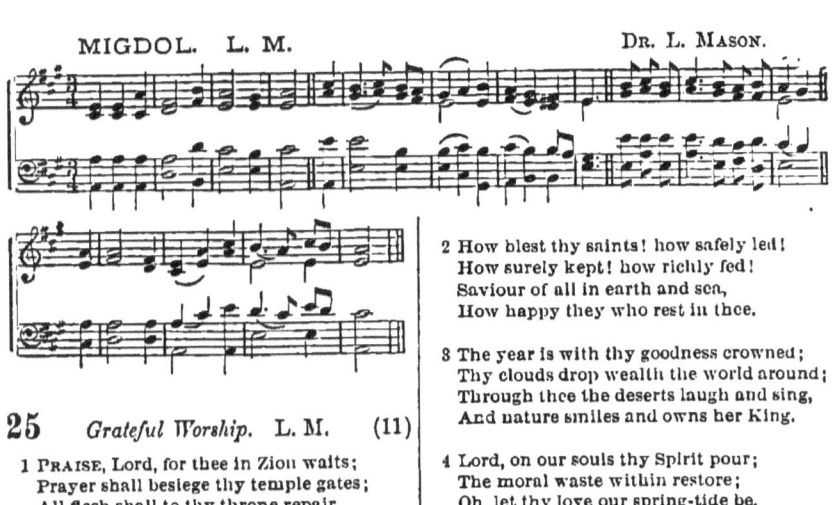

25 *Grateful Worship.* L. M. (11)

1 PRAISE, Lord, for thee in Zion waits;
Prayer shall besiege thy temple gates;
All flesh shall to thy throne repair,
And find through Christ salvation there.

2 How blest thy saints! how safely led!
How surely kept! how richly fed!
Saviour of all in earth and sea,
How happy they who rest in thee.

3 The year is with thy goodness crowned;
Thy clouds drop wealth the world around;
Through thee the deserts laugh and sing,
And nature smiles and owns her King.

4 Lord, on our souls thy Spirit pour;
The moral waste within restore;
Oh, let thy love our spring-tide be,
And make us all bear fruit to thee.

MILGROVE. 7s. MILGROVE.

26 *Praise the Lord.* 7s. (24)

1 PRAISE the Lord, his glories show,
Saints within his courts below,
Angels round his courts above,
All that see and share his love!

2 Earth to heaven, and heaven to earth,
Tell his wonders, sing his worth;
Age to age, and shore to shore,
Praise him, praise him, evermore!

3 Praise the Lord, his mercies trace;
Praise his providence and grace,—
All that he for man hath done,
All he sends us through his Son.

4 Strings and voices, hands and hearts,
In the service bear your parts;
All that breathe, your Lord adore;
Praise him, praise him, evermore!

27 *Songs of Praise.* 7s. (21)

1 SONGS of praise the angels sang,
Heaven with hallelujahs rang,
When Jehovah's work begun,
When he spake, and it was done.

2 Songs of praise awoke the morn,
When the Prince of peace was born;
Songs of praise arose, when he
Captive led captivity.

3 Saints below, with heart and voice,
Still in songs of praise rejoice;
Learning here, by faith and love,
Songs of praise to sing above.

4 Borne upon their latest breath,
Songs of praise shall conquer death;
Then, amid eternal joy,
Songs of praise their powers employ.

FERGUSON. S. M. GEO. KINGSLEY.

28 *Bless the Lord.* S. M. (15)

1 OH, bless the Lord, my soul!
His grace to thee proclaim;
And all that is within me join
To bless his holy name.

2 Oh, bless the Lord, my soul!
His mercies bear in mind:
Forget not all his benefits:
The Lord to thee is kind.

3 He will not always chide;
He will with patience wait;
His wrath is ever slow to rise,
And ready to abate.

4 He pardons all thy sins,
Prolongs thy feeble breath;
He healeth thy infirmities,
And ransoms thee from death.

5 He clothes thee with his love,
Upholds thee with his truth;
And, like the eagle, he renews
The vigor of thy youth.

6 Then bless his holy name,
Whose grace hath made thee whole;
Whose loving-kindness crowns thy days;
Oh, bless the Lord, my soul!

29 *Habitual Devotion.* C. M. (22)

Tune—HEBER, next page.

1 WHILE thee I seek, protecting Power,
Be my vain wishes stilled;
And may this consecrated hour
With better hopes be filled.

2 Thy love the power of thought bestowed;
To thee my thoughts would soar;
Thy mercy o'er my life has flowed;
That mercy I adore.

(CONTINUED.)

HEBER. C. M. GEO. KINGSLEY.

3 In each event of life, how clear
Thy ruling hand I see!
Each blessing to my soul more dear
Because conferred by thee.

4 In every joy that crowns my days,
In every pain I bear,
My heart shall find delight in praise,
Or seek relief in prayer.

5 When gladness wings my favored hour,
Thy love my thoughts shall fill;
Resigned, when storms of sorrow lower,
My soul shall meet thy will

6 My lifted eye, without a tear,
The gathering storm shall see;
My steadfast heart shall know no fear
That heart shall rest on thee.

LOUVAN. L. M. V. C. TAYLOR.

30 L. M. (17)

Prayer of the Heart and Lips.

1 O BLESSED God, to thee I raise
My voice in thankful hymns of praise;
And when my voice shall silent be,
My silence shall be praise to thee.

2 For voice and silence both impart
The filial homage of my heart;
And both alike are understood
By thee, thou Parent of all good,

3 Whose grace is all unsearchable,
Whose care for me no tongue can tell,
Who loves my loudest praise to hear,
And loves to bless my voiceless prayer.

31 *Godly Resolutions.* S. M. (15)

Tune—FERGUSON, No. 28.

1 LET sinners take their course,
And choose the road to death;
But in the worship of my God
I'll spend my daily breath.

2 My thoughts address his throne,
When morning brings the light;
I seek his blessing every noon,
And pay my vows at night.

3 Thou wilt regard my cries,
O my eternal God,
While sinners perish in surprise,
Beneath thy holy rod.

4 But I, with all my cares,
Will lean upon the Lord;
I'll cast my burdens on his arm,
And rest upon his word.

5 His arm shall well sustain
The children of his love;
The ground on which their safety stands
No earthly power can move.

EL PARAN. L. M.

CARMINA SACRA.

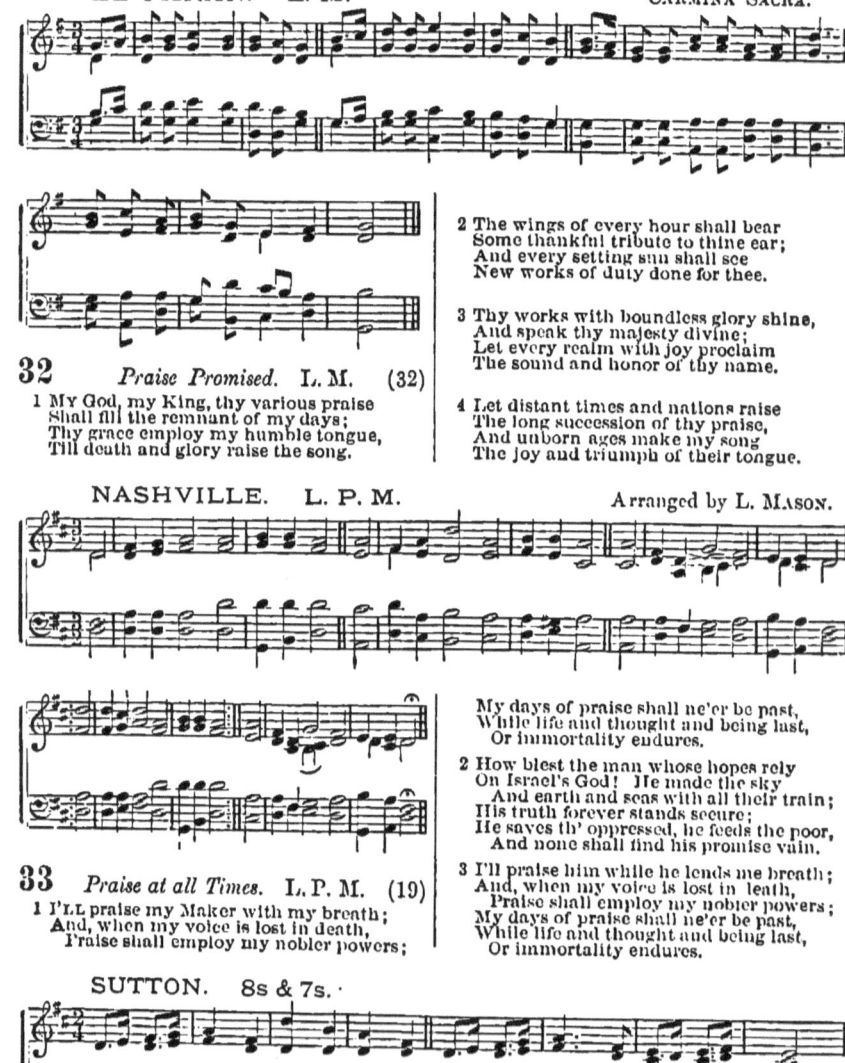

32 *Praise Promised.* L. M. (32)

1 My God, my King, thy various praise
Shall fill the remnant of my days;
Thy grace employ my humble tongue,
Till death and glory raise the song.

2 The wings of every hour shall bear
Some thankful tribute to thine ear;
And every setting sun shall see
New works of duty done for thee.

3 Thy works with boundless glory shine,
And speak thy majesty divine;
Let every realm with joy proclaim
The sound and honor of thy name.

4 Let distant times and nations raise
The long succession of thy praise,
And unborn ages make my song
The joy and triumph of their tongue.

NASHVILLE. L. P. M.

Arranged by L. MASON.

33 *Praise at all Times.* L. P. M. (19)

1 I'LL praise my Maker with my breath;
And, when my voice is lost in death,
Praise shall employ my nobler powers;
My days of praise shall ne'er be past,
While life and thought and being last,
Or immortality endures.

2 How blest the man whose hopes rely
On Israel's God! He made the sky
And earth and seas with all their train;
His truth forever stands secure;
He saves th' oppressed, he feeds the poor,
And none shall find his promise vain.

3 I'll praise him while he lends me breath;
And, when my voice is lost in leath,
Praise shall employ my nobler powers;
My days of praise shall ne'er be past,
While life and thought and being last,
Or immortality endures.

SUTTON. 8s & 7s.

(CONTINUED.)

34 *God of our Salvation.* 8s & 7s. (18)

1 PRAISE to thee, thou great Creator;
Praise be thine from every tongue;
Join, my soul, with every creature,
Join the universal song.

2 Father, source of all compassion,
Free, unbounded grace is thine;
Hail the God of our salvation;
Praise him for his love divine.

3 For ten thousand blessings given,
For the hope of future joy,
Sound his praise through earth and heaven,
Sound Jehovah's praise on high.

4 Joyfully on earth adore him,
Till in heaven our song we raise;
There, enraptured, fall before him,
Lost in wonder, love, and praise.

WARWICK. C. M. STANLEY.

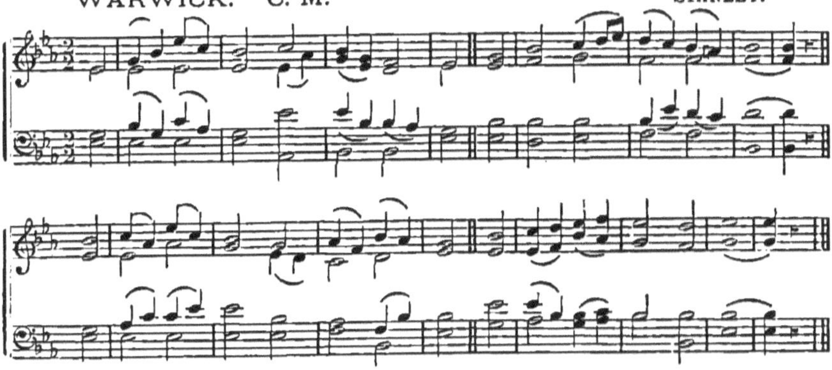

35 C. M. (34)

Praise and Holy Fear.

1 SING to the Lord Jehovah's name,
And in his strength rejoice;
When his salvation is our theme,
Exalted be our voice.

2 With thanks, approach his awful sight,
And psalms of honor sing;
The Lord's a God of boundless might,
The whole creation's King.

3 Come, and with humble souls adore;
Come, kneel before his face;
Oh, may the creatures of his power
Be children of his grace.

4 Now is the time, he bends his ear,
And waits for your request:
Come, lest he rouse his wrath, and swear
"Ye shall not see my rest."

36 L. M. (28)

God's Glory Praised.

Tune—ANVERN, No. 37.

1 COME, O my soul, in sacred lays
Attempt thy great Creator's praise:
But oh, what tongue can speak his fame?
What verse can reach the lofty theme?

2 Enthroned amid the radiant spheres,
He glory like a garment wears;
To form a robe of light divine,
Ten thousand suns around him shine.

3 In all our Maker's grand designs,
Almighty power, with wisdom, shines;
His works, through all this wondrous frame
Declare the glory of his name.

4 Raised on devotion's lofty wing,
Do thou, my soul, his glories sing;
And let his praise employ thy tongue
Till listening worlds shall join the song.

ANVERN. L. M.

DR. L. MASON.

Ritard.

37 L. M. (28)

Praise to God for his Blessings.

1 PRAISE ye the Lord: my heart shall join
In work so pleasant, so divine;
My days of praise shall ne'er be past,
While life and thought and being last.

2 Happy the man whose hopes rely
On Israel's God: he made the sky
And earth and seas with all their train:
And none shall find his promise vain.

3 His truth for ever stands secure;
He saves the oppressed, he feeds the poor,
He helps the stranger in distress,
The widow, and the fatherless.

4 He loves the saints; he knows them well;
But turns the wicked down to hell;
Thy God, O Zion, ever reigns;
Praise him in everlasting strains.

MILGROVE. 7s.

MILGROVE.

38 *God's Holiness praised.* 7s. (24)

1 HOLY, holy, holy Lord,
Be thy glorious name adored!
Lord, thy mercies never fail;
Hail, celestial Goodness, hail!

2 Though unworthy, Lord, thine ear,
Deign our humble songs to hear;
Purer praise we hope to bring,
When around thy throne we sing.

3 While on earth ordained to stay,
Guide our footsteps in thy way,
Till we come to dwell with thee,
Till we all thy glory see.

4 Then with angel-harps again
We will wake a nobler strain;
There, in joyful songs of praise,
Our triumphant voices raise.

LOUVAN. L. M.

V. C. TAYLOR.

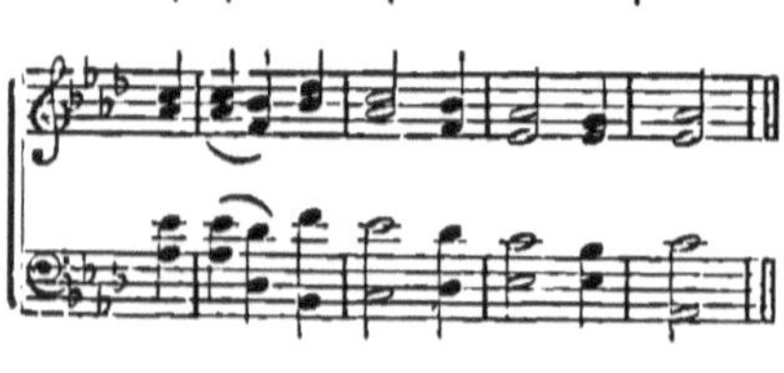

39 *Happiness in Worship.* L. M. (17)

1 FAR from my thoughts, vain world, begone;
Let my religious hours alone;
Fain would my eyes my Saviour see;
I wait a visit, Lord, from thee.

2 Oh, warm my heart with holy fire,
And kindle there a pure desire;
Come, sacred Spirit, from above,
And fill my soul with heavenly love.

(CONTINUED.)

3 Blest Saviour, what delicious fare!
How sweet thy entertainments are!
Ne'er did the angels taste above
Redeeming grace and dying love.

4 Hail, great Immanuel, all divine!
In thee thy Father's glories shine;
Thy glorious name shall be adored,
And every tongue confess thee Lord.

LORD'S DAY.

GOULD. C. M. — J. E. GOULD.

Ritard

40 — C. M. — (23)

The Lord's Day Morning.

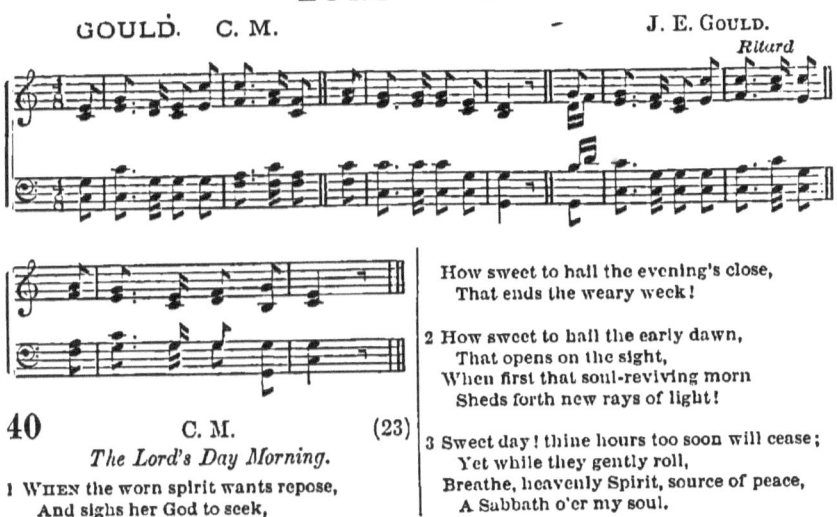

1 WHEN the worn spirit wants repose,
And sighs her God to seek,
How sweet to hail the evening's close,
That ends the weary week!

2 How sweet to hail the early dawn,
That opens on the sight,
When first that soul-reviving morn
Sheds forth new rays of light!

3 Sweet day! thine hours too soon will cease;
Yet while they gently roll,
Breathe, heavenly Spirit, source of peace,
A Sabbath o'er my soul.

ARLINGTON. C. M. — DR. ARNE.

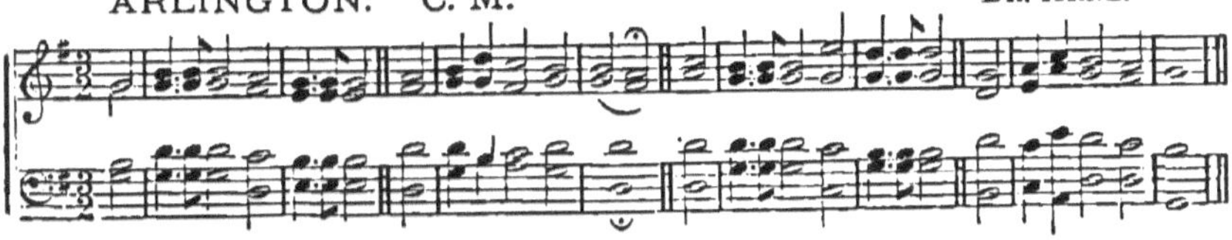

41 — *Praise for the Lord's Day.* C. M. — (31)

1 AGAIN the Lord of life and light
Awakes the kindling ray,
Unseals the eyelids of the morn,
And pours refulgent day.

2 Oh, what a night was that which wrapt
A guilty world in gloom!
Oh, what a Sun, which broke this day,
Triumphant from the tomb!

3 This day be grateful homage paid,
And loud hosannas sung;
Let gladness dwell in every heart,
And praise on every tongue.

4 Ten thousand thousand lips shall join
To hail this happy morn,
Which scatters blessings from its wings
On nations yet unborn.

WARE. L. M. GEO. KINGSLEY.

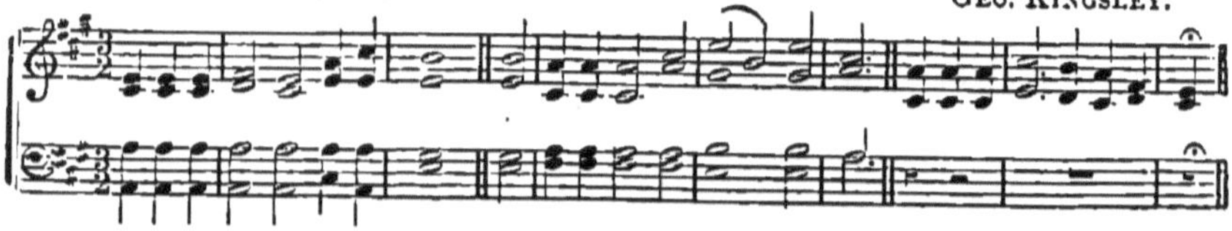

And draw from heaven that sweet repose
Which none but he that feels it knows.

3 A heavenly calm pervades the breast,
The earnest of that glorious rest
Which for the church of God remains,
The end of cares, the end of pains.

4 With joy, great God, thy works we view,
In various scenes, both old and new;
With praise, we think on mercies past;
With hope, we future pleasures taste.

5 In holy duties let the day,
In holy pleasures, pass away;
How sweet, a Sabbath thus to spend,
In hope of one that ne'er shall end!

42 *The Day of Rest.* L. M. (16)

1 ANOTHER six days' work is done,
Another Sabbath is begun;
Return, my soul, enjoy thy rest,
Improve the day that God hath blest.

2 Oh, that our thoughts and thanks may rise,
As grateful incense, to the skies,

LENTWOOD. 10s.

43 *How to spend the Day.* 10s. (36)

1 AGAIN returns the day of holy rest,
Which, when he made the world, Jehovah blest;
When, like his own, he bade our labors cease,
And all be piety, and all be peace.

2 Let us devote this consecrated day
To learn his will, and all we learn obey;
So shall he hear, when fervently we raise
Our supplications and our songs of praise.

3 Father of heaven, in whom our hopes confide,
Whose power defends us, and whose precepts guide,
In life our Guardian, and in death our Friend,
Glory supreme be thine, till life shall end.

44 L. M. (29)

Rejoicing in the Lord's Day.

Tune—DARLEY, next page.

1 MY opening eyes with rapture see
The dawn of thy returning day;
My thoughts, O God, ascend to thee,
While thus my early vows I pay.

2 I yield my heart to thee alone,
Nor would receive another guest.
Eternal King, erect thy throne,
And reign sole monarch in my breast.

3 Oh, bid this trifling world retire,
And drive each carnal thought away;
Nor let me feel one vain desire,
One sinful thought, through all the day.

4 Then, to thy courts when I repair,
My soul shall rise on joyful wing,
The wonders of thy love declare,
And join the strains which angels sing.

DARLEY. L. M. W. W. H. DARLEY.

LISCHER. H. M. DR. L. MASON.

45 *Praise for the sacred Day.* H. M. (21)

1 AWAKE, ye saints, awake,
And hail the sacred day;
In loftiest songs of praise
Your joyful homage pay;
Come bless the day that God hath blest,
The type of heaven's eternal rest.

2 On this auspicious morn
The Lord of life arose,
And burst the bars of death,
And vanquished all our foes;
And now he pleads our cause above,
And reaps the fruit of all his love.

3 All hail, triumphant Lord!
Heaven with hosannas rings;
And earth, in humbler strains,
Thy praise responsive sings:
Worthy the Lamb that once was slain,
Through endless years to live and reign.

THATCHER. S. M. HANDEL.

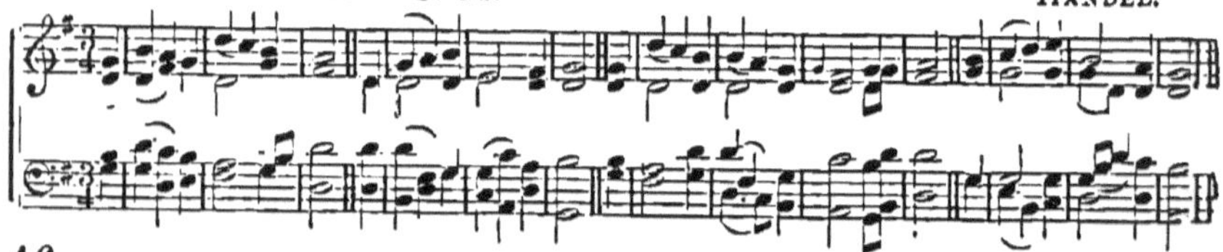

46 *Welcome, sweet Day of Rest.* S. M. (14)

1 WELCOME, sweet day of rest,
That saw the Lord arise;
Welcome to this reviving breast,
And these rejoicing eyes!

2 The King himself comes near,
And feasts his saints to-day;
Here we may sit and see him here,
And love and praise and pray.

3 One day amidst the place
Where my dear God hath seen,
Is sweeter than ten thousand days
Of pleasurable sin.

4 My willing soul would stay
In such a frame as this,
And sit, and sing herself away
To everlasting bliss.

LISCHER. H. M. DR. L. MASON.

47 *Hail to the Day of Rest.* H. M. (21)

1 WELCOME, delightful morn;
Sweet day of sacred rest,
I hail thy kind return;
Lord, make these moments blest:
From low desires | I soar to reach
And fleeting toys, | Immortal joys.

2 Now may the King descend,
And fill his throne of grace;
Thy sceptre, Lord, extend,
While saints address thy face;
Let sinners feel | And learn to know
Thy quickening word, | And fear the Lord.

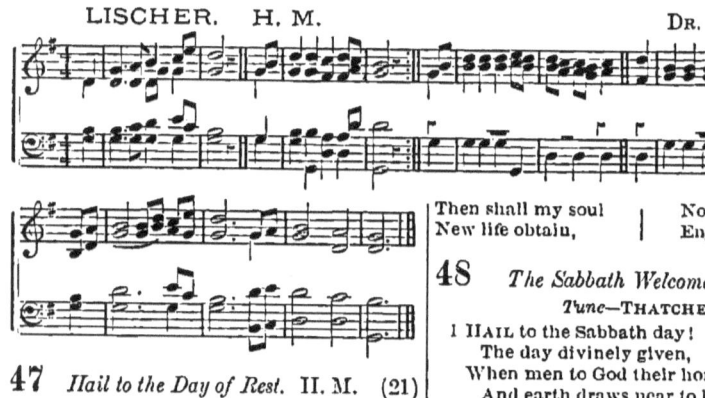

3 Descend, celestial Dove,
With all thy quickening powers,
Disclose a Saviour's love,
And bless the sacred hours:
Then shall my soul | Nor Sabbaths be
New life obtain, | Enjoyed in vain.

48 *The Sabbath Welcome.* S. M. (14)

Tune—THATCHER.

1 HAIL to the Sabbath day!
The day divinely given,
When men to God their homage pay,
And earth draws near to heaven.

2 Lord, in this sacred hour,
Within thy courts we bend,
And bless thy love, and own thy power,
Our Father and our Friend.

3 But thou art not alone
In courts by mortals trod;
Nor only is the day thine own
When man draws near to God.

4 Thy temple is the arch
Of yon unmeasured sky;
Thy Sabbath, the stupendous march
Of grand eternity.

5 Lord, may that holier day
Dawn on thy servant's sight,
And purer worship may we pay
In heaven's unclouded light.

LENTWOOD. 10s.

49 *Joy on the Lord's Day.* 10s. (36)

1 Hail, happy day! thou day of holy rest!
What heavenly peace and transport fill the breast,
When Christ, the God of grace, in love descends,
And kindly holds communion with his friends!

2 Let earth and all its vanities be gone,
Move from my sight, and leave my soul alone;
Its flattering, fading glories I despise,
And to immortal beauties turn my eyes.

3 Fain would I mount and penetrate the skies,
And on my Saviour's glories fix my eyes;
Oh, meet my rising soul, thou God of love,
And waft it to the blissful realms above!

WARE. L. M. Geo. Kingsley.

50 *Offerings of the Heart.* L. M. (16)

1 When, as returns this solemn day,
Man comes to meet his Maker, God,
What rites, what honors shall he pay?
How spread his sovereign name abroad?

2 From marble domes and gilded spires
Shall curling clouds of incense rise,
And gems and gold and garlands deck
The costly pomp of sacrifice?

3 Vain, sinful man! creation's Lord
Thy golden offerings well may spare;
But give thy heart, and thou shalt find
Here dwells a God who heareth prayer.

4 Oh, grant us, in this solemn hour,
From earth and sin's allurements free,
To feel thy love, to own thy power,
And raise each raptured thought to thee.

ARLINGTON. C. M. Dr. Arne.

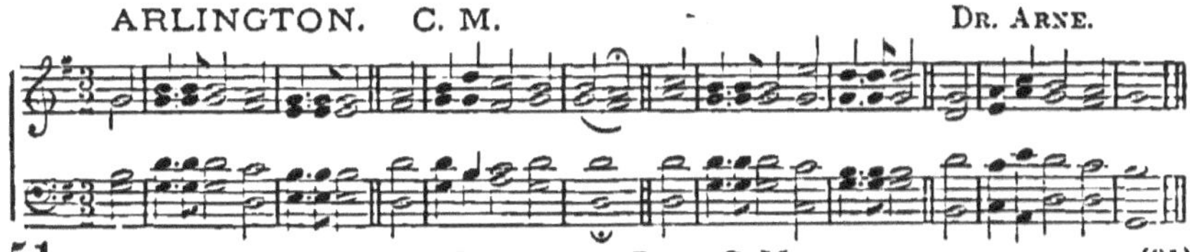

51 *The Resurrection Day.* C. M. (31)

1 This is the day the Lord hath made;
He calls the hours his own:
Let heaven rejoice, let earth be glad,
And praise surround the throne.

(continued.)

2 To-day he rose, and left the dead,
And Satan's empire fell;
To-day the saints his triumph spread,
And all his wonders tell.

3 Hosanna to th' anointed King,
To David's holy Son:
Help us, O Lord! descend, and bring
Salvation from thy throne.

4 Blest be the Lord, who comes to men
With messages of grace;
Who comes, in God his Father's name,
To save our sinful race.

5 Hosanna in the highest strains
The church on earth can raise;
The highest heavens, in which he reigns,
Shall give him nobler praise.

WEBB. 7s & 6s. GEO. J. WEBB.

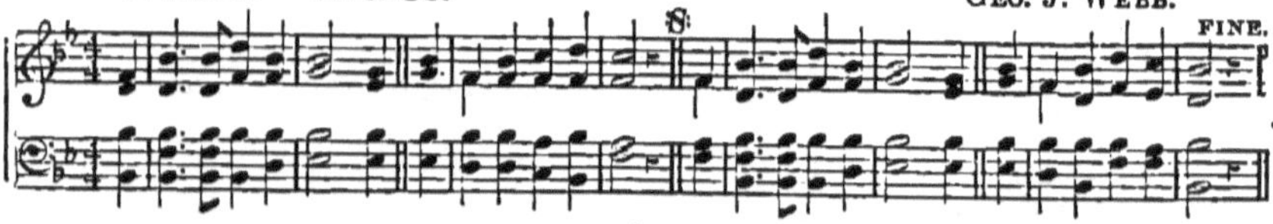
FINE.

D.S.

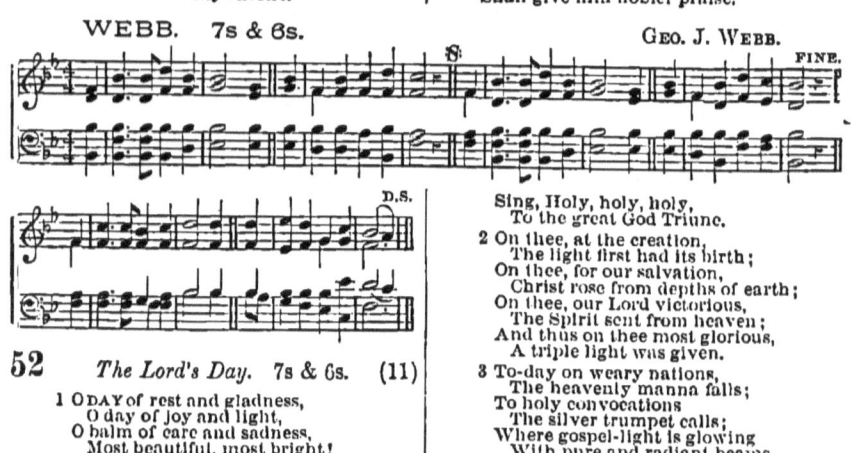

52 *The Lord's Day.* 7s & 6s. (11)

1 O DAY of rest and gladness,
O day of joy and light,
O balm of care and sadness,
Most beautiful, most bright!
On thee, the high and lowly,
Through ages joined in tune,
Sing, Holy, holy, holy,
To the great God Triune.

2 On thee, at the creation,
The light first had its birth;
On thee, for our salvation,
Christ rose from depths of earth;
On thee, our Lord victorious,
The Spirit sent from heaven;
And thus on thee most glorious,
A triple light was given.

3 To-day on weary nations,
The heavenly manna falls;
To holy convocations
The silver trumpet calls;
Where gospel-light is glowing
With pure and radiant beams,
And living water flowing
With soul-refreshing streams.

GOULD. C. M. J. E. GOULD.

Ritard.

53 C. M. (23)

Love of Lord's Day Services.

1 How sweet, upon this sacred day,
The best of all the seven,
To cast our earthly thoughts away,
And think of God and heaven!

2 How sweet to be allowed to pray
Our sins may be forgiven!
With filial confidence to say,
"Father, who art in heaven"!

3 How sweet the words of peace to hear
From him to whom 'tis given
To wake the penitential tear,
And lead the way to heaven!

4 And if, to make our sins depart,
In vain the will has striven,
He who regards the inmost heart
Will send his grace from heaven.

5 Then hail, thou sacred, blessed day,
The best of all the seven,
When hearts unite their vows to pay
Of gratitude to heaven!

HOLLEY. 7s. GEO. HEWS.

54 *Sabbath Evening.* 7s. (39)

1 SOFTLY fades the twilight ray
Of the holy Sabbath day;
Gently as life's setting sun,
When the Christian course is run.

2 Night her solemn mantle spreads
O'er the earth as daylight fades;
All things tell of calm repose,
At the holy Sabbath's close.

3 Peace is on the world abroad;
'Tis the holy peace of God,—
Symbol of the peace within
When the spirit rests from sin.

4 Still the Spirit lingers near,
Where the evening worshipper
Seeks communion with the skies,
Pressing onward to the prize.

5 Saviour! may our Sabbaths be
Days of joy and peace in thee,
Till in heaven our souls repose,
Where the Sabbath ne'er shall close.

55 *The World banished.* C. M. (23)

Tune—GOULD, No. 53.

1 O FATHER, though the anxious fear
May cloud to-morrow's way,
Nor fear nor doubt shall enter here,
All shall be thine to-day.

2 We will not bring divided hearts
To worship at thy shrine;
But each unholy thought departs,
And leaves the temple thine.

3 Sleep, sleep to-day, tormenting cares,
Of earth and folly born;
Ye shall not dim the light that streams
From this celestial morn.

4 To-morrow will be time enough
To feel your harsh control;
Ye shall not desecrate, this day,
The Sabbath of the soul.

DARLEY. L. M. W. W. H. DARLEY.

56 L. M. (29)

Aspirations for the eternal Rest.

1 THINE earthly Sabbaths, Lord, we love;
But there's a nobler rest above;
To that our longing souls aspire,
With cheerful hope and strong desire.

2 No more fatigue, no more distress,
Nor sin, nor death, shall reach the place;
No groans shall mingle with the songs
Which dwell upon immortal tongues.

3 No rude alarms of angry foes;
No cares, to break the long repose;
No midnight shade, no clouded sun,
But sacred, high, eternal noon.

4 O long expected day, begin;
Dawn on these realms of pain and sin;
With joy we'll tread th' appointed road,
And sleep in death, to rest with God.

SABBATH. 7s.

Dr. L. Mason.

SANCTUARY.

57 *Lord's Day Worship.* 7s. (30)

1 Safely through another week,
God has brought us on our way;
Let us now a blessing seek,
Waiting in his courts to-day;
Day of all the week the best,
Emblem of eternal rest.

2 While we seek supplies of grace,
Through the dear Redeemer's name,
Show thy reconciling face,—
Take away our sin and shame;
From our worldly cares set free,
May we rest this day in thee.

3 Here we come thy name to praise;
Let us feel thy presence near;
May thy glory meet our eyes,
While we in thy house appear
Here afford us, Lord, a taste
Of our everlasting rest.

WARWICK. C. M.

Stanley.

58 *Anticipating Worship.* C. M. (34)

1 Lord, in the morning thou shalt hear
My voice ascending high;
To thee will I direct my prayer,
To thee lift up mine eye;

2 Up to the hills where Christ is gone,
To plead for all his saints,
Presenting at his Father's throne
Our songs and our complaints.

3 Thou art a God before whose sight
The wicked shall not stand,
Sinners shall ne'er be thy delight,
Nor dwell at thy right hand.

4 But to thy house will I resort,
To taste thy mercies there;
I will frequent thine holy court,
And worship in thy fear.

5 Oh, may thy Spirit guide my feet
In ways of righteousness,
Make every path of duty straight
And plain before my face.

DARLEY. L. M. W. W. H. DARLEY.

59

Joy in Worship. L. M. (29)

1 SWEET is the work, my God, my King,
To praise thy name, give thanks, and sing;
To show thy love by morning light,
And talk of all thy truth at night.

2 Sweet is the day of sacred rest;
No mortal cares shall seize my breast;
Oh, may my heart in tune be found,
Like David's harp of solemn sound!

3 My heart shall triumph in my Lord,
And bless his works and bless his word;
Thy works of grace, how bright they shine!
How deep thy counsels, how divine!

4 Fools never raise their thoughts so high;
Like brutes they live, like brutes they die;
Like grass they flourish, till thy breath
Blast them in everlasting death.

5 But I shall share a glorious part,
When grace hath well refined my heart
And fresh supplies of joy are shed,
Like holy oil, to cheer my head.

6 Then shall I see and hear and know
All I desired or wished below;
And every power find sweet employ
In that eternal world of joy.

HEBER. C. M. GEO. KINGSLEY.

60

C. M. (22)

Longing for the House of God.

1 EARLY, my God, without delay,
I haste to seek thy face;
My thirsty spirit faints away
Without thy cheering grace.

2 Not all the blessings of a feast
Can please my soul so well
As when thy richer grace I taste,
And in thy presence dwell.

3 Not life itself, with all its joys,
Can my best passions move,
Or raise so high my cheerful voice,
As thy forgiving love.

4 Thus, till my last, expiring day,
I'll bless my God and King;
Thus will I lift my hands to pray,
And tune my lips to sing.

61

Longing for God. H. M. (24)

Tune—LISCHER, No. 47.

1 LORD of the worlds above,
How pleasant and how fair
The dwellings of thy love,
Thine earthly temples are!
To thine abode | With warm desires
My heart aspires, | To see my God.

2 Oh, happy souls, who pray
Where God appoints to hear!
Oh, happy men, who pay
Their constant service there!
They praise thee still; | Who love the way
And happy they | To Zion's hill.

3 They go from strength to strength,
Through this dark vale of tears,
Till each arrives at length,
Till each in heaven appears.
Oh, glorious seat, | Shall thither bring
When God, our King, | Our willing feet!

WARWICK. C. M.

STANLEY.

62 *Prayer for the Sanctuary.* C. M. (34)

1 WITH joy we hail the sacred day
Which God has called his own;
With joy the summons we obey
To worship at his throne.

2 Thy chosen temple, Lord, how fair!
Where willing votaries throng
To breathe the humble, fervent prayer
And pour the choral song.

3 Spirit of grace, oh, deign to dwell
Within thy church below!
Make her in holiness excel,
With pure devotion glow.

4 Let peace within her walls be found;
Let all her sons unite,
To spread with grateful zeal around
Her clear and shining light.

5 Great God, we hail the sacred day
Which thou hast called thine own;
With joy the summons we obey
To worship at thy throne.

MILGROVE. 7s.

MILGROVE.

63 *A Blessing requested.* 7s. (24)

1 SAVIOUR, bless thy word to all;
Quick and powerful let it prove;
Oh, may sinners hear thy call;
Let thy people grow in love.

2 Thine own gracious message bless;
Follow it with power divine;
Give the gospel great success;
Thine the work, the glory thine.

3 Saviour, bid the world rejoice;
Send, oh send thy truth abroad;
Let the nations hear thy voice,
Hear it, and return to God.

BROWN. C. M.

WM. B. BRADBURY.

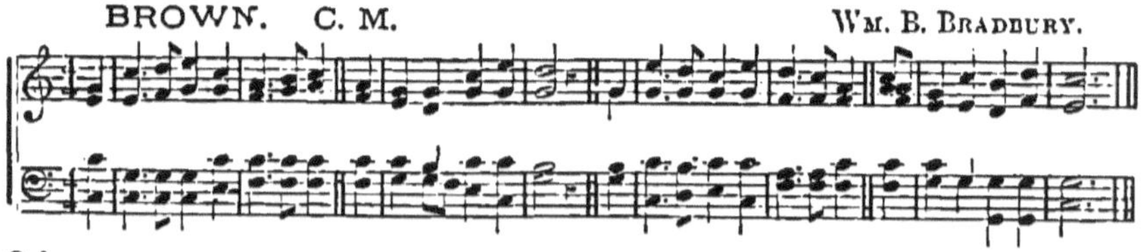

64 *Delight in the House of God.* C. M. (12)

1 How did my heart rejoice to hear
My friends devoutly say,
"In Zion let us all appear,
And keep the solemn day"!

2 I love her gates, I love the road;
The church, adorned with grace,
Stands like a palace built for God,
To show his milder face.

(CONTINUED.)

3 Up to her courts, with joy unknown,
The holy tribes repair;
The Son of David holds his throne,
And sits in judgment there.

4 He hears our praises and complaints;
And, while his awful voice
Divides the sinners from the saints,
We tremble and rejoice.

5 Peace be within this sacred place,
And joy a constant guest;
With holy gifts and heavenly grace
Be her attendants blessed.

6 My soul shall pray for Zion still,
While life or breath remains;
Here my best friends, my kindred, dwell;
Here God, my Saviour, reigns.

ANVERN. L. M. DR. L. MASON.

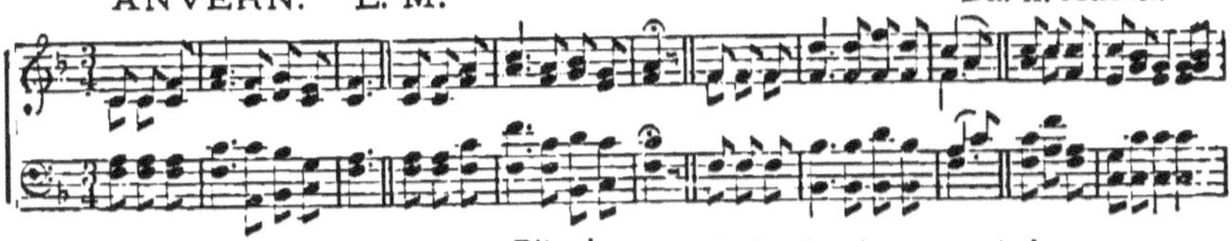

Ritard.

65 L. M. (28)

Joy of the Sanctuary.

1 GREAT God, attend, while Zion sings
The joy that from thy presence springs:
To spend one day with thee on earth,
Exceeds a thousand days of mirth.

2 Might I enjoy the meanest place
Within thy house, O God of grace,
Not tents of ease, nor thrones of power,
Should tempt my feet to leave thy door.

3 God is our sun,—he makes our day;
God is our shield,—he guards our way
From all th' assaults of hell and sin,
From foes without and foes within.

4 All needful grace will God bestow,
And crown that grace with glory too;
He gives us all things, and withholds
No real good from upright souls.

5 O God, our King, whose sovereign sway
The glorious hosts of heaven obey,
Display thy grace, exert thy power,
Till all on earth thy name adore!

DALSTON. S. P. M. A. WILLIAMS.

66 S. P. M. (31)

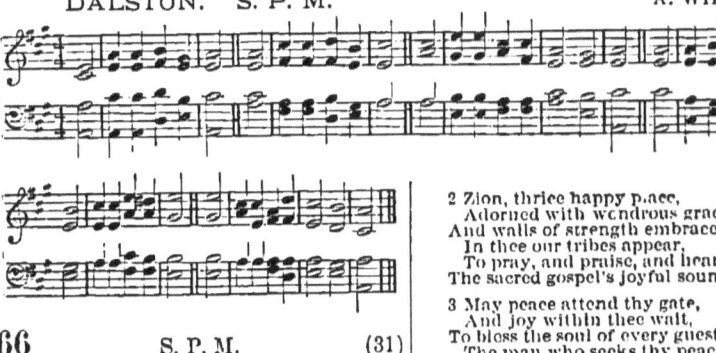

Love for the House of God.

1 How pleased and blest was I
To hear the people cry,
"Come, let us seek our God to-day!"
Yes, with a cheerful zeal,
We haste to Zion's hill,
And there our vows and honors pay.

2 Zion, thrice happy place,
Adorned with wondrous grace,
And walls of strength embrace thee round;
In thee our tribes appear,
To pray, and praise, and hear
The sacred gospel's joyful sound.

3 May peace attend thy gate,
And joy within thee wait,
To bless the soul of every guest;
The man who seeks thy peace,
And wishes thine increase,
A thousand blessings on him rest.

4 My tongue repeats her vows,
"Peace to this sacred house!"
For here my friends and kindred dwell;
And, since my glorious God
Makes thee his blest abode,
My soul shall ever love thee well.

THATCHER. S. M.

HANDEL.

67 *Pleasures of spiritual Worship.* S. M. (14)

1 How sweet to bless the Lord,
And in his praises join,
With saints his goodness to record,
And sing his power divine!

2 These seasons of delight
The dawn of glory seem,
Like rays of pure, celestial light,
Which on our spirits beam.

3 Thus may our joys increase,
Our love more ardent grow,
While rich supplies of Jesus' grace
Refresh our souls below.

4 But, oh, the bliss sublime,
When joy shall be complete,
In that unclouded, glorious clime,
Where all thy servants meet!

LOUVAN. L. M.

V. C. TAYLOR.

68 *The Hour of Prayer.* L. M. (17)

1 BLEST hour, when mortal man retires,
To hold communion with his God,
To send to heaven his warm desires,
And listen to the sacred word.

2 Blest hour, when earthly cares resign
Their empire o'er his anxious breast,
While, all around, the calm divine
Proclaims the holy day of rest.

3 Blest hour, when God himself draws nigh
Well pleased his people's voice to hear,
To hush the penitential sigh,
And wipe away the mourner's tear.

4 Blest hour—for, where the Lord resorts,
Foretastes of future bliss are given,
And mortals find his earthly courts
The house of God, the gate of heaven.

FERGUSON. S. M.

GEO. KINGSLEY.

69 *Enjoyment in Worship.* S. M. (15)

1 SWEET is the work, O Lord,
Thy glorious name to sing,
To praise and pray, to hear thy word,
And grateful offerings bring.

2 Sweet, at the dawning light,
Thy boundless love to tell,
And, when approach the shades of night,
Still on the theme to dwell.

(CONTINUED.)

3 Sweet, on this day of rest,
To join, in heart and voice,
With those who love and serve thee best,
And in thy name rejoice.

4 To songs of praise and joy
Be every Sabbath given,
That such may be our blest employ
Eternally in heaven.

EL PARAN. L. M. CARMINA SACRA.

70 L. M. (32)

Worshipping God in his Temple.

1 How pleasant, how divinely fair,
O Lord of hosts, thy dwellings are!
With long desire my spirit faints
To meet th' assemblies of thy saints.

2 My flesh would rest in thine abode;
My panting heart cries out for God:
My God, my King, why should I be
So far from all my joys and thee?

3 Blest are the men whose hearts are set
To find the way to Zion's gate;
God is their strength; and, through the road,
They lean upon their helper, God.

4 Cheerful they walk, with growing strength,
Till all shall meet in heaven at length;
Till all before thy face appear,
And join in nobler worship there.

HENDON. 7s. DR. MALAN.

71 *The Courts of the Lord.* 7s. (25)

1 LORD of hosts, how bright, how fair,
E'en on earth thy temples are!
Here thy waiting people see
Much of heaven and much of thee.

2 From thy gracious presence nows
Bliss that softens all our woes;
While thy Spirit's holy fire
Warms our hearts with pure desire

3 Here we supplicate thy throne;
Here thou mak'st thy glories known
Here we learn thy righteous ways,
Taste thy love, and sing thy praise.

4 Thus, with sacred songs of joy,
We our happy lives employ;
Love, and long to love thee more,
Till from earth to heaven we soar.

SILVER STREET. S. M. L. SMITH.

72 *Attractions of God's House.* S. M. (27)

1 How charming is the place
Where my Redeemer, God,
Unveils the beauty of his face,
And sheds his love abroad!

2 Not the fair palaces
To which the great resort
Are once to be compared with this,
Where Jesus holds his court.

3 Here on the mercy-seat,
With radiant glory crowned,
Our joyful eyes behold him sit
And smile on all around.

4 Give me, O Lord, a place
Within thy blest abode,
Among the children of thy grace,
The servants of my God.

PETERBORO'. C. M.

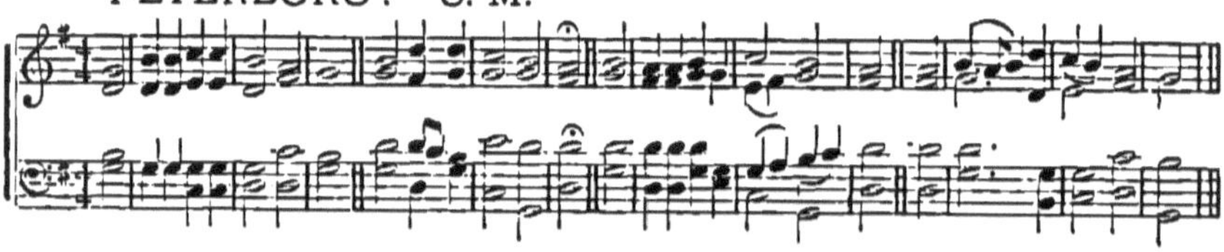

73 *"Increase our Faith."* C. M. (35)

1 FREQUENT the day of God returns
To shed its quickening beams;
And yet, how slow devotion burns;
How languid are its flames!

2 Increase, O Lord, our faith and hope,
And fit us to ascend
Where the assembly ne'er breaks up,
And Sabbaths never end.

3 Where we shall breathe in heavenly air,
With heavenly lustre shine;
Before the throne of God appear,
And feast on love divine.

4 There shall we join, and never tire,
To sing immortal lays;
And, with the bright seraphic choir,
Sound forth Immanuel's praise.

WOODSTOCK. C. M. D. DUTTON, JR.

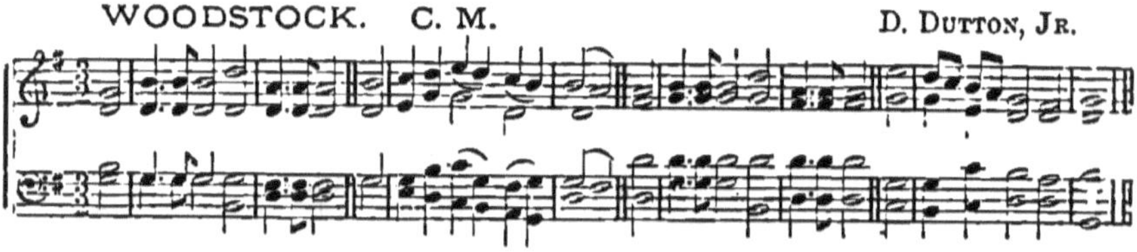

74 *Christ's Presence desired.* C. M. (38)

1 GREAT Shepherd of thy people, hear,
Thy presence now display;
We bow within thy house of prayer;
Oh! give us hearts to pray.

2 The clouds which veil thee from our sight,
In pity, Lord, remove;
Dispose our minds to hear aright
The message of thy love.

3 The feeling heart, the melting eye,
The humble mind, bestow;
And shine upon us from on high,
To make our graces grow.

4 Show us some token of thy love,
Our fainting hopes to raise;
And pour thy blessing from on high,
To aid our feeble praise.

HENDON. 7s. DR. MALAN.

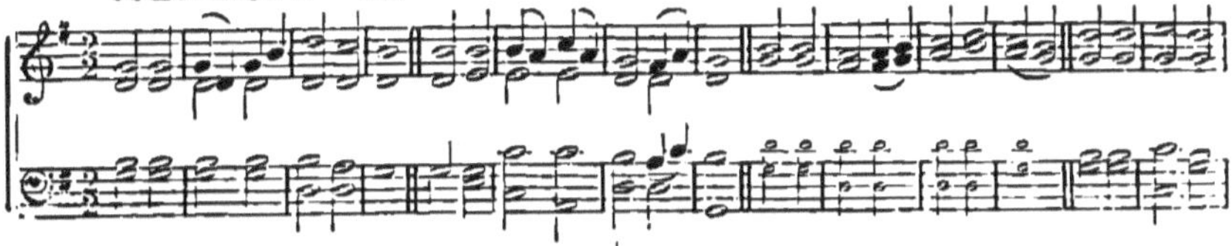

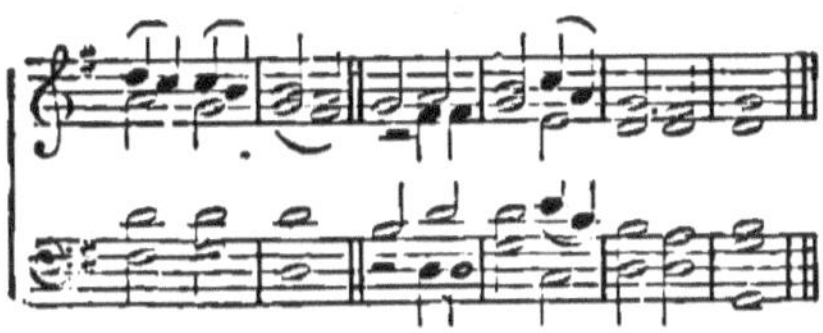

75 *Give us thy Blessing.* 7s. (25)

1 To thy temple we repair,—
Lord, we love to worship there,
When within the vail we meet
Thee upon the mercy-seat.

2 While thy glorious name is sung,
Tune our lips, inspire our tongue,
Then our joyful souls shall bless
Thee, the Lord, our Righteousness.

3 While to thee our prayers ascend,
Let thine ear in love attend;
Hear us, for thy Spirit pleads;
Hear, for Jesus intercedes.

4 While thy word is heard with awe
While we tremble at thy law,
Let thy gospel's wondrous love
Every doubt and fear remove.

5 From thy house, when we return,
Let our hearts within us burn;
That at evening we may say,—
"We have walked with God to-day."

GOULD. C. M. J. E. GOULD.

Ritard.

76 *Delight in Worship.* C. M (23)

1 I LOVE to see the Lord below;
His church displays his grace;
But upper worlds his glory know,
And view him face to face.

2 I love to meet him in his court,
And taste his heavenly love;
But still his visits seem too short,
Or I too soon remove.

3 O Lord, I love thy service now;
Thy church displays thy power
But soon in heaven I hope to bow,
And praise thee evermore.

77 L. M. (16)

Christ ever present in his Churches.

Tune—WARE, No. 42.

1 JESUS, where'er thy people meet
There they behold thy mercy-seat;
Where'er they seek thee, thou art found,
And every place is hallowed ground.

2 For thou within no walls confined,
Dost dwell within the humble mind,
Such ever bring thee where they come,
And going, take thee to their home.

3 Great Shepherd of thy chosen few,
Thy former mercies here renew;
Here, to our waiting hearts, proclaim
The sweetness of thy saving name.

HENDON. 7s. **Dr. Malan.**

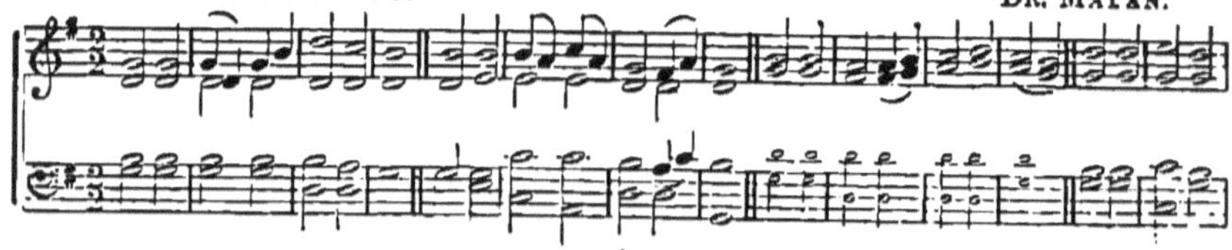

78

7s. (25)

A Blessing humbly requested.

1 Lord, we come before thee now;
At thy feet we humbly bow;
Oh, do not our suit disdain;
Shall we seek thee, Lord, in vain?

2 Lord, on thee our souls depend;
In compassion now descend;
Fill our hearts with thy rich grace,
Tune our lips to sing thy praise.

3 In thine own appointed way
Now we seek thee; here we stay·
Lord, from hence we would not go,
Till a blessing thou bestow.

4 Comfort those who weep and mourn;
Let the time of joy return;
Those that are cast down, lift up;
Make them strong in faith and hope.

5 Grant that all may seek and find
Thee a God supremely kind;
Heal the sick; the captive free;
Let us all rejoice in thee.

THATCHER. S. M. **Handel.**

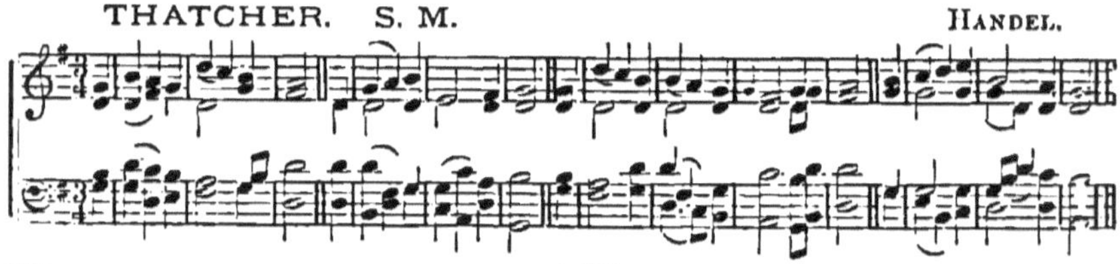

79

S. M. (14)

The Lord revealed

1 Jesus, we look to thee,
Thy promised presence claim;
Thou in the midst of us wilt be,
Assembled in thy name.

2 Thy name salvation is,
Which here we come to prove;
Thy name is life, and health, and peace,
And everlasting love.

3 We meet the grace to take,
Which thou hast freely given;
We meet on earth for thy dear sake,
That we may meet in heaven.

4 Oh, may thy quickening voice
The death of sin remove;
And bid our inmost souls rejoice,
In hope of perfect love.

80

C. M. (38)

God resorted to in Trouble.

Tune—Woodstock, next page.

1 The Lord of glory is my light,
And my salvation, too;
God is my strength, nor will I fear
What all my foes can do.

2 One privilege my heart desires
Oh, grant me an abode
Among the churches of thy saints,
The temples of my God!

3 There shall I offer my requests,
And see thy beauty still;
Shall hear thy messages of love,
And there inquire thy will.

4 When troubles rise, and storms appear,
There may his children hide;
God has a strong pavilion, where
He makes my soul abide.

5 Now shall my head be lifted high
Above my foes around;
And songs of joy and victory
Within thy temple sound.

WOODSTOCK. C. M. D. Dutton, Jr.

GREENVILLE. 8s, 7s, & 4. Rosseau.

D.C.

81 8s, 7s, & 4. (30)

Prayer for the Spirit.

1 Come, thou soul-transforming Spirit,
Bless the sower and the seed;
Let each heart thy grace inherit;
Raise the weak, the hungry feed;
From the gospel
Now supply thy people's need.

2 Oh, may all enjoy the blessing
Which thy word's designed to give;
Let us all, thy love possessing,
Joyfully the truth receive,
And for ever
To thy praise and glory live.

EL PARAN. L. M. Carmina Sacra.

82 *After Sermon.* L. M. (32)

1 Almighty Father, bless the word,
Which through thy grace we now have heard;
Oh, may the precious seed take root,
Spring up, and bear abundant fruit.

2 We praise thee for the means of grace,
Thus in thy courts to seek thy face;
Grant, Lord, that we who worship here,
May all, at length, in heaven appear.

LOUVAN. L. M. — V. C. TAYLOR.

83 L. M. (17)

The Indwelling of God desired.

1 COME, gracious Lord, descend and dwell,
By faith and love, in every breast;
Then shall we know and taste and feel
The joys that cannot be expressed.

2 Come, fill our hearts with inward strength,
Make our enlargéd souls possess,
And learn the height and breadth and length
Of thine eternal love and grace.

3 Now to the God whose power can do
More than our thoughts and wishes know,
Be everlasting honors done.
By all the church, through Christ, his Son

84 *Dismission.* 8s, 7s, & 4. (30)

Tune—GREENVILLE, No. 81.

1 LORD, dismiss us with thy blessing;
Fill our hearts with joy and peace;
Let us each, thy love possessing,
Triumph in redeeming grace:
Oh, refresh us,
Travelling through this wilderness.

2 Thanks we give, and adoration,
For thy gospel's joyful sound;
May the fruits of thy salvation
In our hearts and lives abound;
May thy presence
With us evermore be found.

3 Then, whene'er the signal's given
Us from earth to call away,
Born on angels' wings to heaven,—
Glad the summons to obey,—
May we ever
Reign with Christ in endless day.

HEBRON. L. M. — DR. L. MASON.

85 *Dismission.* L. M. (37)

1 DISMISS us with thy blessing, Lord;
Help us to feed upon thy word;
All that has been amiss forgive,
And let thy truth within us live.

2 Though we are guilty, thou art good;
Wash all our works in Jesus' blood;
Give every burdened soul release,
And bid us all depart in peace.

MORNING.

86 *A Morning Invocation.* L. M. (32)

Tune—EL PARAN, next page.

1 AWAKE, my soul, and with the sun
Thy daily stage of duty run;
Shake off dull sloth, and joyful rise
To pay thy morning sacrifice.

2 Glory to thee, who safe hast kept,
And hast refreshed me while I slept:
Grant, Lord, when I from death shall wake,
I may of endless life partake.

3 Lord, I to thee my vows renew;
Dispel my sins as morning dew;
Guard my first springs of thought and will,
And with thyself my spirit fill.

4 Direct, control, suggest, this day,
All I design or do or say,
That all my powers, with true delight,
In thy sole glory may unite.

EL PARAN. L. M.

CARMINA SACRA.

87 *A Morning Hymn.* L. M. (37)

Tune—HEBRON, No. 85.

1 GOD of the morning, at thy voice
The cheerful sun makes haste to rise,
And like a giant doth rejoice
To run his journey through the skies.

2 Oh, like the sun may I fulfil
Th' appointed duties of the day;
With ready mind and active will
March on and keep my heavenly way.

3 Give me thy counsels for my guide,
And then receive me to thy bliss
All my desires and hopes beside
Are faint and cold compared with this.

BROWNELL. L. M. 6 lines.

HAYDN.

88 *Looking unto Jesus.* L. M. 6 L. (36)

1 WHEN, streaming from the eastern skies,
The morning light salutes mine eyes,
O Sun of righteousness divine,
On me with beams of mercy shine!
Oh! chase the clouds of guilt away,
And turn my darkness into day.

2 And when to heaven's all-glorious King
My morning sacrifice I bring,
And, mourning o'er my guilt and shame,
Ask mercy in my Saviour's name;
Then, Jesus, cleanse me with thy blood,
And be my Advocate with God.

3 When each day's scenes and labors close,
And wearied nature seeks repose,
With pardoning mercy richly blest,
Guard me, my Saviour, while I rest;
And, as each morning sun shall rise,
Oh, lead me onward to the skies!

4 And at my life's last setting sun,
My conflicts o'er, my labors done,
Jesus, thy heavenly radiance shed,
To cheer and bless my dying bed;
And from death's gloom my spirit raise,
To see thy face and sing thy praise.

PETERBORO'. C. M.

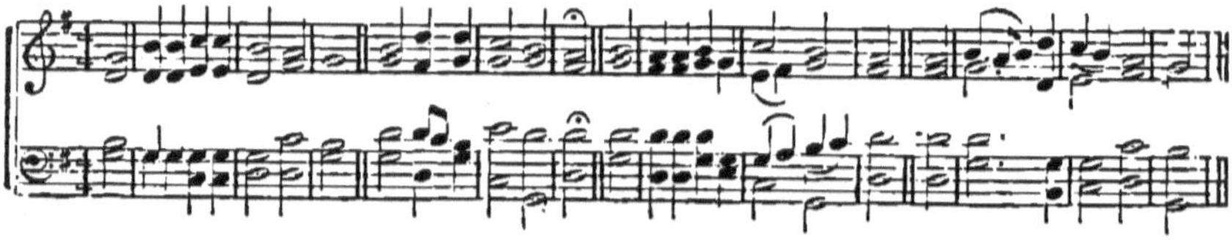

89 *God's Goodness acknowledged.* C. M. (35)

1 Once more, my soul, the rising day
Salutes thy waking eyes;
Once more, my voice, thy tribute pay
To him who rules the skies.

2 Night unto night his name repeats;
The day renews the sound,
Wide as the heavens on which he sits,
To turn the seasons round.

3 'Tis he supports my mortal frame;
My tongue shall speak his praise;
My sins would rouse his wrath to flame,
And yet his wrath delays.

4 Great God, let all my hours be thine,
While I enjoy the light;
Then shall my sun in smiles decline,
And bring a peaceful night.

FEDERAL STREET. L. M. H. K. Oliver.

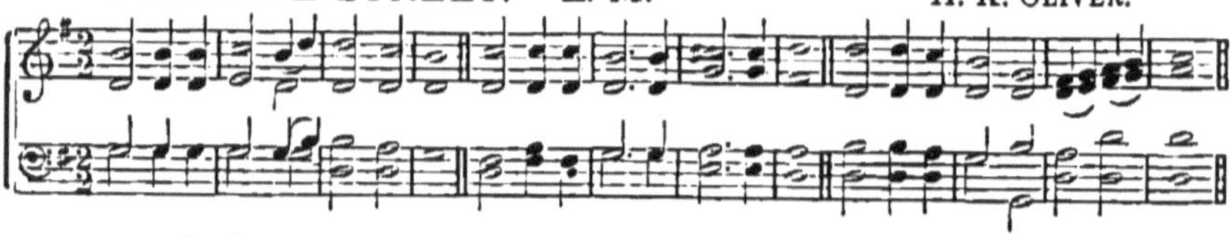

90 *New daily Mercies.* L. M. (33)

1 New every morning is the love
Our wakening and uprising prove;
Through sleep and darkness safely brought,
Restored to life and power and thought.

2 New mercies, each returning day,
Hover around us while we pray;
New perils past, new sins forgiven,
New thoughts of God, new hopes of heaven.

3 Old friends, old scenes, will lovelier be,
As more of heaven in each we see;
Some softening gleam of love and prayer
Shall dawn on every cross and care.

4 Only, O Lord, in thy dear love,
Fit us for perfect rest above,
And keep us this, and every day,
To live more nearly as we pray.

91 C. M. (35)

Keep us, O Lord, this Day.

Tune—Peterboro'.

1 Now that the sun is beaming bright,
Once more to God we pray,
That he, the uncreated Light,
May guide our souls this day.

2 No sinful word, nor deed of wrong,
Nor thoughts that idly rove,
But simple truth be on our tongue,
And in our hearts be love.

3 And while the hours in order flow,
O Christ, securely fence
Our gates beleaguer'd by the foe,
The gate of every sense.

4 And grant that to thine honor, Lord,
Our daily toil may tend;
That we begin it at thy word,
And in thy favor end.

92 L. M. (33)

Morning Prayer to Christ.

1 O Jesus, Lord of heavenly grace,
Thou Brightness of thy Father's face,
Thou Fountain of eternal light,
Whose beams disperse the shades of night!

2 Come, holy Sun of heavenly love,
Send down thy radiance from above;
And to our inmost hearts convey
The Holy Spirit's cloudless ray.

3 Oh, hallowed thus be every day!
Let meekness be our morning ray,
And faithful love our noon-day light,
And hope our sunset, calm and bright.

4 O Christ, with each returning morn,
Thine image to our hearts is borne:
Oh, may we ever clearly see
Our Saviour and our God in thee!

WOODSTOCK. C. M.

D. Dutton, Jr.

93 *Delight in Evening Devotions.* C. M. (38)

1 I love to steal a while away
From every cumbering care,
And spend the hours of setting day
In humble, grateful prayer.

2 I love in solitude to shed
The penitential tear,
And all his promises to plead
Where none but God can hear.

3 I love to think on mercies past,
And future good implore,
And all my cares and sorrows cast
On him whom I adore.

4 I love by faith to take a view
Of brighter scenes in heaven;
The prospect doth my strength renew,
While here by tempests driven.

5 Thus, when life's toilsome day is o'er,
May its departing ray
Be calm as this impressive hour,
And lead to endless day.

FEDERAL STREET. L. M.

H. K. Oliver.

94 L. M. (33)

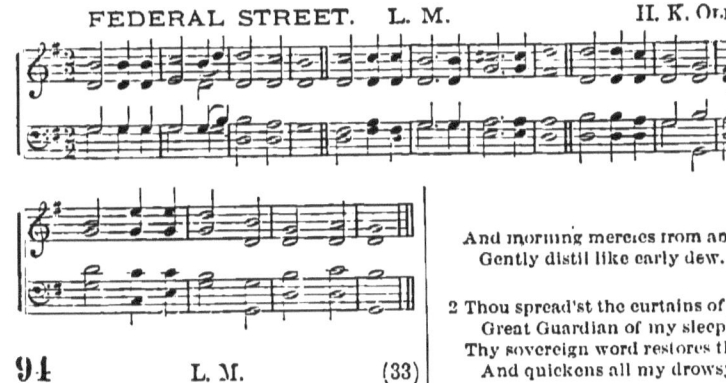

Grateful Acknowledgment.

1 My God, how endless is thy love!
Thy gifts are every evening new
And morning mercies from above
Gently distil like early dew.

2 Thou spread'st the curtains of the night;
Great Guardian of my sleeping hours;
Thy sovereign word restores the light,
And quickens all my drowsy powers.

3 I yield my powers to thy command;
To thee I consecrate my days;
Perpetual blessings from thy hand
Demand perpetual songs of praise.

HOLLEY. 7s.

GEO. HEWS.

95

Prayer at Eventide. 7s. (39)

1 SOFTLY now the light of day
Fades upon my sight away;
Free from care, from labor free,
Lord, I would commune with thee!

2 Thou whose all-pervading eye
Nought escapes, without, within,
Pardon each infirmity,
Open fault, and secret sin.

3 Soon for me the light of day
Shall for ever pass away;
Then, from sin and sorrow free,
Take me, Lord, to dwell with thee!

FEDERAL STREET. L. M.

H. K. OLIVER.

96

Abide with me. L. M. ([illegible])

1 SUN of my soul, thou Saviour dear,
It is not night if thou be near:
Oh, may no earth-born cloud arise
To hide thee from thy servant's eyes!

2 When soft the dews of kindly sleep
My wearied eyelids gently steep,
Be my last thought, how sweet to rest
For ever on my Saviour's breast!

3 Be near to bless me when I wake,
Ere through the world my way I take;
Abide with me till in thy love
I lose myself in heaven above.

PETERBORO'. C. M.

97 *Evening Devotion.* C. M. (35)

1 Now, from the altar of our hearts,
Let holy incense rise;
Assist us, Lord, to offer up
Our evening sacrifice.

2 Minutes and mercies multiplied
Have made up all this day;
Minutes came quick, but mercies were
More swift and free than they.

3 New time, new favor, and new joys
Do a new song require:
Till we shall praise thee as we would,
Accept our hearts' desire.

HEBRON. L. M. Dr. L. Mason.

98 *Evening Reflections.* L. M. (37)

1 Thus far the Lord has led me on;
Thus far his power prolongs my days;
And every evening shall make known
Some fresh memorial of his grace.

2 Much of my time has run to waste,
And I, perhaps, am near my home;
But he forgives my follies past;
He gives me strength for days to come.

3 I lay my body down to sleep;
Peace is the pillow for my head;
While well-appointed angels keep
Their watchful stations round my bed.

4 Thus, when the night of death shall come,
My flesh shall rest beneath the ground,
And wait thy voice to break my tomb,
With sweet salvation in the sound.

99 *Trusting God.* L. M. (37)

1 Glory to thee, my God, this night,
For all the blessings of the light:
Keep me, oh keep me, King of kings,
Beneath the shadow of thy wings.

2 Forgive me, Lord, for thy dear Son,
The ills which I this day have done;
That with the world, myself, and thee,
I, ere I sleep, at peace may be.

3 Teach me to live that I may dread
The grave as little as my bed;
Teach me to die that so I may
With joy behold the judgment day.

4 Be thou my Guardian while I sleep;
Thy watchful station near me keep;
My heart with love celestial fill,
And guard me from th' approach of ill.

SWANWICK. C. M. — Lucas.

100 *Eternity of God.* C. M. (49)

1 Through endless years thou art the same,
O thou eternal God!
Ages to come shall know thy name,
And tell thy works abroad.

2 The strong foundations of the earth
Of old by thee were laid;
By thee the beauteous arch of heaven
With matchless skill was made.

3 Soon shall this goodly frame of things,
Formed by thy powerful hand,
Be, like a vesture, laid aside,
And changed at thy command.

4 But thy perfections, all divine,
Eternal as thy days,
Through everlasting ages shine,
With undiminished rays.

101 *Infinitude of God.* C. M. (49)

1 Great God, how infinite art thou!
What worthless worms are we!
Let all the race of creatures bow,
And pay their praise to thee.

2 Thy throne eternal ages stood,
Ere seas or stars were made;
Thou art the ever-living God,
Were all the nations dead.

3 Eternity, with all its years,
Stands present in thy view;
To thee there's nothing old appears;
Great God, there's nothing new.

4 Our lives through various scenes are drawn
And vexed with trifling cares,
While thine eternal thought moves on
Thine undisturbed affairs.

5 Great God, how infinite art thou!
What worthless worms are we!
Let all the race of creatures bow,
And pay their praise to thee.

NEWBOLD. C. M. — Geo. Kingsley.

102 *Kindness of God.* C. M. (79)

1 What shall I render to my God,
For all his kindness shown?
My feet shall visit thine abode,
My songs address thy throne.

2 Among the saints who fill thy house,
My offering shall be paid;
There shall my zeal perform the vows
My soul in anguish made.

3 How much is mercy thy delight,
Thou ever-blessed God!
How dear thy servants in thy sight;
How precious is their blood!

4 How happy all thy servants are!
How great thy grace to me!
My life, which thou hast made thy care,
Lord, I devote to thee.

5 Now I am thine,—for ever thine,—
Nor shall my purpose move;
Thy hand hath loosed my bonds of pain,
And bound me with thy love.

6 Here, in thy courts, I leave my vow,
And thy rich grace record;
Witness, ye saints, who hear me now,
If I forsake the Lord.

103 *Omniscience.* C. M. (49)

Tune—SWANWICK, No. 100.

1 In all my vast concerns with thee,
In vain my soul would try
To shun thy presence, Lord, or flee
The notice of thine eye.

2 Thine all-surrounding sight surveys
My rising and my rest,
My public walks, my private ways,
And secrets of my breast.

3 My thoughts lie open to the Lord,
Before they're formed within;
And ere my lips pronounce the word,
He knows the sense I mean.

4 Oh, wondrous knowledge, deep and high!
Where can a creature hide?
Within thy circling arms I lie,
Enclosed on every side.

5 So let thy grace surround me still,
And like a bulwark prove,
To guard my soul from every ill,
Secured by sovereign love.

ILLA. L. M. CARMINA SACRA.

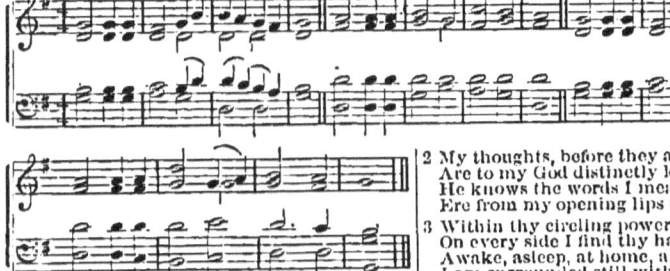

104 *Omniscience.* L. M. (45)

1 Lord, thou hast searched and seen me through;
Thine eye commands, with piercing view,
My rising and my resting hours,
My heart and flesh with all their powers.

2 My thoughts, before they are my own,
Are to my God distinctly known;
He knows the words I mean to speak,
Ere from my opening lips they break.

3 Within thy circling power I stand;
On every side I find thy hand:
Awake, asleep, at home, abroad,
I am surrounded still with God.

4 Amazing knowledge, vast and great!
What large extent! what lofty height!
My soul, with all the powers I boast,
Is in the boundless prospect lost.

5 Oh, may these thoughts possess my breast,
Where'er I rove, where'er I rest;
Nor let my weaker passions dare
Consent to sin, for God is there.

DOANE. L. M. E. L. WHITE.

105 *God with us everywhere.* L. M. (47)

1 O Lord, how full of sweet content
Our years of pilgrimage are spent!
Where'er we dwell, we dwell with thee,
In heaven, in earth, or on the sea.

2 To us remains nor place nor time;
Our country is in every clime:
We can be calm and free from care
On any shore, since God is there.

3 While place we seek, or place we shun,
The soul finds happiness in none;
But with our God to guide our way,
'Tis equal joy to go or stay.

4 Could we be cast where thou art not,
That were indeed a dreadful lot;
But regions none remote we call,
Secure of finding God in all.

ILLA. L. M. CARMINA SACRA.

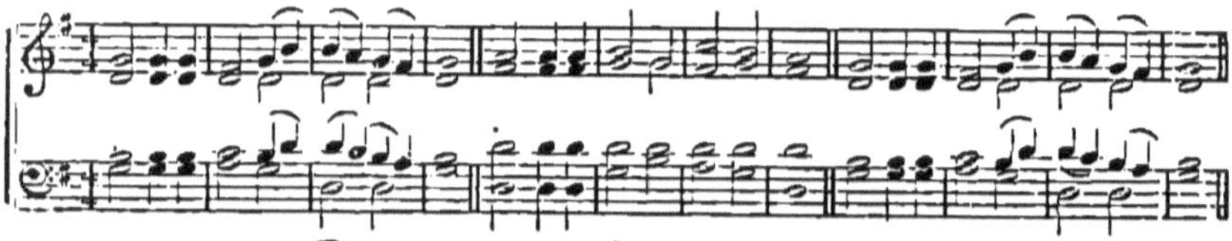

106 *Omnipresence.* L. M. (45)

1 WHERE can we hide, or whither fly,
Lord, to escape thy piercing eye?
With thee it is not day and night,
But darkness shineth as the light.

2 Where'er we go, whate'er pursue,
Our ways are open to thy view,
Our motives read, our thoughts explored,
Our hearts revealed to thee, O Lord.

3 Is there throughout all worlds one spot
One lonely wild, where thou art not?
The hosts of heaven enjoy thy care,
And those of hell know thou art there.

4 Awake, asleep, where none intrude,
Or 'midst the thronging multitude,
In every land, on every sea,
We are surrounded still with thee.

5 Search us, O God, and know each heart;
With every idol bid us part;
Make us to keep thy holy ways,
And live to utter forth thy praise.

DARWIN. C. M. G. HEWS.

107 C. M. (50)

God's Condescension.

1 O THOU, to whom all creatures bow
Within this earthly frame,
Through all the world, how great art thou!
How glorious is thy name!

2 When heaven, thy glorious work on high,
Employs my wondering sight,—
The moon, that nightly rules the sky,
With stars of feebler light,—

3 Lord, what is man, that thou shouldst choose
To keep him in thy mind?
Or what his race, that thou shouldst prove
To them so wondrous kind?

4 O thou, to whom all creatures bow
Within this earthly frame,
Through all the world, how great art thou!
How glorious is thy name!

108 L. M. (58)

God searches the heart.

Tune—WARD, next page.

1 THOU know'st me, Lord; 'tis thine to view
Whate'er I am, whate'er I do,
When up I rise, when down I lie,
I still am in thine awful eye.

2 My inmost thought, my lightest word,
By thee is seen, by thee is heard.
Thy wonder-working hand I find
Around, before me, and behind.

3 Where from thy presence could I flee?
Where find a refuge, Lord, from thee?
From heaven thou shin'st in glory down,
And hell is darkened by thy frown.

4 On morning's wings beyond the sea
I fly, but cannot fly from thee.
I plunge me in the depths of night;
One look from thee makes darkness light.

5 Father of mercy, God of grace,
I cannot, would not, shun thy face.
No, be it rather mine to prove
An Omnipresent God of love.

WARD. L. M. Arr. by Dr. L. Mason.

109 C. M. (65)

Loving-kindness of the Lord.

Tune—AVON.

1 Ye humble souls, approach your God
With songs of sacred praise;
For he is good, supremely good,
And kind are all his ways.

2 All nature owns his guardian care;
In him we live and move;
But nobler benefits declare
The wonders of his love.

3 He gave his well-beloved Son
To save our souls from sin;
'Tis here he makes his goodness known,
And proves it all divine.

4 To this sure refuge, Lord, we come,
And here our hope relies;
A safe defence, a peaceful home,
When storms of trouble rise.

5 Thine eye beholds, with kind regard,
The souls who trust in thee;
Their humble hope thou wilt reward
With bliss divinely free.

AVON. C. M.

PARK STREET. L. M. Venua.

110 *Infinite Perfections of God.* L. M. (51)

1 High in the heavens, eternal God,
Thy goodness in full glory shines;
Thy truth shall break through every cloud
That veils and darkens thy designs.

2 For ever firm thy justice stands,
As mountains their foundations keep,
Wise are the wonders of thy hands;
Thy judgments are a mighty deep.

(CONTINUED.)

3 O God, how excellent thy grace,
  Whence all our hope and comfort spring!
The sons of Adam, in distress,
  Fly to the shadow of thy wing.

4 In the provisions of thy house
  We still shall find a sweet repast;
There mercy, like a river, flows,
  And brings salvation to our taste.

AMES. L. M. Dr. L. Mason.

111 *God of all Goodness.* L. M. (54)

1 God of the world! thy glories shine,
  Through earth and heaven, with rays divine;
Thy smile gives beauty to the flower,
  Thine anger to the tempest power.

2 God of our lives! the throbbing heart
  Doth at thy beck its action start;
Throbs on, obedient to thy will,
  Or ceases at thy fatal chill

3 God of eternal life! thy love
  Doth every stain of sin remove;
The cross, the cross,—its hallowed light
  Shall drive from earth her cheerless night

4 God of all goodness! to the skies
  Our hearts in grateful anthems rise;
And to thy service shall be given
  The rest of life, the whole of heaven.

MANOAH. C. M. Greatorex.

112 *God our Support.* C. M. (64)

1 'Tis faith supports my feeble soul
  In times of deep distress;
When storms arise and billows roll,
  Great God, I trust thy grace.

2 Thy powerful arm still bears me up,
  Whatever griefs befall;
Thou art my life, my joy, my hope,
  And thou my all in all.

3 Bereft of friends, beset with foes,
  With dangers all around,
To thee I all my fears disclose;
  In thee my help is found.

4 In every want, in every strait,
  To thee alone I fly;
When other comforters depart,
  Thou art for ever nigh.

113 *God worthy of all Praise.* L. M. (53)

Tune—Alfreton, next page.

1 Be thou exalted, O my God,
  Above the heavens where angels dwell;
Thy power on earth be known abroad,
  And land to land thy wonders tell.

2 My heart is fixed; my song shall raise
  Immortal honors to his name;
Awake, my tongue, to sound his praise,
  His wondrous goodness to proclaim.

3 High o'er the earth his mercy reigns,
  And reaches to the utmost sky;
His truth to endless years remains,
  When lower worlds dissolve and die.

4 Be thou exalted, O my God,
  Above the heavens, where angels dwell;
Thy power on earth be known abroad,
  And land to land thy wonders tell.

ALFRETON. L. M. — Beastall.

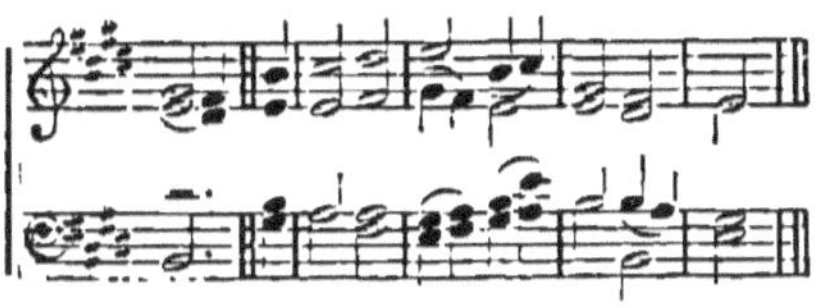

114 *Goodness of God.* C. M. (43)

Tune—Mount Auburn.

1 Thy goodness, Lord, our souls confess;
Thy goodness we adore;
A spring whose blessings never fail,
A sea without a shore.

2 Sun, moon, and stars thy love declare,
In every golden ray;
Love draws the curtains of the night,
And love brings back the day.

3 Thy bounty every season crowns
With all the bliss it yields,
With joyful clusters loads the vines,
With strengthening grain the fields.

4 But chiefly, thy compassion, Lord,
Is in the gospel seen;
There, like a sun, thy mercy shines,
Without a cloud between.

5 There pardon, peace, and holy joy,
Through Jesus' name are given;
He on the cross was lifted high,
That we might reign in heaven.

MOUNT AUBURN. C. M. — G. Kingsley.

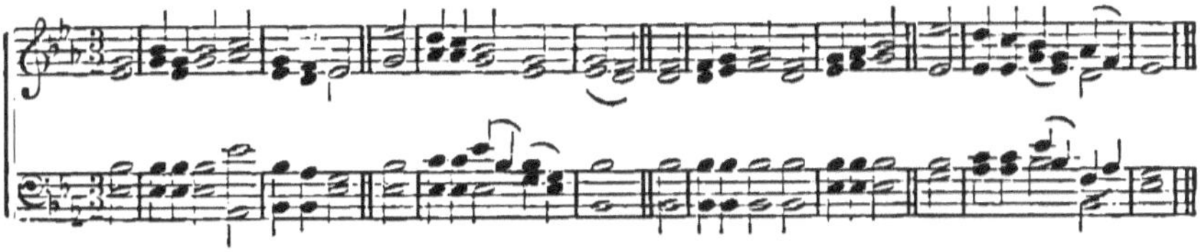

DARWIN. C. M. — G. Hews.

115 *Gratitude.* C. M. (50)

1 When all thy mercies, O my God,
My rising soul surveys,
Transported with the view, I'm lost
In wonder, love, and praise.

2 Unnumbered comforts on my soul
Thy tender care bestowed,
Before my infant heart conceived
From whom those comforts flowed.

3 When in the slippery paths of youth
With heedless steps I ran,
Thine arm, unseen, conveyed me safe,
And led me up to man.

4 Ten thousand thousand precious gifts
My daily thanks employ;
Nor is the least a cheerful heart,
That tastes those gifts with joy.

5 Through every period of my life,
Thy goodness I'll pursue;
And after death, in distant worlds,
The glorious theme renew.

6 Through all eternity, to thee
A grateful song I'll raise;
But, oh, eternity's too short
To utter all thy praise.

DESIRE. L. M.

116 L. M. (48)

God's Blessings everywhere.

1 THERE'S not a bird with lonely nest,
In pathless wood or mountain crest,
Nor meaner thing which does not share,
O God, in thy continual care.

2 Each barren crag, each desert rude,
Holds thee within its solitude;
And thou dost bless the wanderer there
Who makes his solitary prayer.

3 In busy mart and crowded street,
No less than in the still retreat,
Thou, Lord, art near, our souls to bless
With all a parent's tenderness.

4 And every moment still doth bring
Thy blessings on its loaded wing;
Widely they spread through earth and sky,
And last to all eternity.

ELIZABETHTOWN. C. M. GEO. KINGSLEY.

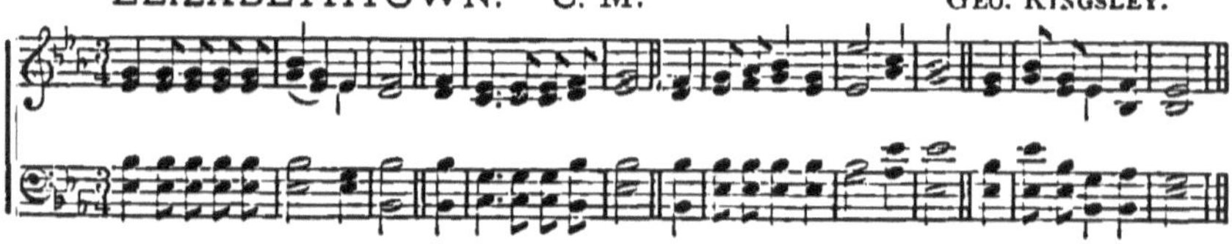

117 *Our Father.* C. M. (63)

1 FATHER of mercies! God of Love!
My Father and my God!
I'll sing the honors of thy name,
And spread thy praise abroad.

2 In every period of my life
Thy thoughts of love appear;
Thy mercies gild each transient scene,
And crown each passing year.

3 In all thy mercies, may my soul
A Father's bounty see;
Nor let the gifts thy grace bestows
Estrange my heart from thee.

4 Teach me, in times of deep distress,
To own thy hand, O God!
And in submissive silence learn
The lessons of thy rod.

5 Through every period of my life,
Each bright, each clouded scene,
Give me a meek and humble mind,
Still equal and serene.

118 *Divine Perfections.* L. M. (46)

Tune—ERNAN, next page.

1 THE Lord! how wondrous are his ways!
How firm his truth! how large his grace!
He takes his mercy for his throne,
And thence he makes his glories known.

2 Not half so high his power hath spread
The starry heavens above our head,
As his rich love exceeds our praise,
Exceeds the highest hopes we raise.

3 Not half so far has nature placed
The rising morning from the west,
As his forgiving grace removes
The daily guilt of those he loves.

4 How slowly doth his wrath arise!
On swifter wings salvation flies:
Or, if he lets his anger burn,
How soon his frowns to pity turn!

5 His everlasting love is sure
To all his saints, and shall endure;
From age to age his truth shall reign,
Nor children's children hope in vain.

ERNAN. L. M. — Dr. L. Mason.

119 *The Mercy of God.* S. M. (72)

Tune—Boylston.

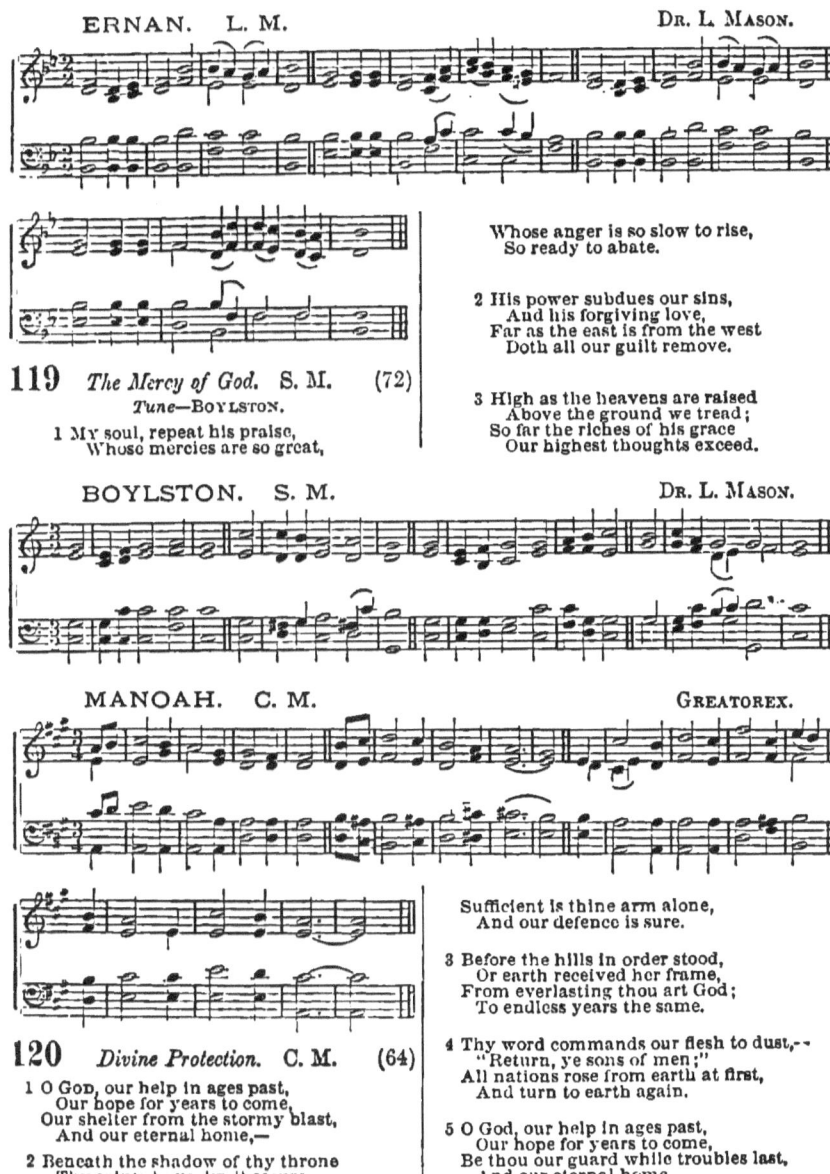

1 My soul, repeat his praise,
  Whose mercies are so great,
Whose anger is so slow to rise,
  So ready to abate.

2 His power subdues our sins,
  And his forgiving love,
Far as the east is from the west
  Doth all our guilt remove.

3 High as the heavens are raised
  Above the ground we tread;
So far the riches of his grace
  Our highest thoughts exceed.

BOYLSTON. S. M. — Dr. L. Mason.

MANOAH. C. M. — Greatorex.

120 *Divine Protection.* C. M. (64)

1 O God, our help in ages past,
  Our hope for years to come,
Our shelter from the stormy blast,
  And our eternal home,—

2 Beneath the shadow of thy throne
  Thy saints have dwelt secure;
Sufficient is thine arm alone,
  And our defence is sure.

3 Before the hills in order stood,
  Or earth received her frame,
From everlasting thou art God;
  To endless years the same.

4 Thy word commands our flesh to dust,—
  "Return, ye sons of men;"
All nations rose from earth at first,
  And turn to earth again.

5 O God, our help in ages past,
  Our hope for years to come,
Be thou our guard while troubles last,
  And our eternal home.

ALFRETON. L. M. BEASTALL.

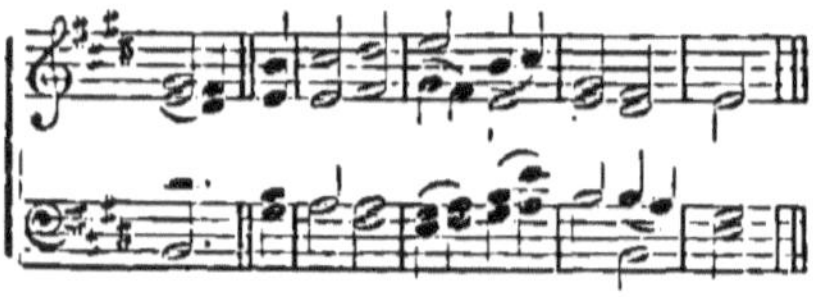

121 *Grateful Praise.* L. M. (53)

1 WITH all my powers of heart and tongue,
I'll praise my Maker in my song;
Angels shall hear the notes I raise,
Approve the song, and join the praise.

2 To God I cried, when troubles rose;
He heard me, and subdued my foes;
He did my rising fears control,
And strength diffused through all my soul.

3 Amid a thousand snares I stand,
Upheld and guarded by his hand;
His words my fainting soul revive,
And keep my dying faith alive.

4 I'll sing thy truth and mercy, Lord;
I'll sing the wonders of thy word;
Not all the works and names below
So much thy power and glory show.

122 *God's Perfections.* L. M. (53)

1 THY mercy, Lord, the sinner's hope,
The highest orb of heaven transcends:
Thy sacred truth's unmeasured scope
Through all eternity extends.

2 Thy justice like the hills remains,
Unfathomed depths thy judgments are,
Thy providence the world sustains,
The whole creation is thy care.

3 Thy saints shall to thy courts be led
To banquet on thy love's repast,
And drink, as from a fountain head,
Of joys that shall for ever last.

4 The streams of life with thee abound;
Thy presence is eternal day;
Oh, shower thy gifts the world around,
Thy glorious face to all display.

BYEFIELD. C. M. DR. T. HASTINGS.

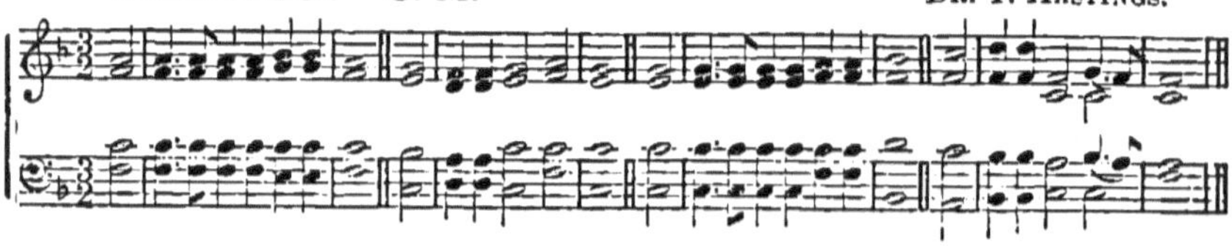

123 C. M. (56)

Truth and Goodness of God.

1 FAITHFUL, O Lord, thy mercies are,
A rock that cannot move;
A thousand promises declare
Thy constancy of love.

2 Thou waitest to be gracious still;
Thou dost with sinners bear,
That, saved, we may thy goodness feel,
And all thy grace declare.

3 Its streams the whole creation reach,
So plenteous is the store;
Enough for all, enough for each,
Enough for evermore.

4 Throughout the universe it reigns;
It stands for ever sure;
And while thy truth, O God, remains,
Thy goodness shall endure.

124 C. M. (63)

Praise for God's Goodness.

Tune—ELIZABETHTOWN, next page.

1 SWEET is the memory of thy grace
My God, my heavenly King;
Let age to age thy righteousness
In songs of glory sing.

2 God reigns on high, but ne'er confines
His goodness to the skies;
Through all the earth his bounty shines,
And every want supplies.

3 How kind are thy compassions, Lord!
How slow thine anger moves!
But soon he sends his pardoning word,
To cheer the souls he loves.

4 Sweet is the memory of thy grace,
My God, my heavenly King;
Let age to age thy righteousness
In songs of glory sing.

ELIZABETHTOWN. C. M. GEO. KINGSLEY.

BOYLSTON. S. M. DR. L. MASON.

125 *The Mercies of God.* S. M. (73)

1 Oh, bless the Lord, my soul;
Let all within me join,
And aid my tongue to bless his name
Whose favors are divine.

2 Oh, bless the Lord, my soul;
Nor let his mercies lie
Forgotten in unthankfulness,
And without praises die.

3 'Tis he forgives thy sins;
'Tis he relieves thy pain;
'Tis he that heals thy sicknesses,
And gives thee strength again.

4 He crowns thy life with love,
When ransomed from the grave;
He, who redeemed my soul from hell,
Hath sovereign power to save.

126 *Divine Compassion.* S. M. (72)

1 THE pity of the Lord,
To those that fear his name,
Is such as tender parents feel;
He knows our feeble frame.

2 He knows we are but dust,
Scattered with every breath;
His anger, like a rising wind,
Can send us swift to death.

3 Our days are as the grass,
Or like the morning flower;
When blasting winds sweep o'er the field,
It withers in an hour.

4 But thy compassions, Lord,
To endless years endure;
And children's children ever find
Thy word of promise sure.

NEWBOLD. C. M. GEO. KINGSLEY.

127 *God protects his People.* C. M. (79)

1 THROUGH all the changing scenes of life,
In trouble and in joy,
The praises of my God shall still
My heart and tongue employ.

2 The hosts of God encamp around
The dwellings of the just;
Protection he affords to all
Who make his name their trust.

3 Oh, make but trial of his love!
Experience will decide
How blest are they, and only they,
Who in his truth confide.

4 Fear him, ye saints, and you will then
Have nothing else to fear:
Make you his service your delight,
He'll make your wants his care.

DESIRE. L. M.

128 L. M. (48)

"Return unto thy Rest, O my Soul!"

1 Return, my soul, and sweetly rest
On thy almighty Father's breast;
The bounties of his grace adore,
And count his wondrous mercies o'er.

2 Thy mercy, Lord, preserved my breath,
And snatched my fainting soul from death;
Removed my sorrows, dried my tears,
And saved me from surrounding snares.

3 What shall I render to the Lord?
Or how his wondrous grace record?
To him my grateful voice I'll raise,
With just thanksgiving to his praise.

4 O Zion, in thy sacred courts,
Where glory dwells and joy resorts,
To notes divine I'll tune the song,
And praise shall flow from every tongue.

LYDIA. C. M.

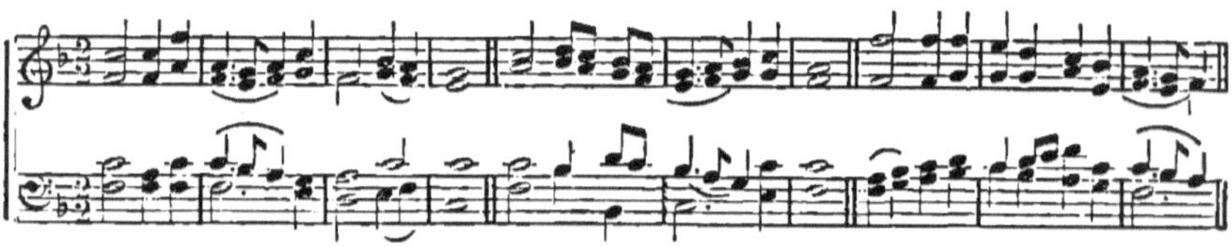

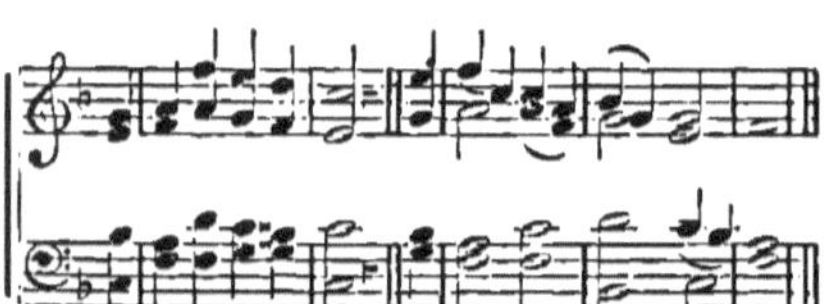

129 *A faithful God.* C. M. (71)

1 Begin, my tongue, some heavenly theme,
And speak some boundless thing,—
The mighty works, or mightier name,
Of our eternal King.

2 Tell of his wondrous faithfulness,
And sound his power abroad;
Sing of the glory and the grace
Of our Redeemer, God.

3 Proclaim "salvation from the Lord,
For wretched, dying men;"
His hand inscribed the sacred word
With an immortal pen.

4 Recorded by eternal love,
Each promise clearly shines;
Nor can the powers of hell remove
Those everlasting lines.

5 His every word of grace is strong
As that which built the skies;
The voice that rolls the stars along
Speaks all the promises.

6 Oh, might I hear his heavenly tongue
But whisper, "Thou art mine,"
The gentle words should raise my song
To notes almost divine.

130 8s. (62)

Our God for ever and ever.

Tune—Foster, next page.

1 This God is the God we adore,
Our faithful, unchangeable Friend,
Whose love is as large as his power,
And neither knows measure nor end.

2 'Tis Jesus, the first and the last,
Whose Spirit shall guide us safe home;
We'll praise him for all that is past,
And trust him for all that's to come.

FOSTER. 8s. WM. B. BRADBURY.

CHANNING. H. M. MODERN HARP.

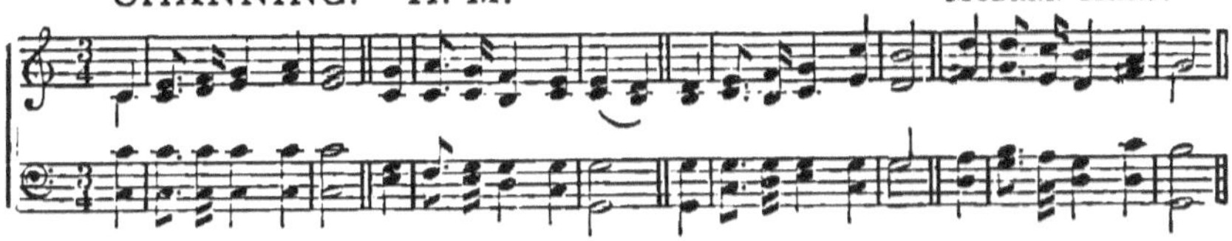

131 *Faithfulness of God.* H. M. (60)

1 THE promises I sing,
Which sovereign mercy spoke;
Nor will th' eternal King
His words of grace revoke:
They stand secure | Not Zion's hill
And steadfast still; | Abides so sure.

2 The mountains melt away,
When once the Judge appears,
And sun and moon decay,
That measure mortal years;
But still the same, | The promise shines
In radiant lines | Through all the flame.

3 Their harmony shall sound
Through my attentive ears,
When thunders cleave the ground,
And dissipate the spheres:
'Midst all the shock | I stand serene,
Of that dread scene, | Thy word my rock.

MARLOW. C. M. DR. L. MASON.

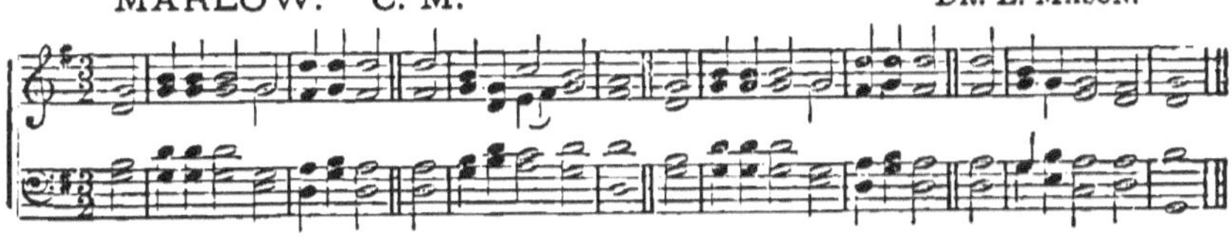

132 *Holiness of God.* C. M. (55)

1 HOLY and reverend is the name
Of our eternal King;
"Thrice holy Lord," the angels cry;
"Thrice holy," let us sing.

2 The deepest reverence of the mind
Pay, O my soul, to God;
Lift with thy hands, a holy heart
To his sublime abode.

3 With sacred awe pronounce his name,
Whom words nor thoughts can reach;
A contrite heart shall please him more
Than noblest form of speech.

4 Thou holy God, preserve my soul
From all pollution free;
The pure in heart are thy delight,
And they thy face shall see.

SPANISH HYMN. 7s Double.

FINE.
D.C.

133 *Thou only art holy.* 7s. (61)

1 Holy, holy, holy Lord,
God of hosts, in heaven adored,
Earth with awe has heard thy name,
Men thy majesty proclaim.

2 Just and true are all thy ways,
Great thy works above our praise;
Humbled in the dust, we own,
Thou art holy, thou alone.

3 In thy sight, the angel band
Justly charged with folly stand;
Holiest deeds of creatures lie
Meritless before thine eye.

4 How shall sinners worship thee,
God of spotless purity?
To thy grace all hope we owe:
Thine own righteousness bestow.

134 *Holiness of God.* 7s. (61)

1 Holy, holy, holy Lord
God of hosts! when heaven and earth,
Out of darkness, at thy word
Issued into glorious birth,
All thy works before thee stood,
And thine eye beheld them good,
While they sung with sweet accord,
Holy, holy, holy Lord!

2 Holy, holy, holy! thee,
One Jehovah evermore,
Father, Son, and Spirit! we,
Dust and ashes, would adore;
Lightly by the world esteemed,
From that world by thee redeemed,
Sing we here with glad accord,
Holy, holy, holy Lord!

3 Holy, holy, holy! all
Heaven's triumphant choir shall sing,
While the ransomed nations fall
At the footstool of their King:
Then shall saints and seraphim,
Harps and voices, swell one hymn,
Blending in sublime accord,
Holy, holy, holy Lord!

ARIEL. C. P. M. Dr. L. Mason.

135 *The Love of God.* C. P. M. (59)

1 My God, thy boundless love I praise;
How bright, on high, its glories blaze!
How sweetly bloom below!
It streams from thine eternal throne;
Through heaven its joys for ever run,
And o'er the earth they flow.

2 But in the gospel it appears
In sweeter, fairer characters,
And charms the ravished breast;
There, love immortal leaves the sky,
To wipe the drooping mourner's eye,
And give the weary rest.

3 Then let the love that makes me blest,
With cheerful praise inspire my breast,
And ardent gratitude;
And all my thoughts and passions tend
To thee, my Father and my Friend,
My soul's eternal good.

MARLOW. C. M. DR. L. MASON.

136 *Herein is Love.* C. M. (55)

1 My God, how wonderful thou art,
Thy majesty how bright!
How glorious is thy mercy-seat,
In depths of burning light!

2 Yet I may love thee too, O Lord,
Almighty as thou art;
For thou hast stooped to ask of me
The love of my poor heart.

3 No earthly father loves like thee,
No mother half so mild
Bears and forbears, as thou hast done
With me, thy sinful child.

4 My God, how wonderful thou art,
Thou everlasting Friend!
On thee I stay my trusting heart,
Till faith in vision end.

137 *The Love of God.* C. P. M. (59)

Tune—ARIEL, No. 135.

1 OH, wondrous, vast, surpassing love,
The theme of heavenly hosts above,
And of the saints below!
We only know in part while here;
But when in glory we appear,
Then shall we fully know.

2 It is a mystery divine
Where justice, mercy, truth, combine
God's glory to display!
His righteousness is satisfied,
Since Christ for us in love hath died,
And borne our curse away.

3 'Midst all the changing scenes around,
In this no change can e'er be found,
For God himself is love.
Though earthly things shall all decay,
And heaven and earth shall pass away,
Yet this shall ne'er remove.

4 Once loved in Christ, for ever loved!
God's counsel'd purpose stands unmov'd,
Eternally the same:
And when we change this house of clay,
We shall throughout eternal day
God's endless love proclaim!

ILLA. L. M. CARMINA SACRA.

138 L. M. (45)

Not that we loved God, but that he loved us.

1 ERE earth's foundations yet were laid,
Or heaven's fair roof was spread abroad;
Ere man a living soul was made,
Love stirred within the heart of God.

2 Thy loving counsel gave to me
True life in Christ, thy only Son,
Whom thou hast made my way to thee,
From whom all grace flows ever down.

3 I am not worthy, Lord, that thou
Shouldst such compassion on me show;
That he who made the world should bow
To cheer with love a wretch so low.

4 Could I but honor thee aright,
Noble and sweet my song should be;
That earth and heaven should learn thy might,
And what my God hath done for me.

DESIRE. L. M.

139 L. M. (48)

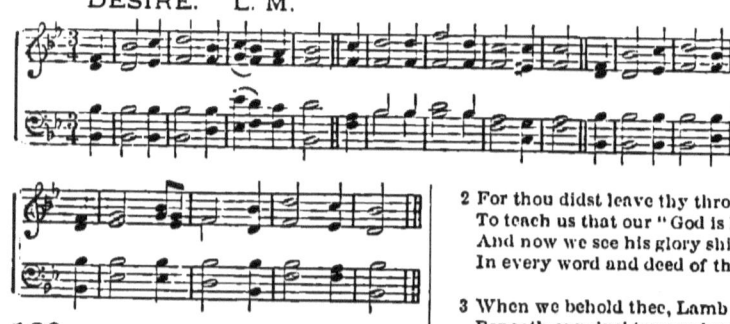

God's Love revealed by Christ.

1 O SPOTLESS Lamb of God, in thee
The Father's holiness we see;
And with delight thy children trace
In thee his wondrous love and grace.

2 For thou didst leave thy throne above,
To teach us that our "God is love;"
And now we see his glory shine
In every word and deed of thine.

3 When we behold thee, Lamb of God,
Beneath our sins' tremendous load,
Expiring on th' accursed tree,
How great our guilt, with grief we see!

4 There we with joy thy grace behold,
Its height and depth can ne'er be told!
It bursts our chains and sets us free,
And sweetly draws our souls to thee!

MOUNT AUBURN. C. M. G. KINGSLEY.

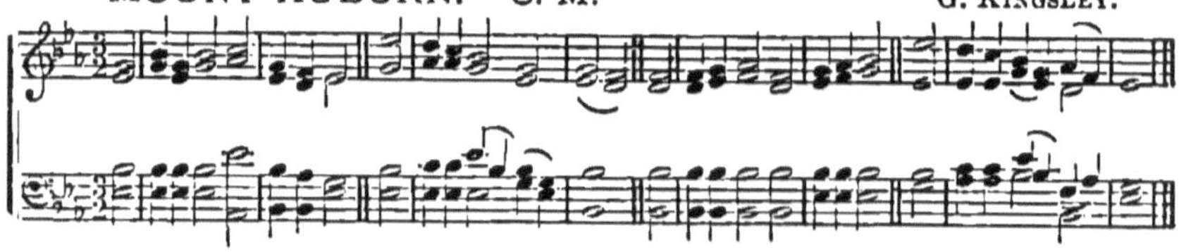

140 C. M. (43)

God is Love.

1 COME, ye that know and fear the Lord,
And raise your souls above;
Let every heart and voice accord
To sing that God is love.

2 This precious truth his word declares,
And all his mercies prove;
While Christ, th' atoning Lamb, appears,
To show that God is love.

3 Behold, his loving kindness waits
For those who from him rove,
And calls of mercy reach their hearts,
To teach them God is love.

4 Oh, may we all, while here below,
This best of blessings prove;
Till warmer hearts, in brighter worlds,
Shall shout that God is love.

141 L. M. (57)

He led them forth by the right Way.

Tune—UXBRIDGE, next page.

1 GIVE thanks to God; he reigns above;
Kind are his thoughts, his name is love;
His mercy ages past have known,
And ages long to come shall own.

2 From age to age exalt his name;
God and his grace are still the same;
He fills the hungry soul with food,
And feeds the poor with every good.

3 He feeds and clothes us all the way,
He guides our footsteps, lest we stray,
He guards us with a powerful hand,
And brings us to the heavenly land.

4 Oh, let the saints with joy record
The truth and goodness of the Lord;
How great his works! how kind his ways!
Let every tongue pronounce his praise.

UXBRIDGE. L. M. DR. L. MASON.

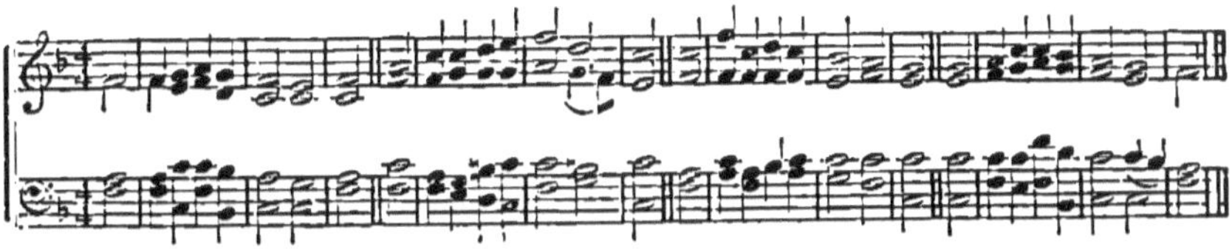

THORNTON. 8s & 7s. E. L. WHITE.

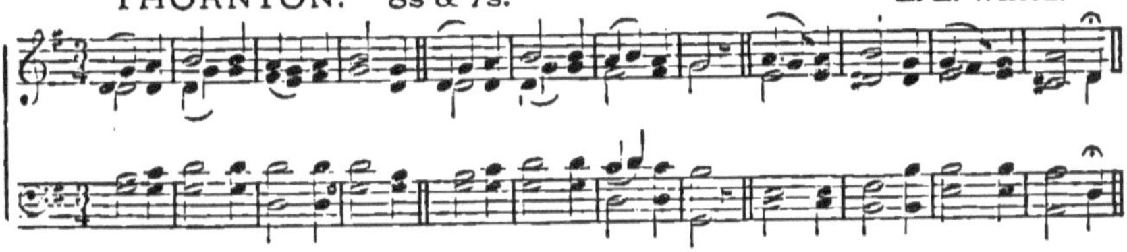

142 *God is Love.* 8s & 7s. (61)

1 GOD is love; his mercy brightens
All the path in which we rove;
Bliss he wakes, and woe he lightens:
God is wisdom, God is love.

2 Death and change are busy ever,
Man decays and ages move;
But his mercy waneth never:
God is wisdom, God is love.

3 E'en the hour that darkest seemeth
Will his changeless goodness prove;
From the gloom his brightness streameth:
God is wisdom, God is love.

4 He with earthly cares entwineth
Hope and comfort from above;
Everywhere his glory shineth:
God is wisdom, God is love.

ERNAN. L. M. DR. L. MASON.

143 L. M. (46)

God's Love seen in Christ.

1 O LOVE of God, how strong and true!
Eternal, and yet ever new;
Uncomprehended and unbought,
Beyond all knowledge and all thought.

2 We read thee best in him who came
To bear for us the cross of shame;
Sent by the Father from on high,
Our life to live, our death to die.

3 We read thy power to bless and save,
E'en in the darkness of the grave;
Still more in resurrection light,
We read the fulness of thy might.

4 O love of God, our shield and stay,
Through all the perils of our way
Eternal love, in thee we rest,
For ever safe, for ever blest!

144 *The Heavens declare God's Glory.* L. M. (57)

Tune—UXBRIDGE, preceding page.

1 The spacious firmament on high,
With all the blue ethereal sky,
And spangled heavens, a shining frame,
Their great original proclaim.

2 Th' unwearied sun, from day to day,
Does his Creator's power display,
And publishes to every land
The work of an Almighty hand.

3 Soon as the evening shades prevail,
The moon takes up the wondrous tale,
And nightly to the listening earth
Repeats the story of her birth;—

4 While all the stars that round her burn,
And all the planets in their turn,
Confirm the tidings as they roll,
And spread the truth from pole to pole.

5 What though, in solemn silence, all
Move round this dark terrestrial ball?
What though no real voice nor sound
Amid their radiant orbs be found?

6 In reason's ear they all rejoice,
And utter forth a glorious voice;
For ever singing, as they shine,
"The hand that made us is Divine."

LYDIA. C. M.

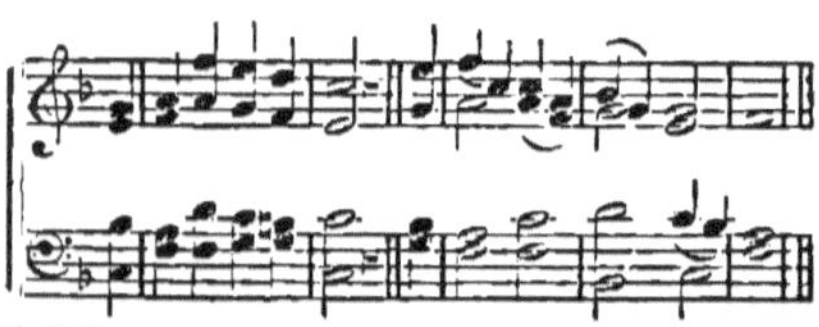

145 C. M. (71)

The Creation praises God.

1 Eternal Wisdom, thee we praise,
Thee the creation sings;
With thy loved name, rocks, hills, and seas,
And heaven's high palace rings.

2 How wide thy hand hath spread the sky!
How glorious to behold!
Tinged with a blue of heavenly dye,
And starred with sparkling gold.

3 Infinite strength and equal skill
Shine through the world abroad,
Our souls with vast amazement fill,
And speak the builder, God.

NEWBOLD. C. M. Geo. Kingsley.

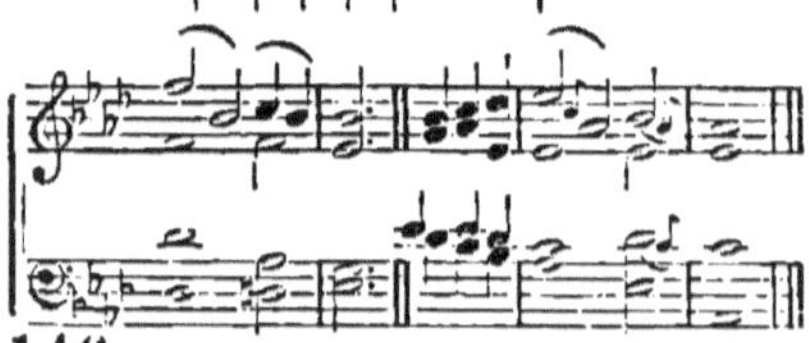

146 C. M. (79)

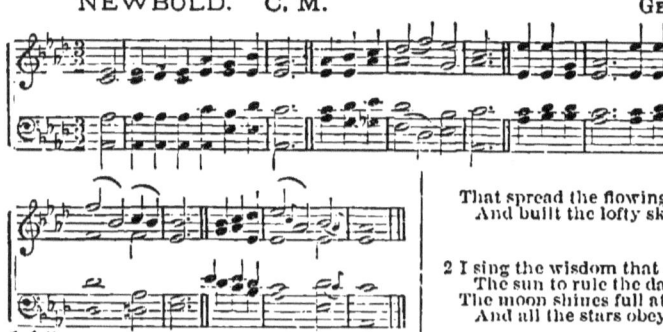

God the Builder of all Things.

1 I sing th' almighty power of God,
That made the mountains rise,
That spread the flowing seas abroad,
And built the lofty skies.

2 I sing the wisdom that ordained
The sun to rule the day;
The moon shines full at his command,
And all the stars obey.

3 I sing the goodness of the Lord,
That filled the earth with food;
He formed the creatures with his word,
And then pronounced them good.

4 There's not a plant or flower below
But makes thy glories known;
And clouds arise and tempests blow,
By order from thy throne.

5 Creatures that borrow life from thee
Are subject to thy care:
There's not a place where we can flee,
But God is present there.

AMES. L. M. Dr. L. Mason.

147 L. M. (54)

O Lord, my God, thou art very great.

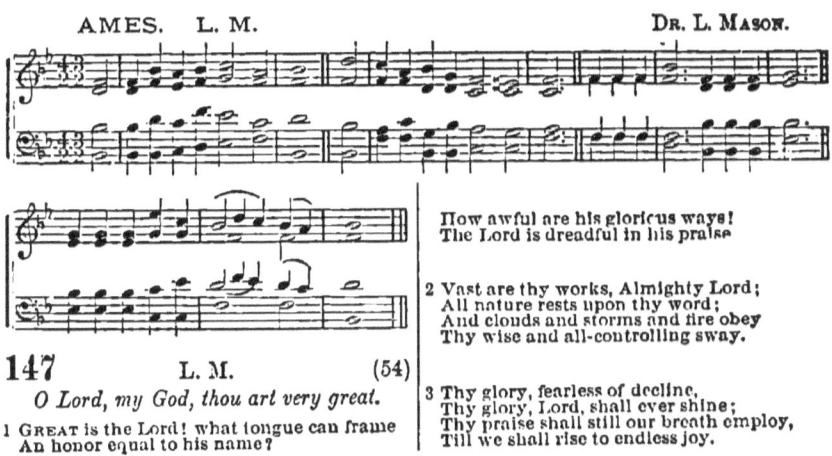

1 Great is the Lord! what tongue can frame
An honor equal to his name?
How awful are his glorious ways!
The Lord is dreadful in his praise.

2 Vast are thy works, Almighty Lord;
All nature rests upon thy word;
And clouds and storms and fire obey
Thy wise and all-controlling sway.

3 Thy glory, fearless of decline,
Thy glory, Lord, shall ever shine;
Thy praise shall still our breath employ,
Till we shall rise to endless joy.

GOVERNING.

CHANNING. H. M. Modern Harp.

148 H. M. (60)

Perfections of God's Government.

1 The Lord Jehovah reigns;
His throne is built on high;
The garments he assumes
Are light and majesty;
His glories shine | No mortal eye
With beams so bright | Can bear the sight.

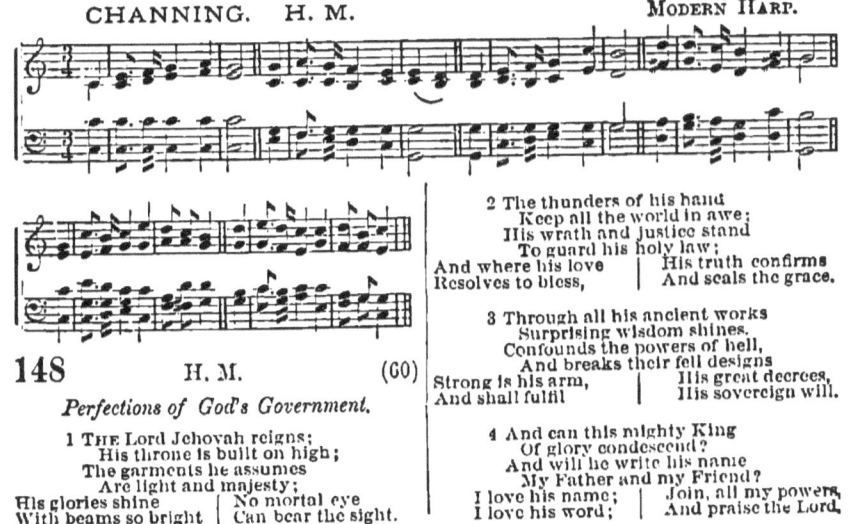

2 The thunders of his hand
Keep all the world in awe;
His wrath and justice stand
To guard his holy law;
And where his love | His truth confirms
Resolves to bless, | And seals the grace.

3 Through all his ancient works
Surprising wisdom shines,
Confounds the powers of hell,
And breaks their fell designs
Strong is his arm, | His great decrees,
And shall fulfil | His sovereign will.

4 And can this mighty King
Of glory condescend?
And will he write his name
My Father and my Friend?
I love his name; | Join, all my powers,
I love his word; | And praise the Lord.

AMES. L. M. DR. L. MASON.

149 L. M. (54)

The Majesty of Jehovah.

1 KINGDOMS and thrones to God belong;
Crown him, ye nations, in your song:
His wondrous name and power rehearse;
His honors shall enrich your verse.

2 He rides and thunders through the sky;
His name, Jehovah, sounds on high:
Praise him aloud, ye sons of grace;
Ye saints, rejoice before his face.

3 God is our shield, our joy, our rest;
God is our King; proclaim him blest:
When terrors rise, when nations faint,
He is the strength of every saint.

DUKE STREET. L. M. J. HATTON.

150 L. M. (52)

Rejoice, for the Lord reigneth.

1 THE Lord is King; lift up thy voice,
O earth, and all ye heavens, rejoice!
From world to world the joy shall ring,
The Lord Omnipotent is King!

2 The Lord is King; child of the dust,
The Judge of all the earth is just:
Holy and true are all his ways;
Let every creature speak his praise.

3 He reigns; ye saints, exalt your strains:
Your God is King, your Father reigns;
And he is at the Father's side,
The Man of love, the Crucified.

4 Come make your wants, your burdens known,
He will present them at the throne;
And angel bands are waiting there,
His messages of love to bear.

5 Oh, when his wisdom can mistake,
His might decay, his love forsake;
Then may his children cease to sing,
The Lord Omnipotent is King!

151 L. M. (52)

Perfections of God combined in his Government.

1 JEHOVAH reigns; his throne is high;
His robes are light and majesty;
His glory shines with beams so bright,
No mortal can sustain the sight.

2 His terrors keep the world in awe;
His justice guards his holy law;
His love reveals a smiling face;
His truth and promise seal the grace.

3 Through all his works his wisdom shines,
And baffles Satan's deep designs;
His power is sovereign to fulfil
The noblest counsels of his will.

4 And will this glorious Lord descend
To be my Father and my friend?
Then let my songs with angels' join;
Heaven is secure, if God be mine.

152 *The eternal Throne of God.* L. M. (52)

Tune—Duke Street, No. 150.

1 Jehovah reigns; he dwells in light,
Girded with majesty and might;
The world, created by his hands,
Still on its firm foundation stands.

2 But ere this spacious world was made,
Or had its first foundation laid,
Thy throne eternal ages stood,
Thyself the ever-living God.

3 Like floods the angry nations rise,
And aim their rage against the skies;
Vain floods that aim their rage so high!
At thy rebuke the billows die.

4 For ever shall his throne endure;
His promise stands for ever sure;
And everlasting holiness
Becomes the dwelling of his grace.

BYEFIELD. C. M. — Dr. T. Hastings.

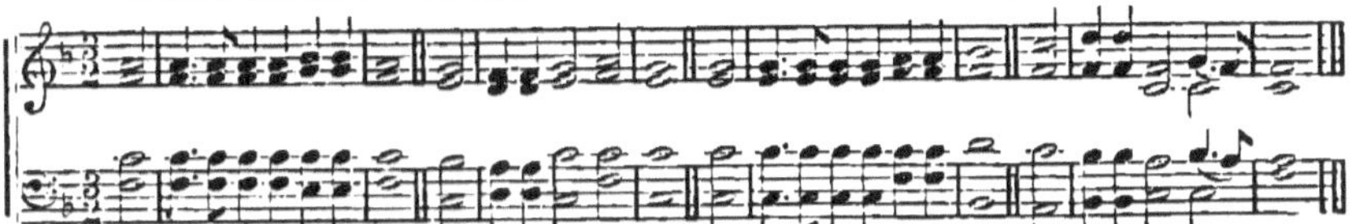

153 *Purposes of God developed by his Providence.* C. M. (56)

1 God moves in a mysterious way,
His wonders to perform;
He plants his footsteps in the sea,
And rides upon the storm.

2 Ye fearful saints, fresh courage take;
The clouds ye so much dread
Are big with mercy, and shall break
With blessing on your head.

3 Judge not the Lord by feeble sense,
But trust him for his grace;
Behind a frowning providence
He hides a smiling face.

4 His purposes will ripen fast,
Unfolding every hour;
The bud may have a bitter taste,
But sweet will be the flower.

5 Blind unbelief is sure to err,
And scan his work in vain;
God is his own interpreter,
And he will make it plain.

ELIZABETHTOWN. C. M. — Geo. Kingsley.

154 C. M. (63)

Benevolence of God's Decrees.

1 Since all the varying scenes of time
God's watchful eye surveys,
Oh, who so wise to choose our lot,
Or to appoint our ways!

2 Good, when he gives, supremely good;
Nor less when he denies:
E'en crosses, from his sovereign hand,
Are blessings in disguise.

3 Why should we doubt a father's love,
So constant and so kind?
To his unerring, gracious will
Be every wish resigned.

155 *God our Defence.* C. M. (56)

Tune—Byefield.

1 No change of time shall ever shock
My trust, O Lord, in thee;
For thou hast always been my rock,
A sure defence to me.

2 Thou our deliverer art, O God;
Our trust is in thy power;
Thou art our shield from foes abroad,
Our safeguard and our tower.

3 To thee we will address our prayer,
To whom all praise we owe;
Oh, may we, by thy watchful care,
Be saved from every foe.

4 Then let Jehovah be adored,
On whom our hopes depend;
For who, except the mighty Lord,
His people can defend?

ERNAN. L. M. DR. L. MASON.

156 L. M. (46)

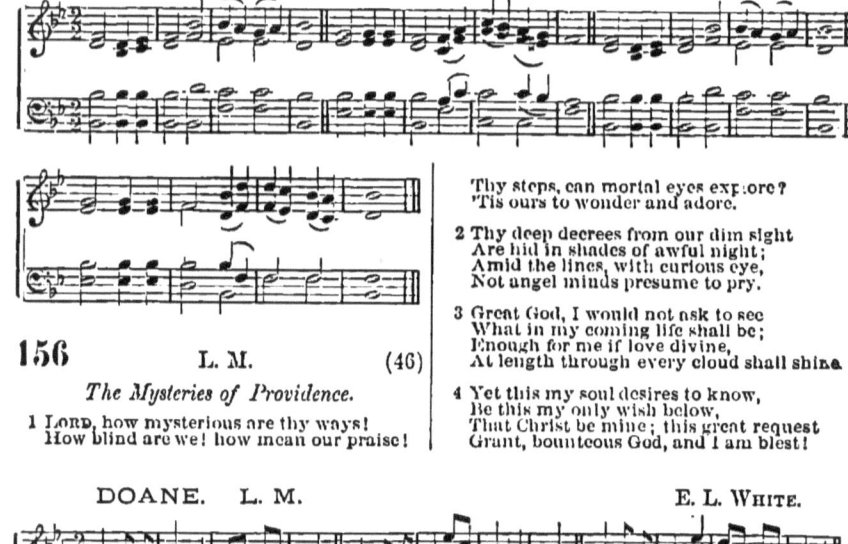

The Mysteries of Providence.

1 LORD, how mysterious are thy ways!
How blind are we! how mean our praise!
Thy steps, can mortal eyes explore?
'Tis ours to wonder and adore.

2 Thy deep decrees from our dim sight
Are hid in shades of awful night;
Amid the lines, with curious eye,
Not angel minds presume to pry.

3 Great God, I would not ask to see
What in my coming life shall be;
Enough for me if love divine,
At length through every cloud shall shine.

4 Yet this my soul desires to know,
Be this my only wish below,
That Christ be mine; this great request
Grant, bounteous God, and I am blest!

DOANE. L. M. E. L. WHITE.

157 L. M. (47)

The Darkness of Providence.

1 LORD, we adore thy vast designs,
Th' obscure abyss of providence,
Too deep to sound with mortal lines,
Too dark to view with feeble sense.

2 When thou dost clothe thine awful face
In angry frowns, without a smile,
We, through the clouds, believe thy grace,
Secure of thy compassion still.

3 Through seas and storms of deep distress
We sail by faith and not by sight;
Faith guides us, in the wilderness,
Through all the terrors of the night.

4 Dear Father, if thy lifted rod
Resolves to scourge us here below,
Still let us lean upon our God;
Thine arm shall bear us safely through.

158 L. M. (58)

Submission to God's Decrees.

Tune—WARD, No. 160.

1 WAIT, O my soul, thy Maker's will;
Tumultuous passions, all be still;
Nor let a murmuring thought arise;
His ways are just, his counsels wise.

2 He in the thickest darkness dwells,
Performs his work, the cause conceals,
But, though his methods are unknown,
Judgment and truth support his throne.

3 In heaven and earth and air and seas
He executes his firm decrees;
And by his saints it stands confessed,
That what he does is ever best.

4 Wait, then, my soul, submissive wait,
Prostrate before his awful seat;
And, 'midst the terrors of his rod,
Trust in a wise and gracious God.

DARWIN. C. M. G. Hews.

159 *God the Trust of his Saints.* C. M. (50)

1 O thou, my light, my life, my joy,
My glory, and my all;
Unsent by thee, no good can come,
Nor evil can befall.

2 Such are thy schemes of providence,
And methods of thy grace,
That I may safely trust in thee
Through all this wilderness.

3 'Tis thine outstretch'd and pow'rful arm
Upholds me in the way;
And thy rich bounty well supplies
The wants of every day.

4 For such compassion, O my God,
Ten thousand thanks are due;
For such compassion I esteem
Ten thousand thanks too few.

WARD. L. M. Arr. by Dr. L. Mason.

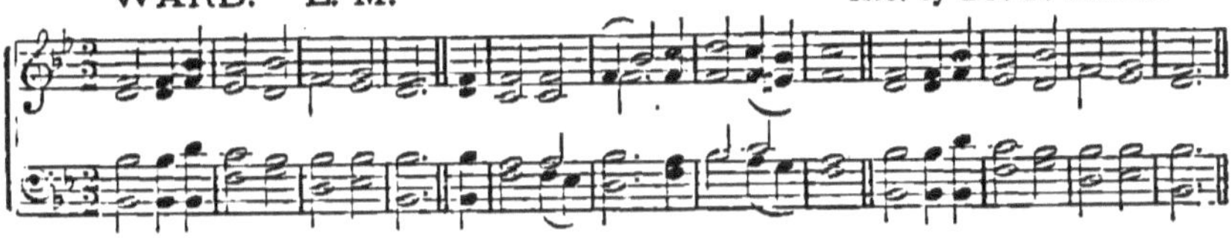

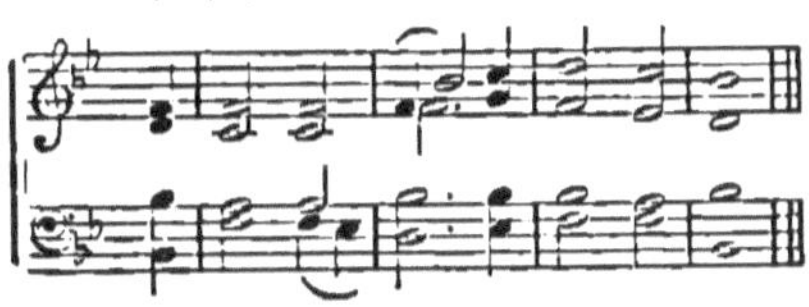

160 *God our Refuge.* L. M. (58)

1 God is the refuge of his saints,
When storms of sharp distress invade;
Ere we can offer our complaints,
Behold him present with his aid.

2 Let mountains from their seats be hurled
Down to the deep, and buried there,
Convulsions shake the solid world,
Our faith shall never yield to fear.

3 Loud may the troubled ocean roar;
In sacred peace our souls abide,
While every nation, every shore,
Trembles and dreads the swelling tide.

4 There is a stream, whose gentle flow
Supplies the city of our God,
Life, love, and joy still gliding through,
And watering our divine abode.

5 That sacred stream, thine holy word
Our grief allays, our fear controls;
Sweet peace thy promises afford,
And give new strength to fainting souls.

CHANNING. H. M. Modern Harp.

161 *God a sure Protection.* H. M. (60)

1 To heaven I lift mine eyes;
From God is all my aid,—
The God who built the skies,
And earth and nature made:
God is the tower | His grace is nigh
To which I fly; | In every hour.

2 My feet shall never slide,
And fall in fatal snares,
Since God, my guard and guide
Defends me from my fears.
Those wakeful eyes | Shall Israel keep
Which never sleep | When dangers rise.

3 No burning heats by day,
Nor blasts of evening air,
Shall take my health away,
If God be with me there:
Thou art my sun, | To guard my head
And thou my shade, | By night or noon.

4 Hast thou not pledged thy word
To save my soul from death?
And I can trust my Lord
To keep my mortal breath:
I'll go and come, | Till from on high
Nor fear to die, | Thou call me home.

MANOAH. C. M. Greatorex.

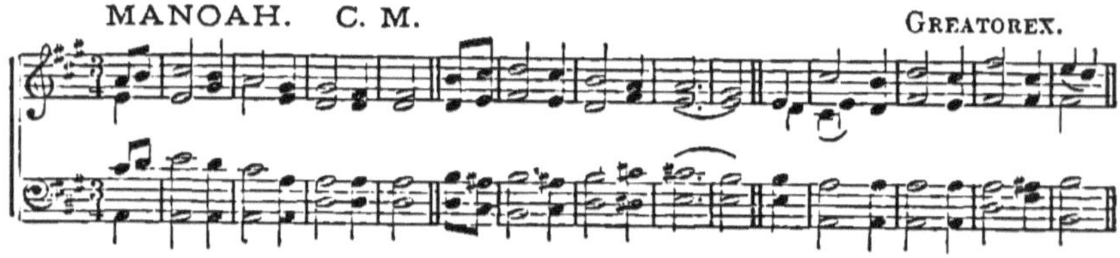

162 C. M. (64)

Submission to a Father's Rule.

1 My God, my Father,—blissful name,—
Oh, may I call thee mine?
May I with sweet assurance claim
A portion so divine?

2 This only can my fears control,
And bid my sorrows fly;
What harm can ever reach my soul,
Beneath my Father's eye?

3 Whate'er thy holy will denies,
I calmly would resign;
For thou art good and just and wise;
Oh, bend my will to thine.

4 Whate'er thy sacred will ordains,
Oh, give me strength to bear;
And let me know my Father reigns,
And trust his tender care.

163 S. M. (72)

The Lord is my Shepherd.

Tune—Boylston, next page.

1 The Lord my shepherd is;
I shall be well supplied:
Since he is mine, and I am his,
What can I want beside?

2 He leads me to the place
Where heavenly pasture grows,
Where living waters gently pass,
And full salvation flows.

3 If e'er I go astray,
He doth my soul reclaim,
And guides me, in his own right way,
For his most holy name.

4 While he affords his aid,
I cannot yield to fear;
Though I should walk through death's dark shade,
My shepherd's with me there.

(continued.)

BOYLSTON. S. M. Dr. L. Mason.

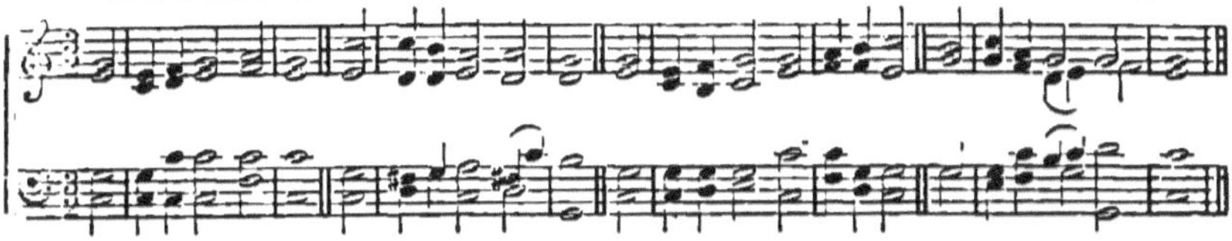

5 In sight of all my foes,
Thou dost my table spread;
My cup with blessings overflows,
And joy exalts my head.

6 The bounties of thy love
Shall crown my future days;
Nor from thy house will I remove,
Nor cease to speak thy praise.

AVON. C. M.

164 *Sovereign Purposes of God.* C. M. (65)

1 Keep silence, all created things,
And wait your Maker's nod;
My soul stands trembling while she sings
The honors of her God.

2 Life, death, and hell, and worlds unknown,
Hang on his firm decree;
He sits on no precarious throne,
Nor borrows leave to be.

3 His providence unfolds a book,
In which his counsels shine;
Each opening leaf, and every stroke,
Fulfils some deep design.

4 Here, he exalts neglected worms
To sceptres and a crown;
And there, the following page he turns,
And casts the monarch down.

5 In thy fair book of life and grace
Oh, may I find my name,
Recorded in some humble place,
Beneath my Lord, the Lamb.

BELVILLE. L. M. 6 lines.

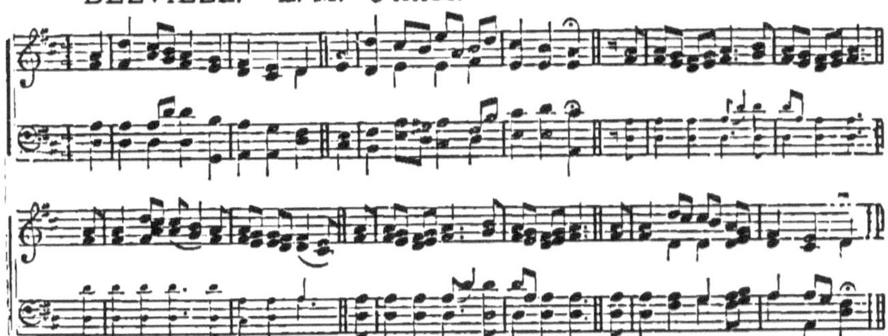

165 *Jehovah the Shepherd of his People.* L. M. 6 L. (62)

1 The Lord my pasture shall prepare,
And feed me with a shepherd's care;
His presence shall my wants supply,
And guard me with a watchful eye;
My noonday walks he shall attend,
And all my midnight hours defend

(CONTINUED.)

2 When in the sultry glebe I faint,
Or on the thirsty mountain pant,
To fertile vales and dewy meads
My weary, wandering steps he leads,
Where peaceful rivers, soft and slow,
Amid the verdant landscape flow.

3 Though in the paths of death I tread,
With gloomy horrors overspread,
My steadfast heart shall fear no ill,
For thou, O Lord, art with me still:
Thy friendly rod shall give me aid,
And guide me through the dreadful shade.

4 Though in a bare and rugged way,
Through devious, lonely wilds I stray,
Thy presence shall my pains beguile;
The barren wilderness shall smile,
With sudden green and herbage crowned,
And streams shall murmur all around.

AMES. L. M. DR. L. MASON.

166 L. M. (54)

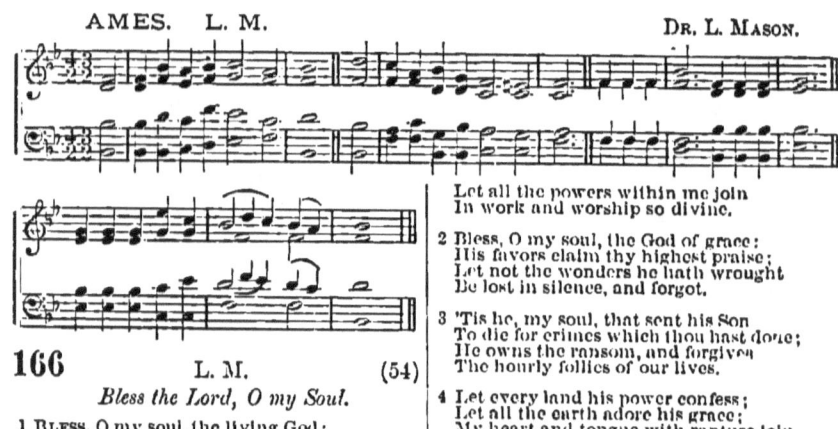

Bless the Lord, O my Soul.

1 BLESS, O my soul, the living God;
Call home thy thoughts that rove abroad:
Let all the powers within me join
In work and worship so divine.

2 Bless, O my soul, the God of grace:
His favors claim thy highest praise;
Let not the wonders he hath wrought
Be lost in silence, and forgot.

3 'Tis he, my soul, that sent his Son
To die for crimes which thou hast done;
He owns the ransom, and forgives
The hourly follies of our lives.

4 Let every land his power confess;
Let all the earth adore his grace;
My heart and tongue with rapture join
In work and worship so divine.

PARK STREET. L. M. VENUA.

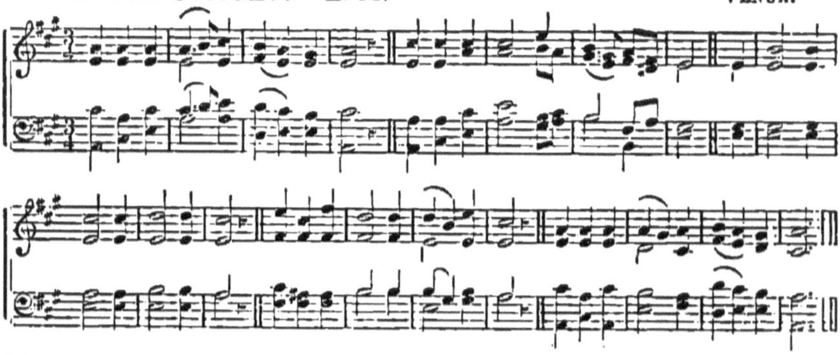

167 *Praise for redeeming Grace.* L. M (51)

1 AWAKE, my tongue; thy tribute bring
To him who gave thee power to sing;
Praise him who has all praise above,
The source of wisdom and of love.

2 How vast his knowledge! how profound!
A depth where all our thoughts are drowned!
The stars he numbers, and their names
He gives to all those heavenly flames.

3 Through each bright world above, behold
Ten thousand thousand charms unfold;
Earth, air, and mighty seas combine
To speak his wisdom all divine.

4 But in redemption, oh, what grace!
Its wonders, oh, what thought can trace!
Here wisdom shines for ever bright;
Praise him, my soul, with sweet delight.

168 *Praise for Christ.* L. M. (51)

Tune—PARK STREET, No. 167.

1 Now to the Lord a noble song!
Awake, my soul, awake, my tongue,
Hosanna to th' eternal name,
And all his boundless love proclaim.

2 See where it shines in Jesus' face,—
The brightest image of his grace;
God, in the person of his Son,
Has al. his mightiest works outdone.

3 Grace! 'tis a sweet, a charming theme;
My thoughts rejoice at Jesus' name;
Ye angels, dwell upon the sound;
Ye heavens, reflect it to the ground.

4 Oh, may I reach the happy place,
Where he unveils his lovely face,
His beauties there may I behold,
And sing his name to harps of gold.

LYDIA. C. M.

169 C. M. (71)

Triumphing in the Grace of God.

1 ARISE, my soul, my joyful powers,
And triumph in my God;
Awake, my voice, and loud proclaim
His glorious grace abroad.

2 He raised me from the deeps of sin,
The gates of gaping hell,
And fixed my standing more secure
Than 'twas before I fell.

3 The arms of everlasting love
Beneath my soul he placed,
And on the Rock of Ages set
My slippery footsteps fast.

4 The city of my bless'd abode
Is walled around with grace;
Salvation for a bulwark stands
To shield the sacred place.

5 Arise, my soul; awake, my voice,
And tunes of pleasure sing;
Loud hallelujahs shall address
My Saviour and my King.

AVON. C. M.

170 *God the Author of Salvation.* C. M. (65)

1 LORD, we confess our numerous faults,
How great our guilt has been:
Foolish and vain were all our thoughts,
And all our lives were sin.

2 But, O my soul, for ever praise,
For ever love his name,
Who turns thy feet from dangerous ways
Of folly, sin, and shame.

3 'Tis not by works of righteousness
Which our own hands have done;
But we are saved by sovereign grace,
Abounding through his Son.

4 Raised from the dead, we live anew;
And, justified by grace,
We shall appear in glory too,
And see our Father's face.

GOD.

DOANE. L. M. E. L. White.

171 L. M. (47)

The Cross shows the Love of God.

1 Inscribed upon the cross we see,
In glowing letters, "God is love;"
He bears our sins upon the tree;
He brings us mercy from above.

2 The cross! it takes our guilt away;
It holds the fainting spirit up;
It cheers with hope the gloomy day,
And sweetens every bitter cup;—

3 The balm of life, the cure of woe,
The measure and the pledge of love,
The sinner's refuge here below,
The angel's theme in heaven above.

172 L. M. (47)

Sovereignty of God in Conversion.

1 May not the sovereign Lord on high
Dispense his favors as he will;
Choose some to life, while others die,
And yet be just and gracious still?

2 Shall man reply against the Lord,
And call his Maker's ways unjust,
The thunder of whose dreadful word
Can crush a thousand worlds to dust?

3 But, O my soul, if truth so bright
Should dazzle and confound thy sight,
Yet still his written will obey,
And wait the great decisive day.

4 Then shall he make his justice known,
And the whole world before his throne,
With joy or terror, shall confess
The glory of his righteousness.

CHRIST.

ORTONVILLE. C. M. Dr. T. Hastings.

173 *Altogether lovely.* C. M. (81)

1 To Christ the Lord let every tongue
Its noblest tribute bring:
When he's the subject of the song,
Who can refuse to sing?

2 Majestic sweetness sits enthroned
Upon his awful brow;
His head with radiant glories crown'd,
His lips with grace o'erflow.

3 No mortal can with him compare,
Among the sons of men;
Fairer he is than all the fair
That fill the heavenly train.

4 He saw me plunged in deep distress,
He flew to my relief;
For me he bore the shameful cross,
And carried all my grief.

5 Since from his bounty I receive
Such proofs of love divine,
Had I a thousand hearts to give,
Lord, they should all be thine.

LUTON. L. M. BURDER.

174

Equal with God. L. M. (89)

1 BRIGHT King of glory! dreadful God!
Our spirits bow before thy seat;
To thee we lift an humble thought,
And worship at thine awful feet.

2 A thousand seraphs, strong and bright,
Stand round the glorious Deity;
But who, among the sons of light,
Pretends comparison with thee?

3 Yet there is one of human frame,
Jesus, arrayed in flesh and blood,
Thinks it no robbery to claim
A full equality with God.

4 Then, let the name of Christ, our King
With equal honors be adored:
His praise let every angel sing,
And all the nations own him Lord

MESSIAH. 7s. J. NETHERCLIFT.

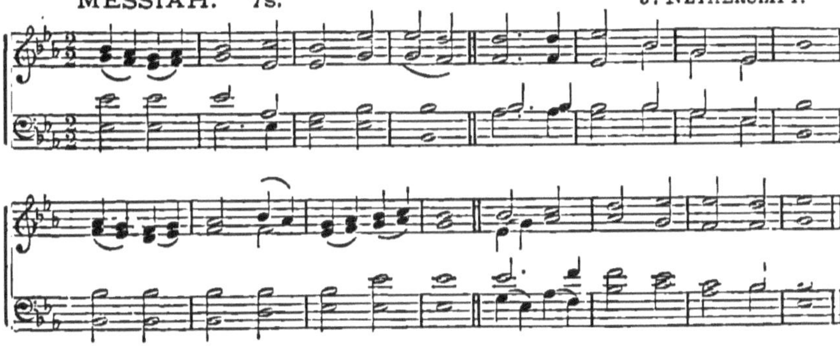

175

Immanuel. 7s. (97)

1 GOD with us! oh, glorious name!
Let it shine in endless fame;
God and man in Christ unite—
Oh, mysterious depth and height!

2 God with us! amazing love
Brought him from his courts above;
Now, ye saints, his grace admire,
Swell the song with holy fire.

3 God with us! oh, wondrous grace!
Let us see him face to face;
That we may Immanuel sing,
As we ought, our God and King.

LEYDEN. L. M. COSTELLO.

1st time.
2d time.

176 *God incarnate.* L. M. (75)

1 Go, worship at Immanuel's feet;
See in his face what wonders meet;
Earth is too narrow to express
His worth, his glory, or his grace.

2 Nor earth, nor seas, nor sun, nor stars,
Nor heaven, his full resemblance bears;
His beauties we can never trace,
Till we behold him face to face.

3 Oh, let me climb those higher skies,
Where storms and darkness never rise:
There he displays his power abroad,
And shines, and reigns, th' incarnate God.

WARNER. L. M.

177 *A Man of Sorrows.* L. M. (92)

1 THE Lord of glory, moved by love,
Descends in mercy from above;
And he, before whom angels bow,
Is found a man of grief below.

2 Such love is great, too great for thought;
Its length and breadth in vain are sought;
No tongue can tell its depth and height;
The love of Christ is infinite.

3 But though his love no measure knows,
The Saviour to his people shows
Enough to give them joy when known,
Enough to make their hearts his own.

4 Constrained by this, they walk with him;
His love their most delightful theme;
To glorify him here, their aim;
Their hope, in heaven to praise his name.

178 *Christ's Commission.* C. M. (67)

Tune—ANTIOCH, next page.

1 COME, happy souls, approach your God,
With new, melodious songs;
Come, render to almighty grace
The tribute of your tongues.

2 So strange, so boundless was the love
That pitied dying men,
The Father sent his equal Son
To give them life again.

3 Here, sinners, you may heal your wounds,
And wipe your sorrows dry;
Trust in the mighty Saviour's name,
And you shall never die.

4 See, dearest Lord, our willing souls
Accept thine offered grace;
We bless the great Redeemer's love,
And give the Father praise.

ANTIOCH. C. M. HANDEL.

179 C. M. (81)

Unto you which believe he is precious.

Tune—ORTONVILLE, No. 173.

1 THE Saviour! oh, what endless charms
Dwell in that blissful sound!
Its influence every fear disarms,
And spreads delight around.

2 Here pardon, life, and joy divine
In rich profusion flow
For guilty rebels, lost in sin,
And doomed to endless woe.

3 The mighty Former of the skies
Descends to our abode,
While angels view with wondering eyes,
And hail th' incarnate God.

4 How rich the depths of love divine!
Of bliss, a boundless store!
Dear Saviour, let me call thee mine;
I cannot wish for more.

180 C. M. (81)

Praise to the Saviour.

Tune—ORTONVILLE, No. 173.

1 COME, ye that love the Saviour's name,
And joy to make it known,
The Sovereign of your hearts proclaim,
And bow before his throne.

2 When in his earthly courts we view
The glories of our King,
We long to love as angels do,
And wish like them to sing.

3 And shall we long and wish in vain?
Lord, teach our songs to rise:
Thy love can raise our humble strain,
And bid it reach the skies.

4 Oh, happy period! glorious day!
When heaven and earth shall raise,
With all their powers, their raptured lay,
To celebrate thy praise.

ROLLAND. L. M. WM. B. BRADBURY.

181 L. M. (69)

Thy Throne, O God, is for ever and ever.

1 Now be my heart inspired to sing
The glories of my Saviour King:
Jesus, the Lord,—how heavenly fair
His form! how bright his beauties are!

2 O'er all the sons of human race
He shines with a superior grace;
Love from his lips divinely flows,
And blessings all his state compose.

3 Thy throne, O God, for ever stands:
Grace is the sceptre in thy hands:
Thy laws and works are just and right:
Justice and grace are thy delight.

CHRISTMAS. C. M. HANDEL.

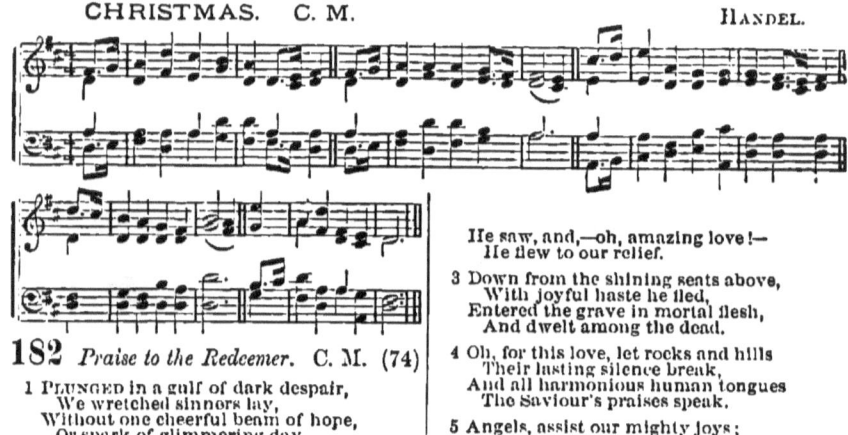

182 *Praise to the Redeemer.* C. M. (74)

1 PLUNGED in a gulf of dark despair,
We wretched sinners lay,
Without one cheerful beam of hope,
Or spark of glimmering day.

2 With pitying eyes the Prince of grace
Beheld our helpless grief;
He saw, and,—oh, amazing love!—
He flew to our relief.

3 Down from the shining seats above,
With joyful haste he fled,
Entered the grave in mortal flesh,
And dwelt among the dead.

4 Oh, for this love, let rocks and hills
Their lasting silence break,
And all harmonious human tongues
The Saviour's praises speak.

5 Angels, assist our mighty joys;
Strike all your harps of gold;
But when you raise your highest notes,
His love can ne'er be told.

ANTIOCH. C. M. HANDEL.

183 C. M. (67)

The Blessings which Christ brings.

1 JOY to the world; the Lord is come!
Let earth receive her King;
Let every heart prepare him room,
And heaven and nature sing.

2 Joy to the earth; the Saviour reigns;
Let men their songs employ;
While fields and floods, rocks, hills, and plains,
Repeat the sounding joy.

3 No more let sins and sorrows grow,
Nor thorns infest the ground;
He comes to make his blessings flow
Far as the curse is found.

4 He rules the world with truth and grace,
And makes the nations prove
The glories of his righteousness,
And wonders of his love.

184 C. M. (67)

Object of Christ's Advent.

1 HARK, the glad sound! the Saviour comes,
The Saviour promised long;
Let every heart prepare a throne,
And every voice a song.

2 He comes, the prisoner to release,
In Satan's bondage held:
The gates of brass before him burst
The iron fetters yield.

3 He comes, the broken heart to bind,
The bleeding soul to cure,
And, with the treasures of his grace,
Enrich the humble poor.

4 Our glad hosannas, Prince of peace,
Thy welcome shall proclaim,
And heaven's eternal arches ring
With thy beloved name.

CHRIST.—BORN.

COLCHESTER. C. M. A. WILLIAMS.

185 C. M. (98)

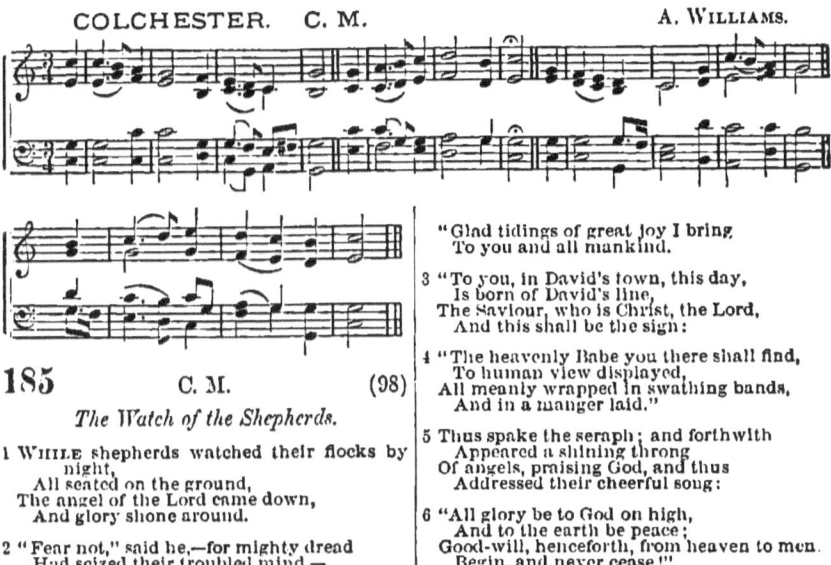

The Watch of the Shepherds.

1 WHILE shepherds watched their flocks by night,
All seated on the ground,
The angel of the Lord came down,
And glory shone around.

2 "Fear not," said he,—for mighty dread
Had seized their troubled mind,—
"Glad tidings of great joy I bring
To you and all mankind.

3 "To you, in David's town, this day,
Is born of David's line,
The Saviour, who is Christ, the Lord,
And this shall be the sign:

4 "The heavenly Babe you there shall find,
To human view displayed,
All meanly wrapped in swathing bands,
And in a manger laid."

5 Thus spake the seraph; and forthwith
Appeared a shining throng
Of angels, praising God, and thus
Addressed their cheerful song:

6 "All glory be to God on high,
And to the earth be peace;
Good-will, henceforth, from heaven to men.
Begin, and never cease!"

HARWELL. 8s & 7s. DR. L. MASON.

186 8s & 7s. (100)

The Song of the Angels.

1 HARK! what mean those holy voices,
Sweetly sounding through the skies?
Lo! th' angelic host rejoices;
Heavenly hallelujahs rise.

2 Hear them tell the wondrous story;
Hear them chant, in hymns of joy,
"Glory in the highest,—glory!
Glory be to God most high!

3 "Peace on earth, good-will from heaven,
Reaching far as man is found;
Souls redeemed, and sins forgiven,"
Loud our golden harps shall sound.

4 "Christ is born, the great Anointed;
Heaven and earth his praises sing;
Oh, receive whom God appointed,
For your Prophet, Priest, and King.'

5 Haste, ye mortals, to adore him;
Learn his name, and taste his joy;
Till in heaven ye sing before him,
"Glory be to God most high!"

HOSANNA. 11s, 12s, & 10s. MODERN HARP

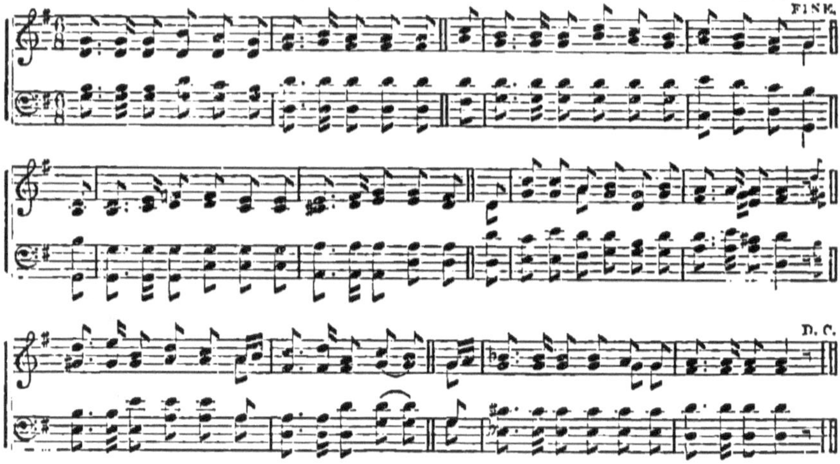
FINE.
D. C.

187

Hosanna to the King. 11s, 12s, & 10s. (73)

1 ZION, the marvellous story be telling,
The Son of the Highest, how lowly his birth!
The brightest of angels in glory excelling,
He stoops to redeem thee, he reigns upon earth.
Shout the glad tidings! exultingly sing,
Jerusalem triumphs! Messiah is King!

2 Tell how he cometh from nation to nation,
The heart-cheering news let the earth echo round,
How free to the sinner he offers salvation,
How his people with joy everlasting are crown'd.
Shout the glad tidings! exultingly sing,
Jerusalem triumphs! Messiah is King!

3 Mortals, your homage be gratefully bringing,
And sweet let the gladsome hosanna arise;
Ye angels, the full hallelujah be singing,
One chorus resound through the earth and the skies.
Shout the glad tidings! exultingly sing,
Jerusalem triumphs! Messiah is King!

TELEMANS. 7s. C. ZEUNER.

188

Christ welcomed. 7s. (105)

1 HARK! the herald angels sing,
"Glory to the new-born King!
Peace on earth, and mercy mild;
God and sinners reconciled."

2 See, he lays his glory by;
Born that man no more may die;
Born to raise the sons of earth;
Born to give them second birth.

3 Hail, the holy Prince of peace!
Hail, the Sun of righteousness!
Light and life to all he brings,
Risen with healing in his wings.

4 Let us then with angels sing,
"Glory to the new-born King!
Peace on earth, and mercy mild,
God and sinners reconciled!"

WARDLAW. C. M.

W. B. BRADBURY.

189

A Light to lighten the Gentiles. C. M. (80)

1 The race that long in darkness pined
Have seen a glorious light;
The people dwell in day, who dwelt
In death's surrounding night.

2 To us a Child of hope is born,
To us a Son is given;
And him shall all the earth obey,
And all the hosts of heaven.

3 His name shall be the Prince of peace,
For evermore adored,
The Wonderful, the Counsellor,
The great and mighty Lord.

4 His power increasing still shall spread;
His reign no end shall know;
His throne shall justice guard above,
And peace abound below.

MISSIONARY CHANT. L. M.

CHARLES ZEUNER.

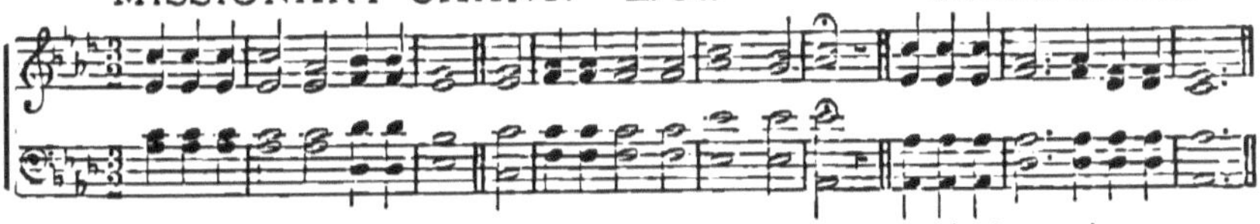

190

Praise to Christ. L. M. (76)

1 Oh, wake our hearts, in gladness sing,
And raise hosannas to our King,
Till living song, from loving souls,
Like sound of mighty waters rolls.

2 O holy Child, thy manger streams
Till earth and heaven glow with its beams,
Till midnight noon's broad light has won,
And Jacob's Star outshines the sun.

3 Thou patriarchs' joy, thou prophets' song,
Thou heavenly Day-spring, looked for long,
Thou Son of man, incarnate Word,
Great David's Son, great David's Lord!

4 Come, Jesus, glorious, heavenly Guest,
Make thine own temple in our breast,
Then David's harp-strings, hushed so long,
Shall swell our jubilee of song.

DORRANCE. 8s & 7s.

I. B. WOODBURY.

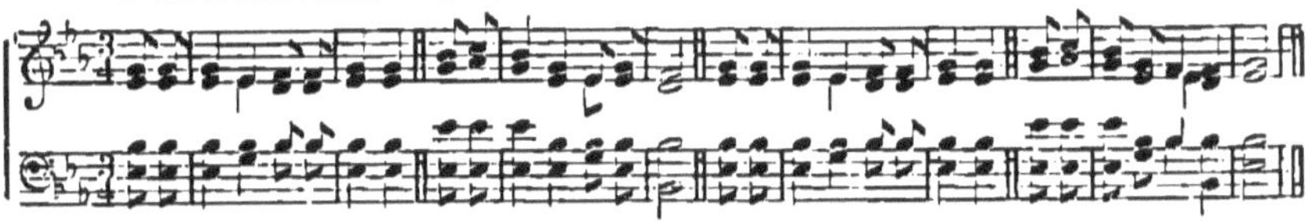

191

Object of Christ's Coming. 8s & 7s. (106)

1 Hail, thou long-expected Jesus,
Born to set thy people free!
From our sins and fears release us;
Let us find our rest in thee.

2 Israel's strength and consolation;
Hope of all the saints thou art;
Long desired of every nation,
Joy of every waiting heart.

3 Born thy people to deliver,
Born a child,—yet God our King,—
Born to reign in us for ever,
Now thy gracious kingdom bring.

4 By thine own eternal Spirit,
Rule in all our hearts alone;
By thine all-sufficient merit,
Raise us to thy glorious throne.

LA MIRA. C. M. Wm. B. Bradbury.

192

The Star of Bethlehem. C. M. (96)

1 Bright was the guiding star that led,
With mild, benignant ray,
The Gentiles to the lowly shed
Where the Redeemer lay.

2 But lo! a brighter, clearer light
Now points to his abode;
It shines through sin and sorrow's night,
To guide us to our God.

3 Oh, haste to follow where it leads;
The gracious call obey,
Be rugged wilds or flowery meads
The Christian's destined way.

4 Oh, gladly tread the narrow path,
While light and grace are given:
Who meekly follow Christ on earth
Shall reign with him in heaven.

BRIGHTEST AND BEST. 11s & 10s. Dr. L. Mason.

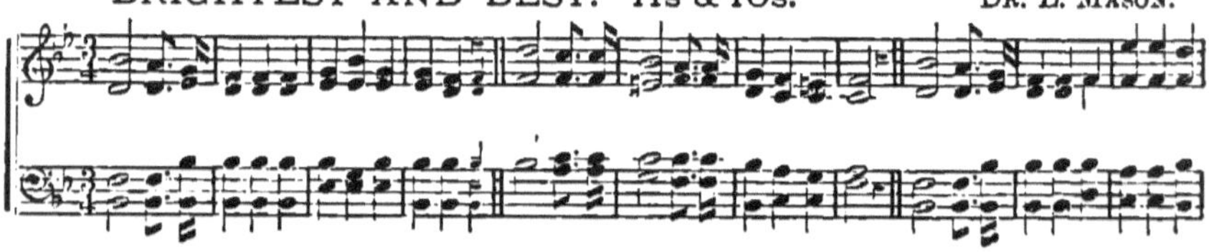

193

The Infant Saviour. 11s & 10s. (96)

1 Brightest and best of the sons of the morning,
Dawn on our darkness, and lend us thine aid;
Star of the east, the horizon adorning,
Guide where the infant Redeemer is laid.

2 Cold, on his cradle, the dew-drops are shining;
Low lies his bed with the beasts of the stall;
Angels adore him in slumber reclining,
Maker and Monarch and Saviour of all.

3 Say, shall we yield him, in costly devotion,
Odors of Eden and offerings divine?
Gems of the mountain, and pearls of the ocean,
Myrrh from the forest, and gold from the mine?

4 Vainly we offer each ample oblation;
Vainly with gifts would his favor secure;
Richer by far is the heart's adoration;
Dearer to God are the prayers of the poor.

194

The Birth of Christ. (75)

Tune—Leyden, No. 195.

1 All praise to thee, eternal Lord!
Clothed in a garb of flesh and blood;
Choosing a manger for thy throne,
While worlds on worlds are thine alone.

2 A little child, thou art our guest,
That weary ones in thee may rest;
Forlorn and lowly is thy birth,
That we may rise to heaven from earth.

3 Thou comest in the darksome night,
To make us children of the light,—
To make us, in the realms divine,
Like thine own angels round thee shine.

4 All this for us thy love hath done;
By this to thee our love is won:
For this we tune our cheerful lays,
And shout our thanks in ceaseless praise.

COSTELLO.

LEYDEN. L. M.

1st time.
2d time.

195 L. M. (75)

Blessed are our Eyes, for they see.

1 ALL glory, worship, thanks, and praise,
That thou art come in these, our days:
Thou heavenly Guest, expected long,
We hail thee with a joyful song.

2 For thee, since first the world was made,
Men's hearts have waited, watched, and prayed;
Prophets and patriarchs, year by year,
Have longed to see thy light appear.

3 Thou art our Head: then, Lord, of thee
True, living members we will be;
And, in the strength thy grace shall give,
Will live as thou wouldst have us live.

4 As each short year goes quickly round,
Our hallelujahs shall resound;
And, when we reckon years no more,
May we in heaven thy name adore.

HAMBURG. L. M. GREGORIAN.

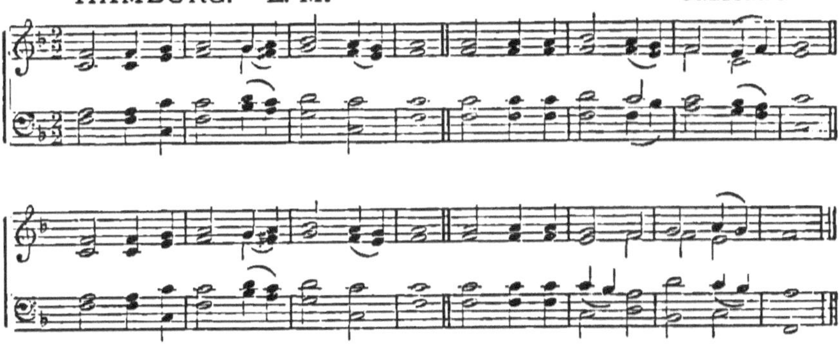

196 *Object of Christ's Advent.* L. M. (88)

1 NOT to condemn the sons of men,
Did Christ, the Son of God, appear;
No weapons in his hands are seen,
No flaming sword nor thunder there.

2 Such was the pity of our God,
He loved the race of man so well,
He sent his Son to bear our load
Of sin, and save our souls from hell.

3 Sinners, believe the Saviour's word;
Trust in his mighty name, and live;
A thousand joys his lips afford,
His hands a thousand blessings give.

SALEM. L. M. PSALMODIST.

197 L. M. (70)

The Cry of the Forerunner.

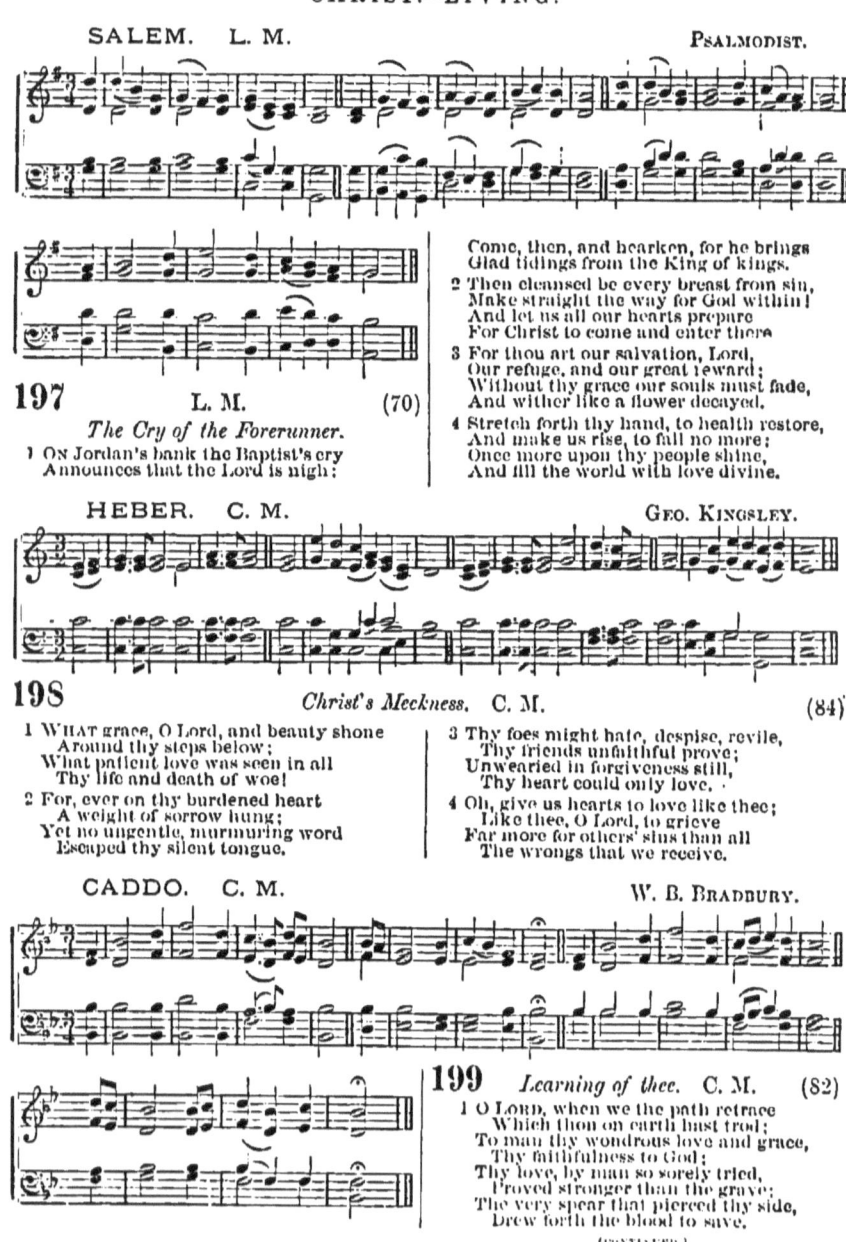

1 On Jordan's bank the Baptist's cry
Announces that the Lord is nigh:
Come, then, and hearken, for he brings
Glad tidings from the King of kings.

2 Then cleansed be every breast from sin,
Make straight the way for God within!
And let us all our hearts prepare
For Christ to come and enter there.

3 For thou art our salvation, Lord,
Our refuge, and our great reward;
Without thy grace our souls must fade,
And wither like a flower decayed.

4 Stretch forth thy hand, to health restore,
And make us rise, to fall no more;
Once more upon thy people shine,
And fill the world with love divine.

HEBER. C. M. GEO. KINGSLEY.

198 *Christ's Meekness.* C. M. (84)

1 What grace, O Lord, and beauty shone
Around thy steps below;
What patient love was seen in all
Thy life and death of woe!

2 For, ever on thy burdened heart
A weight of sorrow hung;
Yet no ungentle, murmuring word
Escaped thy silent tongue.

3 Thy foes might hate, despise, revile,
Thy friends unfaithful prove;
Unwearied in forgiveness still,
Thy heart could only love.

4 Oh, give us hearts to love like thee;
Like thee, O Lord, to grieve
Far more for others' sins than all
The wrongs that we receive.

CADDO. C. M. W. B. BRADBURY.

199 *Learning of thee.* C. M. (82)

1 O Lord, when we the path retrace
Which thou on earth hast trod;
To man thy wondrous love and grace,
Thy faithfulness to God;
Thy love, by man so sorely tried,
Proved stronger than the grave;
The very spear that pierced thy side,
Drew forth the blood to save.

(CONTINUED.)

2 O Lord, with sorrow and with shame,
Before thee we confess
How little we, who bear thy name,
Thy mind, thy ways express.

Give us thy meek, thy lowly mind:
We would obedient be;
And all our rest and pleasure find
In learning, Lord, of thee.

SILOAM. C. M. I. B. WOODBURY.

200 C. M. (44)

The Man of Sorrows.

1 A PILGRIM through this lonely world,
The blessed Saviour passed;
A mourner all his life was he,
A dying lamb at last.

2 That tender heart which felt for all,
For us its life-blood gave;
It found on earth no resting-place,
Save only in the grave.

3 Such was our Lord; and shall we fear
The cross with all its scorn?
Or love a faithless, evil world,
That wreathed his brow with thorn?

4 No; facing all its frowns or smiles,
Like him, obedient still,
We homeward press, through storm or calm,
To Zion's blessed hill.

201 C. M. (82)

When he shall appear we shall be like him.

Tune—CADDO, No. 199.

1 OH! mean may seem this house of clay,
Yet 'twas the Lord's abode;
Our feet may mourn this thorny way,
Yet here Immanuel trod.

2 This fleshly robe the Lord did wear;
This watch the Lord did keep;
These burdens sore the Lord did bear;
These tears the Lord did weep.

3 But not these fleshly robes alone
Shall link us, Lord, to thee;
Nor always in the tear and groan
Shall the dear kindred be.

4 We shall be reckoned for thine own,
Because thy heaven we share;
Because we sing around thy throne,
And thy bright raiment wear.

202 *Christ our Example.* L. M. (70)

Tune—SALEM, No. 197.

1 How beauteous were the marks divine,
That in thy meekness used to shine;
That lit thy lonely pathway, trod
In wondrous love, O Son of God!

2 Oh, who like thee, so calm, so bright,
So pure, so made to live in light—
Oh, who like thee did ever go
So patient through a world of woe?

3 Oh, who like thee so humbly bore
The scorn, the scoffs of men, before?
So meek, forgiving, godlike, high,
So glorious in humility?

4 Oh, in thy light be mine to go,
Illuming all my way of woe:
And give me ever on the road
To trace thy footsteps, Son of God.

WELTON. L. M. DR. MALAN.

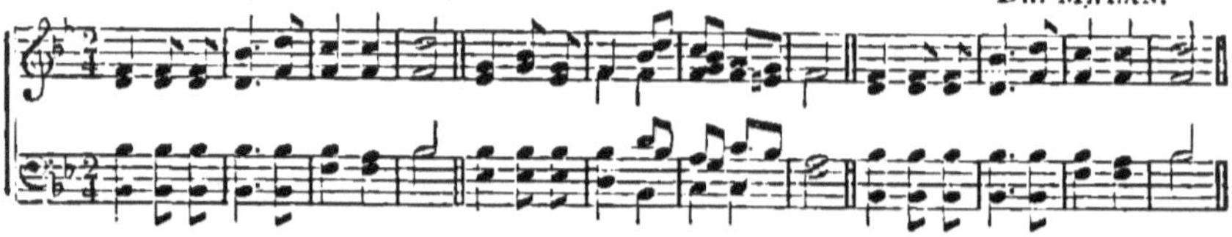

203 L. M. (99)

Following the Example of Christ.

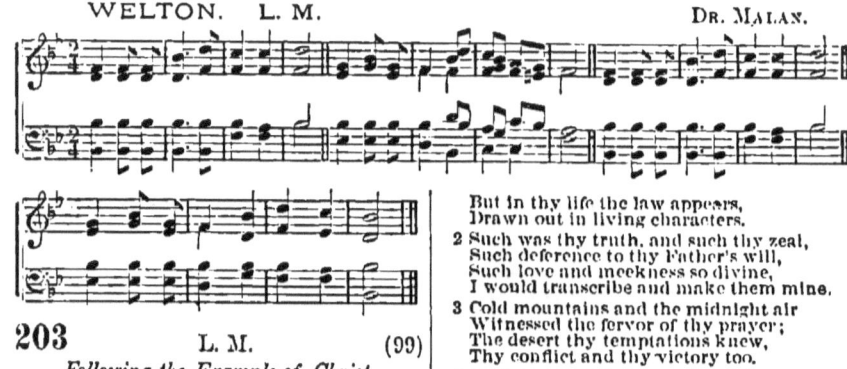

1 My dear Redeemer and my Lord,
I read my duty in thy word;
But in thy life the law appears,
Drawn out in living characters.

2 Such was thy truth, and such thy zeal,
Such deference to thy Father's will,
Such love and meekness so divine,
I would transcribe and make them mine.

3 Cold mountains and the midnight air
Witnessed the fervor of thy prayer;
The desert thy temptations knew,
Thy conflict and thy victory too.

4 Be thou my pattern; make me bear
More of thy gracious image here;
Then God, the Judge, shall own my name
Among the followers of the Lamb.

ELMWOOD. L. M. 6 lines.

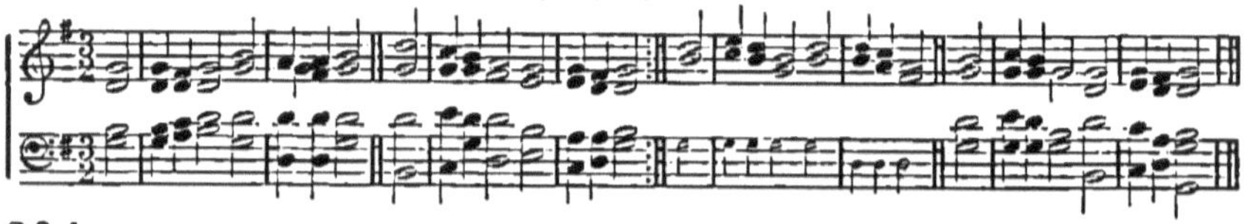

204 *Sympathy of Jesus.* L. M. 6l. (85)

1 When gathering clouds around I view,
And days are dark, and friends are few,
On him I lean, who not in vain
Experienced every human pain;
He sees my wants, allays my fears,
And counts and treasures up my tears.

2 If aught should tempt my soul to stray
From heavenly wisdom's narrow way,
To fly the good I would pursue,
Or do the ill I would not do;
Still he who felt temptation's power
Will guard me in that dangerous hour.

3 When sorrowing o'er some stone I bend,
Which covers all that was a friend,
And from his hand, his voice, his smile,
Divides me for a little while;
Thou, Saviour, seest the tears I shed,
For thou didst weep o'er Lazarus dead.

4 And, oh, when I have safely passed
Through every conflict but the last,
Still, still unchanging, watch beside
My painful bed, for thou hast died;
Then point to realms of cloudless day,
And wipe the latest tear away.

205 C. M. (44)

Imitation of Christ in Self-denial.

Tune—SILOAM, No. 200.

1 We tread the path our master trod;
We bear the cross he bore;
And every thorn that wounds our feet
His temples pierced before.

2 Oft do our eyes with joy o'erflow,
And oft are bathed in tears;
Yet naught but heaven our hopes can raise,
And naught but sin our fears.

3 We purge our mortal dross away,
Refining as we run;
And while we die to earth and sense,
Our heaven is here begun.

206 C. M. (41)

Imitation of Christ.

Tune—SILOAM, No. 200.

1 In duties and in suffering too,
Thy path, my Lord, I'd trace;
As thou hast done, so would I do,
Depending on thy grace.

2 Inflamed with zeal, 'twas thy delight
To do thy Father's will;
Oh, may that zeal my soul excite
Thy precepts to fulfil.

3 Unsullied meekness, truth, and love
Through all thy conduct shine;
Oh, may my whole deportment prove
A copy, Lord, of thine.

ROLLAND. L. M. WM. B. BRADBURY.

4 With shining face and bright array
Christ deigns to manifest to-day
What glory shall be theirs above
Who joy in God with perfect love.

207 *The Transfiguration.* L. M. (69)

1 OH, wondrous type! oh, vision fair
Of glory that the church shall share,
Which Christ upon the mountain shows,
Where brighter than the sun he glows!

2 From age to age the tale declare,
How with the three disciples there,
Where Moses and Elias meet,
The Lord holds converse high and sweet.

3 The Law and Prophets there have place,
Two chosen witnesses of grace;
The Father's voice, from out the cloud,
Proclaims his only Son aloud.

208 *Miracles of Christ.* C. M. (84)

Tune—HEBER, No. 198.

1 AND didst thou, Jesus, condescend,
When veiled in human clay,
To heal the sick, the lame, the blind,
And drive disease away?

2 Didst thou regard the beggar's cry,
And cause the blind to see?
Thou Son of David, hear, oh, hear,
Have mercy, too, on me.

3 And didst thou pity mortal woe,
And sight and health restore?
Oh, pity, Lord, and save my soul,
Which needs thy mercy more.

4 Didst thou thy trembling servant raise,
When sinking in the wave?
I perish, Lord; oh, save my soul;
For thou alone canst save.

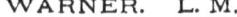

WARNER. L. M.

209 L. M. (92)

It is I; be not afraid.

1 WHEN power divine, in mortal form,
Hushed with a word the raging storm,
In soothing accents, Jesus said,
"Lo, it is I; be not afraid."

2 So, when in silence nature sleeps,
And his lone watch the mourner keeps,
One thought shall every pang remove,
Trust, feeble man, thy Maker's love.

3 God calms the tumult and the storm;
He rules the seraph and the worm;
No creature is by him forgot
Of those who know or know him not.

4 And when the last, dread hour shall come,
While trembling Nature waits her doom,
This voice shall wake the pious dead,
"Lo, it is I; be not afraid."

210

Christ with us. C. M. (85)

Tune—HEBER, No. 198.

1 OH, where is he that trod the sea?
Oh, where is he that spake,
And demons from their victims flee,
The dead their slumbers break?

2 The palsied rise in freedom strong,
The dumb men talk and sing,
And from blind eyes, benighted long,
Bright beams of morning spring.

3 Oh, where is he that trod the sea?
My soul, the Lord is here,
Let all thy fears be hushed in thee:
To leap, to look, to hear,

4 Be thine: thy needs he'll satisfy;
Art thou diseased or dumb,
Or dost thou in thy hunger cry?
"I come," saith Christ, "I come!"

DORRANCE. 8s & 7s. I. B. WOODBURY.

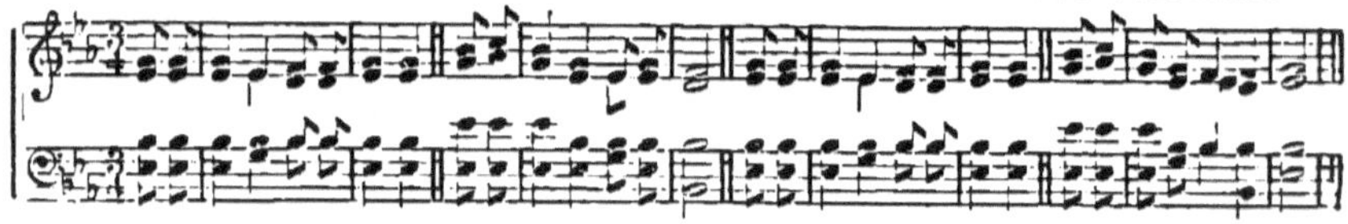

211

Cry of Bartimeus. 8s & 7s. (106)

1 "MERCY, O thou Son of David,"
Thus blind Bartimeus prayed,
"Others by thy word are saved,
Now to me afford thine aid."

2 Many for his crying chid him,
But he called the louder still,
Till the gracious Saviour bid him
"Come, and ask me what you will."

3 "Lord, remove this grievous blindness,
Let mine eyes behold the day!"
Straight he saw, and, won by kindness,
Followed Jesus in the way.

4 Oh, methinks I hear him praising,
Publishing to all around,
"Friends, is not my case amazing?
What a Saviour I have found!"

UXBRIDGE. L. M. DR. L. MASON.

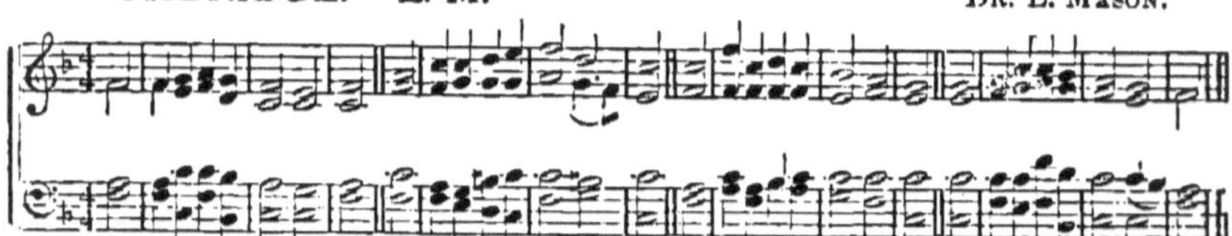

212

L. M. (57)

Christ's Entry into Jerusalem.

1 RIDE on! ride on in majesty!
Hark! all the tribes hosanna cry:
O Saviour meek, pursue thy road
With palms and scattered garments strewed.

2 Ride on! ride on in majesty!
In lowly pomp, ride on to die:
O Christ, thy triumphs now begin
O'er captive death and conquered sin.

3 Ride on! ride on in majesty!
The last and fiercest strife is nigh:
The Father on his sapphire throne
Awaits his own anointed Son.

4 Ride on! ride on in majesty!
In lowly pomp, ride on to die;
Bow thy meek head to mortal pain,
Then take, O God, thy power, and reign.

213

L. M (76)

The Entry into Jerusalem.

Tune—MISSIONARY CHANT, next page

1 WHAT are those soul-reviving strains,
Which echo thus from Salem's plains?
What anthems loud, and louder still,
So sweetly sound from Zion's hill?

2 Lo! 'tis an infant chorus sings
Hosanna to the King of kings:
The Saviour comes; and babes proclaim
Salvation, sent in Jesus' name.

(CONTINUED.)

MISSIONARY CHANT. L. M.

CHARLES ZEUNER

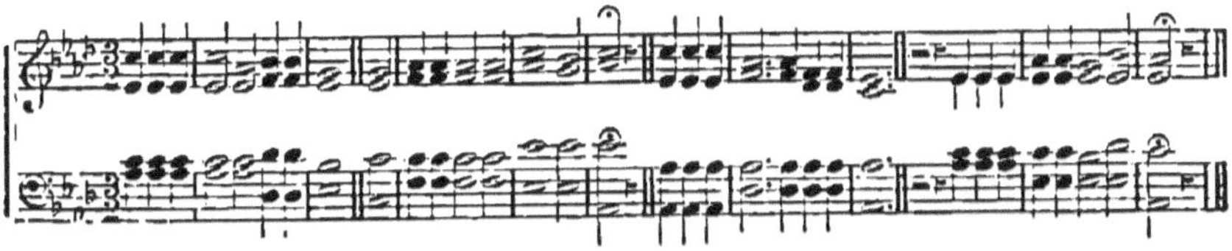

3 Messiah's name shall joy impart
Alike to Jew and Gentile heart:
He bled for us, he bled for you,
And we will sing hosanna too.

4 Proclaim hosannas loud and clear;
See David's Son and Lord appear;
All praise on earth to him be given,
And glory shout through highest heaven

BOYLSTON. S. M.

DR. L. MASON.

214 *Prayer for Likeness to Christ.* S. M. (73)

1 Thou art, O Christ, the way:
Thyself reveal to me;
And let me humbly, day by day,
Live, move, and walk in thee.

2 Thou art the Truth divine:
Its fulness may I see;
Believe, and find the promise mine,—
"The Truth shall make you free."

3 Thou art the Life of God;
By thee the dying live:
In me diffuse thyself abroad,
And life eternal give.

4 Thus, by thyself, the Way,
I to the Father come;
Led by the Truth, I cannot stray:
The Life and I are one.

COLCHESTER. C. M.

A. WILLIAMS.

215 C. M. (98)

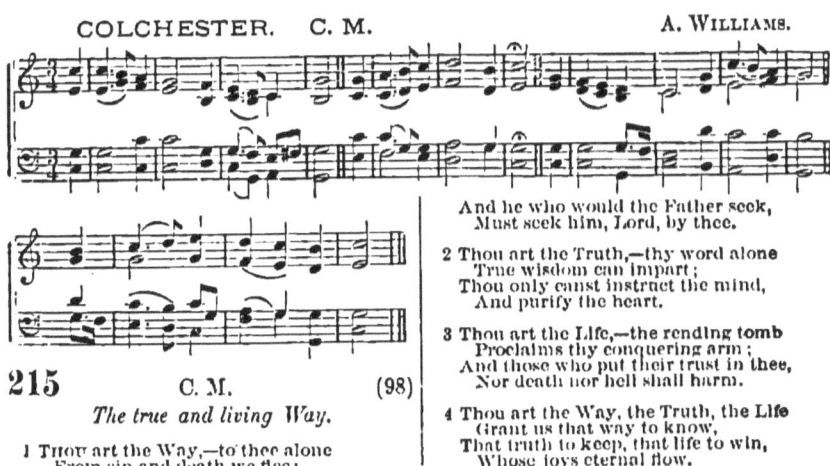

The true and living Way.

1 Thou art the Way,—to thee alone
From sin and death we flee:
And he who would the Father seek,
Must seek him, Lord, by thee.

2 Thou art the Truth,—thy word alone
True wisdom can impart;
Thou only canst instruct the mind,
And purify the heart.

3 Thou art the Life,—the rending tomb
Proclaims thy conquering arm;
And those who put their trust in thee,
Nor death nor hell shall harm.

4 Thou art the Way, the Truth, the Life
Grant us that way to know,
That truth to keep, that life to win,
Whose joys eternal flow.

OLIVE'S BROW. L. M. Wm. B. Bradbury.

216

Christ in Gethsemane. L. M. (101)

1 'Tis midnight; and on Olive's brow
The star is dimmed that lately shone;
'Tis midnight; in the garden, now,
The suffering Saviour prays alone.

2 'Tis midnight; and, from all removed,
The Saviour wrestles lone with fears;
E'en that disciple whom he loved
Heeds not his Master's grief and tears.

3 'Tis midnight; and for others' guilt
The Man of sorrows weeps in blood;
Yet he that hath in anguish knelt
Is not forsaken by his God.

4 'Tis midnight; and from ether plains
Is borne the song that angels know;
Unheard by mortals are the strains
That sweetly soothe the Saviour's woe.

MUSTIN. 8s & 6. Dr. T. Hastings.

217

Gethsemane. 8s & 6. (102)

1 Beyond where Kedron's waters flow,
Behold the suffering Saviour go
To sad Gethsemane;
His countenance is all divine,
Yet grief appears in every line.

2 He bows beneath the sins of men;
He cries to God, and cries again,
In sad Gethsemane;
He lifts his mournful eyes above,
"My Father, can this cup remove?"

3 With gentle resignation still,
He yielded to his Father's will,
In sad Gethsemane;
"Behold me here, thine only Son;
And, Father, let thy will be done."

4 The Father heard; and angels, there,
Sustained the Son of God in prayer
In sad Gethsemane;
He drank the dreadful cup of pain,
Then rose to life and joy again.

5 When storms of sorrow round us sweep,
And scenes of anguish make us weep,
To sad Gethsemane
We'll look, and see the Saviour there,
And humbly bow, like him, in prayer.

BALERMA. C. M.

218 *The Agony of the Garden.* C. M. (83)

1 Dark was the night, and cold the ground
  On which the Lord was laid;
His sweat like drops of blood ran down;
  In agony he prayed:

2 "Father, remove this bitter cup,
  If such thy sacred will;
If not, content to drink it up,
  Thy pleasure I fulfil."

3 Go to the garden, sinner: see
  Those precious drops that flow;
The heavy load he bore for thee;
  For thee he lies so low.

4 Then learn of him the cross to bear;
  Thy Father's will obey;
And when temptations press thee near
  Awake to watch and pray.

GETHSEMANE. 7s. 6 lines. E. L. White.

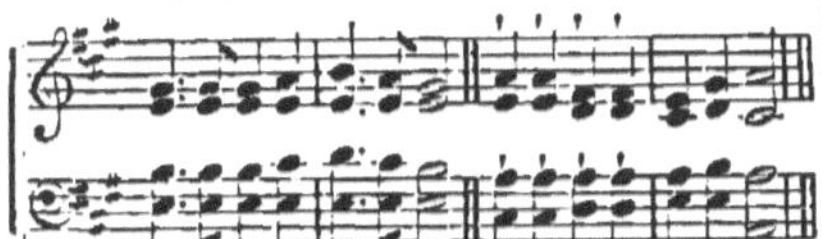

219 7s. 6l. (102)

Christ our Example in Suffering.

1 Go to dark Gethsemane,
  Ye that feel temptation's power;
Your Redeemer's conflict see;
  Watch with him one bitter hour:
Turn not from his griefs away:
Learn of Jesus Christ to pray.

2 Follow to the judgment hall;
  View the Lord of life arraigned;
Oh, the wormwood and the gall!
  Oh, the pangs his soul sustained!
Shun not suffering, shame, or loss;
Learn of him to bear the cross.

3 Calvary's mournful mountain climb;
  There, admiring at his feet,
Mark that miracle of time,
  God's own sacrifice complete:
"It is finished," hear him cry;
Learn of Jesus Christ to die.

220 *Salvation by Christ.* L. M. (101)

Tune—Olive's Brow, No. 216.

1 Behold the sin-atoning Lamb,
  With wonder, gratitude, and love;
To take away our guilt and shame,
  See him descending from above.

2 Our sins and griefs on him were laid;
  He meekly bore the mighty load;
Our ransom-price he fully paid,
  In groans and tears, in sweat and blood.

3 To save a guilty world, he dies;
  Sinners, behold the bleeding Lamb;
To him lift up your longing eyes,
  And hope for mercy in his name.

4 Pardon and peace through him abound;
  He can the richest blessings give;
Salvation in his name is found;
  He bids the dying sinner live.

221 *Looking unto Jesus.* L. M. (101)

Tune—Olive's Brow, No. 216.

1 Saviour, I think upon that hour,
  When thou, the Shepherd of the flock,
The Prince of peace, the Lord of power,
  Wert the priests' scorn, the soldiers' mock.

2 And bleeding from the Roman rod,
  And scoffed at by the heartless Jew,
I hear thee plead for them to God,—
  "Father, they know not what they do."

3 And then I lift my trembling eyes
  To that bright seat, where, placed on high
The great, the atoning sacrifice,
  For me, for all, is ever nigh.

4 Be thou my guard on peril's brink;
  Be thou my guide through weal or woe;
And teach me of thy cup to drink;
  And make me in thy path to go.

GRIFFITH. 7s & 6s. JOHN M. EVANS.

222

Sin wounding Jesus. 7s & 6s. (111)

1 My sins, my sins, my Saviour,
How sad on thee they fall!
Seen through thy gentle patience,
I tenfold feel them all.

2 I know they are forgiven,
But still their pain to me
Is all the grief and anguish
They laid, my Lord, on thee.

3 My sins, my sins, my Saviour,—
Their guilt I never knew,
Till with thee in the desert
I near thy passion drew;

4 Till with thee in the garden
I heard thy pleading prayer,
And saw the sweat-drops bloody
That told thy sorrows there.

MELODY. C. M.

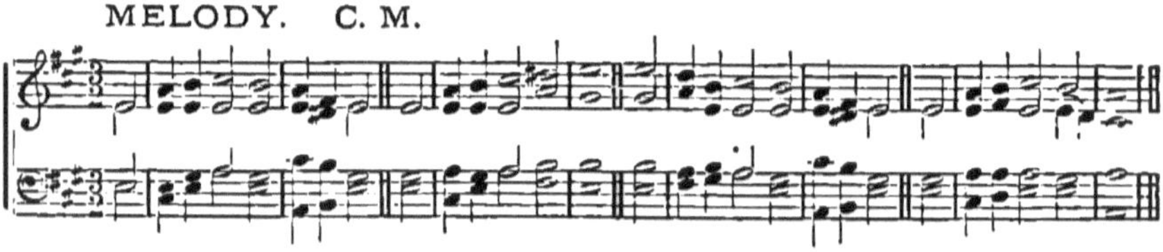

223

C. M. (86)

Humiliation of Christ.

1 And did the holy and the just,
The Sovereign of the skies,
Stoop down to wretchedness and dust,
That guilty man might rise?

2 Yes, the Redeemer left his throne,
His radiant throne on high,—
Surprising mercy! love unknown!—
To suffer, bleed, and die.

3 He took the dying traitor's place,
And suffered in his stead;
For sinful man,—oh, wondrous grace!—
For sinful man he bled.

4 O Lord, what heavenly wonders dwell
In thine atoning blood!
By this are sinners saved from hell,
And rebels brought to God.

224

Christ on the Cross. S. M. (103)

Tune—DENNIS, next page.

1 Behold th' amazing sight,
The Saviour lifted high;
Behold the Son of God's delight
Expire in agony.

2 For whom, for whom, my heart,
Were all these sorrows borne?
Why did he feel that painful smart,
And meet that various scorn?

3 For us he hung and bled,
For us in torture died
'Twas love that bowed his fainting head,
And oped his gushing side.

4 I see, and I adore
In sympathy of love;
I feel the strong, attractive power
To lift my soul above.

5 In thee our hearts unite,
Nor share thy griefs alone,
But from the cross pursue their flight
To thy triumphant throne.

DENNIS. S. M. Arr. from NAGELI.

225

My Saviour. 7s & 6s. (111)

Tune—GRIFFITH, No. 222.

1 O SACRED Head, now wounded!
  With grief and shame bowed down;
O sacred brow, surrounded
  With thorns, thine only crown!
Once on a throne of glory,
  Adorned with light divine,
Now all despised and gory,
  I joy to call thee mine.

2 On me, as thou art dying,
  Oh, turn thy pitying eye!
To thee for mercy crying
  Before thy cross I lie.
Thine, thine the bitter passion,
  Thy pain is all for me;
Mine, mine the deep transgression
  My sins are all on thee.

3 What language can I borrow
  To thank thee, dearest Friend,
For all this dying sorrow,
  Of all my woes the end?
Oh, can I leave thee ever?
  Then do not thou leave me:
Lord, let me never, never
  Outlive my love to thee

PHILLIPS. C. M. I. B. WOODBURY.

226

C. M. (66)

Of whom I am Chief.

1 I SEE the crowd in Pilate's hall,
  I mark their wrathful mien;
Their shouts of "crucify" appal,
  With blasphemy between.

2 And of that shouting multitude
  I feel that I am one;
And in that din of voices rude
  I recognize my own.

3 I see the scourges tear his back,
  I see the piercing crown,
And of that crowd who smite and mock,
  I feel that I am one.

4 'Twas I that shed the sacred blood;
  I nailed him to the tree;
I crucified the Christ of God,
  I joined the mockery.

5 Yet not the less that blood avails
  To cleanse away my sin;
And not the less that cross prevails
  To give me peace within.

227

Sufferings of Christ. L. M. (87)

Tune—WINDHAM, next page.

1 DEEP in our hearts let us record
The deeper sorrows of our Lord;
Behold, the rising billows roll,
To overwhelm his holy soul.

2 Yet, gracious God, thy power and love
Have made the curse a blessing prove;
Those dreadful sufferings of thy Son
Atoned for sins that we had done.

3 The pangs of our expiring Lord
The honors of thy law restored;
His sorrows made thy justice known
And paid for follies not his own.

4 Oh, for his sake our guilt forgive,
And let the mourning sinner live:
The Lord will hear us in his name,
Nor shall our hope be turned to shame.

WINDHAM. L. M. DANIEL READ.

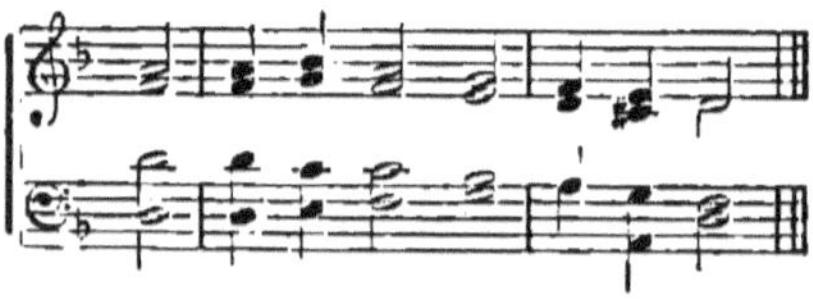

228 *He gave himself for me.* C. M. (83)

Tune—BALERMA, No. 218.

1 ALAS! and did my Saviour bleed?
And did my Sovereign die?
Would he devote that sacred head
For such a worm as I?

2 Was it for crimes that I had done
He groaned upon the tree?
Amazing pity! grace unknown!
And love beyond degree!

3 Well might the sun in darkness hide,
And shut his glories in,
When Christ, the mighty Maker, died
For man the creature's sin.

4 Thus might I hide my blushing face
While his dear cross appears,
Dissolve my heart in thankfulness,
And melt mine eyes to tears.

5 But drops of grief can ne'er repay
The debt of love I owe:
Here, Lord, I give myself away;
'Tis all that I can do.

DENNIS. S. M. Arr. from NAGELI.

229 S. M. (103)

Christ gives his Life for the Sheep.

1 LIKE sheep we went astray,
And broke the fold of God;
Each wandering in a different way,
But all the downward road.

2 How dreadful was the hour
When God our wanderings laid,
And did at once his vengeance pour
Upon the shepherd's head!

3 How glorious was the grace,
When Christ sustained the stroke!
His life and blood the Shepherd pays,
A ransom for the flock.

230 *A dying Saviour.* L. M. (88)

Tune—HAMBURG, next page.

1 STRETCHED on the cross, the Saviour dies,
Hark! his expiring groans arise:
See, from his hands, his feet, his side,
Descends the sacred, crimson tide.

2 And didst thou bleed?—for sinners bleed?
And could the sun behold the deed?
No; he withdrew his cheering ray,
And darkness veiled the mourning day.

3 Can I survey this scene of woe,
Where mingling grief and mercy flow,
And yet my heart so hard remain,
Unmoved by either love or pain?

4 Come, dearest Lord, thy grace impart,
To warm this cold, this stupid heart,
Till all its powers and passions move
In melting grief and ardent love.

HAMBURG. L. M. GREGORIAN.

231

It is finished. C. M. (86)

Tune—MELODY, No. 223.

1 BEHOLD the Saviour of mankind
Upon the shameful tree!
How vast the love that him inclined
To bleed and die for thee!

2 "My God!" he cries; all nature shakes,
And earth's strong pillars bend,
The gate of death in sunder breaks,
The solid marbles rend.

3 "'Tis finished; now the ransom's paid!
Receive my soul!" he cries:
Behold, he bows his sacred head,
He bows his head and dies!

4 But soon he'll break death's tyrant chain,
And in full glory shine:
O Lamb of God, was ever pain,
Was ever love like thine?

PHILLIPS. C. M. I. B. WOODBURY.

232

Christ's great Love. C. M. (66)

1 How condescending and how kind
Was God's eternal Son!
Our misery reached his heavenly mind,
And pity brought him down.

2 He sunk beneath our heavy woes,
To raise us to his throne;
There's ne'er a gift his hand bestows,
But cost his heart a groan.

3 This was compassion, like a God,
That when the Saviour knew
The price of pardon was his blood,
His pity ne'er withdrew.

4 Now, though he reigns exalted high,
His love is still as great;
Well he remembers Calvary,
Nor let his saints forget.

ARAVESTA. 7s.

233 7s. (109)

Sufficiency of Grace in Christ.

1 Weeping saint, no longer mourn;
Surely Christ thy griefs hath borne;
Jesus, best of friends, for thee,
Numbered with transgressors, see!

2 He the wine-press trod alone;
Hear the Man of sorrows groan;
Mocked and bruised, and crowned with thorns,
He his Father's absence mourns.

3 All thy sins, when Jesus bled,
Met on his devoted head;
All thy hope on Jesus place;
Plead his promise, trust his grace.

4 At his feet thy burden lay;
Christ shall smile thy fears away;
He thy guilt and sorrow bore;
Weeping saint, lament no more.

CADDO. C. M. W. B. Bradbury.

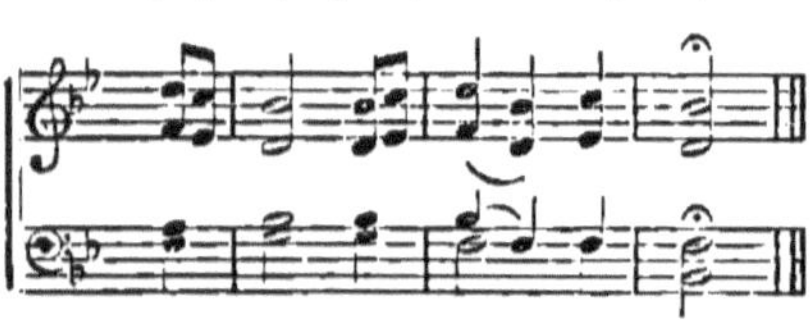

234 C. M. (82)

Redemption by Christ.

1 Behold what pity touched the heart
Of God's eternal Son;
Descending from the heavenly court,
He left his Father's throne.

2 His living power and dying love
Redeemed unhappy men,
And raised the ruins of our race
To life and God again.

3 To thee, O Lord, our noblest powers
We joyfully resign;
Blest Jesus, take us for thy own,
For we are doubly thine.

235 L. M. (99)

The Grace of God in Christ.

Tune—Welton, next page.

1 Nature with open volume stands,
To spread her Maker's praise abroad;
And every labor of his hands
Shows something worthy of a God.

2 But in the grace that rescued man
His brightest form of glory shines,
Here, on the cross, 'tis fairest drawn,
In precious blood and crimson lines.

3 Here I behold his inmost heart,
Where truth and mercy strangely join
To pierce his Son with keenest smart,
And make the purchased pleasures mine.

4 Oh, the sweet wonders of that cross,
Where God, the Saviour, loved and died!
Her noblest life my spirit draws
From his dear wounds and bleeding side.

5 I would for ever speak his name,
In sounds to mortal ears unknown,
With angels join to praise the Lamb,
And worship at his Father's throne.

WELTON. L. M. DR. MALAN.

236 8s, 7s, & 4. (107)

The Voice from Calvary.

Tune—FINNEY.

1 HARK! the voice of love and mercy
Sounds aloud from Calvary;
See! it rends the rocks asunder,
Shakes the earth, and veils the sky:
"It is finished!"
Hear the dying Saviour cry.

2 "It is finished!" Oh, what pleasure
Do these charming words afford!
Heavenly blessings, without measure,
Flow to us from Christ, the Lord:
"It is finished!"
Saints, the dying words record.

3 Tune your harps anew, ye seraphs;
Join to sing the pleasing theme;
All on earth and all in heaven,
Join to praise Immanuel's name;
Hallelujah!
Glory to the bleeding Lamb!

FINNEY. 8s, 7s, & 4. W. B. BRADBURY.

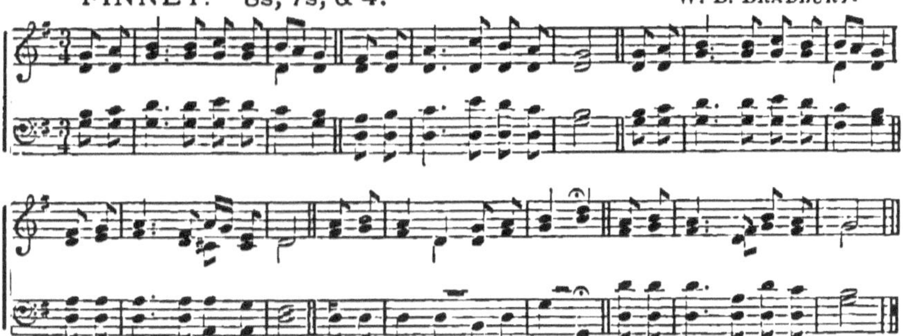

237 *Christ expiring upon the Cross.* L. M. (87)

Tune—WINDHAM, No. 28.

1 "'Tis finished!"—so the Saviour cried,
And meekly bowed his head and died;
"'Tis finished!"—yes, the race is run,
The battle fought, the victory won.

2 "'Tis finished!"—this his dying groan
Shall sins of deepest hue atone,
And millions be redeemed from death
By Jesus' last, expiring breath.

3 "'Tis finished!"—Heaven is reconciled,
And all the powers of darkness spoiled;
Peace, love, and happiness again
Return, and dwell with sinful men.

4 "'Tis finished!"—let the joyful sound
Be heard through all the nations round:
"'Tis finished!"—let the triumph rise,
And swell the chorus of the skies.

SEYMOUR. 7s. GREATOREX.

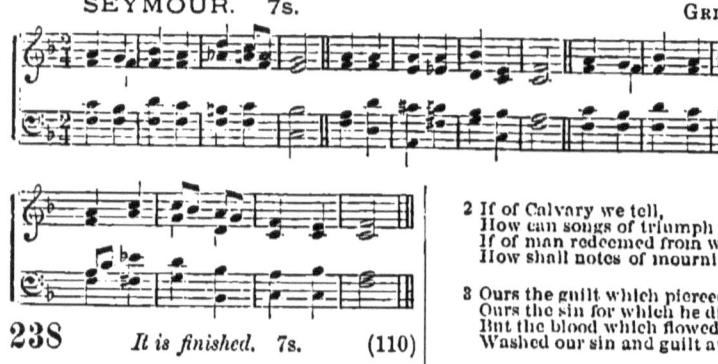

238 *It is finished.* 7s. (110)

1 "IT is finished!" shall we raise
Songs of sorrow, or of praise?
Mourn to see the Saviour die,
Or proclaim his victory?

2 If of Calvary we tell,
How can songs of triumph swell?
If of man redeemed from woe,
How shall notes of mourning flow?

3 Ours the guilt which pierced his side;
Ours the sin for which he died;
But the blood which flowed that day
Washed our sin and guilt away.

4 Lamb of God! thy death hath given
Pardon, peace, and hope of heaven:
"It is finished!" let us raise
Songs of thankfulness and praise.

ZEBULON. H. M. DR. L. MASON.

239 H. M. (94)

The efficacious Fountain.

1 FROM thy dear, piercèd side,
Unspotted Lamb of God,
Came forth a mingled stream
Of water and of blood:
My sinful soul | Till every stain
There I would lay, | Is washed away.

2 'Tis from this sacred spring
A sovereign virtue flows,
To heal my painful wounds,
And cure my deadly woes:
Here, then, I'll bathe, | Till not a wound
And bathe again, | Or woe remain.

3 A fountain 'tis, unsealed,
Divinely rich and free,
Open for all who come,
And open, too, for me:
To this pure fount | Come, sinners, come,
Will I repair; | There's mercy there.

240 *He died for me.* C. M. (83)

Tune—BALERMA, No. 218.

1 O JESUS! sweet the tears I shed,
While at thy cross I kneel,
Gaze at thy wounded, fainting head,
And all thy sorrows feel.

2 My heart dissolves to see thee bleed,
This heart so hard before;
I hear thee for the guilty plead,
And grief o'erflows the more.

3 I know this cleansing blood of thine
Was shed, dear Lord, for me,—
For me, for all,—oh, grace divine!—
Who look by faith on thee.

4 O Christ of God! O spotless Lamb!
By love my soul is drawn;
Henceforth, for ever, thine I am;
Here life and peace are born.

241 *Gazing on Christ's Suffering.* 7s & 6s. (111)

Tune—GRIFFITH, No. 222.

1 O CHRIST! what consolation
Doth in our hearts take place,
When we thy toil and passion
Can joyfully retrace.

2 Ah! should we, while thus musing
On our Redeemer's cross,
E'en life itself be losing,
Great gain would be that loss.

3 We give thee thanks unfeigned,
O Jesus! friend in need,
For what thy soul sustainèd,
When thou for us didst bleed.

4 Grant us to lean unshaken
Upon thy faithfulness,
Until to glory taken
We see thee face to face.

HAMBURG. L. M. GREGORIAN.

242 L. M. (88)

O Death, where is thy Sting?

1 HE dies!—the Friend of sinners dies:
Lo! Salem's daughters weep around;
A solemn darkness veils the skies;
A sudden trembling shakes the ground.

2 Here's love and grief beyond degree:
The Lord of glory dies for men!
But, lo! what sudden joys we see,—
Jesus, the dead, revives again!

3 The rising God forsakes the tomb;
Up to his Father's court he flies;
Cherubic legions guard him home,
And shout him welcome to the skies.

4 Break off your tears, ye saints, and tell
How high our great Deliverer reigns;
Sing how he spoiled the hosts of hell,
And led the tyrant Death in chains.

5 Say, "Live for ever, glorious King;
Born to redeem, and strong to save!"
Then ask, "O Death, where is thy sting?
And where thy vict'ry, boasting Grave?"

TELEMANS. 7s. C. ZEUNER.

243 7s. (104)

Sing, O Heavens.

1 SING, O heavens! O earth, rejoice!
Angel harp and human voice,
Round him, as he rises, raise
Your ascending Saviour's praise.

2 Bruisèd is the serpent's head,
Hell is vanquished, Death is dead,
And to Christ, gone up on high,
Captive is Captivity.

3 All his work and warfare done,
He into his heaven is gone,
And beside his Father's throne,
Now is pleading for his own.

244 7s. (105)

Praise for the Resurrection.

1 ANGELS, roll the rock away;
Death, yield up thy mighty prey:
See! he rises from the tomb,—
Rises with immortal bloom.

2 'Tis the Saviour; seraphs, raise
Your triumphant shouts of praise;
Let the earth's remotest bound
Hear the joy inspiring sound.

3 Lift, ye saints, lift up your eyes;
Now to glory see him rise;
Hosts of angels on the road
Hail and sing th' incarnate God.

4 Praise him, all ye heavenly choirs,
Praise him with your golden lyres;
Praise him in your noblest songs;
Praise him from ten thousand tongues.

HADDAM. H. M.

DR. L. MASON.

245 *Captivity led captive.* H. M. (93)

1 THE happy morn is come:
Triumphant o'er the grave,
The Saviour leaves the tomb,
Omnipotent to save:
Captivity is captive led;
For Jesus liveth that was dead.

2 Who now accuseth them,
For whom their Ransom died?
Who now shall those condemn
Whom God hath justified?
Captivity is captive led;
For Jesus liveth that was dead

3 Christ hath the ransom paid;
The glorious work is done;
On him our help is laid,
By him our victory won:
Captivity is captive led;
For Jesus liveth that was dead.

HEBER. C. M.

GEO. KINGSLEY.

246 *The Resurrection Morning.* C. M. (85)

1 BLEST morning, whose young dawning rays
Beheld our rising God,
That saw him triumph o'er the dust,
And leave his dark abode.

2 A silent prisoner in the tomb
The great Redeemer lay,
Till the revolving skies had brought
The third, th' appointed day.

3 Hell and the grave unite their force
To hold our God, in vain;
The sleeping Conqueror arose,
And burst their feeble chain.

4 To thy great name, almighty Lord,
These sacred hours we pay,
And loud hosannas shall proclaim
The triumph of the day.

TELEMANS. 7s.

C. ZEUNER.

247 *The Conqueror of Death.* 7s. (104)

1 CHRIST, the Lord, is risen to-day;
Sons of men and angels say:
Raise your joys and triumphs high;
Sing, ye heavens, and, earth, reply.

2 Love's redeeming work is done,
Fought the fight, the battle won:
Lo! our Sun's eclipse is o'er;
Lo! he sets in blood no more.

(CONTINUED.)

3 Vain the stone, the watch, the seal,
Christ hath burst the gates of hell:
Death in vain forbids his rise,
Christ hath opened paradise.

4 Soar we now where Christ hath led,
Following our exalted head:
Made like him, like him we rise;
Ours the cross, the grave, the skies.

RIALTO. S. M. G. F. Root.

248

He rose for our Justification. S. M. (78)

1 To-day the Saviour rose,
Our Jesus left the dead,
He conquered our malignant foes,
And Satan captive led.

2 He left his glorious throne,
To make our peace with God;
Blessings for ever on his name,
He bought us with his blood.

3 For us his life he paid,
For us the law fulfilled;
On him our load of guilt was laid;
We by his stripes are healed.

4 Ye saints, adore his name,
Who hath such mercy shown;
Ye sinners, love the bleeding Lamb,
And make his praises known.

SILOAM. C. M. I. B. Woodbury.

249

For our Sakes. C. M. (44)

1 Thou, Lord of all, on earth hast dwelt,
Rejected and unknown;
What bitter grief thy heart hath felt,
Endured by thee alone!

2 Thou on the cross didst suffer, too,
More than man's eye could see;
For then the wrath that was our due
Was poured, O Lord, on thee.

3 But thou art risen, and now we know
That thou, in heaven above,
For all God's children here below
Dost feel a brother's love.

4 Oh, may we ever look to thee
For needed grace and strength,
Till we thy face in glory see,
And reign with thee at length.

HOSANNA. 11s, 12s, & 10s. MODERN HARP.

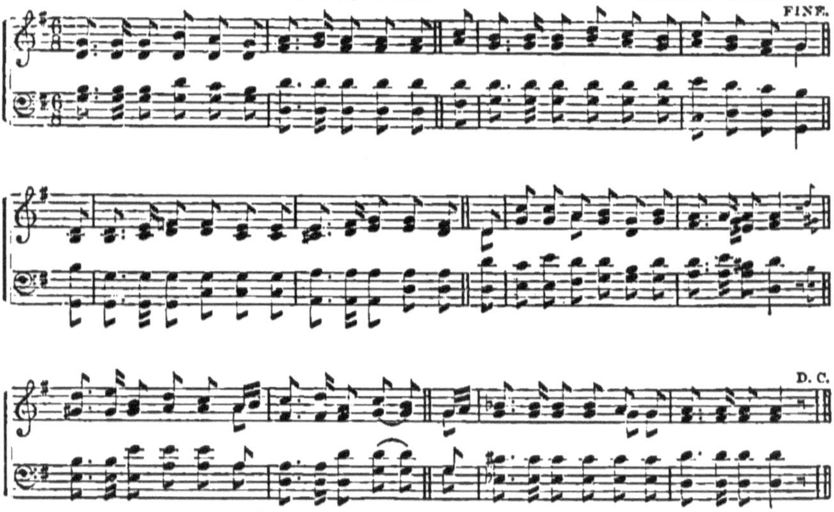
FINE.
D. C.

250 10s, 11s, & 12s. (73)

Death conquered and his Captives rescued.

1 PRAISE the Redeemer, almighty to save;
Immanuel has triumphed o'er Death and the Grave!
Sing, for the door of the dungeon is open,
The Captive came forth at the dawn of the day.
How vain the precautions! the signet is broken;
The watchmen in terror have fled far away.
Praise the Redeemer, almighty to save,
Immanuel has triumphed o'er Death and the Grave.

2 Praise the Redeemer; oh, tell of his love!
In pity to mortals he came from above.
Who shall rebuild for the tyrant his prison?
The sceptre lies broken that fell from his hands.
His dominion is ended; the Lord has arisen,
The helpless shall soon be released from their bands.
Praise the Redeemer, almighty to save,
Immanuel has triumphed o'er Death and the Grave.

251 C. P. M. (59)

The Reviving of Jesus.

Tune—ARIEL, next page.

1 OH, joyful day! oh, glorious hour!
When Jesus, by almighty power,
Revived and left the grave;
In all his works behold him great,
Before, almighty to create,
Almighty now to save.

2 The first begotten from the dead,
He's risen now, his people's head,
And thus our life's secure;
What though this earthly house should fail,
Almighty power will yet prevail,
Our resurrection's sure.

3 Ye ransom'd, let your praise resound,
And in your Master's work abound,
His blessed work of love:
Be sure your labor's not in vain,
For we with Jesus soon shall reign,
With Jesus dwell above.

ARIEL. C. P. M. DR. L. MASON.

CHRISTMAS. C. M. HANDEL.

252 *The Resurrection and Ascension of Christ.* C. M. (74)

1 HOSANNA to the Prince of Light,
Who clothed himself in clay,
Entered the iron gates of death,
And tore the bars away.

2 Now our exalted Saviour reigns,
And scatters blessings down;
Now Jesus fills the middle seat
Of the celestial throne.

3 Raise your devotion, mortal tongues,
To reach his blest abode;
Sweet be the accents of your song
To our incarnate God.

4 Bright angels, strike your loudest strings
Your sweetest voices raise;
Let heaven and all created things
Sound our Immanuel's praise.

MESSIAH. 7s. J. NETHERCLIFT.

253 7s. (97)

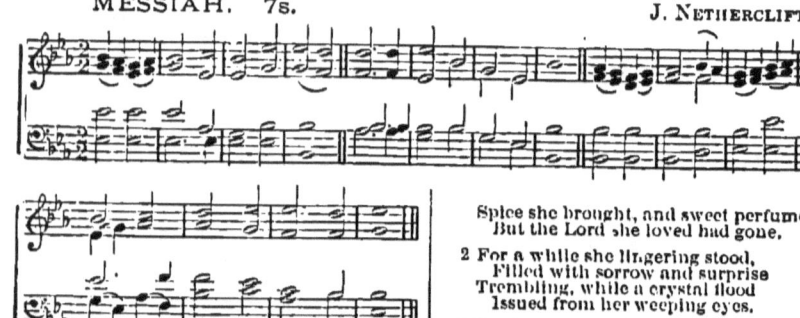

Mary at the Saviour's Tomb.

1 MARY to the Saviour's tomb
Hasted at the early dawn;
Spice she brought, and sweet perfume,
But the Lord she loved had gone.

2 For a while she lingering stood,
Filled with sorrow and surprise
Trembling, while a crystal flood
Issued from her weeping eyes.

3 But her sorrows quickly fled
When she heard his welcome voice:
Christ had risen from the dead;
Now he bids her heart rejoice.

4 What a change his word can make,
Turning darkness into day!
Ye who weep for Jesus' sake,
He will wipe your tears away

CORONATION. C. M. O. HOLDEN.

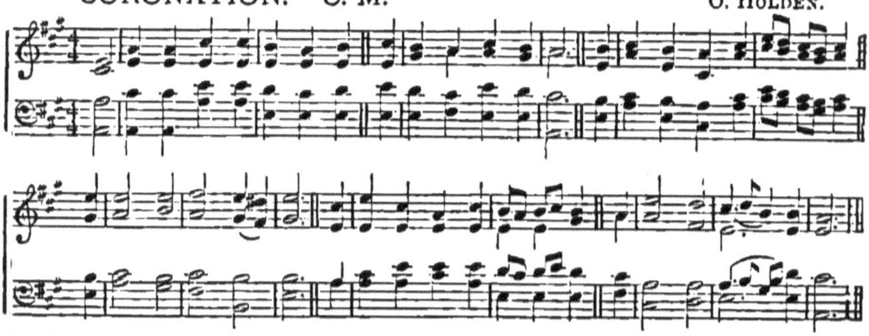

254 *The joyful Tidings.* C. M. (68)

1 "THE Lord is risen,"—oh, what joy
These blessed tidings give!
He died, our enemies to destroy
He lives; we therefore live.

2 "The Lord is risen,"—death and sin
And hell all conquer'd are;
He's gone the holiest within
Our mansion to prepare.

3 "The Lord is risen,"—risen too
With him from sin and death,
Let us the heavenly things pursue,
And die to all beneath.

4 Our place is with him on the throne,
There, with the Lord we love;
As strangers here ourselves we own,
Our hearts, our home above.

255 *A living Saviour.* L. M. (67)

Tune—ROLLAND, next page.

1 THE Saviour lives, no more to die;
He lives, the Lord enthroned on high;
He lives, triumphant o'er the grave;
He lives, eternally to save.

2 He lives, to still his servants' fears;
He lives, to wipe away their tears;
He lives, their mansions to prepare;
He lives, to bring them safely there.

3 Ye mourning souls, dry up your tears;
Dismiss your gloomy doubts and fears;
With cheerful hope your hearts revive,
For Christ, the Lord, is yet alive.

4 His saints he loves, and never leaves;
The contrite sinner he receives:
Abundant grace will he afford,
Till all are present with the Lord.

ROLLAND. L. M. Wm. B. Bradbury.

256 CHANT.—"Jesus Lives." (95)

Behold, I am alive for evermore.

1 Jesus lives!—henceforth is death
But the gate of | life im- | mortal ;‖
This shall calm our trembling breath,
When we | pass its gloomy | portal.

CHANT.—"Jesus Lives." John M. Evans.

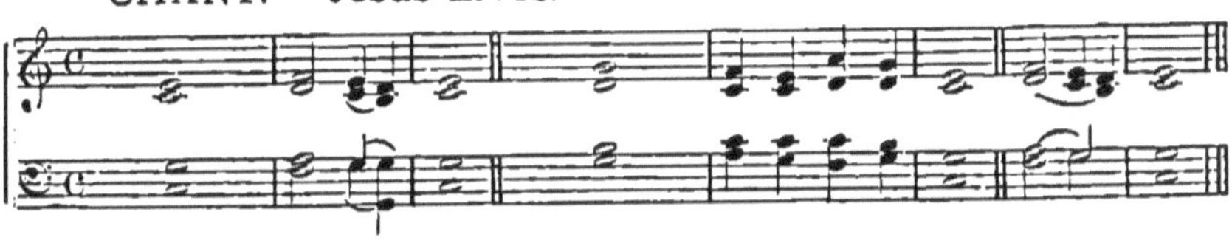

2 Jesus lives!—for us he died;
Then, alone to | Jesus | living,‖
Pure in heart may we abide,
Glory | to our Saviour | giving.

3 Jesus lives!—our hearts know well,
Naught from us his | love shall | sever ;‖
Life, nor death, nor powers of hell,
Tear us | from his keeping | ever.

4 Jesus lives!—to him the throne
Over all the | world is | given :‖
May we go where he is gone,
Rest and | reign with him in | heaven.

PURVES. S. M. Geo. Kingsley.

257 *Redemption completed.* S. M. (77)

1 "The Lord is risen indeed;
He lives to die no more;
He lives the sinners' cause to plead,
Whose curse and shame he bore.

2 "The Lord is risen indeed;"
Then hell has lost his prey;
With him has risen the ransomed seed,
To reign in endless day.

3 "The Lord is risen indeed;"
Attending angels, hear;
Up to the courts of heaven, with speed,
The joyful tidings bear.

4 Then wake your golden lyres,
And strike each cheerful chord;
Join, all ye bright, celestial choirs,
To sing our risen Lord.

LEYDEN. L. M. COSTELLO.

1st time.
2d time.

258 L. M. (75)

Glories attending Christ's Ascension.

1 LORD, when thou didst ascend on high,
Ten thousand angels filled the sky;
Those heavenly guards around thee wait,
Like chariots, that attend thy state.

2 Not Sinai's mountain could appear
More glorious, when the Lord was there;
While he pronounced his holy law,
And struck the chosen .ribes with awe.

3 How bright the triumph none can tell,
When all the rebel powers of hell,
That thousand souls had captive made,
Were all in chains, like captives led.

4 Raised by his Father to the throne,
He sent his promised Spirit down,
With gifts and grace for rebel men,
That God might dwell on earth again.

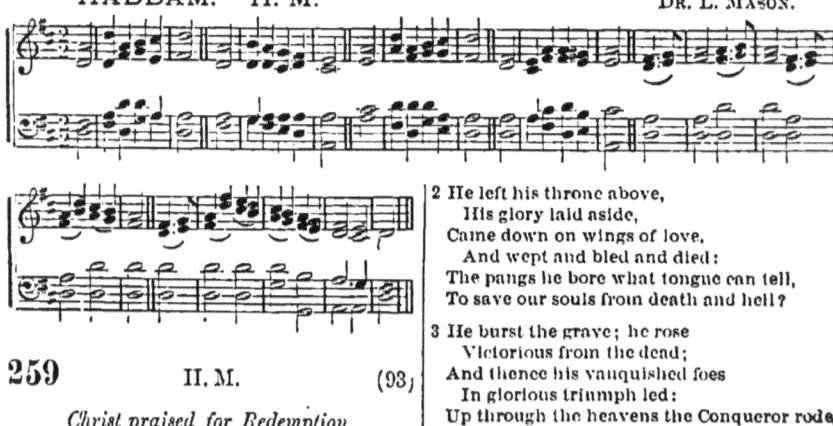

HADDAM. H. M. DR. L. MASON.

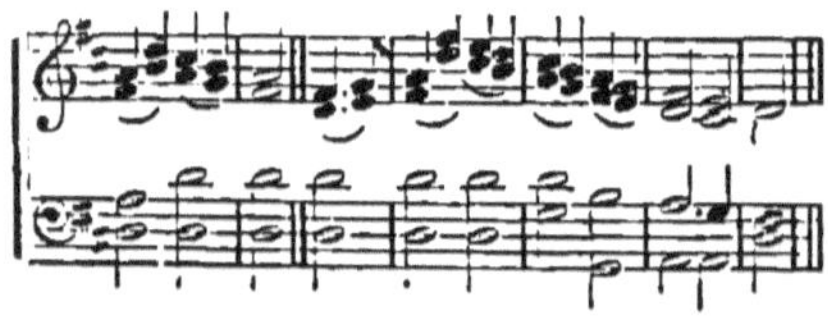

259 H. M. (93)

Christ praised for Redemption

1 COME, ye who love the Lord,
And feel his quickening power,
Unite, with one accord,
His goodness to adore:
To heaven and earth aloud proclaim
Your great Redeemer's glorious name.

2 He left his throne above,
His glory laid aside,
Came down on wings of love,
And wept and bled and died:
The pangs he bore what tongue can tell,
To save our souls from death and hell?

3 He burst the grave; he rose
Victorious from the dead;
And thence his vanquished foes
In glorious triumph led:
Up through the heavens the Conqueror rode,
Triumphant to the throne of God.

4 Soon he again will come,—
His chariot will not stay,—
To take his children home
To realms of endless day:
There shall we see him face to face,
And sing the triumphs of his grace.

MIGDOL. L. M. DR. L. MASON.

260 *Christ's Ascension.* L. M. (105)

1 O SAVIOUR, who for man hast trod
The winepress of the wrath of God,
Ascend and claim again on high
Thy glory left for us to die.

2 A radiant cloud is now thy seat,
And earth lies stretched beneath thy feet;
Ten thousand thousands round thee sing,
And share the triumph of their King.

3 The angel host enraptured waits:
Lift up your heads, eternal gates!
O God and Man, the Father's throne
Is now, for evermore, thine own!

4 Our great High Priest and Shepherd, thou
Within the veil art entered now,
To offer there thy precious blood,
Once poured on earth, a cleansing flood.

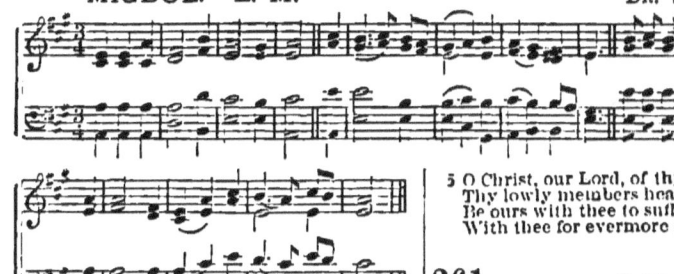

5 O Christ, our Lord, of thy dear care
Thy lowly members heavenward bear;
Be ours with thee to suffer pain,
With thee for evermore to reign.

261 C. M. (68)

Let all the Earth praise Christ.

Tune—CORONATION, No. 254.

1 OH, for a shout of sacred joy
To God, the sovereign King!
Let every land their tongues employ,
And hymns of triumph sing.

2 Jesus, our God, ascends on high;
His heavenly guards around
Attend him rising through the sky,
With trumpets' joyful sound.

3 While angels shout and praise their King,
Let mortals learn their strains;
Let all the earth his honors sing;
O'er all the earth he reigns.

4 Speak forth his praise with awe profound;
Let knowledge guide the song;
Nor mock him with a solemn sound,
Upon a thoughtless tongue.

TELEMANS. 7s. C. ZEUNER.

262 *The King of Glory shall come in.* 7s. (104)

1 HAIL the day that sees him rise
To his throne above the skies;
Christ, the Lamb for sinners given,
Enters now the highest heaven.

2 Lo! the heaven its Lord receives,
Yet he loves the earth he leaves;
Though returning to his throne,
Still he calls mankind his own.

3 Still for us he intercedes,
His prevailing death he pleads,
Near himself prepares our place,
Great Forerunner of our race.

4 Lord, though parted from our sight,
Far above the starry height,
Grant our hearts may thither rise,
Seeking thee above the skies.

BERA. L. M. J. E. GOULD.

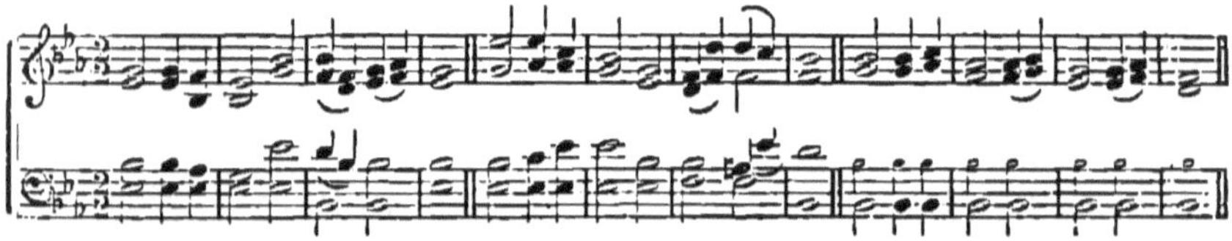

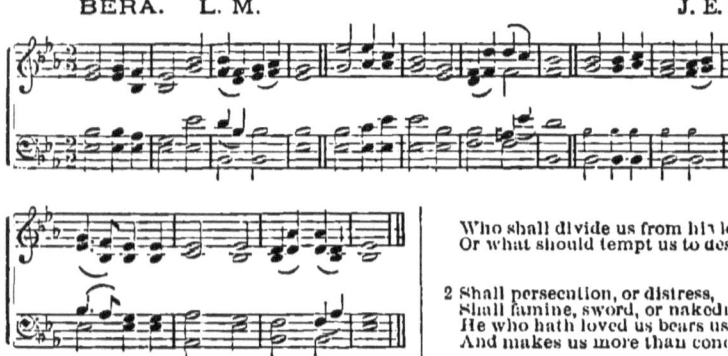

263 *Faithfulness.* L. M. (91)

1 HE lives! he lives! and sits above,
For ever interceding there;
Who shall divide us from his love,
Or what should tempt us to despair?

2 Shall persecution, or distress,
Shall famine, sword, or nakedness?
He who hath loved us bears us through,
And makes us more than conquerors too.

3 Faith hath an overcoming power;
It triumphs in the dying hour:
Christ is our life, our joy, our hope;
Nor can we sink with such a prop.

ZEBULON. H. M. DR. L. MASON.

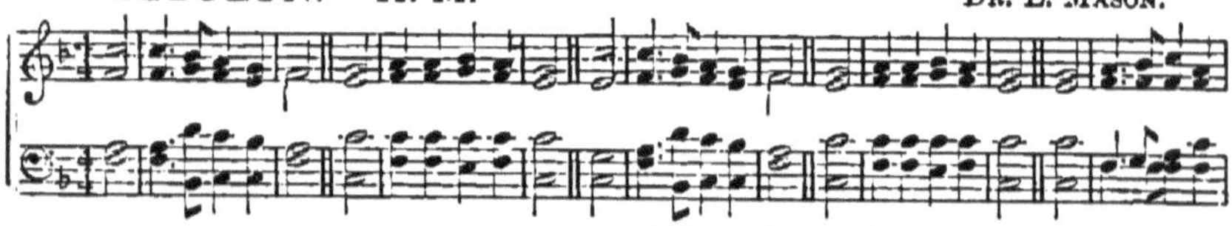

264 H. M. (94)

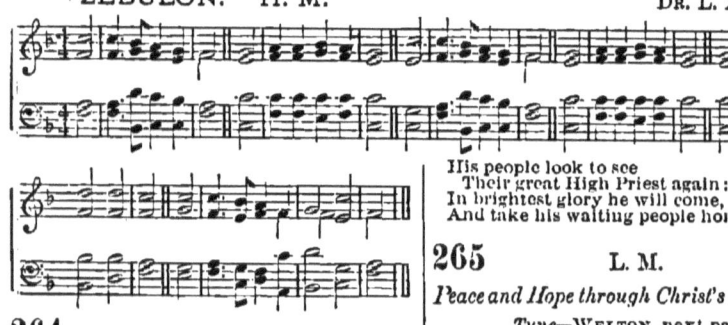

A great High Priest in the Heavens.

1 TH' atoning work is done,
The victim's blood is shed,
And Jesus now is gone
His people's cause to plead:
He stands in heaven, their great High Priest,
And bears their names upon his breast.

No temple made with hands
His place of service is;
In heaven itself he stands,
A heavenly priesthood his:
In him the shadows of the law
Are all fulfilled, and now withdraw.

3 And though awhile he be
Hid from the eyes of men,
His people look to see
Their great High Priest again:
In brightest glory he will come,
And take his waiting people home.

265 L. M. (99)

Peace and Hope through Christ's Intercession.

Tune—WELTON, next page.

1 HE lives! the great Redeemer lives!
What joy the blest assurance gives!
And now, before his Father, God,
He pleads the merits of his blood.

2 Repeated crimes awake our fears,
And justice, armed with frowns, appears;
But in the Saviour's lovely face
Sweet mercy smiles, and all is peace.

3 Hence, then, ye dark, despairing thoughts;
Above our fears, above our faults,
His powerful intercessions rise;
And guilt recedes, and terror dies.

4 Great Advocate, almighty Friend,
On thee our humble hopes depend;
Our cause can never, never fail,
For thou dost plead, and must prevail

WELTON. L. M. — Dr. Malan.

KENNARD. 7s, 8s, & 7s. — Dr. T. Hastings.

266 *Jesus, my Hope and Trust.* 7s, 8s, & 7s. (108)

1 Jesus lives, and so shall I;
 Death, thy sting is gone for ever:
He who deigned for me to die,
 Lives the bands of death to sever.
He shall raise me with the just:
Jesus is my hope and trust.

2 Jesus lives, and God extends
 Grace to each returning sinner;
Rebels he receives as friends,
 And exalts to highest honor.
God is true as he is just;
Jesus is my hope and trust.

3 Jesus lives, and death is now
 But my entrance into glory.
Courage, then, my soul, for thou
 Hast a crown of life before thee:
Thou shalt find thy hopes were just:
Jesus is my hope and trust.

CHRISTMAS. C. M. — Handel.

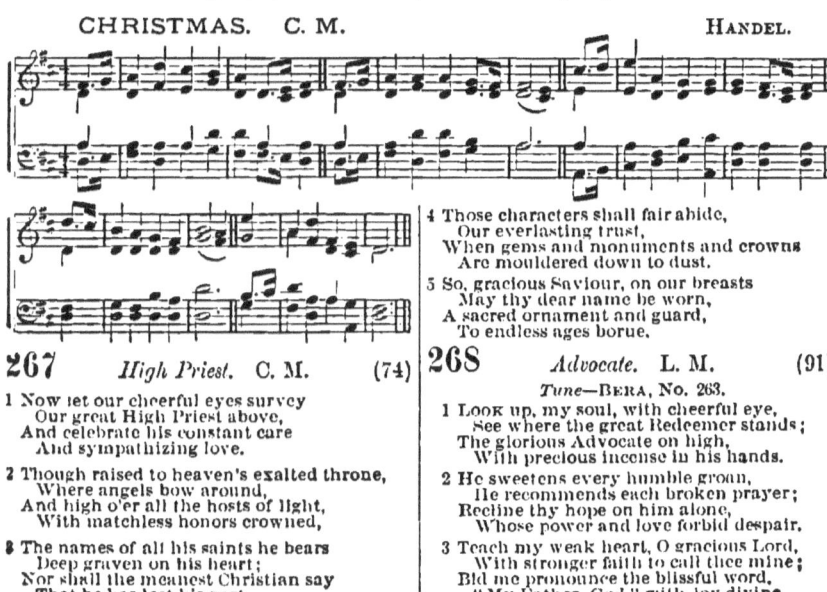

4 Those characters shall fair abide,
 Our everlasting trust,
When gems and monuments and crowns
 Are mouldered down to dust.

5 So, gracious Saviour, on our breasts
 May thy dear name be worn,
A sacred ornament and guard,
 To endless ages borne.

267 *High Priest.* C. M. (74)

1 Now let our cheerful eyes survey
 Our great High Priest above,
And celebrate his constant care
 And sympathizing love.

2 Though raised to heaven's exalted throne,
 Where angels bow around,
And high o'er all the hosts of light,
 With matchless honors crowned,

3 The names of all his saints he bears
 Deep graven on his heart;
Nor shall the meanest Christian say
 That he has lost his part.

268 *Advocate.* L. M. (91)

Tune—Bera, No. 263.

1 Look up, my soul, with cheerful eye,
 See where the great Redeemer stands;
The glorious Advocate on high,
 With precious incense in his hands.

2 He sweetens every humble groan,
 He recommends each broken prayer;
Recline thy hope on him alone,
 Whose power and love forbid despair.

3 Teach my weak heart, O gracious Lord,
 With stronger faith to call thee mine;
Bid me pronounce the blissful word,
 "My Father, God," with joy divine.

LA MIRA. C. M. Wm. B. Bradbury.

269 *Christ a merciful High Priest.* C. M. (96)

1 With joy we meditate the grace
  Of our High Priest above;
His heart is full of tenderness;
  His bosom glows with love.

2 Touched with a sympathy within,
  He knows our feeble frame;
He knows what sore temptations mean,
  For he has felt the same.

3 He, in the days of feeble flesh,
  Poured out his cries and tears,
And in his measure feels afresh
  What every member bears.

4 Then let our humble faith address
  His mercy and his power;
We shall obtain delivering grace
  In each distressing hour.

WARDLAW. C. M. W. B. Bradbury.

270 *A Name above every Name.* C. M. (80)

1 Jesus, in thy transporting name
  What glories meet our eyes!
Thou art the seraphs' lofty theme,
  The wonder of the skies.

2 Well might the heavens with wonder view
  A love so strange as thine;
No thought of angels ever knew
  Compassion so divine.

3 And didst thou, Saviour, leave the sky,
  To sink beneath our woes?
Didst thou descend to bleed and die
  For thy rebellious foes?

4 Oh, may our willing hearts confess
  Thy sweet, thy gentle sway;
Glad captives of thy matchless grace
  Thy righteous rule obey.

CHRIST.—REIGNING.

271 *Christ's Coronation.* C. M. (68)

Tune—Coronation, No. 254.

1 All hail the power of Jesus' name,
  Let angels prostrate fall;
Bring forth the royal diadem,
  And crown him Lord of all.

2 Ye chosen seed of Israel's race,
  A remnant weak and small,
Hail him, who saves you by his grace,
  And crown him Lord of all.

3 Ye Gentile sinners, ne'er forget
  The wormwood and the gall;
Go, spread your trophies at his feet,
  And crown him Lord of all.

4 Let every kindred, every tribe,
  On this terrestrial ball,
To him all majesty ascribe,
  And crown him Lord of all.

5 Oh that, with yonder sacred throng,
  We at his feet may fall!
We'll join the everlasting song,
  And crown him Lord of all.

RIALTO. S. M. G. F. ROOT.

272

Hail to the King. S. M. (78)

1 AWAKE, my soul, and sing
Of him who died for thee;
And hail him as thy matchless King
Through all eternity.

2 Crown him, the Lord of peace,
Whose power a sceptre sways,
From pole to pole, that wars may cease,
Absorbed in prayer and praise.

3 His reign shall know no end;
And round his pierced feet
Fair flowers of Paradise extend
Their fragrance ever sweet.

COLCHESTER. C. M. A. WILLIAMS.

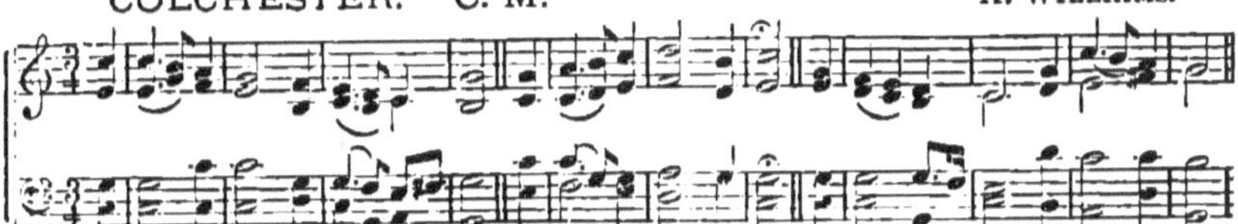

273

C. M. (98)

The Lamb on the Throne.

1 BEHOLD the glories of the Lamb,
Amid his Father's throne;
Prepare new honors for his name,
And songs before unknown.

2 Let elders worship at his feet,
The church adore around,
With vials full of odors sweet,
And harps of sweeter sound.

3 Now to the Lamb that once was slain,
Be endless blessings paid;
Salvation, glory, joy, remain
For ever on thy head!

4 Thou hast redeemed our souls with blood,
Hast set the prisoners free,
Hast made us kings and priests to God,
And we shall reign with thee.

ROCKINGHAM. L. M. DR. L. MASON.

274

L. M. (90)

Blessing and Honor to the Lamb.

1 WHAT equal honors shall we bring
To thee, O Lord our God, the Lamb,
When all the notes that angels sing
Are far inferior to thy name?

2 Worthy is he that once was slain,
The Prince of life that groaned and died
Worthy to rise, and live and reign
At his almighty Father's side.

(CONTINUED.)

3 Honor immortal must be paid,
Instead of scandal and of scorn;
While glory shines around his head,
He wears a crown without a thorn.

4 Blessings for ever on the Lamb,
Who bore the curse for wretched men!
Let angels sound his sacred name,
And every creature say "Amen."

PURVES. S. M. Geo. Kingsley.

275

Song of Moses and the Lamb. S. M. (77)

1 Awake, and sing the song
Of Moses and the Lamb;
Wake, every heart and every tongue,
To praise the Saviour's name.

2 Sing of his dying love;
Sing of his rising power;
Sing, how he intercedes above
For those whose sins he bore.

3 Sing on your heavenly way,
Ye ransomed sinners, sing;
Sing on, rejoicing every day,
In Christ, the eternal King.

4 Soon shall we hear him say,—
"Ye blessed children, come;"
Soon will he call us hence away,
To our eternal home.

5 There shall our raptured tongue
His endless praise proclaim;
And sweeter voices tune the song
Of Moses and the Lamb.

HARWELL. 8s & 7s. Dr. L. Mason.

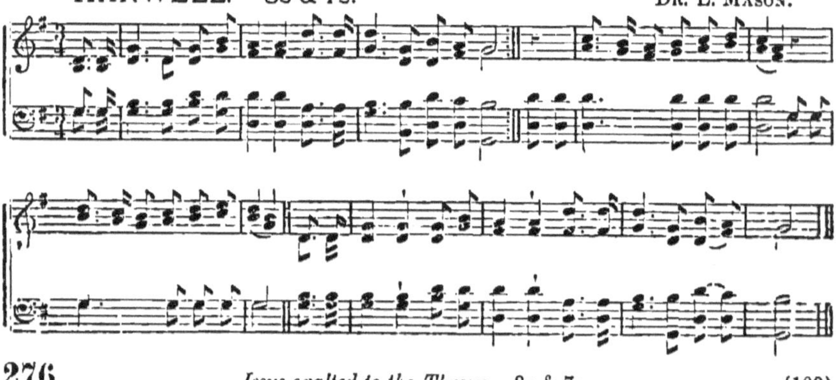

276

Jesus exalted to the Throne. 8s & 7s. (100)

1 Jesus, hail! enthroned in glory,
There for ever to abide;
All the heavenly hosts adore thee,
Seated at thy Father's side.

2 There for sinners thou art pleading;
There thou dost our place prepare;
Ever for us interceding,
Till in glory we appear.

3 Worship, honor, power, and blessing,
Thou art worthy to receive;
Loudest praises, without ceasing,
Meet it is for us to give.

ROLLAND. L. M. WM. B. BRADBURY.

277 L. M. (69)

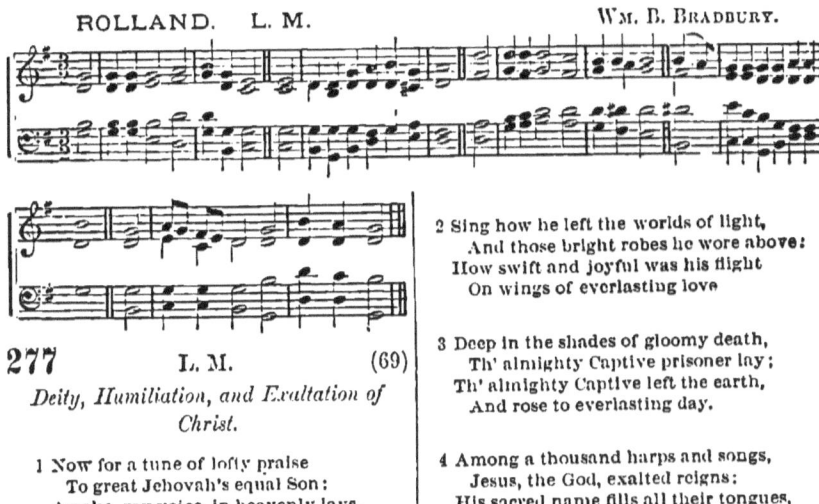

Deity, Humiliation, and Exaltation of Christ.

1 Now for a tune of lofty praise
To great Jehovah's equal Son:
Awake, my voice, in heavenly lays,
And tell the wonders he hath done.

2 Sing how he left the worlds of light,
And those bright robes he wore above:
How swift and joyful was his flight
On wings of everlasting love.

3 Deep in the shades of gloomy death,
Th' almighty Captive prisoner lay;
Th' almighty Captive left the earth,
And rose to everlasting day.

4 Among a thousand harps and songs,
Jesus, the God, exalted reigns:
His sacred name fills all their tongues,
And echoes through the heavenly plains.

ZEBULON. H. M. DR. L. MASON.

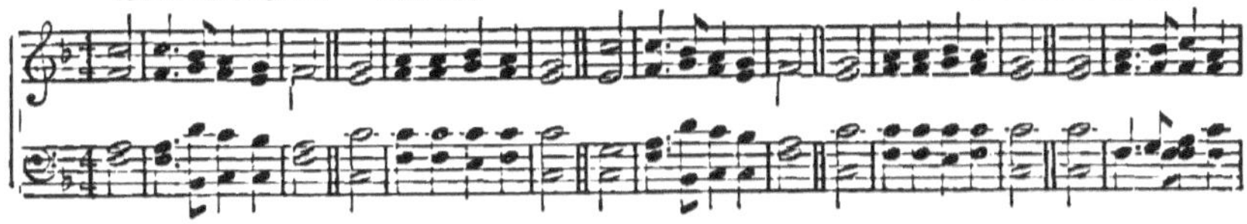

278 H. M. (95)

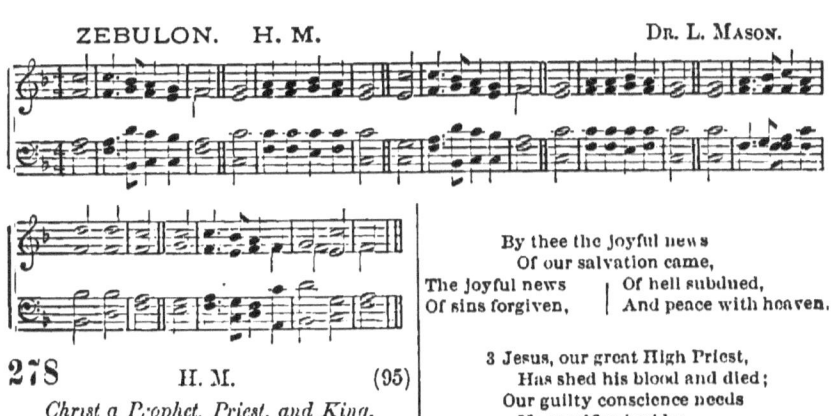

Christ a Prophet, Priest, and King.

1 JOIN all the glorious names
Of wisdom, love, and power,
That ever mortals knew,
Or angels ever bore:
All are too mean | Too mean to set
To speak his worth, | The Saviour forth.

2 Great Prophet of our God,
Our tongues shall bless thy name;
By thee the joyful news
Of our salvation came,
The joyful news | Of hell subdued,
Of sins forgiven, | And peace with heaven.

3 Jesus, our great High Priest,
Has shed his blood and died;
Our guilty conscience needs
No sacrifice beside:
His precious blood | And now it pleads
Did once atone, | Before the throne.

4 O thou almighty Lord
Our Conqueror and our King,
Thy sceptre and thy sword,
Thy reigning grace we sing.
Thine is the power; | In willing bonds
Oh, make us sit | Beneath thy feet.

ARIEL. C. P. M. — Dr. L. Mason.

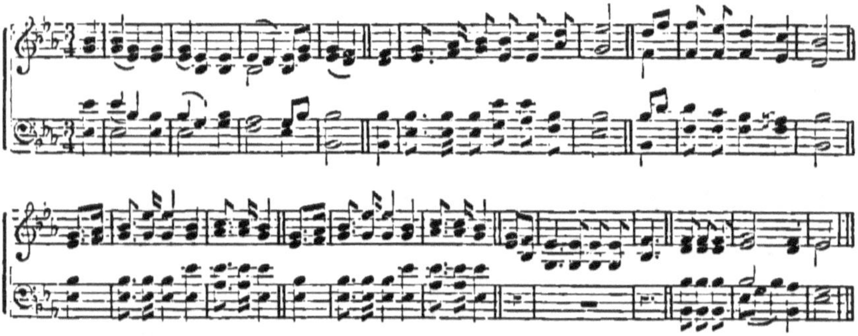

279

The exaltation of Jesus. C. P. M. (59)

1 O blessed Jesus, Lamb of God,
Who hast redeemed us with thy blood,
From sin and death and shame;
With joy and praise thy people see
The crown of glory worn by thee,
And worthy thee proclaim.

2 Exalted by the Father's love,
All thrones and powers and names above,
In earth below or heaven:
Wisdom and riches, power divine,
Blessing and honor, Lord, are thine,
All things to thee are given.

3 Head of the church, thou sittest there,
Thy bride shall all thy glory share:
Thy fulness, Lord, is ours;
Our life thou art, thy grace sustains,
Thy strength in us the vict'ry gains
O'er sin and Satan's powers.

WARDLAW. C. M. — W. B. Bradbury.

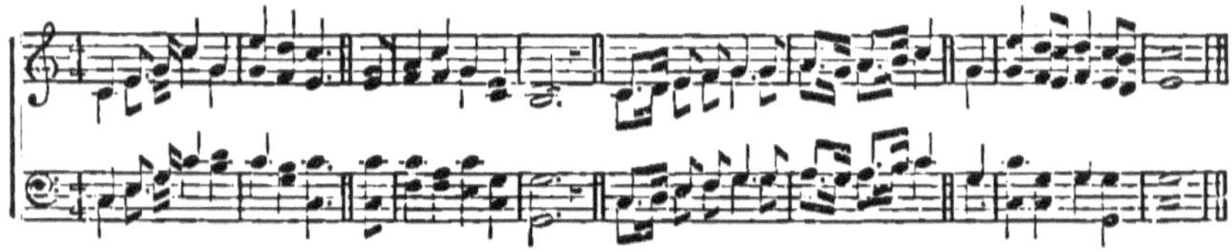

280

One Song in Heaven and Earth. C. M. (50)

1 Come, let us join our cheerful songs
With angels' round the throne;
Ten thousand thousand are their tongues,
But all their joys are one.

2 "Worthy the Lamb that died," they cry,
"To be exalted thus:"
"Worthy the Lamb," our lips reply,
"For he was slain for us."

3 Jesus is worthy to receive
Honor and power divine;
And blessings, more than we can give,
Be, Lord, for ever thine.

4 Let all that dwell above the sky,
And air and earth and seas,
Conspire to lift thy glories high,
And speak thy endless praise.

5 The whole creation join in one
To bless the sacred name
Of him who sits upon the throne,
And to adore the Lamb.

281 *Christ enthroned and worshipped.* 8s & 7s. (100)

Tune—HARWELL, No. 276.

1 HARK! ten thousand harps and voices
Sound the note of praise above;
Jesus reigns, and heaven rejoices;
Jesus reigns, the God of love;
See, he sits on yonder throne;
Jesus rules the world alone.

2 Jesus, hail! whose glory brightens
All above, and gives it worth:
Lord of life, thy smile enlightens,
Cheers, and charms thy saints on earth:
When we think of love like thine,
Lord, we own it love divine.

3 King of glory, reign for ever;
Thine an everlasting crown:
Nothing from thy love shall sever
Those whom thou hast made thine own;
Happy objects of thy grace,
Destined to behold thy face.

4 Saviour, hasten thine appearing;
Bring, oh, bring the glorious day,
When the awful summons hearing,
Heaven and earth shall pass away:
Then, with golden harps, we'll sing,
"Glory, glory to our King."

TELEMANS. 7s. C. ZEUNER.

282 *A victorious Saviour.* 7s. (101)

1 CROWNS of glory ever bright
Rest upon the Conqueror's head;
Crowns of glory are his right,—
His, "who liveth and was dead."

2 He subdued the powers of hell;
In the fight he stood alone:
All his foes before him fell,
By his single arm o'erthrown.

3 His the battle, his the toil;
His the honors of the day;
His the glory and the spoil;
Jesus bears them all away.

4 Now proclaim his deeds afar;
Fill the world with his renown:
His alone the victor's car;
His the everlasting crown.

LUTON. L. M. BURDER.

283 *An ancient Hymn to the Redeemer.* L. M. (89)

1 O CHRIST, our King, Creator, Lord,
Saviour of all who trust thy word,
To them who seek thee ever near,
Now to our praises bend thine ear.

2 In thy dear cross a grace is found,—
It flows from every streaming wound,—
Whose power our inbred sin controls,
Breaks the firm bond, and frees our souls.

3 When thou didst hang upon the tree,
The quaking earth acknowledged thee;
When thou didst there yield up thy breath,
The world grew dark as shades of death.

4 Now in the Father's glory high,
Great Conqueror, never more to die,
Us by thy mighty power defend,
And reign through ages without end.

FINNEY. 8s, 7s, & 4. W. B. BRADBURY.

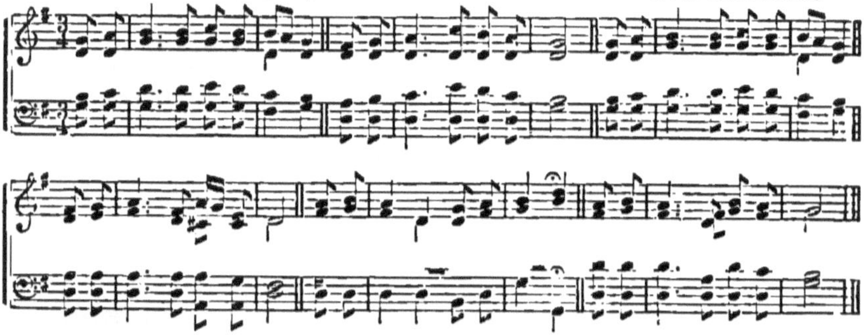

284

Coronation of the King of Kings. 8s, 7s, & 4. (107)

1 LOOK, ye saints; the sight is glorious,
See the Man of sorrows now;
From the fight returned victorious,
Every knee to him shall bow:
Crown him, crown him;
Crowns become the Victor's brow.

2 Crown the Saviour, angels, crown him;
Rich the trophies Jesus brings:
In the seat of power enthrone him,
While the heavenly concave rings:
Crown him, crown him;
Crown the Saviour King of kings.

3 Sinners in derision crowned him,
Mocking thus the Saviour's claim;
Saints and angels crowd around him,
Own his title, praise his name:
Crown him, crown him;
Spread abroad the Victor's fame.

4 Hark! those bursts of acclamation!
Hark! those loud triumphant chords!
Jesus takes the highest station;
Oh, what joy the sight affords!
Crown him, crown him,
King of kings and Lord of lords.

WARNER. L. M.

285

All for us. L. M. (92)

1 OH love, how deep, how broad, how high!
It fills the heart with ecstasy,
That God, the Son of God, should take
Our mortal form for mortals' sake.

2 For us he was baptized, and bore
His holy fast, and hunger'd sore;
For us temptation sharp he knew
For us the tempter overthrew.

3 For us he pray'd, for us he taught,
For us his daily works he wrought
By words and signs and actions, thus
Still seeking, not himself, but us.

4 For us to wicked men betray'd,
Scourged, mock'd, in purple robe array'd,
He bore the shameful cross and death;
For us at length gave up his breath.

5 For us he rose from death again,
For us he went on high to reign,
For us he sent his Spirit here
To guide, to strengthen, and to cheer.

RIALTO. S. M. G. F. Root

286

"The Lord is King." S. M. (78)

1 The Lord our God is King;
His rule, his name is love:
Let earth with hallelujahs ring,
And heaven respond above!

2 His counsels he may keep
Hidden from mortal sight;
His ends may be a soundless deep;
But all he wills is right.

3 Never shall wrong prevail,
Whate'er his foes may do:
His word is given, and shall not fail;
For all he saith is true.

4 Dread storms may mark his path;
Darkness may o'er it brood;
The round world shake as with his wrath;
But all he doth is good.

5 Then sing, the Lord is King;
Sing, for his name is love;
Let earth with hallelujahs ring,
And heaven respond above.

THE HOLY SPIRIT.

ROCKINGHAM. L. M. Dr. L. Mason.

287

L. M. (90)

The Spirit enlightening and renewing.

1 Eternal Spirit, we confess
And sing the wonders of thy grace;
Thy power conveys our blessings down
From God the Father and the Son

2 Enlightened by thine heavenly ray,
Our shades and darkness turn to day;
Thine inward teachings make us know
Our danger and our refuge too.

3 Thy power and glory work within,
And break the chains of reigning sin;
Our wild, imperious lusts subdue,
And form our wretched hearts anew.

4 The troubled conscience knows thy voice;
Thy cheering words awake our joys;
Thy words allay the stormy wind,
And calm the surges of the mind.

288

S. M. (72)

The Guidance of the Spirit.

Tune—Boylston, next page.

1 'Tis God the Spirit leads
In paths before unknown;
The work to be performed is ours,
The strength is all his own.

2 Supported by his grace,
We still pursue our way;
And hope at last to reach the prize,
Secure in endless day.

3 'Tis he that works to will,
'Tis he that works to do;
His is the power by which we act,
His be the glory too.

BOYLSTON. S. M. Dr. L. Mason.

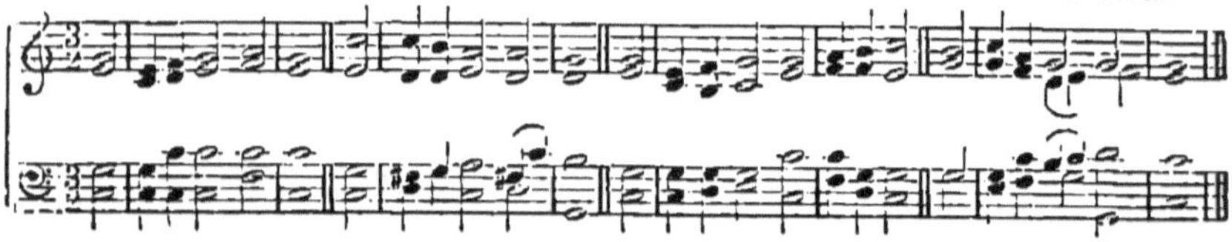

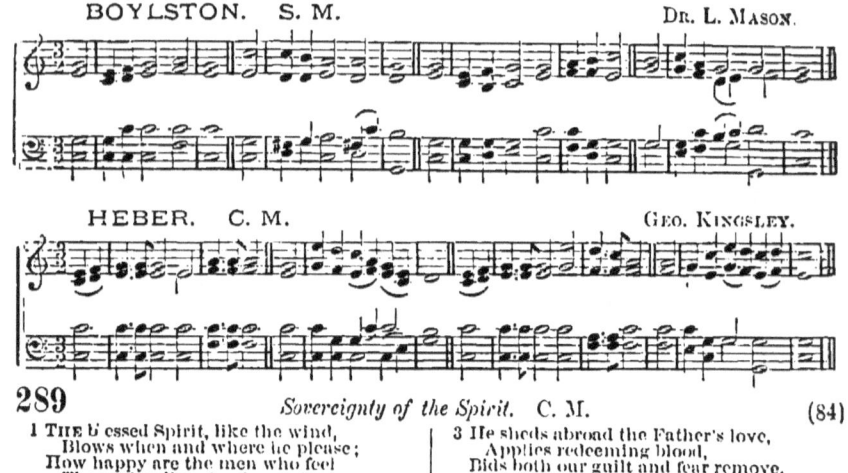

HEBER. C. M. Geo. Kingsley.

289 *Sovereignty of the Spirit.* C. M. (84)

1 The blessed Spirit, like the wind,
Blows when and where he please;
How happy are the men who feel
The soul-enlivening breeze!

2 He moulds the carnal mind afresh,
Subdues the power of sin,
Transforms the heart of stone to flesh,
And plants his grace within.

3 He sheds abroad the Father's love,
Applies redeeming blood,
Bids both our guilt and fear remove,
And brings us home to God.

4 Lord, fill each dead, benighted soul
With light and life and joy;
None can thy mighty power control,
Or shall thy work destroy.

MARLOW. C. M. Dr. L. Mason.

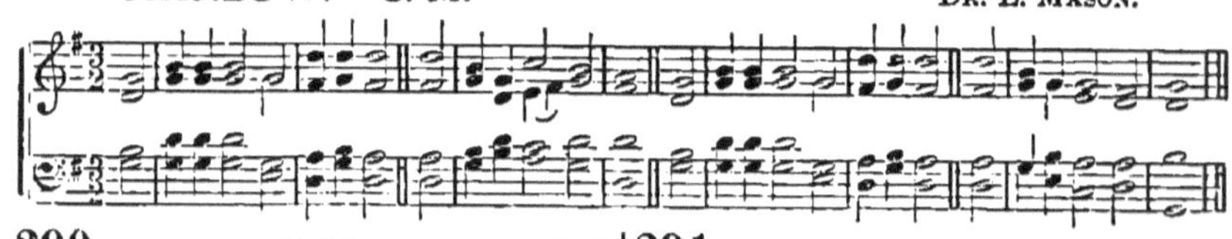

290 C. M. (55)

Regeneration by the Spirit.

1 Not all the outward forms on earth,
Nor rites that God has given,
Nor will of man, nor blood, nor birth,
Can raise a soul to heaven.

2 The sovereign will of God alone
Creates us heirs of grace,
Born in the image of his Son,
A new, peculiar race.

3 The Spirit, like some heavenly wind,
Breathes on the sons of flesh,
Creates anew the carnal mind,
And forms the man afresh.

4 Our quickened souls awake and rise
From their long sleep of death;
On heavenly things we fix our eyes,
And praise employs our breath.

291 C. M. (66)

Dependence upon the Spirit.

Tune—Phillips, next page.

1 How helpless guilty nature lies,
Unconscious of its load!
The heart, unchanged, can never rise
To happiness and God.

2 Can aught beneath a power divine
The stubborn will subdue?
'Tis thine, eternal Spirit, thine
To form the heart anew.

3 'Tis thine the passions to recall,
And upward bid them rise,
And make the scales of error fall
From reason's darkened eyes;

4 To chase the shades of death away,
And bid the sinner live;
A beam of heaven, a vital ray,
'Tis thine alone to give.

5 Oh, change these wretched hearts of ours,
And give them life divine;
Then shall our passions and our powers,
Almighty Lord, be thine.

PHILLIPS. C. M. I. B. WOODBURY.

DORRANCE. 8s & 7s. I. B. WOODBURY.

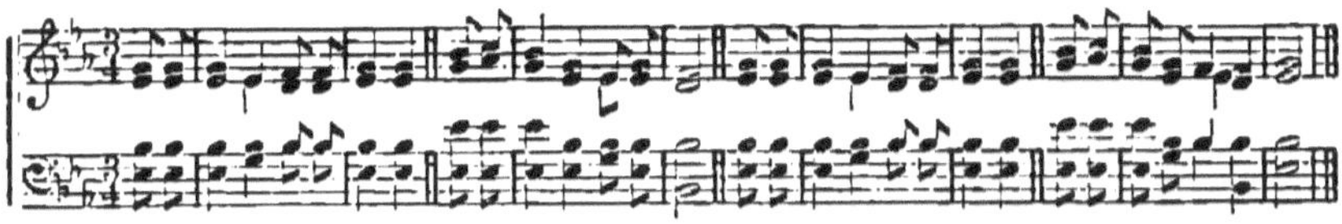

292 8s & 7s. (106)

Prayer for the Spirit.

1 HOLY source of consolation,
Light and life thy grace imparts;
Visit us in thy compassion;
Guide our minds and fill our hearts.

2 Heavenly blessings, without measure,
Thou canst bring us from above;
Lord, we ask that heavenly treasure,
Wisdom, holiness, and love.

3 Dwell within us, blessed Spirit;
Where thou art no ill can come;
Bless us now, through Jesus' merit;
Reign in every heart and home.

293 L. M. (87)

The Spirit entreated not to depart.

Tune—WINDHAM, No. 312.

1 STAY, thou insulted Spirit, stay,
Though I have done thee such despite;
Cast not a sinner quite away,
Nor take thine everlasting flight.

2 Though I have most unfaithful been
Of all who e'er thy grace received,
Ten thousand times thy goodness seen,
Ten thousand times thy goodness grieved

3 Yet, oh, the chief of sinners spare,
In honor of my great High Priest;
Nor, in thy righteous anger, swear
I shall not see thy people's rest.

4 My weary soul, O God, release;
Uphold me with thy gracious hand;
Oh, guide me into perfect peace,
And bring me to the promised land.

DENNIS. S. M. Arr. from NAGELI.

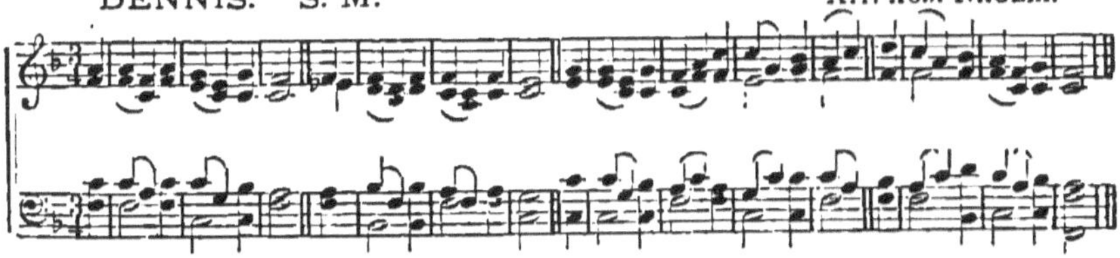

294 *The Holy Ghost is here.* S. M. (103)

1 THE Holy Ghost is here,
Where saints in prayer agree,
As Jesus' parting gift he's near
Each pleading company.

2 He dwells within our soul,
An ever welcome guest:
He reigns with absolute control,
As monarch in the breast.

3 Our bodies are his shrine,
And he th' indwelling Lord;
All hail, thou Comforter divine,
Be evermore adored.

4 Obedient to thy will,
We wait to feel thy power,
O Lord of life, our hopes fulfil,
And bless this hallowed hour!

ROCKINGHAM. L. M. DR. L. MASON.

295 L. M. (90)

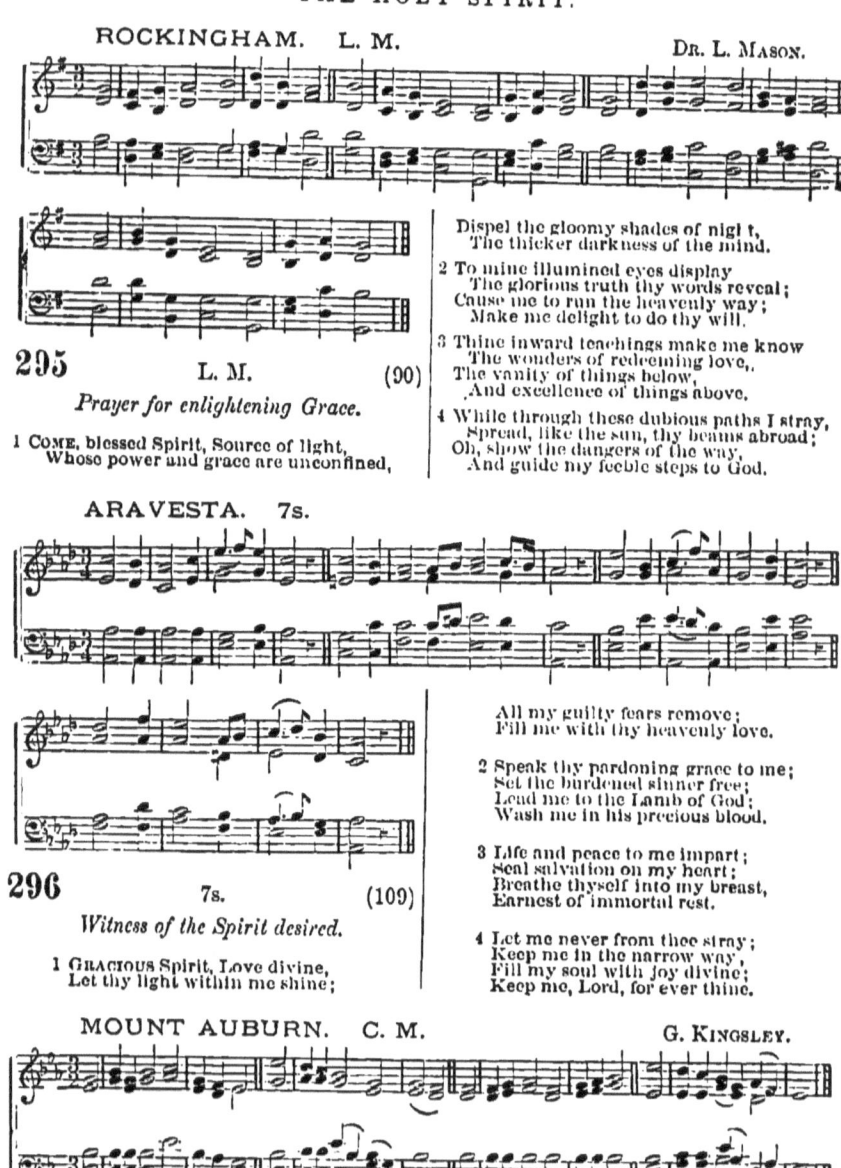

Prayer for enlightening Grace.

1 COME, blessed Spirit, Source of light,
Whose power and grace are unconfined,
Dispel the gloomy shades of night,
The thicker darkness of the mind.

2 To mine illumined eyes display
The glorious truth thy words reveal;
Cause me to run the heavenly way;
Make me delight to do thy will.

3 Thine inward teachings make me know
The wonders of redeeming love,
The vanity of things below,
And excellence of things above.

4 While through these dubious paths I stray,
Spread, like the sun, thy beams abroad;
Oh, show the dangers of the way,
And guide my feeble steps to God.

ARAVESTA. 7s.

296 7s. (109)

Witness of the Spirit desired.

1 GRACIOUS Spirit, Love divine,
Let thy light within me shine;
All my guilty fears remove;
Fill me with thy heavenly love.

2 Speak thy pardoning grace to me;
Set the burdened sinner free;
Lead me to the Lamb of God;
Wash me in his precious blood.

3 Life and peace to me impart;
Seal salvation on my heart;
Breathe thyself into my breast,
Earnest of immortal rest.

4 Let me never from thee stray;
Keep me in the narrow way;
Fill my soul with joy divine;
Keep me, Lord, for ever thine.

MOUNT AUBURN. C. M. G. KINGSLEY.

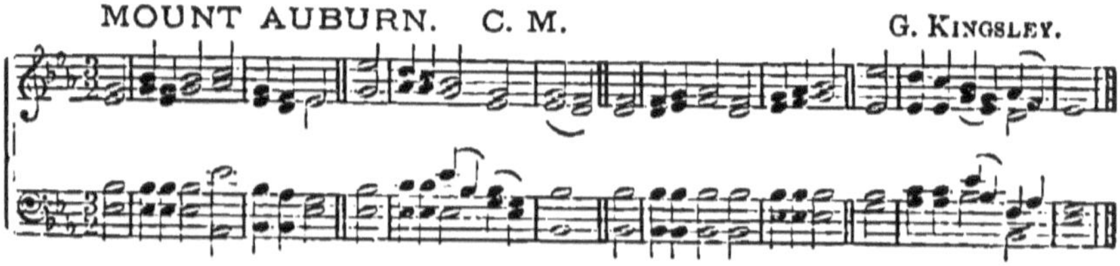

297 *Spirit of Holiness.* C. M. (43)

1 SPIRIT of holiness, descend;
Thy people wait for thee;
Thine ear, in kind compassion, lend;
Let us thy mercy see.

2 Behold, thy weary churches wait
With wishful, longing eyes;
Let us no more lie desolate;
Oh, bid thy light arise.

3 Thy light, that on our souls hath shone,
Leads us in hope to thee·
Let us not feel its rays alone,
Alone thy people be.

4 Oh, bring our dearest friends to God
Remember those we love;
Fit them on earth for thine abode;
Fit them for joys above.

5 Spirit of holiness, 'tis thine
To hear our feeble prayer;
Come, for we wait thy power divine,
Let us thy mercy share

DENNIS. S. M. Arr. from NAGELI.

298 *Sanctifying Power.* S. M. (103)

1 COME, Holy Spirit, come,
With energy divine,
And on this poor, benighted soul
With beams of mercy shine.

2 Melt, melt this frozen heart;
This stubborn will subdue;
Each evil passion overcome,
And form me all anew.

3 Mine will the profit be,
But thine shall be the praise;
And unto thee will I devote
The remnant of my days.

MELODY. C. M.

299 *Prayer for the Spirit.* C. M. (65)

1 COME, Holy Spirit, heavenly Dove,
With all thy quickening powers,
Kindle a flame of sacred love
In these cold hearts of ours.

2 Look! how we grovel here below,
Fond of these trifling toys;
Our souls can neither fly nor go
To reach eternal joys.

3 In vain we tune our formal songs;
In vain we strive to rise;
Hosannas languish on our tongues,
And our devotion dies.

4 Dear Lord, and shall we ever live
At this poor dying rate,
Our love so faint, so cold to thee,
And thine to us so great?

5 Come, Holy Spirit, heavenly Dove,
With all thy quickening powers;
Come, shed abroad a Saviour's love,
And that shall kindle ours.

BERA. L. M. J. E. GOULD.

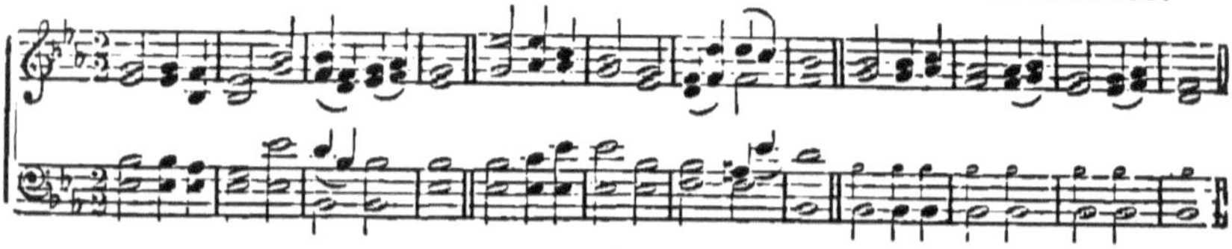

300 L. M. (91)

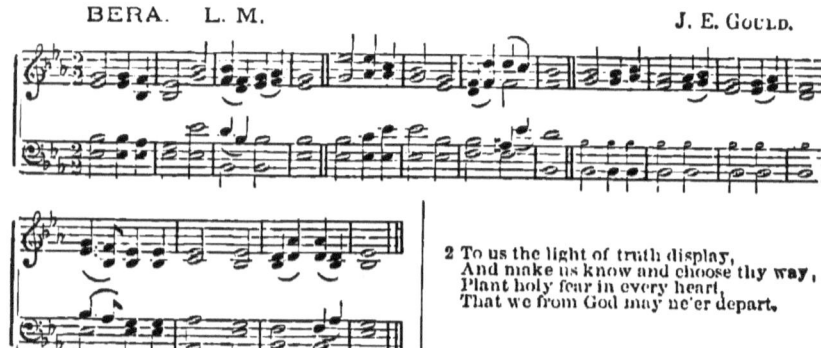

Our Guardian and Guide.

1 COME, gracious Spirit, heavenly Dove,
With light and comfort from above;
Be thou our Guardian, thou our Guide;
O'er every thought and step preside.

2 To us the light of truth display,
And make us know and choose thy way,
Plant holy fear in every heart,
That we from God may ne'er depart.

3 Lead us to holiness, the road
Which we must take to dwell with God,
Lead us to Christ, the living way,
Nor let us from his pastures stray.

4 Lead us to God, our final rest,
To be with him for ever blest;
Lead us to heaven, its bliss to share,
Fulness of joy for ever there.

ZEBULON. H. M. DR. L. MASON.

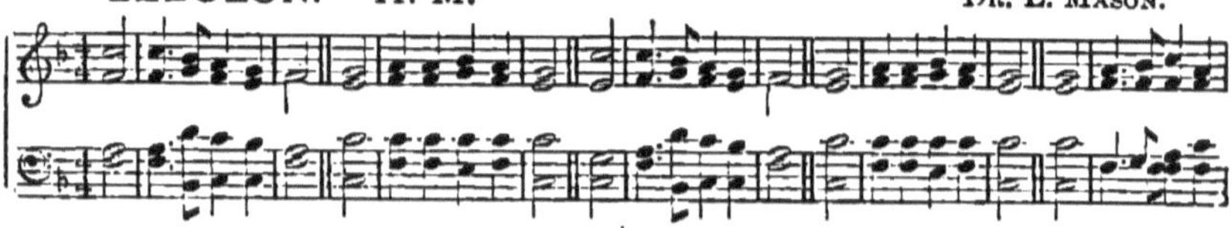

301 H. M. (95)

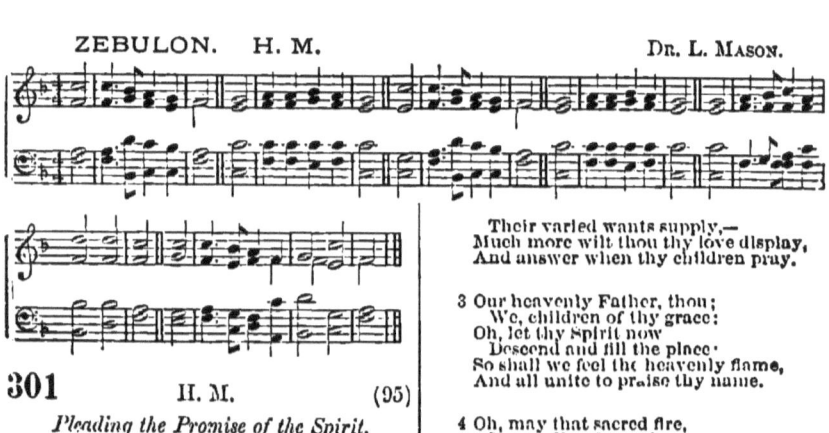

Pleading the Promise of the Spirit.

1 O THOU that hearest prayer,
Attend our humble cry,
And let thy servants share
Thy blessing from on high:
We plead the promise of thy word;
Grant us thy Holy Spirit, Lord.

2 If earthly parents hear
Their children when they cry;
If they, with love sincere,
Their varied wants supply,—
Much more wilt thou thy love display,
And answer when thy children pray.

3 Our heavenly Father, thou;
We, children of thy grace:
Oh, let thy Spirit now
Descend and fill the place:
So shall we feel the heavenly flame,
And all unite to praise thy name.

4 Oh, may that sacred fire,
Descending from above,
Our languid hearts inspire
With fervent zeal and love:
Enlighten our beclouded eyes,
And teach our grovelling souls to rise.

5 And send thy Spirit down
On all the nations, Lord,
With great success to crown
The preaching of thy word;
Till heathen lands shall own thy sway,
And cast their idol gods away.

ARAVESTA. 7s.

302 7s. (109)

Breathings after the Spirit.

1 Holy Ghost, with light divine,
Shine upon this heart of mine;
Chase the shades of night away:
Turn the darkness into day.

2 Holy Ghost, with power divine,
Cleanse this guilty heart of mine;
Long has sin, without control,
Held dominion o'er my soul.

3 Holy Ghost, with joy divine,
Cheer this saddened heart of mine;
Bid my many woes depart;
Heal my wounded, bleeding heart.

4 Holy Spirit, all divine
Dwell within this heart of mine;
Cast down every idol throne;
Reign supreme, and reign alone.

PURVES. S. M. Geo. Kingsley.

303 S. M. (77)

Sanctifying Power.

1 Come, Holy Spirit, come;
Let thy bright beams arise:
Dispel the sorrow from our minds,
The darkness from our eyes.

2 Convince us all of sin;
Then lead to Jesus' blood,
And to our wondering view reveal
The mercies of our God.

3 Revive our drooping faith,
Our doubts and fears remove,
And kindle in our breasts the flame
Of never-dying love.

4 'Tis thine to cleanse the heart,
To sanctify the soul,
To pour fresh life in every part,
And new-create the whole.

5 Dwell, Spirit, in our hearts;
Our minds from bondage free:
Then shall we know and praise and love
The Father, Son, and thee.

304 *Come and dwell in us.* L. M. (91)

Tune—Bera, No. 300.

1 Come, O Creator, Spirit blest,
And in our souls take up thy rest;
Come, with thy grace and heavenly aid,
To fill the hearts which thou hast made.

2 Great Comforter, to thee we cry:
O highest gift of God most high,
O fount of life, O fire of love,
And sweet anointing from above.

3 Kindle our senses from above,
And make our hearts o'erflow with love;
With patience firm, and virtue high,
The weakness of our flesh supply.

4 Far from us drive the foe we dread,
And grant us thy true peace instead;
So shall we not, with thee for guide,
Turn from the path of life aside.

SEYMOUR. 7s. GREATOREX.

305 *Prayer for the Spirit.* 7s. (110)

1 HOLY Spirit, from on high,
Bend o'er us a pitying eye;
Now refresh the drooping heart;
Bid the power of sin depart.

2 Light up every dark recess
Of our hearts' ungodliness;
Show us every devious way
Where our steps have gone astray.

3 Teach us, with repentant grief,
Humbly to implore relief;
Then the Saviour's blood reveal,
And our broken spirits heal.

4 May we daily grow in grace,
And pursue the heavenly race,
Trained in wisdom, led by love,
Till we reach our rest above.

TRINITY.

FINNEY. 8s, 7s, & 4. W. B. BRADBURY.

306 *Glory to the Trinity.* 8s, 7s, & 4 (107)

1 GLORY be to God the Father,
Glory be to God the Son,
Glory be to God the Spirit,
Great Jehovah, Three in One;
Glory, glory,
While eternal ages run!

2 Glory be to him who loved us,
Washed us from each spot and stain;
Glory be to him who bought us,
Made us kings with him to reign;
Glory, glory,
To the Lamb that once was slain.

3 "Glory, blessing, praise eternal!"
Thus the choir of angels sings;
"Honor, riches, power, dominion!"
Thus its praise creation brings;
Glory, glory,
Glory to the King of kings!

HADDAM. H. M. DR. L. MASON.

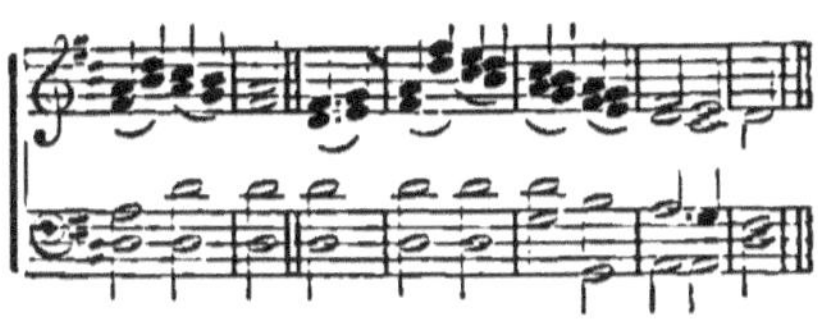

307 *Praise to the Trinity.* H. M. (93)

1 WE give immortal praise
For God the Father's love,
For all our comforts here,
And better hopes above;
He sent his own | To die for sins
Eternal Son | That we had done.

2 To God the Son belongs
Immortal glory too,
Who bought us with his blood
From everlasting woe:
And now he lives, | And sees the fruit
And now he reigns, | Of all his pains.

3 To God the Spirit's name
Immortal worship give,
Whose new-creating power
Makes the dead sinner live:
His work completes | And fills the soul
The great design, | With joy divine.

4 Almighty God, to thee
Be endless honors done,
The undivided Three,
The great and glorious One:
Where reason fails, | There faith prevails,
With all her powers, | And love adores.

MESSIAH. 7s. J. NETHERCLIFT.

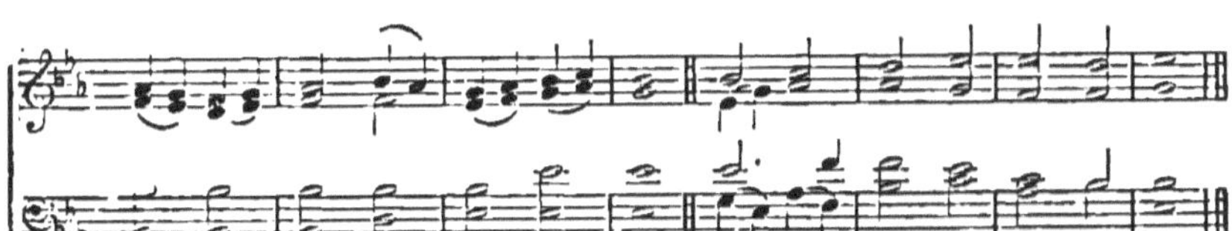

308 *Honor to God's Name.* 7s. (97)

1 To the name of God on high,
God of might and majesty,
God of heaven and earth and sea,
Blessing, praise, and glory be.

2 To the name of Christ the Lord,
Son of God, incarnate Word,
Christ, by whom all things were made
Be an endless honor paid.

3 To the Holy Spirit be
Equal praise eternally,
With the Father and the Son,
One in name, in glory one.

4 This, the song of ages past,
Song that shall for ever last;
Let the ages yet to be
Join the joyful melody.

ITALIAN HYMN. 6s & 4s. GIARDINI.

309 *The Presence of the Trinity desired.* 6s & 4s. (108)

1 COME, thou almighty King,
Help us thy name to sing,
Help us to praise:
Father, all-glorious,
O'er all victorious,
Come, and reign over us,
Ancient of days.

2 Come, thou incarnate Word,
Gird on thy mighty sword;
Our prayer attend;
Come, and thy people bless,
And give thy word success:
Spirit of holiness,
On us descend.

3 Come, holy Comforter,
Thy sacred witness bear,
In this glad hour:
Thou, who almighty art,
Now rule in every heart,
And ne'er from us depart,
Spirit of power.

4 To the great One in Three,
The highest praises be,
Hence evermore;
His sovereign majesty
May we in glory see,
And to eternity
Love and adore.

MISSIONARY CHANT. L. M. CHARLES ZEUNER.

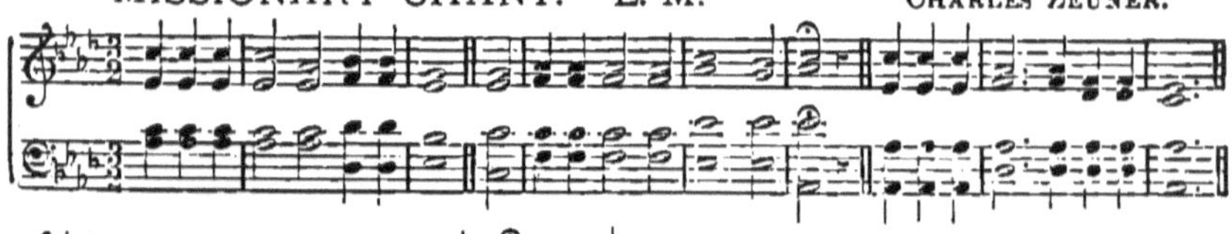

310 L. M. (76)

Praise to Father, Son, and Spirit.

1 PRAISES to him whose love has given,
In Christ his Son, the Life of heaven;
Who for our darkness gives us light,
And turns to day our deepest night.

2 Praises to him, in grace who came,
To bear our woe and sin and shame;
Who lived to die, who died to rise,
The God-accepted sacrifice.

3 Praises to him who sheds abroad
Within our hearts the love of God,—
The Spirit of all truth and peace,
Fountain of joy and holiness.

4 To Father, Son, and Spirit, now
Our hands we lift, our knees we bow;
To Jah-Jehovah thus we raise
The sinner's endless song of praise.

SALEM. L. M. PSALMODIST.

311 L. M. (70)

Praise to the Trinity.

Tune—SALEM.

1 BLEST be the Father and his love,
To whose celestial source we owe
Rivers of endless joy above,
And rills of comfort here below.

2 All praise to thee, great Son of God,
From whose dear, wounded body rolls
A precious stream of vital blood,
The fount of life for dying souls.

3 We give thee, sacred Spirit, praise,
Who, in our hearts of sin and woe,
Mak'st living springs of grace arise,
And into boundless glory flow.

4 Thus God the Father, God the Son,
And God the Spirit, we adore,
That sea of life and love unknown,
Without a bottom or a shore.

312 L. M. (89)

Prayer to Father, Son, and Spirit.

Tune—LUTON.

1 FATHER of heaven, whose love profound
A ransom for our souls hath found,
Before thy throne we sinners bend;
To us thy pardoning love extend.

2 Almighty Son, incarnate Word,
Our Prophet, Priest, Redeemer, Lord,
Before thy throne we sinners bend:
To us thy saving grace extend.

3 Eternal Spirit, by whose breath
The soul is raised from sin and death,
Before thy throne we sinners bend:
To us thy quickening power extend.

4 Jehovah, Father, Spirit, Son,
Eternal Godhead, three in one,—
Before thy throne we sinners bend:
Grace, pardon, life, to us extend.

LUTON. L. M. BURDER.

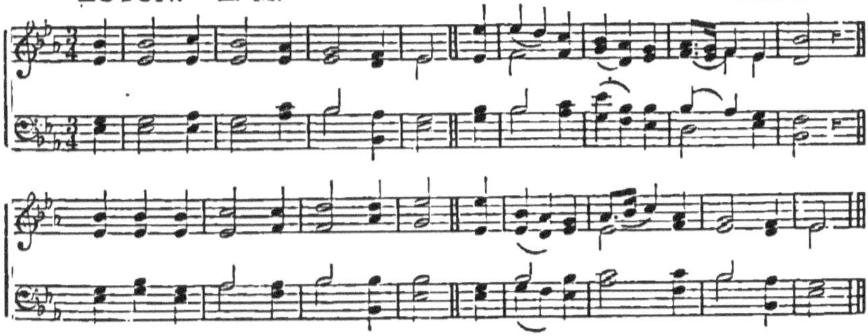

ZEBULON. H. M. Dr. L. Mason.

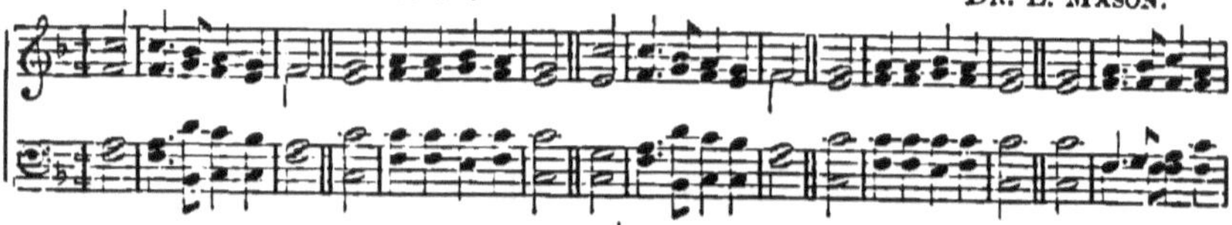

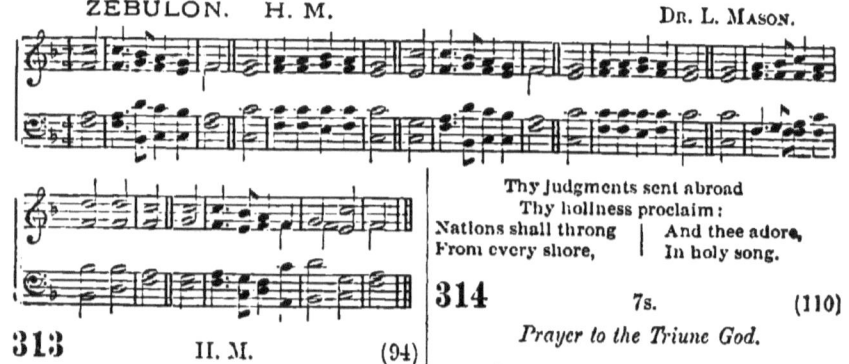

Thy judgments sent abroad
Thy holiness proclaim:
Nations shall throng | And thee adore,
From every shore, | In holy song.

313 H. M. (94)

"Holy, holy, holy, Lord God Almighty."

1 O holy, holy Lord,
Creation's sovereign King,
Thy majesty adored,
Let all thy creatures sing:
Who wast, and art, | Nor time shall see
And art to be; | Thy sway depart.

2 Great are thy works of praise,
O God of boundless might;
And just and true thy ways,
Thou King of saints in light.
Let all above, | Conspire to show
And all below, | Thy power and love.

3 Who shall not fear thee, Lord,
And magnify thy name?

314 7s. (110)

Prayer to the Triune God.

1 Holy Father, hear my cry;
Holy Saviour, bend thine ear;
Holy Spirit, come thou nigh;
Father, Saviour, Spirit, hear.

2 Father, save me from my sin;
Saviour, I thy mercy crave;
Gracious Spirit, make me clean;
Father, Son, and Spirit, save.

3 Father, let me taste thy love;
Saviour, fill my soul with peace;
Spirit, come my heart to move;
Father, Son, and Spirit, bless.

4 Father, Son, and Spirit—thou
One Jehovah, shed abroad
All thy grace within me now;
Be my Portion and my God.

SEYMOUR. 7s. Greatorex.

BARBY. C. M.

A. WILLIAMS.

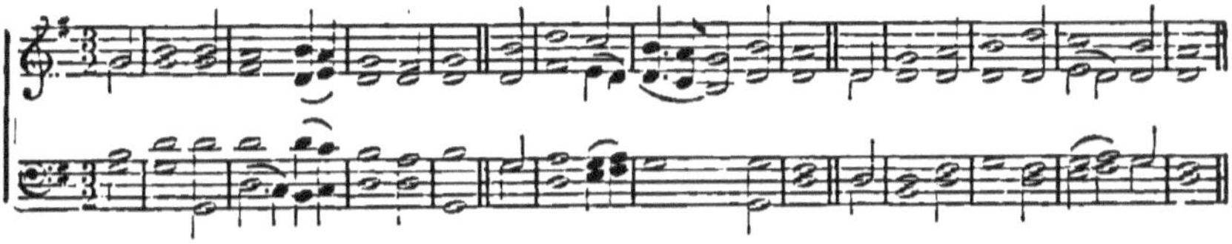

315 C. M. (115)

Sense of Depravity.

1 GREAT King of glory and of grace,
We own with humble shame,
How vile is our degenerate race,
And our first father's name.

2 We live estranged, afar from God,
And love the distance well;
With haste we run the dangerous road
That leads to death and hell.

3 And can such rebels be restored?
Such natures made divine?
Let sinners see thy glory, Lord,
And feel this power of thine

4 We raise our Father's name on high,
Who his own Spirit sends
To bring rebellious strangers nigh,
And turn his foes to friends.

WOODWORTH. L. M.

WM. B. BRADBURY.

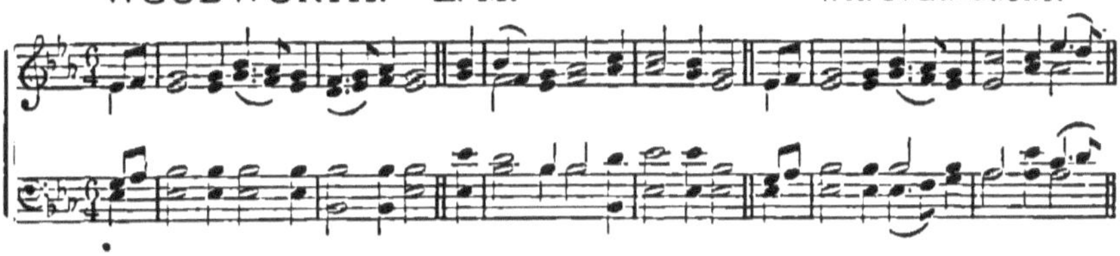

316 L. M. (118)

Shapen in Iniquity.

1 LORD, I am vile,—conceived in sin,
And born unholy and unclean;
Sprung from the man whose guilty fall
Corrupts the race, and taints us all.

2 Soon as we draw our infant breath,
The seeds of sin grow up for death;
Thy law demands a perfect heart;
But we're defiled in every part.

3 O Lord, I fall before thy face;
My only refuge is thy grace;
No outward forms can make me clean,
The leprosy lies deep within.

4 Jesus, my God, thy blood alone
Hath power sufficient to atone:
Thy blood can make me white as snow;
No human power could cleanse me so.

5 While guilt disturbs and breaks my peace,
Nor flesh nor soul hath rest or ease:
Lord, let me hear thy pard'ning voice,
And make my broken bones rejoice.

OLMUTZ. S. M.

Arr. by Dr. L. Mason.

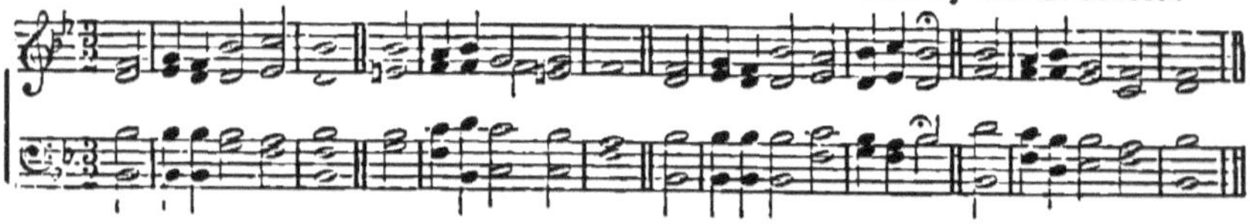

317

None righteous. S. M. (179)

1 Ah! how shall fallen man
Be just before his God?
If he contend in righteousness,
We fall beneath his rod.

2 If he our ways should mark
With strict, inquiring eyes,
Could we for one of thousand faults
A just excuse devise?

3 The mountains, in thy wrath,
Their ancient seats forsake;
The trembling earth deserts her place:
Her rooted pillars shake.

4 Ah! how shall guilty man
Contend with such a God?
None, none can meet him, and escape,
But through the Saviour's blood.

BLANDNER. S. M.

John M. Evans.

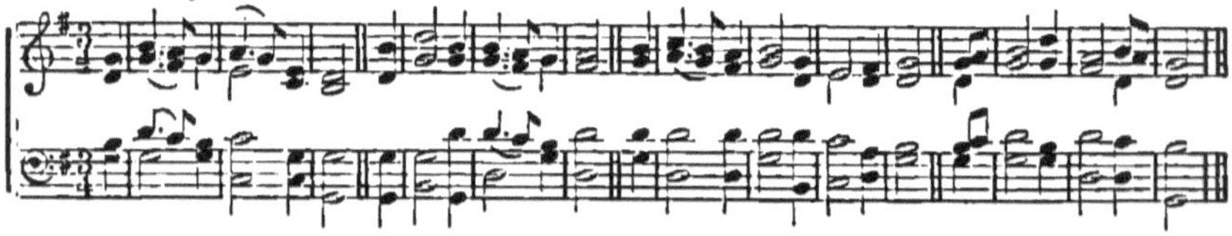

318

Man's State by Nature. S. M. (116)

1 How heavy is the night
That hangs upon our eyes,
Till Christ, with his reviving light,
O'er our dark souls arise.

2 Our guilty spirits dread
To meet the wrath of Heaven;
But, in his righteousness arrayed,
We see our sins forgiven.

3 Unholy and impure
Are all our thoughts and ways
His hands infected nature cure
With sanctifying grace.

4 The powers of hell agree
To hold our souls in vain;
He sets the sons of bondage free,
And breaks the cruel chain.

5 Lord, we adore thy ways
To bring us near to God,
Thy sovereign power, thy healing grace,
And thine atoning blood.

BYEFIELD. C. M.

Dr. T. Hastings.

319

The Sinner alive without the Law. C. M. (168)

1 Lord, how secure my conscience was
And felt no inward dread!
I was alive without the law,
And thought my sins were dead.

2 My hopes of heaven were firm and bright;
But since the precept came
With a convincing power and light,
I find how vile I am.

(CONTINUED.)

3 My guilt appeared but small before,
Till I with terror saw
How perfect, holy, just, and pure,
Is thine eternal law.

4 Then felt my soul the heavy load;
My sins revived again:
I had provoked a dreadful God,
And all my hopes were slain.

5 My God, I cry with every breath,
For some kind power to save;
Oh, break the yoke of sin and death,
And thus redeem the slave.

HEBER. C. M. Geo. Kingsley.

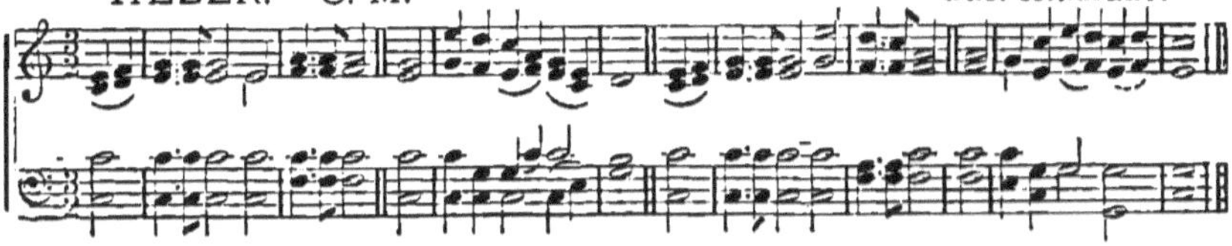

320

Self-righteousness renounced. C. M. (135)

1 Vain are the hopes the sons of men
On their own works have built;
Their hearts by nature all unclean,
And all their actions guilt.

2 Let Jew and Gentile silent bow,
Without a murmuring word;
Let all the race of man confess
Their guilt before the Lord.

3 In vain we ask God's righteous law
To justify us now;
Since to convince and to condemn
Is all the law can do.

4 Jesus, how glorious is thy grace!
When in thy name we trust,
Our faith receives a righteousness
That makes the sinner just.

FEDERAL STREET. L. M. H. K. Oliver.

321

Lost without Christ. L. M. (175)

1 Buried in shadows of the night
We lie, till Christ restores the light,
Till he descends to heal the blind,
And chase the darkness of the mind.

2 Our guilty souls are drowned in tears,
Till his atoning blood appears;
Then we awake from deep distress,
And sing the Lord our Righteousness.

3 Jesus beholds where Satan reigns
And binds his slaves in heavy chains;
He sets the prisoners free, and breaks
The iron bondage from our necks.

4 Poor, helpless worms in thee possess
Grace, wisdom, power, and righteousness.
Thou art our mighty All, and we
Give our whole selves, O Lord, to thee.

322

C. P. M. (206)

Necessity of Regeneration.

Tune—Meribah, next page

1 Awaked by Sinai's awful sound,
My soul in bonds of guilt I found,
And knew not where to go;
Eternal truth did loud proclaim,
"The sinner must be born again,
Or sink in endless woe."

2 Amazed I stood, but could not tell
Which way to shun the gates of hell,
For death and hell drew near;
I strove, indeed, but strove in vain·
"The sinner must be born again"
Still sounded in my ear.

(continued.)

MERIBAH. C. P. M.

DR. L. MASON.

3 When to the law I trembling fled,
It poured its curses on my head;
I no relief could find:
This fearful truth increased my pain;
"The sinner must be born again"
O'erwhelmed my tortured mind.

4 But while I thus in anguish lay,
Jesus of Naz'reth passed that way,
And felt his pity move:
The sinner, by his justice slain,
Now by his grace is born again,
And sings redeeming love.

ORWELL. L. M.

DR. L. MASON.

323

Union of Pleas. L. M. (121)

1 WHY will ye waste on trifling cares
That life which God's compassion spares;
While, in the various range of thought,
The one thing needful is forgot?

2 Shall God invite you from above?
Shall Jesus urge his dying love?
Shall troubled conscience give you pain,
And all these pleas unite in vain?

3 Not so your eyes will always view
Those objects which you now pursue;
Not so will heaven and hell appear,
When death's decisive hour is near.

4 Almighty God, thy grace impart;
Fix deep conviction on each heart;
Nor let us waste on trifling cares
That life which thy compassion spares.

VINTON. 7s.

S. P. TUCKERMAN.

324

The Sinner pointed to the Judgment. 7s. (187)

1 WHEN thy mortal life is fled,
When the death-shades o'er thee spread,
When is finished thy career,
Sinner, where wilt thou appear?

2 When the world has passed away,
When draws near the judgment day,
When the awful trump shall sound,
Say, oh, where wilt thou be found?

3 When the Judge descends in light,
Clothed in majesty and might,
When the wicked quail with fear,
Where, oh, where wilt thou appear?

4 What shall soothe thy bursting heart,
When the saints and thou must part?
When the good with joy are crowned,
Sinner, where wilt thou be found?

5 While the Holy Ghost is nigh,
Quickly to the Saviour fly;
Then shall peace thy spirit cheer;
Then in heaven shalt thou appear.

325 C. M. (134)

Anticipations of the Judgment.

Tune—HEBER, No. 289.

1 WHEN rising from the bed of death,
O'erwhelmed with guilt and fear,
I see my Maker face to face,
Oh, how shall I appear?

2 If yet, while pardon may be found,
And mercy may be sought,
My heart with inward terror shrinks,
And trembles at the thought:

3 When thou, O Lord, shalt stand disclosed
In majesty severe,
And sit in judgment on my soul,
Oh, how shall I appear?

4 But there's forgiveness, Lord, with thee;
Thy nature is benign;
Thy pardoning mercy I implore,
For mercy, Lord, is thine.

326 L. M. (117)

Eternity anticipated.

Tune—WINDHAM, No. 342.

1 ETERNITY is just at hand;
And shall I waste my ebbing sand,
And careless view departing day,
And throw my inch of time away?

2 Eternity! tremendous sound!
To guilty souls a dreadful wound;
But, oh, if Christ and heaven be mine,
How sweet the accents, how divine!

3 Be this my chief, my only care,
My high pursuit, my ardent prayer,
An interest in the Saviour's blood,
My pardon sealed, my peace with God

4 Search, Lord, oh search my inmost heart,
And light and hope and joy impart;
From guilt and error set me free,
And guide me safe to heaven and thee.

SESSIONS. L. M. L. O. EMERSON.

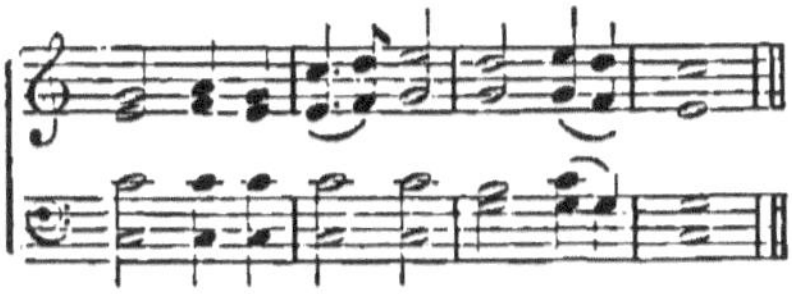

327 L. M. (120)

Expostulation with the Sinner.

1 O SINNER, why so thoughtless grown?
Why in such dreadful haste to die?
Daring to leap to worlds unknown;
Heedless against thy God to fly?

2 Wilt thou despise eternal fate,
Urged on by sin's delusive dreams?
Madly attempt th' infernal gate,
And force thy passage to the flames?

3 Stay, sinner, on the gospel plains,
And hear the Lord of life unfold
The glories of his dying pains,
For ever telling, yet untold.

328 *Life and Death.* S. M. (116)

Tune—BLANDNER, No. 318.

1 OH, where shall rest be found,—
Rest for the weary soul?
'Twere vain the ocean depths to sound,
Or pierce to either pole.

2 The world can never give
The bliss for which we sigh:
'Tis not the whole of life to live,
Nor all of death to die.

3 Beyond this vale of tears
There is a life above,
Unmeasured by the flight of years;
And all that life is love.

4 There is a death whose pang
Outlasts the fleeting breath:
Oh, what eternal horrors hang
Around the second death!

5 Lord God of truth and grace,
Teach us that death to shun;
Lest we be banished from thy face,
And evermore undone.

CARPENTER. 7s. BLUMENTHAL.

329

Pleading with the Sinner. 7s. (191)

1 SINNERS, turn, why will ye die?
God, your Maker, asks you why;
God, who did your being give,
Made you with himself to live.

2 Sinners, turn; why will ye die?
God, your Saviour, asks you why.
Will ye not in him believe?
He has died that ye might live.

3 Sinners, turn; why will ye die?
God, the Spirit, asks you why.
Often with you has he strove,
Wooed you to embrace his love.

4 Will ye not his grace receive?
Will ye still refuse to live?
O ye dying sinners, why,
Why will ye for ever die?

TO-DAY. 6s & 4s. DR. L. MASON.

330

The Call to-day. 6s & 4s. (194)

1 TO-DAY the Saviour calls;
Ye wanderers, come;
Oh, ye benighted souls,
Why longer roam?

2 To-day the Saviour calls:
Oh, hear him now;
Within these sacred walls
To Jesus bow.

3 To-day the Saviour calls:
For refuge fly;
The storm of justice falls,
And death is nigh.

4 The Spirit calls to-day:
Yield to his power;
Oh, grieve him not away:
'Tis mercy's hour.

VINTON. 7s. S. P. TUCKERMAN.

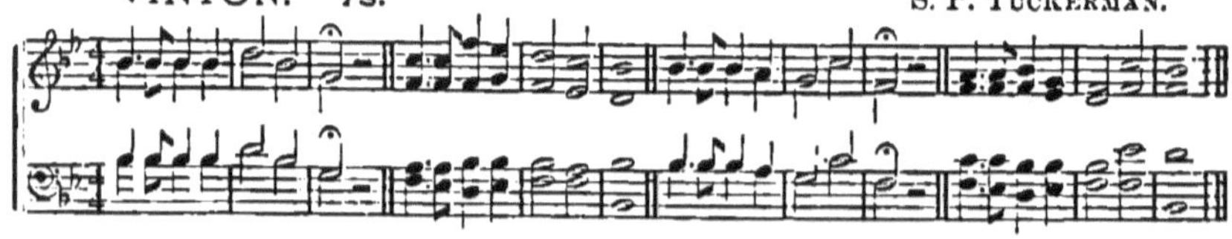

331

Important Questions. 7s. (187)

1 SINNER, what hast thou to show
Like the joys believers know?
Is thy path, of fading flowers,
Half so bright, so sweet, as ours?

2 Doth a skilful, healing friend
On thy daily path attend,
And, where thorns and stings abound,
Shed a balm on every wound?

3 When the tempest rolls on high,
Hast thou still a refuge nigh?
Can, oh, can thy dying breath
Summon one more strong than death?

4 Canst thou, in that awful day,
Fearless tread the gloomy way,
Plead a glorious ransom given,
Burst from earth, and soar to heaven?

ROSEFIELD. 7s. 6 lines. DR. MALAN.

332 *Who is it that smote thee?* 7s, 61 (133)

1 HEART of stone, relent, relent;
  Break, by Jesus' cross subdued;
See his body mangled, rent,
  Covered with a gore of blood:
Sinful soul, what hast thou done?
Crucified th' eternal Son.

2 Yes, thy sins have done the deed,
  Driven the nails that fixed him there,
Crowned with thorns his sacred head,
  Plunged into his side the spear
Made his soul a sacrifice,
While for sinful man he dies.

3 Wilt thou let him bleed in vain?
  Still to death thy Lord pursue?
Open all his wounds again?
  And the shameful cross renew?
No; with all my sins I'll part;
Break, oh, break, my bleeding heart.

UNAM. 8s, 7s, & 4. CARMINA SACRA.

333 8s, 7s & 4. (222)

Sinners entreated.

1 SINNERS, will you scorn the message
  Sent in mercy from above?
Every sentence, oh, how tender!
  Every line is full of love:
    Listen to it;
  Every line is full of love.

2 Hear the heralds of the gospel
  News from Zion's King proclaim
"Pardon to each rebel sinner;
  Free forgiveness in his name:"
    How important!
  "Free forgiveness in his name."

3 Tempted souls, they bring you succor;
  Fearful hearts, they quell your fears;
And, with news of consolation
  Chase away the falling tears;
    Tender heralds,
  Chase away the falling tears.

4 Who hath our report believed?
  Who received the joyful word?
Who embraced the news of pardon
  Offered to you by the Lord?
    Can you slight it,
  Offered to you by the Lord?

CROSS AND CROWN. C. M.

WESTERN MELODY.

334 *Exhortation to Repentance.* C. M. (161)

1 "REPENT!" the voice celestial cries;
  No longer dare delay:
The soul that scorns the mandate dies,
  And meets a fiery day.

2 No more the sovereign eye of God
  O'erlooks the crimes of men;
His heralds now are sent abroad
  To warn the world of sin.

3 O sinners, in his presence bow,
  And all your guilt confess;
Embrace the offered Saviour now
  Nor trifle with his grace.

4 Bow ere the awful trumpet sound,
  And call you to his bar;
His mercy knows th' appointed bound
  And yields to justice there.

5 Amazing love, that yet will call,
  And yet prolong our days!
Our hearts, subdued by goodness, fall,
  And weep and love and praise.

BRADEN. S. M.

WM. B. BRADBURY.

Ritard.

335 *Do not delay.* S. M. (139)

1 AND canst thou, sinner, slight
  The call of love divine?
Shall God with tenderness invite,
  And gain no thought of thine?

2 Wilt thou not cease to grieve
  The Spirit from thy breast,
Till he thy wretched soul shall leave
  With all thy sins oppressed?

3 To-day a pardoning God
  Will hear the suppliant pray;
To-day, a Saviour's cleansing blood
  Will wash thy guilt away.

4 But grace so dearly bought
  If yet thou wilt despise,
Thy fearful doom, with sorrow fraught,
  Will fill thee with surprise.

DUHRING. C. M.

WM. B. BRADBURY.

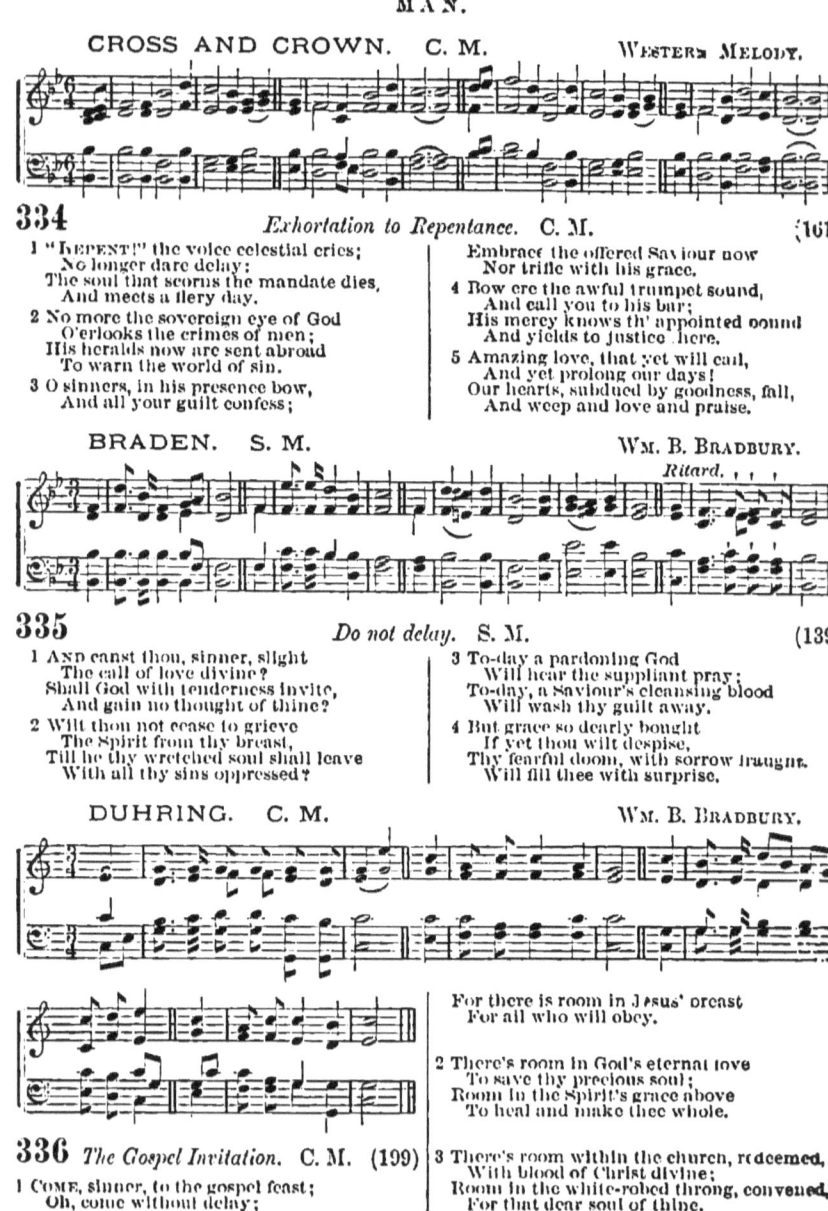

336 *The Gospel Invitation.* C. M. (199)

1 COME, sinner, to the gospel feast;
  Oh, come without delay;
For there is room in Jesus' breast
  For all who will obey.

2 There's room in God's eternal love
  To save thy precious soul;
Room in the Spirit's grace above
  To heal and make thee whole.

3 There's room within the church, redeemed,
  With blood of Christ divine;
Room in the white-robed throng, convened,
  For that dear soul of thine.

(CONTINUED.)

4 There's room in heaven among the choir,
And harps and crowns of gold,
And glorious palms of victory there,
And joys that ne'er were told.

5 There's room around thy Father's board
For thee and thousands more;
Oh, come and welcome to the Lord;
Yea, come this very hour.

ORWELL. L. M. DR. L. MASON.

337 *Sinners invited to immediate Repentance.* L. M. (121)

1 WHILE life prolongs its precious light,
Mercy is found, and peace is given;
But soon, ah, soon, approaching night
Shall blot out every hope of heaven.

2 While God invites, how blest the day!
How sweet the gospel's charming sound!
Come, sinners, haste, oh, haste away,
While yet a pardoning God is found.

3 Soon, borne on time's most rapid wing,
Shall death command you to the grave,
Before his bar your spirits bring,
And none be found to hear or save.

4 In that lone land of deep despair,
No Sabbath's heavenly light shall rise,
No God regard your bitter prayer,
No Saviour call you to the skies.

5 While God invites, how blest the day!
How sweet the gospel's charming sound!
Come, sinners, haste, oh, haste away,
While yet a pardoning God is found.

SESSIONS. L. M. L. O. EMERSON.

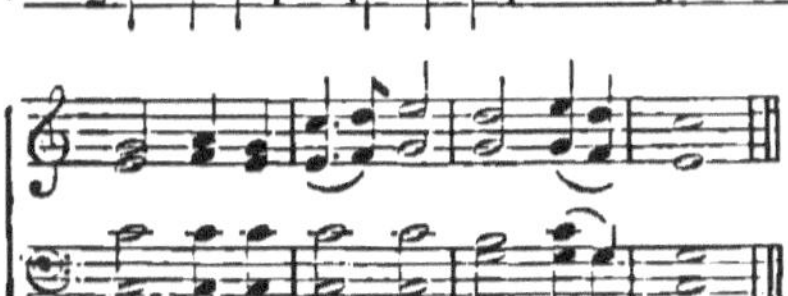

338 L. M. (120)

The Sinner urged.

1 HASTE, traveller, haste; the night comes on;
And many a shining hour is gone;
The storm is gathering in the west,
And thou far off from home and rest.

2 The rising tempest sweeps the sky:
The rains descend, the winds are high,
The waters swell, and death and fear
Beset thy path, nor refuge near.

3 Oh, yet a shelter you may gain,
A covert from the wind and rain,
A hiding-place, a rest, a home,
A refuge from the wrath to come!

4 Then linger not in all the plain;
Flee for thy life; the mountain gain;
Look not behind; make no delay;
Oh, speed thee, speed thee on thy way!

VINTON. 7s. S. P. TUCKERMAN.

339

Delay deprecated. 7s. (187)

1 HASTE, O sinner; now be wise;
Stay not for the morrow's sun;
Wisdom if you still despise
Harder is it to be won.

2 Haste, and mercy now implore;
Stay not for the morrow's sun,
Lest thy season should be o'er
Ere this evening's stage be run.

3 Haste, O sinner; now return,
Stay not for the morrow's sun,
Lest thy lamp should cease to burn
Ere salvation's work is done.

4 Haste, O sinner; now be blest;
Stay not for the morrow's sun,
Lest perdition thee arrest
Ere the morrow is begun.

EXPOSTULATION. 11s.

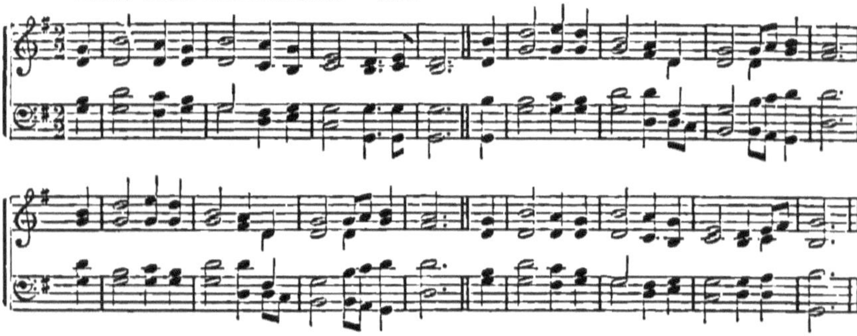

340

The Sinner warned against Delay. 11s. (127)

1 DELAY not, delay not; O sinner, draw near;
The waters of life are now flowing for thee;
No price is demanded; the Saviour is here;
Redemption is purchased, salvation is free.

2 Delay not, delay not; why longer abuse
The love and compassion of Jesus, thy God?
A fountain is opened; how canst thou refuse
To wash and be cleansed in his pardoning blood?

3 Delay not, delay not, O sinner, to come,
For Mercy still lingers, and calls thee to-day;
Her voice is not heard in the shades of the tomb;
Her message, unheeded, will soon pass away.

4 Delay not, delay not, the Spirit of grace,
Long grieved and resisted, may take his sad flight,
And leave thee in darkness to finish thy race,
To sink in the gloom of eternity's night.

5 Delay not, delay not; the hour is at hand;
The earth shall dissolve, and the heavens shall fade,
The dead, small and great, in the judgment shall stand;
What helper, then, sinner, shall lend thee his aid?

341 *Come to-day.* S. M. (138)

Tune—BRADEN, No. 335.

1 YE sinners, fear the Lord,
While yet 'tis called to-day;
Soon will the awful voice of death
Command your souls away.

2 Soon will the harvest close,
The summer soon be o'er;
O sinners, then your injured God
Will heed your cries no more.

3 Then, while 'tis called to-day,
Oh, hear the gospel's sound;
Come, sinners, haste, oh, haste away,
While pardon may be found

WINDHAM. L. M. DANIEL READ.

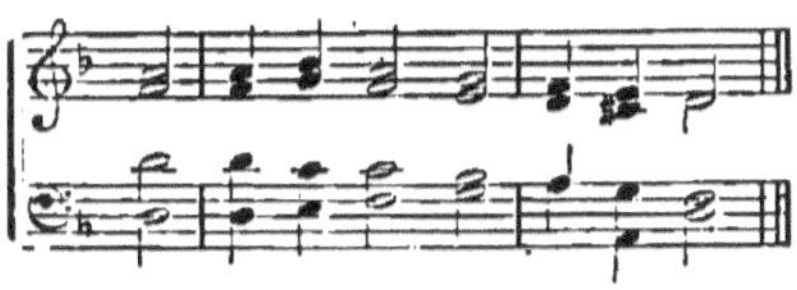

342 *While Life lasts.* L. M. (117)

1 LIFE is the time to serve the Lord,
The time to insure the great reward,
And while the lamp holds out to burn,
Oh, hasten, sinner, to return!

2 Life is the hour that God has giv'n,
To 'scape from hell and fly to heav'n,
The day of grace when mortals may
Secure the blessings of the day.

3 The living know that they must die,
Beneath the clods their dust must lie;
Then have no share in all that's done
Beneath the circle of the sun.

4 Then what my thoughts design to do,
My hands, with all your might pursue;
Since no device nor work is found,
Nor faith nor hope, beneath the ground.

CARPENTER. 7s. BLUMENTHAL.

343 *The Sinner entreated to awake.* 7s. (197)

1 SINNER, rouse thee from thy sleep;
Wake, and o'er thy folly weep;
Raise thy spirit, dark and dead;
Jesus waits his light to shed.

2 Wake from sleep; arise from death;
See the bright and living path;
Watchful, tread that path; be wise;
Leave thy folly; seek the skies.

3 Leave thy folly; cease from crime.
From this hour redeem thy time:
Life secure without delay;
Evil is thy mortal day.

4 Oh, then, rouse thee from thy sleep
Wake, and o'er thy folly weep;
Jesus calls from death and night;
Jesus waits to shed his light.

BRADEN. S. M. WM. B. BRADBURY.

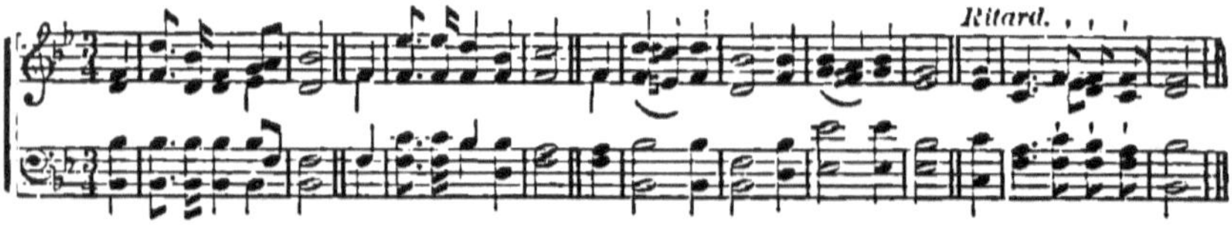
Ritard.

344 *Importance of To-day.* S. M. (139)

To-MORROW, Lord, is thine,
Lodged in thy sovereign hand;
And if its sun arise and shine,
It shines by thy command.

2 The present moment flies,
And bears our life away;
Oh, make thy servants truly wise,
That they may live to-day.

3 Since on this fleeting hour
Eternity is hung,
Awake, by thy almighty power,
The aged and the young.

4 One thing demands our care;
Oh, be it still pursued,
Lest, slighted once, the season fair
Should never be renewed.

5 To Jesus may we fly,
Swift as the morning light,
Lest life's young, golden beams should die
In sudden, endless night.

345 *The Evening's Lesson.* S. M. (138)

1 THE swift declining day,
How fast its moments fly,
While evening's broad and gloomy shade
Gains on the western sky!

2 Ye mortals, mark its pace,
And use the hours of light;
For, know, its Maker can command
An instant, endless night.

3 Give glory to the Lord,
Who rules the rolling sphere:
Submissive, at his footstool bow,
And seek salvation there.

346 *The accepted Time.* S. M. (138)

1 Now is th' accepted time;
Now is the day of grace;
Now, sinners, come, without delay,
And seek the Saviour's face.

2 Now is th' accepted time;
The Saviour calls to-day;
To-morrow it may be too late;
Then why should you delay?

3 Now is th' accepted time;
The gospel bids you come,
And every promise in his word
Declares there yet is room.

4 Lord, draw reluctant souls,
And feast them with thy love;
Then will the angels swiftly fly
To bear the news above.

347 S. M. (138)

To-day harden not your Hearts

1 THE Lord Jehovah calls;
Be every ear inclined;
May such a voice awake each heart,
And captivate the mind.

2 If he in thunder speak,
Earth trembles at his nod:
But milder accents here proclaim
The condescending God.

3 Oh, harden not your hearts,
But hear his voice to-day;
Lest, ere to-morrow's earliest dawn,
He call your souls away.

4 Almighty God, pronounce
The word of conquering grace:
So shall the flint dissolve to tears,
And scorners seek thy face.

348 *Expostulation.* L. M. (120)

Tune—SESSIONS, next page.

1 OH, do not let the word depart,
And close thine eyes against the light;
Poor sinner, harden not thy heart:
Thou wouldst be saved; why not to-night?

2 To-morrow's sun may never rise
To bless thy long deluded sight;
This is the time; oh, then be wise!
Thou wouldst be saved; why not to-night?

3 Our God in pity lingers still;
And wilt thou thus his love requite?
Renounce at length thy stubborn will:
Thou wouldst be saved; why not to-night?

4 Our blessed Lord refuses none
Who would to him their souls unite;
Then be the work of grace begun:
Thou wouldst be saved; why not to-night?

SESSIONS L. M. L. O. EMERSON.

349 L. M. (124)

Hardness of Heart lamented.

Tune—WARE.

1 LORD, shed a beam of heavenly day
To melt this stubborn stone away;
Now thaw, with rays of love divine,
This heart, this frozen heart, of mine.

2 The rocks can rend; the earth can quake;
The seas can roar; the mountains shake:
Of feeling all things show some sign
But this unfeeling heart of mine.

3 To hear the sorrows thou hast felt,
All but an adamant would melt;
Goodness and wrath in vain combine
To move this stupid heart of mine.

4 But One can yet perform the deed;
That One in all his grace I need;
Thy Spirit can from dross refine
And melt this stubborn heart of mine.

5 O Breath of life, breathe on my soul!
On me let streams of mercy roll;
Now thaw, with rays of love divine,
This heart, this frozen heart, of mine.

WARE. L. M. GEO. KINGSLEY.

350 S. M. (180)

Hope from the Gospel only.

Tune—EVANS.

1 GOD'S holy law, transgressed,
Speaks nothing but despair;
Convinced of guilt, with grief oppressed
We find no comfort there.

2 Not all our groans and tears,
Nor works which we have done,
Nor vows, nor promises, nor prayers,
Can e'er for sin atone.

3 Relief alone is found
In Jesus' precious blood:
'Tis this that heals the mortal wound,
And reconciles to God.

4 High lifted on the cross
The spotless Victim dies;
This is salvation's only source;
Hence all our hopes arise.

EVANS. S. M. W. A. TARBUTTON.

351 *Pardon penitently implored.* L. M. (117)

Tune—WINDHAM, No. 312.

1 Show pity, Lord; O Lord, forgive;
Let a repenting rebel live;
Are not thy mercies large and free?
May not a sinner trust in thee?

2 My crimes, though great, cannot surpass
The power and glory of thy grace:
Great God, thy nature hath no bound;
So let thy pardoning love be found.

3 Oh, wash my soul from every sin,
And make my guilty conscience clean
Here, on my heart, the burden lies,
And past offences pain mine eyes.

4 My lips, with shame, my sins confess,
Against thy law, against thy grace:
Lord, should thy judgment grow severe,
I am condemned, but thou art clear.

5 Should sudden vengeance seize my breath,
I must pronounce thee just in death;
And if my soul were sent to hell,
Thy righteous law approves it well.

6 Yet save a trembling sinner, Lord,
Whose hope, still hovering round thy word
Would light on some sweet promise there,
Some sure support against despair.

WOODWORTH. L. M. Wm. B. Bradbury.

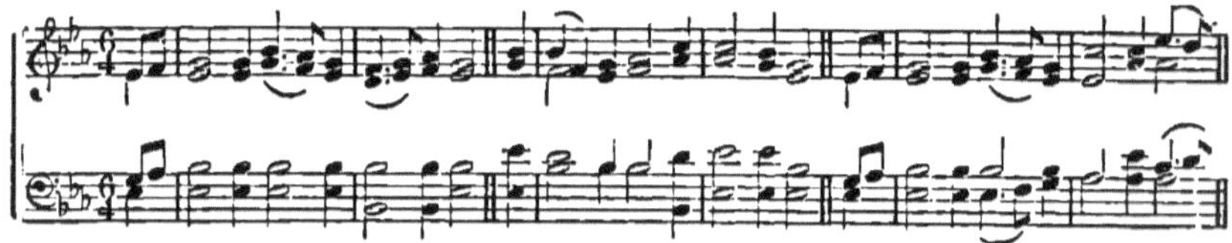

352 L. M. (118)

Prayer of the Publican.

1 With broken heart and contrite sigh,
A trembling sinner, Lord, I cry:
Thy pardoning grace is rich and free:
O God, be merciful to me!

2 I smite upon my troubled breast,
With deep and conscious guilt oppressed:
Christ and his cross my only plea:
O God, be merciful to me!

3 Far off I stand with tearful eyes,
Nor dare uplift them to the skies;
But thou dost all my anguish see:
O God, be merciful to me!

4 Nor alms, nor deeds that I have done,
Can for a single sin atone;
To Calvary alone I flee:
O God, be merciful to me

5 And when, redeemed from sin and hell,
With all the ransomed throng I dwell,
My raptured song shall ever be,
God has been merciful to me!

ROMBERG. C. M. Dr. T. Hastings.

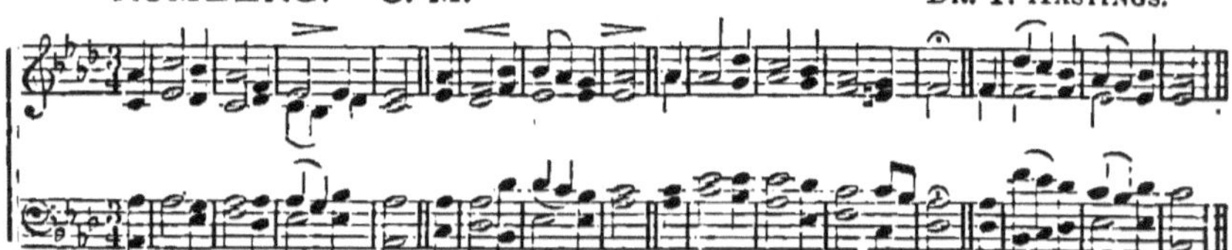

353 *A new Heart desired.* C. M. (155)

1 With guilt oppressed, bowed down with sin,
Beneath its load I groan;
Give me, O Lord, a heart of flesh;
Remove this heart of stone.

2 A burdened sinner, lo! I come,
In dread of death and hell;
Oh, seal my pardon with thy blood,
And all my fears dispel.

3 Nor peace nor rest my soul can find
Till thy dear cross I see;
Till there in humble faith I cry,
"The Saviour died for me."

4 Oh, give this true and living faith,
This soul-supporting view;
Till old things be for ever past,
And all within be new

354 *Seeking perfect Rest in Christ.* L. M. (119)

Tune—WOODWORTH, No. 352.

1 OH that my load of sin were gone!
Oh that I could at last submit,
At Jesus' feet to lay it down,
To lay my soul at Jesus' feet!

2 Rest for my soul I long to find;
Saviour of all, if mine thou art,
Give me thy meek and lowly mind,
And stamp thine image on my heart.

3 Fain would I learn of thee, my God,
Thy light and easy burden prove;
The cross, all stain'd with hallow'd blood,
The labor of thy dying love.

4 I would, but thou must give the power;
My heart from every sin release;
Bring near, bring near the joyful hour,
And fill me with thy perfect peace.

ALETTA. 7s. WM. B. BRADBURY.

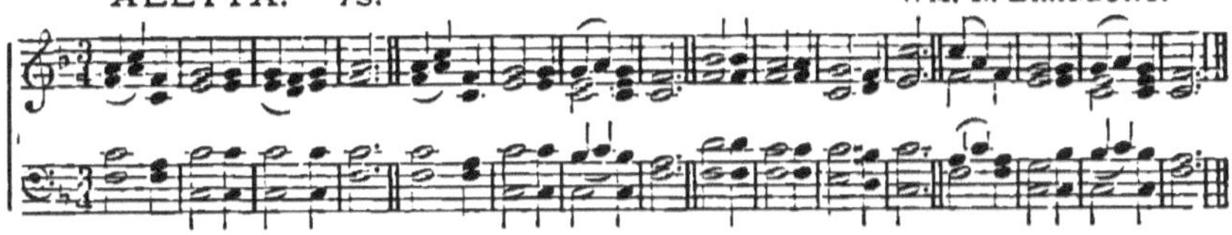

355 *"Humbled in the Dust."* 7s. (188)

1 SOVEREIGN Ruler, Lord of all,
Prostrate at thy feet we fall;
Hear, oh, hear our earnest cry!
Frown not, lest we faint and die.

2 Justly might the fatal dart
Pierce our guilty, broken heart;
Justly might thy righteous breath
Doom us to eternal death.

3 Jesus, save our dying soul;
Make our broken spirit whole:
Humbled in the dust we lie;
Saviour, leave us not to die.

OZREM. S. M. I. B. WOODBURY.

356 *Mercy implored.* S. M. (154)

1 THOU Lord of all above,
And all below the sky,
Before thy feet I prostrate fall,
And for thy mercy cry.

2 Forgive my follies past,
The crimes which I have done;
Oh, bid a contrite sinner live,
Through thy incarnate Son.

3 Guilt, like a heavy load,
Upon my conscience lies;
To thee I make my sorrows known,
And lift my weeping eyes.

4 The burden which I feel,
Thou only canst remove;
Display, O Lord, thy pardoning grace,
And thy unbounded love.

5 One gracious look of thine
Will ease my troubled breast;
Oh, let me know my sins forgiven,
And I shall then be blest.

357 *The Penitent's Inquiry.* 7s. (188)

Tune—ALETTA.

1 DEPTH of mercy! can there be
Mercy still reserved for me?
Can my God his wrath forbear
And the chief of sinners spare?

2 I have long withstood his grace;
Long provoked him to his face;
Would not hear his gracious calls;
Grieved him by a thousand falls.

3 Jesus, answer from above:
Is not all thy nature love?
Wilt thou not the wrong forget?
Lo, I fall before thy feet.

4 Now incline me to repent;
Let me now my fall lament;
Deeply my revolt deplore;
Weep, believe, and sin no more.

FULTON. 7s. Wm. B. Bradbury.

358 *Confession of Sin.* 7s. (137)

1 God of mercy, God of grace,
Hear our sad, repentant songs;
Oh, restore thy suppliant race,
Thou, to whom our praise belongs.

2 Deep regret for follies past,
Talents wasted, time misspent;
Hearts debased by worldly cares,
Thankless for the blessings lent;—

3 Foolish fears and fond desires,
Vain regrets for things as vain,
Lips too seldom taught to praise,
Oft to murmur and complain;—

4 These, and every secret fault,
Filled with grief and shame, we own;
Humbled at thy feet we lie,
Seeking pardon from thy throne.

HEBER. C. M. Geo. Kingsley.

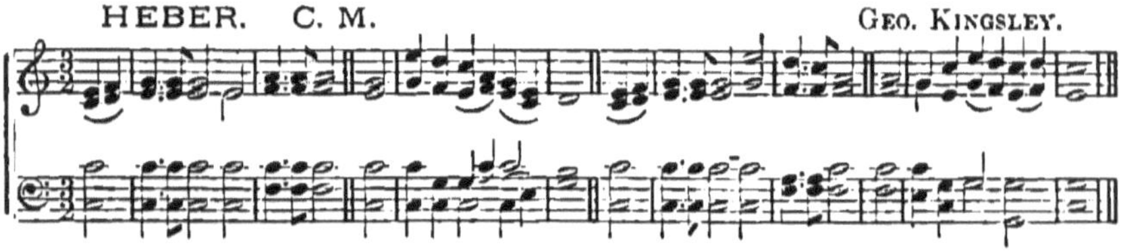

359 *Past Sins acknowledged.* C. M. (134)

1 As o'er the past my memory strays,
Why heaves the secret sigh?
'Tis that I mourn departed days,
Still unprepared to die.

2 The world and worldly things beloved
My anxious thoughts employed;
And time, unhallowed, unimproved,
Presents a fearful void.

3 Yet, holy Father, wild despair
Chase from my laboring breast:
Thy grace it is which prompts the prayer;
That grace can do the rest.

4 My life's brief remnant all be thine;
And when thy sure decree
Bids me this fleeting breath resign,
Oh, speed my soul to thee.

HAVERGAL. C. M. Havergal.

360 *The Sinner's Plea.* C. M. (156)

1 Dear Saviour, prostrate at thy feet
A guilty rebel lies,
And upward to thy mercy-seat
Presumes to lift his eyes.

2 If tears of sorrow would suffice
To pay the debt I owe,
Tears should from both my weeping eyes
In ceaseless torrents flow.

(continued.)

3 But no such sacrifice I plead
To expiate my guilt;
No tears but those which thou hast shed,
No blood but thou hast spilt.

4 I plead thy sorrows, gracious Lord,
Do thou my sins forgive;
Thy justice will approve the word
That bids the sinner live.

361 *The Sinner's Request.* L. M. (119)

Tune—WOODWORTH, No. 352.

1 O THOU that hear'st when sinners cry,
Though all my sins before thee lie,
Behold them not with angry look,
But blot their memory from thy book.

2 Create my nature pure within,
And form my soul averse to sin;
Let thy good Spirit ne'er depart,
Nor hide thy presence from my heart.

3 I cannot live without thy light,
Cast out and banished from thy sight;
Thy holy joys, my God, restore,
And guard me, that I fall no more.

4 Though I have grieved thy Spirit, Lord,
His help and comfort still afford,
And let a wretch come near thy throne,
To plead the merits of thy Son.

362 C. M. (156)

Pleading the Death of Christ.

Tune—HAVERGAL, No. 360.

1 O GOD of mercy, hear my call;
My load of guilt remove;
Break down this separating wall
That bars me from thy love.

2 Give me the presence of thy grace;
Then my rejoicing tongue
Shall speak aloud thy righteousness,
And make thy praise my song.

3 No blood of goats, nor heifer slain,
For sin could e'er atone;
The death of Christ shall still remain
Sufficient and alone.

4 A soul, oppressed with sin's desert,
My God will ne'er despise;
A broken and a contrite heart
Is our best sacrifice.

363 L. M. (118)

Returning to God.

Tune—WOODWORTH, No. 352.

1 A BROKEN heart, my God, my King,
Is all the sacrifice I bring;
The God of grace will ne'er despise
A broken heart for sacrifice.

2 My soul is humbled in the dust,
And owns thy dreadful sentence just;
Look down, O Lord, with pitying eye,
And save the soul condemned to die.

3 Then will I teach the world thy ways;
Sinners shall learn thy sovereign grace;
I'll lead them to my Saviour's blood,
And they shall praise a pardoning God.

4 Oh, may thy love inspire my tongue;
Salvation shall be all my song;
And all my powers shall join to bless
The Lord, my strength and righteousness.

INVITED.

UNAM. 8s, 7s, & 4. CARMINA SACRA.

364 8s, 7s, & 4. (222)

The Sinner entreated.

1 HEAR, O sinner; Mercy hails you;
Now with sweetest voice she calls;
Bids you haste to seek the Saviour,
Ere the hand of Justice falls:
Trust in Jesus;
'Tis the voice of Mercy calls.

2 Haste, O sinner, to the Saviour;
Seek his mercy while you may,
Soon the day of grace is over;
Soon your life will pass away;
Haste to Jesus;
You must perish if you stay.

LENOX. H. M. EDSON.

365 *The Jubilee proclaimed.* H. M. (132)

1 BLOW ye the trumpet, blow,
The gladly solemn sound;
Let all the nations know,
To earth's remotest bound,
The year of jubilee is come;
Return, ye ransomed sinners, home.

2 Exalt the Lamb of God,
The sin-atoning Lamb;
Redemption by his blood
Through all the lands proclaim:
The year of jubilee is come;
Return, ye ransomed sinners, home.

3 Ye slaves of sin and hell,
Your liberty receive,
And safe in Jesus dwell,
And blest in Jesus live:
The year of jubilee is come;
Return, ye ransomed sinners, home.

4 The gospel trumpet hear,
The news of pardoning grace;
Ye happy souls, draw near;
Behold your Saviour's face;
The year of jubilee is come;
Return, ye ransomed sinners, home.

5 Jesus, our great High Priest,
Has full atonement made;
Ye weary spirits, rest;
Ye mourning souls, be glad:
The year of jubilee is come;
Return, ye ransomed sinners, home.

BROWN. C. M. WM. B. BRADBURY.

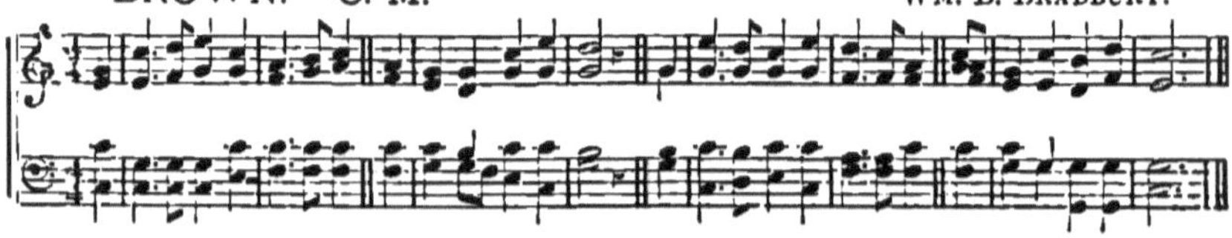

366 *The Gospel Offer.* C. M. (162)

1 LET every mortal ear attend,
And every heart rejoice;
The trumpet of the gospel sounds,
With an inviting voice.

2 Ho! all ye hungry, starving souls,
That feed upon the wind,
And vainly strive with earthly toys
To fill an empty mind,—

3 Eternal wisdom has prepared
A soul-reviving feast,
And bids your longing appetites
The rich provision taste.

4 Ho! ye that pant for living streams,
And pine away and die,
Here you may quench your raging thirst
With springs that never dry.

5 The happy gates of gospel grace
Stand open night and day;
Lord, we are come to seek supplies,
And drive our wants away.

ADAMS. C. M. GEO. KINGSLEY.

367 *The Gospel Feast.* C. M. (196)

1 YE wretched, hungry starving poor,
Behold a royal feast,
Where Mercy spreads her bounteous store
For every humble guest.

2 There Jesus stands with open arms,
He calls, he bids you come:
Though guilt restrains, and fear alarms,
Behold, there yet is room.

3 Oh, come, and with his children taste
The blessings of his love;
While hope expects the sweet repast
Of nobler joys above.

4 There, with united heart and voice,
Before th' eternal throne,
Ten thousand thousand souls rejoice,
In songs on earth unknown.

5 And yet ten thousand thousand more
Are welcome still to come;
Ye longing souls, the grace adore,
And enter while there's room.

SCOTLAND. 12s. DR. CLARKE.

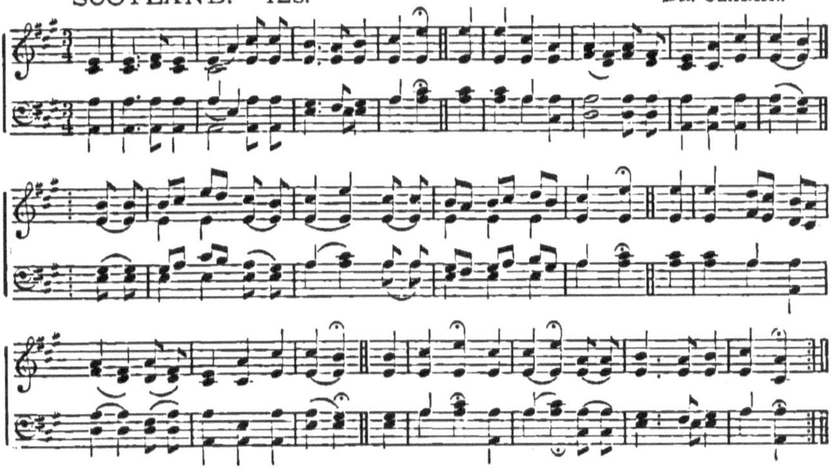

368 *Free Grace.* 12s. (131)

1 THE voice of free grace cries, Escape to the mountain;
For Adam's lost race Christ has opened a fountain:
For sin and uncleanness, for every transgression,
His blood flows most freely in streams of salvation.
Hallelujah to the Lamb! he hath purchased our pardon;
We'll praise him again when we pass over Jordan.

2 Ye souls that are wounded, oh, flee to the Saviour!
He calls you in mercy, 'tis infinite favor!
Your sins are increasing; escape to the mountain;
His blood can remove them, which flows from the fountain.
Hallelujah to the Lamb, etc.

3 O Jesus, ride on, triumphantly glorious;
O'er sin, death, and hell, thou art more than victorious;
Thy name is the theme of the great congregation,
While angels and men raise the shout of salvation:
Hallelujah to the Lamb, etc.

ROMBERG. C. M. DR. T. HASTINGS.

369 *Provisions of Grace.* C. M. (155)

1 AMAZING sight! the Saviour stands
And knocks at every door;
Ten thousand blessings in his hands,
To satisfy the poor.

2 "Behold," he saith, "I bleed and die
To bring you to my rest:
Hear, sinners, while I'm passing by,
And be for ever blest.

3 "Will you despise my bleeding love,
And choose the way to hell?
Or in the glorious realms above,
With me, for ever dwell?

4 "Say, will you hear my gracious voice,
And have your sins forgiven?
Or will you make that wretched choice,
And bar yourselves from heaven?"

FINNEY. 8s, 7s, & 4. W. B. BRADBURY.

370 *Sinners called.* 8s, 7s, & 4. (221)

1 COME, ye sinners, poor and wretched,
Come in mercy's gracious hour;
Jesus ready stands to save you,
Full of pity, love, and power:
He is able,
He is willing, doubt no more.

2 Let not conscience make you linger,
Nor of fitness fondly dream;
All the fitness he requireth
Is to feel your need of him:
This he gives you;
'Tis the Spirit's rising beam.

3 Agonizing in the garden,
Lo! your Maker prostrate lies;
On the bloody tree behold him;
Hear him cry before he dies:
"It is finished;"
Sinners, will not this suffice?

4 Lo! th' incarnate God, ascended,
Pleads the merit of his blood;
Venture on him, venture wholly;
Let no other trust intrude:
None but Jesus
Can do helpless sinners good.

371 *The last Resolve.* C. M. (161)

Tune—CROSS AND CROWN, next page.

1 COME, weary sinner, in whose breast
A thousand thoughts revolve;
Come, with your guilt and fear oppressed,
And make this last resolve:

2 "I'll go to Jesus, though my sin
Hath like a mountain rose;
I know his courts; I'll enter in,
Whatever may oppose.

3 "I'll prostrate lie before his throne,
And there my guilt confess;
I'll tell him I'm a wretch undone,
Without his sovereign grace.

4 "I'll to the gracious King approach,
Whose sceptre pardon gives:
Perhaps he may command my touch,
And then the suppliant lives.

(CONTINUED.)

CROSS AND CROWN. C. M. WESTERN MELODY.

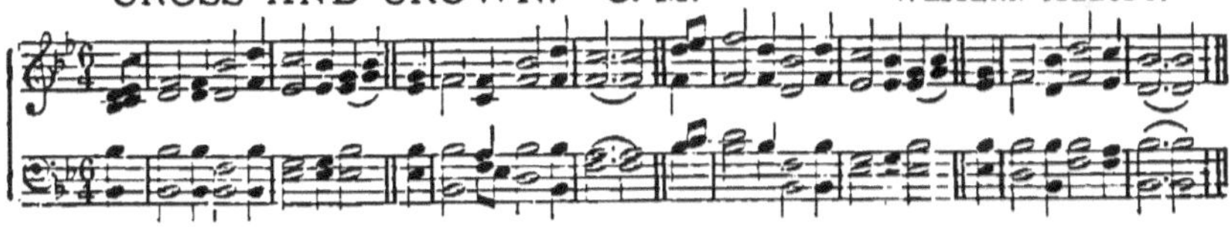

5 "Perhaps he will admit my plea,
Perhaps will hear my prayer;
But, if I perish, I will pray,
And perish only there.

6 "I can but perish if I go;
I am resolved to try;
For if I stay away, I know
I must for ever die."

ELLIOT. 8s & 6. DR. L. MASON.

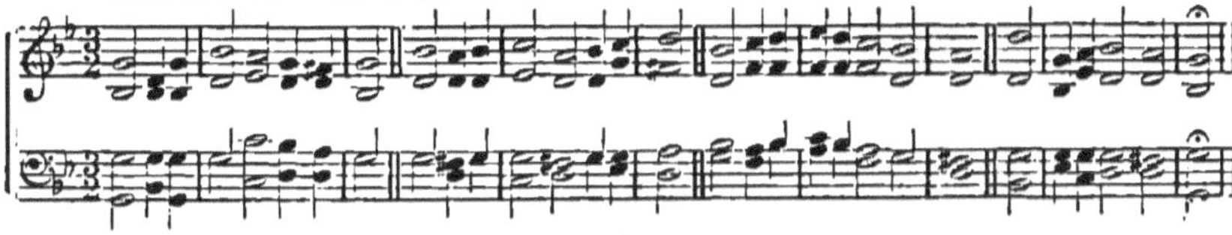

372 *The Invitation.* 8s & 6. (176)

1 JUST as thou art,—without one trace
Of love, or joy, or inward grace,
Or fitness for the heavenly place,—
O guilty sinner, come!

2 Thy sins I bore on Calvary's tree;
The stripes, thy due, were laid on me,
That peace and pardon might be free,—
O wretched sinner, come!

3 Come, leave thy burden at the cross;
Count all thy gains but empty dross;
My grace repays all earthly loss,—
O needy sinner, come!

4 Come, hither bring thy boding fears,
Thy aching heart, thy bursting tears;
'Tis Mercy's voice salutes thine ears,—
O trembling sinner, come!

5 The Spirit and the bride say, "Come!"
Rejoicing saints re-echo, "Come!"
Who faints, who thirsts, who will, may come,
Thy Saviour bids thee come.

373 *Sinners invited.* C. M. (163)

Tune—BROWN, No. 366.

1 OH, what amazing words of grace
Are in the gospel found!
Suited to every sinner's case
Who hears the joyful sound.

2 Come, then, with all your wants and wounds;
Your every burden bring;
Here love, unchanging love abounds,
A deep, celestial spring.

3 This spring with living water flows,
And heavenly joy imparts:
Come, thirsty souls, your wants disclose,
And drink with thankful hearts.

4 A host of sinners, vile as you,
Have here found life and peace;
Come, thou, and prove its virtues too,
And drink, adore, and bless.

374 L. M. (119)

The Saviour's Invitation.

Tune—WOODWORTH, No. 352.

1 "COME hither, all ye weary souls,
Ye heavy-laden sinners, come:
I'll give you rest from all your toils,
And raise you to my heavenly home.

2 "They shall find rest who learn of me:
I'm of a meek and lowly mind;
But passion rages like the sea,
And pride is restless as the wind.

3 "Blest is the man whose shoulders take
My yoke, and bear it with delight:
My yoke is easy to the neck;
My grace shall make the burden light."

4 Jesus, we come at thy command;
With faith and hope and humble zeal,
Resign our spirits to thy hand,
To mould and guide us at thy will.

"LOOKING UNTO JESUS." 6s.

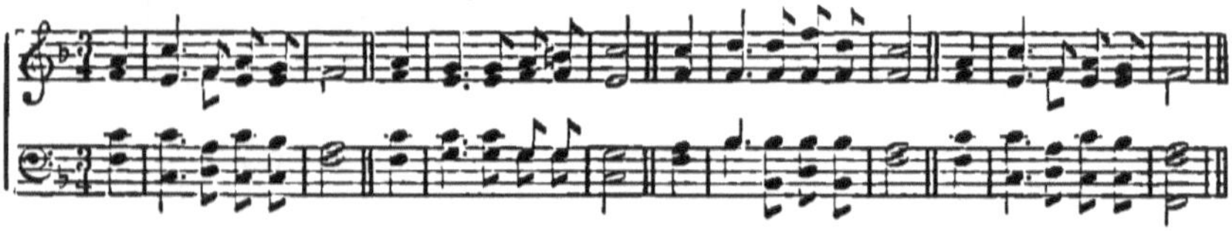

375 *"Looking unto Jesus."* 6s. (148)

1 Come to the blood-stained tree
The victim bleeding lies;
God sets the sinner free,
Since Christ a ransom dies.

2 Look not within for peace;
Within there's naught to cheer;
Look up and find release
From sin and self and fear.

3 Rest to the weary soul
And aching breast is given;
Balm makes the wounded whole;
Love fills the heart with heaven.

4 For thee, dear soul, for thee,
These priceless joys were bought;
Accept the mercy free
That Christ to earth hath brought.

WOODWORTH. L. M.

Wm. B. Bradbury.

376 *Gospel Grace.* L. M. (119)

1 Come, weary souls, with sins distressed,
Come, and accept the promised rest;
The Saviour's gracious call obey,
And cast your gloomy fears away.

2 Oppressed with guilt, a painful load,
Oh, come and spread your woes abroad:
Divine compassion, mighty love,
Will all that painful load remove.

3 Here mercy's boundless ocean flows,
To cleanse your guilt and heal your woes;
Pardon and life and endless peace,—
How rich the gift, how free the grace!

4 Dear Saviour, let thy wondrous love
Confirm our faith, our fears remove;
Oh, sweetly influence every breast,
And guide us to eternal rest.

377 *"Come to me."* L. M. (146)

Tune—Retreat, next page.

1 With tearful eyes I look around;
Life seems a dark and stormy sea;
Yet, 'mid the gloom, I hear a sound,
A heavenly whisper, "Come to me."

2 It tells me of a place of rest;
It tells me where my soul may flee:
Oh, to the weary, faint, oppressed,
How sweet the bidding, "Come to me!"

3 "Come, for all else must fail and die;
Earth is no resting place for thee;
To heaven direct thy weeping eye,
I am thy portion; come to me."

4 O voice of mercy, voice of love,
In conflict, grief, and agony,
Support me, cheer me from above;
And gently whisper, "Come to me."

378 *All Things are ready.* C. M. (163)

Tune—Brown, No. 366.

1 The Saviour calls; let every ear
Attend the heavenly sound;
Ye doubting souls, dismiss your fear;
Hope smiles reviving round.

2 For every thirsty, longing heart,
Here streams of bounty flow;
And life and health and bliss impart,
To banish mortal woe.

3 Ye sinners, come; 'tis mercy's voice;
That gracious voice obey;
'Tis Jesus calls to heavenly joys;
And can you yet delay?

4 Dear Saviour, draw reluctant hearts;
To thee let sinners fly,
And take the bliss thy love imparts,
And drink, and never die.

RETREAT. L. M. DR. T. HASTINGS.

379 L. M. (119)

Behold, I stand at the Door and knock.

Tune—WOODWORTH, No. 376.

1 BEHOLD a Stranger at the door:
He gently knocks, has knocked before;
Has waited long, is waiting still:
You treat no other friend so ill.

2 Oh, lovely attitude! he stands
With melting heart and open hands:
Oh, matchless kindness! and he shows
This matchless kindness to his foes.

3 Rise, touched with gratitude divine,
Turn out his enemy and thine;
Turn out thy soul-enslaving sin,
And let the heavenly Stranger in.

4 Oh, welcome him, the Prince of peace!
Now may his gentle reign increase!
Throw wide the door, each willing mind
And be his empire all mankind.

ROSEFIELD. 7s. 6 lines. DR. MALAN.

380 *Substitution.* 7s. 6l. (133)

1 SURELY Christ thy griefs hath borne,
Weeping soul, no longer mourn·
View him bleeding on the tree,
Pouring out his life for thee:
There thy every sin he bore;
Weeping soul, lament no more.

2 Cast thy guilty soul on him,
Find him mighty to redeem;
At his feet thy burden lay;
Look thy doubts and cares away;
Now by faith the Son embrace;
Plead his promise, trust his grace.

3 Lord, thy arm must be reveal'd,
Ere I can by faith be heal'd;
Since I scarce can look to thee,
Cast a gracious eye on me.
At thy feet myself I lay;
Shine, oh, shine my fears away.

381 *Jesus paid it all.* 7s & 6s. (129)

Tune next page.

1 NOTHING, either great or small,
Remains for me to do;
Jesus died and paid it all,
Yes, all the debt I owe.

Jesus paid it all,
All the debt I owe;
Jesus died and paid it all,
Yes, all the debt I owe.

2 When he from his lofty throne
Stooped down to do and die,
Everything was fully done;
Yes, "finished!" was his cry.

3 Weary, working, plodding one,
Oh, wherefore toil you so?
Cease your "doing:" all was done,
Yes, ages long ago.

(CONTINUED.)

JESUS PAID IT ALL. 7s & 6s.

WM. B. BRADBURY.

CHORUS.

4 Till to Jesus' work you cling,
Alone by simple faith,
"Doing" is a deadly thing,
All "doing" ends in death.

5 Cast your deadly "doing" down,
Down, all at Jesus' feet;
Stand in him, in him alone,
All glorious and complete.

TELEMANS. 7s.

C. ZEUNER.

382 *The Sinner welcomed.* 7s. (177)

1 WELCOME, welcome! sinner, hear!
Draw not back through shame or fear;
Doubt not, nor distrust the call;
Mercy is proclaimed to all.

2 Welcome to the offered peace;
Welcome, prisoner, to release;
Burst thy bonds; be saved; be free;
Rise and come,—He calleth thee.

3 Welcome to the cleansing fount,
Springing from the sacred mount;
Welcome to the feast divine,
Bread of life, and living wine.

4 All ye weary and distrest,
Welcome to relief and rest:
All is ready; hear the call;
There is ample room for all.

EXPOSTULATION. 11s.

383 *Expostulation.* 11s. (127)

1 Oh, turn ye oh, turn ye, for why will ye die,
When God in great mercy is coming so nigh?
Now Jesus invites you, the Spirit says, "Come,"
And angels are waiting to welcome you home.

2 How vain the delusion, that while you delay,
Your hearts may grow better, your chains melt away;
Come guilty, come wretched, come just as you are;
All helpless and dying, to Jesus repair.

3 The contrite in heart he will freely receive,
Oh! why will you not the glad message believe?
If sin be your burden, why will you not come?
'Tis you he makes welcome; he bids you come home.

LOWRY. L. M. 6 lines. C. F. BLANDNER.

384 *"Come unto me, all ye that labor."* L. M. (147)

1 PEACE, troubled soul, whose plaintive moan
Hath taught the rocks the notes of woe;
Cease thy complaint, suppress thy groan,
And let thy tears forget to flow:
Behold, the precious balm is found,
To lull thy pain, to heal thy wound.

2 Come, freely come, by sin oppressed;
Unburden here thy weighty load;
Here find thy refuge and thy rest,
And trust the mercy of thy God:
Thy God's thy Saviour—glorious word!
For ever love and praise the Lord!

ARCADIA. C. M. DR. T. HASTINGS.

385 *Come to the Ark.* C. M. (218)

1 COME to the ark, come to the ark;
To Jesus come away;
The pestilence walks forth by night,
The arrow flies by day.

2 Come to the ark: the waters rise,
The seas their billows rear;
While darkness gathers o'er the skies,
Behold a refuge near!

3 Come to the ark, all, all that weep
Beneath the sense of sin:
Without, deep calleth unto deep,
But all is peace within.

4 Come to the ark, ere yet the flood
Your lingering steps oppose:
Come, for the door which open stood
Is now about to close.

OLNEY. S. M. DR. L. MASON.

386

The urgent Invitation. S. M. (192)

1 THE Spirit, in our hearts,
Is whispering, "Sinner, come;"
The bride, the church of Christ, proclaims
To all his children, "Come!"

2 Let him that heareth say
To all about him, "Come;"
Let him that thirsts for righteousness
To Christ, the fountain, come.

3 Yes, whosoever will,
Oh, let him freely come,
And freely drink the stream of life;
'Tis Jesus bids him come.

4 Lo! Jesus, who invites,
Declares, "I quickly come;"
Lord, even so; we wait thy hour;
O blest Redeemer, come.

FOREST. L. M. CHAPIN.

387

Christ the only Refuge. L. M. (126)

1 WHAT shall the dying sinner do,
Who seeks relief for all his woe?
Where shall the guilty sufferer find
A balm to soothe his anguished mind?

2 In vain we search, in vain we try,
Till Jesus brings his gospel nigh;
'Tis there we find a sure relief,
A soothing balm for inward grief.

3 Be this the pillar of our hope;
This bears the fainting spirit up;
We read the grace, we trust the word,
And find salvation in the Lord.

4 Then let his name, who shed his blood
To bring the guilty nigh to God,
Be great in all the earth, and sung
In every land, by every tongue.

WOODWORTH. L. M. WM. B. BRADBURY.

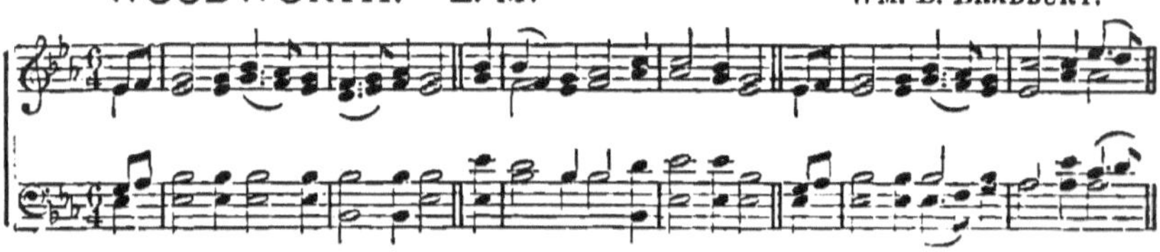

388

L. M. (119)

Christ the Physician of the Soul.

1 DEEP are the wounds which sin has made;
Where shall the sinner find a cure?
In vain, alas! is Nature's aid;
The work exceeds her utmost power.

2 But can no sovereign balm be found?
And is no kind physician nigh,
To ease the pain and heal the wound,
Ere life and hope for ever fly?

3 There is a great Physician near;
Look up, O fainting soul, and live;
See, in his heavenly smiles appear
Such help as nature cannot give.

4 See, in the Saviour's dying blood,
Life, health, and bliss abundant flow:
'Tis only that dear, sacred flood
Can ease thy pain, and heal thy woe.

COMING TO CHRIST.

ROSEFIELD. 7s. 6 lines. DR. MALAN.

389 *The finished Work.* 7s. 6l. (188)

1 FROM the cross uplifted high,
Where the Saviour deigns to die,
What melodious sounds we hear,
Bursting on the ravished ear!
"Love's redeeming work is done;
Come and welcome, sinner, come.

2 "Sprinkled now with blood the throne,
Why beneath thy burdens groan?
On my pierced body laid,
Justice owns the ransom paid;
Bow the knee, embrace the Son;
Come and welcome, sinner, come.

3 "Spread for thee, the festal board
See, with richest dainties stored;
To thy Father's bosom pressed,
Yet again a child confessed,
Never from his house to roam,
Come and welcome, sinner, come.

4 "Soon the days of life shall end;
Lo, I come, your Saviour, Friend,
Safe your spirits to convey
To the realms of endless day,
Up to my eternal home;
Come and welcome, sinner, come.

COMING TO CHRIST.

BYEFIELD. C. M. DR. T. HASTINGS.

390 *Fleeing to Christ.* C. M. (168)

1 How sad our state by nature is!
Our sin, how deep it stains!
And Satan binds our captive minds
Fast in his slavish chains.

2 But, hark! a voice of sovereign love!
'Tis Christ's inviting word:
"Ho! ye despairing sinners, come,
And trust upon the Lord."

3 My soul obeys the almighty call,
And runs to this relief;
I would believe thy promise, Lord;
Oh, help my unbelief.

4 To the dear fountain of thy blood,
Incarnate God, I fly;
Here let me wash my spotted soul
From stains of deepest dye.

5 A guilty, weak, and helpless worm,
On thy kind arms I fall;
Be thou my strength and righteousness,
My Saviour and my all

WILLMARTH. L. M. I. B. WOODBURY.

391 *God calling yet.* L. M. (145)

1 GOD calling yet! shall I not hear?
Earth's pleasures shall I still hold dear?
Shall life's swift passing years all fly,
And still my soul in slumbers lie?

2 God calling yet! shall I not rise?
Can I his loving voice despise,
And basely his kind care repay?
He calls me still; can I delay?

3 God calling yet! and shall he knock,
And I my heart the closer lock?
He still is waiting to receive,
And shall I dare his Spirit grieve?

4 God calling yet! and shall I give
No heed, but still in bondage live?
I wait, but he does not forsake;
He calls me still! my heart, awake!

5 God calling yet! I cannot stay;
My heart I yield without delay:
Vain world, farewell; from thee I part;
The voice of God hath reached my heart.

PEDDIE. 7s. 6 lines. GREGORIAN.

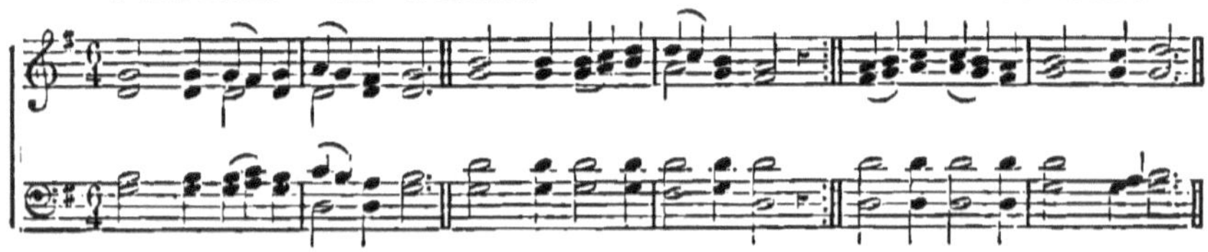

392 *Invitation accepted.* 7s. (136)

1 AM I called? and can it be?
Has my Saviour chosen me?
Guilty, wretched as I am,
Has he named my worthless name?
Vilest of the vile am I;
Dare I raise my hopes so high?

2 Am I called? I dare not stay,
May not, must not disobey;
Here I lay me at thy feet,
Clinging to the mercy-seat.
Thine I am, and thine alone;
Lord, with me thy will be done.

3 Am I called? an heir of God?
Wash'd, redeem'd, by precious blood?
Father, lead me by thy hand,
Guide me to that better land,
Where my soul shall be at rest,
Pillow'd on my Saviour's breast.

FULTON. 7s. Wm. B. Bradbury.

393

7s. (137)

Christ the Source of Happiness.

1 Object of my first desire,
Jesus, crucified for me,
I to happiness aspire
Only to be found in thee:
Thee to praise, and thee to know,
Constitute our bliss below:
Thee to see, and thee to love,
Constitute our bliss above.

2 Lord, it is not life to live,
If thy presence thou deny:
Lord, if thou thy presence give,
'Tis no longer death to die:
Source and Giver of repose,
Singly from thy smile it flows;
Peace and happiness are thine;
Mine they are, if thou art mine.

394

S. M. (192)

The Soul given up to Christ.

Tune—Olney, No. 386.

1 And can I yet delay
My little all to give?
To tear my soul from earth away,
And Jesus to receive?

2 Nay, but I yield, I yield!
I can hold out no more:
I sink, by dying love compelled,
And own thee Conqueror.

3 Though late, I all forsake;
My friends, my all resign:
Gracious Redeemer, take, oh, take,
And seal me ever thine.

4 Come, and possess me whole,
Nor hence again remove:
Settle and fix my wavering soul
With all thy weight of love.

5 My one desire be this,
Thy only love to know;
Freely to yield all other bliss,
All other good, below.

COMPASSION. S. M. G. O. Robinson.

395

Filial Confidence. S. M. (234)

1 Lord, I would come to thee,
A sinner all defiled;
Oh, take the stain of guilt away,
And own me as thy child.

2 I cannot live in sin,
And feel a Saviour's love;
Thy blood can make my spirit clean,
And write my name above.

3 Blest Shepherd, I am thine;
Still keep me in thy fear;
Now fill my heart with grace divine;
Bring thy salvation near.

COLBURN. L. M. W. B. BRADBURY

Ritard.

396 *The only Plea.* L. M. (122)

1 JESUS, the sinner's Friend, to thee,
Lost and undone, for aid I flee;
Weary of earth, myself, and sin,
Open thine arms and take me in.

2 Pity and save my ruined soul;
'Tis thou alone canst make me whole;
Dark, till in me thine image shine,
And lost I am till thou art mine.

3 At last I own it cannot be
That I should fit myself for thee:
Here, then, to thee I all resign;
Thine is the work, and only thine.

4 What can I say thy grace to move?
Lord, I am sin,—but thou art love:
I give up every plea beside,
Lord, I am lost,—but thou hast died!

BLANDNER. S. M. JOHN M. EVANS.

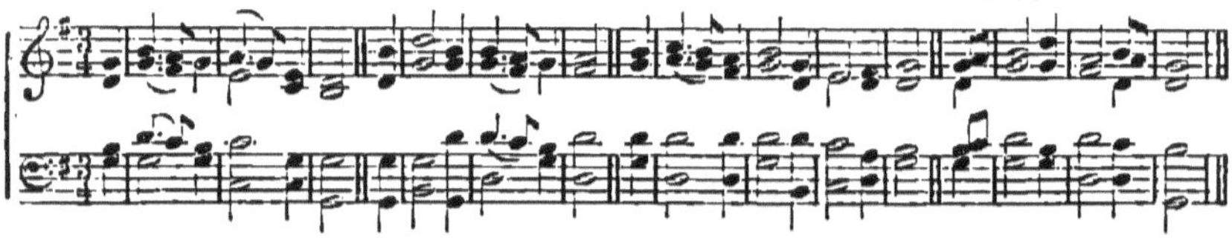

397 *The only Refuge.* S. M. (116)

1 JESUS, I come to thee,
A sinner doomed to die;
My only refuge is thy cross,
Here at thy feet I lie.

2 Can mercy reach my case,
And all my sins remove?
Break, O my God, this heart of stone,
And melt it by thy love.

3 Thy blood can cleanse my heart,
Thy hand can wipe my tears;
Oh! send thy blessed Spirit down
To banish all my fears.

4 Then shall my soul arise,
From sin and Satan free;
Redeemed from hell and every foe,
I'll trust alone in thee.

398 L. M. (174)

The Joy of Forgiveness.

Tune—FEDERAL STREET, next page.

1 TREMBLING before thine awful throne,
O Lord, in dust my sins I own:
Justice and mercy for my life
Contend: thy blood must heal the strife!

2 In thee I trust!—upon my soul
New tides of hope tumultuous roll—
Thy voice proclaims my pardon found;
Seraphic transport wings the sound.

3 Earth has a joy unknown in heaven,
The new-born peace of sin forgiven:
Tears of such pure and deep delight,
Ye angels, never dimmed your sight.

4 But I amid your choirs shall shine,
And all your knowledge will be mine:
Ye on your harps must lean to hear
A secret chord that mine will bear.

399 7s. (137)

Lord, save us: we perish.

Tune—FULTON, next page.

1 GRACIOUS Lord, incline thine ear
My requests vouchsafe to hear;
Hear my never-ceasing cry:
Give me Christ, or else I die.

2 Lord, deny me what thou wilt,
Only ease me of my guilt:
Suppliant at thy feet I lie;
Give me Christ, or else I die.

3 All unholy and unclean,
I am nothing else but sin:
On thy mercy I rely;
Give me Christ, or else I die.

4 Thou dost freely save the lost,
In thy grace alone I trust:
With my earnest suit comply;
Give me Christ, or else I die.

FEDERAL STREET. L. M. H. K. OLIVER.

FULTON. 7s. WM. B. BRADBURY.

400 *Coming to Christ.* L. M. (122)

Tune—COLBURN, No. 398.

1 JESUS, my Lord, my life, my all,
Prostrate before thy throne I fall;
Fain would my soul look up, and see
My hope, my heaven, my all, in thee.

2 Here, in this world of sin and woe,
I'm filled with tossings to and fro,
Burdened with sin, with fear oppressed;
And nothing here can give me rest.

3 In vain from creatures help I seek:
Thou, only thou, the word canst speak,
To heal my wounds, and calm my grief,
Or give my mournful heart relief.

4 Oh, speak and bid my soul rejoice!
I long to hear thy pardoning voice;
Say, "Peace, be still! look up and live;
Life, peace, and heaven are mine to give."

401 *Cry to Christ.* C. P. M. (206)

Tune—MERIBAH, No. 322.

1 O THOU that hear'st the prayer of faith,
Wilt thou not save a soul from death
That casts itself on thee?
I have no refuge of my own,
But fly to what my Lord hath done
And suffered once for me.

2 Slain in the guilty sinner's stead,
His spotless righteousness I plead,
And his availing blood;
That righteousness my robe shall be;
That merit shall atone for me,
And bring me near to God.

3 Then save me from eternal death;
The Spirit of adoption breathe;
His consolations send;
By him some word of life impart,
And sweetly whisper to my heart,
"Thy Maker is thy Friend."

402 C. M. (169)

Faith the Gift of God.

Tune—BYEFIELD, No. 310.

1 FATHER, I stretch my hands to thee;
No other help I know;
If thou withdraw thyself from me,
Ah, whither shall I go?

2 What did thine only Son endure
Before I drew my breath!
What pain, what labor, to secure
My soul from endless death!

3 Author of faith, to thee I lift
My weary, longing eyes;
Oh, may I now receive that gift;
My soul, without it, dies.

FOREST. L. M.

CHAPIN.

403 *For Jesus' Sake.* L. M. (126)

1 When at thy footstool, Lord, I bend,
And plead with thee for mercy there,
Oh, think thou of the sinner's Friend,
And for his sake receive my prayer!

2 Oh, think not of my shame and guilt,
My thousand stains of deepest dye;
Think of the blood which Jesus spilt,
And let that blood my pardon buy!

3 Oh, think not of my doubts and fears,
My strivings with thy grace divine;
Think upon Jesus' woes and tears,
And let his merits stand for mine!

4 Thine eye, thine ear, they are not dull;
Thine arm can never shortened be;
Behold me here, my heart is full;
Behold and spare and succor me.

5 No claim, no merits, Lord, I plead;
I come, a humbled, helpless slave;
But, ah! the more my guilty need,
The more thy glory, Lord, to save.

COLBURN. L. M.

W. B. BRADBURY.

Ritard.

404 L. M. (122)

Lord, undertake for me.

1 Lord, I'm oppressed; oh, undertake
For me, for my Redeemer's sake!
Unclean, unworthy, I confess,
Yet, oh, accept his righteousness!

2 On him alone I dare repose;
From him alone my comfort flows;
And all I am or hope to be,
I owe, through him, my God, to thee.

3 A wanderer, his mercy sought;
A slave, his blood my freedom bought;
And dead in trespasses and sin,
His voice awoke life's pulse within.

4 Since faint and feeble, weak and low,
I cannot stay, yet dare not go:
I have no strength, no hope, no plea,
Unless thou undertake for me.

405 *Yielding to Christ.* C. P. M. (206)

Tune—MERIBAH, No. 322.

1 Lord, thou hast won: at length I yield;
My heart, by mighty grace compelled,
Surrenders all to thee;
Against thy terrors long I strove,
But who can stand against thy love?
Love conquers even me.

2 Yes, since thou hast thy love revealed,
And shown my soul a pardon sealed,
I can resist no more;
Couldst thou for such a sinner bleed?
Canst thou for such a rebel plead?
I wonder and adore.

3 Now, Lord, I would be thine alone;
Come, take possession of thine own,—
For thou hast set me free;
Released from Satan's hard command,
See, all my powers in waiting stand,
To be employed by thee.

406 *Jesus! Master!* 7s. (137)

Tune—FULTON, No. 358.

1 JESUS, Master, hear my cry;
Save me, heal me with a word;
Fainting at thy feet I lie,
Thou my whisper'd plaint hast heard.

2 Jesus, Master, mercy show;
Thou art passing near my soul,
Thou my inward grief dost know,
Thou alone canst make me whole

3 Jesus, Master, as of yore
Thou didst bid the blind man see
Light upon my soul restore:
Jesus, Master, heal thou me.

FOUNTAIN. C. M. DR. L. MASON.

407 C. M. (143)

"Lord, remember me."

1 JESUS, thou art the sinner's Friend;
As such I look to thee;
Now, in the fulness of thy love,
O Lord, remember me.

2 Remember thy pure word of grace,
Remember Calvary,
Remember all thy dying groans,
And then remember me.

3 Thou wondrous Advocate with God!
I yield myself to thee;
While thou art sitting on thy throne,
Dear Lord, remember me.

4 I own I'm guilty, own I'm vile,
Yet thy salvation's free;
Then, in thy all-abounding grace,
Dear Lord, remember me.

5 And when I close my eyes in death,
When earthly helps all flee,
Then, O my dear Redeemer God
I pray, remember me.

ELLIOT. 8s & 6. DR. L. MASON.

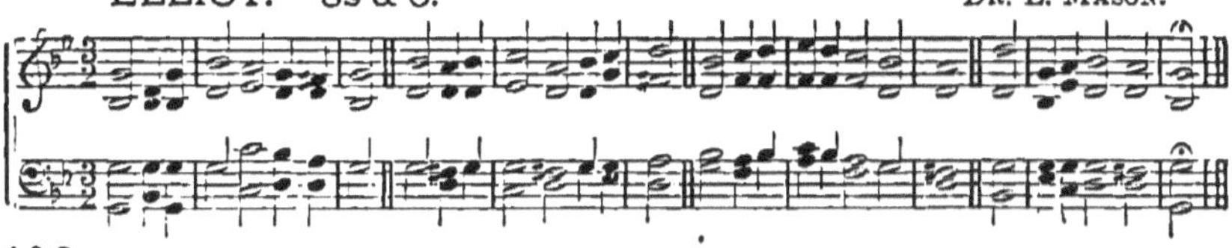

408 *Just as I am.* 8s & 6. (176)

1 JUST as I am, without one plea,
But that thy blood was shed for me,
And that thou bid'st me come to thee,
O Lamb of God, I come!

2 Just as I am, and waiting not
To rid my soul of one dark blot,
To thee, whose blood can cleanse each spot,
O Lamb of God, I come!

3 Just as I am, though tossed about
With many a conflict, many a doubt,
Fightings within, and fears without,
O Lamb of God, I come!

4 Just as I am,—poor, wretched, blind;
Sight, riches, healing of the mind,
Yea, all I need, in thee to find,
O Lamb of God, I come!

5 Just as I am,—thou wilt receive,
Wilt welcome, pardon, cleanse, relieve;
Because thy promise I believe,
O Lamb of God, I come!

6 Just as I am,—thy love unknown
Has broken every barrier down;
Now, to be thine, yea, thine alone,
O Lamb of God, I come!

ROMBERG. C. M. — Dr. T. Hastings.

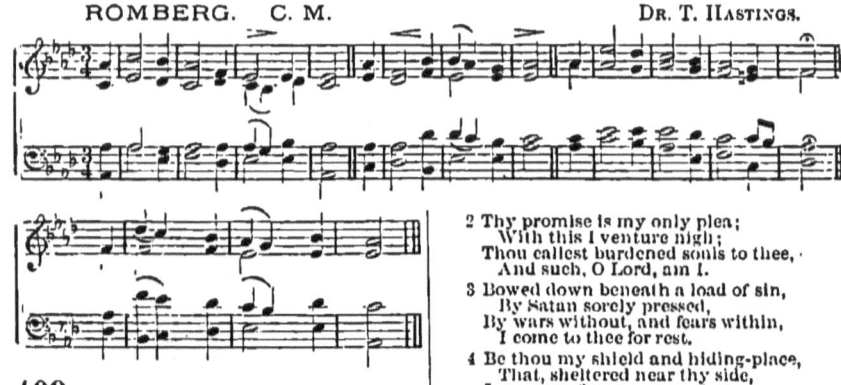

409 *The burdened Soul.* C. M. (155)

1 Lord, I approach the mercy-seat,
Where thou dost answer prayer;
There humbly fall before thy feet,
For none can perish there.

2 Thy promise is my only plea;
With this I venture nigh;
Thou callest burdened souls to thee,
And such, O Lord, am I.

3 Bowed down beneath a load of sin,
By Satan sorely pressed,
By wars without, and fears within,
I come to thee for rest.

4 Be thou my shield and hiding-place,
That, sheltered near thy side,
I may my fierce accuser face,
And tell him thou hast died.

5 Oh, wondrous love! to bleed and die,
To bear the cross and shame,
That guilty sinners, such as I,
Might plead thy gracious name.

TRUSTING IN CHRIST.

FOUNTAIN. C. M. — Dr. L. Mason.

410 C. M. (143)

Sufficiency of the Atonement.

1 There is a fountain, filled with blood,
Drawn from Immanuel's veins;
And sinners, plunged beneath that flood,
Lose all their guilty stains.

2 The dying thief rejoiced to see
That fountain, in his day;
And there have I, as vile as he,
Washed all my sins away.

3 Thou dying Lamb, thy precious blood
Shall never lose its power,
Till all the ransomed church of God
Be saved to sin no more.

4 E'er since, by faith, I saw the stream
Thy flowing wounds supply,
Redeeming love has been my theme,
And shall be, till I die.

5 And when this feeble, faltering tongue
Lies silent in the grave,
Then, in a nobler, sweeter song,
I'll sing thy power to save.

411 H. M. (132)

The sufficient Sacrifice.

Tune—Lenox, next page.

1 Arise, my soul, arise;
Shake off thy guilty fears;
The bleeding Sacrifice
In my behalf appears:
Before the throne my Surety stands;
My name is written on his hands.

2 The bleeding wounds he bears,
Received on Calvary,
Now pour effectual prayers,
And strongly speak for me:
"Forgive him, oh, forgive," they cry,
"Nor let that ransomed sinner die."

(continued.)

LENOX. H. M. EDSON.

3 The Father hears him pray,
The dear Anointed One;
He cannot turn away
The pleading of his Son:
His Spirit answers to the blood,
And tells me I am born of God.

4 To God I'm reconciled;
His pardoning voice I hear;
He owns me for his child;
I can no longer fear:
With filial trust I now draw nigh,
And "Father, Abba Father," cry

DUANE STREET. L. M. G. COLES.

FINE.

412

Looking unto Jesus. L. M. (130)

1 JESUS, my all, to heaven is gone,
He whom I fix my hopes upon;
His track I see, and I'll pursue
The narrow way till him I view.

2 The way the holy prophets went;
The road that leads from banishment:
The King's highway of holiness,
I'll go, for all his paths are peace.

3 This is the way I long have sought,
And mourned because I found it not;
My grief, my burden, long have been,
Because I could not cease from sin.

4 The more I strove against its power,
I sinned and stumbled but the more,
Till late I heard my Saviour say,
"Come hither, soul, I am the way!"

5 Lo! glad I come; and thou, dear **Lamb**,
Shalt take me to thee, as I am:
My sinful self to thee I give;
Nothing but love shall I receive

MARTYN. 7s. Double. MARSH.

FINE.
D.C.

413 *Refuge in Christ.* 7s. (153)

1 JESUS! lover of my soul,
Let me to thy bosom fly,
While the raging billows roll,
While the tempest still is high.
Hide me, O my Saviour! hide,
Till the storm of life is past;
Safe into the haven guide;
Oh, receive my soul at last!

2 Other refuge have I none;
Hangs my helpless soul on thee;
Leave, ah! leave me not alone,
Still support and comfort me.
All my trust on thee is stayed;
All my help from thee I bring;
Cover my defenceless head
With the shadow of thy wing.

3 Thou, O Christ, art all I want;
All in all in thee I find;
Raise the fallen, cheer the faint,
Heal the sick, and lead the blind.
Just and holy is thy name,
I am all unrighteousness;
Vile and full of sin I am,
Thou art full of truth and grace.

SOLID ROCK. L. M. 6 lines. W. B. BRADBURY.

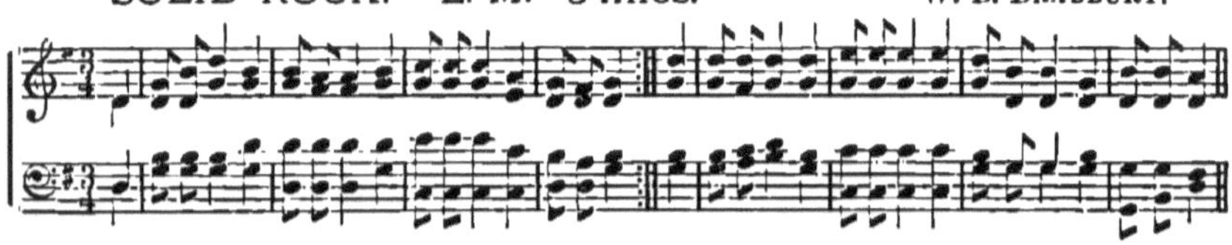

414 *The solid Rock.* L. M. 6l. (128)

1 MY hope is built on nothing less
Than Jesus' blood and righteousness,
I dare not trust the sweetest frame,
But wholly lean on Jesus' name:
On Christ, the solid rock, I stand;
All other ground is sinking sand.

2 When darkness seems to veil his face,
I rest on his unchanging grace;
In every high and stormy gale,
My anchor holds within the veil:
On Christ, the solid rock, I stand:
All other ground is sinking sand

3 His oath, his covenant and blood,
Support me in the whelming flood:
When all around my soul gives way,
He then is all my hope and stay:
On Christ, the solid rock, I stand;
All other ground is sinking sand.

415 *Security in the Cross.* L. M. (126)

Tune– FOREST, next page.

1 HERE at thy cross, incarnate God,
I lay my soul beneath thy love,
Beneath the droppings of thy blood,
Nor shall it, Jesus, e'er remove

2 Should worlds conspire to drive me thence,
Unmoved and firm this heart should lie;
Resolved,—for that's my last defence,—
If I must perish, there to die.

3 But speak, my Lord, and calm my fear;
Am I not safe beneath thy shade?
Thy justice will not strike me here,
Nor Satan dare my soul invade.

4 Yes, I'm secure beneath thy blood,
And all my foes shall lose their aim,
Hosanna to my Saviour God,
And my best honors to his name.

FOREST. L. M. CHAPIN.

416

Hidden in Christ. 7s. (152)

Tune—TOPLADY.

1 Rock of ages, cleft for me,
Let me hide myself in thee;
Let the water and the blood,
From thy side, a healing flood,
Be of sin the double cure,
Save from wrath, and make me pure.

2 Should my tears for ever flow,
Should my zeal no languor know,
All for sin could not atone;
Thou must save, and thou alone:
In my hand no price I bring;
Simply to thy cross I cling.

3 While I draw this fleeting breath,
When mine eyelids close in death,
When I rise to worlds unknown,
See thee on thy judgment throne—
Rock of ages, cleft for me,
Let me hide myself in thee.

TOPLADY. 7s. 6 lines. DR. T. HASTINGS.

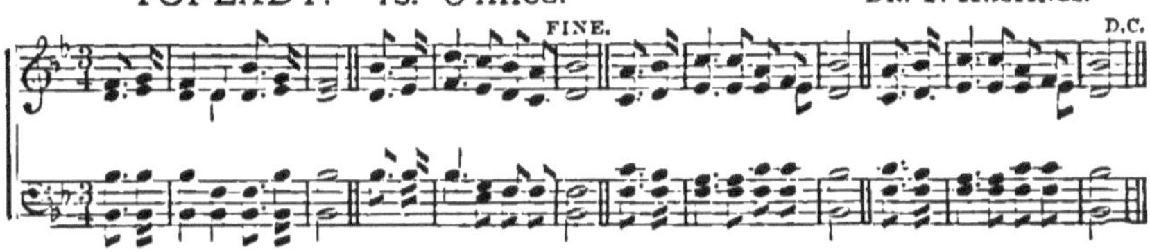
FINE.
D.C.

BRADEN. S. M. WM. B. BRADBURY.

Ritard.

417

Resting on Christ's Promise. S. M. (133)

1 My soul, with joy attend,
While Jesus silence breaks:
No angel's harp such music yields
As what my Shepherd speaks.

2 "I know my sheep," he cries;
"My soul approves them well:
Vain is the world's delusive guise,
And vain the rage of hell.

3 "I freely feed them now
With tokens of my love;
But richer pastures I prepare,
And sweeter streams above.

4 "Unnumbered years of bliss
I to my people give;
And while my throne unshaken stands
Shall all my chosen live.

5 "This tried, almighty hand
Is raised for their defence;
Where is the power shall reach them there,
Or what shall force them thence?"

6 "Enough, my gracious Lord,"
Let faith triumphant cry;
"My heart can on this promise live—
Can with this promise die."

COLBURN. L. M. W. B. BRADBURY.

Ritard.

418 *Jesus a Friend.* L. M. (122)

1 POOR, weak, and worthless though I am,
I have a rich, almighty Friend;
Jesus, the Saviour, is his name,
He freely loves, and without end.

2 He ransomed me from hell with blood,
And by his power my foes controlled;
He found me wandering far from God,
And brought me to his chosen fold.

3 He cheers my heart, my wants supplies,
And says that I shall shortly be
Enthroned with him above the skies:
Oh, what a friend is Christ to me!

SOLID ROCK. L. M. 6 lines. W. B. BRADBURY.

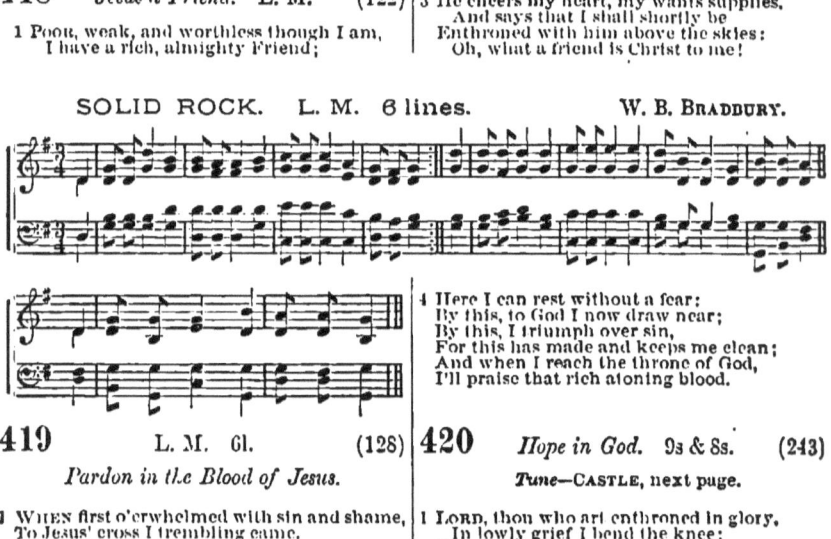

4 Here I can rest without a fear:
By this, to God I now draw near;
By this, I triumph over sin,
For this has made and keeps me clean;
And when I reach the throne of God,
I'll praise that rich atoning blood.

419 L. M. 6l. (128)

Pardon in the Blood of Jesus.

1 WHEN first o'erwhelmed with sin and shame,
To Jesus' cross I trembling came,
Burden'd with guilt, and full of fear,
Yet drawn by love, I ventured near,
And pardon found, and peace with God,
In Jesus' rich atoning blood.

2 My sin is gone, my fear is o'er,
I shun his presence now no more;
He sits upon the throne of grace,
He bids me boldly seek his face;
Sprinkled upon the throne of God,
I see that rich atoning blood.

3 Before his face my Priest appears;
My Advocate the Father hears;
That precious blood, before his eyes,
Both day and night for mercy cries;
It speaks, it ever speaks to God,
The voice of that atoning blood.

420 *Hope in God.* 9s & 8s. (243)

Tune—CASTLE, next page.

1 LORD, thou who art enthroned in glory,
In lowly grief I bend the knee:
No claim have I to come before thee,
For deep is sin and guilt in me.
Thy law, how pure its righteousness!
My soul, how vile its dark abyss!

2 In deepest need, in anguish sighing,
I cry to thee, to thee alone.
Were I to other help applying,
Vain were each prayer, each suppliant groan.
My plaints, O Lord, ascend to thee!
Oh, graciously give ear to me!

3 O Father, for thy tender mercy!
O Son, for thy atoning blood!
O Spirit, comfort of the weary!
For all thy gifts of heavenly good,
Accept a life of grateful praise,
And make me thine, and thine always.

CASTLE. 9s & 8s. DR. T. HASTINGS.

HAVERGAL. C. M. HAVERGAL.

421 *Close to thy bleeding Side.* C. M. (156)

1 FOR ever here my rest shall be,
Close to thy bleeding side;
This all my hope, and all my plea:
For me the Saviour died.

2 My dying Saviour and my God,
Fountain for guilt and sin,
Sprinkle me ever with thy blood,
And cleanse and keep me clean.

3 Wash me, and make me thus thine own;
Wash me, and mine thou art;
Wash me, but not my feet alone,
My hands, my head, my heart.

4 Th' atonement of thy blood apply,
Till faith to sight improve;
Till hope in full fruition die,
And all my soul be love.

NEWMAN. H. M. CARMINA SACRA.

422 H. M. (205)

Thine, O Christ, not mine.

1 THY works, not mine, O Christ,
Speak gladness to this heart;
They tell me all is done;
They bid my fear depart:
To whom, save thee, | For sin atone,
Who canst alone | Lord, shall I flee?

2 Thy wounds, not mine, O Christ,
Can heal my bruiséd soul;
Thy stripes, not mine, contain
The balm that makes me whole.
To whom, save thee, | For sin atone,
Who canst alone | Lord, shall I flee?

3 Thy cross, not mine, O Christ,
Has borne the awful load
Of sins that none could bear
But the incarnate God:
To whom, save thee, | For sin atone,
Who canst alone | Lord, shall I flee?

4 Thy death, not mine, O Christ,
Has paid the ransom due;
Ten thousand deaths like mine
Would have been all too few:
To whom, save thee, | For sin atone,
Who canst alone | Lord, shall I flee?

WILLMARTH. L. M. I. B. Woodbury.

423 *One believing Look.* L. M. (145)

1 Could I recall the buried past,
And all its richest offerings cast
Before thee, Lord, what wouldst thou see
But sin in them, and guilt in me?

2 A backward glance,—shame paints my cheek;
An inward,—all is vile and weak;
But looking upward, clear and long,
Light streams o'er all—for there I'm strong;

3 Strong in the strength of him who died—
The Righteous, yet the Crucified!—
Strong in the strength of him who lives,
And grace to help in weakness gives.

PHILLIPS. C. M. I. B. Woodbury.

424 *All due to Grace.* C. M. (164)

1 All that I was, my sin, my guilt,
My death, was all mine own;
All that I am, I owe to thee,
My gracious God, alone.

2 The evil of my former state
Was mine, and only mine;
The good in which I now rejoice
Is thine, and only thine.

3 The darkness of my former state,
The bondage—all was mine;
The light of life in which I walk,
The liberty—is thine.

4 Thy grace that made me feel my sin,
It taught me to believe;
Then, in believing, peace I found,
And now I live, I live.

5 All that I am, e'en here on earth,
All that I hope to be,
When Jesus comes and glory dawns,
I owe it, Lord, to thee.

425 L. M. (124)

Self-righteousness renounced.

Tune—Ware, next page.

1 No more, my God, I boast no more
Of all the duties I have done;
I quit the hopes I held before,
To trust the merits of thy Son.

2 Now, for the love I bear his name,
What was my gain, I count my loss,
My former pride I call my shame,
And nail my glory to his cross.

3 Yes, and I must and will esteem
All things but loss for Jesus' sake;
Oh, may my soul be found in him,
And of his righteousness partake.

4 The best obedience of my hands
Dares not appear before thy throne:
But faith can answer thy demands
By pleading what my Lord has done.

WARE. L. M. Geo. Kingsley.

426 S. M. (180)

Salvation through Christ.

Tune—Evans.

1 Not what I feel or do
  Can give me peace with God,
Not all my prayers and sighs and tears
  Can bear my awful load.

2 Thy work alone, O Christ,
  Can ease this weight of sin;
Thy blood alone, O Lamb of God,
  Can give me peace within.

3 Thy love to me, O God,
  Not mine, O Lord, to thee,
Can rid me of this dark unrest,
  And set my spirit free.

4 'Tis Christ who saveth me,
  And freely pardon gives;
I love because he loveth me,
  I live because he lives.

EVANS. S. M. W. A. Tarbutton.

427 C. M. (143)

Pleading Christ's Death.

Tune—Fountain, No. 410.

1 Great God, when I approach thy throne,
  And all thy glory see,
This is my stay, and this alone,
  That Jesus died for me.

2 How can a soul condemned to die,
  Escape the just decree?
Helpless, and full of sin am I,
  But Jesus died for me.

3 Burdened with sin's oppressive chain,
  Oh, how can I get free?
No peace can all my efforts gain,
  But Jesus died for me.

4 And, Lord, when I behold thy face,
  This must be all my plea;
Save me by thy almighty grace,
  For Jesus died for me.

428 L. M. 6l. (128)

The Death of Christ sufficient.

Tune—Solid Rock, No. 419

1 When time seems short and death is near
And I am pressed by doubt and fear,
And sins, an overflowing tide,
Assail my peace on every side,
This thought my refuge still shall be,
I know the Saviour died for me.

2 If grace were bought, I could not buy;
If grace were coined, no wealth have I;
By grace alone I draw my breath,
Held up from everlasting death;
Yet, since I know his grace is free,
I know the Saviour died for me.

3 My faith is weak, but 'tis thy gift;
Thou canst my helpless soul uplift,
And say, "Thy bonds of death are riven,
Thy sins by me are all forgiven;
And thou shalt live from guilt set free,
For I, thy Saviour, died for thee."

ARIEL. C. P. M. DR. L. MASON.

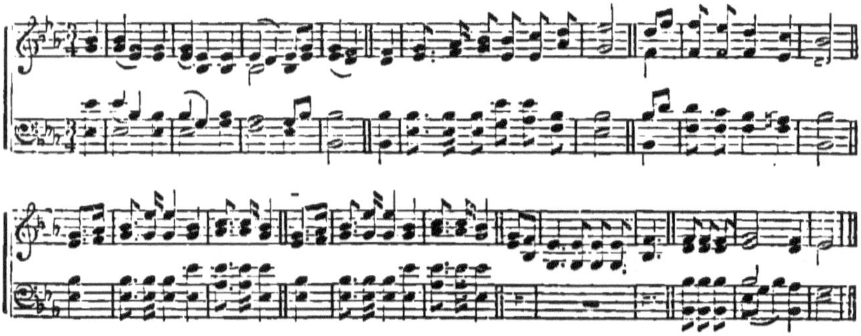

429 *The only Foundation.* C. P. M. (226)

1 HAD I ten thousand gifts beside,
I'd cleave to Jesus crucified,
And build on him alone;
For no foundation is there giv'n
On which to place my hopes of heav'n,
But Christ, the corner-stone.

2 Possessing Christ I all possess,
Wisdom and strength and righteousness,
And holiness complete;
Bold in his name, I dare draw nigh
Before the Ruler of the sky,
And all his justice meet.

3 There is no path to heav'nly bliss,
To solid joy or lasting peace,
But Christ, th' appointed road;
Oh, may we tread the sacred way,
By faith rejoice and praise and pray,
Till we sit down with God.

BARBY. C. M. A. WILLIAMS.

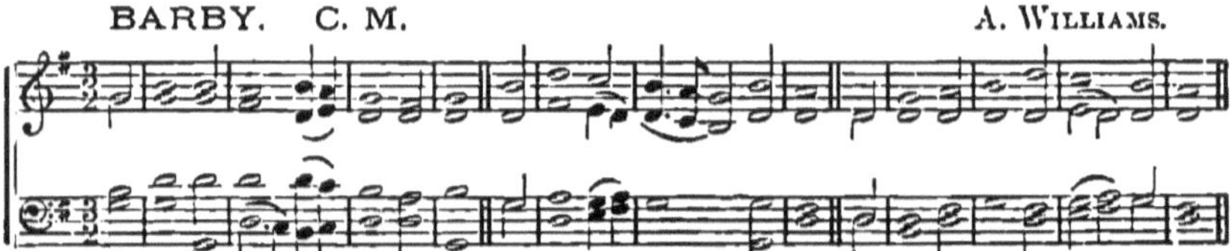

430 C. M. (115)

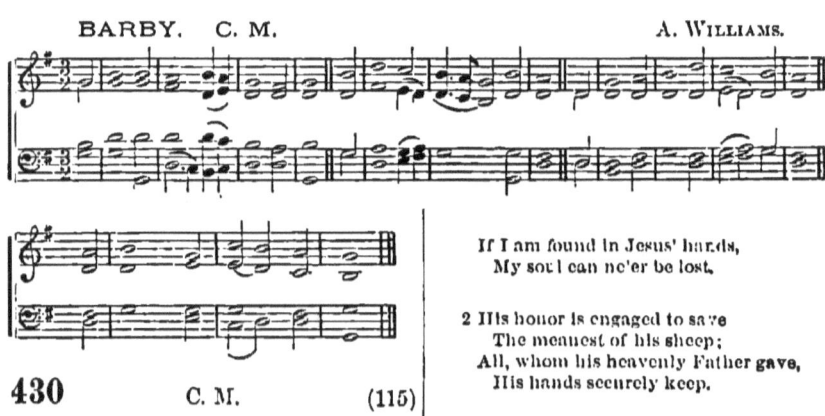

Saints in the Hands of Christ.

1 FIRM as the earth thy gospel stands,
My Lord, my hope, my trust;
If I am found in Jesus' hands,
My soul can ne'er be lost.

2 His honor is engaged to save
The meanest of his sheep;
All, whom his heavenly Father gave,
His hands securely keep.

3 Nor death nor hell shall e'er remove
His favorites from his breast;
Within the bosom of his love
They must for ever rest.

TOPLADY. 7s. 6 lines. DR. T. HASTINGS

FINE.
D.C.

431 *Christ all in all.* 7s. 6l. (152)

1 Chief of sinners though I be,
Jesus shed his blood for me;
Died that I might live on high,
Died that I might never die;
As the branch is to the vine,
I am his and he is mine.

2 Oh, the height of Jesus' love!
Higher than the heavens above,
Deeper than the depths of sea,
Lasting as eternity;
Love that found me, wondrous thought!
Found me when I sought him not!

3 Chief of sinners though I be,
Christ is all in all to me;
All my wants to him are known,
All my sorrows are his own;
Safe with him from earthly strife,
He sustains the hidden life.

TAPPAN. C. M. GEO. KINGSLEY.

432 C. M. (141)

My Saviour died for me.

1 Thou art my hiding-place, O Lord:
In thee I put my trust,
Encouraged by thy holy word,
A feeble child of dust.

2 I have no argument beside,
I urge no other plea;
And 'tis enough the Saviour died,
The Saviour died for me.

3 When storms of fierce temptation beat,
And furious foes assail,
My refuge is the mercy-seat,
My hope within the veil.

4 From strife of tongues and bitter words,
My spirit flies to thee;
Joy to my heart the thought affords,
My Saviour died for me.

433 *My Hiding Place.* C. M. (141)

1 Thou art, O Lord, my hiding place,
In danger and distress;
My weary spirit turns to thee
When thronging terrors press.

2 And, oh, with bounding heart I praise
Thy free, exhaustless grace;
Thou never to my needy cry
Turn'st an upbraiding face.

3 Thy ready hand applies the blood
That makes the conscience clean;
Thy gentle voice the pardon breathes
That stills the storm within.

4 Good Shepherd, thy most helpless lamb
Within thy bosom hide;
Set me a seal upon thy heart,
And let me there abide.

DUANE STREET. L. M. G. COLES.

FINE.

434 *Robe of Righteousness.* L. M. (130)

1 JESUS, thy robe of righteousness
My beauty is, my glorious dress;
'Mid flaming worlds, in this arrayed,
With joy shall I lift up my head.

2 When from the dust of death I rise
To claim my mansion in the skies,
E'en then shall this be all my plea,—
"Jesus hath lived and died for me."

3 This spotless robe the same appears,
When ruined nature sinks in years;
No age can change its glorious hue;
The robe of Christ is ever new.

4 Oh, let the dead now hear thy voice;
Now bid thy banished ones rejoice;
Their beauty this, their glorious dress,
Jesus, the Lord, our Righteousness.

WEIMAR. 7s & 6s. GERMAN.

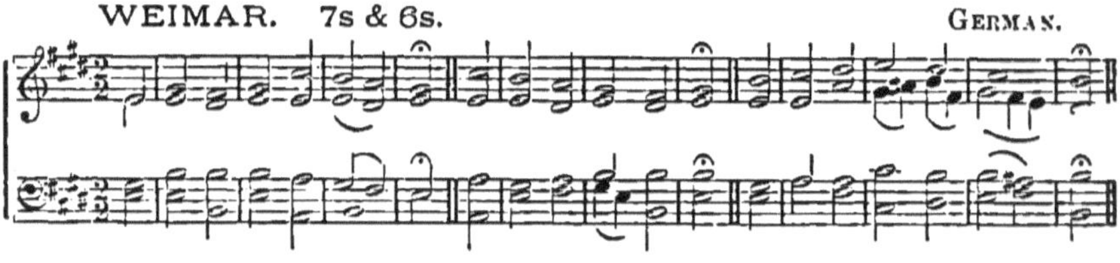

435 7s & 6s. (172)

He hath borne our Griefs.

1 I LAY my sins on Jesus,
The spotless Lamb of God;
He bears them all and frees us
From the accursed load.

2 I bring my guilt to Jesus,
To wash my crimson stains
White in his blood most precious,
Till not a stain remains.

3 I lay my wants on Jesus;
All fulness dwells in him;
He heals all my diseases,
He doth my soul redeem.

4 I lay my griefs on Jesus,
My burdens and my cares;
He from them all releases,
He all my sorrow shares.

436 7s & 6s. (172)

Resting on Jesus.

1 I REST my soul on Jesus,
This weary soul of mine,
His right hand me embraces,
I on his breast recline.

2 I love the name of Jesus,
Immanuel, Christ, the Lord;
Like fragrance on the breezes,
His name abroad is poured.

3 I long to be like Jesus,
Meek, loving, lowly, mild;
I long to be like Jesus,
The Father's holy child.

4 I long to be with Jesus,
Amid the heavenly throng,
To sing with saints his praises,
To learn the angels' song.

ELLIOT. 8s & 6. DR. L. MASON.

437 8s & 6. (176)

Prayer for Christ's Intercession.

1 O THOU, the contrite sinner's Friend,
Who, loving, lov'st them to the end,
On this alone my hopes depend,
That thou wilt plead for me.

2 When weary in the Christian race,
Far off appears my resting place,
And, fainting, I mistrust thy grace,
Then, Saviour, plead for me.

3 When I have erred and gone astray,
Afar from thine and wisdom's way,
And see no glimmering, guiding ray,
Still, Saviour, plead for me.

4 When Satan, by my sins made bold,
Strives from thy cross to loose my hold,
Then with thy pitying arms enfold,
And plead, oh, plead for me!

5 And when my dying hour draws near,
Darkened with anguish, guilt, and fear,
Then to my fainting sight appear,
Pleading in heaven for me.

438 S. M. (193)

The Safety of the Christian.

Tune—OLNEY, No. 386

1 I STAND on Zion's mount,
And view my starry crown;
No power on earth my hope can shake
Nor hell can thrust me down.

2 The lofty hills and towers,
That lift their heads on high,
Shall all be levelled low in dust—
Their very names shall die.

3 The vaulted heavens shall fall,
Built by Jehovah's hands;
But firmer than the heavens, the Rock
Of my salvation stands.

NEWMAN. H. M. CARMINA SACRA.

439 *The finished Work.* H. M. (205)

1 DONE is the work that saves;
Once and for ever done:
Finished the righteousness
That clothes the unrighteous one.
The love that blesses us below
Is flowing freely to us now.

2 The sacrifice is o'er;
The veil is rent in twain;
The mercy-seat is red
With blood of victim slain;
Why stand we then without, in fear?
The blood divine invites us near.

3 Upon the mercy-seat
The High Priest sits within;
The blood is in his hand
Which makes and keeps us clean.
With boldness let us now draw near,
That blood has banished every fear.

DARLEY. L. M. W. W. H. DARLEY.

440 L. M. (149)

Trust in Christ.

1 LORD Jesus Christ, my life, my light,
My strength by day, my trust by night,
On earth I'm but a passing guest,
And sorely with my sins oppressed.

2 Since thou hast died, the pure, the just,
I take my homeward way in trust;
The gates of heaven, Lord, open wide,
When here I may no more abide.

3 And when the last great day is come,
And thou, our Judge, shall speak the doom,
Let me with joy behold the light,
And set me then upon thy right.

4 Ah! then I have my heart's desire,
When, singing with the angels' choir,
Among the ransomed of thy grace
For ever I behold thy face.

441 L. M. (145)

Jesus pleads for me.

Tune—WILLMARTH, No. 423.

1 BEFORE the throne of God above
I have a strong, a perfect plea;
A great High Priest, whose name is Love
Who ever lives and pleads for me.

2 My name is graven on his hands,
My name is written on his heart;
I know that while in heaven he stands
No tongue can bid me thence depart.

3 Because the sinless Saviour died,
My sinful soul is counted free;
For God, the Just, is satisfied
To look on him and pardon me.

4 One with himself, I cannot die;
My soul is purchased by his blood;
My life is hid with Christ on high,
With Christ, my Saviour and my God.

DARWIN. C. M. G. HEWS.

442 *Suretyship of Jesus.* C. M. 61. (183)

1 O CHRIST, what burdens bowed thy head;
Our load was laid on thee;
Thou stoodest in the sinner's stead,
Barest all my ill for me:
A victim led, thy blood was shed;
Now there's no load for me.

2 Death and the curse were in our cup,
O Christ, 'twas full for thee;
But thou hast drained the last dark drop;
'Tis empty now for me.
That bitter cup, love drank it up;
Now blessing's draught for me.

3 For me, Lord Jesus, thou hast died
And I have died in thee;
Thou'rt risen; my bands are all untied
And now thou liv'st in me.
When purified, made white, and tried,
Thy glory then for me.

WARE. L. M. Geo. Kingsley.

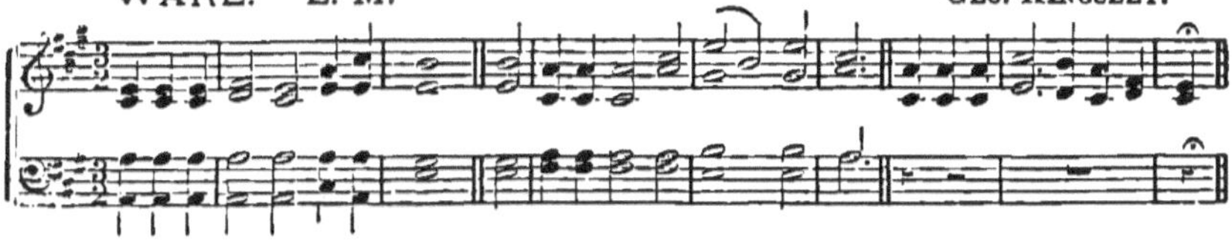

443 *Completeness.* L. M. (125)

1 Complete in thee,—no work of mine
May take, dear Lord, the place of thine;
Thy blood has pardon bought for me,
And I am now complete in thee.

2 Complete in thee,—no more shall sin,
Thy grace has conquered, reign within;
Thy voice will bid the tempter flee,
And I shall stand complete in thee.

3 Complete in thee,—each want supplied,
And no good thing to me denied,
Since thou my portion, Lord, wilt be,
I ask no more,—complete in thee.

4 Dear Saviour, when, before thy bar,
All tribes and tongues assembled are,
Among thy chosen may I be
At thy right hand,—complete in thee.

444 C. M. 61. (183)

The Fearlessness of the Believer.

Tune—Darwin, No. 442.

1 In all the impotence of need,
My God, I count on thee;
And in the Name of names I plead,
Intent thy power to see.
The foe is near, I will not fear,
Thou standest up for me.

2 I watch the wonders of thy grace,
I dwell beneath thy wings:
Thy wisdom undertakes my case,
Thine arm salvation brings.
My Shield art thou, my Buckler now,
My victor spirit sings.

3 My God, thou hast vouchsafed to be
My Father and my Guide;
The sprinkled blood assureth me
How well thou dost provide.
At peace and free, I walk with thee,
No more to leave thy side.

SHINING SHORE. 8s & 7s. G. F. Root.

FINE.
D.S.

445 *Trusting in Jesus.* 8s & 7s. (190)

1 Who trusts in God a strong abode
In heaven and earth possesses;
Who looks in love to Christ above,
No fear his heart oppresses.

2 In only thee, dear Lord, I see
Sweet hope and consolation,
My shield from foes, my balm for woes,
My great and sure salvation.

3 In all the strife of mortal life
My foot shall stand securely;
Temptation's hour shall lose its power,
For thou wilt guard me surely.

4 O God, renew with heavenly dew,
My body, soul, and spirit,
And be thou mine and keep me thine
For Jesus' saving merit.

WARE. L. M. GEO. KINGSLEY.

446 L. M. (125)

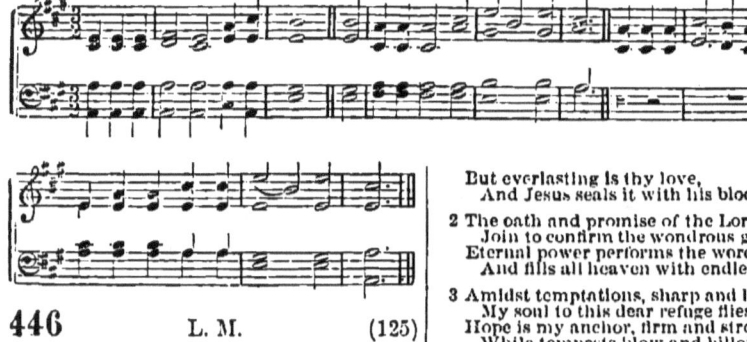

Security of the Believer.

1 How oft have sin and Satan strove
To rend my soul from thee, my God!
But everlasting is thy love,
And Jesus seals it with his blood

2 The oath and promise of the Lord
Join to confirm the wondrous grace;
Eternal power performs the word,
And fills all heaven with endless praise.

3 Amidst temptations, sharp and long,
My soul to this dear refuge flies;
Hope is my anchor, firm and strong,
While tempests blow and billows rise.

4 The gospel bears my spirit up;
A faithful and unchanging God
Lays the foundation for my hope
In oaths and promises and blood.

LOUVAN. L. M. V C. TAYLOR.

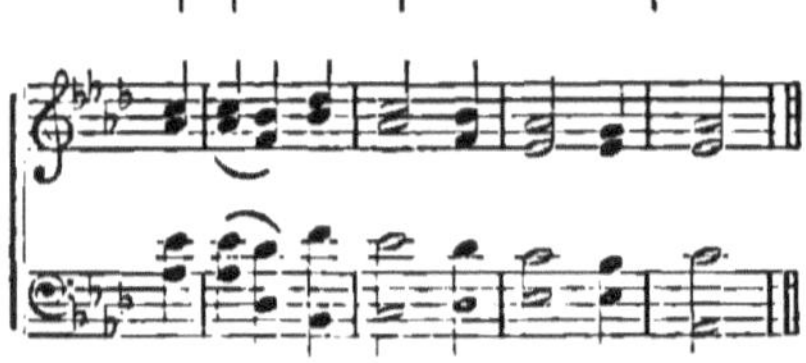

447 *All Things in Christ.* L. M. (219)

1 FOUNTAIN of grace, rich, full, and free,
What need I that is not in thee?
Full pardon, strength to meet the day,
And peace which none can take away.

2 Doth sickness fill the heart with fear?
'Tis sweet to know that thou art near.
Am I with dread of justice tried?
'Tis sweet to feel that Christ hath died.

3 In life, thy promises of aid
Forbid my heart to be afraid;
In death, peace gently veils the eyes;
Christ rose, and I shall surely rise.

4 O all-sufficient Saviour, be
This all-sufficiency to me;
Nor pain nor sin nor death can harm
The weakest shielded by thine arm.

448 C. M. (158)

The New Covenant sealed.

Tune—GEER, next page.

1 "THE promise of my Father's love
Shall stand for ever good;"
He said, and gave his soul to death,
And sealed the grace with blood.

2 To this dear covenant of thy word
I set my worthless name;
I seal the promise to my Lord,
And make my humble claim.

3 I call that legacy my own,
Which Jesus did bequeath;
'Twas purchased with a dying groan,
And ratified in death.

4 The light and strength, the pardoning grace,
And glory shall be mine:
My life and soul, my heart and flesh,
And all my powers are thine.

GEER. C. M. H. W. GREATOREX.

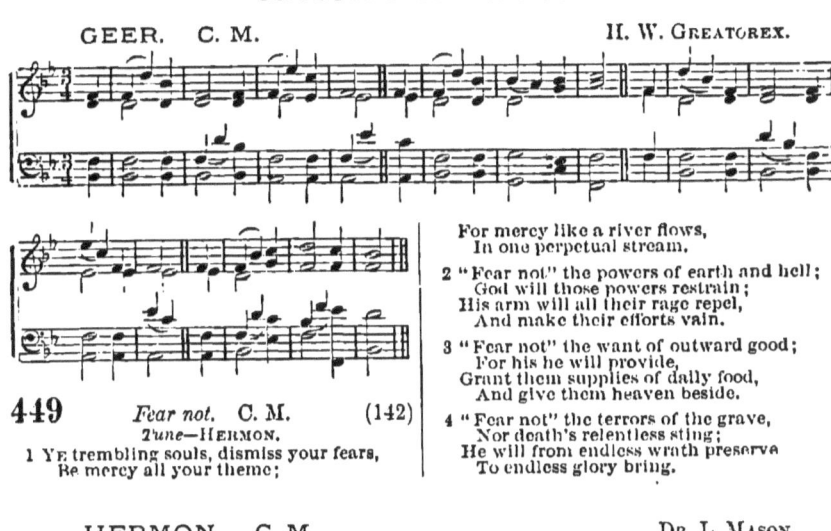

449 *Fear not.* C. M. (142)

Tune—HERMON.

1 YE trembling souls, dismiss your fears,
Be mercy all your theme;
For mercy like a river flows,
In one perpetual stream.

2 "Fear not" the powers of earth and hell;
God will those powers restrain;
His arm will all their rage repel,
And make their efforts vain.

3 "Fear not" the want of outward good;
For his he will provide,
Grant them supplies of daily food,
And give them heaven beside.

4 "Fear not" the terrors of the grave,
Nor death's relentless sting;
He will from endless wrath preserve
To endless glory bring.

HERMON. C. M. DR. L. MASON.

KEDRON. C. M. DR. T. HASTINGS.

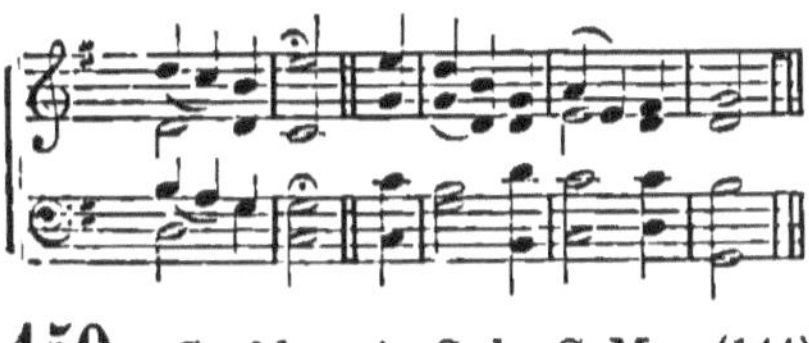

450 *Confidence in God.* C. M. (144)

1 SOON as I heard my Father say,
"Ye children, seek my grace,"
My heart replied, without delay,
"I'll seek my Father's face."

2 Let not thy face be hid from me,
Nor frown my soul away;
God of my life, I fly to thee
In each distressing day.

3 Should friends and kindred, near and dear,
Leave me to want, or die,
My God will make my life his care,
And all my need supply.

4 Wait on the Lord, ye trembling saints,
And keep your courage up;
He'll raise your spirit when it faints,
And far exceed your hope.

TOPLADY. 7s. 6 lines. DR. T. HASTINGS.

FINE.
D.C.

451 *Only the Crucified.* 7s. 51. (152)

1 Ask ye what great thing I know
That delights and stirs me so?
What the high reward I win?
Whose the name I glory in?
Jesus Christ, the Crucified.

2 What is faith's foundation strong?
What awakes my lips to song?
He who bore my sinful load,
Purchased for me peace with God.
Jesus Christ, the Crucified.

3 Who is life in life to me?
Who the death of death will be?
Who will place me on his right,
With the countless hosts of light?
Jesus Christ, the Crucified.

4 This is that great thing I know;
This delights and stirs me so;
Faith in him who died to save,
Him who triumphed o'er the grave,
Jesus Christ, the Crucified.

WARE. L. M. GEO. KINGSLEY.

452 L. M. (125)

The Grasp of Faith.

1 When sins and fears, prevailing, rise,
And fainting hope almost expires,
To thee, O Lord, I lift my eyes;
To thee I breathe my soul's desires.

2 Art thou not mine, my living Lord?
And can my hope, my comfort, die?
'Tis fixed on thine almighty word,
That word which built the earth and sky.

3 If my immortal Saviour lives,
Then my immortal life is sure;
His word a firm foundation gives;
Here I may build, and rest secure.

4 Here let my faith unshaken dwell;
For ever sure the promise stands;
Not all the powers of earth or hell
Can e'er dissolve the sacred bands.

5 Here, O my soul, thy trust repose;
If Jesus is for ever mine,
Not death itself, that last of foes,
Shall break a union so divine.

453 7s & 6s. (170)

The old, old Story.

Tune next page.

1 Tell me the old, old story,
Of unseen things above,
Of Jesus and his glory,
Of Jesus and his love.
Tell me the story simply,
As to a little child,
For I am weak and weary,
And helpless and defiled.

2 Tell me the story slowly,
That I may take it in—
That wonderful redemption,
God's remedy for sin.
Tell me the story often,
For I forget so soon!
The "early dew" of morning
Has passed away at noon.

3 Tell me the same old story,
When you have cause to fear
That this world's empty glory
Is costing me too dear.
Yes, and when that world's glory
Is dawning on my soul,
Tell me the old, old story:
"Christ Jesus makes thee whole."

"THE OLD, OLD STORY." 7s & 6s.

W. H. DOANE.

From "Songs of Devotion," by permission.

FINE.
D.S.
CHORUS.

HERMON. C. M.

DR. L. MASON.

454 *The Gospel a Savor of Life or Death.* C M (142)

1 CHRIST and his cross are all our theme;
The mysteries that we speak
Are scandal in the Jews' esteem,
And folly to the Greek.

2 But souls enlightened from above
With joy receive the word;
They see what wisdom, power, and love
Shine in their dying Lord.

3 The vital savor of his name
Restores their fainting breath;
But unbelief perverts the same
To guilt, despair, and death.

4 Till God diffuse his graces down,
Like showers of heavenly rain,
In vain Apollos sows the ground,
And Paul may plant in vain.

SEYMOUR. 7s. GREATOREX.

455 *Winning Souls to Christ.* 7s. (212)

1 WOULD you win a soul to God?
Tell him of a Saviour's blood,
Once for dying sinners spilt,
To atone for all their guilt.

2 Tell him how the streams did glide
From his hands, his feet, his side;
How his head with thorns was crowned,
And his heart in sorrow drowned.

3 How he yielded up his breath;
How he agonized in death;
How he lives to intercede:
Christ our Advocate and Head.

4 Tell him of that liberty
Wherewith Jesus makes us free;
Sweetly speak of sins forgiven,
Earnest of the joys of heaven.

OVIO. 8s & 7s. DR. L. MASON.

456 *Glorying in the Cross.* 8s & 7s. (201)

1 IN the cross of Christ I glory,
Towering o'er the wrecks of time;
All the light of sacred story
Gathers round its head sublime.

2 When the woes of life o'ertake me,
Hopes deceive and fears annoy,
Never shall the cross forsake me:
Lo! it glows with peace and joy.

3 When the sun of bliss is beaming
Light and love upon my way,
From the cross the radiance streaming
Adds new lustre to the day.

4 Bane and blessing, pain and pleasure,
By the cross are sanctified;
Peace is there, that knows no measure,
Joys that through all time abide.

HEBER. C. M. GEO. KINGSLEY.

457 *Prayer for Faith.* C. M. (135)

1 O GOD of our salvation, Lord
Of wondrous power and love,
May faith, whereby we look to thee,
Be sent us from above.

2 'Tis faith that gives us strength to fight,
That we our foes may quell;
'Tis with the shield of faith we quench
The fiery darts of hell.

3 By faith we make our prayers to thee
In that most holy name,
On which, for mercy and for peace,
We rest our humble claim.

4 For thy dear sake, assist us, Lord,
To run our heavenward race;
And, oh, may no unholy life
Our holy faith disgrace!

HERMON. C. M. — Dr. L. Mason.

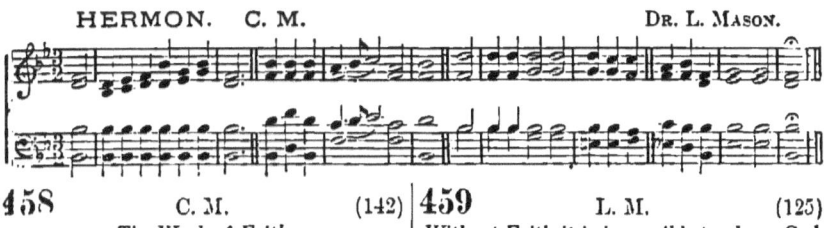

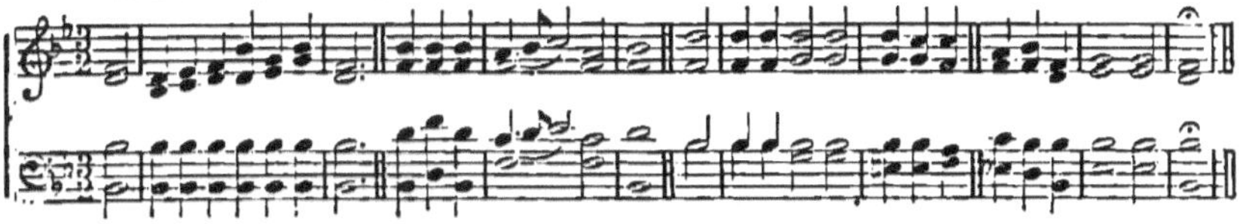

458 C. M. (142)

The Work of Faith.

1 Faith adds new charms to earthly bliss,
And saves us from its snares;
It yields support in all our toils,
And softens all our cares.

2 The wounded conscience knows its power
The healing balm to give;
That balm the saddest heart can cheer,
And make the dying live.

3 Faith shows the promise fully sealed
With our Redeemer's blood;
It helps our feeble hope to rest
Upon a faithful God.

4 There, still unshaken, would we rest,
Till this frail body dies,
And then, on faith's triumphant wing,
To endless glory rise.

459 L. M. (125)

Without Faith it is impossible to please God.

Tune—Ware, No. 452.

1 Faith is a living power from heaven,
Which grasps the promise God has given;
A trust that cannot be o'erthrown,
Securely fixed on Christ alone.

2 Faith finds in Christ whate'er we need,
To save and strengthen, guide and feed;
Strong in his grace, it joys to share
His cross, in hope his crown to wear.

3 Faith feels the Spirit's kindling breath,
In hope and love that conquer death;
Faith brings us to delight in God,
And blesses e'en his smiting rod.

4 Such faith in us, O God, implant,
And to our prayers thy favor grant,
In Jesus Christ, thy saving Son,
Who is our Fount of health alone.

TAPPAN. C. M. — Geo. Kingsley.

460 C. M. (141)

Lord, I believe; help thou my Unbelief.

1 Lord, I believe; thy power I own,
Thy word I would obey;
I wander comfortless and lone,
When from thy truth I stray.

2 Lord, I believe; but gloomy fears
Sometimes bedim my sight;
I look to thee with prayers and tears,
And cry for strength and light.

3 Lord, I believe; but oft, I know,
My faith is cold and weak:
My weakness strengthen, and bestow
The confidence I seek.

4 Yes, I believe; and only thou
Canst give my soul relief:
Lord, to thy truth my spirit bow;
"Help thou my unbelief!"

MAN.

WARE L. M. — Geo. Kingsley.

461 *Thou art mine.* L. M. (124)

1 Yes, thou art mine, my blessed Lord;
For ever and for ever mine:
And, purchased with thy precious blood,
My Lord and Saviour, I am thine.

2 Thy spotless righteousness is mine,
Resplendent now before the throne;
In thee I stand accepted there—
In thee, O Son of God, alone.

3 Thy Spirit, Lord, is mine, for thou
Didst send him, never to depart,
Thine own sweet Comforter, to dwell
Within the temple of my heart.

4 Thy rich inheritance is mine;
Joint heir with thee of worlds above,
Lord, in thy kingdom I shall shine,
And reign with thee in endless love.

LOVING CHRIST.

NAOMI. C. M. — Dr. L. Mason.

462 C. M. (215)

Love to the Lord declared.

1 I love the Lord: he heard my cries,
And pitied every groan:
Long as I live, when troubles rise,
I'll hasten to his throne.

2 I love the Lord: he bowed his ear,
And chased my grief away:
Oh, let my heart no more despair,
While I have breath to pray.

3 The Lord beheld me sore distressed;
He bade my pains remove;
Return, my soul, to God, thy rest,
For thou hast known his love.

463 *Christ is all.* C. M. (144)

Tune—Kedron, next page.

1 Compared with Christ, in all beside
No comeliness I see;
The one thing needful, dearest Lord,
Is to be one with thee.

2 The sense of thy expiring love
Into my soul convey:
Thyself bestow; for thee alone
My all in all I pray.

3 Less than thyself will not suffice
My comfort to restore;
More than thyself I cannot crave,
And thou canst give no more.

4 Whate'er consists not with thy love,
Oh, teach me to resign;
I'm rich to all th' intents of bliss,
If thou, O God, art mine.

KEDRON. C. M. — DR. T. HASTINGS.

464 *I would love thee.* 8s & 7s. (201)

Tune—OVIO, No. 456.

1 I WOULD love thee, God and Father,
My Redeemer, and my King;
I would love thee; for, without thee,
Life is but a bitter thing.

2 I would love thee; every blessing
Flows to me from out thy throne:
I would love thee; he who loves thee
Never feels himself alone.

3 I would love thee; look upon me,
Ever guide me with thine eye:
I would love thee; if not nourished
By thy love, my soul would die.

4 I would love thee; I have vowed it,
On thy love my heart is set:
While I love thee, I will never
My Redeemer's blood forget.

AUTUMN. 8s & 7s. Double.

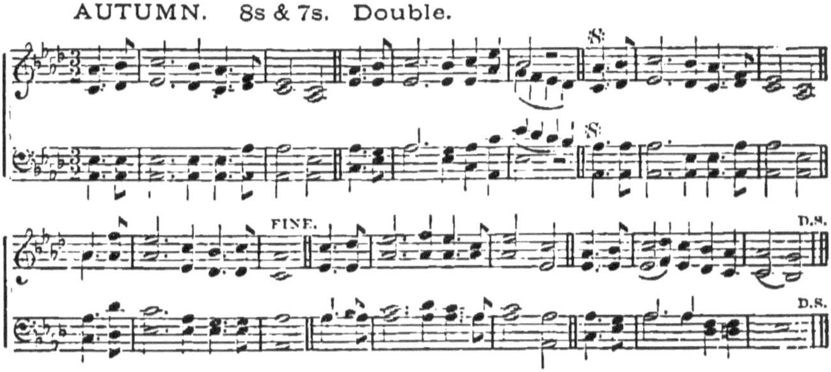

FINE.
D.S.
D.S.

465 *Thou knowest that I love thee.* 8s, 7s, & 7s. (202)

1 I WILL love thee, all my treasure;
I will love thee, all my strength,
I will love thee without measure,
And without a stain at length:
I will love thee, Light divine,
Till I die and find thee mine.

2 Be my heart more warmly glowing,
Sweet and calm the tears I shed;
And its love, its ardor, showing,
Let my spirit onward tread:
Near to thee, and nearer still,
Draw this heart, this mind, this will.

3 I will love in joy or sorrow,
While I in this body dwell;
I will love to-day, to-morrow,
With a love no words can tell:
I will love thee, Light divine,
Till I die and find thee mine.

IDDO. C. M. Double. NAGELI.

466

Gratitude to Christ. C. M. (184)

1 I LOVE thee, O my God, but not
For what I hope thereby;
Nor yet because who love thee not,
Must die eternally:
I love thee, O my God, and still
I ever will love thee,
Solely because my God thou art,
Who first hast lovèd me.

2 For me, to lowest depths of woe
Thou didst thyself abase:
For me didst bear the cross, the shame,
And manifold disgrace.
For me didst suffer pains unknown,
Blood-sweat and agony,
Yea, death itself,—all, all for me,
For me, thine enemy.

3 Then shall I not, O Saviour mine!
Shall I not love thee well?
Not with the hope of winning heaven,
Nor of escaping hell;
Not with the hope of earning aught,
Nor seeking a reward,
But freely, fully, as thyself
Hast lovèd me, O Lord!

NETTLETON. 8s & 7s. Double.

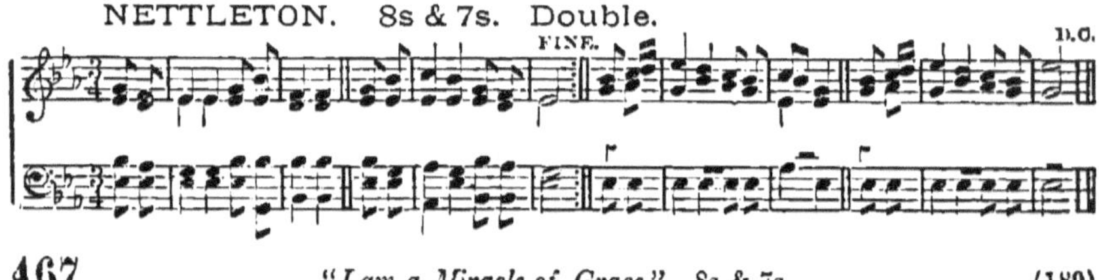
FINE.
D.C.

467

"I am a Miracle of Grace." 8s & 7s. (189)

1 HAIL, my ever blessed Jesus!
Only thee I wish to sing;
To my soul thy name is precious,
Thou my Prophet, Priest, and King;
Oh, what mercy flows from heaven!
Oh, what joy and happiness!
Love I much? I've much forgiven,—
I'm a miracle of grace!

2 Once with Adam's race in ruin,
Unconcerned in sin I lay;
Swift destruction still pursuing,
Till my Saviour passed that way:
Witness, all ye hosts of heaven,
My Redeemer's tenderness:
Love I much? I've much forgiven,—
I'm a miracle of grace!

3 Shout, ye bright angelic choir!
Praise the Lamb enthroned above!
While, astonished, I admire
God's free grace and boundless love:
That blest moment I received him
Filled my soul with joy and peace:
Love I much? I've much forgiven,—
I'm a miracle of grace!

468 *Jesus only.* 7s. 6l. (153)

Tune—TOPLADY, No. 451.

1 BLESSED Saviour, thee I love
All my other joys above;
All my hopes in thee abide,
Thou my hope, and naught beside:
Ever let my glory be
Only, only, only thee.

2 Once again beside the cross
All my gain I count but loss;
Earthly pleasures fade away,
Clouds they are that hide my day:
Hence, vain shadows! let me see
Jesus crucified for me.

3 Blessed Saviour, thine am I,
Thine to live and thine to die;
Height or depth or earthly pow'r
Ne'er shall hide my Saviour more:
Ever shall my glory be
Only, only, only thee.

469 C. P. M. (226)

The Fulness of Christ's Love.

Tune—ARIEL, No. 429.

1 O LOVE divine, how sweet thou art!
When shall I find my willing heart
All taken up by thee?
I thirst, I faint, I die, to prove
The greatness of redeeming love,
The love of Christ to me.

2 Stronger his love than death or hell:
No mortal can its riches tell,
Nor first-born sons of light:
In vain they long its depths to see;
They cannot reach the mystery,
The length, the breadth, the height.

3 Oh that I could for ever sit
In transport at my Saviour's feet!
Be this my happy choice:
My only care, delight, and bliss;
My joy, my heaven on earth, be this,
To hear my Saviour's voice.

470 *The Teaching of Jesus.* L. M. (125)

Tune—WARE, No. 461.

1 How sweetly flowed the gospel sound
From lips of gentleness and grace,
When listening thousands gathered round,
And joy and gladness filled the place!

2 From heaven he came, of heaven he spoke,
To heaven he led his followers' way;
Dark clouds of gloomy night he broke,
Unveiling an immortal day.

3 "Come, wanderers, to my Father's home,
Come, all ye weary ones, and rest:"
Yes, sacred Teacher, we will come,
Obey thee, love thee, and be blest.

4 Decay, then, tenements of dust;
Pillars of earthly pride, decay;
A nobler mansion waits the just,
And Jesus has prepared the way.

471 7s. 6l. (136)

Obligation to Christ manifested.

Tune—PEDDIE, No. 392.

1 CHOSEN, not for good in me,
Wakened up from wrath to flee,
Hidden in the Saviour's side,
By the Spirit sanctified,—
Teach me, Lord, on earth to show,
By my love, how much I owe.

2 Oft the nights of sorrow reign;
Weeping, sickness, sighing, pain;
But a night thine anger burns:
Morning comes, and joy returns.
God of comforts, bid me show
To thy poor how much I owe.

3 When in flowery paths I tread,
Oft by sin I'm captive led;
Oft I fall, but still arise;
Jesus comes, the tempter flies:
Blessed Jesus, bid me show
Weary sinners all I owe.

BADEN. L. M. DR. T. HASTINGS.

472 *Enjoyment of Christ's Love.* L. M. (171)

1 JESUS, thy boundless love to me
No thought can reach, no tongue declare;
Unite my thankful heart to thee,
And reign without a rival there.

2 Thy love, now cheering is its ray!
All pain before its presence flies;
Care, anguish, sorrow, melt away,
Where'er its healing beams arise.

3 Oh, let thy love my soul inflame,
And to thy service sweetly bind;
Transfuse it through my inmost frame,
And mould me wholly to thy mind.

4 Thy love, in sufferings, be my peace;
Thy love, in weakness, make me strong;
And, when the storms of life shall cease,
Thy love shall be in heaven my song.

MONSON. C. M.

BROWN.

473 *Christ's Love unseen.* C. M. (157)

1 JESUS, these eyes have never seen
 That radiant form of thine;
The veil of sense hangs dark between
 Thy blessed face and mine.

2 I see thee not, I hear thee not,
 Yet art thou oft with me;
And earth hath ne'er so dear a spot,
 As where I meet with thee.

3 Yet though I have not seen, and still
 Must rest in faith alone,
I love thee, dearest Lord, and will,
 Unseen, but not unknown.

4 When death these mortal eyes shall seal,
 And still this throbbing heart,
The rending veil shall thee reveal,
 All glorious as thou art.

WEIMAR. 7s & 6s.

GERMAN.

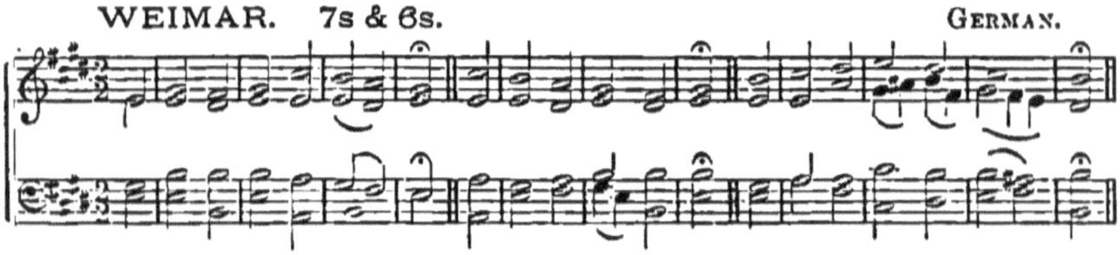

474 7s & 6s. (172)

The exceeding Riches of his Grace.

1 O LORD, thy love's unbounded;
 So full, so sweet, so free,
Our thoughts are all confounded,
 Whene'er we think on thee.

2 For us, thou cam'st from heaven,
 For us to bleed and die;
That, purchased and forgiven,
 We might ascend on high.

3 Oh, let this love constrain us
 To give our hearts to thee;
Let nothing henceforth pain us,
 But that which paineth thee.

4 Our joy, our one endeavor,
 Through suffering, conflict, shame,
To serve thee, gracious Saviour,
 And magnify thy name.

475 *More Love desired.* L. M. 6l. (129)

Tune next page.

1 JESUS, my Lord, my God, my all,
Hear me, blest Saviour, when I call;
Hear me, and from thy dwelling place
Pour down the riches of thy grace.
Jesus, my Lord, I thee adore;
Oh, make me love thee more and more.

2 Jesus, too late I thee have sought;
How can I love thee as I ought?
And how extol thy matchless fame,
The glorious beauty of thy name?
Jesus, my Lord, I thee adore;
Oh, make me love thee more and more.

(CONTINUED.)

3 Jesus, what didst thou find in me,
That thou hast dealt so lovingly?
How great the joy that thou hast brought,
So far exceeding hope or thought!
Jesus, my Lord, I thee adore;
Oh make me love thee more and more.

4 Jesus, of thee shall be my song:
To thee my heart and soul belong
All that I have or own is thine,
And thou, blest Saviour, thou art mine.
Jesus, my Lord, I thee adore;
Oh, make me love thee more and more.

SOLID ROCK. L. M. 6 lines. Wm. B. Bradbury.

OLIVET. 6s & 4s. Dr. L. Mason.

476 6s & 4s. (181)

The Name of Jesus praised.

1 Jesus, thy name I love,
All other names above,
Jesus, my Lord.
Oh, thou art all to me;
Nothing to please I see,
Nothing apart from thee,
Jesus, my Lord.

2 Thou, blessed Son of God,
Hast bought me with thy blood,
Jesus, my Lord.
Oh, wondrous is thy love,
All other loves above,
Love that I daily prove,
Jesus, my Lord.

3 When unto thee I flee,
Thou wilt my refuge be,
Jesus, my Lord.
What need I now to fear?
What earthly grief or care,
Since thou art ever near?
Jesus, my Lord.

SHINING SHORE. 8s & 7s. G. F. ROOT.

S:
FINE.
D.S.

477

The Name of Jesus. 8s & 7s. (190)

1 THERE is no name so sweet on earth,
No name so sweet in heaven,
The name before his wondrous birth
To Christ the Saviour given.

We love to sing around our King,
And hail him blessed Jesus;
For there's no word ear ever heard
So dear, so sweet, as Jesus.

2 And when he hung upon the tree,
They wrote this name above him,
That all might see the reason we
For evermore must love him.

3 So now, upon the Father's throne,
Almighty to release us
From sin and pains, he ever reigns,
The Prince and Saviour Jesus.

4 O Jesus, by that matchless name,
Thy grace shall fail us never;
To-day as yesterday the same,
Thou art the same for ever.

BROWN. C. M. WM. B. BRADBURY.

478

C. M. (162)

Christ precious.

1 JESUS, delightful, charming name!
It spreads a fragrance round;
Justice and mercy, truth and peace,
In union here are found.

2 He is our life, our joy, our strength;
In him all glories meet;
He is a shade above our heads,
A light to guide our feet.

3 The thickest clouds are soon dispersed,
If Jesus shows his face;
To weary, heavy-laden souls
He is the resting-place.

4 When storms arise and tempests blow,
He speaks the stilling word;
The threatening billows cease to flow,
The winds obey their Lord.

479

L. M. (171)

A Name above every Name.

Tune next page.

1 THERE is none other name than thine,
Jehovah Jesus, name divine,
On which to rest for sins forgiven,
For peace with God, for hope of heaven.

2 There is none other name than thine,
When cares and fears and griefs are mine,
That, with a gracious power, can heal
Each care and fear and grief I feel.

3 There is none other name than thine,
When called my spirit to resign,
To bear me through that latest strife,
And even in death to be my life.

4 Name above every name, thy praise
Shall fill the remnant of my days:
Jehovah Jesus, name divine,
Rock of salvation, thou art mine.

BADEN. L. M. DR. T. HASTINGS.

CLARENDON. C. M. TUCKER.

480 *God in Christ.* C. M. (166)

1 DEAREST of all the names above,
My Saviour and my God,
Who can resist thy heavenly love,
Or trifle with thy blood?

2 'Tis by the merits of thy death
The Father smiles again;
'Tis by thine interceding breath
The Spirit dwells with men.

3 Till God in human flesh I see,
My thoughts no comfort find;
The holy, just, and sacred Three
Are terrors to my mind.

4 But if Immanuel's face appear,
My hope, my joy, begin;
His name forbids my slavish fear;
His grace removes my sin.

HELENA. C. M. W. B. BRADBURY.

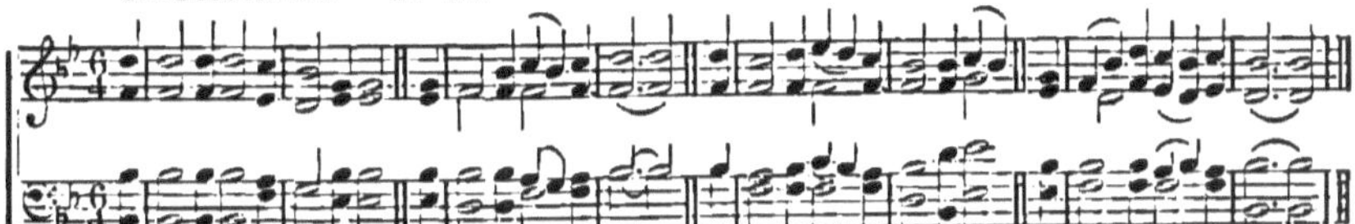

481 *Praise for Mediation.* C. M. (203)

1 FATHER, I sing thy wondrous grace;
I bless my Saviour's name:
He bought salvation for the poor,
And bore the sinner's shame.

2 His deep distress has raised us high;
His duty and his zeal
Fulfilled the law which mortals broke,
And finished all thy will.

3 Zion is thine, most holy God;
Thy Son shall bless her gates;
And glory, purchased by his blood,
For thine own Israel waits.

4 Let heaven and all that dwell on high,
To God their voices raise;
While lands and seas assist the sky,
And join t' advance his praise.

DUHRING. C. M. Wm. B. Bradbury.

482 *The Name of Jesus.* C. M. (199)

1 There is a name I love to hear,
I love to sing its worth;
It sounds like music in mine ear
The sweetest name on earth.

2 It tells me of a Saviour's love,
Who died to set me free·
It tells me of his precious blood,
The sinner's perfect plea.

3 Jesus, the name I love so well,
The name I love to hear!
No saint on earth its worth can tell,
No heart conceive how dear.

4 This name shall shed its fragrance still
Along this thorny road;
Shall sweetly smooth the rugged hill
That leads me up to God.

GEER. C. M. H. W. Greatorex.

483 C. M. (158)

The Name of Jesus precious.

1 How sweet the name of Jesus sounds
In a believer's ear!
It soothes his sorrows, heals his wounds,
And drives away his fear.

2 It makes the wounded spirit whole,
And calms the troubled breast;
'Tis manna to the hungry soul,
And to the weary rest.

3 Weak is the effort of my heart,
And cold my warmest thought;
But when I see thee as thou art,
I'll praise thee as I ought.

4 Till then, I would thy love proclaim
With every fleeting breath;
And may the music of thy name
Refresh my soul in death.

SESSIONS. L. M. L. O. Emerson.

484 *"No other Friend can I desire."* L. M. (120)

1 My precious Lord, for thy dear name
I bear the cross, despise the shame;
Nor do I faint while thou art near;
I lean on thee; how can I fear?

2 No other name but thine is given
To cheer my soul in earth or heaven;
No other wealth will I require;
No other friend can I desire.

3 Yea, into nothing would I fall
For thee alone, my All in all;
To feel thy love, my only joy;
To tell thy love, my sole employ.

485 *The Name of Jesus loved.* C. M. (162)

Tune—BROWN, No. 478.

1 JESUS, I love thy charming name;
'Tis music to my ear;
Fain would I sound it out so loud
That earth and heaven might hear.

2 Yes, thou art precious to my soul,
My transport and my trust:
Jewels to thee are gaudy toys,
And gold is sordid dust.

3 All my capacious powers can wish
In thee doth richly meet;
Nor to my eyes is light so dear,
Nor friendship half so sweet.

4 Thy grace shall dwell upon my heart,
And shed its fragrance there,—
The noblest balm of all its wounds,
The cordial of its care.

5 I'll speak the honors of thy name
With my last, laboring breath,
And, dying, clasp thee in my arms,
The antidote of death.

ALETTA. 7s. WM. B. BRADBURY.

486 *Searching Inquiry.* 7s. (188)

1 HARK, my soul, it is the Lord;
'Tis the Saviour; hear his word:
Jesus speaks, and speaks to thee:
"Say, poor sinner, lov'st thou me?

2 "I delivered thee when bound,
And, when wounded, healed thy wound,
Sought thee wandering, set thee right,
Turned thy darkness into light.

3 "Can a woman's tender care
Cease toward the child she bare?
Yes, she may forgetful be;
Yet will I remember thee.

4 "Mine is an unchanging love,
Higher than the heights above,
Deeper than the depths beneath,
Free and faithful, strong as death.

5 "Thou shalt see my glory soon,
When the work of grace is done;
Partner of my throne shall be:
Say, poor sinner, lovest thou me?"

6 Lord, it is my chief complaint
That my love is weak and faint;
Yet I love thee, and adore;
Oh, for grace to love thee more!

ADAMS. C. M. GEO. KINGSLEY.

487 *Most glorious King.* C. M. (197)

1 O JESUS, King most wonderful,
Thou Conqueror renown'd,
Thou sweetness most ineffable,
In whom all joys are found!

2 When once thou visitest the heart,
Then truth begins to shine,
Then earthly vanities depart,
Then kindles love divine.

3 O Jesus, Light of all below,
Thou Fount of living fire,
Surpassing all the joys we know,
And all we can desire.

4 Jesus, may all confess thy name,
Thy wondrous love adore;
And, seeking thee, themselves inflame
To seek thee more and more.

NETTLETON. 8s & 7s. Double.

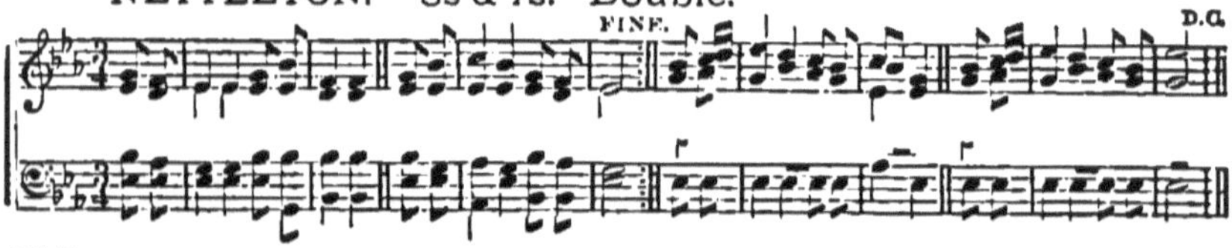
FINE.
D.C.

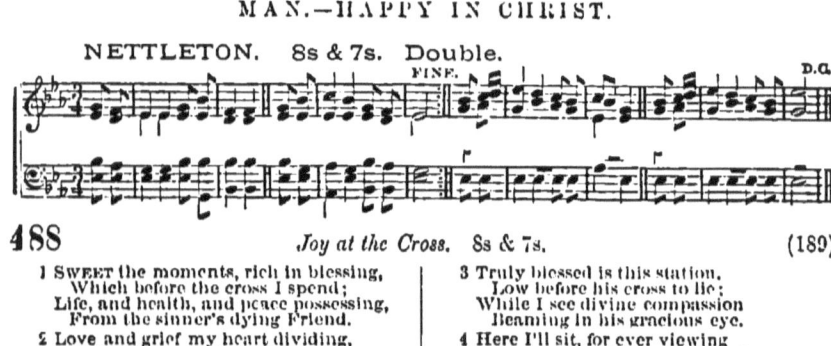

488 *Joy at the Cross.* 8s & 7s. (189)

1 SWEET the moments, rich in blessing,
Which before the cross I spend;
Life, and health, and peace possessing,
From the sinner's dying Friend.

2 Love and grief my heart dividing,
With my tears his feet I'll bathe;
Constant still, in faith abiding,
Life deriving from his death.

3 Truly blessed is this station,
Low before his cross to lie;
While I see divine compassion
Beaming in his gracious eye.

4 Here I'll sit, for ever viewing
Mercy streaming in his blood;
Precious drops, my soul bedewing,
Plead, and claim my peace with God.

MOUNT AUBURN. C. M. G. KINGSLEY.

489 C. M. (204)

The Christian's Happiness.

1 How happy's every child of grace,
Who knows his sins forgiven!
"This earth," he cries, "is not my place,
I seek my home in heaven.

2 "A country far from mortal sight—
Yet, oh, by faith, I see
The land of rest, the saints' delight,
The heaven prepared for me."

3 Oh, what a blessed hope is ours,
While here on earth we stay!
We more than taste the heavenly powers,
And antedate that day.

4 We feel the resurrection near,
Our life in Christ concealed,
And with his glorious presence here
Our earthen vessels filled.

490 *Supporting Grace.* C. M. (204)

1 How happy is the Christian's state!
His sins are all forgiven;
A cheering ray confirms the grace,
And lifts his hopes to heaven.

2 Though, in the rugged path of life
He heaves the pensive sigh,
Yet, trusting in the Lord, he finds
Supporting grace is nigh.

3 If, to prevent his wandering steps,
He feels the chastening rod,
The gentle stroke shall bring him back
To his forgiving God.

4 And when the welcome message comes,
To call his soul away,
His soul in raptures will ascend
To everlasting day.

491 *Joy of a Convert.* 6s & 9s. (167)

Tune, next page.

1 OH, how happy are they
Who their Saviour obey,
And have laid up their treasure above!
Tongue can never express
The sweet comfort and peace
Of a soul in its earliest love.

2 That sweet comfort was mine
When the favor divine
I had found in the blood of the Lamb.
When at first I believed,
What true joy I received!
What a heaven in Jesus' sweet name!

3 'Twas a heaven below
My Redeemer to know;
And the angels could do nothing more
Than to fall at his feet,
And the story repeat,
And the Lover of sinners adore.

4 Jesus all the day long
Was my joy and my song;
Oh, that all his salvation might see!
"He hath loved me," I cried,
"He hath suffered and died
To redeem such a rebel as me."

5 Oh, the rapturous height
Of that holy delight
Which I felt in the life-giving blood!
Of my Saviour possessed,
I was perfectly blest,
As if filled with the fulness of God.

OH, HOW HAPPY ARE THEY. 6s & 9s.

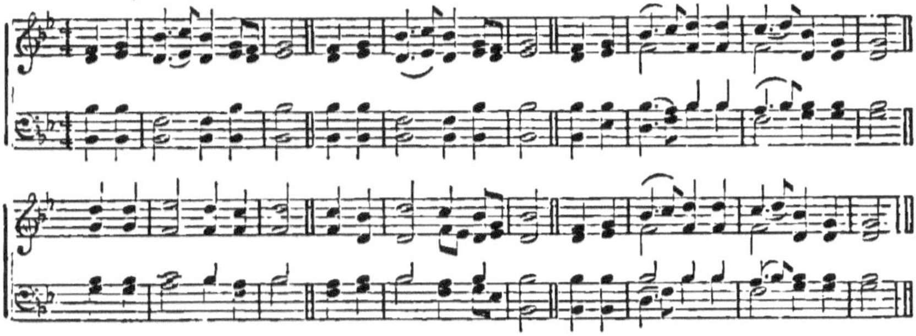

ADAMS. C. M. GEO. KINGSLEY.

492 *The Crown of Jesus.* C. M. (197)

1 THE head that once was crowned with thorns,
Is crowned with glory now:
A royal diadem adorns
The mighty Victor's brow.

2 The joy of all who dwell above,
The joy of all below,
To whom he manifests his love,
And grants his name to know.

3 To them the cross, with all its shame,
With all its grace, is given;
Their name, an everlasting name,
Their joy the joy of heaven.

4 They suffer with their Lord below,
They reign with him above:
Their profit and their joy to know
The mystery of his love.

5 The cross he bore is life and health,
Though shame and death to him,
His people's hope, his people's wealth,
Their everlasting theme.

REPOSE. 8s & 7s. NOAH K. DA

493 *The elder Brother.* 8s & 7s. (186)

1 YES, for me, for me he careth
With a brother's tender care;
Yes, with me, with me he shareth
Every burden, every fear.

2 Yes, for me he standeth pleading
At the mercy-seat above;
Ever for me interceding,
Constant in untiring love.

3 Yes, in me abroad he sheddeth
Joys unearthly, love and light
And to cover me he spreadeth
His paternal wing of might.

4 Yes, in me, in me he dwelleth;
I in him, and he in me,
And my empty soul he filleth,
Here and through eternity.

5 Thus I wait for his returning,
Singing all the way to heaven:
Such the joyful song of morning,
Such the tranquil song of even.

PEDDIE. 7s. 6 lines. GREGORIAN.

494 7s. 6l. (136)

Blessedness of Trust in Christ.

1 SAVIOUR, happy should I be,
Could I always trust in thee;
Trust thy wisdom me to guide;
Trust thy goodness to provide;
Trust thy saving love and power;
Trust thee every day and hour.

2 Trust thee as the only light
In the darkest hour of night:
Trust in sickness, trust in health;
Trust in poverty and wealth;
Trust in joy, and trust in grief;
Trust thy promise for relief.

3 Trust thy blood to cleanse my soul;
Trust thy grace to make me whole;
Trust thee living, dying too;
Trust thee all my journey through;
Trust thee till my feet shall be
Planted on the crystal sea.

TIOGA. S. M. DR. T. HASTINGS.

495 *The Rest of Faith.* S. M. (159)

1 IF Jesus be my friend,
And I to him belong,
I care not what my foes intend,
Though fierce they be and strong.

2 I rest upon the ground
Of Jesus and his blood;
For I in him alone have found
The true, eternal good.

3 My heart for gladness springs;
It cannot more be sad;
For very joy it smiles and sings,
Sees naught but sunshine glad.

4 The sun that lights mine eyes,
Is Christ, the Lord I love;
I sing for joy of that which lies
Stored up for me above.

JUDEA. C. M.

496 *Perfect Peace.* C. M. (232)

1 A MIND at perfect peace with God,
Oh, what a word is this!
A sinner, reconciled through blood,
This, this indeed is peace.

2 By nature and by practice far,
How very far from God!
Yet now, by grace, brought nigh to him,
Through faith in Jesus' blood.

3 So nigh, so very nigh to God,
I cannot nearer be;
For in the person of his Son
I am as near as he.

4 So dear, so very dear to God,
More dear I cannot be;
The love wherewith he loves the Son,
Such is his love to me.

AMBOY. 7s.

FINE.
D.C.

497 *Joy in Christ.* 7s. (207)

1 JOYFUL be the hours to-day;
Joyful let the seasons be;
Let us sing, for well we may;
Jesus, we will sing of thee.

2 Should thy people silent be,
Then the very stones would sing:
What a debt we owe to thee,
Thee, our Saviour, thee, our King!

3 Joyful are we now to own,
Rapture thrills us as we trace
All the deeds thy love hath done,
All the riches of thy grace.

4 'Tis thy grace alone can save;
Every blessing comes from thee:
All we have and hope to have,
All we are and hope to be.

JESUS IS MINE. 6s & 4s. WM. B. BRADBURY.

498 *My Beloved is mine.* 6s & 4s. (185)

1 Now I have found a friend,
Jesus is mine;
Whose love shall never end;
Jesus is mine.
Though earthly joys decrease,
Though human friendships cease,
Now I have lasting peace·
Jesus is mine.

2 Though I grow poor and old,
Jesus is mine;
He will my faith uphold;
Jesus is mine.
He shall my wants supply;
His precious blood is nigh;
Naught can my hope destroy;
Jesus is mine.

3 When earth shall pass away,
Jesus is mine.
In the great judgment day,
Jesus is mine.
Oh, what a glorious thing,
Then to behold my King,
On tuneful harps to sing,
Jesus is mine!

GLORIA PATRI. TALLIS.

GLORY be to the Father, and | to the | Son: ‖
And | to the | Holy | Ghost: ‖

As it was in the beginning, is now, and | ever shall | be, ‖
World without | end. A- | men, A- | men. ‖

HAYDN. S. M. HAYDN.

499 *Peace with God.* S. M. (233)

1 I HEAR the words of love,
I gaze upon the blood,
I see the mighty sacrifice,
And I have peace with God.

2 'Tis everlasting peace,
Sure as Jehovah's name;
'Tis stable as his steadfast throne,
For evermore the same.

3 The clouds may go and come,
And storms may sweep my sky,
This blood-sealed friendship changes not
The cross is ever nigh.

4 I change, he changes not,
The Christ can never die;
His love, not mine, the resting place
His truth, not mine, the tie.

5 I know he liveth now
At God's right hand above;
I know the throne on which he sits;
I know his truth and love.

GEER. C. M. H. W. GREATOREX.

500 *The Heart at Rest.* C. M. (158)

1 My heart is resting, O my God;
I will give thanks and sing,
My heart has found the secret source
Of every precious thing.

2 I thirst for springs of heavenly life,
And from thyself they rise;
I seek the treasure of thy love,
And close at hand it lies.

3 Thus a new song is in my mouth,
To long loved music set:
Glory to thee for all the grace
I have not tasted yet.

4 I have a heritage of joy
That yet I cannot see;
But he who bled to make it mine
Is keeping it for me.

5 My heart is resting, O my God;
My heart is in thy care;
And while it finds its joy in thee,
Can trust thee everywhere.

501 S. M. (197)

Forgiveness of Sin upon Confession.

Tune—DENNIS, No. 298.

1 OH, blessed souls are they
Whose sins are covered o'er;
Divinely blest, to whom the Lord
Imputes their guilt no more.

2 They mourn their follies past,
And keep their hearts with care;
Their lips and lives, without deceit,
Shall prove their faith sincere.

3 While I concealed my guilt,
I felt the festering wound,
Till I confessed my sins to thee,
And ready pardon found.

4 Let sinners learn to pray;
Let saints keep near the throne;
Our help in times of deep distress
Is found in God alone.

502 C. M. (135)

The Change effected by Grace.

Tune—HEBER, No. 457.

1 WHEN God revealed his gracious name,
And changed my mournful state,
My rapture seemed a pleasing dream,
The grace appeared so great.

2 The world beheld the glorious change,
And did thy hand confess;
My tongue broke out in unknown strains,
And sung surprising grace.

3 "Great is the work," my neighbors cried,
And owned thy power divine;
"Great is the work," my heart replied,
"And be the glory thine."

4 The Lord can clear the darkest skies,
Can give us day for night,
Make drops of sacred sorrow rise
To rivers of delight.

LABAN. S. M. Dr. L. Mason.

503 S. M. (243)

Heavenly Joy on Earth.

1 Come, we that love the Lord,
And let our joys be known;
Join in a song with sweet accord,
And thus surround the throne.

2 The sorrows of the mind
Be banished from the place;
Religion never was designed
To make our pleasures less.

3 Let those refuse to sing
Who never knew our God;
But children of the heavenly King
May speak their joys abroad.

4 The hill of Zion yields
A thousand sacred sweets,
Before we reach the heavenly fields
Or walk the golden streets.

5 Then let our songs abound,
And every tear be dry;
We're marching through Immanuel's ground,
To fairer worlds on high.

504 *Delight in Christ.* L. M. (149)

Tune—Darley, No. 440.

1 Jesus, thou joy of loving hearts,
Thou Fount of life, thou Light of men,
From the best bliss that earth imparts
We turn unfilled to thee again.

2 Thy truth unchanged hath ever stood;
Thou savest those that on thee call;
To them that seek thee thou art good,
To them that find thee, All in all.

3 We taste thee, O thou living bread,
And long to feast upon thee still;
We drink of thee, the fountain head,
And thirst our souls from thee to fill.

4 Our restless spirits yearn for thee,
Where'er our changeful lot is cast;
Glad when thy gracious smile we see,
Blest when our faith can hold thee fast.

5 O Jesus, ever with us stay;
Make all our moments calm and bright;
Chase the dark night of sin away;
Shed o'er the world thy holy light.

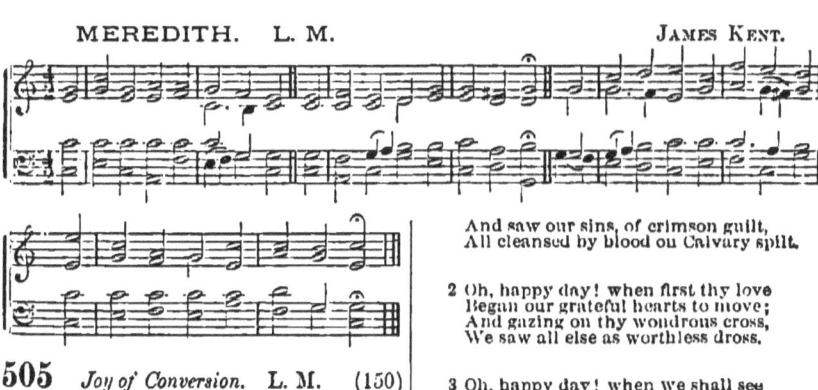

MEREDITH. L. M. James Kent.

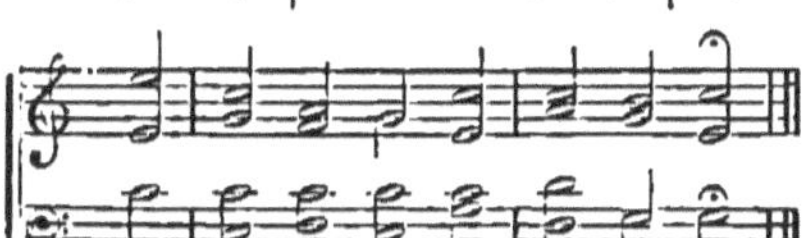

505 *Joy of Conversion.* L. M. (150)

1 Oh, happy day! when first we felt
Our souls with deep contrition melt,
And saw our sins, of crimson guilt,
All cleansed by blood on Calvary spilt.

2 Oh, happy day! when first thy love
Began our grateful hearts to move;
And gazing on thy wondrous cross,
We saw all else as worthless dross.

3 Oh, happy day! when we shall see
And fix our longing eyes on thee,
On thee, our Light, our Life, our Love,
Our All below, our Heaven above.

KEDRON. C. M. DR. T. HASTINGS.

506 C. M. (144)

No Joy without God.

1 GOD, my supporter and my hope,
My help for ever near,
Thine arm of mercy held me up,
When sinking in despair.

2 Thy counsels, Lord, shall guide my feet
Through this dark wilderness:
Thy hand conduct me near thy seat,
To dwell before thy face.

3 Were I in heaven without my God,
'Twould be no joy to me;
And while this earth is my abode,
I long for none but thee.

4 What if the springs of life were broke,
And flesh and heart should faint?
God is my soul's eternal rock,
The strength of every saint.

5 Then, to draw near to thee, my God,
Shall be my sweet employ:
My tongue shall sound thy works abroad,
And tell the world my joy.

IDDO. C. M. Double. NAGELI.

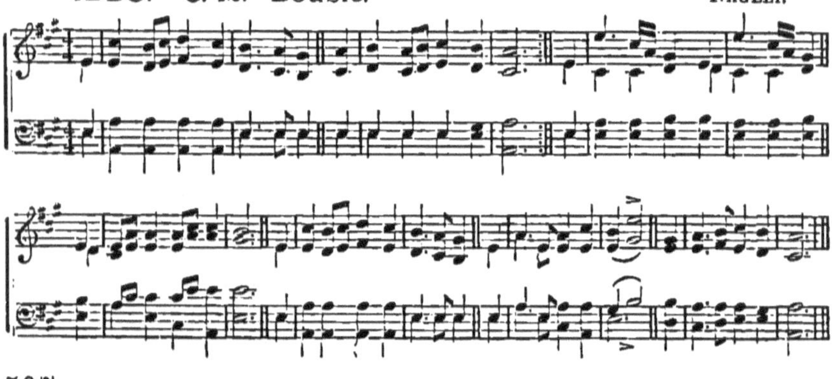

507 *All Things in Christ.* C. M. (185)

1 I HEARD the voice of Jesus say,
"Come unto me and rest;
Lay down, thou weary one, lay down
Thy head upon my breast."
I came to Jesus as I was,
Weary and worn and sad;
I found in him a resting-place,
And he has made me glad.

2 I heard the voice of Jesus say,
"Behold I freely give
The living water, thirsty one,
Stoop down, and drink, and live."
I came to Jesus, and I drank
Of that life-giving stream;
My thirst was quenched, my soul revived,
And now I live in him.

3 I heard the voice of Jesus say,
"I am this dark world's Light;
Look unto me, thy morn shall rise,
And all thy day be bright."
I looked to Jesus, and I found
In him my Star, my Sun;
So in that Light of life I'll walk
Till travelling days are done.

AMBOY. 7s.

FINE.
D.C.

508 7s. (207)

The Pleasures of Religion.

1 'Tis religion that can give
Sweetest pleasures while we live;
'Tis religion must supply
Solid comfort when we die.

2 After death, its joys will be
Lasting as eternity:
Be the living God my Friend,
Then my bliss shall never end.

509 *Christ our only Joy.* C. M. (134)

Tune—Heber, No. 350 or 457.

1 Jesus, the very thought of thee
With gladness fills my breast;
But sweeter far thy face to see,
And in thy presence rest.

2 Nor voice can sing, nor heart can frame,
Nor can the memory find
A sweeter sound than thy blest name,
O Saviour of mankind!

3 And those who find thee, find a bliss
Nor tongue nor pen can show:
The love of Jesus, what it is,
None but his loved ones know.

4 Jesus, our only joy be thou,
As thou our prize wilt be;
Jesus, be thou our glory now,
And through eternity.

OBERLIN. S. H. M. Modern Harp.

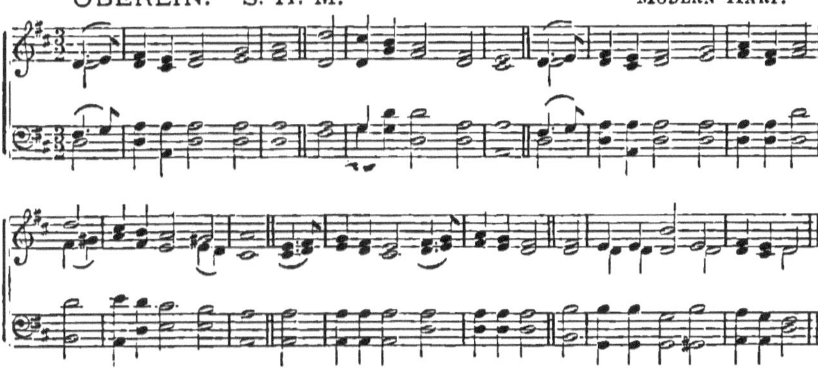

510 *Resting in Jesus.* S. H. M. (205)

1 Jesus, we rest in thee,
In thee ourselves we hide;
Laden with guilt and misery,
Where could we rest beside?
'Tis on thy meek and lowly breast
Our weary souls alone can rest.

2 The slaves of sin and fear,
Thy truth our bondage broke;
Our happy spirits love to wear
Thy light and easy yoke:
The love which fills our grateful breast
Makes duty joy, and labor rest.

3 Soon the bright, glorious day,
The rest of God, shall come;
Sorrow and sin shall pass away,
And we shall reach our home:
Then, of the promised land possess'd,
Our souls shall know eternal rest.

IDDO. C. M. Double. NAGELI.

511 *Our Blessings.* C. M. (184)

1 Oh, praise our great and gracious Lord,
And call upon his name;
To strains of joy tune every chord,
His mighty acts proclaim.
Tell how he led his chosen race
To Canaan's promised land;
Tell how his covenant of grace
Unchanged shall ever stand.

2 We, too, have manna from above,—
The bread that came from heaven;
To us the same kind hand of love
Hath living waters given.
A rock we have, from whence the spring
In rich abundance flows;
That rock is Christ, our Priest, our King,
Who life and health bestows.

3 Oh, let us prize this blessed food,
And trust our heavenly Guide,
So shall we find death's fearful flood
Serene as Jordan's tide;
And safely reach that happy shore,
The land of peace and rest,
Where angels worship and adore,
In God's own presence bless'd.

SAVANNAH. 10s. 6 lines. PLEYEL.

512 *My Beloved is mine, and I am his.* 10s. (195)

1 Yes, he is mine! and naught of earthly things,
Not all the charms of pleasure, wealth, or power,
The fame of heroes, or the pomp of kings,
Could tempt me to forego his love an hour.
"Go, worthless world," I cry, "with all that's thine!
Go! I my Saviour's am, and he is mine."

2 Whate'er may change, in him no change is seen;
A glorious sun, that wanes not, nor declines;
Above the clouds and storms he walks serene,
And on his people's inward darkness shines.
All may depart; I fret not, nor repine,
While I my Saviour's am, while he is mine.

513 *One with Christ.* C. M. (135)

Tune—HEBER, No. 457.

1 LORD Jesus, are we one with thee?
Oh, height, oh, depth of love!
With thee we died upon the tree;
In thee we live above.

2 Such was thy grace that for our sake
Thou didst from heaven come down,
Our mortal flesh and blood partake,
In all our misery one

3 Our sins, our guilt, in love divine,
Were borne on earth by thee;
The pain, the curse, the wrath were thine
To set thy members free.

4 Ascended now in glory bright,
Still one with us thou art;
Nor life nor death nor depth nor height
Thy saints and thee can part.

CLARENDON. C. M. TUCKER.

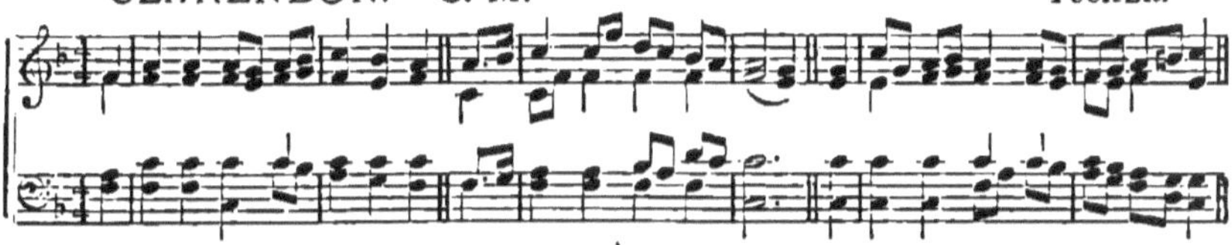

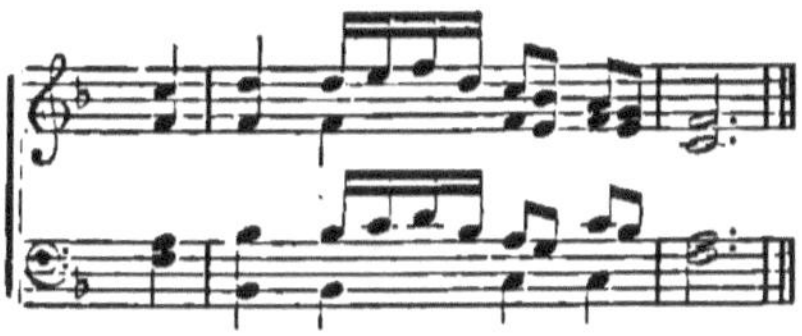

514 *God our Portion.* C. M. (166)

1 MY God, my portion and my love,
Mine everlasting all,
I've none but thee in heaven above,
Or on this earthly ball.

2 How vain a toy is glittering wealth,
If once compared to thee!
Or what's my safety, or my health,
Or all my friends to me?

3 Were I possessor of the earth,
And called the stars mine own,
Without thy graces and thyself,
I were a wretch undone.

4 Let others stretch their arms like seas,
And grasp in all the shore;
Grant me the visits of thy grace,
And I desire no more.

HELENA. C. M. W. B. BRADBURY.

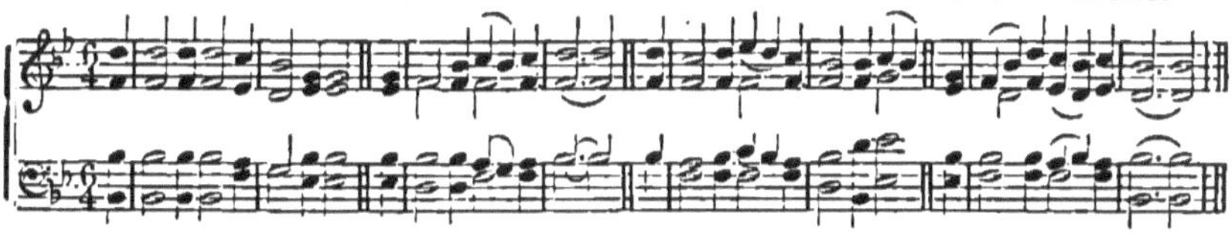

515 *Security and Comfort in God.* C. M. (203)

1 THIS world would be a wilderness,
If banished, Lord, from thee;
And heaven without thy smiling face,
Would be no heaven to me.

2 My Friend art thou where'er I go,
The object of my love,
My kind Protector here below,
And my reward above.

3 'Midst rising winds and beating storms,
Reclining on thy breast,
I find in thee a hiding-place,
And there securely rest.

ADAMS. C. M. GEO. KINGSLEY.

516 *God's Presence is Light in Darkness.* C. M. (197)

1 MY God, the spring of all my joys,
The life of my delights,
The glory of my brightest days,
And comfort of my nights!

2 In darkest shades, if he appear,
My dawning is begun;
He is my soul's bright morning star,
And he my rising sun.

3 The opening heavens around me shine
With beams of sacred bliss,
While Jesus shows his love is mine,
And whispers, I am his.

4 My soul would leave this heavy clay,
At that transporting word,
And run with joy the shining way,
To meet my gracious Lord.

5 Fearless of hell and ghastly death,
I break through every foe:
The wings of love and arms of faith
Shall bear me conqueror through.

GERMANY. L. M. BEETHOVEN.

517 L. M. (178)

The Righteous and the Wicked.

1 How blest the man whose cautious feet
Avoid the way that sinners go;
Who hates the place where atheists meet
And fears to talk as scoffers do.

2 He loves t'employ his morning light
Among the statutes of the Lord,
And spends the wakeful hours of night
With pleasure pondering o'er the word.

3 He, like a plant by gentle streams,
Shall flourish in immortal green;
And heaven will shine with kindest beams,
On every work his hands begin.

4 But sinners find their counsels crossed:
As chaff before the tempest flies,
So shall their hopes be blown and lost,
When the last trumpet shakes the skies.

518 C. M. (135)

Mourning over departed Comforts.

Tune—HEBER, next page.

1 SWEET was the time when first I felt
The Saviour's pardoning blood,
Applied to cleanse my soul from guilt,
And bring me home to God.

2 Soon as the morn the light revealed,
His praises tuned my tongue;
And when the evening shades prevailed,
His love was all my song.

3 In prayer my soul drew near the Lord,
And saw his glory shine;
And when I read his holy word,
I called each promise mine.

4 But now, when evening shade prevails,
My soul in darkness mourns;
And when the morn the light reveals,
No light to me returns.

5 Rise, Lord, and help me to prevail;
Oh, make my soul thy care:
I know thy mercy cannot fail;
Let me that mercy share.

HAPPY IN CHRIST.

HEBER. C. M. Geo. Kingsley.

DE FLEURY. 8s. Double. De Fleury.

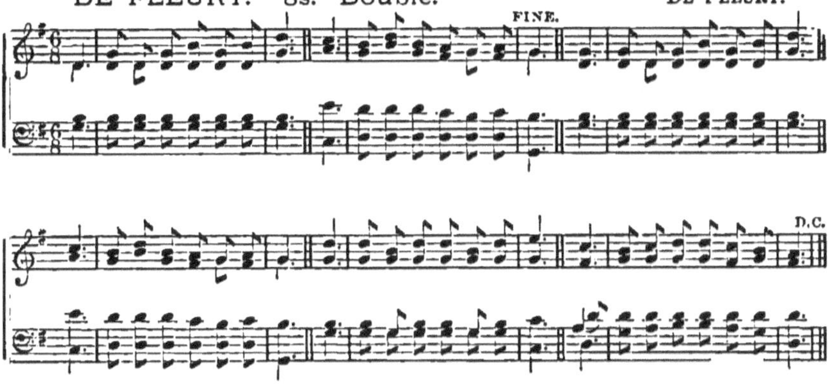
FINE.
D.C.

519 *No Joy without Christ.* 8s. Double. (198)

1 How tedious and tasteless the hours
When Jesus no longer I see!
Sweet prospects, sweet birds, and sweet flowers,
Have all lost their sweetness with me.
The midsummer sun shines but dim;
The fields strive in vain to look gay;
But when I am happy in him,
December's as pleasant as May.

2 His name yields the richest perfume,
And sweeter than music his voice;
His presence disperses my gloom,
And makes all within me rejoice:
I should, were he always thus nigh,
Have nothing to wish or to fear;
No mortal so happy as I;
My summer would last all the year.

3 Content with beholding his face,
My all to his pleasure resigned,
No changes of season or place
Would make any change in my mind:
While blest with a sense of his love,
A palace a toy would appear;
And prisons would palaces prove,
If Jesus would dwell with me here.

4 Dear Lord, if indeed I am thine,
If thou art my sun and my song,
Say, why do I languish and pine,
And why are my winters so long?
Oh, drive these dark clouds from my sky,
Thy soul-cheering presence restore;
Or take me unto thee on high,
Where winter and clouds are no more.

AUTUMN. 8s & 7s. Double.

FINE.
D.S.
D.S.

520 *Rejoicing in Hope of the Glory of God.* 8s & 7s. (202)

1 Know, my soul, thy full salvation;
Rise o'er sin and fear and care;
Joy to find, in every station,
Something still to do or bear:
Think what Spirit dwells within thee;
Think what Father's smiles are thine;
Think what Jesus did to win thee:
Child of heaven, canst thou repine?

2 Haste thee on from grace to glory,
Armed by faith and winged by prayer;
Heaven's eternal day's before thee;
God's own hand shall guide thee there:
Soon shall close thy earthly mission;
Soon shall pass thy pilgrim days;
Hope shall change to glad fruition,
Faith to sight, and prayer to praise.

TIOGA. S. M. DR. T. HASTINGS.

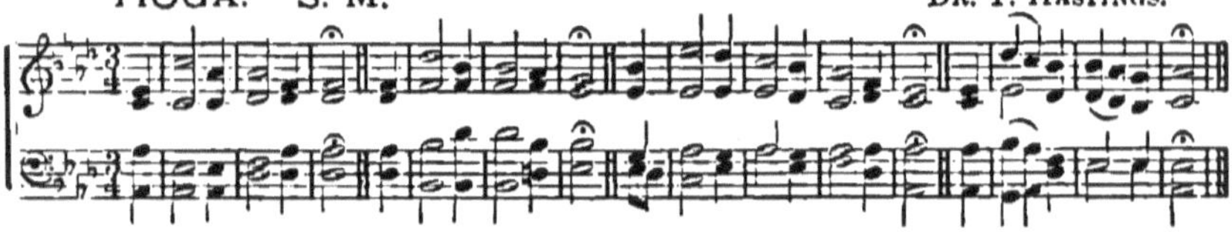

521 *The Sons of God.* S. M. (159)

1 Behold, what wondrous grace
The Father has bestowed
On sinners of a mortal race,
To call them sons of God!

2 Nor doth it yet appear
How great we must be made;
But when we see our Saviour here,
We shall be like our Head.

3 A hope so much divine
May trials well endure;
May purify our souls from sin,
As Christ, the Lord, is pure.

4 If in my Father's love
I share a filial part,
Send down thy Spirit like a dove,
To rest upon my heart.

5 We would no longer lie
Like slaves beneath the throne;
Our faith shall Abba, Father, cry,
And thou the kindred own.

BROWN. C. M. WM. B. BRADBURY.

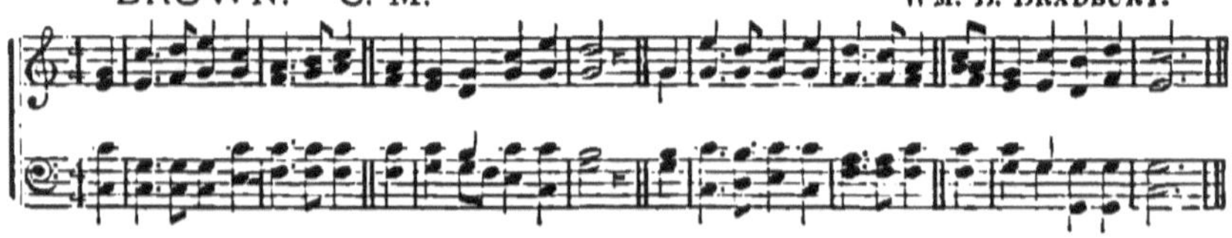

PRAISING CHRIST.

522 *Delight in praising Christ.* C. M. (163)

Tune—BROWN, preceding page.

1 OH, for a thousand tongues to sing
My dear Redeemer's praise,
The glories of my God and King,
The triumphs of his grace!

2 My gracious Master and my God,
Assist me to proclaim,
To spread through all the earth abroad
The honors of thy name.

3 Jesus, the name that calms my fears,
That bids my sorrows cease;
'Tis music in the sinner's ears;
'Tis life and health and peace.

4 He breaks the power of reigning sin,
He sets the prisoner free;
His blood can make the foulest clean;
His blood availed for me.

VANHALL. L. M.

523 L. M. (209)

The Rock of my Strength.

1 REJOICE, ye saints, rejoice and praise
The blessings of redeeming grace.
Jesus, your everlasting tower,
Stands firm against the tempest's power.

2 He is a refuge ever nigh:
His love endures as mountains high:
His name's a rock, which winds above
And waves below can never move.

3 While all things change, he changes not;
He ne'er forgets, though oft forgot;
His love will ever be the same;
His word, enduring as his name.

524 C. M. (204)

Ye are complete in him.

Tune—MOUNT AUBURN, No 189.

1 I'VE found the pearl of greatest price;
My heart doth sing for joy;
And sing I must, for Christ is mine,
Christ shall my song employ.

2 Christ is my Prophet, Priest, and King:
My Prophet full of light;
My great High Priest before the throne:
My King of heavenly might.

3 Christ is my Peace: he died for me,
For me he gave his blood;
And, as my wondrous sacrifice,
Offered himself to God.

4 Christ Jesus is my All in all,
My comfort and my love;
My life below, and he shall be
My joy and crown above.

525 S. M. (192)

What shall we render unto the Lord?

Tune—OLNEY, No. 386.

1 LORD of the realms above,
Our Prophet, Priest, and King,
How shall our souls return thy love,
And all thy glories sing?

2 Oh, love divine indeed,
Oh, rich surpassing grace,
Which brought the Saviour down to bleed
For man's apostate race!

3 Great King of glory, gird
Thy sword upon thy thigh;
Speed on, speed on thy conquering word,
Till all that live comply.

4 The world is all thine own;
Oh, spread thy sway abroad,
Till every heart becomes thy throne,
And owns a present God.

WILLMARTH. L. M. I. B. WOODBURY.

526 *I desire none but thee.* L. M. (145)

1 JESUS, my Lord, 'tis sweet to rest
Upon thy tender, loving breast;
Thy love, my Saviour, dries my tears,
Expels my griefs, and calms my fears.

2 Blest foretaste this of joys to come,
In thy eternal, heavenly home,
Where I shall see thy smiling face,
And know thy rich, unfathomed grace.

3 Help me to praise thee day by day,
Till earth's dark scenes are passed away,
Till, in thine own unclouded light,
Thy glory satisfies my sight.

DUANE STREET. L. M. G. COLES.

FINE.

527 *The Hiding-place.* L. M. (130)

1 HAIL, sovereign love, that first began
The scheme to rescue fallen man.
Hail, matchless, free, eternal grace,
That gave my soul a hiding-place.

2 Against the God that rules the sky,
I fought with hands uplifted high;
Despised the offers of his grace,
Too proud to seek a hiding-place.

3 But thus th' eternal counsel ran:
"Almighty love, arrest the man;"
I felt the arrows of distress,
And found I had no hiding-place.

4 Vindictive Justice stood in view;
To Sinai's fiery mount I flew;
But Justice cried, with frowning face,
"This mountain is no hiding-place."

5 But, lo! a heavenly voice I heard,
And Mercy's angel soon appeared;
Who led me on, a pleasing pace,
To Jesus Christ, my hiding-place.

528 *Grace.* C. M. (163)

Tune—BROWN, No. 522.

1 AWAKE, my heart, arise, my tongue,
Prepare a tuneful voice;
In God, the life of all my joys,
Aloud will I rejoice.

2 'Tis he adorned my naked soul,
And made salvation mine;
Upon a poor polluted worm
He makes his graces shine.

3 And, lest the shadow of a spot
Should on my soul be found,
He took the robe the Saviour wrought,
And cast it all around.

4 Strangely, my soul, art thou arrayed,
By the great sacred Three:
In sweetest harmony of praise,
Let all thy powers agree.

529 *None but Christ.* C. M. (199)

Tune—DUHRING, No. 482.

1 MY Saviour, my Almighty Friend,
When I begin thy praise,
Where will the growing numbers end,
The numbers of thy grace?

2 Thou art my everlasting trust;
Thy goodness I adore;
And since I knew thy graces first,
I speak thy glories more.

3 When I am filled with sore distress
For some surprising sin,
I'll plead thy perfect righteousness,
And mention none but thine.

4 How will my lips rejoice to tell
The victories of my King!
My soul, redeemed from sin and hell,
Shall thy salvation sing.

MEREDITH. L. M. JAMES KENT.

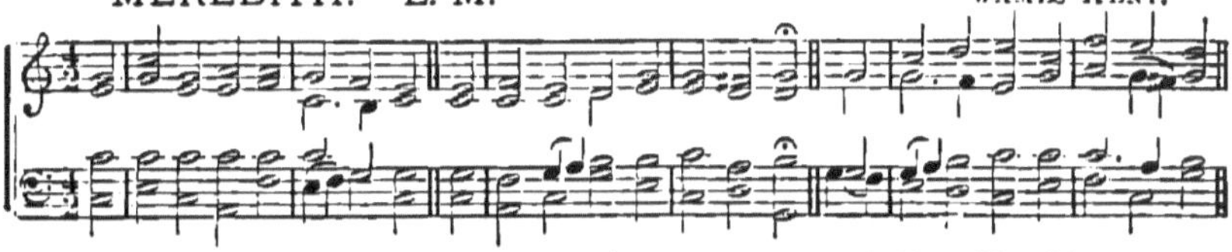

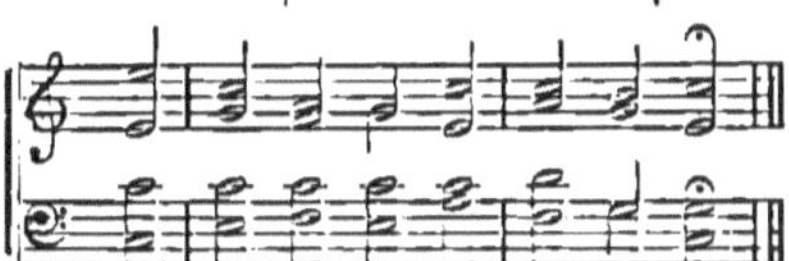

530 L. M. (150)

Salvation through Christ only.

1 Now to the power of God supreme
Be everlasting honors given;
He saves from hell, we bless his name,
He guides our wandering feet to heaven.

2 Not for our duties or deserts,
But of his own abundant grace,
He works salvation in our hearts,
And forms a people for his praise.

3 'Twas his own purpose that begun
To rescue rebels doomed to die;
He gave us grace in Christ his Son,
Before he spread the starry sky.

4 Jesus, the Lord, appears at last,
And makes his Father's counsels known,
Declares the great transaction past,
And brings immortal blessings down.

OZREM. S. M. I. B. WOODBURY.

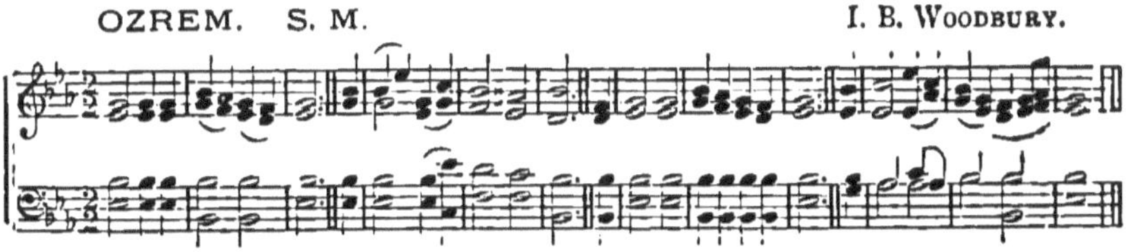

531 *Christ of God.* S. M. (154)

1 JESUS, the Lamb of God,
Who us from hell to raise
Hast shed thy reconciling blood
We give thee endless praise.

2 To thee, the Christ of God,
Thy saints exulting sing:
The bearer of our heavy load,
Our own anointed King.

3 True Lover of the lost,
From heaven thou camest down,
To pay for souls the righteous cost,
And claim them for thine own.

4 Rest of the weary, thou;
To thee, our rest, we come;
In thee to find our dwelling now,
Our everlasting home.

MEREDITH. L. M. JAMES KENT.

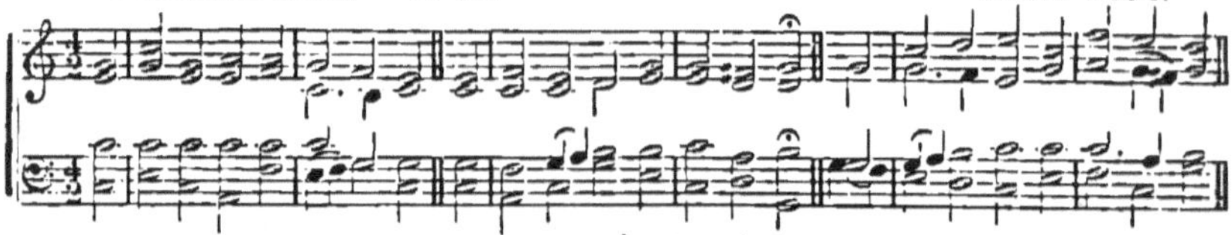

532 L. M. (150)

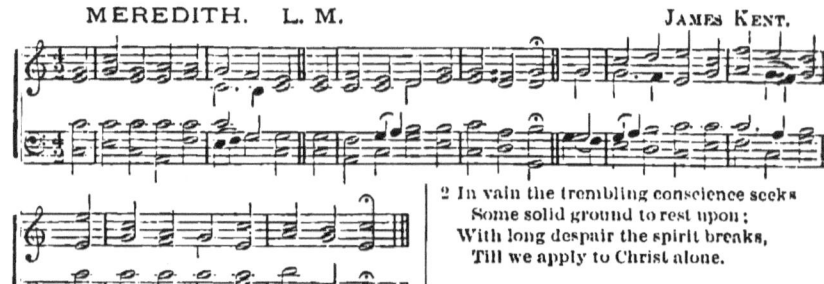

Excellency of the Knowledge of Christ.

1 LET everlasting glories crown
Thy head, my Saviour and my Lord;
Thy hands have brought salvation down,
And stored the blessings in thy word.

2 In vain the trembling conscience seeks
Some solid ground to rest upon;
With long despair the spirit breaks,
Till we apply to Christ alone.

3 How well thy blessed truths agree
How wise and holy thy commands!
Thy promises, how firm they be!
How firm our hope and comfort stands!

4 Should all the forms that men devise
Assault my faith with treacherous art,
I'd call them vanity and lies,
And bind the gospel to my heart.

TOPLADY. 7s. 6 lines. DR. T. HASTINGS.

FINE.
D.C.

533 *How much I owe!* 7s. (152)

1 WHEN this passing world is done;
When has sunk yon glorious sun;
When the pearly gates I gain,
Never to go out again;
Then, Lord, shall I fully know—
Not till then—how much I owe!

2 When I stand before the throne,
Clothed in beauty not my own;
When I see thee as thou art,
Love thee with unsinning heart;
Then, Lord, shall I fully know—
Not till then—how much I owe!

3 When the praise of heaven I hear
Loud as thunders to the ear,
Loud as many waters' noise,
Sweet as harp's melodious voice,
Then, Lord, shall I fully know—
Not till then—how much I owe!

AMBOY. 7s.

FINE.
D.C.

CLARENDON. C. M. TUCKER.

534 *The Lost found.* C. M. (166)

1 OH, how divine, how sweet the joy,
When but one sinner turns,
And, with a humble, broken heart,
His sins and errors mourns!

2 Pleased with the news, the saints below
In songs their tongues employ;
Beyond the skies the tidings go,
And heaven is filled with joy.

3 Well pleased, the Father sees and hears
The conscious sinner's moan;
Jesus receives him in his arms,
And claims him for his own.

535 7s. (207)

Every precious Name in one.

Tune—AMBOY, preceding page.

1 SWEETER sounds than music knows
Charm me in Immanuel's name;
All her hopes my spirit owes
To his birth and cross and shame.

2 When he came, the angels sang,
"Glory be to God on high;"
Lord, unloose my stammering tongue,
Who should louder sing than I?

3 Did the Lord a man become,
That he might the law fulfil,
Bleed and suffer in my room,
And canst thou, my tongue, be still?

4 No; I must my praises bring,
Though they worthless are, and weak;
For, should I refuse to sing,
Sure the very stones would speak.

5 O my Saviour, Shield, and Sun,
Shepherd, Brother, Lord, and Friend,
Every precious name in one,
I will love thee without end.

CRANBROOK. S. M. CLARK.

536 *Salvation by Grace.* S. M. (208)

1 GRACE! 'tis a charming sound,
Harmonious to the ear;
Heaven with the echo shall resound,
And all the earth shall hear.

2 Grace first contrived the way
To save rebellious man;
And all the steps that grace display
Which drew the wondrous plan.

(CONTINUED.)

3 Grace led my roving feet
To tread the heavenly road;
And new supplies each hour I meet,
While pressing on to God.

4 Grace all the work shall crown,
Through everlasting days;
It lays in heaven the topmost stone,
And well deserves the praise.

ADAMS. C. M. Geo. Kingsley.

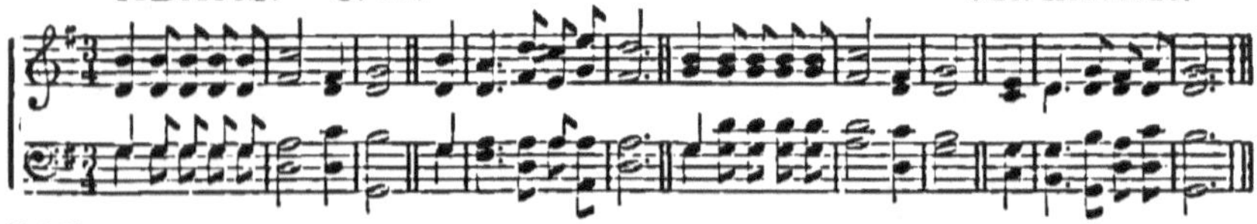

537 *The Love that God hath to us.* C. M. (196)

1 Oh, love beyond the reach of thought,
That form'd the sovereign plan,
Ere Adam had our ruin wrought,
Of saving fallen man!

2 God has so loved our rebel race
As his own Son to give,
That whoso will,—amazing grace!—
May look to him and live.

3 Blest be the Father of our Lord,
From whom all blessings spring!
And blessed be th' incarnate Word,
Our Saviour and our King!

4 We know and have believed the love
Which God through Christ displays:
And when we see his face above,
We'll nobler anthems raise.

BROWN. C. M. Wm. B. Bradbury.

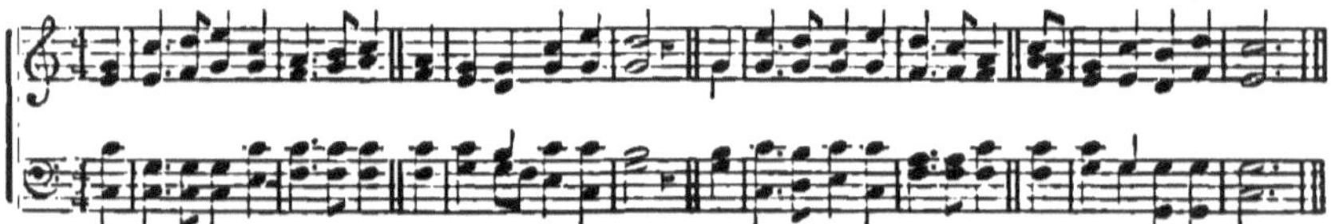

538 *Salvation.* C. M. (163)

1 Salvation! oh, the joyful sound!
'Tis pleasure to our ears,
A sovereign balm for every wound,
A cordial for our fears.

2 Buried in sorrow and in sin,
At hell's dark door we lay;
But we arise, by grace divine,
To see a heavenly day.

3 Salvation! let the echo fly
The spacious earth around,
While all the armies of the sky
Conspire to raise the sound.

PHILLIPS. C. M. I. B. Woodbury.

539 *Subdued by the Cross.* C. M. (164)

1 In evil long I took delight,
Unawed by shame or fear,
Till a new object struck my sight,
And stopped my wild career.

2 I saw one hanging on a tree,
In agonies and blood;
He fixed his languid eyes on me,
As near his cross I stood.

3 Oh, never, till my latest breath,
Shall I forget that look;
It seemed to charge me with his death,
Though not a word he spoke.

4 My conscience felt and owned the guilt;
It plunged me in despair;
I saw my sins his blood had spilt,
And helped to nail him there.

5 A second look he gave, which said,
"I freely all forgive;
This blood is for thy ransom paid;
I die that thou mayest live."

540 *Electing Love acknowledged.* 7s & 6s. (173)

Tune—WEIMAR, NO. 474.

1 'Tis not that I did choose thee,
For, Lord, that could not be;
This heart would still refuse thee,
But thou hast chosen me;

2 Thou from the sin that stain'd me
Washed me and set me free,
And to this end ordain'd me,
That I should live to thee.

3 'Twas sovereign mercy called me,
And taught my opening mind;
The world had else enthrall'd me,
To heavenly glories blind.

4 My heart owns none above thee;
For thy rich grace I thirst;
This knowing: if I love thee,
Thou must have loved me first.

NUREMBURG. 7s.

541 *Redeeming Love.* 7s. (211)

1 Now begin the heavenly theme;
Sing aloud in Jesus name;
Ye who his salvation prove,
Triumph in redeeming love.

2 Mourning souls, dry up your tears;
Banish all your guilty fears;
See your guilt and curse remove,
Cancelled by redeeming love.

3 Welcome, all by sin oppressed,
Welcome to his sacred rest;
Nothing brought him from above,
Nothing but redeeming love.

4 Hither, then, your music bring;
Strike aloud each cheerful string;
Mortals, join the host above,
Join to praise redeeming love.

542 C. M. (163)

Praise to the Lamb.

Tune—BROWN, No. 538.

1 JESUS, with all thy saints above,
My tongue would bear her part,
Would sound aloud thy saving love,
And sing thy bleeding heart.

2 Blest be the Lamb, my dearest Lord,
Who bought me with his blood,
And quenched his Father's flaming sword
In his own vital flood.

3 All glory to the dying Lamb,
And never-ceasing praise,
While angels live to know his name,
Or saints to feel his grace.

JUDEA. C. M.

543 *Amazing Grace.* C. M. (232)

1 AMAZING grace, how sweet the sound,
That saved a wretch like me!
I once was lost, but now am found:
Was blind, but now I see.

2 'Twas grace that taught my heart to fear,
And grace my fears relieved;
How precious did that grace appear,
The hour I first believed!

3 Through many dangers, toils, and snares,
I have already come;
'Tis grace has brought me safe thus far,
And grace will lead me home.

STAR OF BETHLEHEM. L. M.

D.S.

544 *The Revelation of Christ.* L. M (220)

1 When, marshalled on the nightly plain,
The glittering host bestud the sky,
One star alone of all the train,
Can fix the sinner's wandering eye.

2 Hark! hark! to God the chorus breaks,
From every host, from every gem;
But one alone the Saviour speaks,—
It is the Star of Bethlehem!

3 Once on the raging seas I rode;
The storm was loud, the night was dark;
The ocean yawned, and rudely blowed
The wind that tossed my foundering bark.

4 Deep horror then my vitals froze;
Death-struck, I ceased the tide to stem;
When suddenly a star arose,—
It was the Star of Bethlehem!

5 It was my guide, my light, my all;
It bade my dark forebodings cease;
And, through the storm and danger's thrall,
It led me to the port of peace.

6 Now, safely moored, my perils o'er,
I'll sing, first in night's diadem,
For ever, and for evermore,—
The Star, the Star of Bethlehem!

BARBY. C. M. A. Williams.

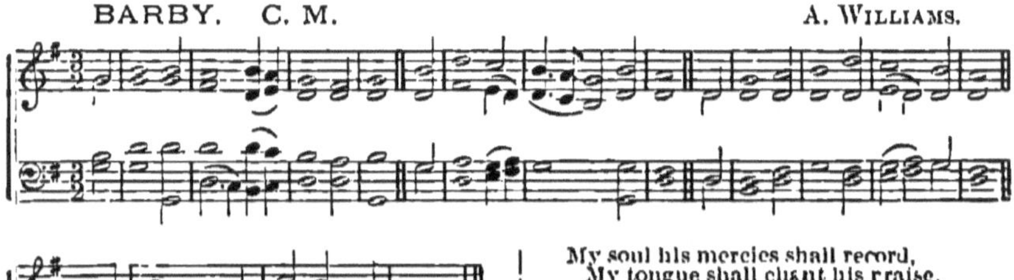

545 C. M. (115)

Oh, magnify the Lord with me!

1 I'll bless the Lord, I'll bless the Lord,
In all his wondrous ways;
My soul his mercies shall record,
My tongue shall chant his praise.

2 Beset with darkness, pressed with cares,
To him, in grief, I cried;
His mercy listened to my prayers,
His hand my wants supplied.

3 With angel hosts encamped around,
To guard them from their foes,
What peace, what glory, have they found,
Who in his name repose!

4 Oh, magnify the Lord with me!
His might, his mercies, prove;
How blest his sway! oh, taste and see
How vast, how kind, his love!

HELENA. C. M. W. B. BRADBURY.

546 *What shall I render unto the Lord.* C. M. (203)

1 For mercies countless as the sands,
Which daily I receive
From Jesus my Redeemer's hands,
My soul, what canst thou give?

2 The best return for one like me,
So wretched and so poor,
Is from his gifts to draw a plea,
And ask him still for more.

3 I cannot serve him as I ought;
No works have I to boast;
Yet would I glory in the thought
That I shall owe him most.

LEBANON. S. M. Double. J. ZUNDEL.

547 S. M. Double. (193)

Christ sought me.

1 I was a wandering sheep,
I did not love the fold;
I did not love my Shepherd's voice,
I would not be controlled;
I was a wayward child,
I did not love my home,
I did not love my Father's voice,
I loved afar to roam.

2 The Shepherd sought his sheep,
The Father sought his child;
He followed me o'er vale and hill,
O'er deserts waste and wild;
He found me nigh to death,
Famished and faint and lone;
He bound me with the bands of love,
He saved the wandering one.

3 Jesus my Shepherd is,
'Twas he that loved my soul,
'Twas he that washed me in his blood,
'Twas he that made me whole;
'Twas he that sought the lost,
That found the wandering sheep;
'Twas he that brought me to the fold;
'Tis he that still doth keep.

548 L. M. (150)

Recognizing God as a Father.

Tune—MEREDITH, No. 532.

1 Great God, indulge my humble claim,
Thou art my hope, my joy, my rest;
The glories that compose thy name
Stand all engaged to make me blest.

2 Thou great and good, thou just and wise,
Thou art my Father and my God;
And I am thine, by sacred ties,
Thy son, thy servant, bought with blood.

3 With early feet I love t' appear
Among thy saints, and seek thy face;
Oft have I seen thy glory there,
And felt the power of sovereign grace.

4 I'll lift my hands, I'll raise my voice,
While I have breath to pray or praise;
This work shall make my heart rejoice,
And bless the remnant of my days.

LENTWOOD. 10s.

549 10s. (182)

The Love that passeth Knowledge.

1 Not what I am, O Lord, but what thou art!
That, that alone, can be my soul's true rest:
Thy love, not mine, bids fear and doubt depart,
And stills the tempest of my tossing breast.

2 Thy name is love;—I hear it from yon cross,
Thy name is love;—I read it in yon tomb;
All meaner love is perishable dross,
But this shall light me thro' time's thickest gloom.

3 It blesses now, and shall for ever bless:
It saves me now, and shall for ever save;
It holds me up in days of helplessness;
It bears me safely o'er each swelling wave.

4 More of thyself, oh, show me hour by hour,
More of thy glory, O my God and Lord;
More of thyself in all thy grace and power,
More of thy love and truth, incarnate Word!

AMBOY. 7s.

FINE.
D.C.

550 *Singing Christians.* 7s. (207)

1 Children of the heavenly King,
As ye journey, sweetly sing;
Sing your Saviour's worthy praise,
Glorious in his works and ways.

2 Ye are travelling home to God,
In the way the fathers trod:
They are happy now, and ye
Soon their happiness shall see.

3 Shout, ye little flock, and blest;
You on Jesus' throne shall rest;
There your seat is now prepared,
There your kingdom and reward

4 Lord, submissive make us go,
Gladly leaving all below;
Only thou our Leader be,
And we still will follow thee.

551 *The Work of Grace.* S. M. (208)

Tune—Cranbrook, next page.

1 Raise your triumphant songs
To an immortal tune;
Let all the earth resound the deeds
Celestial grace has done.

2 Sing how eternal love
Its chief Beloved chose,
And bade him raise our ruined race
From their abyss of woes.

3 Now, sinners, dry your tears;
Let hopeless sorrow cease;
Bow to the sceptre of his love,
And take the offered peace.

4 Lord, we obey thy call;
We lay a humble claim
To the salvation thou hast brought,
And love and praise thy name.

CRANBROOK. S. M. CLARK.

UNAM. 8s, 7s, & 4. CARMINA SACRA.

552 *Security in Jesus.* 8s, 7s, & 4. (222)

1 SOVEREIGN grace, o'er sin abounding!
Ransom'd souls the tidings swell;
'Tis a deep that knows no sounding—
Who its breadth or length can tell?
On its glories
Let my soul for ever dwell!

2 What from Christ the soul can sever,
Bound by everlasting bands?
Once in him, in him for ever,
Thus the eternal covenant stands;
None shall pluck thee
From the Strength of Israel's hands.

3 Heirs of God, joint-heirs with Jesus,
Long ere time its race begun,
To his name eternal praises!
Oh, what wonders love hath done!
One with Jesus,
By eternal union one.

553 C. P. M. (226)

Longing to Praise Christ.

Tune—ARIEL, No. 429.

1 OH, could we speak the matchless worth,
Oh, could we sound the glories forth,
Which in our Saviour shine,
We'd soar, and touch the heavenly strings,
And vie with Gabriel, while he sings
In notes almost divine.

2 We'd sing the precious blood he spilt—
Our ransom from the dreadful guilt
Of sin and wrath divine;
We'd sing his glorious righteousness,
In which all-perfect, heavenly dress
We shall for ever shine.

3 We'd sing the characters he bears,
And all the forms of love he wears,
Exalted on his throne:
In loftiest songs of sweetest praise,
We would, to everlasting days,
Make all his glories known.

4 Well, the delightful day will come,
When our dear Lord will bring us home,
And we shall see his face:
Then with our Saviour, Brother, Friend,
A blest eternity we'll spend,
Triumphant in his grace.

OLNEY. S. M. Dr. L. Mason.

554

Blessed be his Name. S. M. (193)

1 I bless the Christ of God;
I rest on love divine;
And with unfaltering lip and heart,
I call this Saviour mine.

2 His cross dispels each doubt;
I bury in his tomb
Each thought of unbelief and fear,
Each lingering shade of gloom.

3 I praise the God of grace;
I trust his truth and might;
He calls me his, I call him mine,
My God, my joy, my light.

4 'Tis he who saveth me,
And freely pardon gives;
I love because he loveth me,
I live because he lives.

5 My life with him is hid,
My death has passed away,
My clouds have melted into light,
My midnight into day.

LOVING KINDNESS. L. M.

555

L. M. (148)

Christ's loving Kindness.

1 Awake, my soul, in joyful lays,
And sing thy great Redeemer's praise;
He justly claims a song from me;
His loving kindness, oh, how free!

2 He saw me ruined by the fall,
Yet loved me, notwithstanding all;
He saved me from my lost estate;
His loving kindness, oh, how great!

3 Though numerous hosts of mighty foes,
Though earth and hell my way oppose
He safely leads my soul along;
His loving kindness, oh, how strong!

4 I often feel my sinful heart
Prone from my Saviour to depart;
But though I oft have him forgot,
His loving kindness changes not.

5 Soon shall I pass the gloomy vale;
Soon all my mortal powers must fail;
Oh, may my last, expiring breath
His loving kindness sing in death.

6 Then let me mount and soar away
To the bright world of endless day;
And sing, with rapture and surprise,
His loving kindness in the skies.

556

The Believer safe. 8s. (198)

Tune—De Fleury, No. 519.

1 A debtor to mercy alone,
Of covenant mercy I sing;
Nor fear, with thy righteousness on,
My person and offering to bring.
The terrors of law and of God
With me can have nothing to do;
My Saviour's obedience and blood
Hide all my transgressions from view

2 The work which his goodness began,
The arm of his strength will complete;
His promise is yea and amen,
And never was forfeited yet.
Things future, nor things that are now,
Not all things, below nor above,
Can make him his purpose forego,
Or sever my soul from his love.

3 My name from the palms of his hands,
Eternity will not erase;
Impressed on his heart it remains,
In marks of indelible grace:
Yes, I to the end shall endure,
As sure as the earnest is given;
More happy, but not more secure,
The glorified spirits in heaven.

STATE STREET. S. M. J. C. WOODMAN.

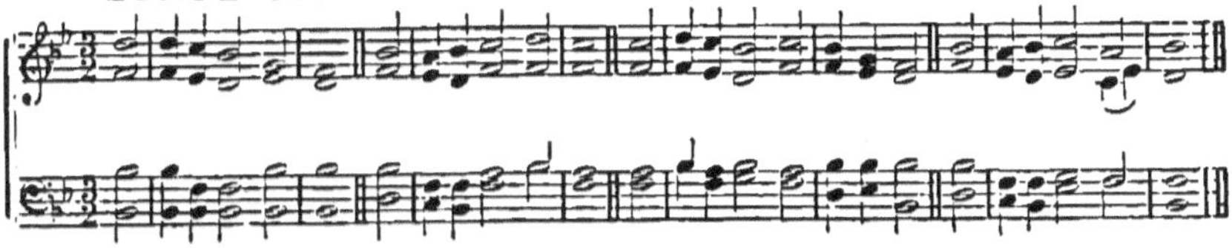

557

Entire Surrender. S. M. (151)

1 O LORD, thou art my Lord,
My portion and delight;
All other lords I now reject,
And cast them from my sight.

2 Thy sovereign right I own,
Thy glorious power confess;
Thy law shall ever rule my heart,
While I adore thy grace.

3 Too long my feet have strayed
In sin's forbidden way;
But since thou hast my soul reclaimed,
To thee my vows I'll pay.

4 My soul, to Jesus joined
By faith and hope and love,
Now seeks to dwell among thy saints,
And rest with them above.

5 Accept, O Lord, my heart;
To thee myself I give;
Nor suffer me from hence to stray,
Or cause thy saints to grieve.

JAZER. C. M. WM. B. BRADBURY.

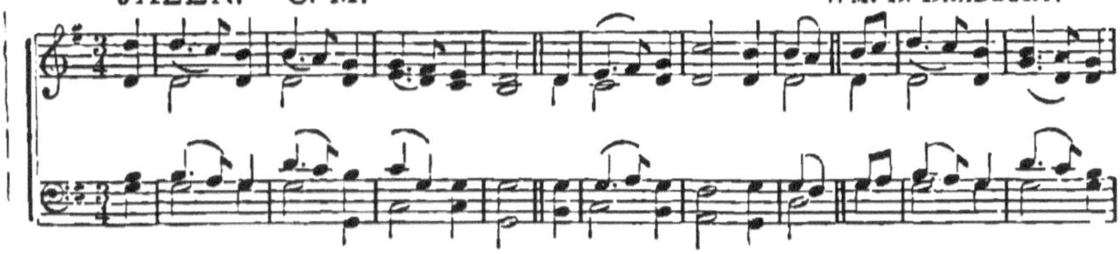

558

C. M. (217)

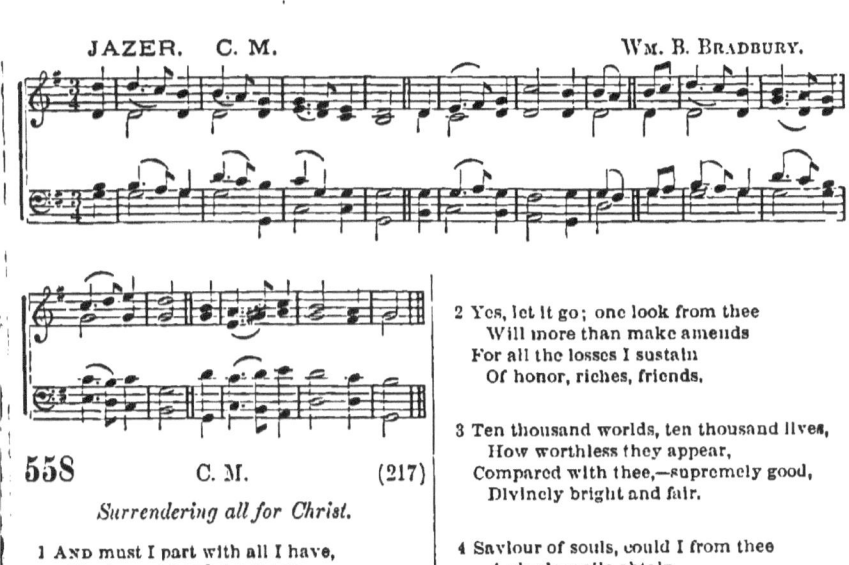

Surrendering all for Christ.

1 AND must I part with all I have,
My dearest Lord, for thee?
It is but right, since thou hast done
Much more than this for me.

2 Yes, let it go; one look from thee
Will more than make amends
For all the losses I sustain
Of honor, riches, friends.

3 Ten thousand worlds, ten thousand lives,
How worthless they appear,
Compared with thee,—supremely good,
Divinely bright and fair.

4 Saviour of souls, could I from thee
A single smile obtain,
The loss of all things I could bear,
And glory in my gain.

HORTON. 7s. SCHNYDER.

559 *A living Sacrifice.* 7s. (140)

1 JESUS, who upon the tree
Wast an offering for me,
Take this throbbing heart of mine,
Lay it on thy holy shrine.

2 As thy love accepteth naught
Save what love itself hath wrought,
Offer thou my sacrifice,
Else to heaven it cannot rise.

3 Take away my erring will;
All my wayward passions kill;
Tear my sins from out my heart,
Though it cost me bitter smart.

4 Fain were I of self bereft,
Naught but thee within me left;
Living sacrifice I am,
Offered only in thy name.

NUREMBURG. 7s.

560 *Prayer for Consecration.* 7s. (211)

1 THINE for ever! God of love,
Hear us from thy throne above;—
Thine for ever may we be,
Here and in eternity.

2 Thine for ever! Lord of life,
Shield us through our earthly strife;
Thou, the Life, the Truth, the Way,
Guide us to the realms of day.

3 Thine for ever! oh, how blest
They who find in thee their rest;
Saviour, Guardian, heavenly Friend,
Oh, defend us to the end!

4 Thine for ever! thou our Guide,
All our wants by thee supplied,
All our sins by thee forgiven,
Led by thee from earth to heaven.

561 *I am his.* C. M. (217)

Tune—JAZER, next page.

1 I'M thine, O Lord, and thine alone,
I'm thine by every tie;
By duty's claims, by love's glad choice,
For thee to live or die.

2 There's not an angel blest in heaven
So bound to thee as I;
To them thy love its gifts has given
For me Love's self did die.

3 My life, my time, my strength, my all,
I'd hold and spend for thee;
Oh, set my heart as free from earth
As saints in glory be.

4 With single eye and fervent heart
Let this poor life be spent:
Eager to use for thy great name
Whatever thou hast lent.

JAZER. C. M. Wm. B. Bradbury.

562 C. M. (161)

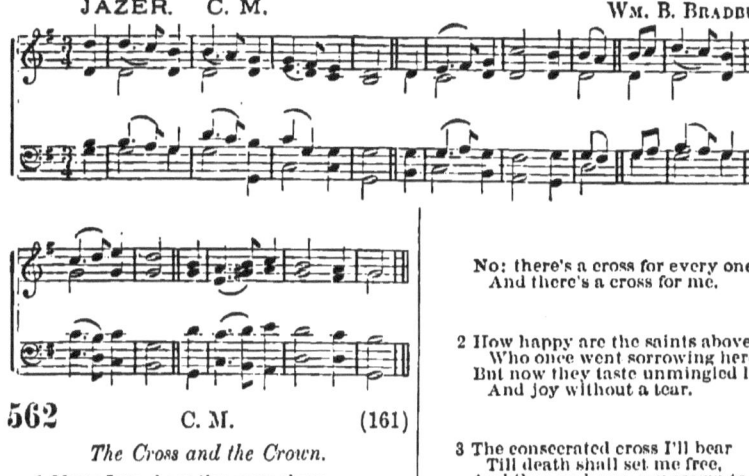

The Cross and the Crown.

1 Must Jesus bear the cross alone,
And all the world go free?
No: there's a cross for every one,
And there's a cross for me.

2 How happy are the saints above,
Who once went sorrowing here;
But now they taste unmingled love,
And joy without a tear.

3 The consecrated cross I'll bear
Till death shall set me free,
And then go home my crown to wear,
For there's a crown for me.

CROSS AND CROWN. C. M. Western Melody.

FEDERAL STREET. L. M. H. K. Oliver.

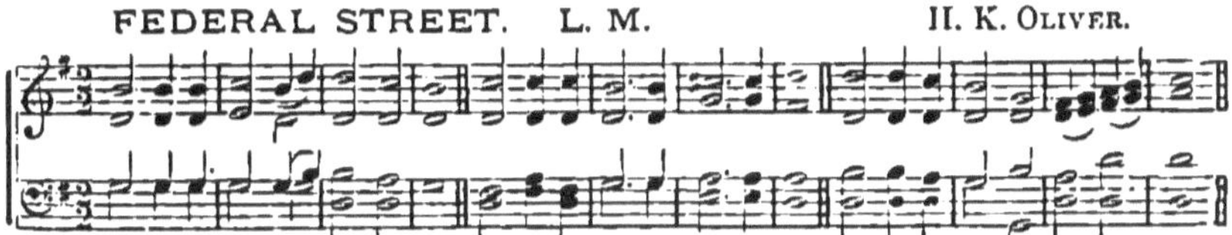

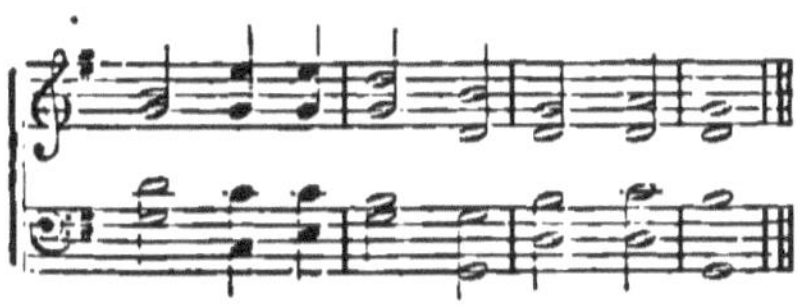

563 *Living to Christ.* L. M. (175)

1 My gracious Lord, I own thy right
To every service I can pay,
And call it my supreme delight
To hear thy dictates and obey.

2 What is my being but for thee,
Its sure support, its noblest end?
'Tis my delight thy face to see,
And serve the cause of such a friend.

3 I would not sigh for worldly joy,
Or to increase my worldly good,
Nor future days nor powers employ
To spread a sounding name abroad.

4 'Tis to my Saviour I would live,
To him who for my ransom died;
Nor could all worldly honor give
Such bliss as crowns me at his side.

5 His work my hoary age shall bless,
When youthful vigor is no more,
And my last hour of life confess
His saving love, his glorious power.

OVIO. 8s & 7s. DR. L. MASON.

564 *Forsaking all to follow Christ.* 8s & 7s. (201)

1 JESUS, I my cross have taken,
All to leave, and follow thee;
Naked, poor, despised, forsaken,
Thou from hence my all shalt be.

2 Perish every fond ambition,
All I've sought and hoped and known,
Yet, how rich is my condition,
God and heaven are still my own.

3 Man may trouble and distress me;
'Twill but drive me to thy breast:
Life with trials hard may press me;
Heaven will bring me sweeter rest.

4 Oh, 'tis not in grief to harm me,
While thy love is left to me;
Oh, 'twere not in joy to charm me,
Were that joy unmixed with thee.

STATE STREET. S. M. J. C. WOODMAN.

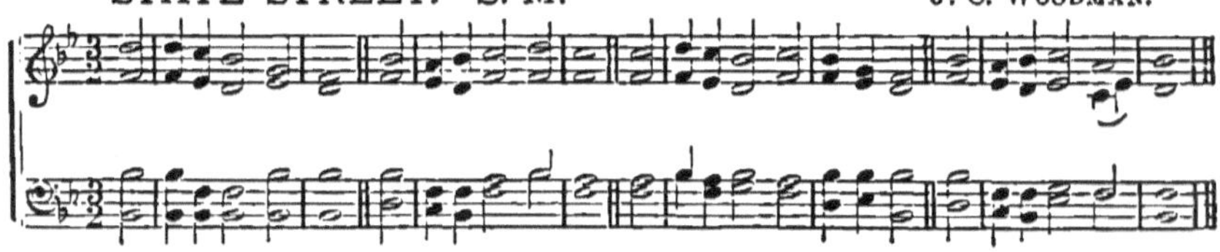

565 *We are his.* S. M. (151)

1 NOT to ourselves again,
Not to the flesh we live;
Not to the world henceforth shall we
Our strength, our being give.

2 Our life is hid with Christ,
With Christ in God above;
Upward our heart would go to him,
Whom, seeing not, we love.

3 Not to ourselves we live,
Not to ourselves we die;
Unto the Lord we die or live,
With him are we on high.

4 We seek the things above,
For we are only his;
Like him we soon shall be, for we
Shall see him as he is.

BARBY. C. M. A. WILLIAMS.

566 *Self-Dedication.* C. M. (115)

1 O SAVIOUR, welcome to my heart;
Possess thy humble throne;
Bid every rival hence depart,
And claim me for thy own.

2 The world and Satan I forsake;
To thee I all resign:
My longing heart, O Saviour, take,
And fill with love divine.

3 Oh, may I never turn aside,
Nor from thy bosom flee;
Let nothing here my heart divide;
I give it all to thee.

567 *Grateful Acknowledgment.* S. M. (159)

Tune—TIOGA, No. 521.

1 My Maker and my King,
To thee my all I owe;
Thy sovereign bounty is the spring
Whence all my blessings flow.

2 The creature of thy hand,
On thee alone I live;
My God, thy benefits demand
More praise than I can give.

3 Lord, what can I impart,
When all is thine before?
Thy love demands a thankful heart.
The gift, alas! how poor!

4 Shall I withhold thy due!
And shall my passions rove?
Lord, form this wretched heart anew,
And fill it with thy love

5 Oh, let thy grace inspire
My soul with strength divine;
Let all my powers to thee aspire,
And all my days be thine.

VANMETER. C. M. I. B. WOODBURY.

568 *The eternal God is thy Refuge.* C. M. (165)

1 How can I sink with such a prop
As my eternal God,
Who bears the earth's huge pillars up,
And spreads the heavens abroad?

2 How can I die while Jesus lives,
Who rose and left the dead?
Pardon and grace my soul receives
From my exalted Head?

3 All that I am, and all I have,
Shall be for ever thine;
Whate'er my duty bids me give,
My cheerful hands resign.

4 Yet if I might make some reserve,
And duty did not call,
I love my God with zeal so great,
That I should give him all.

FEDERAL STREET. L. M. H. K. OLIVER.

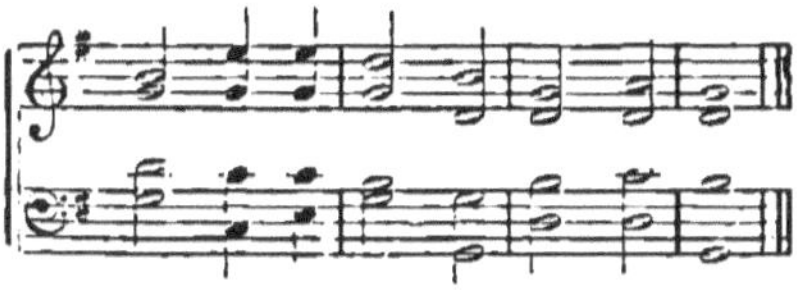

569 *Bought with a Price.* L. M. (174)

1 LORD, I am thine, entirely thine,
Purchased and saved by blood divine;
With full consent thine would I be,
And own thy sovereign right in me.

2 Grant one poor sinner more a place
Among the children of thy grace;
A wretched sinner, lost to God,
But ransomed by Immanuel's blood.

3 Thine would I live, thine would I die,
Be thine through all eternity;
The vow is past beyond repeal,
Now will I set the solemn seal.

4 Do thou assist a feeble worm
The great engagement to perform;
Thy grace can full assistance lend,
And on that grace I dare depend.

HORTON. 7s. SCHNYDER.

570 *Jesus, I am thine.* 7s. (140)

1 JESUS, spotless Lamb of God,
Thou hast bought me with thy blood,
I would value naught beside
Jesus, Jesus crucified.

2 I am thine, and thine alone,
This I gladly, fully own;
And, in all my works and ways,
Only now would seek thy praise.

3 Help me to confess thy name,
Bear with joy thy cross and shame;
Only seek to follow thee,
Though reproach my portion be.

4 When thou shalt in glory come,
And I reach my heavenly home,
Louder still my lips shall own
I am thine, and thine alone.

SEYMOUR. 7s. GREATOREX.

571 *To me to live is Christ.* 7s. (212)

1 CHRIST, of all my hopes the ground,
Christ, the spring of all my joy,
Still in thee let me be found,
Still for thee my powers employ.

2 Fountain of o'erflowing grace,
Freely from thy fulness give;
Till I close my earthly race,
Be it "Christ for me to live."

3 Firmly trusting in thy blood,
Nothing shall my heart confound;
Safely I shall pass the flood,
Safely reach Immanuel's ground.

4 Thus, oh, thus an entrance give
To the land of cloudless sky!
Having known it "Christ to live,"
Let me know it "gain to die."

CLARENDON. C. M. TUCKER.

FEDERAL STREET. L. M. H. K. OLIVER.

572 *Wholly Christ's.* L. M. (175)

1 LORD, we are thine: bought by thy blood,
Once the poor guilty slaves of sin;
But thou hast brought us nigh to God
And made thy Spirit dwell within.

2 Thou hast our sinful wanderings borne
With love and patience all divine;
As brands then from the burning torn,
We own that we are wholly thine.

3 Lord, we are thine: thy claims we own,
Ourselves to thee we wholly give;
Reign thou within our hearts alone,
And let us to thy glory live.

4 Here let us each thy mind display,
In all thy gracious image shine,
And haste that long-expected day
When thou shalt own us wholly thine.

573 C. M. (166)

Renouncing the World.

Tune—CLARENDON, preceding page.

1 LET worldly minds the world pursue;
It has no charms for me;
Once I admired its trifles, too,
But grace has set me free.

2 Its pleasures now no longer please,
Nor more content afford;
Far from my heart be joys like these,
Now I have seen the Lord.

3 As by the light of opening day
The stars are all concealed;
So earthly pleasures fade away
When Jesus is revealed.

4 Creatures no more divide my choice;
I bid them all depart;
His name and love and gracious voice
Have fixed my roving heart.

CARPENTER. 7s. BLUMENTHAL.

574 *Consecration.* 7s. (191)

1 JESUS, all-atoning Lamb,
Thine, and only thine, I am;
Take my body, spirit, soul;
Only thou possess the whole.

2 Thou my one thing needful be;
Let me ever cleave to thee;
Let me choose the better part;
Let me give thee all my heart.

3 Whom have I on earth below;
Thee, and only thee, I know;
Whom have I in heaven but thee?
Thou art all in all to me.

ORWELL. L. M. DR. L. MASON.

575

Desires after Consecration. L. M. (121)

1 O THOU, to whose all-searching sight
The darkness shineth as the light,
Search, prove my heart, it pants for thee:
Oh, burst these bonds, and set it free.

2 Wash out its stains, refine its dross;
Nail my affections to the cross;
Hallow each thought; let all within
Be clean, as thou, my Lord, art clean.

3 If in this darksome wild I stray,
Be thou my light, be thou my way;
No foes, no violence I fear,
No fraud, while thou, my God, art near.

4 When rising floods my soul o'erflow,
When sinks my heart in waves of woe,
Jesus, thy timely aid impart,
And raise my head, and cheer my heart.

5 Saviour, where'er thy steps I see,
Dauntless, untired, I follow thee:
Oh, let thy hand support me still,
And lead me to thy holy hill.

COMMUNING WITH CHRIST.

REPOSE. 8s & 7s. NOAH K. DAVIS.

576

8s & 7s. (186)

Contribution.

1 WITH my substance I will honor
My Redeemer and my Lord;
Were ten thousand worlds my manor,
All were nothing to his word.

2 While the heralds of salvation
His abounding grace proclaim,
Let his friends, of every station,
Gladly join to spread his fame.

3 Be his kingdom now promoted,
Let the earth her Monarch know;
Be my all to him devoted;
To my Lord my all I owe.

577

S. M. (151)

Blessings sought in Prayer.
Tune—STATE STREET, No. 565.

1 BEHOLD the throne of grace!
The promise calls me near;
There Jesus shows a smiling face
And waits to answer prayer

2 Thine image, Lord, bestow,
Thy presence and thy love;
I ask to serve thee here below,
And reign with thee above.

3 Teach me to live by faith;
Conform my will to thine;
Let me victorious be in death,
And then in glory shine.

4 If thou these blessings give,
And wilt my portion be,
All worldly joys I'll cheerful leave,
And find my heaven in thee.

SWEET HOUR OF PRAYER. L. M. Double.

WM. B. BRADBURY.

FINE.
D.C.

578 *Sweet Hour of Prayer.* L. M. Double. (195)

1 SWEET hour of prayer! sweet hour of prayer!
That calls me from a world of care,
And bids me at my Father's throne
Make all my wants and wishes known.
In seasons of distress and grief,
My soul has often found relief,
And oft escaped the tempter's snare
By thy return, sweet hour of prayer.

2 Sweet hour of prayer! sweet hour of prayer!
Thy wings shall my petition bear,
To him whose truth and faithfulness
Engage the waiting soul to bless;
And since he bids me seek his face,
Believe his word and trust his grace,
I'll cast on him my every care,
And wait for thee, sweet hour of prayer.

3 Sweet hour of prayer! sweet hour of prayer!
May I thy consolation share,
Till from Mount Pisgah's lofty height,
I view my home, and take my flight:
This robe of flesh I'll drop, and rise
To seize the everlasting prize;
And shout, while passing through the air,
Farewell, farewell, sweet hour of prayer.

WEBB. 7s & 6s.

GEO. J. WEBB.

FINE.

D.S.

579 *Prayer at all Times.* 7s & 6s. (223)

1 Go when the morning shineth,
Go when the noon is bright,
Go when the eve declineth,
Go in the hush of night;
Go with pure mind and feeling,
Fling earthly thought away,
And, in thy closet kneeling,
Do thou in secret pray.

2 Remember all who love thee,
All who are loved by thee;
Pray, too, for those who hate thee,
If any such there be;
Then for thyself, in meekness,
A blessing humbly claim,
And blend with each petition
Thy great Redeemer's name.

3 Oh, not a joy or blessing
With this can we compare,—
The grace . ur Father gave us
To pour our souls in prayer;
Whene'er thou pin'st in sadness,
Before his footstool fall;
Remember, in thy gladness,
His love who gave thee all.

BYEFIELD. C. M. DR. T. HASTINGS.

580 *A Throne of Grace.* C. M. (169)

1 A THRONE of grace! then let us go
And offer up our prayer;
A gracious God will mercy show
To all that worship there.

2 A throne of grace! oh, at that throne
Our knees have often bent,
And God has showered his blessings down
As often as we went.

3 A throne of grace! rejoice, ye saints;
That throne is open still;
To God unbosom your complaints,
And then inquire his will.

4 A throne of grace we yet shall need
Long as we draw our breath,
A Saviour, too, to intercede,
Till we are changed by death.

5 The throne of glory then shall glow
With beams of Jesus' face,
And we no longer want shall know,
Nor need a throne of grace.

581 *Prayer.* C. M. (169)

1 PRAYER is the breath of God in man,
Returning whence it came;
Love is the sacred fire within,
And prayer the rising flame.

2 It gives the burdened spirit ease,
And soothes the troubled breast;
Yields comfort to the mourners here,
And to the weary rest.

3 When God inclines the heart to pray,
He hath an ear to hear;
To him there's music in a groan,
And beauty in a tear.

4 The humble suppliant cannot fail
To have his wants supplied,
Since he for sinners intercedes
Who once for sinners died.

582 C. M. (168)

The Nature of Prayer.

1 PRAYER is the soul's sincere desire,
Unuttered or expressed,
The motion of a hidden fire,
That trembles in the breast.

2 Prayer is the burden of a sigh,
The falling of a tear,
The upward glancing of an eye,
When none but God is near.

3 Prayer is the simplest form of speech
That infant lips can try;
Prayer, the sublimest strains that reach
The Majesty on high.

4 Prayer is the Christian's vital breath,
The Christian's native air,
His watchword at the gates of death;
He enters heaven with prayer.

583 *Teach us to pray.* C. M. (169)

1 PRAYER is the contrite sinner's voice
Returning from his ways,
While angels in their songs rejoice
And cry, "Behold, he prays."

2 The saints in prayer appear as one
In word and deed and mind,
While with the Father and the Son
Sweet fellowship they find.

3 Nor prayer is made on earth alone:
The Holy Spirit pleads,
And Jesus, on th' eternal throne,
For sinners intercedes.

4 O thou, by whom we come to God,—
The Life, the Truth, the Way,—
The path of prayer thyself hast trod,
Lord, teach us how to pray.

584 *The Mercy-seat.* L. M. (148)

Tune—RETREAT, next page.

1 FROM every stormy wind that blows,
From every swelling tide of woes,
There is a calm, a sure retreat,—
'Tis found beneath the mercy-seat.

2 There is a place where Jesus sheds
The oil of gladness on our heads,—
A place of all on earth most sweet;
It is the blood-bought mercy-seat.

3 There is a scene where spirits blend,
Where friend holds fellowship with friend;
Though sundered far, by faith they meet
Around one common mercy-seat.

4 There, there on eagle wings we soar,
And sin and sense molest no more,
And heaven comes down our souls to greet,
And glory crowns the mercy-seat.

RETREAT. L. M. DR. T. HASTINGS.

585 *Hindrances to prayer.* L. M. (146)

1 WHAT various hindrances we meet
In coming to a mercy-seat!
Yet who that knows the worth of prayer
But wishes to be often there?

2 Prayer makes the darkened clouds withdraw;
Prayer climbs the ladder Jacob saw;
Gives exercise to faith and love;
Brings every blessing from above.

3 Restraining prayer, we cease to fight;
Prayer makes the Christian's armor bright;
And Satan trembles when he sees
The weakest saint upon his knees.

4 Have you no words? Ah! think again;
Words flow apace when you complain,
And fill your fellow-creature's ear
With the sad tale of all your care.

5 Were half the breath thus vainly spent
To heaven in supplication sent,
Your cheerful song would often be,
"Hear what the Lord hath done for me!"

EVENTIDE. 11s. ENGLISH.

586 *I have set the Lord always before me.* 11s & 10s. (225)

1 STILL, still with thee when purple morning breaketh,
When wake the birds, and all the shadows flee,
Fairer than morning, lovelier than the daylight,
Dawns the sweet consciousness, I am with thee.

2 When sinks the soul, subdued by toil, to slumber,
Its closing eye looks up to thee in prayer;
Sweet the repose, beneath thy wings o'ershading,
But sweeter still to wake and find thee there.

3 So shall it be at last, in that bright morning,
When the soul waketh, and life's shadows flee:
Oh, in that hour, fairer than daylight dawning,
Shall rise the glorious thought, I am with thee.

COME, YE DISCONSOLATE. 11s & 10s. S. WEBBE.

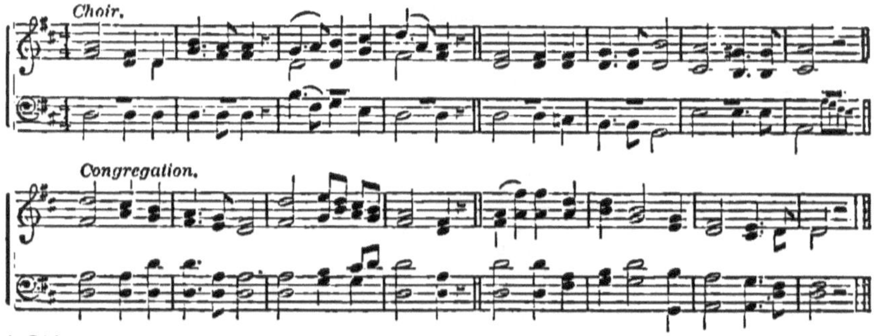
Choir.
Congregation.

587 *The Disconsolate invited to pray.* 11s & 10s. (182)

1 COME, ye disconsolate, where'er ye languish,
Come to the mercy seat, fervently kneel;
Here bring your wounded hearts, here tell your anguish,
Earth has no sorrow that heaven cannot heal.

2 Joy of the desolate, light of the straying,
Hope of the penitent, fadeless and pure,
Here speaks the Comforter, tenderly saying,
Earth has no sorrow that heaven cannot cure.

3 Here see the bread of life; see waters flowing
Forth from the throne of God, pure from above;
Come to the feast of love; come, ever knowing
Earth has no sorrow but heaven can remove.

HAYDN. S. M. HAYDN.

588 *Pray and not faint.* S. M. (233)

1 JESUS, who knows full well
The heart of every saint,
Invites us all our grief to tell,
To pray and never faint.

2 He bows his gracious ear;
We never plead in vain;
Then let us wait till he appear,
And pray, and pray again.

3 Though unbelief suggest
"Why should we longer wait?"
He bids us never give him rest,
But knock at Mercy's gate.

4 Jesus, the Lord, will hear
His chosen when they cry;
Yes, though he may a while forbear,
He'll help them from on high.

5 Then let us earnest cry,
And never faint in prayer;
He sees, he hears, and from on high
Will make our cause his care.

HELENA. C. M. W. B. BRADBURY.

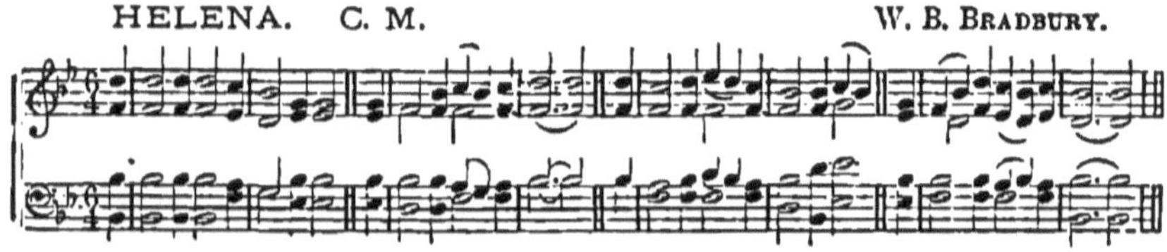

589 *Divine Sympathy.* C. M. (203)

Tune—HELENA, preceding page.

1 THERE is no sorrow, Lord, too light
To bring in prayer to thee;
There is no anxious care too slight
To wake thy sympathy.

2 Thou who hast trod the thorny road
Wilt share each small distress;
The love which bore the greater load
Will not refuse the less.

3 There is no secret sigh we breathe
But meets thine ear divine;
And every cross grows light beneath
The shadow, Lord, of thine.

4 Life's ills without, sin's strife within,
The heart would overflow,
But for that love which died for sin,
That love which wept with woe.

590 7s. (213)

Encouragement to Prayer.

Tune—SEYMOUR, No. 571.

1 COME, my soul, thy suit prepare,
Jesus loves to answer prayer;
He himself has bid thee pray;
Rise and ask without delay.

2 Thou art coming to a King,
Large petitions with thee bring;
For his grace and power are such,
None can ever ask too much.

3 With my burden I begin;
Lord, remove this load of sin;
Let thy blood, for sinners spilt,
Set my conscience free from guilt.

4 Lord, I come to thee for rest;
Take possession of my breast;
There thy blood-bought right maintain,
And without a rival reign.

591 *Prayer for Grace.* 7s. (211)

Tune—NUREMBURG, No. 560.

1 SON of God, thy blessing grant;
Still supply mine every want;
Tree of life, thine influence shed;
From thy fulness I am fed.

2 Unsustained by thee, I fall;
Send the strength for which I call;
Weaker than a bruisèd reed,
Help I every moment need.

3 All my hopes on thee depend,
Love me, save me to the end;
Still preserve me by thy grace;
Take the everlasting praise.

FINNEY. 8s, 7s, & 4. W. B. BRADBURY.

592 *Prayer for Guidance.* 8s, 7s, & 4. (221)

1 GENTLY, Lord, oh, gently lead us
Through this gloomy vale of tears,
And, O Lord, in mercy give us
Thy rich grace in all our fears.
Oh, refresh us,
Travelling through this wilderness.

2 When temptation's darts assail us,
When in devious paths we stray,
Let thy goodness never fail us,
Lead us in thy perfect way.
Oh, refresh us, etc.

3 In the hour of pain and anguish,
In the hour when death draws near,
Suffer not our hearts to languish
Suffer not our souls to fear.
Oh, refresh us, etc.

4 When this mortal life is ended,
Bid us in thine arms to rest,
Till, by angel bands attended,
We awake among the blest.
Oh, refresh us, etc.

NURENBURG. 7s.

593 *Importunity in Prayer.* 7s. (210)

1 LORD, I cannot let thee go,
Till a blessing thou bestow;
Do not turn away thy face,
Mine's an urgent, pressing case.

2 Once a sinner, near despair,
Sought thy mercy-seat by prayer;
Mercy heard and set him free:
Lord, that mercy came to me.

3 Thou hast helped in every need;
This emboldens me to plead;
After so much mercy past,
Canst thou let me sink at last?

4 No; I must maintain my hold;
'Tis thy goodness makes me bold;
I can no denial take,
Since I plead for Jesus' sake.

EVENTIDE. 11s. ENGLISH.

594 10s. (225)

Prayer for Christ's Presence.

1 ABIDE with me! fast falls the eventide;
The darkness deepens; Lord, with me abide;
When other helpers fail, and comforts flee,
Help of the helpless, oh, abide with me!

2 Swift to its close ebbs out life's little day;
Earth's joys grow dim, its glories pass away;
Change and decay on all around I see;
O thou who changest not, abide with me!

3 I need thy presence every passing hour:
What but thy grace can foil the tempter's power?
Who, like thyself, my guide and stay can be?
Through cloud and sunshine, Lord, abide with me!

4 I fear no foe, with thee at hand to bless;
Ills have no weight, and tears no bitterness.
Where is death's sting, and where his victory?
I triumph still, if thou abide with me.

5 Hold thou thy cross before my closing eyes,
Shine through the gloom, and point me to the skies;
Heaven's morning breaks, and earth's vain shadows flee.
In life, in death, O Lord, abide with me!

595 *Seeking God.* C. M. (216)

1 OH, that I knew the secret place
Where I might find my God!
I'd spread my wants before his face,
And pour my woes abroad.

2 I'd tell him how my sins arise;
What sorrows I sustain;
How grace decays, and comfort dies,
And leaves my heart in pain.

(CONTINUED.)

3 He knows what arguments I'd take
 To wrestle with my God;
I'd plead for his own mercy's sake,
 And for my Saviour's blood.

4 My God will pity my complaints,
 And heal my broken bones;
He takes the meaning of his saints,
 The language of their groans.

5 Arise, my soul, from deep distress,
 And banish every fear;
He calls thee to his throne of grace,
 To spread thy sorrows there.

NAOMI. C. M. DR. L. MASON.

596 *The Fount of Blessing.* 8s & 7s. (189)

Tune—NETTLETON, No. 488.

1 COME, thou Fount of every blessing,
 Tune my heart to sing thy grace;
Streams of mercy, never ceasing,
 Call for songs of loudest praise:
Teach me some melodious sonnet,
 Sung by flaming tongues above;
Praise the mount,—oh fix me on it,
 Mount of God's unchanging love.

2 Here I raise my Ebenezer;
 Hither by thy help I'm come;
And I hope, by thy good pleasure,
 Safely to arrive at home:
Jesus sought me when a stranger,
 Wandering from the fold of God;
He, to save my soul from danger,
 Interposed his precious blood.

3 Oh, to grace how great a debtor
 Daily I'm constrained to be!
Let that grace, Lord, like a fetter,
 Bind my wandering heart to thee.
Prone to wander, Lord, I feel it;
 Prone to leave the God I love;
Here's my heart; Lord, take and seal it;
 Seal it from thy courts above.

BADEN. L. M. DR. T. HASTINGS.

597 L. M. (171)

Trusting Christ the only Refuge.

BADEN.

1 THOU only Sovereign of my heart,
 My refuge, my almighty Friend,
And can my soul from thee depart,
 On whom alone my hopes depend?

2 Whither, ah, whither shall I go,
 A wretched wanderer from my Lord?
Can this dark world of sin and woe
 One glimpse of happiness afford?

3 Eternal life thy words impart;
 On these my fainting spirit lives;
Here sweeter comforts cheer my heart
 Than all the round of nature gives.

4 Let earth's alluring joys combine;
 While thou art near, in vain they call;
One smile, one blissful smile, of thine,
 My gracious Lord, outweighs them all.

5 Low at thy feet my soul would lie;
 Here safety dwells, and peace divine
Still let me live beneath thine eye,
 For life, eternal life, is thine.

598 *Sun of Righteousness.* 7s. (153)

Tune—MARTYN, No. 413.

1 CHRIST, whose glory fills the skies,
 Christ, the true, the only light,
Sun of righteousness, arise,
 Triumph o'er the shades of night:
Dayspring from on high, be near;
Daystar, in my heart appear.

2 Dark and cheerless is the morn,
 If thy light is hid from me;
Joyless is the day's return,
 Till thy mercy's beams I see,—
Till they inward light impart,
Warmth and gladness to my heart.

3 Visit, then, this soul of mine;
 Pierce the gloom of sin and grief;
Fill me, radiant Sun divine;
 Scatter all my unbelief;
More and more thyself display,
Shining to the perfect day.

599 *Taking Christ as a King.* 7s. (210)

Tune—NUREMBURG, No. 593.

1 KING of kings, and wilt thou deign
O'er this wayward heart to reign?
Henceforth take it for thy throne;
Rule here, Lord, and rule alone.

2 Then, like heaven's angelic bands,
Waiting for thy high commands,
All my powers shall wait on thee,
Captive, yet divinely free.

3 Tuned by thee in sweet accord,
All shall sing their gracious Lord
Love, the leader of the choir,
Breathing round her seraph fire.

4 Be it so: my heart's thy throne.
All my powers thy sceptre own,
And, with them or thine own hill,
Live rejoicing in thy will.

BETHANY. 6s & 4s. DR. L. MASON

600 *Nearer to God.* 6s & 4s. (228)

1 NEARER, my God, to thee,—
Nearer to thee!
E'en though it be a cross
That raiseth me;
Still all my song shall be,
Nearer, my God, to thee,
Nearer to thee!

2 Though like a wanderer,
The sun gone down,
Darkness comes over me,
My rest a stone,
Yet in my dreams I'd be
Nearer, my God, to thee,
Nearer to thee!

3 There let my way appear
Steps unto heaven;
All that thou sendest me
In mercy given;
Angels to beckon me
Nearer, my God, to thee,
Nearer to thee!

4 Then with my waking thoughts
Bright with thy praise,
Out of my stony griefs
Bethel I'll raise;
So by my woes to be
Nearer, my God, to thee,
Nearer to thee!

5 And when on joyful wing
Cleaving the sky,
Sun, moon, and stars forgot,
Upward I fly:
Still all my song shall be,
Nearer, my God, to thee,
Nearer to thee!

601 6s & 4s. (181)

Breathings after Christ.

Tune—OLIVET, next page.

1 MY faith looks up to thee,
Thou Lamb of Calvary;
Saviour divine,
Now hear me while I pray;
Take all my guilt away;
Oh, let me, from this day,
Be wholly thine.

2 May thy rich grace impart
Strength to my fainting heart,
My zeal inspire;
As thou hast died for me,
Oh, may my love to thee
Pure, warm, and changeless be
A living fire.

3 While life's dark maze I tread,
And griefs around me spread,
Be thou my Guide;
Bid darkness turn to day,
Wipe sorrow's tears away,
Nor let me ever stray
From thee aside.

4 When ends life's transient dream,
When death's cold, sullen stream
Shall o'er me roll,
Blest Saviour, then, in love,
Fear and distress remove;
Oh, bear me safe above,
A ransomed soul!

OLIVET. 6s & 4s. DR. L. MASON.

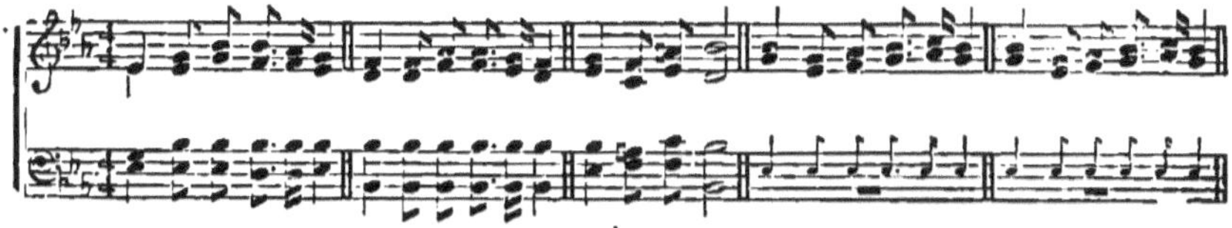

602

7s & 6s. (173)

My Spirit hath rejoiced in God my Saviour.

Tune—WEIMAR, No. 474.

1 To thee, O dear, dear Saviour,
My spirit turns for rest;
My peace is in thy favor,
My pillow on thy breast.

2 O thou whose mercy found me,
From bondage set me free,
And then for ever bound me
With threefold cords to thee.

3 Oh for a heart to love thee
More truly as I ought,
And nothing place above thee,
In deed or word or thought.

4 Oh for that choicest blessing
Of living in thy love,
And thus on earth possessing
The peace of heaven above.

AUTUMN. 8s & 7s. Double.

FINE.
D.S.
D.S.

603

Desiring Sanctification. 8s & 7s. (202)

1 LOVE divine, all love excelling,
Joy of heaven, to earth come down;
Fix in us thy humble dwelling;
All thy faithful mercies crown:
Jesus, thou art all compassion;
Pure, unbounded love thou art;
Visit us with thy salvation;
Enter every trembling heart.

2 Breathe, oh, breathe thy Holy Spirit
Into every troubled breast;
Let us all thy grace inherit;
Let us find thy promised rest:
Take away the love of sinning;
Take our load of guilt away;
End the work of thy beginning;
Bring us to eternal day.

3 Carry on thy new creation;
Pure and holy may we be;
Let us see our whole salvation
Perfectly secured by thee:
Change from glory into glory,
Till in heaven we take our place,
Till we cast our crowns before thee,
Lost in wonder, love, and praise.

CARPENTER. 7s. BLUMENTHAL.

604

All in all. 7s. (191)

1 JESUS, merciful and mild,
Lead me as a helpless child;
On no other arm but thine
Would my weary soul recline.

2 I am weakness, thou art might;
I am darkness, thou art light;
I am all defiled with sin,
Thou canst make me pure within.

3 Jesus, Saviour all divine,
Hast thou made me truly thine?
Hast thou bought me by thy blood?
Reconciled my heart to God?

4 Hearken to my humble prayer,
Let me thine own image bear;
Let me love thee more and more,
Till I reach the blissful shore.

ELMSFORD. 7s & 6s.

605

7s & 6s. (186)

The Spirit witnesseth with our Spirits.

1 SAVIOUR, I thy word believe;
My unbelief remove;
Now thy quickening Spirit give,
The unction from above.

2 Show me, Lord, how good thou art;
Now thy gracious word fulfil;
Send the witness to my heart;
The Holy Ghost reveal.

3 Blessed Comforter, come down,
And live and move in me;
Make my every deed thine own,
In all things led by thee.

4 Bid my sin and fear depart,
And within, oh, deign to dwell;
Faithful witness in my heart,
Thy perfect light reveal.

606

C. M. 61. (183)

The Spirit of a little Child.

Tune—DARWIN, next page

1 FATHER, I know that all my life
Is portioned out for me;
The changes that will surely come
I do not fear to see:
I ask thee for a present mind,
Intent on pleasing thee.

2 I ask thee for a thoughtful love,
Through constant watching wise,
To meet the glad with joyful smiles,
And wipe the weeping eyes;
A heart at leisure from itself,
To soothe and sympathize.

3 I ask thee for the daily strength,
To none that ask denied,
A mind to blend with outward life,
While keeping at thy side;
Content to fill a little space,
If thou be glorified.

DARWIN. C. M. 6 lines. G. Hews.

607 *Purer and purer.* 11s. (225)

Tune—Eventide, No. 594.

1 Purer yet and purer I would be in mind,
Dearer yet and dearer every duty find;
Hoping still and trusting God without a fear,
Patiently believing he will make all clear.

2 Calmer yet and calmer, trial bear and pain,
Surer yet and surer peace at last to gain:
Suffering still and doing, to his will resigned,
And to God subduing heart and will and mind.

3 Higher yet and higher out of clouds and night,
Nearer yet and nearer rising to the light—
Light serene and holy, where my soul may rest,
Purified and lowly, sanctified and blest.

4 Quicker yet and quicker ever onward press,
Firmer yet and firmer step as I progress:
Oft these earnest longings swell within my breast,
Yet their inner meaning ne'er can be expressed.

OZREM. S. M. I. B. Woodbury.

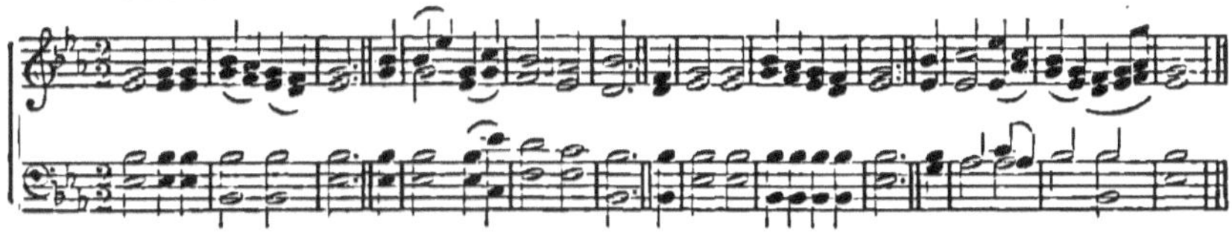

608 *Union with Christ.* S. M. (154)

1 Dear Saviour, we are thine
By everlasting bands;
Our hearts, our souls, we would resign
Entirely to thy hands.

2 To thee we still would cleave
With ever-growing zeal;
If millions tempt us Christ to leave,
Oh, let them ne'er prevail.

3 Thy Spirit shall unite
Our souls to thee, our Head;
Shall form us to thy image bright,
And teach thy paths to tread.

4 Death may our souls divide
From these abodes of clay;
But love shall keep us near thy side,
Through all the gloomy way.

5 Since Christ and we are one,
Why should we doubt or fear?
If he in heaven hath fixed his throne,
He'll fix his members there.

HEBER. C. M. Geo. Kingsley.

609 *Conformity to Jesus.* C. M. (135)

1 Lord, I desire to live as one
Who bears a blood-bought name,
As one who fears but grieving thee,
And knows no other shame.

2 As one by whom thy walk below
Should never be forgot;
As one who fain would keep apart
From all thou lovest not.

3 As one who daily speaks to thee,
And hears thy voice divine
With depths of tenderness declare,
"Beloved, thou art mine."

MORE LIKE JESUS. 7s. Double.

W. H. Doane.
From "Silver Spray," by permission.

S
FINE.
D.S.

610 7s. (224)

More like Jesus.

1 More like Jesus would I be,
Let my Saviour dwell with me;
Fill my soul with peace and love,
Make me gentle as a dove;
More like Jesus, while I go,
Pilgrim in this world below,
Poor in spirit would I be,
Let my Saviour dwell in me.

2 If he hears the raven's cry,
If his ever watchful eye
Marks the sparrows when they fall,
Surely he will hear my call.
He will teach me how to live,
All my sinful thoughts forgive;
Pure in heart I still would be,—
Let my Saviour dwell in me.

3 More like Jesus when I pray,
More like Jesus day by day,
May I rest me by his side,
Where the tranquil waters glide.
Born of him, through grace renewed,
By his love my will subdued,
Rich in faith I still would be,—
Let my Saviour dwell in me.

611 7s, 6s, & 8. (213)

Nothing, save Christ and him crucified

1 Vain, delusive world, adieu,
With all of creature good!
Only Jesus I pursue,
Who bought me with his blood!
All thy pleasures I forego,
I trample on thy wealth and pride;
Only Jesus will I know,
And Jesus crucified.

2 Him to know is life and peace,
And pleasure without end;
This is all my happiness,
On Jesus to depend;
Daily in his grace to grow,
And ever in his faith abide:
Only Jesus will I know,
And Jesus crucified.

3 Oh, that I could all invite
This saving truth to prove,
Show the length, the breadth, the height
And depth of Jesus' love!
Fain would I to sinners show
The precious blood by faith applied.
Only Jesus will I know,
And Jesus crucified.

ROCKPORT. 7s, 6s, & 8s.

I. B. Woodbury.

FINE.
D.C.
D.C.

612 *Parting with earthly Joys.* L. M. (149)

Tune—DARLEY, No. 410.

1 I SEND the joys of earth away;
Away, ye tempters of the mind,
False as the smooth, deceitful sea,
And empty as the whistling wind.

2 Your streams were floating me along
Down to the gulf of dark despair;
And while I listened to your song,
Your streams had e'en conveyed me there.

3 Lord, I adore thy matchless grace,
That warned me of that dark abyss,
That drew me from those treacherous seas,
And bade me seek superior bliss.

4 Now to the shining realms above
I stretch my hands and glance my eyes;
Oh, for the pinions of a dove,
To bear me to the upper skies!

5 There, from the bosom of my God,
Oceans of endless pleasure roll;
There would I fix my last abode,
And drown the sorrows of my soul.

GERMANY. L. M. BEETHOVEN.

613 *Emptied of Earth.* L. M. (178)

1 EMPTIED of earth I fain would be,
Of sin, myself, and all but thee;
Only reserved for Christ that died,
Surrender'd to the Crucified.

2 Sequester'd from the noise and strife
The lust, the pomp, and pride of life;
For heaven alone my heart prepare,
And have my conversation there.

3 Nothing, save Jesus, would I know;
My friend and my companion thou:
Lord, seize my heart, assert thy right,
And put all other loves to flight.

4 Larger communion let me prove
With thee, blest object of my love;
But, oh, for this no power have I;
My strength is at thy feet to lie.

COLBURN. L. M. W. B. BRADBURY.

Ritard.

614 L. M. (123)

Longing to be like God.

1 WHAT sinners value I resign;
Lord, 'tis enough that thou art mine;
I shall behold thy blissful face,
And stand complete in righteousness.

2 This life's a dream, an empty show;
But that bright world to which I go
Hath joys substantial and sincere;
When shall I wake and find me there?

3 Oh, glorious hour! oh, blest abode!
I shall be near and like my God;
And flesh and sin no more control
The sacred pleasures of the soul.

4 My flesh shall slumber in the ground,
Till the last trumpet's joyful sound,
Then burst the chains with sweet surprise,
And in my Saviour's image rise.

HARMONY GROVE. L. M. H. K. OLIVER.

615 *Holy Aspiration.* L. M. (235)

1 MY God, permit me not to be
A stranger to myself and thee;
Amidst a thousand thoughts I rove,
Forgetful of my highest love.

2 Why should my passions mix with earth,
And thus debase my heavenly birth?
Why should I cleave to things below,
And let my God, my Saviour, go?

3 Call me away from flesh and sense;
One sovereign word can draw me thence;
I would obey the voice divine,
And all inferior joys resign.

4 Be earth, with all her scenes, withdrawn;
Let noise and vanity be gone:
In secret silence of the mind
My heaven, and there my God, I find.

EVANS. S. M. W. A. TARBUTTON.

616 *God, All and in All.* S. M. (180)

1 MY God, my life, my love,
To thee, to thee I call;
I cannot live if thou remove,
For thou art all in all.

2 To thee, and thee alone,
The angels owe their bliss;
They sit around thy gracious throne,
And dwell where Jesus is.

3 Nor earth, nor all the sky,
Can one delight afford,
No, not a drop of real joy,
Without thy presence, Lord.

4 Thou art the sea of love,
Where all my pleasures roll,
The circle where my passions move,
And centre of my soul.

DARIEN. L. M. DR. L. MASON.

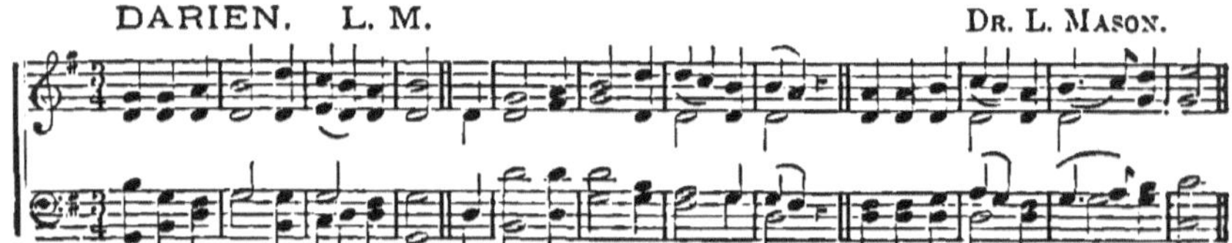

617 *Sufficiency of Grace.* L. M. (214)

1 IN vain my roving thoughts would find
A port'on wo-thy of the mind;
On earth my soul can never rest,
For earth can never make me blest.

2 Can lasting happiness be found
Where seasons roll their hasty round,
And days and hours, with rapid flight,
Sweep cares and pleasures out of sight?

3 Arise, my thoughts; my heart, arise;
Leave this vain world, and seek the skies;
There purest joys for ever last,
When seasons, days, and hours are past.

4 Come, Lord, thy powerful grace impart;
Thy grace can raise my wandering heart
To pleasure, perfect and sublime,
Unmeasured by the wing of time.

MONSON. C. M. BROWN.

618 C. M. (157)

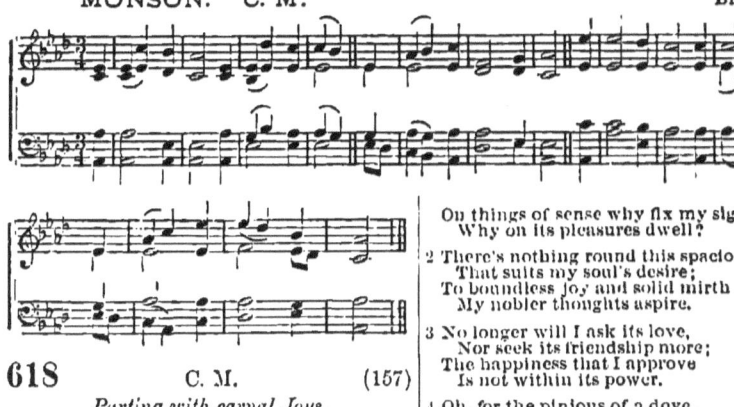

Parting with carnal Joys.

1 My soul forsakes her vain delight,
And bids the world farewell;
Ou things of sense why fix my sight?
Why on its pleasures dwell?

2 There's nothing round this spacious earth
That suits my soul's desire;
To boundless joy and solid mirth
My nobler thoughts aspire.

3 No longer will I ask its love,
Nor seek its friendship more;
The happiness that I approve
Is not within its power.

4 Oh, for the pinions of a dove,
To mount the heavenly road;
There shall I share my Saviour's love,
There shall I dwell with God.

JAZER. C. M. WM. B. BRADBURY.

619 C. M. (217)

Earthly Pleasures dangerous.

1 How vain are all things here below!
How false, and yet how fair!
Each pleasure hath its poison too,
And every sweet a snare.

2 The brightest things below the sky
Shine with deceiving light:
We should suspect some danger nigh,
Where we possess delight.

3 Our dearest joys, our nearest friends,
The partners of our blood,
How they divide our wavering minds
And leave but half for God!

4 The fondness of a creature's love,
How strong it strikes the sense!
'Tis there the warm affections move,
Nor can we call them thence.

5 Dear Saviour, let thy beauties be
My soul's eternal food,
And grace command my heart away
From all created good.

620 *Living to Christ.* C. M. (215)

Tune—NAOMI, No. 462.

1 FATHER, whate'er of earthly bliss
Thy sovereign will denies,
Accepted at thy throne of grace,
Let this petition rise:—

2 Give me a calm, a thankful heart,
From every murmur free;
The blessings of thy grace impart,
And make me live to thee.

3 Let the sweet hope that thou art mine
My life and death attend:
Thy presence through my journey shine,
And crown my journey's end.

ARCADIA. C. M. DR. T. HASTINGS.

621 C. M. (218)

Parting with all for Christ.

1 YE glittering toys of earth, adieu;
A nobler choice be mine;
A heavenly prize attracts my view,
A treasure all divine.

2 Jesus, to multitudes unknown,—
Oh, name divinely sweet!—
Jesus, in thee, in thee alone,
True wealth and honor meet.

3 Should earth's vain treasures all depart,
Of this dear gift possessed,
I'd clasp it to my joyful heart,
And be for ever blest.

4 Dear portion of my soul's desires,
Thy love is bliss divine;
Accept the wish that love inspires,
And let me call thee mine.

622 *Desires for Holiness.* C. M. (216)

BALERMA.

1 OH, could I find from day to day,
A nearness to my God,
Then would my hours glide sweet away,
While leaning on his word.

2 Lord, I desire with thee to live
Anew from day to day,
In joys the world can never give,
Nor ever take away.

3 Blest Jesus, come, and rule my heart,
And make me wholly thine,
That I may never more depart,
Nor grieve thy love divine.

4 Thus, till my last, expiring breath,
Thy goodness I'll adore;
And when my frame dissolves in death,
My soul shall love thee more.

623 *Purity of Heart.* C. M. (218

ARCADIA.

1 OH for a heart to praise my God,
A heart from sin set free;
A heart that's sprinkled with the blood
So freely shed for me.

2 Oh for a heart submissive, meek,
My great Redeemer's throne,
Where only Christ is heard to speak,
Where Jesus reigns alone.

3 Oh for a humble, contrite heart,
Believing, true, and clean,
Which neither life nor death can part
From him that dwells within.

4 Thy temper, gracious Lord, impart,
Come quickly from above;
Oh, write thy name upon my heart!
Thy name, O God, is Love.

BALERMA. C. M.

VANHALL. L. M.

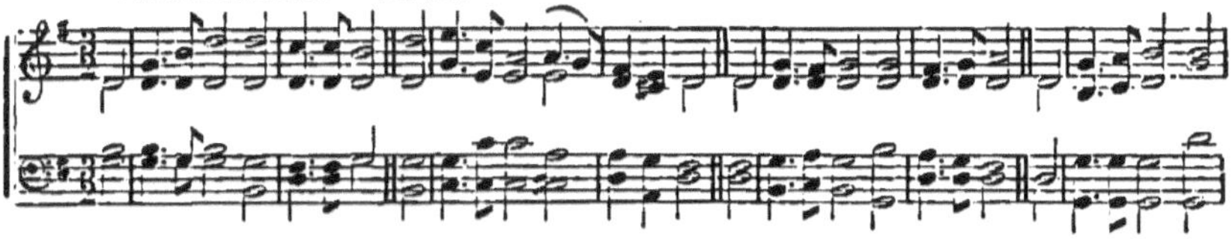

624 *Christian Stability.* L. M. (209)

1 O Lord, thy heavenly grace impart,
And fix my frail, inconstant heart;
Henceforth my chief desire shall be,
To dedicate myself to thee.

2 Whate'er pursuits my time employ,
One thought shall fill my soul with joy;
That silent, secret thought shall be,
That all my hopes are fixed on thee.

3 Thy glorious eye pervadeth space;
Thy presence, Lord, fills every place;
And, wheresoe'er my lot may be,
Still shall my spirit cleave to thee.

4 Renouncing every worldly thing,
And safe beneath thy spreading wing,
My sweetest thought henceforth shall be,
That all I want I find in thee.

FEDERAL STREET. L. M. H. K. Oliver.

625 L. M. (174)

Cast me not away from thy Presence.

1 Oh, turn, great Ruler of the skies,
Turn from my sin thy searching eyes;
Nor let th' offences of my hand
Within thy book recorded stand.

2 Give me a will to thine subdued,
A conscience pure, a soul renewed;
Nor let me, wrapt in endless gloom,
An outcast from thy presence roam.

3 Oh, let thy Spirit to my heart
Once more its quickening aid impart;
My mind from every fear release,
And soothe my troubled thoughts to peace.

626 C. M. (216)

Longing for God.

Tune—Balerma, preceding page.

1 Oh, for a closer walk with God,
A calm and heavenly frame,
A light to shine upon the road
That leads me to the Lamb.

2 Where is the blessedness I knew
When first I saw the Lord?
Where is the soul-refreshing view
Of Jesus and his word?

3 What peaceful hours I then enjoyed!
How sweet their memory still!
But now I find an aching void
The world can never fill.

4 Return, O holy Dove, return,
Sweet messenger of rest:
I hate the sins that made thee mourn,
And drove thee from my breast.

5 The dearest idol I have known,
Whate'er that idol be,
Help me to tear it from thy throne,
And worship only thee.

6 So shall my walk be close with God,
Calm and serene my frame;
So purer light shall mark the road
That leads me to the Lamb.

GOLDEN HILL. S. M.

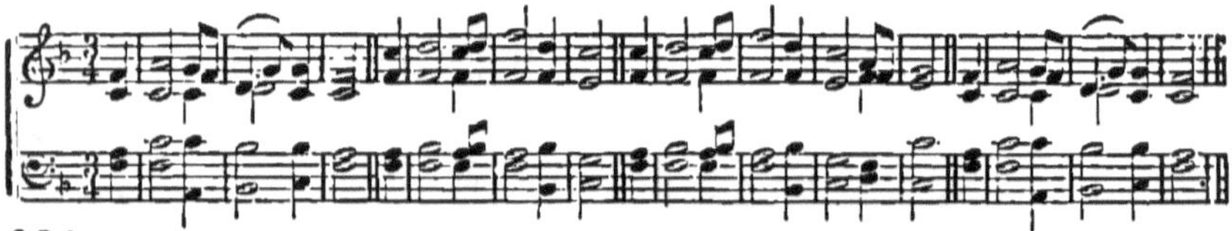

627 *Renouncing Sin.* S. M. (160)

1 SHALL we go on to sin,
Because thy grace abounds?
Or crucify the Lord again,
And open all his wounds?

2 Forbid it, mighty God;
Nor let it e'er be said
That we, whose sins are crucified,
Should raise them from the dead.

3 We will be slaves no more,
Since Christ has made us free,
Has nailed our tyrants to his cross,
And bought our liberty.

628 C. M. (216)

Complaints of Coldness.

Tune—BALERMA, No. 622.

1 WITH tears of anguish I lament,
Here, at thy feet, my God,
My passion, pride, and discontent,
And vile ingratitude.

2 Sure there was ne'er a heart so base,
So false as mine has been;
So faithless to its promises,
So prone to every sin.

3 How long, dear Saviour, shall I feel
These struggles in my breast?
When wilt thou bow my stubborn will,
And give my conscience rest?

4 Break, sovereign grace, oh, break the charm,
And set the captive free;
Reveal, almighty God, thine arm,
And haste to rescue me.

629 C. M. (231)

Delight in God and his Word.

TAMACH.

1 THOU art my portion, O my God;
Soon as I know thy way,
My heart makes haste t' obey thy word,
And suffers no delay.

2 I choose the path of heavenly truth,
And glory in my choice;
Not all the riches of the earth
Could make me so rejoice.

3 Thy precepts and thy heavenly grace
I set before my eyes;
Thence I derive my daily strength,
And there my comfort lies.

4 Now I am thine, for ever thine;
Oh, save thy servant, Lord;
Thou art my shield, my hiding-place;
My hope is in thy word.

TAMACH. C. M. CARMINA SACRA.

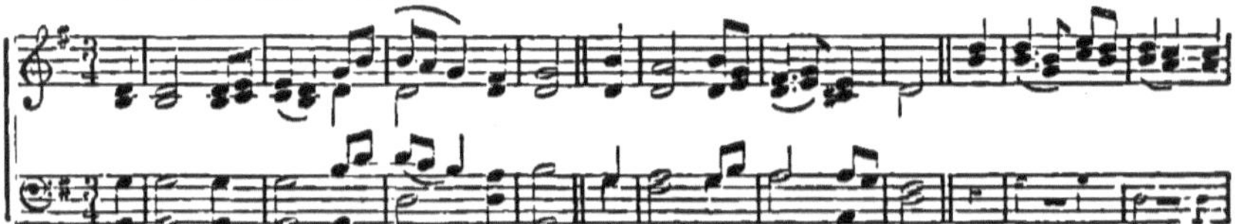

630 *A living Faith.* C. M. (169)

Tune—BYEFIELD, No. 580.

1 MISTAKEN souls, that dream of heaven,
And make their empty boast
Of inward joys, and sins forgiven,
While they are slaves to lust!

2 How vain are fancy's airy flights,
If faith be cold and dead!
None but a living power unites
To Christ, the living Head.

3 'Tis faith that purifies the heart;
'Tis faith that works by love;
That bids all sinful joys depart,
And lifts the thoughts above.

4 This faith shall every fear contro.
By its celestial power,
With holy triumph fill the soul
In death's approaching hour.

631 *Difficulty and Dependence.* C. M. (231)

Tune—TAMACH, preceding page.

1 STRAIT is the way, the door is strait,
That leads to joys on high;
'Tis but a few that find the gate,
While crowds mistake and die.

2 Beloved self must be denied.
The mind and will renewed,
Passion suppressed, and patience tried,
And vain desires subdued.

3 Lord, can a feeble, helpless worm
Fulfil a task so hard?
Thy grace must all the work perform,
And give the free reward.

NUREMBURG. 7s.

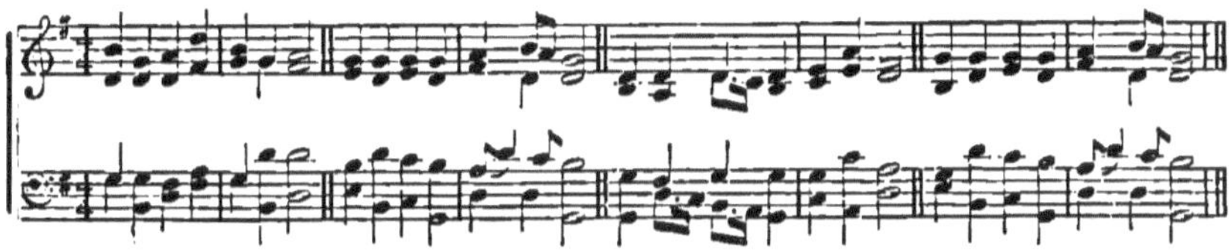

632 *The anxious Inquiry.* 7s. (210)

1 'TIS a point I long to know,—
Oft it causes anxious thought,—
Do I love the Lord, or no?
Am I his, or am I not?

2 If I love, why am I thus?
Why this dull and lifeless frame?
Hardly, sure, can they be worse
Who have never heard his name.

3 When I turn my eyes within,
All is dark and vain and wild;
Filled with unbelief and sin,
Can I deem myself a child?

4 Yet I mourn my stubborn will,
Find my sin a grief and thrall;
Should I grieve for what I feel,
If I did not love at all?

5 Let me love thee more and more,
If I love at all, I pray;
If I have not loved before,
Help me to begin to-day.

COLBURN. L. M. W. B. BRADBURY.

Ritard.

633 L. M. (123)

The Road to Life and Death.

1 BROAD is the road that leads to death,
And thousands walk together there;
But wisdom shows a narrow path,
With here and there a traveller.

2 "Deny thyself and take thy cross,"
Is the Redeemer's great command:
Nature must count her gold but dross,
If she would gain this heavenly land.

3 The fearful soul that tires and faints,
And walks the ways of God no more,
Is but esteemed almost a saint,
And makes his own destruction sure.

4 Lord, let not all my hopes be vain,
Create my heart entirely new,—
Which hypocrites could ne'er attain,
Which false apostates never knew.

DARIEN. L. M. DR. L. MASON.

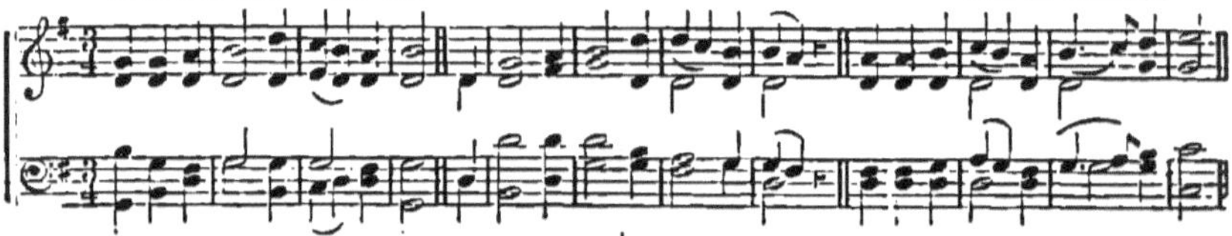

634 L. M. (214)

Exemplifying the Gospel.

1 So let our lips and lives express
The holy gospel we profess;
So let our works and virtues shine,
To prove the doctrine all divine.

2 Thus shall we best proclaim abroad
The honors of our Saviour God,
When his salvation reigns within,
And grace subdues the power of sin.

3 Our flesh and sense must be denied,
Ambition, envy, lust, and pride;
While justice, temperance, truth, and love
Our inward piety approve.

4 Religion bears our spirits up,
While we expect that blessed hope,
The bright appearance of the Lord,
And faith stands leaning on his word.

VANMETER. C. M. I. B. WOODBURY.

635 C. M. (165)

Prayer for Direction.

1 Oh, that the Lord would guide my ways
To keep his statutes still!
Oh, that my God would grant me grace
To know and do his will!

2 From folly turn away my eyes;
Let no corrupt design
Nor covetous desire arise
Within this soul of mine.

3 Direct my footsteps by thy word,
And make my heart sincere;
Let sin have no dominion, Lord,
But keep my conscience clear.

4 Make me to walk in thy commands,—
'Tis a delightful road,—
Nor let my head nor heart nor hands
Offend against my God.

636 S. M. (160)

Prayer for Self-Consecration.

1 O God, my strength, my hope,
On thee I cast my care;
With humble confidence look up,
And know thou hearest prayer.

2 Oh for a godly fear,
A quick-discerning eye,
That looks to thee when sin is near,
And sees the tempter fly!

3 A spirit still prepared,
And armed with jealous care,
For ever standing on its guard,
And watching unto prayer.

4 Lord, let me still abide,
Nor from my hope remove,
Till thou my patient spirit guide
To better worlds above.

GOLDEN HILL. S. M.

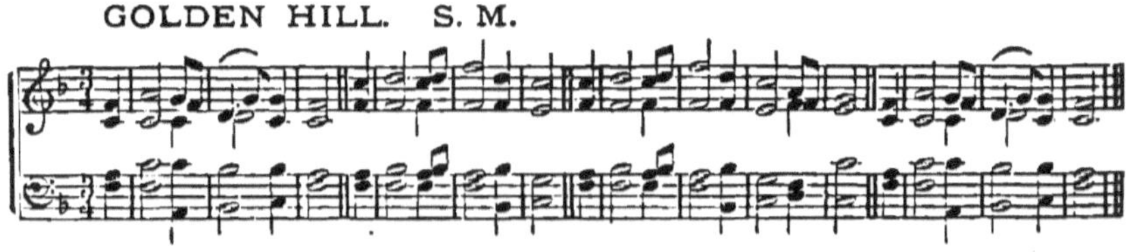

LABAN. S. M. DR. L. MASON.

637 *Attachment to the Church.* S. M. (208)

1 I LOVE thy kingdom, Lord,
The house of thine abode,
The Church our blest Redeemer saved
With his own precious blood.

2 I love thy church, O God;
Her walls before thee stand,
Dear as the apple of thine eye,
And graven on thy hand.

3 For her my tears shall fall;
For her my prayers ascend;
To her my cares and toils be given,
Till toils and cares shall end.

4 Beyond my highest joy
I prize her heavenly ways,
Her sweet communion, solemn vows,
Her hymns of love and praise.

5 Jesus, thou Friend divine,
Our Saviour and our King,
Thy hand, from every snare and foe,
Shall great deliverance bring.

6 Sure as thy truth shall last,
To Zion shall be given
The brightest glories earth can yield,
And brighter bliss of heaven.

UNION. 8s.

638 *The Union of Saints.* 8s. (173)

1 FROM whence doth this union arise,
That hatred is conquered by love?
It fastens our souls in such ties
As distance and time can't remove.

2 It cannot in Eden be found,
Nor yet in a Paradise lost;
It grows on Immanuel's ground,
And Jesus' dear blood it did cost.

3 My brethren are dear unto me,
Our hearts all united in love;
Where Jesus is gone we shall be,
In yonder blest mansions above.

4 Why, then, so unwilling to part,
Since there we shall all meet again?
Engraved on Immanuel's heart,
At a distance we cannot remain.

5 With Jesus we ever shall reign,
And all his bright glories shall see,
Singing, Hallelujah! amen!
Amen! even so let it be.

MONSON. C. M. BROWN.

639 C. M. (157)

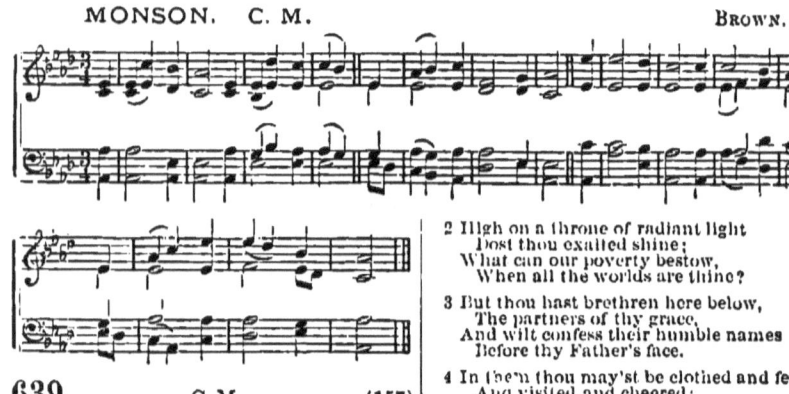

Ye have done it unto Me.

1 JESUS, our Lord, how rich thy grace!
Thy bounties how complete!
How can we count the matchless sum?
How pay the mighty debt?

2 High on a throne of radiant light
Dost thou exalted shine;
What can our poverty bestow,
When all the worlds are thine?

3 But thou hast brethren here below,
The partners of thy grace,
And wilt confess their humble names
Before thy Father's face.

4 In them thou may'st be clothed and fed
And visited and cheered;
And, in their accents of distress
Our Saviour's voice is heard.

5 Thy face, with reverence and with love,
We in thy poor would see;
Oh, rather let us beg our bread,
Than hold it back from thee.

GOLDEN HILL. S. M.

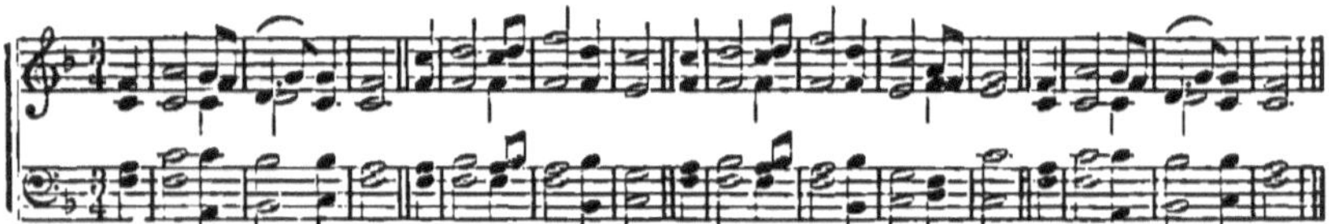

640 *Christian Fellowship.* S. M. (160)

1 BLEST be the tie that binds
Our hearts in Christian love:
The fellowship of kindred minds
Is like to that above.

2 Before our Father's throne
We pour our ardent prayers:
Our fears, our hopes, our aims are one,
Our comforts and our cares.

3 We share our mutual woes,
Our mutual burdens bear;
And often for each other flows
The sympathizing tear.

4 When we asunder part,
It gives us inward pain;
But we shall still be joined in heart,
And hope to meet again.

641 *Love as Brethren.* C. M. (229)

Tune—BOARDMAN, No. 641.

1 How sweet, how heavenly, is the sight,
When those who love the Lord
In one another's peace delight,
And thus fulfil his word;—

2 When each can feel his brother's sigh,
And with him bear a part;
When sorrow flows from eye to eye,
And joy from heart to heart;—

3 When, free from envy, scorn, and pride,
Our wishes all above,
Each can his brother's failings hide,
And show a brother's love!

4 Love is the golden chain that binds
The happy souls above;
And he's an heir of heaven that finds
His bosom glow with love.

642 *Brotherly Love.* C. M. (229)

1 OUR souls, by love together knit,
Cemented, mixed in one,
One hope, one heart, one mind, one voice,
'Tis heaven on earth begun.

2 Our hearts have often burned within,
And glowed with sacred fire,
While Jesus spoke, and fed, and blessed,
And filled the enlarged desire.

3 And when thou mak'st thy jewels up,
And sett'st thy starry crown;
When all thy sparkling gems shall shine,
Proclaimed by thee thine own;—

4 May we, a little band of love,
We sinners, saved by grace,
From glory unto glory changed,
Behold thee face to face.

VANHALL. L. M.

643

L. M. (209)

Religion nothing without Love.

1 HAD I the tongues of Greeks and Jews,
And nobler speech than angels use,
If love be absent, I am found,
Like tinkling brass, an empty sound.

2 Were I inspired to preach and tell
All that is done in heaven and hell,
Or could my faith the world remove,
Still I am nothing without love.

3 Should I distribute all my store
To feed the hungry, clothe the poor;
Or give my body to the flame,
To gain a martyr's glorious name,—

4 If love to God and love to men
Be absent, all my hopes are vain;
Nor tongues nor gifts nor fiery zeal
The work of love can e'er fulfil.

BOARDMAN. C. M.

644

C. M. (229)

Importance and Influence of Love.

1 HAPPY the heart where graces reign,
Where love inspires the breast;
Love is the brightest of the train,
And strengthens all the rest.

2 Knowledge, alas! 'tis all in vain,
And all in vain our fear;
Our stubborn sins will fight and reign,
If love be absent there.

3 'Tis love that makes our cheerful feet
In swift obedience move;
The devils know, and tremble too,
But they can never love.

4 This is the grace that lives and sings
When faith and hope shall cease;
'Tis this shall strike our joyful strings
In brightest realms of bliss.

LOGAN. C. M. E. L. White.

645 C. M. (237)

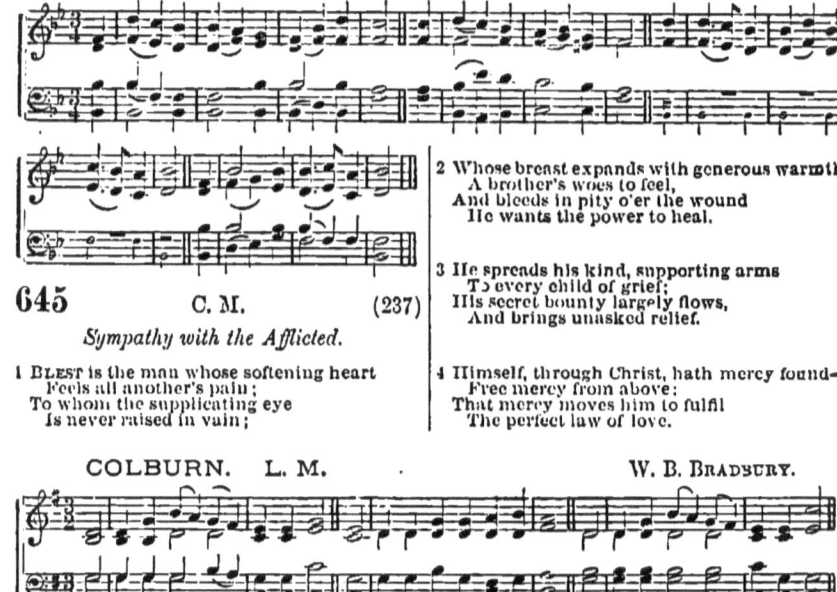

Sympathy with the Afflicted.

1 Blest is the man whose softening heart
Feels all another's pain;
To whom the supplicating eye
Is never raised in vain;

2 Whose breast expands with generous warmth
A brother's woes to feel,
And bleeds in pity o'er the wound
He wants the power to heal.

3 He spreads his kind, supporting arms
To every child of grief;
His secret bounty largely flows,
And brings unasked relief.

4 Himself, through Christ, hath mercy found—
Free mercy from above:
That mercy moves him to fulfil
The perfect law of love.

COLBURN. L. M. W. B. Bradbury.

Ritard.

646 L. M. (123)

Grief for the Sins and Miseries of Men.

1 Arise, my tenderest thoughts, arise,
To torrents melt my streaming eyes;
And thou, my heart, with anguish fee.
Those evils which thou canst not heal.

2 See human nature sunk in shame;
See scandals poured on Jesus' name;
The Father wounded through the Son;
The world abused; the soul undone.

3 See the short course of vain delight
Closing in everlasting night,
In flames that no abatement know,
Though briny tears for ever flow.

4 My God, I feel the mournful scene;
My spirit yearns o'er dying men;
And fain my pity would reclaim,
And snatch the firebrands from the flame.

5 But feeble my compassion proves,
And can but weep where most it loves:
Thy own all-saving arm employ,
And turn these drops of grief to joy.

647 *Christian Affection.* L. M. (209)

Tune—Vanhall, next page.

1 How blest the sacred tie that binds,
In sweet communion, kindred minds!
How swift the heavenly course they run,
Whose hearts, whose faith, whose hopes, are one!

2 To each the soul of each how dear!
What tender love, what holy fear!
How doth the generous flame within
Refine from earth, and cleanse from sin!

3 Nor shall the glowing flame expire,
When dimly burns frail nature's fire;
Then shall they meet in realms above,
A heaven of joy, a heaven of love.

VANHALL. L. M.

4 Small are the offerings we can make;
Yet thou hast taught us, Lord,
If given for the Saviour's sake,
They lose not their reward.

648 C. M. (237)

Imitation of Christ's Kindness.

Tune—LOGAN, No. 615.

1 LORD, lead the way the Saviour went,
By lane and cell obscure,
And let our treasures still be spent,
Like his, upon the poor.

2 Like him, through scenes of deep distress,
Who bore the world's sad weight,
We, in their gloomy loneliness,
Would seek the desolate.

3 For thou hast placed us side by side,
In this wide world of ill;
And that thy followers may be tried,
The poor are with us still.

649 L. M. (123)

Blessedness of the Righteous.

Tune—COLBURN, No. 646.

1 BLEST are the men whose mercies move
To acts of kindness and of love;
From Christ, the Lord, shall they obtain
Like sympathy and love again.

2 Blest are the pure, whose hearts are clean,
Who never tread the ways of sin;
With endless pleasure they shall see
A God of spotless purity.

3 Blest are the men of peaceful life,
Who quench the coals of growing strife;
They shall be called the heirs of bliss,
The sons of God,—the God of peace.

4 Blest are the faithful who partake
Of pain and shame for Jesus' sake;
Their souls shall triumph in the Lord;
Eternal life is their reward.

NUREMBURG. 7s.

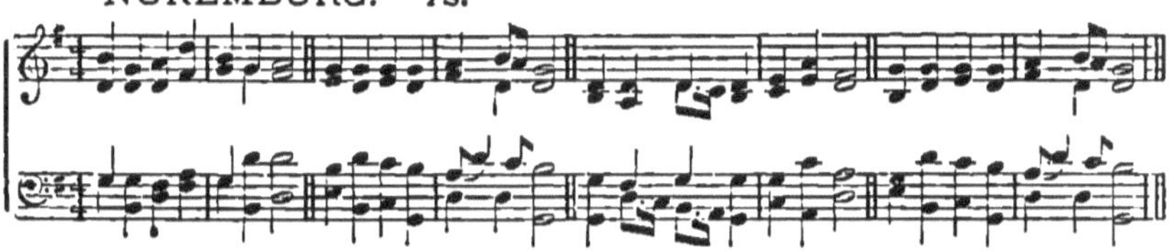

650 *Save our Children.* 7s. (211)

1 GOD of mercy, hear our prayer
For the children thou hast given;
Let them all thy blessings share,—
Grace on earth and bliss in heaven.

2 In the morning of their days
May their hearts be drawn to thee;
Let them learn to lisp thy praise
In their earliest infancy.

3 Cleanse their souls from every stain,
Through the Saviour's precious blood;
Let them all be born again,
And be reconciled to God.

4 For this mercy, Lord, we cry;
Bend thine ever gracious ear;
While on thee our souls rely,
Hear our prayer, in mercy hear.

GRIGG. C. M. GRIGG.

651

Prayer for Children's Conversion. C. M. (230)

1 O LORD, behold us at thy feet,
A needy, sinful band;
As suppliants round thy mercy-seat,
We come at thy command.

2 'Tis for our children we would plead,
The offspring thou hast given;
Where shall we go, in time of need,
But to the God of heaven?

3 We ask not for them wealth or fame,
Amid the worldly strife;
But, in the all-prevailing Name,
We ask eternal life.

4 We seek the Spirit's quickening grace,
To make them pure in heart,
That they may stand before thy face,
And see thee as thou art.

HARMONY GROVE. L. M. H. K. OLIVER.

652

L. M. (235)

Parents' Prayer for their Children.

1 FATHER of all, before thy throne,
Grateful but anxious parents bow;
Look in paternal mercy down,
And yield the boon we ask thee now.

2 'Tis not for wealth, or joys of earth,
Or life prolonged, we seek thy face;
'Tis for a new and heavenly birth,
'Tis for the treasures of thy grace.

3 'Tis for the soul's eternal joy,
For rescue from the coming woe:
Do not our earnest suit deny;
We cannot, cannot let thee go.

653

S. M. (234)

Compassion of Christ.

1 DID Christ o'er sinners weep,
And shall our cheeks be dry?
Let floods of penitential grief
Burst forth from every eye.

2 The Son of God in tears
The wondering angels see;
Be thou astonished, O my soul,
He shed those tears for thee.

3 He wept that we might weep;
Each sin demands a tear;
In heaven alone no sin is found,
And there's no weeping there.

COMPASSION. S. M. G. O. ROBINSON.

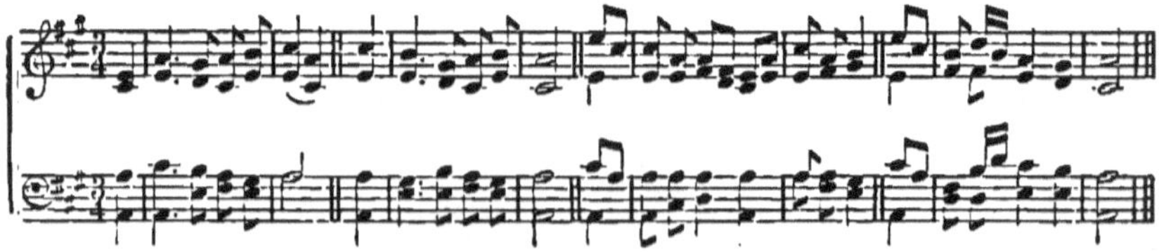

REFUGE IN CHRIST.

GERMANY. L. M. BEETHOVEN.

654 L. M. (178)

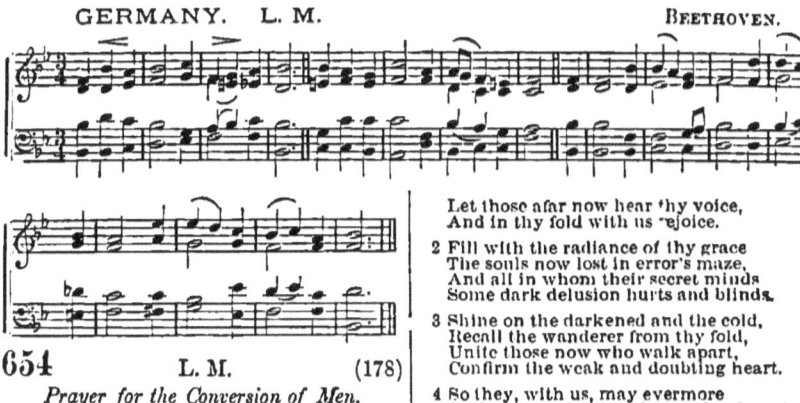

Prayer for the Conversion of Men.

1 O CHRIST, our true and only light,
Illumine those who sit in night;
Let those afar now hear thy voice,
And in thy fold with us rejoice.

2 Fill with the radiance of thy grace
The souls now lost in error's maze,
And all in whom their secret minds
Some dark delusion hurts and blinds.

3 Shine on the darkened and the cold,
Recall the wanderer from thy fold,
Unite those now who walk apart,
Confirm the weak and doubting heart.

4 So they, with us, may evermore
Such grace, with wondering thanks, adore·
And endless praise to thee be given,
By all thy church, in earth and heaven.

REFUGE IN CHRIST.

LANSINGBURG. 6s & 5s. GERMAN.

655 6s & 5s. (194)

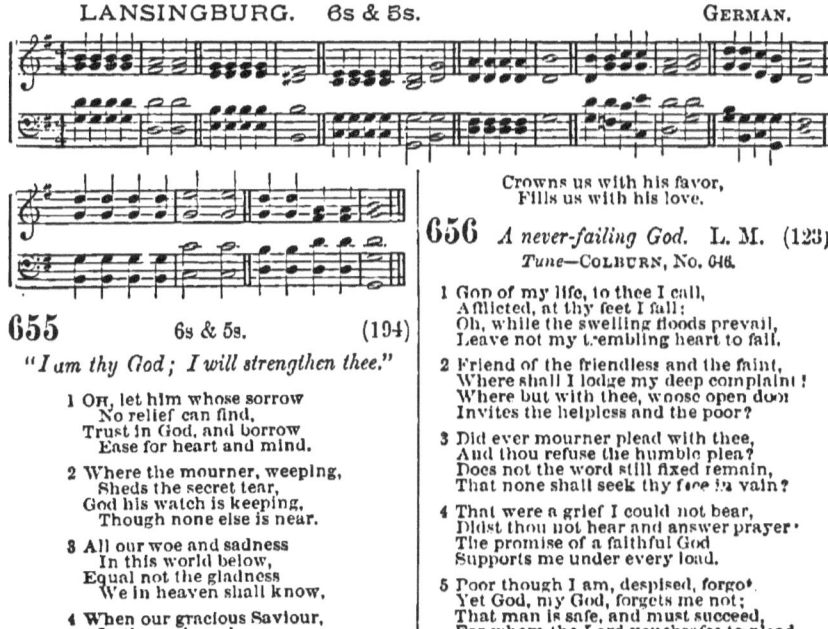

"I am thy God; I will strengthen thee."

1 OH, let him whose sorrow
No relief can find,
Trust in God, and borrow
Ease for heart and mind.

2 Where the mourner, weeping,
Sheds the secret tear,
God his watch is keeping,
Though none else is near.

3 All our woe and sadness
In this world below,
Equal not the gladness
We in heaven shall know.

4 When our gracious Saviour,
In the realms above,
Crowns us with his favor,
Fills us with his love.

656 *A never-failing God.* L. M. (123)

Tune—COLBURN, No. 646.

1 GOD of my life, to thee I call,
Afflicted, at thy feet I fall;
Oh, while the swelling floods prevail,
Leave not my trembling heart to fail.

2 Friend of the friendless and the faint,
Where shall I lodge my deep complaint!
Where but with thee, whose open door
Invites the helpless and the poor?

3 Did ever mourner plead with thee,
And thou refuse the humble plea?
Does not the word still fixed remain,
That none shall seek thy face in vain?

4 That were a grief I could not bear,
Didst thou not hear and answer prayer·
The promise of a faithful God
Supports me under every load.

5 Poor though I am, despised, forgot,
Yet God, my God, forgets me not;
That man is safe, and must succeed,
For whom the Lord vouchsafes to plead.

FEDERAL STREET. L. M. H. K. OLIVER.

657 L. M. (174)

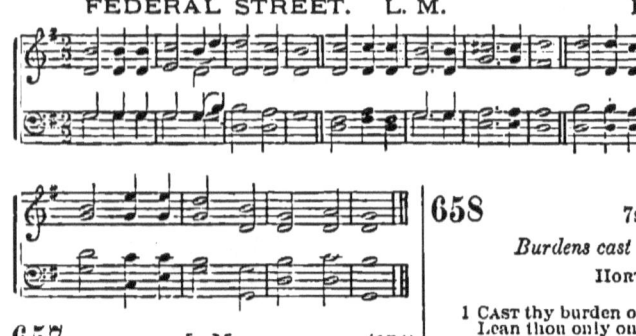

Why art thou cast down?

1 Be still, my heart! these anxious cares
To thee are burdens, thorns, and snares;
They cast dishonor on thy Lord,
And contradict his gracious word.

2 Brought safely by his hand thus far,
Why wilt thou now give place to fear?
How canst thou want, if he provide,
Or lose thy way with such a guide?

3 Though rough and thorny be the road,
It leads thee home apace to God;
Then count thy present trials small,
For heaven will make amends for all.

658 7s. (110)

Burdens cast on the Lord.

HORTON.

1 Cast thy burden on the Lord;
Lean thou only on his word:
Ever will he be thy stay,
Though the heavens shall melt away.

2 Ever in the raging storm,
Thou shalt see his cheering form,
Hear his pledge of coming aid
"It is I, be not afraid."

3 Cast thy burden at his feet;
Linger near his mercy seat:
He will lead thee by the hand
Gently to the better land.

4 He will gird thee by his power,
In thy weary, fainting hour;
Lean, then, loving, on his word;
Cast thy burden on the Lord.

HORTON. 7s. SCHNYDER.

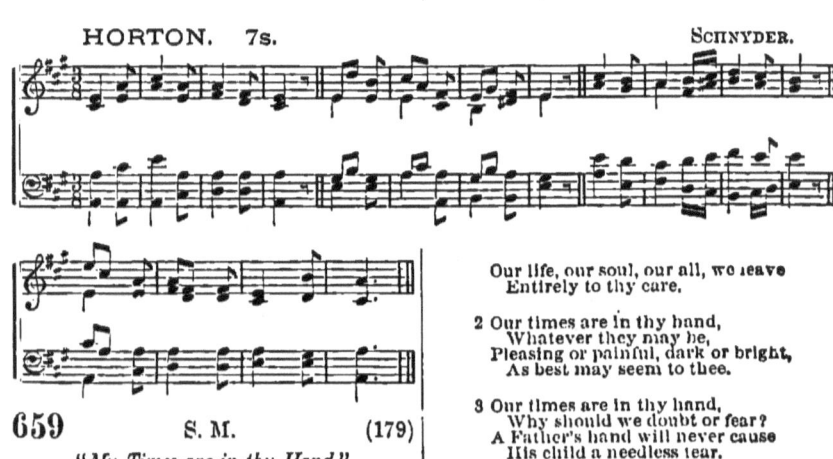

659 S. M. (179)

"My Times are in thy Hand."

Tune—OLMUTZ, next page.

1 Our times are in thy hand,
Father, we wish them there,
Our life, our soul, our all, we leave
Entirely to thy care.

2 Our times are in thy hand,
Whatever they may be,
Pleasing or painful, dark or bright,
As best may seem to thee.

3 Our times are in thy hand,
Why should we doubt or fear?
A Father's hand will never cause
His child a needless tear.

4 Our times are in thy hand,
We'll always trust in thee
Till we have left this weary land,
And all thy glory see.

OLMUTZ. S. M. Arr. by Dr. L. Mason.

660 L. M. (235)

"Welcome to me the darkest Night."

Tune—Harmony Grove, No. 652.

1 Welcome to me the darkest night,
If there the Saviour's presence bright
Beam forth upon the soul dismayed,
And say, "'Tis I, be not afraid."

2 Welcome the fiercest waves that roll
Their deepening floods to whelm my soul,
If he rebuke the storm of ill,
And bid the tempest, "Peace, be still."

3 Welcome the thorniest path, if there
The print-marks of his feet appear;
If in his footsteps we may tread,
And follow where our Lord hath led.

4 I will not ask what else is mine,
If thou, O Lord, account me thine;
For what but joy can be my lot,
If God, my God, reject me not?

661 S. M. (238)

Gentleness of God's Command.

Tune—Haydn, No. 588.

1 How gentle God's commands!
How kind his precepts are!
Come, cast your burdens on the Lord,
And trust his constant care.

2 Beneath his watchful eye
His saints securely dwell;
That hand which bears creation up,
Shall guard his children well.

3 Why should this anxious load
Press down your weary mind?
Haste to your heavenly Father's throne,
And peace and comfort find.

4 His goodness stands approved,
Unchanged from day to day:
I'll drop my burden at his feet,
And bear a song away.

LOWRY. L. M. 6 lines. C. F. Blandner.

662 *Christ, All and in All.* L. M. 6l. (147)

1 Jesus, thou source of calm repose,
All fulness dwells in thee divine;
Our strength, to quell the proudest foes;
Our light, in deepest gloom to shine;
Thou art our fortress, strength, and tower,
Our trust and portion, evermore.

2 Jesus, our Comforter thou art;
Our rest in toil, our ease in pain;
The balm to heal each broken heart
In storms our peace, in loss our gain;
Our joy beneath the worldling's frown
In shame our glory and our crown.

3 In want, our plentiful supply;
In weakness, our almighty power;
In bonds, our perfect liberty;
Our refuge in temptation's hour;
Our comfort, 'midst all grief and thrall;
Our life in death; our all in all.

OLMUTZ. S. M. Arr. by Dr. L. Mason.

663 *Comfort in Darkness.* S. M. (179)

1 Your harps, ye trembling saints,
Down from the willows take,
Loud to the praise of love divine
Bid every string awake.

2 Though in a foreign land,
We are not far from home;
And nearer to our house above
We every moment come.

3 His grace will to the end
Stronger and brighter shine;
Nor present things nor things to come
Shall quench the spark divine.

4 When we in darkness walk,
Nor feel the heavenly flame,
Then is the time to trust our God,
And rest upon his name.

664 *Strength from Christ.* L. M. (211)

1 Let me but hear my Saviour say,
"Strength shall be equal to thy day,"
Then I rejoice in deep distress,
Upheld by all-sufficient grace.

2 I can do all things, or can bear
All sufferings, if my Lord be there:
Sweet pleasures mingle with the pains,
While he my sinking head sustains.

3 I glory in infirmity,
That Christ's own power may rest on me;
When I am weak then am I strong,
Grace is my shield, and Christ my song.

DARIEN. L. M. Dr. L. Mason.

665 S. M. (160)

Resignation to the Lord's Will.

1 If on a quiet sea
Toward heaven we calmly sail,
With grateful hearts, O God, to thee,
We'll own the favoring gale.

2 But should the surges rise,
And rest delay to come,
Blest be the sorrow, kind the storm,
Which drives us nearer home.

3 Teach us, in every state,
To make thy will our own,
And, when the joys of sense depart,
To live by faith alone.

GOLDEN HILL. S. M.

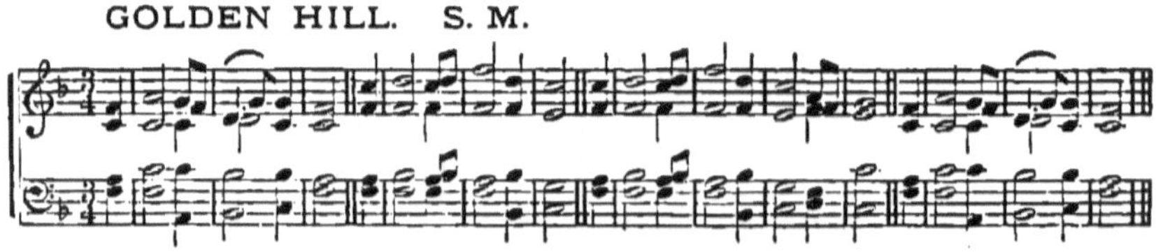

666 S. M. (234)

Security and Comfort in God.

Tune—Compassion, No. 653.

1 When, overwhelmed with grief,
My heart within me dies,
Helpless, and far from all relief,
To heaven I lift mine eyes.

2 Oh, lead me to the Rock
That's high above my head,
And make the covert of thy wings
My shelter and my shade.

3 Within thy presence, Lord,
For ever I'll abide;
Thou art the tower of my defence,
The refuge where I hide.

667 L. M. (214)

Walking by Faith, not by Sight.

Tune—Darien, No. 664.

1 'Tis by the faith of joys to come
We walk through deserts dark as night;
Till we arrive at heaven, our home,
Faith is our guide, and faith our light.

2 The want of sight she well supplies;
She makes the pearly gates appear;
Far into distant worlds she pries,
And brings eternal glories near.

3 With joy we tread the desert through,
While faith inspires a heavenly ray,
Though lions roar and tempests blow,
And rocks and dangers fill the way.

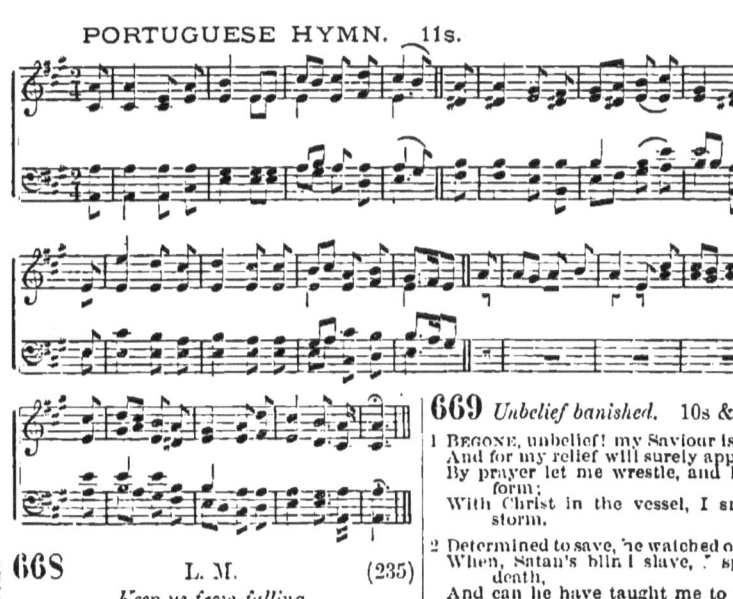

PORTUGUESE HYMN. 11s.

668 L. M. (235)

Keep us from falling.

Tune—Harmony Grove, No. 652.

1 Lord, through the desert drear and wide,
Our erring footsteps need a guide;
Keep us, oh, keep us near thy side;
Let us not fall; let us not fall.

2 We have no fear that thou shouldst lose
One whom eternal love could choose;
But we would ne'er this grace abuse.
Let us not fall; let us not fall.

3 All thy good work in us complete,
And seat us daily at thy feet;
Thy love, thy words, thy name, how sweet.
Let us not fall; let us not fall.

669 *Unbelief banished.* 10s & 11s. (236)

1 Begone, unbelief! my Saviour is near;
And for my relief will surely appear;
By prayer let me wrestle, and he will perform;
With Christ in the vessel, I smile at the storm.

2 Determined to save, he watched o'er my path,
When, Satan's blind slave, I sported with death,
And can he have taught me to trust in his name,
And thus far have brought me to put me to shame?

3 Though dark be my way, since he is my guide,
'Tis mine to obey, 'tis his to provide;
His way was much rougher and darker than mine;
Did Jesus thus suffer, and shall I repine?

4 His love, in time past, forbids me to think
He'll leave me at last in trouble to sink;
Though painful at present, 'twill cease before long,
And then, oh, how pleasant the conqueror's song!

FEDERAL STREET. L. M. H. K. OLIVER.

670 L. M. (175)

Rocked in the Cradle of the Deep.

1 ROCKED in the cradle of the deep,
I lay me down in peace to sleep;
Secure I rest upon the wave,
For thou, O Lord, hast power to save.

2 I know thou wilt not slight my call,
For thou dost mark the sparrow's fall;
And calm and peaceful is my sleep,
Rocked in the cradle of the deep.

3 And such the trust that still were mine,
Though stormy winds swept o'er the brine,
Or though the tempest's fiery breath
Roused me from sleep to wreck and death.

4 In ocean caves still safe with thee,
The germs of immortality;
And calm and peaceful is my sleep,
Rocked in the cradle of the deep.

JUDEA. C. M.

NAOMI. C. M. DR. L. MASON.

671 C. M. (232)

Deliverance from deep Distress.

JUDEA.

1 I WAITED patient for the Lord;
He bowed to hear my cry;
He saw me resting on his word,
And brought salvation nigh.

2 He raised me from a gloomy pit,
Where, mourning, long I lay,
And from my bonds released my feet,—
Deep bonds of miry clay.

3 Firm on a rock he made me stand,
And taught my cheerful tongue
To praise the wonders of his hand,
In new and thankful song.

4 How many are thy thoughts of love!
Thy mercies, Lord, how great!
We have not words nor hours enough
Their numbers to repeat.

672 C. M. (215)

The safe Retreat.

NAOMI.

1 DEAR Father, to thy mercy-seat
My soul for shelter flies:
'Tis here I find a safe retreat
When storms and tempests rise.

2 My cheerful hope can never die,
If thou, my God, art near;
Thy grace can raise my comforts high,
And banish every fear.

3 My great Protector and my Lord,
Thy constant aid impart;
Oh, let thy kind, thy gracious word
Sustain my trembling heart!

4 Oh, never let my soul remove
From this divine retreat!
Still let me trust thy power and love,
And dwell beneath thy feet.

HENLY. 11s, 10, & 6. DR. L. MASON.

673

Let not our Faith fail. 11s, 10, & 6. (177)

1 STILL will we trust, though earth seem dark and dreary,
And the heart faint beneath his chastening rod;
Though rough and steep our pathway, worn and weary,
Still will we trust in God.

2 Our eyes see dimly till by faith anointed,
And our blind choosing brings us grief and pain;
Through him alone who hath our way appointed,
We find our peace again.

3 Choose for us, Lord, nor let our weak preferring
Cheat our poor souls of good thou hast designed:
Choose for us, Lord, thy wisdom is unerring,
And we are fools and blind.

ADAMS. C. M. GEO. KINGSLEY.

674

Prayer for strong Faith. C. M. (196)

1 OH, for a faith that will not shrink,
Though pressed by every foe,
That will not tremble on the brink
Of any earthly woe;—

2 That will not murmur nor complain
Beneath the chastening rod,
But, in the hour of grief or pain,
Will lean upon its God;—

3 A faith that shines more bright and clear
When tempests rage without;
That when in danger knows no fear,
In darkness feels no doubt;—

4 A faith that keeps the narrow way
Till life's last hour is fled,
And with a pure and heavenly ray
Lights up a dying bed.

5 Lord, give us such a faith as this,
And then, whate'er may come,
We'll taste, e'en here, the hallowed bliss
Of an eternal home.

LOUVAN. L. M. V. C. TAYLOR.

675 *If thou art with me.* L. M. (219)

1 O LOVE divine, that stooped to share
Our sharpest pang, our bitterest tear,
On thee we cast each earth-born care,
We smile at pain while thou art near.

2 Though long the weary way we tread,
And sorrow crown each lingering year,
No path we shun, no darkness dread,
Our hearts still whispering, thou art near.

3 When drooping pleasure turns to grief,
And trembling faith is changed to fear,
The murmuring wind, the quivering leaf,
Shall softly tell us thou art near.

4 On thee we fling our burdening woe,
O Love divine, for ever dear;
Content to suffer, while we know,
Living or dying, thou art near.

STAR OF BETHLEHEM. L. M.

676 L. M. (220)

Christ the Pilot.

1 THE billows swell; the winds are high;
Clouds overcast my wintry sky;
Out of the depths to thee I call;
My fears are great, my strength is small.

2 O Lord, the pilot's part perform,
And guide and guard me through the storm;
Defend me from each threatening ill;
Control the waves; say, "Peace, be still."

3 Dangers of every shape and name
Attend the followers of the Lamb,
Who leave the world's deceitful shore,
And leave it to return no more.

4 Though tempest-tossed, and half a wreck,
My Saviour through the floods I seek;
Let neither winds nor stormy rain
Force back my shattered bark again.

677 *Comfort in God.* C. M. (230

Tune—GRIGG, No. 651.

1 DEAR Refuge of my weary soul,
On thee, when sorrows rise,
On thee when waves of trouble roll,
My fainting hope relies.

2 To thee I tell each rising grief,
For thou alone canst heal;
Thy word can bring a sweet relief
For every pain I feel.

3 But, oh, when gloomy doubts prevail,
I fear to call thee mine;
The springs of comfort seem to fail,
And all my hopes decline.

4 Yet, gracious God, where shall I flee?
Thou art my only trust;
And still my soul would cleave to thee,
Though prostrate in the dust.

PORTUGUESE HYMN. 11s.

678 *The firm Foundation.* 11s. (236)

PORTUGUESE HYMN.

1 How firm a foundation, ye saints of the Lord,
Is laid for your faith in his excellent word!
What more can he say than to you he hath said,
You who unto Jesus for refuge have fled?

2 In every condition,—in sickness and health,
In poverty's vale, or abounding in wealth,
At home and abroad, on the land, on the sea,—
As thy day may demand, shall thy strength ever be.

3 E'en down to old age, all my people shall prove
My sovereign, eternal, unchangeable love;
And when hoary hairs shall their temples adorn,
Like lambs they shall still in my bosom be borne.

4 The soul that on Jesus hath leaned for repose,
I will not, I will not, desert to its foes;
That soul, though all hell should endeavor to shake,
I'll never, no never, no never, forsake!

679 *The Pilgrim's Song.* 11s. (127)

EXPOSTULATION.

1 My rest is in heaven, my rest is not here,
Then why should I murmur when trials are near?
Be hush'd, my dark spirit; the worst that can come
But shortens thy journey, and hastens thee home.

2 It is not for me to be seeking my bliss,
Or building my hopes in a region like this;
I look for a city that hands have not piled,
I pant for a country by sin undefiled.

3 Afflictions may press me, they cannot destroy;
One glimpse of his love turns them all into joy;
And the bitterest tears, if he smiles but on them,
Like dew in the sunshine, grow diamond and gem.

4 Let trial and danger my progress oppose,
They only make heaven more sweet at its close;
Come joy or come sorrow, whate'er may befall,
An hour with my Saviour will make up for all.

EXPOSTULATION. 11s.

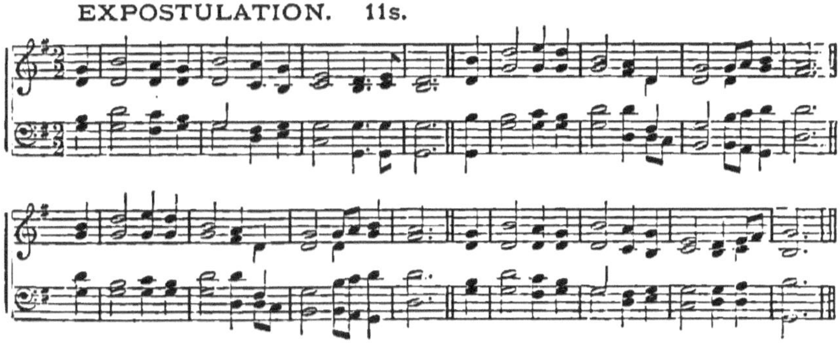

ARIEL. C. P. M. Dr. L. Mason.

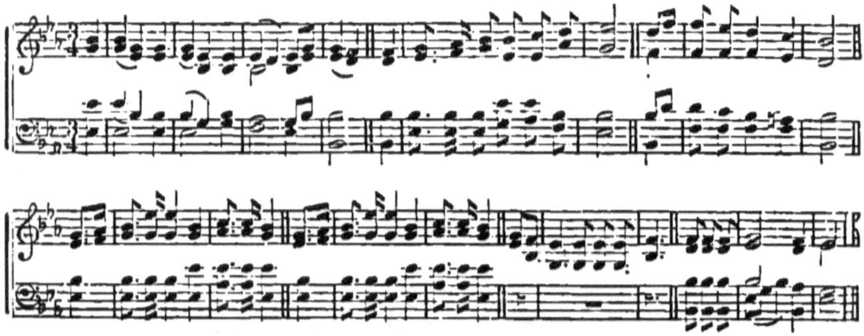

680 C. P. M. (227)

Help in Weakness and Pain.

1 O Lord, our strength and righteousness,
Our hope and refuge in distress,
Our Saviour and our God,
See here, a helpless sinner see;
Weak and in pain, he looks to thee,
For healing in thy blood.

2 In sickness make thou all his bed,
Thy hands support his fainting head,
His feeble soul defend;
Teach him on thee to cast his care,
And all his grief and burden bear,
And love him to the end.

3 Oh, let him look to thee alone;
That all thy will on him be done
His only pleasure be,
Alike resigned to live or die,
As most thy name may glorify,
To live or die to thee.

681 C. P. M. (227)

Casting all your Care upon Him.

1 O Lord, how happy should we be
If we could cast our care on thee;
If we from self could rest,
And feel at heart that One above
In perfect wisdom, perfect love,
Is working for the best!

2 How far from this our daily life,
How oft disturbed by anxious strife,
By sudden wild alarms;
Oh, could we but relinquish all
Our earthly props, and simply fall
On thine almighty arms.

3 Could we but kneel and cast our load,
E'en while we pray, upon our God,
Then rise with lightened cheer;
Sure that the Father, who is nigh
To still the famished raven's cry,
Will hear in that we fear.

NUREMBURG. 7s.

682 *The gracious Promise.* 7s. (211)

1 Wait, my soul, upon the Lord,
To his gracious promise flee,
Laying hold upon his word,
"As thy days thy strength shall be."

2 If the sorrows of thy case
Seem peculiar still to thee,
God has promised needful grace,
"As thy days thy strength shall be."

3 Days of trial, days of grief,
In succession thou mayst see,
This is still thy sweet relief,
"As thy days thy strength shall be."

4 Rock of ages, I'm secure,
With thy promise full and free.
Faithful, positive, and sure—
"As thy days thy strength shall be."

683 *Comfort in Sickness.* C. M. (230)

Tune—Grigg, No. 651.

1 When languor and disease invade
This trembling house of clay,
'Tis sweet to look beyond my pain,
And long to fly away;

2 Sweet to look inward and attend
The whispers of his love;
Sweet to look upward to the place
Where Jesus pleads above;

3 Sweet to look back, and see my name
In life's fair book set down;
Sweet to look forward, and behold
Eternal joys my own;

4 Sweet on his faithfulness to rest,
Whose love can never end;
Sweet on the promise of his grace
For all things to depend;

5 Sweet, in the confidence of faith,
To trust his firm decrees;
Sweet to lie passive in his hands,
And know no will but his.

6 If such the sweetness of the stream,
What must the fountain be,
Where saints and angels draw their bliss
Directly, Lord, from thee!

684 *Holy Contentment.* 7s. (211)

Tune—Nuremburg, preceding page.

1 Lord, my times are in thy hand;
All my fondest hopes have planned
To thy wisdom I resign,
And would make thy purpose mine.

2 Thou my daily task shalt give;
Day by day to thee I live:
So shall added years fulfil,
Not my own, my Father's will.

3 Fond ambition, whisper not;
Happy is my humble lot;
Anxious, busy cares, away;
I'm provided for to-day.

4 Oh, to live exempt from care,
By the energy of prayer,
Strong in faith, with mind subdued,
Yet elate with gratitude.

ACQUIESCING IN THE WILL OF CHRIST.

LOGAN. C. M. E. L. White.

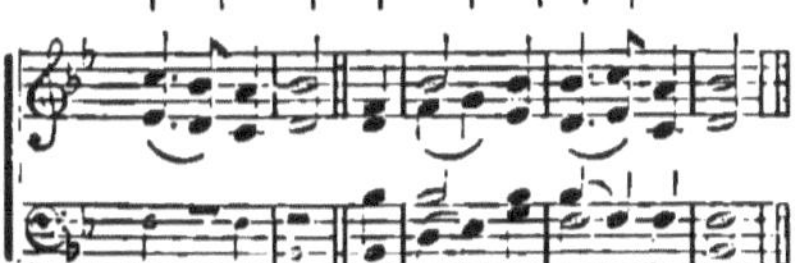

685 *Thy Care, not mine.* C. M. (237)

1 Lord, it belongs not to my care
Whether I die or live;
To love and serve thee is my share,
And this thy grace must give.

2 If life be long, I will be glad
That I may long obey;
If short, yet why should I be sad
To soar to endless day?

3 Christ leads me through no darker rooms
Than he went through before;
No one into his kingdom comes,
But through his opened door.

4 Come, Lord, when grace has made me meet
Thy blessed face to see;
For if thy work on earth be sweet,
What will thy glory be?

5 Then shall I end my sad complaints,
And weary, sinful days,
And join with all triumphant saints
Who sing Jehovah's praise.

6 My knowledge of that life is small;
The eye of faith is dim;
But 'tis enough that Christ knows all,
And I shall be with him.

LOUVAN. L. M. V. C. TAYLOR.

686 L. M. (219)

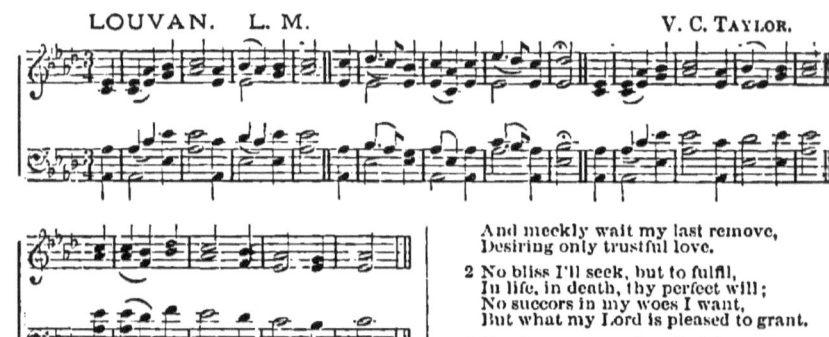

Resignation to Christ's Will.

1 IF life in sorrow must be spent,
So be it; I am well content;
And meekly wait my last remove,
Desiring only trustful love.

2 No bliss I'll seek, but to fulfil,
In life, in death, thy perfect will;
No succors in my woes I want,
But what my Lord is pleased to grant.

3 Our days are numbered: let us spare
Our anxious hearts a needless care:
'Tis thine to number out our days;
'Tis ours to give them to thy praise.

4 Faith is our only business here,—
Faith simple, constant, and sincere;
Oh, blessed days thy servants see!
Thus spent, O Lord, in pleasing thee.

ADAMS. C. M. GEO. KINGSLEY.

687 *Mystery.* C. M. (197)

1 THY way, O Lord, is in the sea;
Thy path I cannot trace,
Nor comprehend the mystery
Of thine unbounded grace.

2 As through a glass I dimly see
The wonders of thy love;
How little do I know of thee,
Or of the joys above!

3 'Tis but in part I know thy will;
I bless thee for the sight:
When will thy love the rest reveal,
In glory's clearer light?

4 With rapture shall I then survey
Thy providence and grace,
And spend an everlasting day
In wonder, love, and praise.

CHANT.—"Thy Will be done." 8s & 6. JOHN M. EVANS.

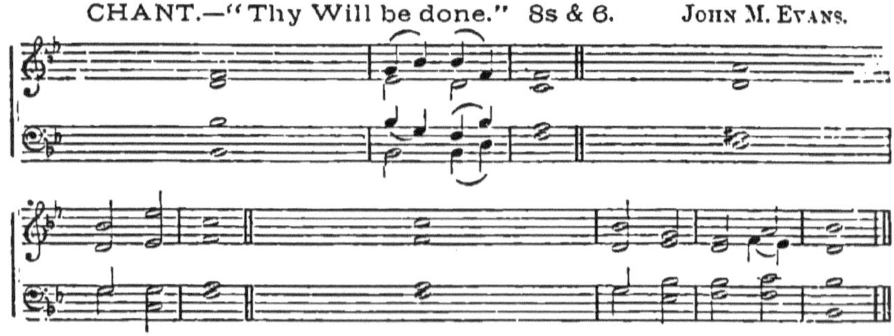

688 *"Thy Will be done."* 8s & 6. (227)

Tune—CHANT, preceding page.

1 MY God, my Father, | while I | stray |
Far from my home, on | life's rough | way, |
Oh, teach me from my heart to say,
"Thy | will, my | God, be | done."

2 Though dark my path, and | sad my | lot, |
Let me be still, and | murmur | not, |
And breathe the prayer divinely taught,
"Thy | will, my | God, be | done."

3 If thou shouldst call me | to re- | sign |
What most I prize,—it | ne'er was | mine,— |
I only yield thee what is thine:
"Thy | will, my | God, be | done.

4 Should pining sickness | waste a- | way |
My life in prema- | ture de- | cay, |
In life or death teach me to say,
"Thy | will, my | God, be | done."

5 Renew my will from | day to | day, |
Blend it with thine, and | take a-way |
Whate'er now makes it hard to say,
"Thy | will, my | God, be | done."

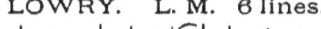

LOWRY. L. M. 6 lines. C. F. BLANDNER.

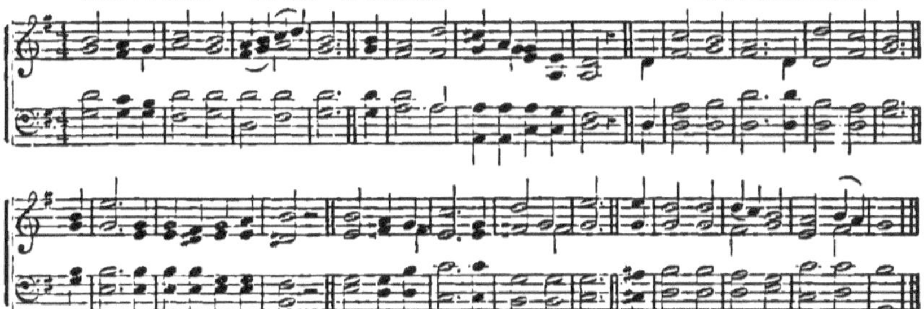

689 L. M. 6l. (147)

Trust in the Lord's Love.

1 OH, let my trembling soul be still,
While darkness veils this mortal eye,
And wait thy wise, thy holy will,
Wrapped yet in fears and mystery;
I cannot, Lord, thy purpose see;
Yet all is well, since ruled by thee.

2 So trusting in thy love, I tread
The narrow path of duty on;
What though some cherished joys are fled?
What though some flattering dreams are gone?
Yet purer, brighter joys remain;
Why should my spirit, then, complain?

690 *Thy Will be done.* 8s & 4s. (227)

Tune—CHANT, No. 688.

1 THY will be done! In | devious | way |
The hurrying stream of | life may | run; |
Yet still our grateful hearts shall say,
Thy | will, thy | will be | done.

2 Thy will be done! If | o'er us | shine |
A gladdening and a | prosperous | sun, |
This prayer shall make it more divine:
Thy | will, thy | will be | done.

3 Thy will be done! Though | shrouded | o'er |
Our path with gloom, one | comfort, | one, |
Is ours,—to breathe, while we adore,
Thy | will, thy | will be | done.

691 S. M. (234)

He shall choose our Inheritance for us.

Tune—COMPASSION, No. 653.

1 THY way, not mine, O Lord,
However dark it be;
Oh, lead me by thine own right hand,
Choose out the path for me.

2 I dare not choose my lot;
I would not if I might;
But choose thou for me, O my God,
So shall I walk aright.

3 Take thou my cup, and it
With joy or sorrow fill;
As ever best to thee may seem,
Choose thou my good and ill.

4 Choose thou for me my friends,
My sickness or my health;
Choose thou my joys and cares for me,
My poverty or wealth.

5 Not mine, not mine the choice,
In things or great or small;
Be thou my guide, my guard, my strength,
My wisdom and my all

692 *God's Will.* C. M. (232)

Tune—JUDEA, No. 671.

1 I WORSHIP thee, sweet will of God,
And all thy ways adore;
And every day I live, I long
To love thee more and more.

2 He always wins who sides with God,
To him no chance is lost;
God's will is sweetest to him when
It triumphs at his cost.

3 Ill that God blesses, is our good,
And unblest good is ill;
And all is right that seems most wrong,
If it be his dear will.

4 When obstacles and trials seem
Like prison-walls to be,
I do the little I can do,
And leave the rest to thee.

LOWRY. L. M. 6 lines. C. F. BLANDNER.

693 *He leadeth me.* L. M. 6l. (147)

1 "HE leadeth me!" oh, blessed thought,
Oh, words with heavenly comfort fraught,
Whate'er I do, whate'er I be,
Still 'tis God's hand that leadeth me.

He leadeth me; he leadeth me;
By his own hand he leadeth me.

2 Sometimes 'midst scenes of deepest gloom,
Sometimes where Eden's bowers bloom;
By waters still, o'er troubled sea,—
Still 'tis his hand that leadeth me.

3 Lord, I would clasp thy hand in mine,
Nor ever murmur nor repine;
Content, whatever lot I see,
Since 'tis my God that leadeth me.

4 And when my task on earth is done,
When, by thy grace, the victory's won;
E'en death's cold wave I will not flee,
Since God through Jordan leadeth me.

FINNEY. 8s, 7s, & 4. W. B. BRADBURY.

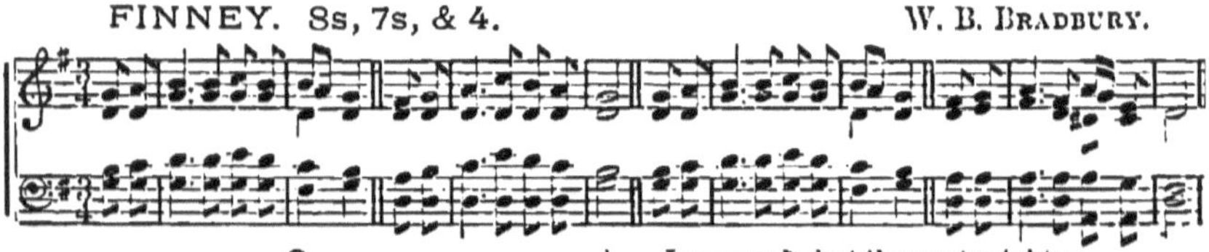

694 8s, 7s, & 4. (221)

God the Pilgrim's Guide and Strength.

1 GUIDE me, O thou great Jehovah,
Pilgrim through this barren land·
I am weak, but thou art mighty:
Hold me with thy powerful hand:
Bread of heaven,
Feed me till I want no more.

2 Open now the crystal fountain
Whence the healing streams do flow;
Let the fiery, cloudy pillar
Lead me all my journey through:
Strong Deliverer,
Be thou still my strength and shield.

3 When I tread the verge of Jordan,
Bid my anxious fears subside;
Bear me through the swelling current;
Land me safe on Canaan's side:
Songs of praises
I will ever give to thee.

LABAN. S. M. Dr. L. Mason.

695

Work in my Vineyard. S. M. (212)

1 Laborers of Christ, arise,
And gird you for the toil;
The dew of promise from the skies
Already cheers the soil.

2 Go where the sick recline,
Where mourning hearts deplore:
And where the sons of sorrow pine,
Dispense your hallowed lore.

3 Urge, with a tender zeal,
The erring child along,
Where peaceful congregations kneel,
And pious teachers throng.

4 Be faith, which looks above,
With prayer, your constant guest;
And wrap the Saviour's changeless love,
A mantle, round your breast.

5 So shall you share the wealth
That earth may ne'er despoil,
And the blest gospel's saving health
Repay your arduous toil.

EVANS. S. M. W. A. Tarbutton.

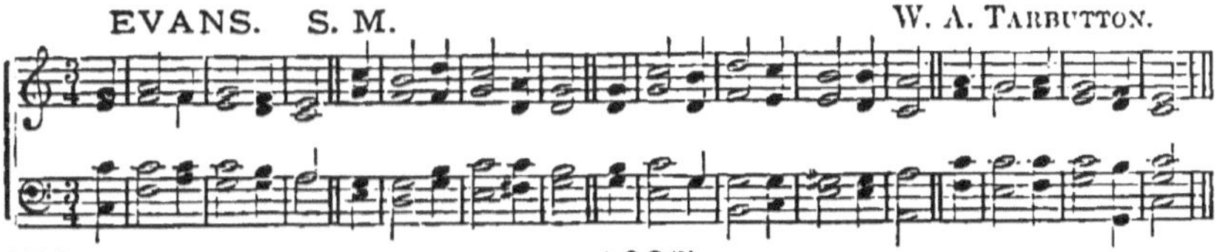

696

S. M. (180)

Heartily as to the Lord.

1 Teach me, my God and King,
In all things thee to see;
And what I do in anything,
To do it as for thee.

2 All may of thee partake;
Nothing so small can be,
But draws, when acted for thy sake,
Greatness and worth from thee.

3 If done beneath thy laws,
E'en servile labors shine:
Hallowed is toil, if this the cause;
The meanest work, divine.

697

God's true Workmen. C. M. (231)

Tune—Tamach, No 629.

1 God's glory is a wondrous thing,
Most strange in all its ways,
And, of all things on earth, least like
What men agree to praise.

2 Oh, blest is he to whom is given
The instinct that can tell
That God is on the field, when he
Is most invisible.

3 And blest is he who can divine
Where real right doth lie,
And dares to take the side that seems
Wrong to man's blinded eye.

BRADEN. S. M. Wm. B. Bradbury.

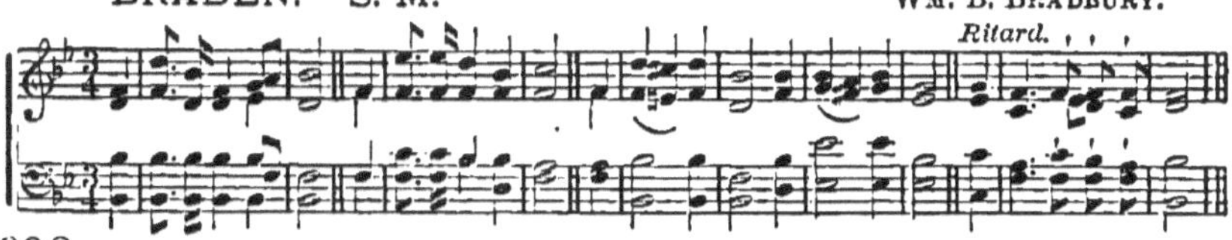
Ritard.

698

Active Effort to do Good. S. M. (139)

1 Sow in the morn thy seed;
At eve hold not thy hand;
To doubt and fear give thou no heed;
Broadcast it o'er the land;

2 And duly shall appear,
In verdure, beauty, strength,
The tender blade, the stalk, the ear,
And the full corn at length.

3 Thou canst not toil in vain;
Cold, heat, and moist and dry
Shall foster and mature the grain
For garners in the sky.

4 Thence, when the glorious end,
The day of God, shall come,
The angel-reapers shall descend,
And heaven cry, "Harvest home!"

NOTHING BUT LEAVES. 8s, 6s, & 4. S. J. VAIL.

699 8s, 6s, & 4. (239)

Nothing but Leaves.

1 NOTHING but leaves!—the Spirit grieves
Over a wasted life;
O'er sins indulged while conscience slept,
O'er vows and promises unkept,
And reaps from years of strife
Nothing but leaves.

2 Nothing but leaves!—no gathered sheaves
Of life's fair ripening grain;
We sow our seeds; lo! tares and weeds,
Words, idle words, for earnest deeds;
We reap with toil and pain
Nothing but leaves.

3 Nothing but leaves!—sad memory weaves
No veil to hide the past;
And as we trace our weary way,
Counting each lost and misspent day,
Sadly we find at last
Nothing but leaves.

4 Ah! who shall thus the Master meet,
Bearing but withered leaves?
Ah! who shall at the Saviour's feet,
Before the awful judgment-seat,
Lay down, for golden sheaves,
Nothing but leaves?

700 7s, 6s, & 5s. (240)

Work while it is called Day.

1 WORK, for the night is coming,
Work thro' the morning hours;
Work while the dew is sparkling,
Work 'mid springing flow'rs:
Work when the day grows brighter;
Work in the glowing sun;
Work, for the night is coming,
When man's work is done.

2 Work, for the night is coming,
Work thro' the sunny noon;
Fill brightest hours with labor,
Rest comes sure and soon.
Give every flying minute
Something to keep in store:
Work, for the night is coming,
When man works no more.

3 Work, for the night is coming,
Under the sunset skies;
While their bright tints are glowing,
Work, for the daylight flies.
Work till the last beam fadeth,
Fadeth to shine no more;
Work while the night is dark'ning,
When man's work is o'er.

WORK, FOR THE NIGHT IS COMING. 7s, 6s, & 5s.

From "Song Garden."

cres.

701 *Clinging to Jesus.* 7s, 6s, & 5. (240)

Tune—WORK, THE NIGHT IS COMING, No. 700.

1 FOLLOW the paths of Jesus,
Walk where his footsteps lead,
Keep in his beaming presence,
Every counsel heed.

2 Watch, while the hours are flying,
Ready some good to do;
Quick, while his voice is calling,
Yield obedience true.

3 Cling to the hand of Jesus,
All through the day and night,
Dark though the way and dreary,
He will guide you right.

4 Live for the good of others,
Helpless, oppressed, and wrong:
Lift them from depths of sorrow,
In his strength be strong.

702 *Go, work.* 6s & 5s. (240)

Tune—WORK, THE NIGHT IS COMING, No. 700.

1 WORK, for time is flying;
Work with heart sincere;
Work, for souls are dying;
Work, for night is near.
In the Master's vineyard
Go and work to-day;
Stand not idly waiting,
Work, without delay.

2 In this glorious calling,
Work till day is o'er;
Work, till, evening falling,
You can work no more.
Then your labor bringing
To the King of kings,
Borne with joy and singing
Home on angels' wings,

3 There where saints adore him,
Where the ransom'd meet,
Lay thy sheaves before him,
Lay them at his feet.
Hear thy Master saying,
From his heavenly throne,
When thy wages paying,
"Laborer, well done!"

WARRING FOR CHRIST.

AZMON. C. M. GLASER.

703 *The Christian Soldier.* C. M. (238)

1 AM I a soldier of the cross,
A follower of the Lamb?
And shall I fear to own his cause,
Or blush to speak his name?

2 Must I be carried to the skies
On flowery beds of ease,
While others fought to win the prize,
And sailed through bloody seas?

3 Are there no foes for me to face?
Must I not stem the flood?
Is this vile world a friend to grace,
To help me on to God?

4 Sure I must fight, if I would reign;
Increase my courage, Lord;
I'll bear the toil, endure the pain,
Supported by thy word.

5 Thy saints in all this glorious war
Shall conquer though they die;
They see the triumph from afar,
And seize it with their eye.

6 When that illustrious day shall rise,
And all thy armies shine
In robes of victory through the skies,
The glory shall be thine.

704 S. M. (242)

Watchfulness and Prayer inculcated.

1 MY soul, be on thy guard;
Ten thousand foes arise;
The hosts of sin are pressing hard
To draw thee from the skies.

2 Oh, watch and fight and pray;
The battle ne'er give o'er;
Renew it boldly every day,
And help divine implore.

3 Ne'er think the victory won,
Nor lay thine armor down;
Thy arduous work will not be done
Till thou obtain thy crown.

4 Fight on, my soul, till death
Shall bring thee to thy God;
He'll take thee, at thy parting breath,
To his divine abode.

LABAN. S. M. DR. L. MASON.

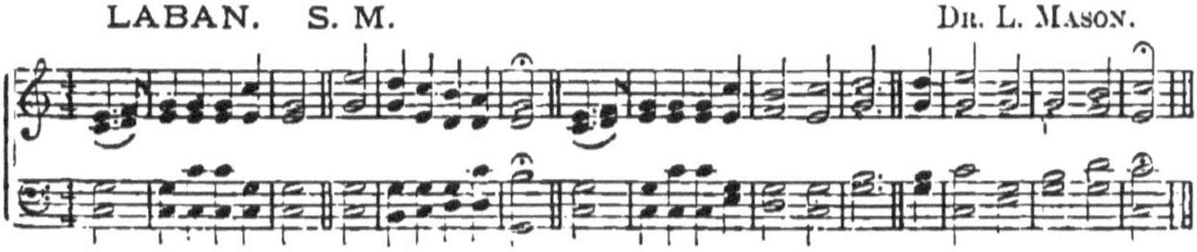

VANMETER. C. M. I. B. WOODBURY.

705 *Watch and pray.* C. M. (1(5)

1 The Saviour bids us watch and pray,
Through life's brief, fleeting hour;
And gives the Spirit's quickening ray
To those who seek his power.

2 The Saviour bids us watch and pray,
Maintain a warrior's strife;
Help, Lord, to hear thy voice to-day;
Obedience is our life.

3 The Saviour bids us watch and pray;
For soon the hour will come
That calls us from the earth away,
To our eternal home.

4 O Saviour, we would watch and pray,
And hear thy sacred voice,
And walk, as thou hast marked the way,
To heaven's eternal joys.

CHRISTMAS. C. M. HANDEL.

706 *The whole Armor.* C. M. (200)

1 Oh, speed thee, Christian, on thy way,
And to thy armor cling;
With girded loins the call obey
That grace and mercy bring.

2 There is a battle to be fought,
An upward race to run,
A crown of glory to be sought,
A victory to be won.

3 The shield of faith repels the dart
That Satan's hand may throw;
His arrow cannot reach thy heart,
If Christ control the bow.

4 The glowing lamp of prayer will light
Thee on thy anxious road;
'Twill keep the goal of heaven in sight,
And guide thee to thy God.

5 Oh, faint not, Christian, for thy sighs
Are heard before his throne;
The race must come before the prize,
The cross before the crown.

707 7s & 6s. (223)

Stand up for Jesus.

Tune—WEBB, next page.

1 Stand up!—stand up for Jesus!
Ye soldiers of the cross;
Lift high his royal banner,
It must not suffer loss:
From victory unto victory
His army shall be led,
Till every foe is vanquished,
And Christ is Lord indeed.

2 Stand up!—stand up for Jesus!
Stand in his strength a one;
The arm of flesh will fail you;
Ye dare not trust your own:
Put on the gospel armor,
And, watching unto prayer,
Where duty calls or danger,
Be never wanting there.

3 Stand up!—stand up for Jesus!
The strife will not be long;
This day the noise of battle,
The next the victor's song:
To him that overcometh,
A crown of life shall be;
He with the King of glory
Shall reign eternally.

WEBB. 7s & 6s. Geo. J. Webb.

FINE.

D.S.

708 C. M. (200)

Following departed Worthies.

Tune—Christmas, No. 706.

1 Rise, O my soul, pursue the path
By ancient worthies trod:
Aspiring, view those holy men
Who lived and walked with God.

2 Though dead, they speak in reason's ear,
And in example live;
Their faith and hope and mighty deeds
Still fresh instruction give.

3 'Twas through the Lamb's most precious blood
They conquered every foe;
To his almighty power and grace
Their crowns of life they owe.

4 Lord, may I ever keep in view
The patterns thou hast given,
And ne'er forsake the blessed road
That led them safe to heaven.

709 *The Saints above.* C. M. (231)

Tune—Tamach, No. 629.

1 Give me the wings of faith to rise
Within the veil, and see
The saints above, how great their joys
How bright their glories be.

2 Once they were mourning here below
And bathed their couch with tears;
They wrestled hard, as we do now,
With sins and doubts and fears.

3 I ask them whence their victory came:
They, with united breath,
Ascribe their conquest to the Lamb,
Their triumph to his death.

4 They marked the footsteps that he trod;
His zeal inspired their breast;
And, following their incarnate God,
Possessed the promised rest.

710 L. M. (241)

Taking the Shield of Faith.

1 Awake, my soul, lift up thine eyes;
See where thy foes against thee rise,
In long array, a numerous host.
Awake, my soul, or thou art lost!

2 Thou tread'st upon enchanted ground;
Perils and snares beset thee round;
Beware of all; guard every part;
But most, the traitor in thy heart.

3 Come, then, my soul, now learn to wield
The weight of thine immortal shield;
Put on the armor, from above,
Of heavenly truth and heavenly love.

4 The terror and the charm repel,
And powers of earth, and powers of hell;
The Man of Calv'ry triumphed here:
Why should his faithful followers fear?

ROTHWELL. L. M.

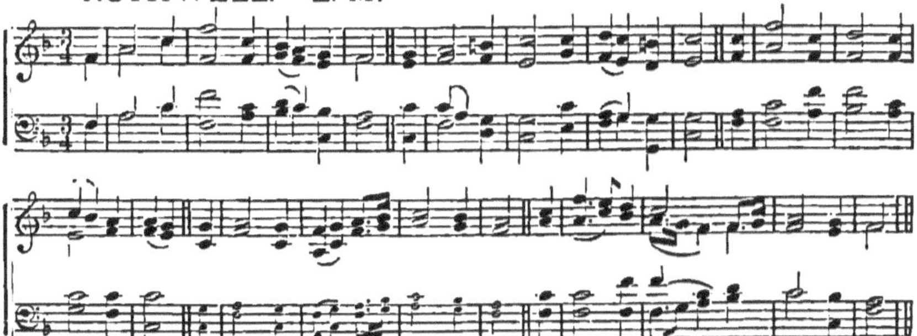

CHRISTMAS. C. M. HANDEL.

711 *The Christian Race.* C. M. (200)

1 AWAKE, my soul; stretch every nerve,
And press with vigor on;
A heavenly race demands thy zeal,
And an immortal crown.

2 A cloud of witnesses around
Hold thee in full survey;
Forget the steps already trod,
And onward urge thy way.

3 'Tis God's all-animating voice
That calls thee from on high;
'Tis his own hand presents the prize
To thine uplifted eye;—

4 That prize, with peerless glories bright,
Which shall new lustre boast,
When victors' wreaths and monarchs' gems
Shall blend in common dust.

ROTHWELL. L. M.

712 *The heavenly Race.* L. M. (241)

1 AWAKE, our souls; away, our fears;
Let every trembling thought be gone;
Awake, and run the heavenly race,
And put a cheerful courage on.

2 True, 'tis a strait and thorny road,
And mortal spirits tire and faint;
But they forget the mighty God,
Who feeds the strength of every saint;—

3 The mighty God, whose matchless power
Is ever new and ever young,
And firm endures, while endless years
Their everlasting circles run.

4 From thee, the overflowing spring,
Our souls shall drink a full supply;
While those who trust their native strength
Shall melt away and droop and die.

5 Swift as an eagle cuts the air,
We'll mount aloft to thine abode;
On wings of love our souls shall fly,
Nor tire amid the heavenly road.

713 *Bearing the Cross.* C. M. (161)

Tune—PHILLIPS. No. 539.

1 DIDST thou, dear Saviour, suffer shame,
And bear the cross for me,
And shall I fear to own thy name,
Or thy disciple be?

2 Inspire my soul with life divine,
And make me truly bold;
Let knowledge, faith, and meekness shine
Nor love nor zeal grow cold.

3 Let mockers scoff, the world defame,
And treat me with disdain;
Still may I glory in thy name,
And count reproach my gain.

714 L. M. (241)

The Christian Warfare.

Tune—ROTHWELL, No. 712.

1 STAND up, my soul, shake off thy fears,
And gird the gospel armor on;
March to the gates of endless joy,
Where Jesus, thy great Captain's gone.

2 Hell and thy sins resist thy course;
But hell and sin are vanquished foes;
Thy Saviour nailed them to the cross,
And sung the triumph when he rose.

3 Then let my soul march boldly on,
Press forward to the heavenly gate;
There peace and joy eternal reign,
And glittering robes for conquerors wait.

4 There shall I wear a starry crown,
And triumph in almighty grace
While all the armies of the skies
Join in my glorious Leader's praise.

715 *Jesus able to keep.* C. M. (238)

Tune—AZMON, next page.

1 I'M not ashamed to own my Lord,
Or to defend his cause,
Maintain the honor of his word,
The glory of his cross.

2 Jesus, my God, I know his name;
His name is all my trust;
Nor will he put my soul to shame,
Nor let my hope be lost.

3 Firm as his throne his promise stands,
And he can well secure
What I've committed to his hands
Till the decisive hour.

4 Then will he own my worthless name
Before his Father's face,
And in the New Jerusalem
Appoint my soul a place.

716 *Not ashamed of Christ.* L. M. (175)

Tune—FEDERAL STREET, No. 670.

1 JESUS, and shall it ever be—
A mortal man ashamed of thee?
Ashamed of thee, whom angels praise,
Whose glories shine through endless days?

2 Ashamed of Jesus!—that dear Friend
On whom my hopes of heaven depend!
No,—when I blush, be this my shame,
That I no more revere his name.

3 Ashamed of Jesus!—yes I may,
When I've no guilt to wash away,
No tear to wipe, no good to crave,
Nor fears to quell, no soul to save.

4 Till then,—nor is my boasting vain,—
Till then, I boast a Saviour slain;
And, oh, may this my glory be,
That Christ is not ashamed of me.

SEYMOUR. 7s. GREATOREX.

717 7s. (212)

Fight the good Fight of Faith.

1 OFT in danger, oft in woe,
Onward, Christians, onward go;
Bear the toil, maintain the strife,
Strengthened with the Bread of life.

2 Let not sorrow dim your eye,
Soon shall every tear be dry;
Let not fear your course impede,
Great your strength, if great your need.

3 Let your drooping hearts be glad;
March in heavenly armor clad;
Fight, nor think the battle long,
Soon shall victory wake your song.

4 Onward then to glory move;
More than conquerors ye shall prove;
Though opposed by many a foe,
Christian soldiers, onward go!

LABAN. S. M. DR. L. MASON.

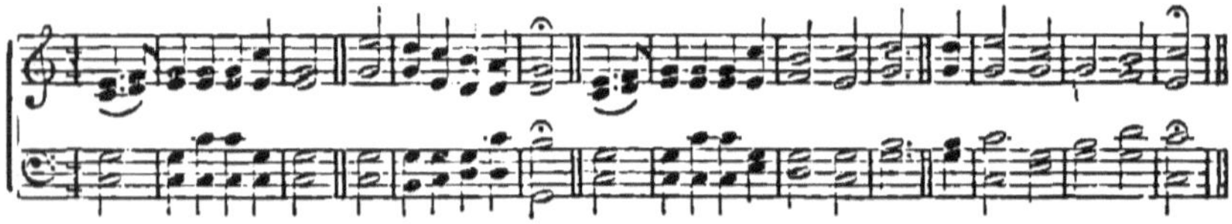

718 *The Christian Soldier's Strength.* S. M. (242)

1 SOLDIERS of Christ, arise,
And gird your armor on,
Strong in the strength which God supplies,
Through his eternal Son.

2 Strong in the Lord of hosts,
And in his mighty power,
The man who in the Saviour trusts
Is more than conqueror.

3 Stand, then, in his great might,
With all his strength endued,
And take, to arm you for the fight,
The panoply of God;

4 That, having all things done,
And all your conflicts past,
You may o'ercome through Christ alone
And stand complete at last.

5 From strength to strength go on;
Wrestle and fight and pray;
Tread all the powers of darkness down,
And win the well-fought day.

6 Still let the Spirit cry,
In all his soldiers, "Come."
Till Christ, the Lord, descends from high,
And takes the conquerors home.

AZMON. C. M. GLASER.

719 C. M. (238)

Succor implored in spiritual Conflicts.

1 ALAS! what hourly dangers rise,
What snares beset my way!
To heaven, oh, let me lift mine eyes,
And hourly watch and pray.

2 How oft my mournful thoughts complain,
And melt in flowing tears!
My weak resistance, ah, how vain!
How strong my foes and fears!

3 O gracious God, in whom I live,
My feeble efforts aid;
Help me to watch and pray and strive,
Though trembling and afraid.

4 Increase my faith, increase my hope,
When foes and fears prevail;
Oh, bear my fainting spirit up,
Or soon my strength will fail.

5 Oh, keep me in thy heavenly way,
And bid the tempter flee;
And let me never, never stray
From happiness and thee.

720 *The Conflict short.* 7s. (224)

Tune—MORE LIKE JESUS, No. 610.

1 BRETHREN, while we sojourn here,
Fight we must, but should not fear;
Foes we have, but we've a Friend,
One that loves us to the end.
Forward, then, with courage go,
Long we shall not dwell below;
Soon the joyful news will come,
"Child, your Father calls,—come home!"

2 In the way a thousand snares
Lie to take us unawares;
Satan, with malicious art,
Watches each unguarded part:
But, from Satan's malice free,
Saints shall soon victorious be;
Soon the joyful news will come,
"Child, your Father calls,—come home!"

3 But, of all the foes we meet,
None so oft mislead our feet,
None betray us into sin,
Like the foes that dwell within:
Yet let nothing spoil your peace,
Christ will also conquer these;
Then the joyful news will come,
"Child, your Father calls,—come home!"

ILLA. L. M. CARMINA SACRA.

721 L. M. (250)

The Glory of God in his Works and Word.

1 THE heavens declare thy glory, Lord:
In every star thy wisdom shines;
But when our eyes behold thy word,
We read thy name in fairer lines.

2 The rolling sun, the changing light,
And nights and days thy power confess;
But that blest volume thou hast writ
Reveals thy justice and thy grace.

3 Great Sun of Righteousness, arise;
Oh, bless the world with heavenly light;
Thy gospel makes the simple wise;
Thy laws are pure, thy judgments right.

4 Thy noblest wonders here we view,
In souls renewed and sins forgiven;
Lord, cleanse my sins, my soul renew,
And make thy word my guide to heaven

WARWICK. C. M. STANLEY.

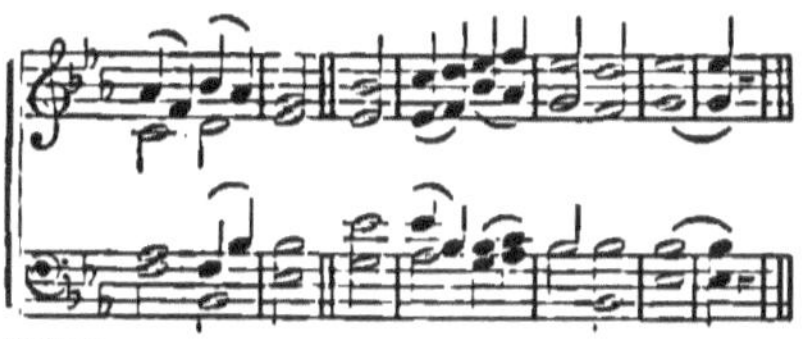

722 C. M. (247)

Sufficiency of the Scripture.

1 GREAT God, with wonder and with praise
On all thy works I look;
But still thy wisdom, power, and grace,
Shine brightest in thy book.

2 Here are my choicest treasures hid;
Here my best comfort lies;
Here my desires are satisfied;
And here my hopes arise.

3 Lord, make me understand thy law:
Show what my faults have been;
And from thy gospel let me draw
The pardon of my sin.

723 L. M. (250)

Superiority of God's Word.

Tune—ILLA.

1 THE starry firmament on high,
And all the glories of the sky,
Yet shine not to thy praise, O Lord,
So brightly as thy written word.

2 The hopes that holy word supplies,
Its truths divine and precepts wise—
In each a heavenly beam I see,
And every beam conducts to thee.

3 Almighty Lord, the sun shall fail,
The moon forget her nightly tale,
And deepest silence hush on high
The radiant chorus of the sky.

4 But fixed for everlasting years,
Unmoved amid the wreck of spheres,
Thy word shall shine in cloudless day,
When heaven and earth have passed away.

724 L. M. (250)

A Saviour seen in the Scripture.

Tune—ILLA.

1 Now let my soul, eternal King,
To thee its grateful tribute bring;
My knee with humble homage bow;
My tongue perform its solemn vow.

2 All nature sings thy boundless love,
In worlds below, and worlds above;
But in thy blessed word I trace
Diviner wonders of thy grace.

3 There what delightful truths I read!
There I behold the Saviour bleed;
His name salutes my listening ear,
Revives my heart, and checks my fear.

4 There Jesus bids my sorrow cease,
And gives my laboring conscience peace;
There lifts my grateful passions high,
And points to mansions in the sky.

WARWICK. C. M. STANLEY.

725 *The Bible suited to our Wants.* C. M. (247)

1 FATHER of mercies, in thy word
What endless glory shines!
For ever be thy name adored
For these celestial lines.

2 'Tis here the tree of knowledge grows,
And yields a free repast;
Here purer sweets than nature knows,
Invite the longing taste.

3 'Tis here the Saviour's welcome voice
Spreads heavenly peace around,
And life and everlasting joys
Attend the blissful sound.

4 Oh, may these heavenly pages be
My ever-dear delight;
And still new beauties may I see,
And still increasing light.

ILLA. L. M. CARMINA SACRA.

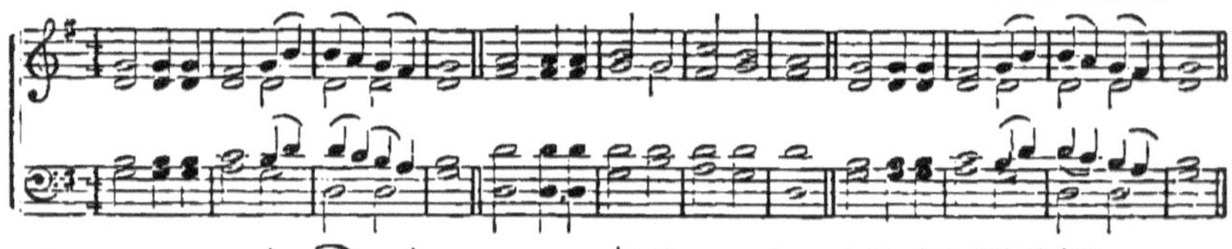

726 L. M. (250)

Thou art my Portion, O Lord.

1 OH, let thy sacred word impart
Its generous influence to my heart;
With power, and light, and love divine,
Assure my soul that thou art mine.

2 Thy blissful word, with joy replete,
Shall bid my gloomy fears retreat;
And heaven-born hope, serenely bright,
Shine cheerful through this mortal night.

3 Then shall my joyful spirit rise,
On wings of faith, above the skies;
And when these transient scenes are o'er,
And this vain world shall tempt no more,—

4 Oh, may I reach the blissful plains,
Where thy unclouded glory reigns,
And dwell for ever near thy throne,
In joys to mortal thought unknown.

727 *The Bible a Light.* C. M. (247)

WARWICK.

1 WHAT glory gilds the sacred page!
Majestic, like the sun,
It gives a light to every age,
It gives, but borrows none.

2 The power that gave it still supplies
The gracious light and heat;
Its truths upon the nations rise;
They rise, but never set.

3 Let everlasting thanks be thine
For such a bright display
As makes a world of darkness shine
With beams of heavenly day.

4 My soul rejoices to pursue
The steps of Him I love,
Till glory breaks upon my view
In brighter worlds above.

728 *Divine Revelation.* L. M. (251)

Tune—ILLA, No. 726.

1 God, in the gospel of his Son,
Makes his eternal counsels known:
Here love in all its glory shines,
And truth is drawn in fairest lines.

2 Here, sinners of a humble frame
May taste his grace, and learn his name,
May read, in characters of blood,
The wisdom, power, and grace of God.

3 Here, faith reveals to mortal eyes
A brighter world beyond the skies;
Here shines the light which guides our way
From earth to realms of endless day.

4 Oh, grant us grace, almighty Lord,
To read and mark thy holy word,
Its truths with meekness to receive,
And by its holy precepts live.

729 *Worth of the Bible.* C. M. (247)

Tune—WARWICK, No. 725.

1 How precious is the book divine,
By inspiration given!
Bright as a lamp its doctrines shine,
To guide our souls to heaven.

2 O'er all the strait and narrow way
Its radiant beams are cast;
A light whose never weary ray
Grows brightest at the last.

3 It sweetly cheers our drooping hearts,
In this dark vale of tears;
Life, light, and joy it still imparts,
And quells our rising fears.

4 This lamp, through all the tedious night
Of life, shall guide our way,
Till we behold the clearer light
Of an eternal day.

DOWNS. C. M. DR. L. MASON.

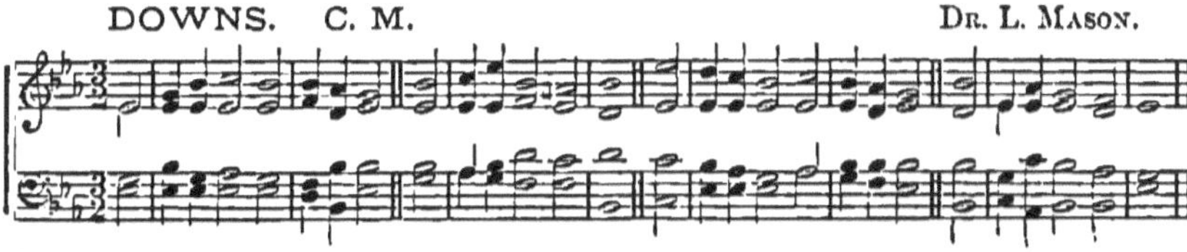

730 *Comfort from the Bible.* C. M. (248)

1 Lord, I have made thy word my choice,
My lasting heritage;
There shall my noblest powers rejoice,
My warmest thoughts engage.

2 I'll read the histories of thy love,
And keep thy laws in sight,
While through the promises I rove,
With ever-fresh delight.

3 'Tis a broad land, of wealth unknown,
Where springs of life arise,
Seeds of immortal bliss are sown,
And hidden glory lies.

4 The best relief that mourners have,
It makes our sorrows blest;
Our fairest hope beyond the grave,
And our eternal rest.

DALLAS. 7s. CHERUBINI.

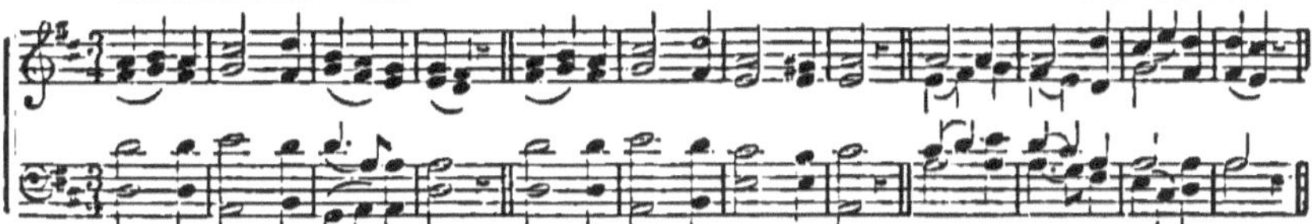

731 7s. (249)

Preciousness of the Scriptures.

1 Holy Bible, book divine,
Precious treasure, thou art mine:
Mine to tell me whence I came,
Mine to teach me what I am;

2 Mine to chide me when I rove;
Mine to show a Saviour's love;
Mine thou art to guide and guard,
Mine to punish or reward;

3 Mine to comfort in distress,
If the Holy Spirit bless;
Mine to show, by living faith,
Man can triumph over death;

4 Mine to tell of joys to come,
And the rebel sinner's doom;
O thou holy book divine,
Precious treasure, thou art mine.

NASHVILLE. L. P. M. Arranged by L. Mason.

732 L. P. M. (251)

Delight and Instruction from the Bible.

1 I love the volume of thy word;
What light and joy those leaves afford
To souls benighted and distressed!
Thy precepts guide my doubtful way;
Thy fear forbids my feet to stray;
Thy promise leads my heart to rest.

2 Thy threatenings wake my slumbering eyes,
And warn me where my danger lies;
But 'tis thy blessed gospel, Lord,
That makes my guilty conscience clean,
Converts my soul, subdues my sin,
And gives a free but large reward.

3 Who knows the errors of his thoughts?
My God, forgive my secret faults,
And from presumptuous sins restrain;
Accept my poor attempts of praise,
That I have read the book of grace,
And book of nature, not in vain.

DOWNS. C. M. Dr. L. Mason.

733 C. M. (248)

Love to the Bible.

1 Oh, how I love thy holy law!
'Tis daily my delight;
And thence my meditations draw
Divine advice by night.

2 My waking eyes prevent the day
To meditate thy word;
My soul with longing melts away
To hear thy gospel, Lord.

3 Thy heavenly words my heart engage,
And well employ my tongue,
And in my weary pilgrimage
Yield me a heavenly song.

4 When nature sinks, and spirits droop,
Thy promises of grace
Are pillars to support my hope,
And there I write thy praise.

734 C. M. (248)

Excellency of the Scripture.

1 Let all the heathen writers join
To form one perfect book;
Great God, if once compared with thine,
How mean their writings look!

2 Not the most perfect rules they gave
Could show one sin forgiven,
Nor lead a step beyond the grave;
But thine conduct to heaven.

3 I've seen an end of what we call
Perfection here below,—
How short the powers of nature fail,
And can no farther go.

4 Our faith and love and every grace
Fall far below thy word;
But perfect truth and righteousness
Dwell only with the Lord.

SHIRLAND. S. M. STANLEY.

735 *Power of God's Word.* S. M. (248)

1 Behold, the morning sun
Begins his glorious way;
His beams through all the nations run,
And life and light convey.

2 But where the gospel comes,
It spreads diviner light;
It calls dead sinners from their tombs,
And gives the blind their sight.

3 How perfect is thy word!
And all thy judgments just;
For ever sure thy promise, Lord
And we securely trust.

4 My gracious God, how plain
Are thy directions given!
Oh, may I never read in vain,
But find the path to heaven.

CHURCH.

SEASONS. L. M. PLEYEL.

736 *Glorious Things spoken of the City of God.* L. M. (261)

1 God in his earthly temple lays
Foundations for his heavenly praise;
He likes the tents of Jacob well,
But still in Zion loves to dwell.

2 His mercy visits every house
That pay their night and morning vows,
But makes a more delightful stay
Where churches meet to praise and pray.

3 What glories are described of old!
What wonders are of Zion told!
Thou city of our God below,
Thy fame shall Tyre and Egypt know.

PURVES. S. M.

GEO. KINGSLEY.

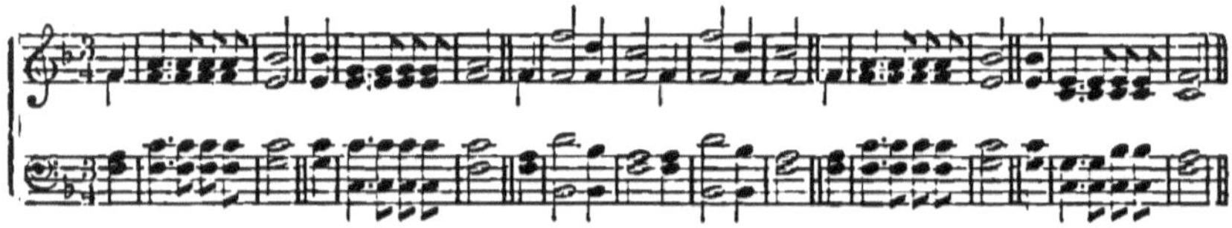

737 S. M. (263)

Safety of the Church.

1 How honored is the place
  Where we adoring stand!
Zion the glory of the earth,
  And beauty of the land.

2 Bulwarks of grace defend
  The city where we dwell,
While walls, of strong salvation made,
  Defy th' assaults of hell.

3 Lift up th' eternal gates;
  The doors wide open fling;
Enter, ye nations that obey
  The statutes of your King.

4 Here taste unmingled joys,
  And live in perfect peace,
You that have known Jehovah's name,
  And ventured on his grace.

738 C. M. (255)

Christ the Foundation of his Church.

1 BEHOLD the sure foundation stone,
  Which God in Zion lays,
To build our heavenly hopes upon,
  And his eternal praise.

2 Chosen of God, to sinners dear,
  Let saints adore the name;
They trust their whole salvation here,
  Nor shall they suffer shame.

3 The foolish builders, scribe and priest,
  Reject it with disdain;
Yet on this rock the church shall rest,
  And envy rage in vain.

4 What though the gates of hell withstood,
  Yet must this building rise:
'Tis thine own work, almighty God,
  And wondrous in our eyes.

AVONDALE. C. M.

CHIMES. C. M.

DR. L. MASON.

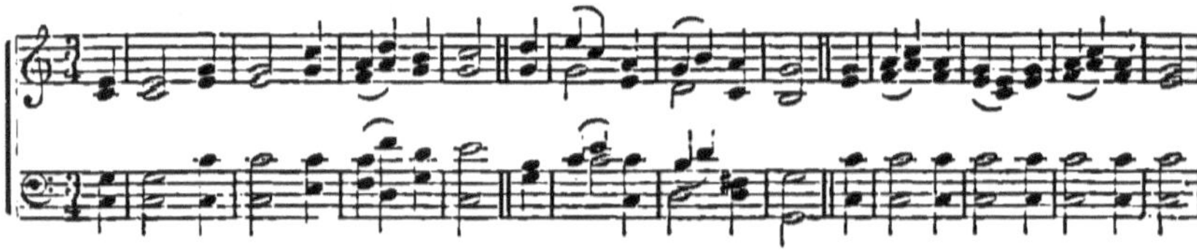

739 C. M. (263)

We are come unto Mount Zion.

1 NOT to the terrors of the Lord,
  The tempest, fire, and smoke;
Not to the thunder of that word
  Which God on Sinai spoke;

(CONTINUED.)

2 But we are come to Zion's hill,
The city of our God,
Where milder words declare his will,
And spread his love abroad.

3 Behold the great, the glorious host
Of angels clothed in light;
Behold the spirits of the just,
Whose faith is turned to sight.

4 Behold the blest assembly there,
Whose names are writ in heaven,
And God, the Judge, who doth declare
Their vilest sins forgiven.

5 The saints on earth, and all the dead,
But one communion make;
All join in Christ the living Head,
And of his grace partake.

6 In such society as this
Our weary souls would rest;
The man who dwells where Jesus is,
Must be for ever blest.

740 *Safety of the Church.* S. M. (263)

Tune—PURVES, No. 737.

1 GREAT is the Lord our God,
And let his praise be great;
He makes his churches his abode,
His most delightful seat.

2 In Zion God is known,
A refuge in distress;
How bright has his salvation shone,
Through all her palaces!

3 When kings against her joined
And saw the Lord was there,
In wild confusion of the mind,
They fled with hasty fear.

4 Oft have our fathers told,
Our eyes have often seen,
How well our God secures the fold
Where his own sheep have been.

5 In every new distress
We'll to his house repair;
We'll call to mind his wondrous grace,
And seek deliverance there.

ELTHAM. 7s. 6 lines. DR. L. MASON.

FINE.
D.C.

741 *Who shall separate?* 7s. 6l. (258)

1 HALLELUJAH! who shall part
Christ's own church from Christ's own heart?
Sever from the Saviour's side
Souls for whom the Saviour died?
Dash one precious jewel down
From Immanuel's blood-bought crown?

2 Hallelujah! shall the sword
Part us from our glorious Lord?
Trouble dark or dire disgrace
E'er the Spirit's seal efface?
Famine, nakedness, or hate
Bride and Bridegroom separate?

3 Hallelujah! life nor death,
Powers above nor powers beneath,
Monarch's might nor tyrant's doom,
Things that are nor things to come,
Men nor angels, e'er shall part
Christ's own church from Christ's own heart.

ROBINSON. 8s & 7s. Double. DR. T. HASTINGS.

FINE.

D.C.

742 8s & 7s. (260)

The Church, God's chosen Residence.

1 GLORIOUS things of thee are spoken,
Zion, city of our God;
He whose word can ne'er be broken
Formed thee for his own abode.

2 Lord, thy church is still thy dwelling,
Still is precious in thy sight,
Judah's temple far excelling,
Beaming with the gospel's light.

3 On the Rock of ages founded,
What can shake her sure repose?
With salvation's walls surrounded,
She can smile at all her foes.

4 Round her habitation hovering,
See the cloud and fire appear,
For a glory and a covering,
Showing that the Lord is near

ANVERN. L. M. DR. L. MASON.

Ritard.

743. L. M. (302)

God is in the Midst of her.

1 HAPPY the church, thou sacred place,
The seat of thy Creator's grace;
Thine holy courts are his abode,
Thou earthly palace of our God.

2 Thy walls are strength, and at thy gates
A guard of heavenly warriors waits;
Nor shall thy deep foundations move,
Fixed on his counsels and his love.

3 Thy foes in vain designs engage;
Against thy throne in vain they rage:
Like rising waves with angry roar,
That dash and die upon the shore.

4 God is our shield, and God our sun;
Swift as the fleeting moments run,
On us he sheds new beams of grace,
And we reflect his brightest praise.

ST. THOMAS. S. M. HANDEL.

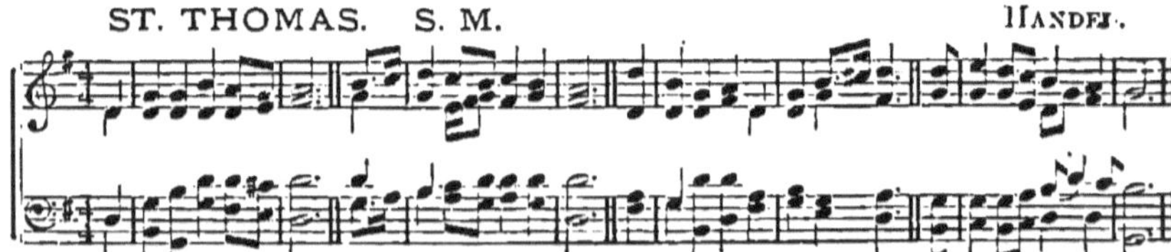

744 *The Beauties of Zion.* S. M. (257)

Tune—St. Thomas.

1 Far as thy name is known
The world declares thy praise;
Thy saints, O Lord, before thy throne,
Their songs of honor raise.

2 With joy thy people stand
On Zion's chosen hill,
Proclaim the wonders of thy hand,
And counsels of thy will.

3 Let strangers walk around
The city where we dwell,
Survey with care thine holy ground,
And mark the building well,—

4 The order of thy house,
The worship of thy court,
The cheerful songs, the solemn vows,
And make a fair report.

5 How decent, and how wise!
How glorious to behold!
Beyond the pomp that charms the eyes,
And rites adorned with gold.

745 S. M. (257)

The Church in the Wilderness.

Tune—St. Thomas, No. 744.

1 Far down the ages now,
Much of her journey done,
The pilgrim church pursues her way,
Until her crown be won.

2 The story of the past
Comes up before her view;
How well it seems to suit her still,—
Old, and yet ever new.

3 No wider is the gate,
No broader is the way,
No smoother is the ancient path,
That leads to life and day.

4 No slacker grows the fight,
No feebler is the foe,
No less the need of armor tried,
Of shield and spear and bow.

5 Still faithful to our God,
And to our Captain true,
We follow where he leads the way,
The kingdom in our view.

746 C. M. (262)

God's Love to the Church.

Tune—Chimes, 730.

1 A mother may forgetful be,
For human love is frail;
But thy Creator's love to thee,
O Zion, cannot fail.

2 No, thy dear name engraven stands,
In characters of love,
On thy almighty Father's hands;
And never shall remove.

3 Before his ever-watchful eye
Thy mournful state appears,
And every groan, and every sigh,
Divine compassion hears.

4 O Zion, learn to doubt no more,
Be every fear suppressed;
Unchanging truth and love and power
Dwell in thy Saviour's breast.

747 C. P. M. (256)

Security of the Church.

1 Fear not, O little flock, the foe
Who madly seeks your overthrow;
Dread not his rage and power.
What tho' your courage sometimes faints,
His seeming triumph o'er God's saints
Lasts but a little hour.

2 Be of good cheer; your cause belongs
To him who can avenge your wrongs;
Leave it to him, our Lord.
Though hidden yet from all our eyes,
He sees the Gideon that shall rise
To save us and his word.

3 Amen, Lord Jesus, grant our prayer;
Great Captain, now thine arm make bare,
Fight for us once again.
So shall thy saints and martyrs raise
A mighty chorus to thy praise,
World without end: Amen.

MEDFORD. C. P. M.

ZION. 8s, 7s, & 4. Dr. T. Hastings.

748

8s, 7s, & 4. (300)

God the Defence of Zion.

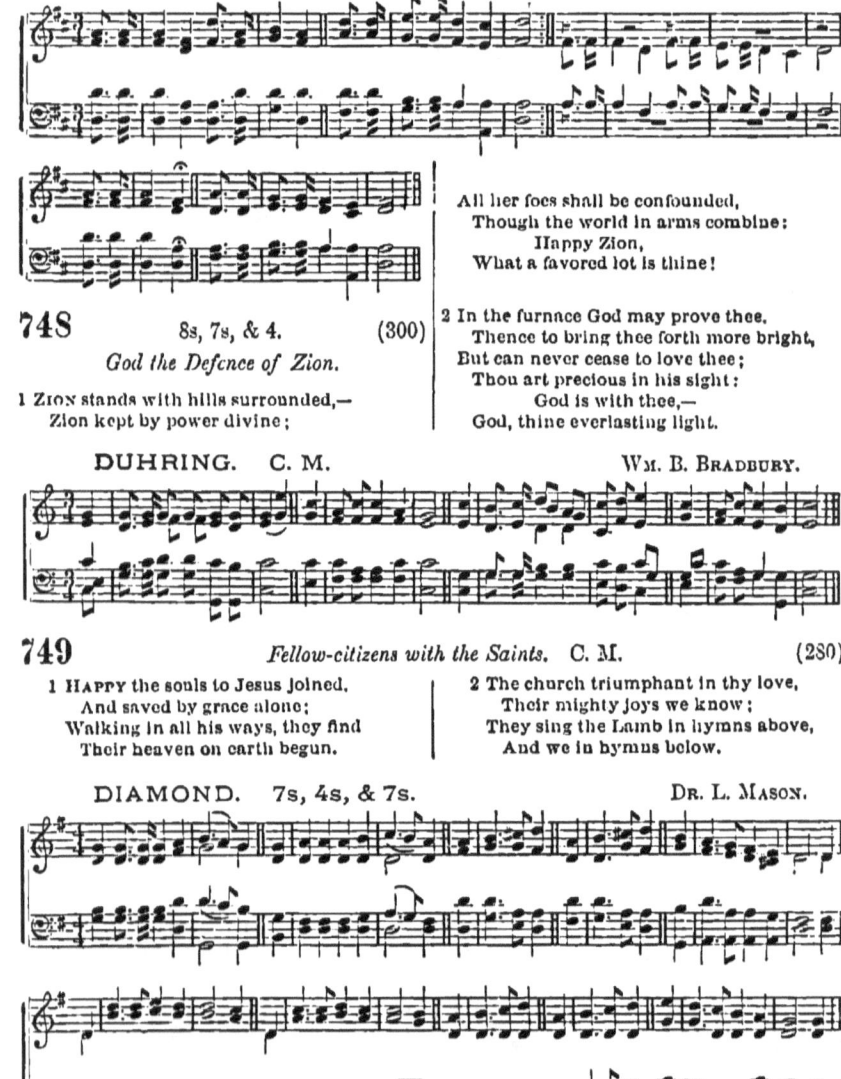

1 Zion stands with hills surrounded,—
Zion kept by power divine;
All her foes shall be confounded,
Though the world in arms combine:
Happy Zion,
What a favored lot is thine!

2 In the furnace God may prove thee,
Thence to bring thee forth more bright,
But can never cease to love thee;
Thou art precious in his sight:
God is with thee,—
God, thine everlasting light.

DUHRING. C. M. Wm. B. Bradbury.

749

Fellow-citizens with the Saints. C. M. (280)

1 Happy the souls to Jesus joined,
And saved by grace alone;
Walking in all his ways, they find
Their heaven on earth begun.

2 The church triumphant in thy love,
Their mighty joys we know;
They sing the Lamb in hymns above,
And we in hymns below.

DIAMOND. 7s, 4s, & 7s. Dr. L. Mason.

750 7s, 4s, & 7s. (259)

The Church triumphant.

Tune—DIAMOND.

1 HEAD of the church triumphant,
We joyfully adore thee;
Till thou appear,
Thy members here
Shall sing like those in glory.
We lift our hearts and voices,
In blest anticipation,
And cry aloud,
And give to God
The praise of our salvation.

2 While in affliction's furnace,
And passing through the fire,
Thy love we praise,
That knows our days,
And ever brings us nigher.
We lift our hands, exulting
In thine almighty favor;
The love divine,
That made us thine,
Shall keep us thine for ever.

3 Thou dost conduct thy people
Through torrents of temptation;
Nor will we fear,
While thou art near,
The fire of tribulation.
The world, with sin and Satan,
In vain our march opposes;
By thee we will
Break through them all,
And sing the song of Moses.

751 *Christian Fellowship.* C. M. (262)

Tune—CHIMES, No. 739.

1 PLANTED in Christ, the living vine,
This day, with one accord,
Ourselves, with humble faith and joy,
We yield to thee, O Lord.

2 Complete in us, whom grace hath called,
Thy glorious work begun,
O thou, in whom the church on earth
And church in heaven are one,

3 Around this feeble, trusting band
Thy sheltering pinions spread,
Nor let the storms of trial beat
Too fiercely on our head.

4 Then, when, among the saints in light,
Our joyful spirits shine,
Shall anthems of immortal praise,
O Lamb of God, be thine.

BAPTISM.

STOCKWELL. 8s & 7s. D. E. JONES.

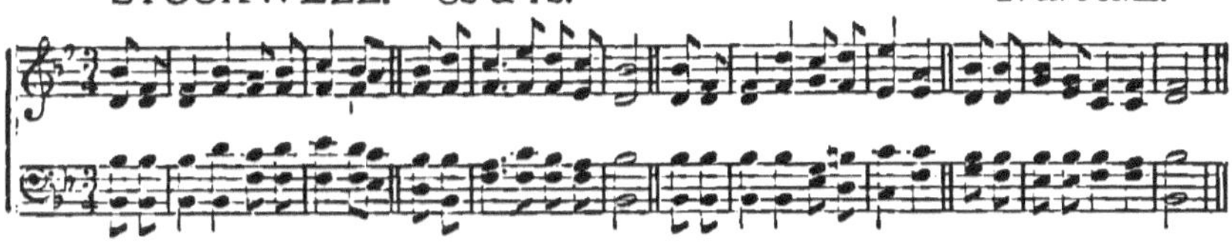

752 *Following Christ.* 8s & 7s. (271)

1 JESUS, mighty King in Zion,
Thou alone our Guide shalt be:
Thy commission we rely on;
We would follow none but thee.

2 As an emblem of thy passion,
And thy victory o'er the grave,
We, who know thy great salvation,
Are baptized beneath the wave

3 Fearless of the world's despising,
We the ancient path pursue,
Buried with our Lord, and rising
To a life divinely new.

753 *Follow Christ.* 8s & 7s. (271)

1 HUMBLE souls, who seek salvation
Through the Lamb's redeeming blood,
Hear the voice of revelation,
Tread the path that Jesus trod.

2 Hear the blest Redeemer call you,
Listen to his heavenly voice;
Dread no ills that can befall you,
While you make his way your choice.

3 Jesus says, "Let each believer
Be baptized in my name;"
He himself, in Jordan's river,
Was immersed beneath the stream.

4 Plainly here his footsteps tracing,
Follow him without delay;
Gladly his command embracing,
Lo! your Captain leads the way.

SHINING SHORE. 8s & 7s. G. F Root.

FINE.
D.S.

754 8s & 7s. (274)

Christ our Example.

1 This rite our blest Redeemer gave
To all in him believing;
He bids us seek this hallowed grave,
To his example cleaving.
I'll follow, then, my glorious Lord,
Whate'er the ties I sever,
He saved my soul, and left his word
To guide me now and ever.

2 For me the cross and shame to bear,
Dear Saviour, thou wast willing:
Nor would I shrink thy yoke to wear,
All righteousness fulfilling.
I'll follow, etc.

3 Jesus, to thee I yield my all;
In thy kind arms enfold me:
My heart is fixed; no fears appal;
Thy gracious power shall hold me.
I'll follow, etc.

755 L. M. (267)

Imitation of Christ.

1 Come, happy souls, adore the Lamb,
Who loved our race ere time began,
Who vailed his Godhead in our clay,
And in an humble manger lay.

2 To Jordan's stream the Spirit led,
To mark the path his saints should tread;
With joy they trace the sacred way,
To see the place where Jesus lay.

3 Immersed by John in Jordan's wave,
The Saviour left his watery grave;
Heaven owned the deed, approved the way
And blessed the place where Jesus lay.

4 Come, all who love his precious name,
Come, tread his steps and learn of him;
Happy beyond expression they
Who find the place where Jesus lay.

HAPPY DAY. L. M.

FINE.
DAL S

STATE STREET. S. M. J. C. WOODMAN.

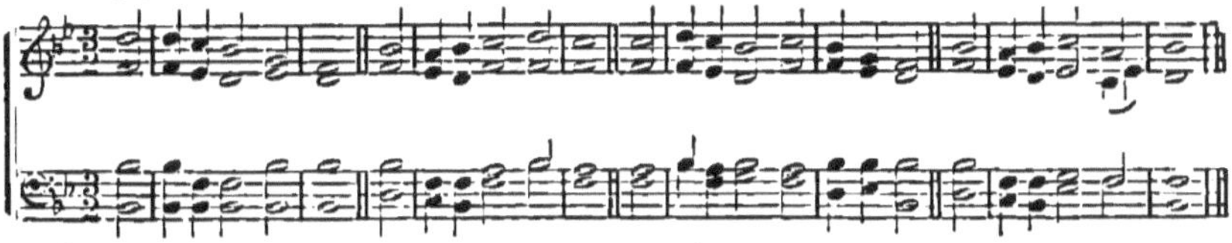

756 S. M (268)

The Baptism of Christ.

1 Down to the sacred wave
The Lord of Life was led;
And he who came our souls to save
In Jordan bowed his head.

2 He taught the solemn way;
He fixed the holy rite;
He bade his ransomed ones obey,
And keep the path of light.

3 Blest Saviour, we will tread
In thy appointed way;
Let glory o'er these scenes be shed,
And smile on us to-day.

757 L. M. (269)

Call to follow Christ in Baptism

1 Behold the grave where Jesus lay,
Before he shed his precious blood.
How plain he marked the humble way
To sinners through the mystic flood!

2 Come, ye redeemed of the Lord,
Come, and obey his sacred word;
He died; and rose again for you;
What more could the Redeemer do?

3 Eternal Spirit, heavenly Dove,
On these baptismal waters move;
And grant that we, through grace divine,
May have the substance with the sign.

MALVERN. L. M. DR. L. MASON.

PUTNEY. 8s, 7s, & 4. CARMINA SACRA.

758 *Following Christ.* 8s, 7s, & 4. (266)

1 Gracious Saviour, we adore thee;
Purchased by thy precious blood,
We present ourselves before thee,
Now to walk the narrow road;
Saviour, guide us,—
Guide us to our heavenly home.

2 Thou didst mark our path of duty;
Thou wast laid beneath the wave;
Thou didst rise in glorious beauty
From the semblance of the grave;
May we follow
In the same delightful way.

MILLENNIUM. 7s & 6s.

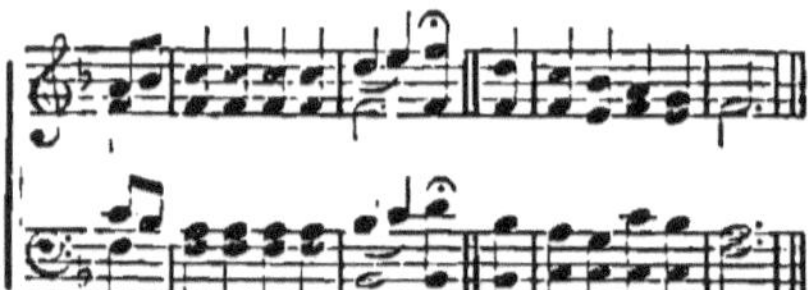

759 7s & 6s. (272)

Buried with Christ.

1 Around thy grave, Lord Jesus,
  Thine empty grave we stand,
With hearts all full of praises,
  To keep thy bless'd command:
By faith our souls rejoicing,
  To trace thy path of love,
Through death's dark angry billows,
  Up to the throne above.

2 Lord Jesus, we remember
  The travail of thy soul,
When, in thy love's deep pity,
  The waves did o'er thee roll;
Baptized in death's cold waters,
  For us thy blood was shed;
For us the Lord of glory
  Was numbered with the dead.

3 Lord, now thou art arisen,
  Thy travail is all o'er,
For sin thou once hast suffer'd,
  Thou livest to die no more;
Sin, death, and hell are vanquish'd,
  By thee, thy church's Head;
And lo! we share thy triumphs,
  Thou first-born from the dead.

4 Into thy death baptizèd,
  We own with thee we died;
With thee, our life, are risen,
  And in thee glorified;
From sin, the world, and Satan,
  We're ransom'd by thy blood,
And now would walk as strangers,
  Alive with thee to God.

MALVERN. L. M. Dr. L. Mason.

STATE STREET. S. M. J. C. Woodman.

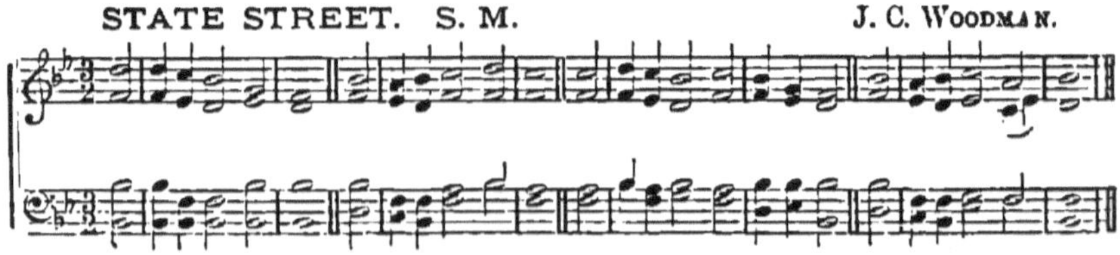

760 *Christ's Example.* L. M. (269)

Tune—MALVERN, preceding page.

1 OUR Saviour bowed beneath the wave,
And meekly sought a watery grave:
Come, see the sacred path he trod—
A path well pleasing to our God.

2 His voice we hear, his footsteps trace,
And hither come to seek his face,
To do his will, to feel his love,
And join our songs with songs above.

3 Hosanna to the Lamb divine!
Let endless glories round him shine;
High o'er the heavens for ever reign,
O Lamb of God, for sinners slain.

761 *Baptism into Christ.* S. M. (268)

Tune—STATE STREET, preceding page.

1 WITH willing hearts we tread
The path the Saviour trod;
We love th' example of our Head,
The glorious Lamb of God.

2 On thee, on thee alone,
Our hope and faith rely,
O thou who didst for sin atone,
Who didst for sinners die.

3 We trust thy sacrifice;
To thy dear cross we flee;
Oh, may we die to sin, and rise
To life and bliss in thee

NEW YORK. C. M.

762 *Hinder me not.* C. M. (264)

1 IN all my Lord's appointed ways
My journey I'll pursue;
"Hinder me not," ye much-loved saints,
For I must go with you.

2 Through floods and flames, if Jesus lead,
I'll follow where he goes;
"Hinder me not," shall be my cry,
Though earth and hell oppose.

3 Through duties, and through trials too,
I'll go at his command;
"Hinder me not;" for I am bound
To my Immanuel's land.

4 And, when my Saviour calls me home,
Still this my cry shall be—
"Hinder me not;" come, welcome, death;
I'll gladly go with thee.

MARTYN. 7s. Double. MARSH.

FINE.
D.C.

763 *Union with Christ.* 7s. (294)

1 CHRIST, who came my soul to save,
Entered Jordan's yielding wave,
Rose from out the crystal flood,
Owned and sealed the Son of God,
By the Father's voice of love,
By the heaven descending Dove;
Saviour, Pattern, Guide for me,
I, like him, baptized would be.

2 In the garden, o'er his soul
Sorrow's whelming waves did roll;
Ah! on Calvary's cruel tree,
Jesus bowed in death for me.
I with him am crucified:
All my hope is,—he hath died:
At his feet my place I take,
Bear the cross for his dear sake.

3 In the new-made tomb he lay,
Taking all its dread away;
Burst he through its rock-bound door,
Glorious now, and evermore.
I with Christ would buried be
In this rite required of me,
Rising from the mystic flood,
Living hence anew to God.

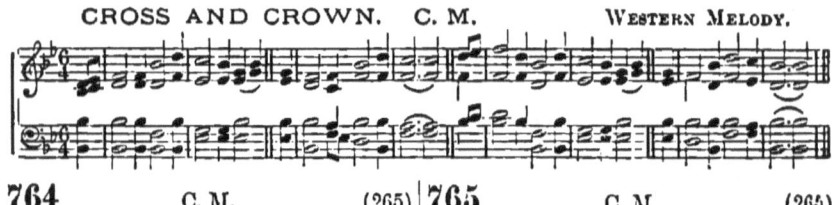

CROSS AND CROWN. C. M.

WESTERN MELODY.

764 C. M. (265)

The Pledge of Fidelity.

1 Ye men and angels, witness now,—
Before the Lord we speak;
To him we make our solemn vow,—
A vow we dare not break,—

2 That long as life itself shall last,
Ourselves to Christ we yield;
Nor from his cause will we depart,
Or ever quit the field.

3 We trust not in our native strength,
But on his grace rely;
May he, with our returning wants,
All needful aid supply.

4 Oh, guide our doubtful feet aright,
And keep us in thy ways;
And, while we turn our vows to prayers,
Turn thou our prayers to praise.

765 C. M. (265)

Delight in Obedience.

1 O Lord, and will thy pardoning love
Embrace a wretch so vile?
Wilt thou my load of guilt remove,
And bless me with thy smile?

2 Hast thou the cross for me endured,
And all its shame despised?
And shall I be ashamed, O Lord,
With thee to be baptized?

3 Didst thou the great example lead,
In Jordan's swelling flood?
And shall my pride disdain the deed
That's worthy of my God?

4 O Lord, the ardor of thy love
Reproves my cold delays;
And now my willing footsteps move
In thy delightful ways.

HAPPY DAY. L. M.

FINE.
DAL 𝄋

NEW YORK. C. M.

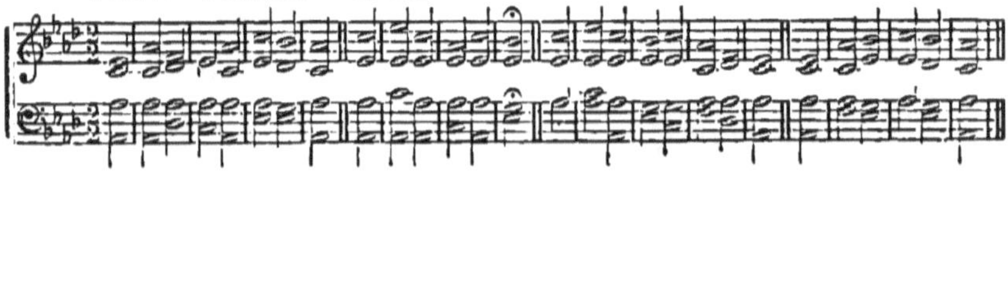

766 *The baptismal Vow.* L. M. (267)

Tune—HAPPY DAY, preceding page.

1 OH, happy day, that fixed my choice
On thee, my Saviour and my God;
Well may this glowing heart rejoice,
And tell its raptures all abroad.

2 'Tis done,—the great transaction's done,
I am my Lord's, and he is mine;
He drew me, and I followed on,
Rejoiced to own the call divine.

3 Now rest, my long-divided heart,
Fixed on this blissful centre, rest;
Here have I found a nobler part,
Here heavenly pleasures fill my breast.

4 High heaven that hears the solemn vow,
That vow renewed shall daily hear;
Till in life's latest hour I bow,
And bless in death a bond so dear.

767 *Baptized into Death.* C. M. (264)

Tune—NEW YORK, preceding page.

1 IMMERSED beneath the closing wave,
We're into death baptized,
And enter thus our Saviour's grave,
Buried with him that died.

2 With Christ we die, that, freed from sin,
With Christ we may arise;
New thoughts, new hopes, new lives to win
To fit us for the skies.

3 O Holy Ghost, to us be given;
And all our converse here
Be waiting for the Lord from heaven,
Till Christ, our Life, appear.

4 And grant our faith the majesty,
The present joy and crown,
With Christ, e'en now, to live on high,
And there with him sit down.

PUTNEY. 8s, 7s, & 4. CARMINA SACRA.

768 8s, 7s, & 4. (266)

Buried with Christ by Baptism.

1 THOU hast said, exalted Jesus,
"Take thy cross and follow me;"
Shall the word with terror seize us?
Shall we from the burden flee?
Lord, I'll take it,
And, rejoicing, follow thee.

2 While this liquid tomb surveying,
Emblem of my Saviour's grave,
Shall I shun its brink, betraying
Feelings worthy of a slave?
No, I'll enter:
Jesus entered Jordan's wave.

3 Blest the sign which thus reminds me,
Saviour, of thy love for me:
But more blest the love that binds me
In its deathless bonds to thee:
Oh, what pleasure,
Buried with my Lord to be!

4 Should it rend some fond connection,
Should I suffer shame or loss,
Yet the fragrant, blest reflection,
I have been where Jesus was,
Will revive me
When I faint beneath the cross.

5 Fellowship with him possessing,
Let me die to earth and sin;
Let me rise t' enjoy the blessing
Which the faithful soul shall win:
May I ever
Follow where my Lord has been.

769 *Baptism an Emblem.* L. M. (269)

Tune—MALVERN, No. 760.

1 Do we not know that solemn word,
That we are buried with the Lord?
Baptized into his death, and then
Put off the body of our sin?

2 Our souls receive diviner breath,
Raised from corruption, guilt, and death;
So from the grave did Christ arise,
And lives to God above the skies.

3 No more let sin or Satan reign
Within our mortal flesh again;
The various lusts we served before
Shall have dominion now no more.

770 S. M. (268)

Death, Burial, and Resurrection.

Tune—STATE STREET, No. 761

1 HERE, O ye faithful, see,
Your Lord baptized in woe,
Immersed in seas of agony,
Which all his soul o'erflow.

2 Here we behold the grave
Which held our buried Head;
We claim a burial in the wave,
Because with Jesus dead.

3 Here, too, we see him rise,
And live no more to die;
And one with him by sacred ties
We rise to live on high.

CROSS AND CROWN. C. M. WESTERN MELODY.

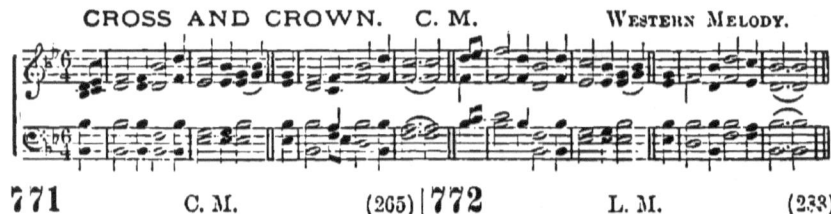

771 C. M. (265)

Glad Obedience.

1 WHILE in the sacred rite of thine,
We yield our spirits now,
Shine o'er the waters, Dove divine,
And seal the cheerful vow.

2 All glory be to him whose life
For ours was freely given,
Who aids us in the spirit's strife,
And makes us meet for heaven.

3 To thee we gladly now resign
Our life and all our powers;
Accept us in this rite divine,
And bless these hallowed hours.

772 L. M. (238)

Obedience to the Gospel.

1 O FATHER, Lord of earth and heaven,
O Son incarnate, Christ our King!
O Spirit for our guidance given!
Hear and accept the vow we bring.

2 We own thee, Saviour, crucified,
We own thee, Saviour, raised to heaven;
With thee our souls to sin have died,
But now would rise as thou art risen.

3 Thy gospel, Lord, we would obey,
We follow, and thy hand shall guide:
We seek through Jordan's wave the way
That leads thy loved ones to thy side.

4 Now in immersion,—wondrous sign!—
We dedicate ourselves to thee;
Now seal the covenant divine,
And own us thine eternally.

HEBRON. L. M. DR. L. MASON.

GOSHEN. 11s.

773 11s. (277)

Baptism a Symbol of Regeneration.

Tune—Goshen.

1 O Thou who in Jordan didst bow thy meek head,
And whelmed in our sorrow, didst sink to the dead,
Then rose from the darkness to glory above,
And claimed for thy chosen the kingdom of love,

2 Thy footsteps we follow, to bow in the tide,
And are buried with thee in the death thou hast died,
Then wake in thy likeness to walk in the way
That brightens and brightens to shadowless day.

3 O Jesus, our Saviour, O Jesus, our Lord,
By the life of thy passion, the grace of thy word,
Accept us, redeem us, dwell ever within,
To keep, by thy Spirit, our spirits from sin.

4 Till crowned with thy glory, and waving the palm,
Our garments all white from the blood of the Lamb,
We join the bright millions of saints gone before,
And bless thee, and wonder, and praise evermore.

774 *"Baptized into Christ."* S. M. (268)

Tune—State Street, No. 761.

1 Baptized into the name
Of my redeeming Lord;
Inspired with loftiest, holiest aim
That grace can man accord;

2 To thee, my God, I raise
A spirit glad and free,
And dedicate once more my days
With firm resolve to thee.

3 I bless the love divine,
That hath thy servant found;
And would for evermore be thine,
And light diffuse around.

4 In word, in thought, in deed,
I yield me to thy will:
O God, my purpose kindly heed,
And help me to fulfil.

775 C. M. (264)

The Descent of the Spirit on Christ.

Tune—New York, No. 767.

1 Meekly in Jordan's holy stream
The great Redeemer bowed;
Bright was the glory's sacred beam
That hushed the wondering crowd.

2 Thus God descended to approve
The deed that Christ had done;
Thus came the emblematic Dove,
And hovered o'er the Son.

3 So, blessed Spirit, come to-day
To our baptismal scene;
Let thoughts of earth be far away,
And every mind serene.

4 This day we give to holy joy;
This day to heaven belongs;
Raised to new life, we will employ
In melody our tongues.

776 *The Spirit desired.* L. M. (269)

Tune—Malvern, No. 760.

1 Come, Holy Spirit, Dove divine,
On these baptismal waters shine.
And teach our hearts, in highest strain,
To praise the Lamb, for sinners slain.

2 We love thy name, we love thy laws,
And joyfully embrace thy cause;
We love thy cross, the shame, the pain,
O Lamb of God, for sinners slain.

3 We sink beneath thy mystic flood:
Oh, bathe us in thy cleansing blood;
We die to sin, and seek a grave,
With thee, beneath the yielding wave.

4 And as we rise, with thee to live,
Oh, let the Holy Spirit give
The sealing unction from above,
The breath of life, the fire of love.

BERTHA. H. M. W. O. Perkins.

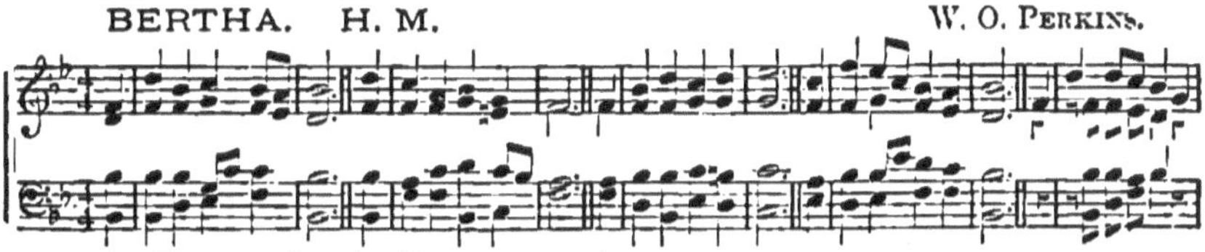

777 H. M. (273)

Prayer for God's Smiles.

1 O glorious God of grace,
Look from thy radiant throne;
And with approving smiles
Thy holy ordinance own:
In strains of rapture may we sing,
While we confess our Lord and King.

2 Inspir'd with love and zeal,
The grateful saints pursue
Th' appointed paths of God,
With Jesus in their view!
They own their Saviour strong to save,
They own him in the watery grave.

3 Now while thy saints attend
This ordinance of thine,
Oh, bless their waiting souls,
With comforts all divine,
Give them a soul-refreshing sight
Of the blest realms of heavenly light.

BERTHA. H. M. W. O. PERKINS.

778 H. M. (273)

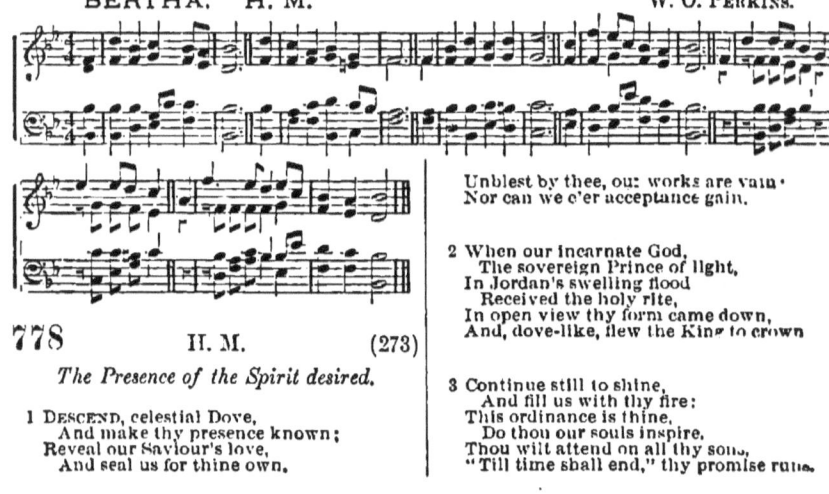

The Presence of the Spirit desired.

1 DESCEND, celestial Dove,
And make thy presence known;
Reveal our Saviour's love,
And seal us for thine own.
Unblest by thee, our works are vain:
Nor can we e'er acceptance gain.

2 When our incarnate God,
The sovereign Prince of light,
In Jordan's swelling flood
Received the holy rite,
In open view thy form came down,
And, dove-like, flew the King to crown

3 Continue still to shine,
And fill us with thy fire:
This ordinance is thine,
Do thou our souls inspire.
Thou wilt attend on all thy sons,
"Till time shall end," thy promise runs.

THE LORD'S SUPPER.

WOODLAND. C. M. N. D. GOULD.

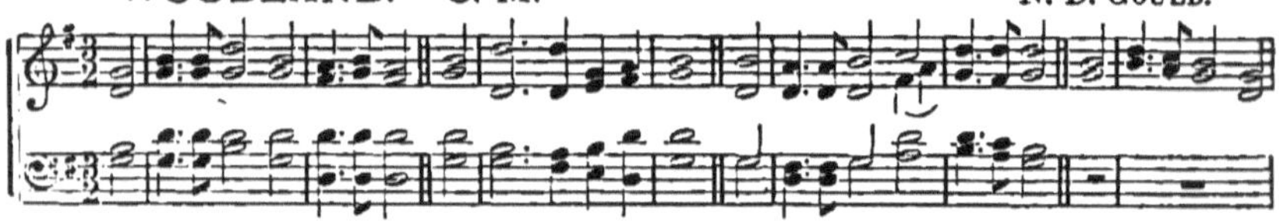

779 *For me.* C. M. (279)

1 HERE at thy table, Lord, we meet,
To feed on food divine;
Thy body is the bread we eat,
Thy precious blood the wine.

2 Here peace and pardon sweetly flow:
Oh, what delightful food!
We eat the bread and drink the wine,
But think on nobler good.

3 Sure, there was never love so free,
Dear Saviour,—so divine;
Well thou mayst claim that heart of me,
Which owes so much to thine.

780 S. M. (278)

Communion with Christ.

Tune—KENTUCKY, next page.

1 JESUS invites his saints
To meet around his board;
Here pardoned rebels sit, and hold
Communion with their Lord.

2 This holy bread and wine
Maintain our fainting breath,
By union with our living Lord,
And interest in his death.

3 Let all our powers be joined
His glorious name to raise;
Let holy love fill every mind,
And every voice be praise.

KENTUCKY. S. M.

OLD MELODY.

781 C. M. (276)

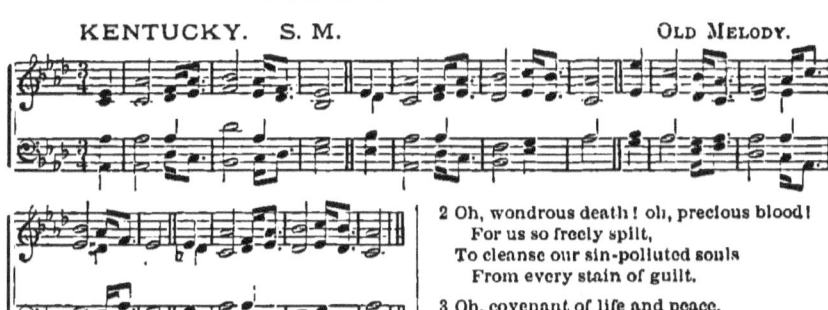

In Remembrance of me.

Tune—MANOAH.

1 OH, love divine! oh, matchless grace!
Which in this sacred rite
Shines forth so full, so free in rays
Of purest living light.

2 Oh, wondrous death! oh, precious blood!
For us so freely spilt,
To cleanse our sin-polluted souls
From every stain of guilt.

3 Oh, covenant of life and peace,
By blood and suffering sealed.
All the rich gifts of gospel grace
Are here to faith revealed.

4 Jesus, we bow our souls to thee,
Our Life, our Hope, our All,
While we, with thankful, contrite hearts,
Thy dying love recall.

5 Oh, may thy pure and perfect love
Be written on our minds;
Nor earth nor self nor sin obscure
The ever-radiant lines.

MANOAH. C. M.

GREATOREX.

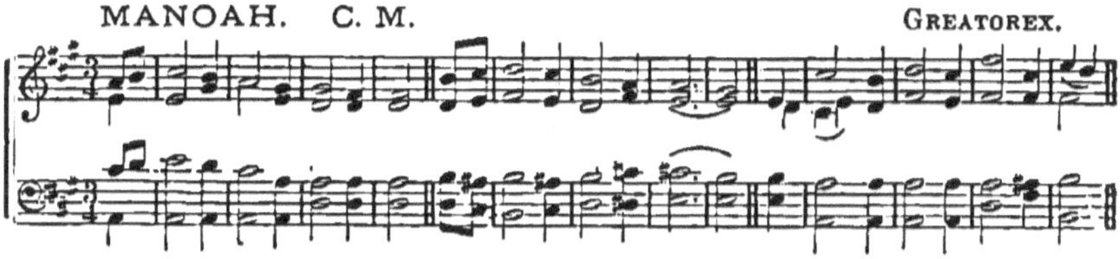

782 C. M. (276)

Humble Acknowledgment.

1 How sweet and awful is the place,
With Christ within the doors,
While everlasting Love displays
The choicest of her stores!

2 While all our hearts, and every song
Join to admire the feast,
Each of us cries, with thankful tongue,
"Lord, why was I a guest?

3 "Why was I made to hear thy voice,
And enter while there's room,
When thousands make a wretched choice
And rather starve than come?"

4 'Twas the same love that spread the feast
That sweetly forced us in;
Else we had still refused to taste,
And perished in our sin.

5 Pity the nations, O our God;
Constrain the earth to come;
Send thy victorious word abroad
And bring the strangers home.

TWILIGHT. 8s & 7s. L. O. EMERSON.

783 *The Banner of Love.* 8s & 7s. (290)

1 JESUS spreads the banner o'er us,
Cheers our fam'shed souls with food;
He the banquet spreads before us,
Of his mystic flesh and blood.

2 Here we feel our sins forgiven,
While upon the Lamb we gaze;
And our thoughts are all of heaven,
And our lips o'erflow with praise.

3 Still in ceaseless contemplation,
Fix our hearts and eyes on thee,
Till we taste thy full salvation,
And, unveiled, thy glories see.

MENDON. L. M. GERMAN.

784 *Forget not Christ.* L. M. (298)

1 O THOU, my soul, forget no more
The Friend who all thy sorrows bore;
Let every idol be forgot;
But, O my soul, forget him not.

2 Renounce thy works and ways with grief,
And fly to this divine relief;
Nor him forget, who left his throne,
And for thy life gave up his own.

3 Eternal truth and mercy shine
In him, and he himself is thine;
And canst thou, then, with sin beset,
Such charms, such matchless charms, forget?

4 Oh, no; till life itself depart,
His name shall cheer and warm my heart;
And, lisping this, from earth I'll rise,
And join the chorus of the skies.

MANOAH. C. M. GREATOREX.

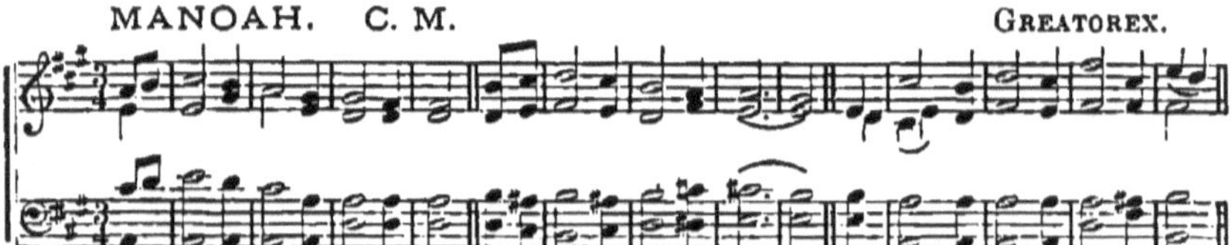

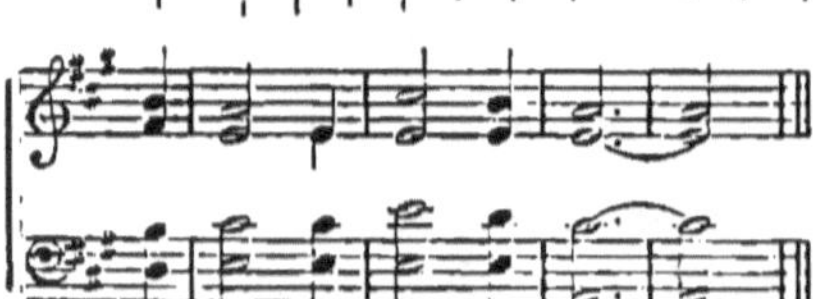

785 *Remembering Christ.* C. M. (276)

1 IF human kindness meets return,
And owns the grateful tie;
If tender thoughts within us burn,
To feel a friend is nigh;

2 Oh, shall not warmer accents tell
The gratitude we owe
To him who died our fears to quell,
And save from endless woe?

(CONTINUED.)

3 While yet his anguished soul surveyed
Those pangs he would not flee,
What love his latest words displayed!—
"Meet and remember me."

4 Remember thee! thy death, thy shame,
The griefs which thou didst bear!
O memory, leave no other name
But his recorded there.

786 *Humble Communion.* C. M. (279)

Tune—WOODLAND, No. 779.

1 LORD, at thy table we behold
The wonders of thy grace,
But most of all admire that we
Should find a welcome place!—

2 We, who were all defiled with sin,
And rebels to our God;
We, who have crucified thy Son,
And trampled on his blood.

3 What strange, surprising grace is this,
That we, so lost, have room!
Jesus our weary souls invites,
And freely bids us come.

4 Ye saints below, and hosts of heaven,
Join all your sacred powers:
No theme is like redeeming love;
No Saviour is like ours.

787 L. M. (28

Consecration in View of the Cross.

1 WHEN I survey the wondrous cross
On which the Prince of glory died,
My richest gain I count but loss,
And pour contempt on all my pride.

2 Forbid it, Lord, that I should boast,
Save in the death of Christ, my God;
All the vain things that charm me most,
I sacrifice them to his blood.

3 See, from his head, his hands, his feet,
Sorrow and love flow mingled down:
Did e'er such love and sorrow meet,
Or thorns compose so rich a crown?

4 Were all the realm of nature mine,
That were a present far too small;
Love so amazing, so divine,
Demands my soul, my life, my all.

WILLMARTH. L. M. I. B. WOODBURY.

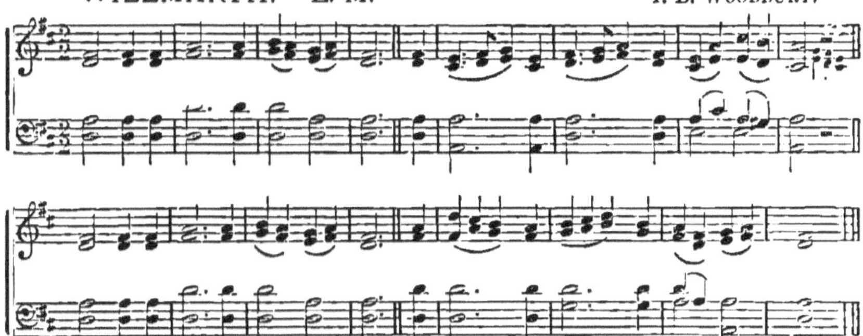

788 *Whom, having not seen, ye love.* C. M. (293)

SILOAM.

1 To Calv'ry, Lord, in spirit, now
Our weary souls repair,
To dwell upon thy dying love,
And taste its sweetness there.

2 Thou suffering Lamb, thy bleeding wounds,
With chords of love divine,
Have drawn our willing hearts to thee,
And linked our life with thine.

SILOAM. C. M. I. B. WOODBURY.

SEASONS. L. M. PLEYEL.

789 *Complete in Christ.* L. M. (261)

1 My soul complete in Jesus stands;
It fears no more the law's demands;
The smile of God is sweet within,
Where all before was guilt and sin.

2 My soul at rest in Jesus lives;
Accepts the peace his pardon gives;
Receives the grace his death secured,
And pleads the anguish he endured.

3 A song of praise my soul shall sing,
To our eternal, glorious King;
Shall worship humbly at his feet,
In whom alone it stands complete.

STOCKWELL. 8s & 7s. D. E. JONES.

790 *Atonement made.* 8s & 7s. (271)

1 Paschal Lamb, by God appointed,
All our sins on thee were laid;
By almighty love anointed,
Thou hast full atonement made.

2 All thy people are forgiven,
Through the virtue of thy blood;
Opened is the gate of heaven;
Peace is made 'twixt man and God.

KENTUCKY. S. M. OLD MELODY.

791 *The Sacrifice.* S. M. (278)

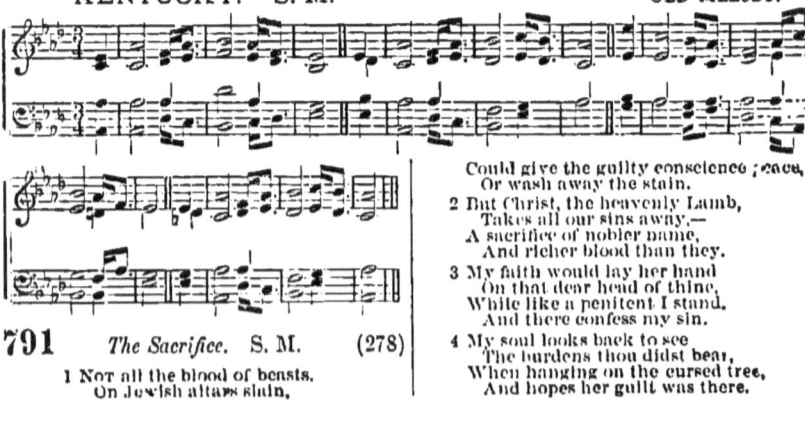

1 Not all the blood of beasts,
On Jewish altars slain,
Could give the guilty conscience peace,
Or wash away the stain.

2 But Christ, the heavenly Lamb,
Takes all our sins away,—
A sacrifice of nobler name,
And richer blood than they.

3 My faith would lay her hand
On that dear head of thine,
While like a penitent I stand,
And there confess my sin.

4 My soul looks back to see
The burdens thou didst bear,
When hanging on the cursed tree,
And hopes her guilt was there.

ROBINSON. 8s & 7s. Double. DR. T. HASTINGS.

FINE.

D.C.

792 8s & 7. (260)

Crying, Abba, Father.

1 "ABBA, Father," we approach thee
In our Saviour's precious name;
We, thy children, here assembling,
Now thy promised blessings claim:
From our sins his blood hath washed us,
'Tis through him our souls draw nigh:
And thy Spirit too hath taught us
"Abba, Father," thus to cry

2 Once as prodigals we wander'd,
In our folly, far from thee;
But thy grace, o'er sin abounding,
Rescued us from misery:
Clothed in garments of salvation,
At thy table is our place;
We rejoice, and thou rejoicest,
In the riches of thy grace.

KOZELUCK. 7s.

793 *Prayer for Christ.* 7s. (256)

1 BREAD of heaven, on thee we feed,
For thy flesh is meat indeed:
Ever let our souls be fed
With this true and living bread.

2 Vine of heaven, thy blood supplies
This blest cup of sacrifice:
Lord, thy wounds our healing give,
To thy cross we look and live.

794 *Christ's Love to us.* C. M. (280)

Tune—DUHRING, No. 749.

1 To our Redeemer's glorious name,
Awake the sacred song.
Oh, may his love,—immortal flame,—
Tune every heart and tongue.

2 His love, what mortal thought can reach,
What mortal tongue display?
Imagination's utmost stretch
In wonder dies away.

3 Dear Lord, while we adoring pay
Our humble thanks to thee,
May every heart with rapture say,
"The Saviour died for me."

795 *Prayer to Christ.* 7s. (256)

1 JESUS, Master, hear me now,
While I would renew my vow,
And record thy dying love;
Hear, and help me from above.

2 And as now I eat and drink,
Let me truly, sweetly think,
Thou didst hang upon the tree,
Broken, bleeding there for me.

TWILIGHT. 8s & 7s. L. O. EMERSON.

796 *Christ the Friend of Sinners.* 8s & 7s. (290)

1 ONE there is, above all others,
Well deserves the name of Friend;
His is love beyond a brother's,
Costly, free, and knows no end.

2 Which of all our friends, to save us,
Could or would have shed his blood?
But our Saviour died, to have us
Reconciled in him to God.

3 When he lived on earth, abasèd,
Friend of sinners was his name;
Now, above all glory raisèd,
He rejoices in the same.

WOODLAND. C. M. N. D. GOULD.

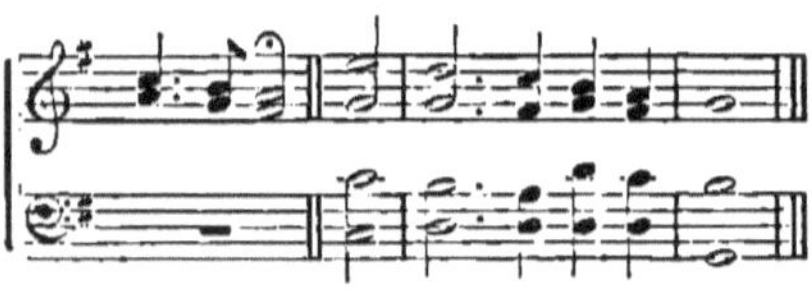

797 *Praise to Christ.* C. M. (279)

1 To him who loved the souls of men,
And washed us in his blood,
To royal honors raised our head,
And made us priests to God—

2 To him let every tongue be praise,
And every heart be love,
All grateful honors paid on earth,
And nobler songs above.

BANES. 8s, 7s, & 4. C. F. BLANDNER.

798 *After Communion.* 8s, 7s, & 4. (306)

Tune—BANES.

1 Now in parting, Father, bless us;
Saviour, still thy peace bestow;
Gracious Comforter, be with us,
As we from thy table go.
Bless us, bless us,
Father, Son, and Spirit now.

2 Bless us here, while still as strangers
Onward to our home we move;
Bless us with eternal blessings,
In our Father's house above,
Ever, ever,
Dwelling in the light of love.

799 *Blessed Feast.* S. M. (278)

Tune—KENTUCKY, No. 791.

1 SWEET feast of love divine;
'Tis grace that makes us free
To feed upon this bread and wine,
In memory, Lord, of thee.

2 Oh, if this glimpse of love
Is so divinely sweet,
What will it be, O Lord, above
Thy gladdening smile to meet?

3 To see thee face to face,
Thy perfect likeness wear,
And all thy ways of wondrous grace
Through endless years declare?

ORDINATION.

MISSIONARY CHANT. L. M. CHARLES ZEUNER.

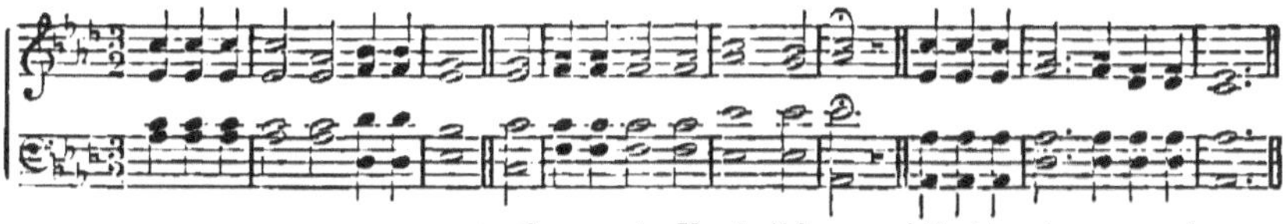

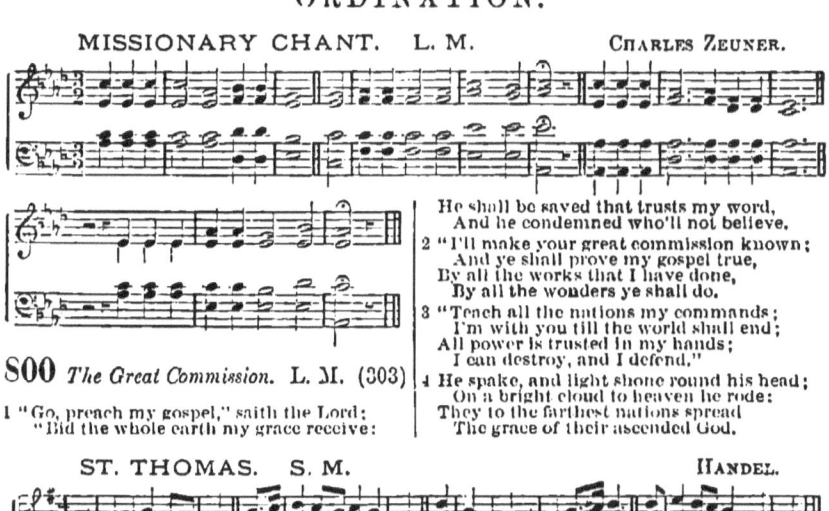

800 *The Great Commission.* L. M. (303)

1 "Go, preach my gospel," saith the Lord;
"Bid the whole earth my grace receive:
He shall be saved that trusts my word,
And he condemned who'll not believe.

2 "I'll make your great commission known;
And ye shall prove my gospel true,
By all the works that I have done,
By all the wonders ye shall do.

3 "Teach all the nations my commands;
I'm with you till the world shall end;
All power is trusted in my hands;
I can destroy, and I defend."

4 He spake, and light shone round his head;
On a bright cloud to heaven he rode:
They to the farthest nations spread
The grace of their ascended God.

ST. THOMAS. S. M. HANDEL.

801 *Ministers the Bearers of Good Tidings.* S. M. (257)

1 How beauteous are their feet
Who stand on Zion's hill:
Who bring salvation on their tongues,
And words of peace reveal!

2 How charming is their voice!
How sweet their tidings are!—
"Zion, behold thy Saviour King;
He reigns and triumphs here."

3 How happy are our ears,
That hear this joyful sound,
Which kings and prophets waited for,
And sought, but never found!

4 How blessed are our eyes,
That see this heavenly light!
Prophets and kings desired it long,
But died without the sight.

5 The watchmen join their voice,
And tuneful notes employ;
Jerusalem breaks forth in songs,
And deserts learn the joy.

6 The Lord makes bare his arm
Through all the earth abroad;
Let every nation now behold
Their Saviour and their God.

HEBRON. L. M. DR. L. MASON.

802 *Prayer for a Minister's Success.* L. M. (283)

1 FATHER of mercies, bow thine ear,
Attentive to our earnest prayer;
We plead for those who plead for thee;
Successful pleaders may they be.

2 How great their work! how vast their charge!
Do thou their anxious souls enlarge:
Their best endowments are our gain;
We share the blessings they obtain.

3 Oh, clothe with energy divine
Their words; and let those words be thine;
To them thy sacred truth reveal;
Suppress their fear, inflame their zeal.

4 Teach them to sow the precious seed;
Teach them thy chosen flock to feed;
Teach them immortal souls to gain,—
And thus reward their toil and pain.

5 Let thronging multitudes around
Hear from their lips the joyful sound;
In humble strains thy grace implore,
And feel thy Spirit's living power.

HEMANS. 6s & 4s. DR. T. HASTINGS.

803 6s & 4s. (294)

Prayer for a Minister.

1 O HOLY Lord, our God,
By heavenly hosts adored,
Hear us, we pray:
To thee the cherubim,
Angels and seraphim,
Unceasing praises bring,
Their homage pay.

2 Here give thy word success,
And this thy servant bless;
His labors own;
And while the sinner's Friend
His life and words commend,
Thy holy Spirit send,
And make him known.

3 May every passing year
More happy still appear
Than this glad day;
With numbers fill the place,
Adorn thy saints with grace,
Thy truth may all embrace,
O Lord, we pray.

804 *Thanks for the Ministry.* L. M. (261)

Tune—SEASONS, next page.

1 FATHER of mercies, in thy house
We pay our homage and our vows,
While with a grateful heart we share
These pledges of our Saviour's care.

2 The Saviour, when to heaven he rose
In splendid triumph o'er his foes,
Conferred his gifts on men below,
And wide his royal bounties flow.

3 Hence sprung th' apostles' honored name,
Sacred beyond all earthly fame;
In lowlier forms to bless our eyes,
Our pastors hence and teachers rise.

4 So shall the bright succession run
Through latest courses of the sun;
While numerous churches, by their care,
Shall rise and flourish, large and fair.

805 *Watching for Souls.* C. M. (280)

Tune—DUHRING, No. 749.

1 LET Zion's watchmen all awake,
And take th' alarm they give;
Now let them from the mouth of God
Their solemn charge receive.

2 'Tis not a cause of small import
The pastor's care demands;
But what might fill an angel's heart,
And filled a Saviour's hands.

3 They watch for souls, for which the Lord
Did heavenly bliss forego,—
For souls, which must for ever live,
In rapture or in woe.

4 May they that Jesus whom they preach,
Their own Redeemer, see;
And watch thou daily o'er their souls,
That they may watch for thee.

SEASONS. L. M. PLEYEL.

806

10s & 4s. (308)

Charge to the Ministry.

MAGOON.

1 APOSTLES of the risen Christ, go forth;
Let love compel.
Go, and in risen power proclaim his worth,
O'er every region of the dead, cold earth,—
His glory tell.

2 Tell how he lived and toiled and wept below;
Tell all his love;
Tell the dread wonders of his awful woe;
Tell how he fought our fight, and smote our foe,
Then rose above.

3 Tell how in weakness he was crucified,
But rose in power;
Went up on high, accepted, glorified;
News of his victory spread far and wide,
From hour to hour.

4 Tell how he sits at the right hand of God
In glory bright,
Making the heaven of heavens his glad abode;
Tell how he cometh with the iron rod
His foes to smite.

5 Tell how his kingdom shall thro' ages stand,
And never cease;
Spreading like sunshine over every land,
All nations bowing to his high command,
Great Prince of peace.

807

L. M. (282)

A Pastor welcomed.

Tune—HEBRON, preceding page.

1 WE bid thee welcome in the name
Of Jesus, our exalted Head:
Come as a servant; so he came;
And we receive thee in his stead.

2 Come as a shepherd: guard and keep
This fold from Satan and from sin;
Nourish the lambs, and feed the sheep,
The wounded heal, the lost bring in.

3 Come as a watchman: take thy stand
Upon the tower on Zion's height;
And when the sword comes on the land,
Warn us to fly, or teach to fight.

4 Come as a teacher sent from God,
Charged his whole counsel to declare;
Lift o'er our ranks the prophet's rod,
While we uphold thy hands with prayer.

5 Come as a messenger of peace,
Filled with the Spirit, fired with love;
Live to behold our large increase,
And die to meet us all above.

MAGOON. 10s & 4s. C. F. BLANDNER.

HEBRON. L. M. DR. L. MASON.

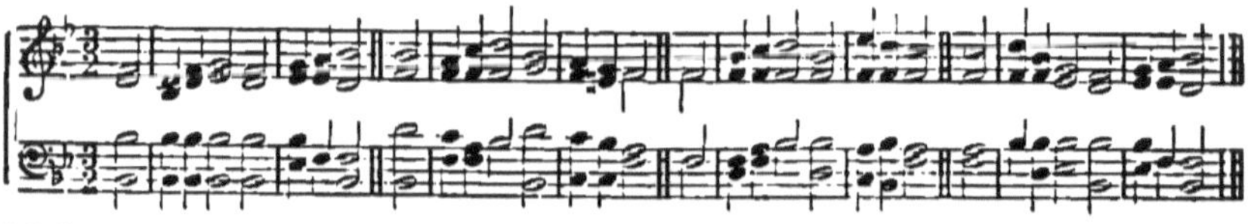

808 L. M. (283)

A Blessing sought upon a Pastor.

1 And now the solemn deed is done;
The vow is pledged, the toil begun;
Seal thou, O God, the choice above,
And ratify the pledge of love.

2 The shepherd of thy people bless;
Gird him with thy own holiness;
In duty may his pleasure be,
His glory in his zeal for thee.

3 Here let the ardent prayer arise,
Faith fix its grasp beyond the skies,
The tear of penitence be shed,
And myriads to the Saviour led.

809 L. M. (282)

Blessings desired for a Pastor.

1 'Tis done—th' important act is done—
Heaven, earth, its solemn purport know;
Its fruits, when time its race has run,
Shall through eternal ages flow.

2 The covenants of this sacred hour,
Great Shepherd of thy people, seal;
Spirit of grace, diffuse thy power,
Our vows accept, thy might reveal.

3 Behold our guide, and deign to crown
His toils, O Lamb of God, with love,
His lips inspire; each effort own;
Breathe, dwell within him, heavenly Dove.

4 Behold his charge; what wealth shall dare
With its most priceless worth to vie?
Suns, systems, worlds,—how mean they are,
Compared with souls, that cannot die!

5 Oh, when, before the judgment-seat,
The wicked quake in dread despair,
May we, all reverent at thy feet,
Pastor and flock, find mercy there.

810 L. M. (282)

Prayer for Pastors and Deacons.

1 Great King of saints, enthroned on high
Under thy care thy churches live;
Thou dost their various wants supply,
And well-appointed elders give.

2 For pastors may thy name be blest,
Who teach the doctrines of the Lord;
On deacons may thy favor rest,
Chosen according to thy word.

3 While they their works assigned fulfil,
Oh, may their souls with grace be crowned!
And patience, sympathy, and zeal,
With meekness, in their lives abound.

4 And when their service here is done,
Their labors and their conflicts o'er,
Then may they wait before thy throne,
In heaven to praise thee evermore.

811 C. M. (311)

Look ye out Men of honest Report.

DUNDEE.

1 O Jesus, in this solemn hour,
Be with thy people here;
Let thine authority and power
To rule thy church appear.

2 Oh, may the choice which we have made
By thee be ratified;
Thy servants' fitness be displayed,
As they are further tried.

3 With faithfulness may they fulfil
The office in their hands,
And seek to know and do thy will
In all that will demands.

DUNDEE. C. M.

SEASONS. L. M. PLEYEL.

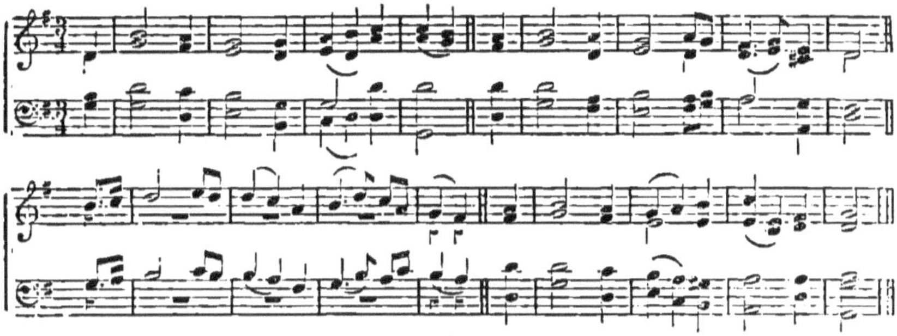

812 L. M. (261)

Prayer for more Laborers.

1 Lord of the harvest, bend thine ear,
In Zion's heritage appear;
Oh! send forth laborers filled with zeal,
Swift to obey their Master's will.

2 Our lifted eyes, O Lord, behold
The ripening harvest tinged with gold;
Wide fields are opening to our view,
The work is great, the laborers few.

3 Led by thine own almighty hand,
Let Zion's sons, in many a band,
Arise to bless the dying race,
As heralds of redeeming grace.

813 *Zeal for Souls.* C. M. (262)

Tune—Chimes, No. 739.

1 Oh, still in accents sweet and strong
Sounds forth the ancient word,—
"More reapers for white harvest fields,
More laborers for the Lord."

2 We hear the call; in dreams no more
In selfish ease we lie,
But girded for our Father's work,
Go forth beneath his sky.

3 Where prophets' word, and martyrs' blood,
And prayers of saints were sown,
We, to their labors entering in,
Would reap where they have strown.

REVIVALS.

ELTHAM. 7s. 6 lines. Dr. L. Mason.

FINE.
D.C.

814 *Prayer for the Unconverted.* 7s. 6l. (258)

1 Saved ourselves by Jesus' blood,
Let us now draw nigh to God;
Many round us blindly stray;
Moved with pity, let us pray,—
Pray that they who now are blind
Soon the way of truth may find.

2 Lord, awaken all around,
Let them know the joyful sound;
Slaves to Satan heretofore,
Let them now be slaves no more;
Lord, we turn our eyes to thee;
Set the captive sinner free.

3 Glorious things of thee are told,
What thine arm has wrought of old;
Thousands once its power confessed;
Oh, for seasons like the past!
Lord, revive the former days;
Thine the power, and thine the praise.

WILLMARTH. L. M. I. B. Woodbury.

815 *Return, O God of Hosts.* L. M. (285)

1 Lord, in the temples of thy grace
Thy saints behold thy smiling face;
And oft have seen thy glory shine,
With power and majesty divine.

2 Come, dearest Lord, thy children cry,
Our graces droop, our comforts die;
Return, and let thy glories rise
Again to our admiring eyes.

3 Till filled with light and joy and love,
Thy courts below, like those above,
Triumphant hallelujahs raise,
And heaven and earth resound thy praise.

ST. MARTINS. C. M. W. Tansur.

816 C. M. (297)

Converting Grace implored.

1 Come, Lord, in mercy come again,
With thy converting power;
The fields of Zion thirst for rain,
Oh, send a gracious shower.

2 Our hearts are filled with sore distress,
While sinners all around
Are pressing on to endless death,
And no relief is found.

3 Dear Saviour, come with quickening power,
Thy mourning people cry;
Salvation bring in mercy's hour,
Nor let the sinner die.

4 Once more let converts throng thy house,
And shouts of victory raise;
Then shall our griefs be turned to joy,
And sighs, to songs of praise.

BOYLE. S. M. Wm. B. Bradbury.

'ed. S. M. (284)

OYLE.

ord,
ce bare;
hat wakes the dead,
e hear.

rd,
thee,
bread of life,
ie!

rd,
ime;
st, our love
nflame.

rd,
showers,
hine own,
e ours.

M. (284)

ival of Religion.

OYLE.

evive
hour,
graces live
power.

ew
prayer;
again renew,
l fear.

l speak
eble clay,
ant shall break,
bey.

ous ear;
cry;
salvation near;
rely.

M. (283)

ase of the Church.

ON, No. 808.

ign, from thy throne,
blessings down:
thou art sought,
word hath taught.

on above,
rt with love;
nty stone,
power be known.

he haughtiest eyes
sorrow rise;
souls are borne
ch now they scorn.

ait
emple gate;
zeal to be
ee.

820 8s & 7s. (290)

Give Times of Refreshing.

Tune—TWILIGHT, No. 786.

1 FATHER, for thy promised blessing,
  Still we plead before thy throne;
For the times of sweet refreshing,
  Which can come from thee alone

2 Blessed earnests thou hast given,
  But in these we would not rest;
Blessings still with thee are hidden,
  Pour them forth, and make us blest

3 Prayer ascendeth to thee ever,
  Answer, Father, answer prayer;
Bless, oh, bless each weak endeavor,
  Blood-bought pardon to declare.

4 Give reviving, give refreshing,
  Give the looked-for jubilee;
To thyself may crowds be pressing,
  Bringing glory unto thee.

821 L. M. (279)

The Breath of the Spirit desired.

Tune—HEBRON, No. 808.

1 SPIRIT of everlasting grace,
  Infinite source of life, come down!
These tombs unlock, these dead upraise,
  Thy glorious power and love make known.

2 Breathe o'er this valley of the dead,
  Send forth thy quickening might abroad
Till rising from their tombs, they spread
  In full array,—the host of God.

3 Thy heritage lies desolate,
  And all thy pleasant places mourn;
Oh, look upon our low estate;
  In loving-kindness, Lord, return.

4 Now let thy glory be revealed;
  Now let thy presence with us rest;
Oh, heal us, and we shall be healed;
  Oh, bless us, and we shall be blest.

822 S. M. (284)

"Descend in all thy Power."

Tune—BOYLE, No. 817.

1 LORD God, the Holy Ghost,
  In this accepted hour,
As on the day of Pentecost,
  Descend in all thy power.

2 Like mighty rushing wind
  Upon the waves beneath,
Move with one impulse every mind;
  One soul, one feeling breathe.

3 The young, the old, inspire
  With wisdom from above;
And give us hearts and tongues of fire,
  To pray and praise and love.

4 Spirit of light, explore
  And chase our gloom away,
With lustre shining more and more
  Unto the perfect day

GARDEN. C. P. M.

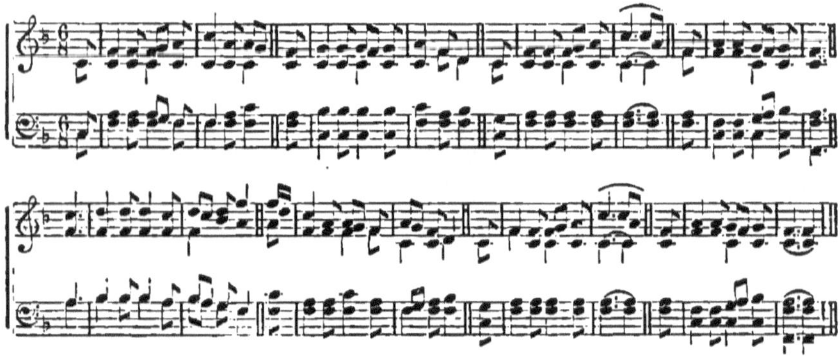

823 *Joy in Revival.* C. P. M. (288)

1 THE Lord into his garden comes,
The spices yield their rich perfumes,
The lilies grow and thrive;
Refreshing showers of grace divine,
From Jesus flow to every vine,
And make the dead revive.

2 Oh, that this dry and barren ground
In springs of water may abound,
A fruitful soil become;
The desert blossoms like the rose,
When Jesus conquers all his foes,
And makes his people one.

3 The glorious time is rolling on,
The gracious work is now begun,
My soul a witness is;
Come taste and see the pardon free
To all mankind, as well as me;
Who come to Christ may live.

INVITATION. 8s, 7s, & 4.

FINE.

D.C.

824 8s, 7s, & 4. (287)

Prayer for Revival.

1 SAVIOUR, visit thy plantation,
Grant us, Lord, a gracious rain;
All will come to desolation,
Unless thou return again.
Lord, revive us;
All our help must come from thee.

2 Keep no longer at a distance,
Shine upon us from on high,
Lest, for want of thine assistance,
Every plant should droop and die.
Lord, revive us;
All our help must come from thee.

3 Let our mutual love be fervent,
Make us prevalent in prayers;
Let each one esteemed thy servant
Shun the world's bewitching snares
Lord, revive us;
All our help must come from thee.

4 Break the tempter's fatal power;
Turn the stony heart to flesh;
And begin, from this good hour,
To revive thy work afresh.
Lord, revive us;
All our help must come from thee

EVEN ME. 8s, 7s, & 3. WM. B. BRADBURY.

825

Longing for divine Favor. 8s, 7s, & 3. (287)

1 LORD, I hear of showers of blessing
Thou art scattering, full and free,—
Showers, the thirsting land refreshing;
Let some droppings fall on me,—
Even me.

2 Pass me not, O God, our Father,
Sinful though my heart may be;
Thou might'st leave me, but the rather
Let thy mercy light on me,—
Even me.

3 Pass me not, O gracious Saviour;
Let me live and cling to thee;
For I'm longing for thy favor;
Whilst thou'rt calling, oh, call me,—
Even me.

4 Pass me not, O mighty Spirit;
Thou canst make the blind to see.
Witnesser of Jesus' merit,
Speak some word of power to me,—
Even me.

5 Love of God, so pure and changeless;
Blood of Christ, so rich, so free;
Grace of God, so strong and boundless
Magnify it all in me,—
Even me.

CHANT.—"Wilt Thou not visit me?" WM. B. BRADBURY.

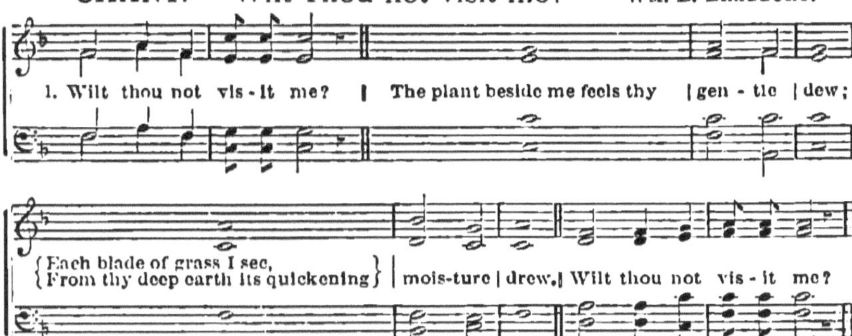
1. Wilt thou not vis - it me? | The plant beside me feels thy | gen - tle | dew; |
{Each blade of grass I see,
{From thy deep earth its quickening} | mois-ture | drew. | Wilt thou not vis - it me?

826

Wilt thou not visit me? 6s & 10s. (255)

2 WILT thou not visit me? |
Thy morning calls on me with | cheering | tone; |
And every hill and tree
Lift but one voice, the voice of | thee a- | lone. |
Wilt thou not visit me?

3 Come, for I need thy love, |
More than the flower the dew, or | grass the | rain; |
Come, like the holy dove,
And let me in thy sight rejoice to | live a- | gain. |
Wilt thou not visit me?

4 Yes, thou wilt visit me; |
Nor plant, nor tree, thine eye de- | lights so | well, |
As when from sin set free,
Man's spirit comes with thine in | peace to | dwell. |
Yes, thou wilt visit me.

KENTUCKY. S. M.

OLD MELODY.

827 S. M. (278)

Ingratitude deplored.

1 Is this the kind return?
Are these the thanks we owe,
Thus to abuse eternal love,
Whence all our blessings flow?

2 To what a stubborn frame
Has sin reduced our mind!
What strange, rebellious wretches we!
And God as strangely kind.

3 Turn, turn us, mighty God,
And mould our souls afresh;
Break, sovereign grace, these hearts of stone
And give us hearts of flesh.

4 Let past ingratitude
Provoke our weeping eyes,
And hourly, as new mercies fall,
Let hourly thanks arise.

SOLITUDE. 7s.

L. T. DOWNES.

828 7s. (295)

My Sheep hear my Voice.

1 JESUS, seek thy wandering sheep;
Bring me back and lead and keep·
Take on thee my every care,
Bear me, on thy bosom bear.

2 Let me know my Shepherd's voice;
More and more in thee rejoice;
More and more of thee receive;
Ever in thy Spirit live,—

3 Live till all thy life I know,
Foll'wing thee, my Lord, below;
Gladly then from earth remove;
Gathered to the fold above.

4 Oh, that I at last may stand
With the sheep at thy right hand,
Take the crown so freely given,
Enter in by thee to heaven!

SILOAM. C. M.

I. B. WOODBURY.

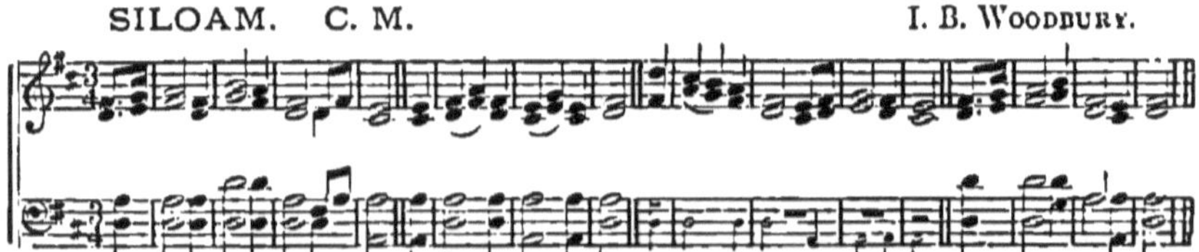

829 *Pardoning Love.* C. M. (293)

Tune—SILOAM

1 How oft, alas, this wretched heart
Has wandered from the Lord!
How oft my roving thoughts depart,
Forgetful of his word!

2 Yet sovereign mercy calls, "Return!"
Dear Lord, and may I come?
My vile ingratitude I mourn;
Oh, take the wanderer home.

3 And canst thou, wilt thou yet forgive,
And bid my crimes remove?
And shall a pardoned rebel live
To speak thy wondrous love?

4 Thy pardoning love, so free, so sweet,
Blest Saviour, I adore;
Oh, keep me at thy sacred feet,
And let me rove no more.

830 L. M. (235)

Dear Lord, to thee I would return.

Tune—WILLMARTH, No. 815.

1 AH, wretched, vile, ungrateful heart,
That can from Jesus thus depart;
Thus, fond of trifles, vainly rove,
Forgetful of a Saviour's love.

2 Dear Lord, to thee I would return,
And at thy feet repenting mourn;
There let me view thy pardoning love,
And never from thy sight remove.

3 Oh, let thy love, with sweet control,
Bind every passion of my soul;
Bid every vain desire depart,
And dwell for ever in my heart.

EXPOSTULATION. 11s.

831 *The Master is coming.* 11s. (289)

1 THE Master is coming, he calleth for thee,
And lov'd ones are hast'ning their Saviour to see;
He's full of compassion, why will you delay?
He's calling, still calling, oh, come, come away!
The Master is coming, he calleth for thee;
Come, trust in his mercy, salvation is free.

2 The Master is coming, receive him and live;
Oh, will you not trust him your sins to forgive?
On Calvary's cross, amid anguish and pain,
Thy ransom was purchased when Jesus was slain.

3 The Master is coming, he calleth to-day;
Awake from thy slumbers, to labor and pray;
The morning is breaking, the noon-tide is near,
And evening's dark shadows will quickly appear.

4 The Master is coming, to call from the grave
His lov'd ones to glory; he's mighty to save;
And all who believe him in rapture shall sing
Salvation thro' Jesus, our Master and King.

832 11s. (288)

Slumbering Professors exhorted.

1 WHY sleep we, my brethren? come, let us arise;
Oh, why should we slumber in sight of the prize?
Salvation is nearer, our days are far spent;
Oh, let us be active; awake, and repent.

2 Oh, how can we slumber? the Master is come,
And calling on sinners to seek them a home;
The Spirit and Bride now in concert unite,
The weary they welcome, the careless invite.

3 Oh, how can we slumber, when so much was done,
To purchase salvation, by Jesus, the Son?
Now mercy is proffered, and justice displayed,
Now God can be honored and sinners be saved.

FERGUSON. S. M.

GEO. KINGSLEY.

833 *Joy in the Salvation of Sinners.* S. M. (270)

1 WHO can forbear to sing,
Who can refuse to praise,
When Zion's high, celestial King,
His saving power displays?—

2 When sinners at his feet,
By mercy conquered, fall?
When grace and truth and justice meet
And peace unites them all?

3 Who can forbear to praise
Our high, celestial King,
When sovereign, rich, redeeming grace
Invites our tongues to sing?

PASS ME NOT. 8s & 5s.

W. H. DOANE.

From "Songs of Devotion," by permission.

CHORUS.
D.S.

834 *Pass me not.* 8s & 5s. (286)

1 PASS me not, O gentle Saviour,
Hear my humble cry;
While on others thou art smiling,
Do not pass me by.

Cho.—Saviour, Saviour, hear my humble cry;
While on others thou art calling
Do not pass me by.

2 Let me at a throne of mercy
Find a sweet relief;
Kneeling there in deep contrition,
Help my unbelief.—*Cho.*

3 Trusting only in thy merit,
Would I seek thy face;
Heal my wounded, broken spirit;
Save me by thy grace.—*Cho.*

4 Thou, the spring of all my comfort,
More than life to me,
Whom have I on earth beside thee?
Whom in heaven but thee?—*Cho.*

835 *Sin confessed.* S. M. (270)

FERGUSON.

1 ONCE more we meet to pray,
Once more our guilt confess;
Turn not, O Lord, thine ear away
From creatures in distress,

2 Our sins to heaven ascend,
And there for vengeance cry;
O God, behold the sinner's Friend,
Who intercedes on high.

3 Though we are vile indeed,
And well deserve thy curse,
The merits of thy Son we plead,
Who lived and died for us.

4 Now let thy bosom yearn,
As it hath done before;
Return to us, O God, return,
And ne'er forsake us more.

836 L. M. (285)

The wandering Soul exhorted.

Tune—WILLMARTH, next page.

1 RETURN, my wandering soul, return,
And seek an injured Father's face;
Those warm desires that in thee burn
Were kindled by redeeming grace.

2 Return, my wandering soul, return,
And seek a Father's melting heart;
His pitying eyes thy grief discern,
His heavenly balm shall heal thy smart.

3 Return, my wandering soul, return;
Thy dying Saviour bids thee live;
Go, view his bleeding side, and learn
How freely Jesus can forgive.

4 Return, my wandering soul, return,
And wipe away the falling tear;
'Tis God who says, "No longer mourn;"
'Tis Mercy's voice invites thee near.

CONVERTS WELCOMED.

WILLMARTH. L. M. I. B WOODBURY.

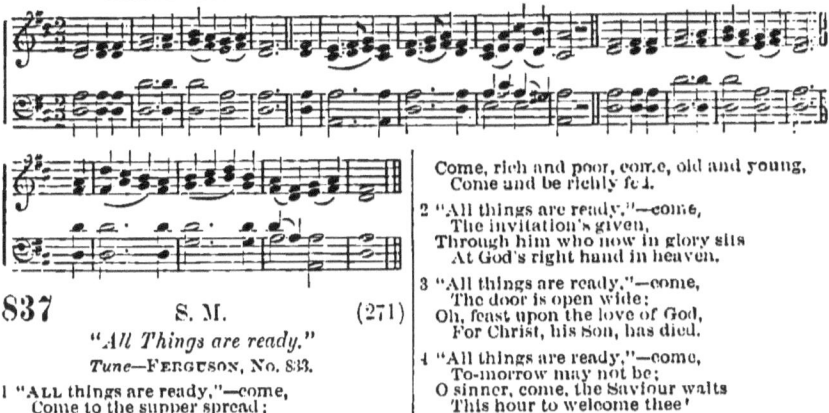

837 S. M. (271)

"All Things are ready."

Tune—FERGUSON, No. 833.

1 "ALL things are ready,"—come,
Come to the supper spread;
Come, rich and poor, come, old and young,
Come and be richly fed.

2 "All things are ready,"—come,
The invitation's given,
Through him who now in glory sits
At God's right hand in heaven.

3 "All things are ready,"—come,
The door is open wide:
Oh, feast upon the love of God,
For Christ, his Son, has died.

4 "All things are ready,"—come,
To-morrow may not be;
O sinner, come, the Saviour waits
This hour to welcome thee!

CONVERTS WELCOMED.

MANOAH. C. M. GREATOREX.

838 *Converts welcomed.* C. M. (277)

1 COME in, thou blessed of the Lord,
Stranger nor foe art thou:
We welcome thee with warm accord,
Our friend, our brother now.

2 The hand of fellowship, the heart
Of love, we offer thee:
Leaving the world, thou dost but part
From lies and vanity.

839 L. M. (283)

On receiving new Members.

Tune—HEBRON, No. 808.

1 KINDRED in Christ, for his dear sake,
A hearty welcome here receive,
May we together now partake
The joys which only he can give.

2 May he, by whose kind care we meet,
Send his good Spirit from above,
Make our communications sweet,
And cause our hearts to burn with love.

3 Forgotten be each worldly theme,
When Christians see each other thus;
We only wish to speak of him
Who lived and died and reigns for us.

4 We'll talk of all he did and said
And suffered for us here below,
The path he marked for us to tread,
And what he's doing for us now.

5 Thus, as the moments pass away
We'll love and wonder and adore,
And long to see the glorious day
When we shall meet to part no more.

ATTICA. L. M.

840 L. M. (291)

Come in, thou blessed of the Lord.

1 Come in, thou blessed of the Lord;
Oh, come in Jesus' precious name;
We welcome thee with one accord,
And trust the Saviour does the same.

2 Those joys which earth cannot afford
We'll seek in fellowship to prove,
Joined in one spirit to our Lord,
Together bound by mutual love.

3 And while we pass this vale of tears,
We'll make our joys and sorrows known;
We'll share each other's hopes and fears,
And count a brother's case our own.

4 Once more our welcome we repeat;
Receive assurance of our love;
Oh, may we all together meet
Around the throne of God above.

841 7s. (295)

The Convert's Choice.

1 People of the living God,
I have sought the world around,
Paths of sin and sorrow trod,
Peace and comfort nowhere found.

2 Now to you my spirit turns,—
Turns, a fugitive unblest;
Brethren, where your altar burns
Oh, receive me into rest.

3 Lonely I no longer roam,
Like the cloud, the wind, the wave;
Where you dwell shall be my home,
Where you die shall be my grave.

4 Mine the God whom you adore;
Your Redeemer shall be mine;
Earth can fill my soul no more;
Every idol I resign.

SOLITUDE. 7s. L. T. Downes.

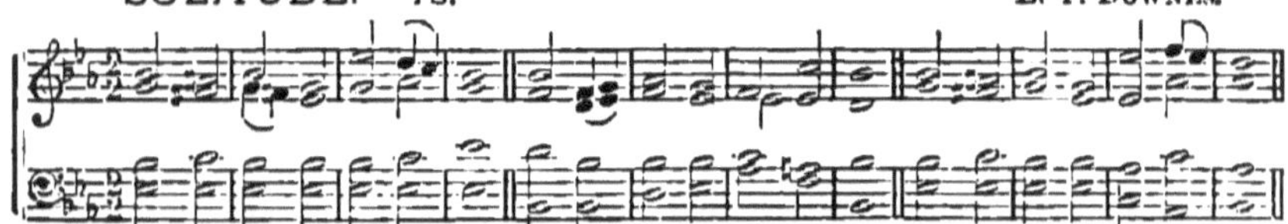

842 L. M. (291)

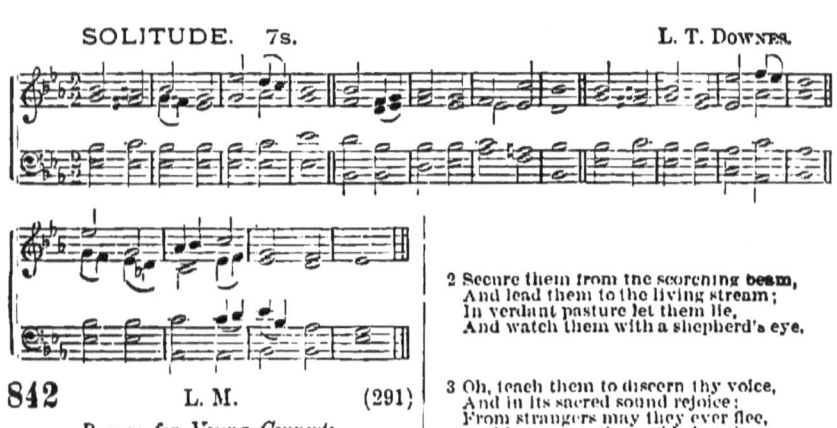

Prayer for Young Converts

Attica.

1 Jesus, thou Shepherd of the sheep,
Thy little flock in safety keep;
These lambs within thine arms now take,
Nor let them e'er thy fold forsake.

2 Secure them from the scorching beam,
And lead them to the living stream;
In verdant pasture let them lie,
And watch them with a shepherd's eye.

3 Oh, teach them to discern thy voice,
And in its sacred sound rejoice;
From strangers may they ever flee,
And know no other guide but thee.

4 Lord, bring thy sheep that wander yet,
And let their number be complete;
Then let the flock from earth remove,
And reach the heavenly fold above.

843 *The Kind Shepherd.* C. M. (293)

Tune—Siloam, No. 829.

1 See Israel's gentle Shepherd stand,
With all-engaging charms;
Hark! how he calls the tender lambs,
And folds them in his arms.

2 "Permit them to approach," he cries,
"Nor scorn their humble name;
For 'twas to bless such souls as these
The Lord of angels came."

3 We bring them, Lord, by fervent prayer,
And yield them up to thee;
With humble trust that we are thine,
Thine let our offspring be.

844 L. M. (302)

Praise offered by Children.

Tune—Anvern, No. 743.

1 We come, we come, with loud acclaim
To sing the praise of Jesus' name;
With joyful heart and smiling face
We gather round the throne of grace,

2 And lowly bend to offer there,
From infant lips, our humble prayer
To him who slept on Mary's knee,
A gentle child as young as we.

3 We come, we come, the song to swell,
To him who loved our world so well,
That, stooping from his Father's throne,
He died to claim it as his own.

4 Oh, thus may we in heaven above
Unite in praises and in love;
And still the angels fill their home
With joyful cry: "They come, they come!"

SALVATORI. 7s & 6s. Arranged by C. F. Blandner.

845 L. M. (302)

The Children cry, Hosanna.

Tune—Anvern, No. 743.

1 Exalted Jesus, heavenly King,
Angels to thee their offerings bring;
And yet thou scornest not the praise,
The simple song that children raise.

2 And hast thou deigned from high to come,
And make this fallen world thy home?
Yea, bow thee to the cross and grave,
And die a sinful worm to save?

3 Crown him with praises, all that live;
To him your ceaseless homage give;
Praises and homage well are due
To him who gave himself for you.

4 Exalted Saviour, risen Lord,
Jesus, by all in heaven adored,
Set up with man thy fallen throne,
And make all hearts on earth thine own.

846 *Children's Praises.* 7s & 6s. (304)

1 Oh, dear and blessed Jesus,
We come with songs of praise,
Our thankful hearts and voices
To thee we gladly raise;
Though thou art high and holy,
'Mid angels bright above,
Yet we on earth so lowly
May reach thee with our love.

2 For thou in thy compassion
Didst leave thy heavenly home,
And didst in Bethlehem's manger
A little child become;
Didst live a life of sorrow,
And die a death of shame,
That thou might'st give salvation
To all who trust thy name.

3 Oh, dear and blessed Jesus,
Accept our loving song,
As we now come to praise thee,
A thankful, happy throng;
As we recount thy story,
We wonder and adore;
Oh, may we sing thy glory
Both now and evermore.

BREAKING AWAY. 10s & 11s. REV. R. LOWRY.

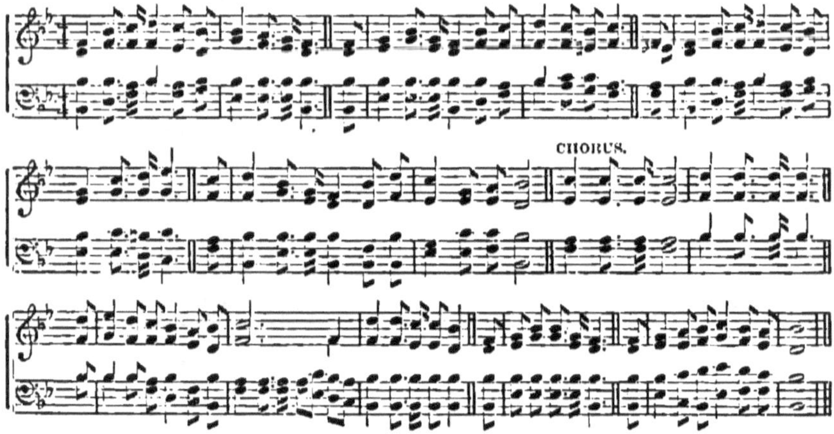
CHORUS.

847

Breaking away. 10s & 11s. (275)

1 PILGRIM, rejoice! for the mantle of sin,
That hung like a pall o'er thy spirit within,
Is yielding at last to the smile of the day;
The gloom and the darkness are breaking away.

Breaking away! breaking away!
The clouds are all breaking away!
The sunshine is coming,
And lighting up the day,
The clouds are all breaking away.

2 Wild was the storm, but thy Saviour was near,
In all thy affliction to comfort and cheer;
His mercy unfolding the brightness of day,
The clouds of thy sorrow are breaking away

3 Nearer the close of thy peril and strife,
And nearer thy home o'er the ocean of life;
Press onward! the angels are guarding thy way;
The mist and the shadow are breaking away.

4 Pilgrim, rejoice! and thy courage renew;
Look up! for the heaven of joy is in view;
One stroke of the oar, and thy spirit can say,
From earth and its toil I have broken away.

SILOAM. C. M. I. B. WOODBURY.

848

Early Piety. C. M. (293)

1 By cool Siloam's shady rill
How fair the lily grows!
How sweet the breath, beneath the hill,
Of Sharon's dewy rose!

2 Lo! such the child whose early feet
The paths of peace hath trod,
Whose secret heart, with influence sweet,
Is upward drawn to God.

3 By cool Siloam's shady rill
The lily must decay;
The rose that blooms beneath the hill
Must shortly fade away.

4 And soon, too soon, the wintry hour
Of man's maturer age
Will shake the soul with sorrow's power,
And stormy passion's rage.

5 O thou who givest life and breath,
We seek thy grace alone,
In childhood, manhood, age, and death,
To keep us still thine own.

JESUS OF NAZARETH. L. M. 6 lines. T. E. PERKINS.

From "Songs of Salvation," by permission.

1st time.
2d time.

849 *Jesus of Nazareth passeth by.* L. M. 6l. (281)

1 WHAT means this eager, anxious throng,
Which moves with busy haste along,—
These wondrous gatherings day by day?
What means this strange commotion, say?
In accents hushed the throng reply:
"Jesus of Nazareth passeth by."

2 Who is this Jesus? why should he
The city move so mightily?
A passing stranger, has he skill
To move the multitude at will?
Again the stirring tones reply:
"Jesus of Nazareth passeth by."

3 Jesus! 'tis he who once below
Man's pathway trod, 'mid pain and woe;
And burdened ones, where'er he came,
Brought out their sick and deaf and lame.
The blind rejoiced to hear the cry:
"Jesus of Nazareth passeth by."

4 Again he comes! From place to place
His holy footprints we can trace.
He pauseth at our threshold,—nay,
He enters,—condescends to stay.
Shall we not gladly raise the cry:
"Jesus of Nazareth passeth by"?

5 Ho! all ye heavy-laden, come!
Here's pardon, comfort, rest, and home.
Ye wanderers from a Father's face,
Return, accept his proffered grace.
Ye tempted, there's a refuge nigh:
"Jesus of Nazareth passeth by."

6 But if you still this call refuse,
And all his wondrous love abuse,
Soon will he sadly from you turn,
Your bitter prayer for pardon spurn.
"Too late! too late!" will be the cry,—
"Jesus of Nazareth *has passed by.*"

KEDESH. 8s, 7s, & 4. DR. L. MASON.

FINE.
D.C.

850 *He shall feed his Flock.* 8s, 7s, & 4. (305)

1 SAVIOUR, like a shepherd lead us;
Much we need thy tenderest care;
In thy pleasant pastures feed us;
For our use thy folds prepare:
Blessed Jesus,
Thou hast bought us, thine we are.

2 Thou hast promised to receive us,
Poor and sinful though we be;
Thou hast mercy to relieve us,
Grace to cleanse, and power to free:
Blessed Jesus,
We will early turn to thee.

3 Early let us seek thy favor;
Early let us do thy will;
Blessed Lord, and only Saviour,
With thy love our bosoms fill:
Blessed Jesus,
Thou hast loved us, love us still.

WELCOME HOME. 8s & 6s. REV. R. LOWRY.

DUET.
CHORUS.

FINE.
D.S.

851 *Welcome Home.* 8s & 6s. (292)

1 THERE is a realm where Jesus reigns,
A home of grace and love,
Where angels wait with sweetest strains
To greet the saints above.

They'll sing their welcome home to me,
They'll sing their welcome home to me,
The angels will stand on the heavenly strand,
And sing their welcome home!

2 There sons of earth will join to bless
The precious Saviour's name,
Clothed in his perfect righteousness,
And saved from sin and shame

3 Yet all, alas! may not be there,
For some will slight his grace;
Tho' now he calls, they do not care
To turn and seek his face.

ATTICA. L. M.

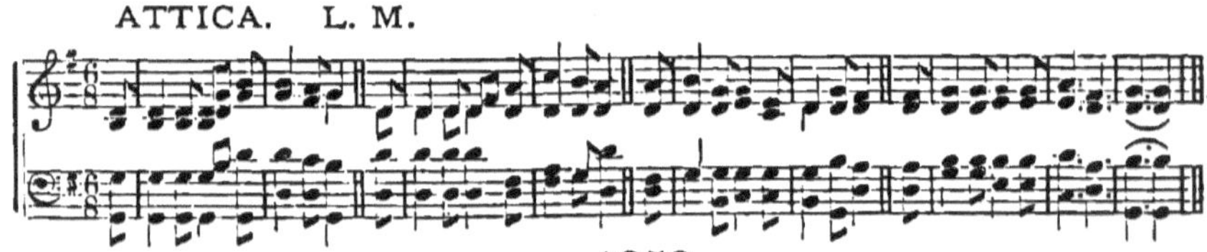

852 *The little Wanderer.* L. M. (291)

1 JESUS, to thy dear arms I flee,
I have no other help but thee;
For thou dost suffer me to come;
Oh, take a little wanderer home.

2 Jesus, I'll try my cross to bear,
I'll follow thee and never fear;
From thy dear fold I would not roam;
Oh, take a little wanderer home.

3 Jesus, I cannot see thee here,
Yet still I know thou'rt very near;
From thy dear fold I would not roam;
Oh, take a little wanderer home.

4 And now, dear Jesus, I am thine;
Oh, be thou ever, ever mine,
And let me never, never roam
From thee, the little wanderer's home.

853 *Children saved.* C. M. (297)

Tune—ST. MARTIN, No 816.

1 AROUND the throne of God in heaven,
Thousands of children stand;
Children, whose sins are all forgiven,
A holy, happy band.

2 What brought them to that world above,
That heaven so bright and fair,
Where all is peace and joy and love?
How came those children there?

3 Because the Saviour shed his blood
To wash away their sin;
Bathed in that pure and precious flood,
Behold them white and clean!

4 On earth they sought their Saviour's grace
On earth they loved his name;
So now they see his blessed face,
And stand before the Lamb.

LEAD THEM, MY GOD, TO THEE. 6s & 4s. R. LOWRY.

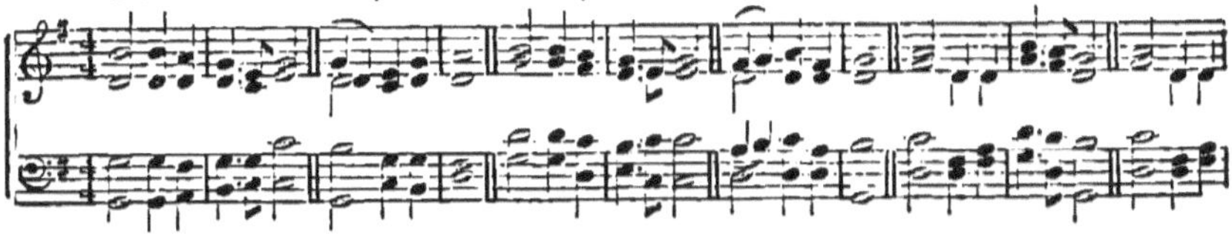

854 6s & 4s. (289)

Lead them, my God, to thee.

1 LEAD them, my God, to thee,
Lead them to thee,
These children dear of mine,
Thou gavest me;
Oh, by thy love divine,
Lead them, my God, to thee;
Lead them, lead them,
Lead them to thee.

2 When earth looks bright and fair
Festive and gay,
Let no delusive snare
Lure them astray;
But from temptation's power
Lead them, my God, to thee

3 E'en for such little ones,
Christ came a child,
And through this world of sin
Moved undefiled;
Oh, for his sake I pray,
Lead them, my God, to thee.

4 Yea, though my faith be dim,
I would believe
That thou this precious gift
Wilt now receive;
Oh, take their young hearts now,
Lead them, my God, to thee.

GO AND TELL JESUS. 10s. T. F. SEWARD.

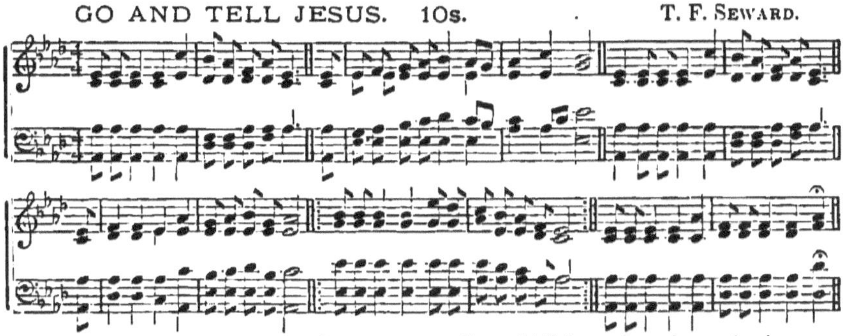

855 *Go and tell Jesus.* 10s. (274)

1 Go and tell Jesus, weary, sin-sick soul;
He'll ease thee of thy burden, make thee whole;
Look up to him, he only can forgive;
Believe on him, and thou shalt surely live.
Go and tell Jesus, he only can forgive;
Go and tell Jesus, oh, turn to him and live;
Go and tell Jesus, he only can forgive.

2 Go and tell Jesus, when your sins arise
Like mountains of deep guilt before your eyes;
His blood was spilt, his precious life he gave,
That mercy, peace, and pardon you might have.
Go and tell Jesus, he only can forgive; etc.

3 Go and tell Jesus, he'll dispel thy fears,
Will calm thy doubts, and wipe away thy tears;
He'll take thee in his arms, and on his breast
Thou may'st be happy, and for ever rest.
Go and tell Jesus, he only can forgive; etc

FERGUSON. S. M. Geo. Kingsley.

856 *Prayer for the Young.* S. M. (270)

1 Great God, now condescend
To bless our rising race;
Soon may their willing spirits bend
To thy victorious grace.

2 Oh, what a vast delight
Their happiness to see;
Our warmest wishes all unite
To lead these souls to thee.

3 Dear Lord, thy Spirit pour
Upon our infant seed;
Oh, bring the long'd-for, happy hour
That makes them thine indeed!

4 May they receive thy word,
Confess the Saviour's name,
Then follow their despisèd Lord
Through the baptismal stream.

5 Thus let our favored race
Surround thy sacred board,
There to adore thy sovereign grace,
And sing their dying Lord.

857 *Prayer for the Children.* 8s & 7s. (290)

1 Saviour, who thy flock art feeding
With the Shepherd's kindest care,
And the feeble gently leading
While the lambs thy bosom share,

2 Now, these little ones receiving,
Fold them in thy gracious arm;
There we know, thy word believing,
Only there, secure from harm.

3 Never, from thy pasture roving,
Let them be the lion's prey;
Let thy tenderness so loving
Keep them all life's dangerous way.

4 Then, within thy fold eternal,
Let them find a resting-place,
Feed in pastures ever vernal,
Drink the rivers of thy grace.

TWILIGHT. 8s & 7s. L. O. Emerson.

CHIMES. C. M. Dr. L. Mason

858 *Happiness of Early Piety.* C. M. (262)

1 How happy is the child who hears
Instruction's warning voice,
And who celestial wisdom makes
His early, only choice!

2 For she has treasures greater far
Than east or west unfold,
And her rewards more precious are
Than all their stores of gold.

3 She guides the young with innocence
In pleasure's path to tread;
A crown of glory she bestows
Upon the hoary head.

4 According as her labors rise,
So her rewards increase;
Her ways are ways of pleasantness,
And all her paths are peace.

859 *Importance of Religion to the Young.* C. M. (264)

Tune—New York, No. 767.

1 Religion is the chief concern
Of mortals here below;
May we its great importance learn,
Its sovereign virtue know.

2 Religion should our thoughts engage
Amid our youthful bloom;
'Twill fit us for declining age,
And for the solemn tomb.

3 Oh, may our hearts, by grace renewed,
Be our Redeemer's throne;
And be our stubborn wills subdued,
His government to own.

DEDICATIONS.

WILLINGTON. L. M. Williams.

860 *Dedication Hymn.* L. M. (296)

1 O God the Father, Christ the Son,
And Holy Spirit, three in one,
Accept this gift our hearts have sought,—
Our hands in Christian love have wrought.

2 Here may the light of gospel truth
Illumine age, enlighten youth:
In many hearts that grace begin,
Which saves from sorrow and from sin,

3 May Jesus here that power display
Which changes darkness into day,
And open wide those gates of love
That lead to blessedness above.

4 O Jesus Christ, our sovereign Lord,
By angels and by saints adored,
Accept this tribute of our praise,
And with thy glory fill this place.

861 *A Blessing implored.* L. M. (296)

1 Here, in thy name, eternal God,
We build this earthly house for thee;
Oh, choose it for thy fixed abode,
And guard it long from error free.

2 Here, when thy people seek thy face,
And dying sinners pray to live,
Hear thou, in heaven, thy dwelling-place,
And when thou hearest, Lord, forgive.

3 Here, when thy messengers proclaim
The blessed gospel of thy Son,
Still by the power of his great name
Be mighty signs and wonders done.

4 When children's voices raise the song,
Hosanna! to their heavenly King,
Let heaven with earth the strain prolong;
Hosanna! let the angels sing.

5 Thy glory never hence depart:
Yet choose not, Lord, this house alone;
Thy kingdom come to every heart;
In every bosom fix thy throne.

862 8s, 7s, & 4. (306)

Prayer for the Holy Trinity.

Tune—Banes, No. 798.

1 God the Father, high in glory,
Seated on the eternal throne,
Lo! thy children, bowed before thee,
Seek thy smile and grace alone.
God the Father,
Make to us thy mercies known.

2 God the Son, our blessed Saviour,
Standing at the mercy-seat,
Thou hast pledged thy gracious favor
Wheresoe'er thy people meet
Blessed Jesus,
Bless us, waiting at thy feet.

3 God the Spirit, Sanctifier,
Light and life and power divine,
O'er us, cloud of hallowed fire,
Let thy sacred presence shine.
Holy Spirit,
Make this tabernacle thine.

4 God the Father, Son, and Spirit,
Love's essential oneness, come:
If we now thy grace inherit,
Make this humble place thy home.
Great Jehovah,
Let the answering glory come.

SOLITUDE. 7s. L. T. DOWNES.

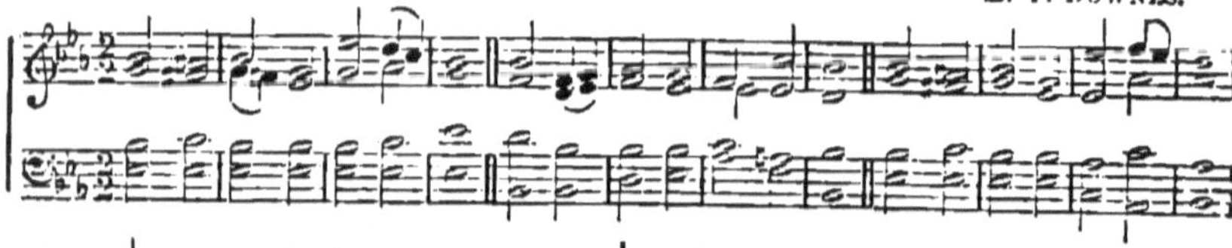

863 7s. (295)

Prayer for divine Blessings.

1 LORD of hosts, to thee we raise
Here a house of prayer and praise;
Thou thy people's hearts prepare
Here to meet for praise and prayer.

2 Let the living here be fed
With thy word, the heavenly bread;
Here, in hope of glory blest,
May the dead be laid to rest.

3 Here to thee a temple stand
While the sea shall gird the land,
Here reveal thy mercy sure
While the sun and moon endure.

4 Hallelujah!—earth and sky
To the joyful sound reply;
Hallelujah!—hence ascend
Prayer and praise till time shall end.

WILLINGTON. L. M. WILLIAMS.

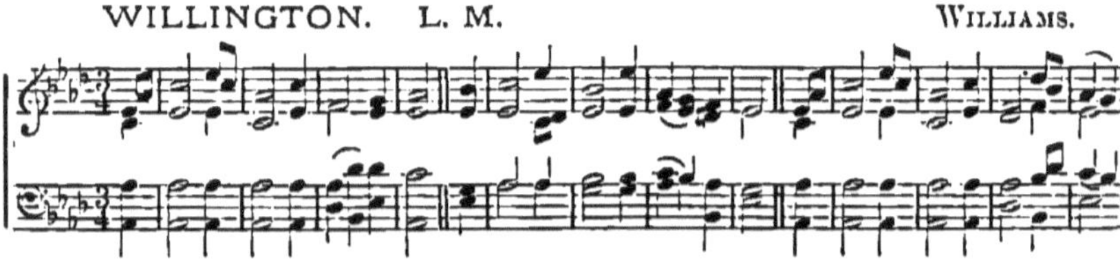

864 *Dedication.* L. M. (296)

1 OH, bow thine ear, Eternal One!
On thee our heart adoring calls;
To thee the followers of thy Son
Have raised and now devote these walls.

2 Here let thy holy day be kept;
And be this place, to worship given,
Like that bright spot where Jacob slept,
The house of God, the gate of heaven.

3 Here may thine honor dwell; and here,
As incense, let thy children's prayer,
From contrite hearts and lips sincere,
Rise on the still and holy air.

4 Here be thy praise devoutly sung;
Here let thy truth beam forth to save,
As when, of old, thy spirit hung,
On wings of light, o'er Jordan's wave.

5 And when the lips, that with thy name
Are vocal now, to dust shall turn,
On others may devotion's flame
Be kindled here, and purely burn.

AVONDALE. C. M.

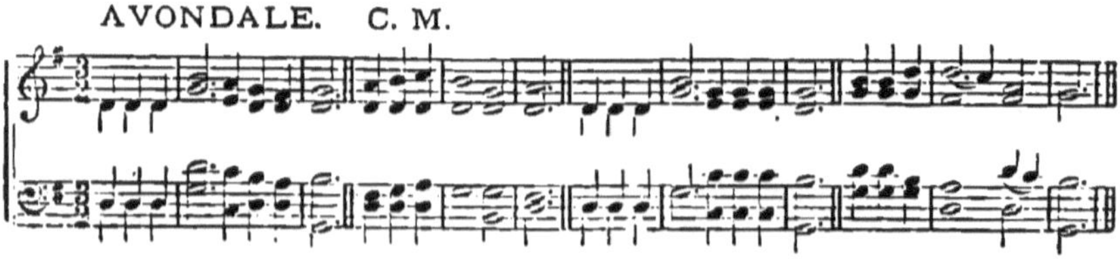

865 *Divine Blessing solicited.* C. M. (255)

AVONDALE.

1 To thee this temple we devote,
Our Father and our God;
Accept it thine, and seal it now
Thy Spirit's blest abode.

2 Here may the prayer of faith ascend,
The voice of praise arise;
Oh, may each lowly service prove
Accepted sacrifice.

3 Here may the sinner learn his guilt,
And weep before his Lord;
Here, pardoned, sing a Saviour's love,
And here his vows record.

4 Here may affliction dry the tear,
And learn to trust in God,
Convinced it is a Father smites,
And love that guides the rod.

5 Peace be within these sacred walls;
Prosperity be here;
Long smile upon thy people, Lord,
And evermore be near.

HILLSIDE. L. M. L. O. EMERSON.

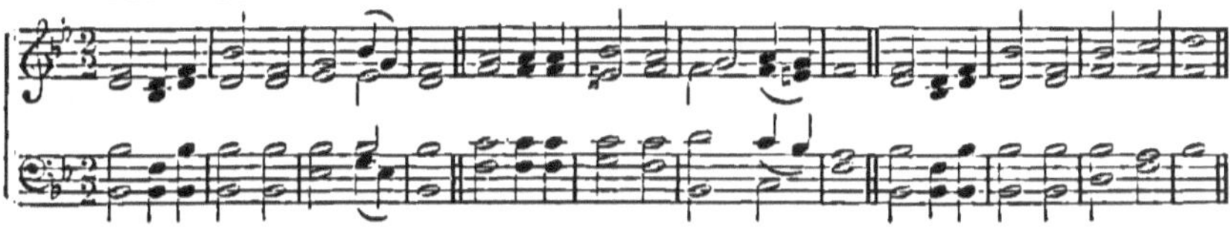

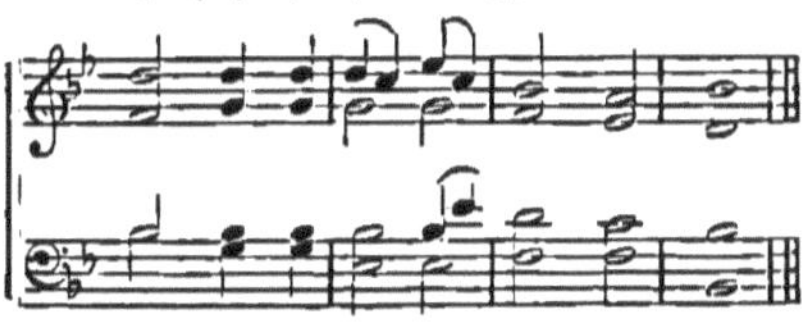

866 *God's Condescension.* L. M. (301)

1 AND will the great, eternal God
On earth establish his abode?
And will he, from his heavenly throne,
Avow our temples for his own?

2 These walls we to thy honor raise;
Long may they echo with thy praise;
And thou, descending, fill the place
With choicest tokens of thy grace.

3 Here let the great Redeemer reign,
With all the graces of his train;
While power divine his words attends,
To conquer foes and cheer his friends.

4 And in the great, decisive day,
When God the nations shall survey,
May it before the world appear
That crowds were born to glory here.

867 *Prayer for the Spirit.* C. M. (277)

Tune—MANOAH, No. 785.

1 SPIRIT divine, attend our prayer,
And make this house thy home;
Descend with all thy gracious power;
Oh, come, Great Spirit, come!

2 Come as the light,—to us reveal
Our sinfulness and woe;
And lead us in the paths of life,
Where all the righteous go.

3 Come as the fire, and purge our hearts,
Like sacrificial flame;
Let every soul an offering be
To our Redeemer's name.

4 Come as the dove, and spread thy wings,
The wings of peaceful love;
And let the church on earth become
Blest as the church above.

868 C. M. (255)

For laying a Corner-stone.

Tune—AVONDALE, No. 865.

1 BUILDER of mighty worlds on worlds,
How poor the house must be,
That with our human, sinful hands,
We may erect for thee!

2 O Christ, thou art our Corner-stone,
On thee our hopes are built;
Thou art our Lord, our light, our life,
Our sacrifice for guilt.

3 In thy blest name we gather here,
And consecrate the ground;
The walls that on this rock shall rise
Thy praises shall resound.

4 May many a soul, from death redeemed
In heavenly regions fair,
With joy exclaim, "I learned the path
To God and glory there."

BERTHA. H. M. W. O. PERKINS.

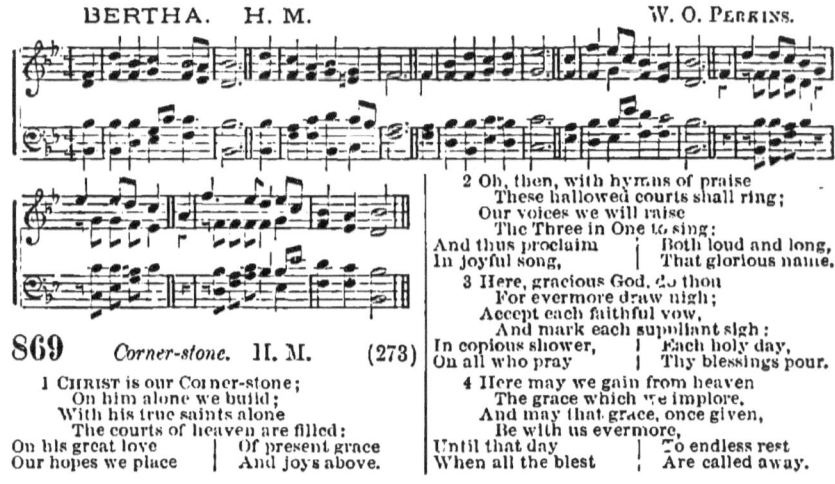

869 *Corner-stone.* H. M. (273)

1 CHRIST is our Corner-stone;
On him alone we build;
With his true saints alone
The courts of heaven are filled:
On his great love | Of present grace
Our hopes we place | And joys above.

2 Oh, then, with hymns of praise
These hallowed courts shall ring;
Our voices we will raise
The Three in One to sing;
And thus proclaim | Both loud and long,
In joyful song, | That glorious name.

3 Here, gracious God, do thou
For evermore draw nigh;
Accept each faithful vow,
And mark each suppliant sigh:
In copious shower, | Each holy day,
On all who pray | Thy blessings pour.

4 Here may we gain from heaven
The grace which we implore,
And may that grace, once given,
Be with us evermore,
Until that day | To endless rest
When all the blest | Are called away.

MISSIONS.

ST. MARTINS. C. M. W. TANSUR.

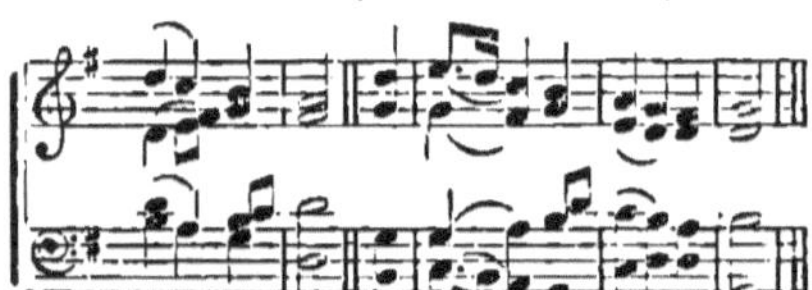

870 C. M. (297)

Prayer for the Success of the Gospel.

1 GREAT God, the nations of the earth
Are by creation thine;
And in thy works, by all beheld,
Thy radiant glories shine.

2 But, Lord, thy greater love has sent
Thy gospel to mankind,
Unveiling what rich stores of grace
Are treasured in thy mind.

3 Oh, when shall these glad tidings spread
The spacious earth around,
Till every tribe and every soul
Shall hear the joyful sound?

4 Smile, Lord, on each divine attempt
To spread the gospel's rays,
And build on sin's demolished throne
The temples of thy praise.

871 L. M. (302)

Subjection of the Nations to Christ prayed for.

Tune—ANVERN.

1 SOON may the last glad song arise
Through all the myriads of the skies;
That song of triumph which records
That all the earth is now the Lord's.

2 Let thrones and powers and kingdoms be
Obedient, mighty God, to thee;
And over land and stream and main
Now wave the sceptre of thy reign.

3 Oh, let the glorious anthem swell;
Let host to host the triumph tell,
That not one rebel heart remains,
But over all the Saviour reigns.

ANVERN. L. M. Dr. L. Mason.

Ritard.

872 L. M. (298)

Christ's universal Reign.

Mendon.

1 Jesus shall reign where'er the sun
Does his successive journeys run;
His kingdom stretch from shore to shore
Till moons shall wax and wane no more.

2 For him shall endless prayer be made,
And endless praises crown his head;
His name, like sweet perfume, shall rise
With every morning sacrifice.

3 People and realms of every tongue
Dwell on his love with sweetest song;
And infant voices shall proclaim
Their early blessings on his name.

4 Blessings abound where'er he reigns;
The joyful prisoner bursts his chains;
The weary find eternal rest,
And all the sons of want are blest.

5 Let every creature rise and bring
Peculiar honors to our King;
Angels descend with songs again,
And earth repeat the loud Amen.

MENDON. L. M. German.

873 *Returning to Zion.* C. M. (280)

1 Daughter of Zion, from the dust
Exalt thy fallen head;
Again in thy Redeemer trust;
He calls thee from the dead.

2 Awake, awake; put on thy strength,
Thy beautiful array;
The day of freedom dawns at length,
The Lord's appointed day.

3 Rebuild thy walls, thy bounds enlarge,
And send thy heralds forth;
Say to the South, "Give up thy charge!"
And, "Keep not back, O North!"

4 They come! they come! thine exiled bands
Where'er they rest or roam,
Have heard thy voice in distant lands,
And hasten to their home.

5 Thus, though the universe shall burn,
And God his works destroy,
With songs thy ransomed shall return,
And everlasting joy.

DUHRING. C. M. Wm. B. Bradbury.

MISSIONARY CHANT. L. M. CHARLES ZEUNER.

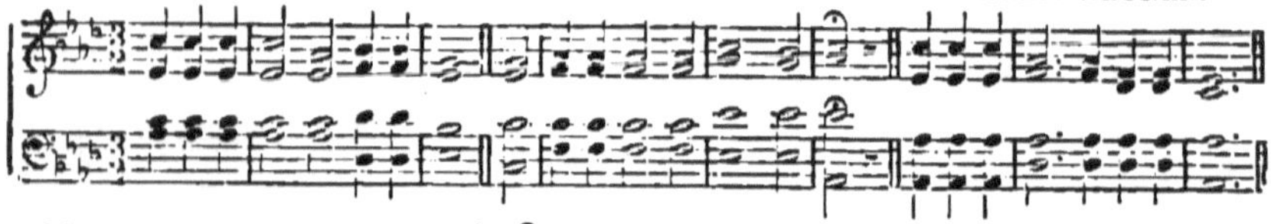

874 L. M. (303)

Prayer for the Heathen.

1 SOVEREIGN of worlds, display thy power;
Be this thy Zion's favored hour:
Oh, bid the morning star arise!
Oh, point the heathen to the skies!

2 Set up thy throne where Satan reigns,
In western wilds and eastern plains;
Far let the gospel's sound be known;
Make thou the universe thine own.

3 Speak, and the world shall hear thy voice;
Speak and the desert shall rejoice;
Dispel the gloom of heathen night;
Bid every nation hail the light.

875 L. M. (303)

Divine Power supplicated.

1 ARM of the Lord, awake, awake;
Put on thy strength, the nations shake;
Now let the world, adoring, see
Triumphs of mercy wrought by thee.

2 Say to the heathen, from thy throne,
"I am Jehovah, God alone:"
Thy voice their idols shall confound,
And cast their altars to the ground.

3 Let Zion's time of favor come;
Oh, bring the tribes of Israel home!
Soon may our wondering eyes behold
Gentiles and Jews in Jesus' fold.

4 Almighty God, thy grace proclaim
Through every clime, of every name,
Let adverse powers before thee fall,
And crown the Saviour Lord of all.

MILLENNIUM. 7s & 6s.

876 *Christ welcomed.* 7s & 6s. (272)

1 HAIL to the Lord's Anointed,
Great David's greater Son!
Hail, in the time appointed,
His reign on earth begun!
He comes to break oppression,
To set the captive free,
To take away transgression,
And rule in equity.

2 He comes, with succor speedy,
To those who suffer wrong;
To help the poor and needy,
And bid the weak be strong;
To give them songs for sighing,
Their darkness turn to light,
Whose souls, condemned and dying,
Were precious in his sight.

3 He shall descend like showers
Upon the fruitful earth,
And love and joy, like flowers,
Spring, in his path, to birth;
Before him, on the mountains,
Shall peace, the herald, go;
And righteousness, in fountains,
From hill to valley flow.

877 L. M. (303)

Missionaries encouraged.

Tune—MISSIONARY CHANT, No. 874.

1 YE Christian heralds, go, proclaim
Salvation in Immanuel's name:
To distant climes the tidings bear,
And plant the rose of Sharon there.

2 He'll shield you with a wall of fire,
With holy zeal your hearts inspire;
Bid raging winds their fury cease,
And calm the savage breast to peace.

3 And when our labors all are o'er,
Then shall we meet to part no more;
Meet, with the blood-bought throng to fall,
And crown the Saviour Lord of all.

878 8s, 7s, & 4. (300)

Glorious Prospects.

Tune—ZION, No. 748.

1 O'ER the gloomy hills of darkness,
Look, my soul, be still and gaze;
See the promises advancing
To a glorious day of grace:
Blessed jubilee,
Let thy glorious morning dawn.

2 Let the dark, benighted pagan,
Let the rude barbarian see
That divine and glorious conquest
Once obtained on Calvary:
Let the gospel
Loud resound from pole to pole.

3 Kingdoms wide, that sit in darkness,
Grant them, Lord, the glorious light;
Now, from eastern coast to western,
May the morning chase the night:
Let redemption,
Freely purchased, win the day.

4 Fly abroad, thou mighty gospel;
Win and conquer,—never cease;
May thy lasting, wide dominions
Multiply and still increase:
Sway thy sceptre,
Saviour, all the world around.

879 *Zion encouraged.* 8s, 7s, & 4. (300)

Tune—ZION, No. 748.

1 ON the mountain's top appearing,
Lo! the sacred herald stands,
Welcome news to Zion bearing,—
Zion, long in hostile lands:
Mourning captive,
God himself will loose thy bands.

2 Has thy night been long and mournful?
Have thy friends unfaithful proved?
Have thy foes been proud and scornful,
By thy sighs and tears unmoved?
Cease thy mourning;
Zion still is well beloved.

3 God, thy God, will now restore thee;
He himself appears thy Friend;
All thy foes shall flee before thee;
Here their boasts and triumphs end:
Great deliverance
Zion's King will surely send.

4 Enemies no more shall trouble,
All thy wrong shall be redress'd;
For thy shame thou shalt have double,
In thy Maker's favor bless'd;
All thy conflicts
End in everlasting rest.

WEBB. 7s & 6s. GEO. J. WEBB.

FINE.
D.S.

880 7s & 6s. (299)

Success of the Gospel.

1 THE morning light is breaking;
The darkness disappears:
The sons of earth are waking
To penitential tears:
Each breeze that sweeps the ocean
Brings tidings from afar
Of nations in commotion,
Prepared for Zion's war.

2 Rich dews of grace come o'er us,
In many a gentle shower,
And brighter scenes before us
Are opening every hour:
Each cry, to heaven going,
Abundant answers brings,
And heavenly gales are blowing,
With peace upon their wings.

3 See heathen nations bending
Before the God we love,
And thousand hearts ascending
In gratitude above;
While sinners, now confessing,
The gospel call obey,
And seek the Saviour's blessing—
A nation in a day.

4 Blest river of salvation,
Pursue thy onward way;
Flow thou to every nation,
Nor in thy richness stay;
Stay not till all the lowly
Triumphant reach their home,
Stay not till all the holy
Proclaim, "The Lord is come."

MISSIONARY HYMN. 7s & 6s. DR. L. MASON.

881

Conversion of the Heathen. 7s & 6s. (307)

1 FROM Greenland's icy mountains,
From India's coral strand,
Where Afric's sunny fountains
Roll down their golden sand,
From many an ancient river,
From many a palmy plain,
They call us to deliver
Their land from error's chain.

2 What though the spicy breezes
Blow soft o'er Ceylon's isle,
Though every prospect pleases,
And only man is vile;
In vain, with lavish kindness,
The gifts of God are strown:
The heathen, in his blindness,
Bows down to wood and stone.

3 Can we, whose souls are lighted
By wisdom from on high,
Can we to men benighted
The lamp of life deny?
Salvation! oh, salvation!
The joyful sound proclaim,
Till earth's remotest nation
Has learned Messiah's name.

4 Waft, waft, ye winds, his story,
And you, ye waters, roll,
Till, like a sea of glory,
It spreads from pole to pole:
Till o'er our ransomed nature
The Lamb, for sinners slain,
Redeemer, King, Creator,
In bliss returns to reign.

WEBB. 7s & 6s. GEO. J. WEBB.

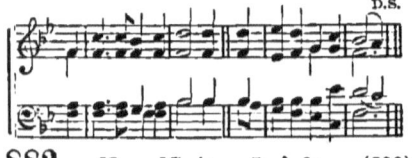

FINE.

D.S.

882

Home Mission. 7s & 6s. (299)

1 Go preach the blest salvation
To every sinful race,
And bid each guilty nation
Accept the Saviour's grace;
But bear, oh, quickly bear it
Where thronging millions roam,
And bid them freely share it,
Who dwell with us at home.

2 Where blooms the broad savanna,
Where mighty waters roll,
There let the gospel banner
Beam hope on every soul;
Go where the West is teeming,
And yet behold they come!
The richest fields are gleaming
For those who reap at home!

3 Our children there are dwelling,
Neglected and astray,
Whose hearts are often swelling
To learn of Zion's way.
Bear, bear to them the treasure,
And bid the exiles come;
There is no sweeter pleasure
Than preaching Christ at home.

883 *Home Missions.* 7s & 6s. (307)

Tune—MISSIONARY HYMN, No. 881.

1 OUR country's voice is pleading,
Ye men of God, arise!
His providence is leading,
The land before you lies;
Day gleams are o'er it brightening,
And promise clothes the soil;
Wide fields for harvest whitening,
Invite the reaper's toil.

2 Go where the waves are breaking,
On California's shore,
Christ's precious gospel taking,
More rich than golden ore;
On Alleghany's mountains,
Through all the Western Vale,
Beside Missouri's fountains,
Rehearse the wondrous tale.

3 The love of Christ unfolding,
Speed on from east to west,
Till all, his cross beholding,
In him are fully blest.
Great Author of salvation,
Haste, haste the glorious day,
When we, a ransomed nation,
Thy sceptre shall obey.

HILLSIDE. L. M. L. O. EMERSON.

884 *Prayer for the Jews.* L. M. (301)

1 DISOWNED of heaven, by man oppressed,
Outcasts from Zion's hallowed ground,
Oh, why should Israel's sons, once blessed,
Still roam the scorning world around?

2 Lord, visit thy forsaken race,
Back to thy fold the wanderers bring;
Teach them to seek thy slighted grace,
And hail in Christ their promised King.

3 The veil of darkness rend in twain,
Which hides their Shiloh's glorious light,
The severed olive branch again
Firm to its parent stock unite.

4 Hail, glorious day, expected long,
When Jew and Greek one prayer shall pour;
With eager feet one temple throng,
With grateful praise one God adore.

KEDESH. 8s, 7s, & 4. DR. L. MASON.

FINE.
D.C.

885 *The Missionary's Farewell.* 8s, 7s, & 4. (305)

1 YES, my native land, I love thee;
All thy scenes, I love them well;
Friends, connections, happy country,
Can I bid you all farewell?
Can I leave you,
Far in heathen lands to dwell?

2 Home, thy joys are passing lovely,—
Joys no stranger heart can tell;
Happy home, indeed I love thee;
Can I, can I say, "Farewell"?
Can I leave thee,
Far in heathen lands to dwell?

3 Scenes of sacred peace and pleasure,
Holy days and Sabbath bell,
Richest, brightest, sweetest treasure,
Can I say a last farewell?
Can I leave you,
Far in heathen lands to dwell?

4 Yes, I hasten from you gladly,
From the scenes I loved so well;
Far away, ye billows, bear me;
Lovely, native land, farewell.
Pleased I leave thee,
Far in heathen lands to dwell.

5 In the deserts let me labor;
On the mountains let me tell
How he died,—the blessed Saviour,—
To redeem a world from hell:
Let me hasten,
Far in heathen lands to dwell.

6 Bear me on, thou restless ocean;
Let the winds my canvas swell;
Heaves my heart with warm emotion,
While I go far hence to dwell:
Glad I bid thee,
Native land, farewell, farewell!

MENDON. L. M.

GERMAN.

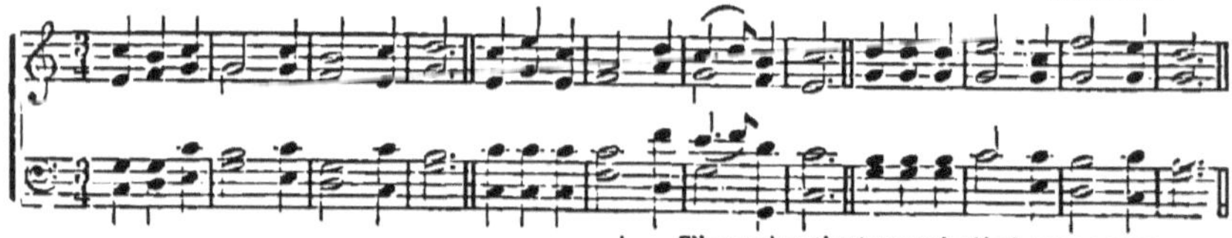

886 *Christians in Convention.* L. M. (298)

1 ASSEMBLED at thy great command,
Before thy face, dread King, we stand;
The voice tha‘ marshalled every star
Has called thy people from afar.

2 We meet, through distant lands to spread
The truth for which the martyrs bled;
Along the line, to either pole,
The anthem of thy praise to roll.

3 Our prayers assist; accept our praise;
Our hopes revive; our courage raise;
Our counsels aid; to each impart
The single eye, the faithful heart.

4 Forth with thy chosen heralds come,
Recall the wandering spirits home:
From Zion's mount send forth the sound,
To spread the spacious earth around.

CROSS AND CROWN. C. M.

WESTERN MELODY.

887 *Prayer for Seamen.* C. M. (265)

1 WE come, O Lord, before thy throne,
And, with united pleas,
We meet and pray for those who roam
Far off upon the seas.

2 Oh, may the Holy Spirit bow
The sailor's heart to thee,
Till tears of deep repentance flow
Like rain-drops in the sea.

3 Then may a Saviour's dying love
Pour peace into his breast,
And waft him to the port above
Of everlasting rest.

888 *Prayer for Mariners.* L. M. (301)

1 GRANT the abundance of the sea
May be converted, Lord, to thee,
And every sailor on the shore
Return to God, to roam no more.

2 The nations, then, with joy shall hail
The Bethel flag in every sail:
And every ship that ploughs the sea
A gospel messenger shall be.

3 Hasten, O Lord, that glorious day
When seamen shall thy word obey,
And safe from port to port be driven
To point a ruined world to heaven.

HILLSIDE. L. M.

L. O. EMERSON.

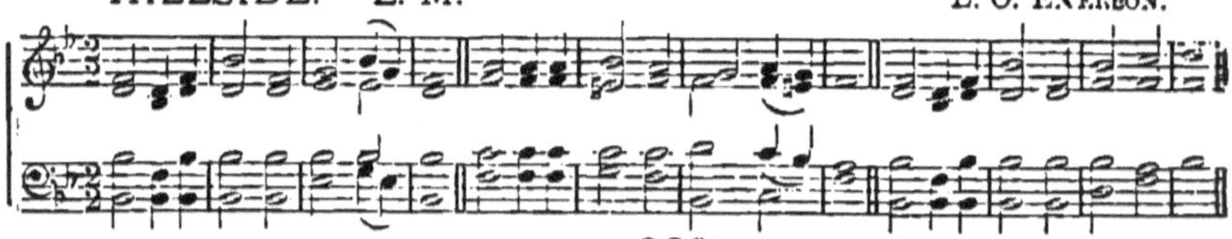

889 *The Restoration of Israel.* L. M. (301)

1 ARISE, great God, and let thy grace
Shed its glad beams on Jacob's race;
Restore the long-lost, scatter'd band,
And call them to their native land.

2 Their misery let thy mercy heal;
Their trespass hide, their pardon seal;
O God of Israel, hear our prayer,
And grant them still thy love to share.

3 How long shall Jacob's offspring prove
The sad suspension of thy love?
Lord, shall thy wrath for ever burn?
And will thy mercy ne'er return?

4 Thy quick'ning Spirit now impart,
And wake to joy each grateful heart;
While Israel's rescued tribes in thee
Their bliss and full salvation see.

OUR COUNTRY.

AMERICA. 6s & 4s.

890 *National Hymn.* 6s & 4s. (314)

1 My country, 'tis of thee,
Sweet land of liberty,
Of thee I sing;
Land where my fathers died,
Land of the pilgrim's pride,
From every mountain side
Let freedom ring.

2 My native country, thee,
Land of the noble free,
Thy name I love;
I love thy rocks and rills,
Thy woods and templed hills;
My heart with rapture thrills,
Like that above.

3 Let music swell the breeze,
And ring from all the trees
Sweet freedom's song:
Let mortal tongues awake;
Let all that breathe partake;
Let rocks their silence break,—
The sound prolong.

4 Our fathers' God, to thee,
Author of liberty,
To thee we sing;
Long may our land be bright
With freedom's holy light;
Protect us by thy might,
Great God, our King.

DUNDEE. C. M.

891 *Our Help is in the Name of the Lord.* C. M. (311)

1 Lord, while for all mankind we pray,
Of every clime and coast,
Oh, hear us for our native land,
The land we love the most.

2 Our fathers' sepulchres are here,
And here our kindred dwell:
Our children too,—how should we love
Another land so well?

3 Oh, guard our shores from every foe,
With peace our borders bless;
With prosperous times our cities crown,
Our fields with plenteousness.

4 Unite us in the sacred love
Of knowledge, truth, and thee;
And let our hills and valleys shout
The songs of liberty.

5 Lord of the nations, thus to thee
Our country we commend:
Be thou her refuge and her trust,
Her everlasting friend.

WIMBORNE. L. M. — WHITTAKER.

892 L. M. (315)

Lord, let thy Goodness lead our Land.

1 Lord, let thy goodness lead our land,
Still sav'd by thine almighty hand,
The tribute of its love to bring
To thee, our Saviour and our King.

2 Let every public temple raise
Triumphant songs of holy praise;
Let every peaceful, private home
A temple, Lord, to thee become.

3 Still be it our supreme delight
To walk as in thy glorious sight;
Still in thy precepts and thy fear,
Till life's last hour, to persevere.

AMERICA. 6s & 4s.

893 6s & 4s. (314)

Prayer for our Country.

1 God bless our native land,
Firm may she ever stand,
Through storm and night;
When the wild tempests rave,
Ruler of winds and wave,
Do thou our country save
By thy great might.

2 For her our prayer shall rise
To God, above the skies;
On him we wait;
Thou who art ever nigh,
Guarding with watchful eye,
To thee aloud we cry,
God save the State.

MOUNT VERNON. 8s & 7s. — DR. L. MASON.

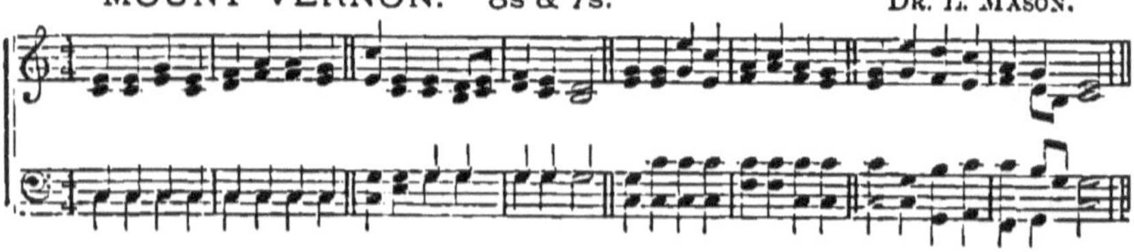

894 *Pardon implored for national Sins.* 8s & 7s. (348)

Tune—MOUNT VERNON.

1 DREAD Jehovah, God of nations,
From thy temple in the skies,
Hear thy people's supplications;
Now for their deliverance rise.

2 Though our sins, our hearts confounding,
Long and loud for vengeance call,
Thou hast mercy more abounding;
Jesus' blood can cleanse them all.

3 Let that love veil our transgressions;
Let that blood our guilt efface;
Save thy people from oppression;
Save from spoil thy holy place.

4 Lo! with deep contrition turning,
Humbly at thy feet we bend;
Hear us, fasting, praying, mourning;
Hear us, spare us, and defend.

GRATITUDE. L. M. BOST.

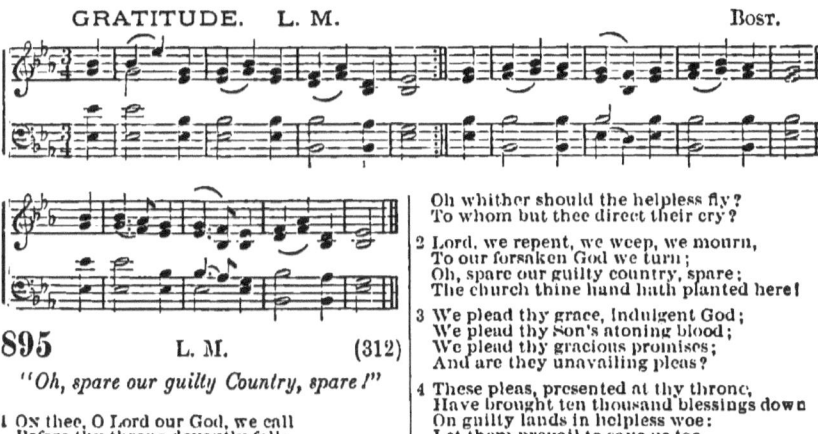

895 L. M. (312)

"Oh, spare our guilty Country, spare!"

1 ON thee, O Lord our God, we call
Before thy throne devoutly fall;
Oh whither should the helpless fly?
To whom but thee direct their cry?

2 Lord, we repent, we weep, we mourn,
To our forsaken God we turn;
Oh, spare our guilty country, spare;
The church thine hand hath planted here!

3 We plead thy grace, indulgent God;
We plead thy Son's atoning blood;
We plead thy gracious promises;
And are they unavailing pleas?

4 These pleas, presented at thy throne,
Have brought ten thousand blessings down
On guilty lands in helpless woe:
Let them prevail to save us too.

FULTON. 7s. WM. B. BRADBURY.

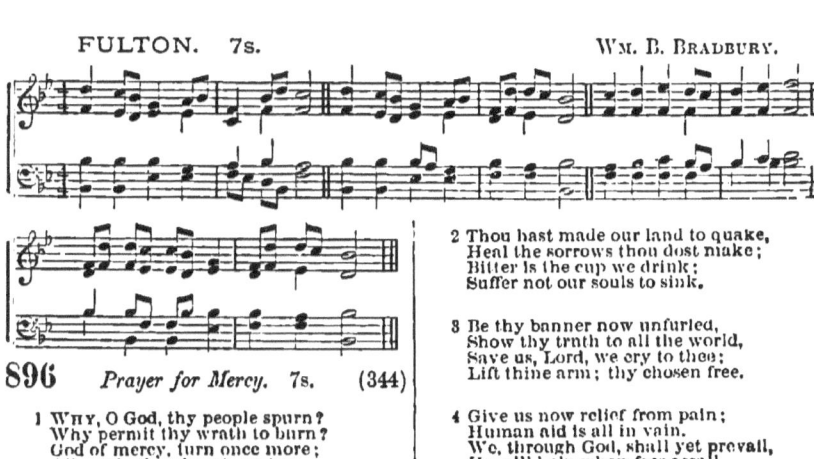

896 *Prayer for Mercy.* 7s. (344)

1 WHY, O God, thy people spurn?
Why permit thy wrath to burn?
God of mercy, turn once more;
All our broken hearts restore.

2 Thou hast made our land to quake,
Heal the sorrows thou dost make;
Bitter is the cup we drink;
Suffer not our souls to sink.

3 Be thy banner now unfurled,
Show thy truth to all the world,
Save us, Lord, we cry to thee;
Lift thine arm; thy chosen free.

4 Give us now relief from pain;
Human aid is all in vain.
We, through God, shall yet prevail,
He will help when foes assail.

DUNDEE. C. M.

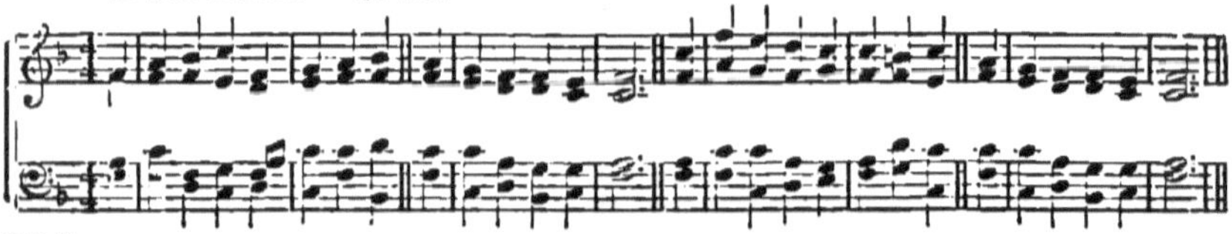

897 *Relief from national Judgments implored.* C. M. (311)

1 Lord, thou hast scourged our guilty land;
Behold, thy people mourn;
Shall vengeance ever guide thy hand,
And mercy ne'er return?

2 Our Zion trembles at thy stroke,
And dreads thy lifted hand;
Oh, heal the people thou hast broke,
And spare our guilty land.

3 Then shall our loud and grateful voice
Proclaim our guardian God,
The nations round the earth rejoice
And sound thy praise abroad.

THANKSGIVING.

AINSWORTH. 7s. Dr. T Hastings.

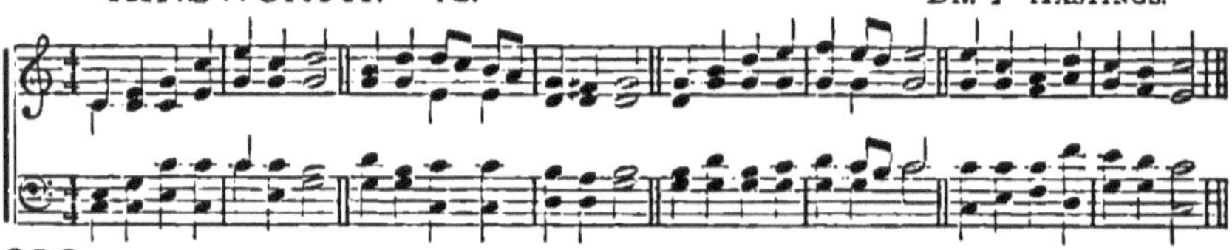

898 *Thanks for all Blessings.* 7s. (316)

1 Praise to God, immortal praise,
For the love that crowns our days;
Bounteous source of every joy,
Let thy praise our tongues employ.

2 Flocks that whiten all the plain,
Yellow sheaves of ripened grain;
Clouds that drop their fattening dews,
Suns that temperate warmth diffuse.

3 All that spring with bounteous hand
Scatters o'er the smiling land;
All that liberal autumn pours
From her rich, o'erflowing stores,—

4 Lord, for these our souls shall raise
Grateful vows and solemn praise;
And when every blessing's flown,
Love thee for thyself alone.

GRATITUDE. L. M. Bost.

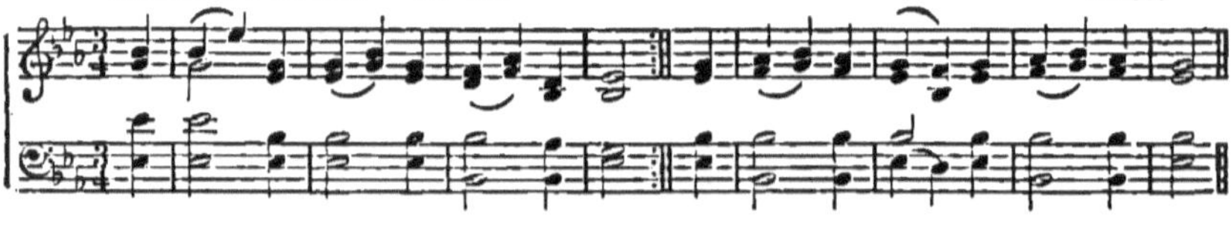

899 L. M. (312)

The Year crowned with Goodness.

1 Eternal Source of every joy,
Thy praise may well our lips employ,
While in thy temple we appear,
Whose goodness crowns the circling year.

2 Wide as the wheels of nature roll,
Thy hand supports the steady pole;
The sun is taught by thee to rise,
And darkness when to veil the skies.

(CONTINUED.)

3 The flowery spring, at thy command,
Embalms the air and paints the land;
The summer rays of vigor shine,
To raise the corn and cheer the vine.

4 Thy hand in autumn richly pours
Through all our coasts abundant stores;
And winters, softened by thy care,
No more a dreary aspect wear.

5 Still be the cheerful homage paid
With morning light and evening shade;
Seasons and months and weeks and days
Demand successive songs of praise.

TELEMANS. 7s. C. ZEUNER.

900 *Thanksgiving.* 7s. (313)

1 SWELL the anthem, raise the song;
Praises to our God belong;
Saints and angels, join to sing
Praises to the heavenly King.

2 Blessings from his liberal hand
Flow around this happy land;
Kept by him, no foes annoy;
Peace and freedom we enjoy.

3 Here, beneath a virtuous sway,
May we cheerfully obey;
Never feel oppression's rod:
Ever own and worship God.

4 Hark! the voice of nature sings
Praises to the King of kings;
Let us join the choral song,
And the grateful notes prolong.

901 6s & 4s. (314)

Praise to the God of Harvest.

Tune—AMERICA, No. 893.

. THE God of harvest praise:
In loud thanksgiving raise
Hand, heart, and voice;
The valleys smile and sing,
Forests and mountains ring,
The plains their tribute bring,
The streams rejoice.

2 Yea, bless his holy name,
And purest thanks proclaim
Through all the earth;
To glory in your lot
Is duty,—but be not
God's benefits forgot,
Amidst your mirth.

3 The God of harvest praise;
Hands, hearts, and voices raise,
With sweet accord;
From field to garner throng,
Bearing your sheaves along,
And in your harvest song
Bless ye the Lord.

902 *Thanksgiving.* L. M. (315)

Tune—WIMBORNE, No. 892.

1 GREAT God, as seasons disappear,
And changes mark the rolling year,
Thy favor still doth crown our days,
And we would celebrate thy praise.

2 The harvest song we would repeat:
"Thou givest us the finest wheat:"
"The joy of harvest" we have known:
The praise, O Lord, is all thine own.

3 Our tables spread, our garners stored,
Oh, give us hearts to bless thee, Lord!
Forbid it, Source of light and love,
That hearts and lives should barren prove.

4 Another harvest comes apace:
Mature our spirits by thy grace,
That we may calmly meet the blow
The sickle gives to lay us low;—

5 That so, when angel reapers come
To gather sheaves to thy blest home,
Our spirits may be borne on high
To thy safe garner in the sky.

903 *Harvest Hymn.* 7s. (313)

TELEMANS.

1 PRAISE, oh, praise our God and King!
Hymns of adoration sing;
For his mercies still endure,
Ever faithful, ever sure.

2 Praise him that he made the sun
Day by day his course to run:
And the silver moon by night,
Shining with her gentle light.

3 Praise him that he gave the rain
To mature the swelling grain;
And hath bid the fruitful field
Crops of precious increase yield.

4 Praise him for our harvest-store,—
He hath filled the garner-floor,—
And for richer food than this,
Pledge of everlasting bliss.

5 Glory to our bounteous King!
Glory let creation sing;
Glory to the Father, Son,
And blest Spirit, Three in One.

904 L. M. (315)

Gratitude for the Past.

Tune—Wimborne, No. 892.

1 Great God, we sing that mighty hand,
By which supported still we stand;
The opening year thy mercy shows;
Let mercy crown it till it close.

2 By day, by night, at home, abroad,
Still we are guarded by our God;
By his incessant bounty fed,
By his unerring counsel led.

3 With grateful hearts the past we own
The future,—all to us unknown,—
We to thy guardian care commit,
And peaceful leave before thy feet.

4 In scenes exalted or depressed,
Be thou our joy, and thou our rest;
Thy goodness all our hopes shall raise,
Adored through all our changing days.

5 When death shall close our earthly songs,
And seal in silence mortal tongues,
Our Helper, God, in whom we trust,
In brighter worlds our souls shall boast.

905 C. M. (334)

Close of the Year.

Avon.

1 Remark, my soul, the narrow bound
Of each revolving year;
How swift the weeks complete their round!
How short the months appear!

2 So fast eternity comes on,
And that important day
When all that mortal life hath done
God's judgment shall survey.

3 Yet like an idle tale we pass
The swift revolving year,
And study artful ways t'increase
The speed of its career.

4 Awake, O God, my careless heart
Its great concerns to see,
That I may act the Christian part,
And give the year to thee.

5 So shall their course more grateful roll,
If future years arise;
Or this shall bear my waiting soul
To joy beyond the skies.

AVON. C. M.

COME, LET US ANEW. 5s & 12s. C. G. Allen.

906 *The New Year.* 5s & 12s. (317)

1 Come, let us anew
Our journey pursue,—
Roll round with the year,
And never stand still till the Master appear;
His adorable will
Let us gladly fulfil,
And our talents improve
By the patience of hope, and the labor of love.

(continued.)

2 Our life is a dream;
Our time, as a stream,
Glides swiftly away.
And the fugitive moment refuses to stay:
The arrow is flown;
The moment is gone;
The millennial year
Rushes on to our view, and eternity's near.

3 Oh that each, in the day
Of his coming, may say,
"I have fought my way through;
I have finished the work thou didst give me to do;"
Oh that each from his Lord
May receive the glad word,
"Well and faithfully done;
Enter into my joy, and sit down on my throne."

907 *Close of the Year.* L. M. (312)

Tune—GRATITUDE, No. 899.

1 OUR helper, God, we bless thy name,
Whose love for ever is the same;
The tokens of whose gracious care
Begin and crown and close the year.

2 Amid ten thousand snares we stand,
Supported by thy guardian hand;
And see, when we review our ways,
Ten thousand monuments of praise.

3 Thus far thine arm has led us on:
Thus far we make thy mercy known;
And while we tread this desert land,
New mercies shall new songs demand.

4 Our grateful souls on Jordan's shore
Shall raise one sacred pillar more,
Then bear, in thy bright courts above,
Inscriptions of immortal love.

908 *Prayer for a Blessing.* C. M. (328)

1 Now, gracious Lord, thine arm reveal,
And make thy glory known;
Now let us all thy presence feel,
And soften hearts of stone.

2 From all the guilt of former sin
May mercy set us free,
And let the year we now begin,
Begin and end with thee.

3 Send down thy Spirit from above,
That saints may love thee more,
And sinners now may learn to love,
Who never loved before.

4 And when before thee we appear,
In our eternal home,
May growing numbers worship here,
And praise thee in our room.

BEMERTON. C. M. H. W. GREATOREX.

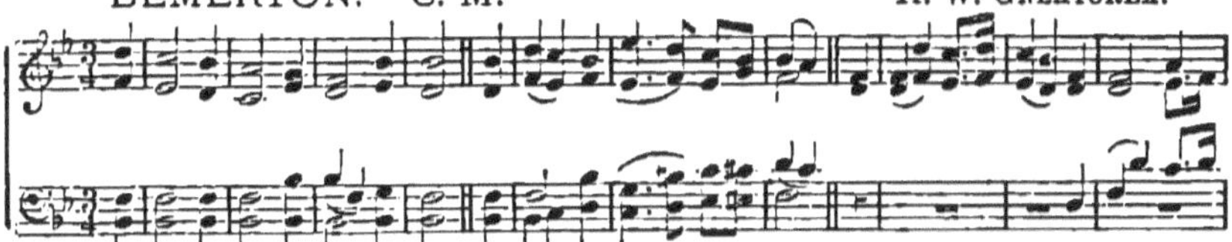

909 *New Year's Day.* 7s. (316)

1 WHILE, with ceaseless course, the sun
Hasted through the former year,
Many souls their race have run,
Nevermore to meet us here:
Fixed in an eternal state,
They have done with all below.
We a little longer wait,
But how little none can know.

2 Thanks for mercies past receive;
Pardon of our sins renew;
Teach us, henceforth, how to live,
With eternity in view,
Bless thy word to old and young;
Fill us with a Saviour's love:
When our life's short race is run,
May we dwell with thee above.

AINSWORTH. 7s. DR. T. HASTINGS.

PARRY. 10s. Dr. L. Mason.

910

New Year's Morning Hymn. 10s. (320)

1 Thanksgiving and the voice of melody,
This New Year's morning, call me from my sleep,
A new sweet song is in my heart for thee,
Thou faithful, tender Shepherd of thy sheep.

2 With voice subdued, my listening spirit sings,
As backward on the trodden path I gaze,
While ministering angels fold their wings
To fill with lowly thoughts my song of praise.

3 Not all that hath been, Lord, henceforth shall be.
A low, sweet, cheering strain is in mine ear;
Thanksgiving and the voice of melody
Are leading in from heaven a blest New Year.

4 Thoughts of thy love,—and oh, how great the sum!
Enduring grief, obtaining bliss for me,—
The world, life, death, things present, things to come,
All swell the New Year's opening melody.

AVON. C. M.

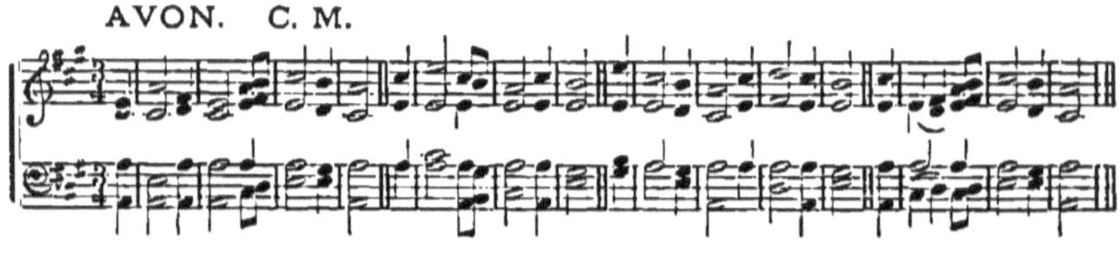

911

Looking forward. C. M. (334)

1 And now, my soul, another year
Of thy short life is past;
I cannot long continue here,
And this may be my last.

2 Awake, my soul; with utmost care
Thy true condition learn:
What are thy hopes? how sure? how fair?
What is thy great concern?

3 Behold, another year begins;
Set out afresh for heaven;
Seek pardon for thy former sins,
In Christ so freely given.

4 Devoutly yield thyself to God,
And on his grace depend;
With zeal pursue the heavenly road,
Nor doubt a happy end.

FULTON. 7s. WM. B. BRADBURY.

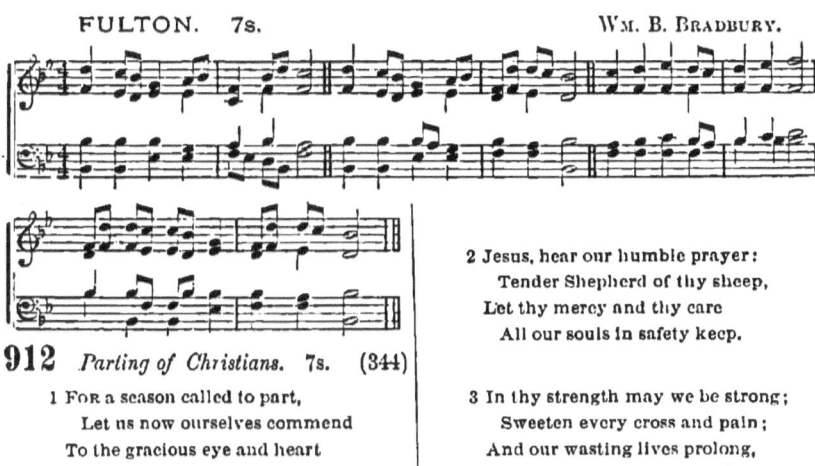

912 *Parting of Christians.* 7s. (344)

1 FOR a season called to part,
Let us now ourselves commend
To the gracious eye and heart
Of our ever-present Friend.

2 Jesus, hear our humble prayer:
Tender Shepherd of thy sheep,
Let thy mercy and thy care
All our souls in safety keep.

3 In thy strength may we be strong;
Sweeten every cross and pain;
And our wasting lives prolong,
Till we meet on earth again.

PARTING SONG. 11s & 10s. W. H. DOANE.

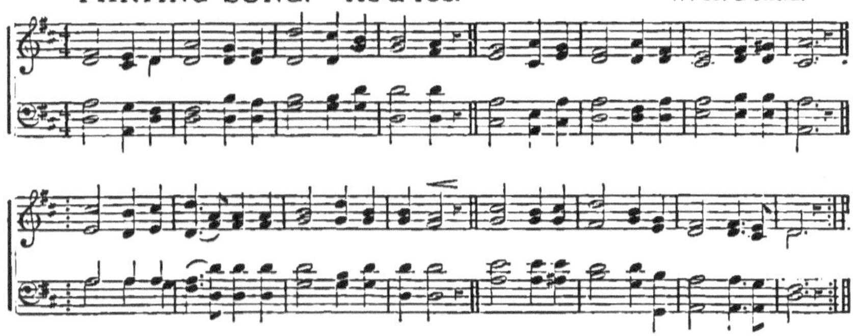

913 *Parting Song.* 11s & 10s. (319)

1 BROTHERS, clasp hands, the brief moments are flying;
Here upon earth but as pilgrims we dwell;
Gladly we met, yet we part without sighing,
Looking beyond the fraternal farewell.
In his dear name, the All-loving, All-seeing,
Hand clasped in hand for him, brothers, farewell.

2 Rich in our faith, in our love, in our union,
Foretastes of heaven together we've known
Ours is the bliss of a saintly communion,
Granted to lovers of Jesus alone.

3 Now to our work again, stronger for meeting,
Pledged to our Master as never before,
Warm are the hearts that are loyally beating,
Longing to serve and to honor him more.

4 Jesus we own as the Lord of our being;
Let our last song rich in gratitude swell;
In his dear name, the All-loving, All-seeing,
Hand clasped in hand for him, brothers farewell.

SHALL WE GATHER AT THE RIVER? 8s & 7s.

REV. R. LOWRY.

CHORUS.
p
p

914 8s & 7s. (348)

Gather at the River.

1 SHALL we gather at the river,
Where bright angel feet have trod;
With its crystal tide for ever
Flowing by the throne of God?

Chorus.—Yes, we'll gather at the river,
The beautiful, the beautiful river,
Gather with the saints at the river
That flows by the throne of God.

2 On the margin of the river,
Washing up its silver spray,
We will walk and worship ever,
All the happy, golden day.

3 On the bosom of the river,
Where the Saviour-King we own,
We shall meet and sorrow never,
'Neath the glory of the throne.

4 Soon we'll reach the shining river,
Soon our pilgrimage will cease;
Soon our happy hearts will quiver
With the melody of peace.

UNITY. 6s & 5s.

DR. L. MASON.

915 *Reunion in Heaven.* 6s & 5s. Peculiar. (318)

Tune—Unity.

1 When shall we meet again?—
Meet ne'er to sever?
When will Peace wreathe her chain
Round us for ever?
Our hearts will ne'er repose
Safe from each blast that blows
In this dark vale of woes,—
Never,—no, never!

2 When shall love freely flow
Pure as life's river?
When shall sweet friendship glow
Changeless for ever?
Where joys celestial thrill,
Where bliss each heart shall fill,
And fears of parting chill
Never—no, never!

3 Up to that world of light
Take us, dear Saviour;
May we all there unite,
Happy for ever:
Where kindred spirits dwell,
There may our music swell,
And time our joys dispel
Never,—no, never.

4 Soon shall we meet again,—
Meet ne'er to sever;
Soon will Peace wreathe her chain
Round us for ever:
Our hearts will then repose
Secure from worldly woes;
Our songs of praise shall close
Never,—no, never!

MORTALITY OF MAN.

ORWELL. L. M. Dr. L. Mason.

916 *Brevity of Life.* L. M. (335)

1 Ere mountains reared their forms sublime,
Or heaven and earth in order stood,
Before the birth of ancient time,
From everlasting thou art God.

2 A thousand ages, in their flight,
With thee are as a fleeting day;
Past, present, future, to thy sight
At once their various scenes display.

3 But our brief life's a shadowy dream,
A passing thought, that soon is o'er,
That fades with morning's earliest beam,
And fills the musing mind no more.

4 To us, O Lord, the wisdom give,
Each passing moment so to spend,
That we at length with thee may live
Where life and bliss shall never end.

GOULD. C. M. J. E. Gould.

Ritard.

917 *Time the Period to prepare for Eternity.* C. M. (326)

1 Thee we adore, Eternal Name,
And humbly own to thee
How feeble is our mortal frame,
What dying worms are we.

2 The year rolls round, and steals away
The breath that first it gave;
Whate'er we do, where'er we stray,
We're travelling to the grave.

3 Great God, on what a slender thread
Hang everlasting things!—
The final state of all the dead
Upon life's feeble strings!

4 Eternal joy, or endless woe,
Attends on every breath;
And yet how unconcerned we go
Upon the brink of death!

5 Awake, O Lord, our drowsy sense,
To walk this dangerous road;
And if our souls are hurried hence,
May they be found with God.

MENDEBAS. 7s & 6s.

918 *Life rapidly passing away.* 7s & 6s. (321)

1 As flows the rapid river,
With channel broad and free,
Its waters rippling ever,
And hasting to the sea,
So life is onward flowing,
And days of offered peace,
And man is swiftly going
Where calls of mercy cease.

2 As moons are ever waning,
As hastes the sun away,
As stormy winds, complaining,
Bring on the wintry day,
So fast the night comes o'er us,
The darkness of the grave;
And death is just before us;
God takes the life he gave.

3 Say, hath thy heart its treasure
Laid up in worlds above?
And is it all thy pleasure
Thy God to praise and love?
Beware, lest death's dark river
Its billows o'er thee roll,
And thou lament for ever
The ruin of thy soul.

BEMERTON. C. M. H. W. GREATOREX.

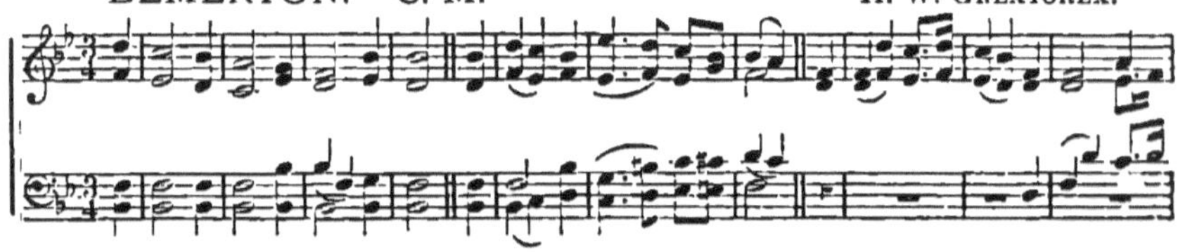

919 C. M. (328)

Life short, and Man frail.

1 TEACH me the measure of my days,
Thou Maker of my frame;
I would survey life's narrow space,
And learn how frail I am.

2 A span is all that we can boast,
An inch or two of time;
Man is but vanity and dust,
In all his flower and prime.

3 What should I wish, or wait for, then,
From creatures, earth and dust?
They make our expectations vain,
And disappoint our trust.

4 Now I forbid my carnal hope,
My fond desire recall;
I give my mortal interest up,
And make my God my all.

GOULD. C. M. J. E. GOULD.

Ritard.

920 C. M. (326)

The Brevity of Life.

1 How short and hasty is our life!
How vast our soul's affairs!
Yet foolish mortals vainly strive
To lavish out their years.

2 Our days run thoughtlessly along,
Without a moment's stay;
Just like a story or a song,
We pass our lives away.

3 God from on high invites us home;
But we march heedless on,
And, ever hastening to the tomb,
Stoop downward as we run.

4 Draw us, O God, with sovereign grace,
And lift our thoughts on high,
That we may end this mortal race,
And see salvation nigh.

921 L. M. (322)

God's Eternity and Man's Frailty.

1 THROUGH every age, eternal God,
Thou art our rest, our safe abode;
High was thy throne e'er heaven was made,
Or earth, thy humble footstool, laid.

2 Long hadst thou reigned ere time began,
Or dust was fashioned into man;
And long thy kingdom shall endure,
When earth and time shall be no more.

3 Death, like an ever-flowing stream,
Sweeps us away; our life's a dream,
An empty tale, a morning flower,
Cut down and withered in an hour.

4 Teach us, O Lord, how frail is man,
And kindly lengthen out our span,
Till, cleansed by grace, we all may be
Prepared to die, and dwell with thee.

REST. L. M. WM. B. BRADBURY.

WHITNEY. C. M. DR. L. MASON.

Dim.

922 C. M. (338)

A warning from the Grave.

1 BENEATH our feet and o'er our head,
Is equal warning given;
Beneath us lie the countless dead,
And far above is heaven.

2 Death rides on every passing breeze,
And lurks in every flower;
Each season has its own disease,
Its perils every hour.

3 Turn, sinner, turn; thy danger know,
Where'er thy feet can tread,
The earth rings hollow from below,
And warns thee of her dead.

4 Turn, Christian, turn; thy soul apply
To truths which hourly tell
That they who underneath thee lie
Shall live in heaven,—or hell.

SALVATORI. 7s & 6s. Arranged by C. F. BLANDNER.

923

Hasting to our Home. 7s & 6s. (304)

1 TIME is winging us away
To our eternal home;
Life is but a winter's day,—
A journey to the tomb;
Youth and vigor soon will flee,
Blooming beauty lose its charms;
All that's mortal soon shall be
Enclosed in death's cold arms.

2 Time is winging us away
To our eternal home;
Life is but a winter's day,—
A journey to the tomb;
But the Christian shall enjoy
Health and beauty soon above,
Where no worldly griefs annoy,
Secure in Jesus' love.

NEARER MY HOME. 6s. JOHN M. EVANS.

CHORUS.

924

Nearer my Home. 6s. (346)

1 ONE sweetly solemn thought
Comes to me o'er and o'er:
I'm nearer my home to-day
Than I've ever been before.

I'm nearer my home, nearer my home,
Nearer my home to-day;
Yes, nearer my home in heaven to-day,
Than ever I've been before.

2 Nearer my Father's house,
Where the many mansions be;
Nearer the great white throne,
Nearer the jasper sea.

3 Nearer the bound of life
Where we lay our burdens down,
Nearer leaving my cross,
Nearer wearing my crown.

4 But lying darkly between,
Winding down through the night,
Is that dim and unknown stream
Which leads at last to light.

5 For even now my feet
May stand upon its brink;
I may be nearer my home,
Nearer now than I think.

WHITNEY. C. M. DR. L. MASON.

Dim.

925 *Heavenly Aspirations.* C. M. (334)

Tune—AVON, No. 911.

1 AND let this feeble body fail,
And let it faint and die;
My soul shall quit this mournful vale,
And soar to worlds on high;

2 Shall join the disembodied saints,
And find its long sought rest,—
That only bliss for which it pants,—
In the Redeemer's breast.

3 Oh, what are all my sufferings here,
If, Lord, thou count me meet
With that enraptured host t' appear,
And worship at thy feet!

4 Give joy or grief, give ease or pain,
Take life or friends away;
But let me find them all again
In that eternal day.

926 *Longing for Heaven.* C. M. (338)

1 SWEET land of rest, for thee I sigh:
When will the moment come,
When I shall lay my armor by,
And dwell with Christ at home?

2 No tranquil joys on earth I know,
No peaceful sheltering dome:
This world's a wilderness of woe,—
This world is not my home.

3 To Jesus Christ I sought for rest.
He bade me cease to roam,
But fly for succor to his breast,
And he'd conduct me home.

4 Weary of wandering round and round
This vale of sin and gloom,
I long to leave th' unhallowed ground
And dwell with Christ at home.

SHINING SHORE. 8s & 7s. G. F. ROOT.

FINE.
D.S.

927 *Flight of Time.* 8s & 7s. (318)

1 MY days are gliding swiftly by,
And I, a pilgrim stranger,
Would not detain them as they fly,—
Those hours of toil and danger:

For now we stand on Jordan's strand,
Our friends are passing over;
And, just before, the shining shore
We may almost discover.

2 Our absent King the watchword gave,—
"Let every lamp be burning:"
We look afar, across the wave,
Our distant home discerning: For now, etc.

3 Should coming days be dark and cold,
We will not yield to sorrow,
For hope will sing, with courage bold,
"There's glory on the morrow:" For now, etc.

4 Let sorrow's rudest tempest blow,
Each chord on earth to sever,
Our King says come, and there's our home,
For ever! oh, for ever! For now, etc.

KINGSLEY. 11s. GEO. KINGSLEY.

928

Longing for Heaven. 11s. (319)

1 I WOULD not live alway: I ask not to stay
Where storm after storm rises dark o'er the way;
The few lucid mornings that dawn on us here
Are followed by gloom or beclouded with fear.

2 I would not live alway thus fettered by sin,—
Temptation without and corruption within;
E'en the rapture of pardon is mingled with fears,
And the cup of thanksgiving with penitent tears.

3 I would not live alway; no—welcome the tomb:
Since Jesus hath lain there, I dread not its gloom:
There sweet be my rest till he bid me arise
To hail him in triumph descending the skies.

4 Who, who would live alway away from his God,—
Away from yon heaven, that blissful abode,
Where rivers of pleasure flow bright o'er the plains,
And the noontide of glory eternally reigns?

5 There saints of all ages in harmony meet,
Their Saviour and brethren transported to greet;
While anthems of rapture unceasingly roll,
And the smile of the Lord is the feast of the soul.

DEATH.

ZEPHYR. L. M. WM. B. BRADBURY.

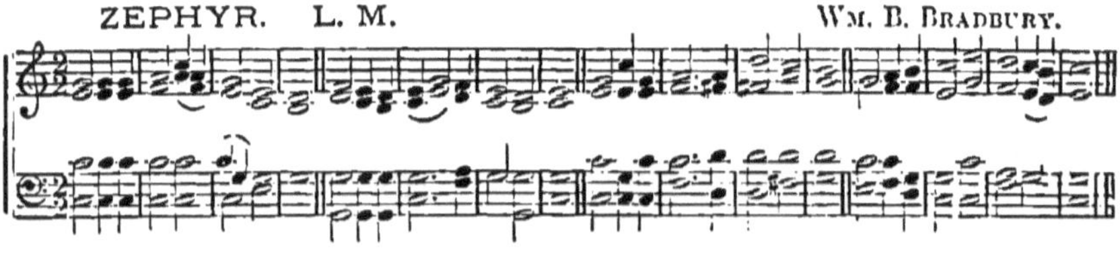

929

Blessedness of the Righteous in Death. L. M. (323)

1 How blest the righteous when he dies!
When sinks a weary soul to rest!
How mildly beam the closing eyes!
How gently heaves th' expiring breast!

2 So fades a summer cloud away;
So sinks the gale when storms are o'er;
So gently shuts the eye of day;
So dies a wave along the shore.

3 A holy quiet reigns around,
A calm which life nor death destroys;
And naught disturbs that peace profound
Which his unfettered soul enjoys.

4 Life's labor done, as sinks the clay,
Light from its load the spirit flies,
While heaven and earth combine to say,
"How blest the righteous when he dies!"

REST. L. M. Wm. B. Bradbury.

930 L. M. (322)

The good Fight fought.

1 The hour of my departure's come;
I hear the voice that calls me home;
Now, O my God, let trouble cease,
And let thy servant die in peace.

2 The race appointed I have run;
The combat's o'er, the prize is won;
And now my witness is on high;
And now my record's in the sky.

3 Not in mine innocence I trust;
I bow before thee in the dust;
And through my Saviour's blood alone
I look for mercy at thy throne.

4 I come, I come, at thy command;
I give my spirit to thy hand;
Stretch forth thine everlasting arms,
And shield me in the last alarms.

931 L. M. (323)

Death not to be feared.

Tune—Zephyr, No. 929.

1 Why should we start and fear to die?
What timorous worms we mortals are!
Death is the gate of endless joy,
And yet we dread to enter there.

2 The pains, the groans, the dying strife,
Fright our approaching souls away;
Still we shrink back again to life,
Fond of our prison and our clay.

3 Oh, if my Lord would come and meet,
My soul should stretch her wings in haste,
Fly fearless through death's iron gate,
Nor feel the terrors as she passed.

4 Jesus can make a dying bed
Feel soft as downy pillows are,
While on his breast I lean my head,
And breathe my life out sweetly there.

932 *Triumph over Death.* L. M. (337)

Tune—Rockingham, No. 295.

1 God of my life, through all my days
I'll tune the grateful notes of praise;
The song shall wake with opening light,
And warble to the silent night.

2 When death o'er nature shall prevail,
And all the powers of language fail,
Joy through my swimming eyes shall break
And mean the thanks I cannot speak.

3 But oh, when that last conflict's o'er,
And I am chained to earth no more,
With what glad accents shall I rise
To join the music of the skies!

4 Then shall I learn the exalted strains
That echo through the heavenly plains,
And emulate, with joy unknown,
The glowing seraphs round thy throne.

HENRY. C. M. S. B. Pond.

933 *Victory over Death.* C. M. (332)

1 Oh, for an overcoming faith,
To cheer my dying hours,
To triumph o'er the monster Death,
And all his frightful powers!

2 Joyful, with all the strength I have,
My quivering lips should sing,—
"Where is thy boasted victory, Grave?
And where, O Death, thy sting?"

3 If sin be pardoned, I'm secure;
Death has no sting beside;
The law gives sin its damning power,
But Christ, my ransom, died.

4 Now to the God of victory
Immortal thanks be paid,
Who makes us conquerors, while we die,
Through Christ, our living Head.

CHINA. C. M. SWAN.

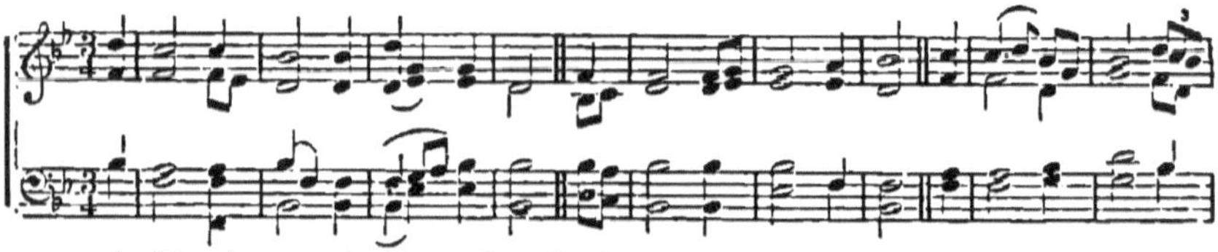

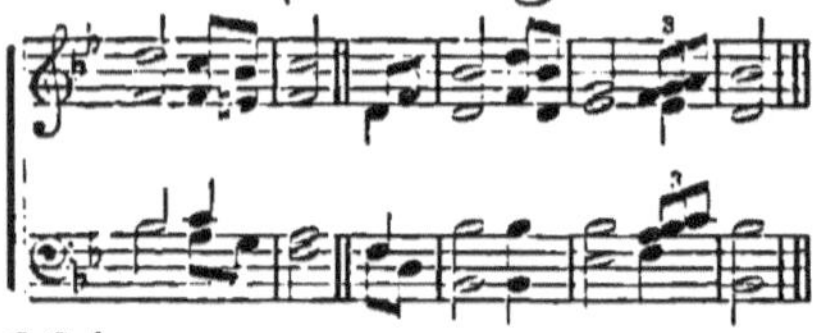

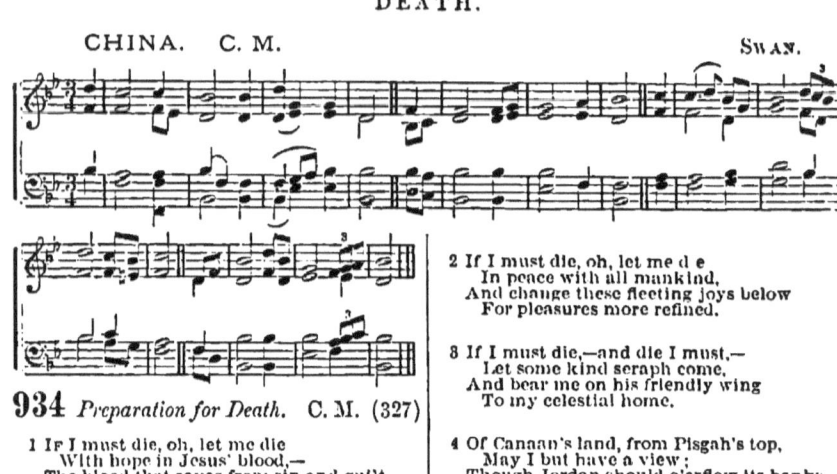

934 *Preparation for Death.* C. M. (327)

1 IF I must die, oh, let me die
With hope in Jesus' blood,—
The blood that saves from sin and guilt,
And reconciles to God.

2 If I must die, oh, let me die
In peace with all mankind,
And change these fleeting joys below
For pleasures more refined.

3 If I must die,—and die I must,—
Let some kind seraph come,
And bear me on his friendly wing
To my celestial home.

4 Of Canaan's land, from Pisgah's top,
May I but have a view;
Though Jordan should o'erflow its banks,
I'll boldly venture through.

HENRY. C. M. S. B. POND.

935 C. M. (332)

God's Presence makes Death easy.

1 DEATH cannot make our souls afraid,
If God be with us there;
We may walk through its darkest shade,
And never yield to fear.

2 I could renounce my all below
If my Redeemer bid;
And run, if I were called to go,
And die, as Moses did.

3 Might I but climb to Pisgah's top,
And view the promised land,
My flesh itself would long to drop,
And welcome the command.

4 Clasped in my heavenly Father's arms,
I would forget my breath,
And lose my life among the charms
Of so divine a death.

936 S. M. (325)

The peaceful Death of the Righteous.

Tune—BLANDNER, next page.

1 OH for the death of those
Who slumber in the Lord!
Oh, be like theirs my last repose,
Like theirs my last reward!

2 Their bodies in the ground,
In silent hope, may lie,
Till the last trumpet's joyful sound
Shall call them to the sky.

3 Their ransomed spirits soar,
On wings of faith and love,
To meet the Saviour they adore,
And reign with him above.

4 Oh for the death of those
Who slumber in the Lord!
Oh, be like theirs my last repose,
Like theirs my last reward!

BLANDNER. S. M. — JOHN M. EVANS.

OBERLIN. S. H. M. — MODERN HARP.

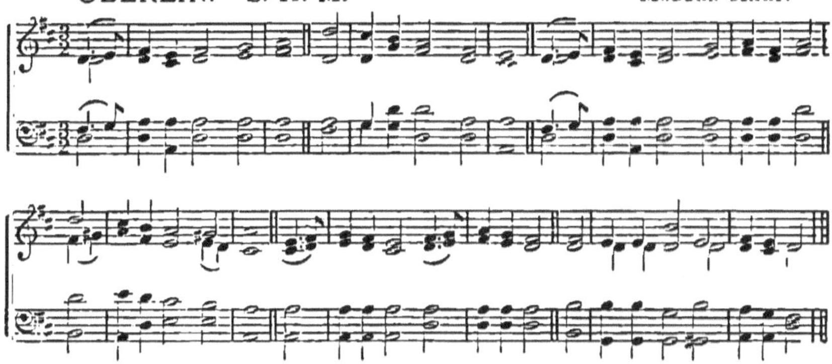

937 S. H. M. (340)

Friends separated by Death.

1 FRIEND after friend departs;
 Who hath not lost a friend?
There is no union here of hearts
 That finds not here an end:
Were this frail world our final rest,
Living or dying, none were blest.

2 There is a world above,
 Where parting is unknown;
A long eternity of love,
 Formed for the good alone;
And faith beholds the dying here
Translated to that glorious sphere.

3 Thus star by star declines,
 Till all are passed away;
As morning high and higher shines
 To pure and perfect day;
Nor sink those stars in empty night,
But hide themselves in heaven's own light.

938 C. M. (332)

Death a temporary Separation.

Tune—HENRY, No. 923.

1 COME, let us join our friends above,
 Who have obtained the prize,
And on the eagle wings of love
 To joy celestial rise.

2 One army of the living God,
 To his command we bow;
Part of the host have crossed the flood,
 And part are crossing now.

3 E'en now to their eternal home
 Some happy spirits fly;
And we are to the margin come,
 And soon expect to die.

4 O Saviour, be our constant Guide;
 Then, when the word is given,
Bid Jordan's narrow stream divide,
 And land us safe in heaven.

939 *Death of a Christian.* C. M. (324)

Tune—BEMERTON, No. 919.

1 DEAR as thou wert, and justly dear,
 We would not weep for thee:
One thought shall check the starting tear:
 It is, that thou art free.

2 And thus shall faith's consoling power
 The tears of love restrain;
Oh, who that saw thy parting hour
 Could wish thee here again?

3 Triumphant in thy closing eye
 The hope of glory shone;
Joy breathed in thy expiring sigh,
 To think the race was run.

4 Gently the passing spirit fled,
 Sustained by grace divine:
Oh, may such grace on us be shed,
 And make our end like thine.

CHINA. C. M. SWAN.

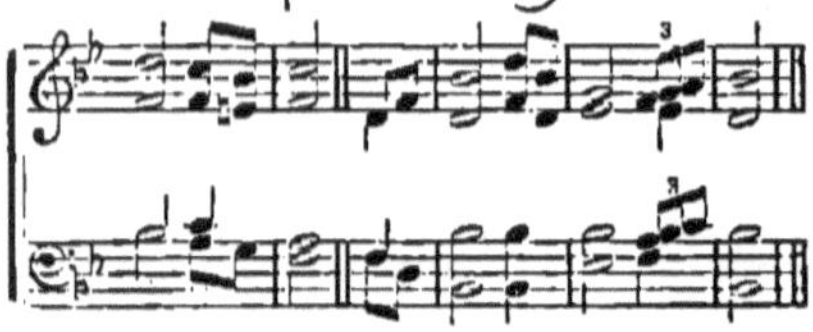

940 C. M. (327)

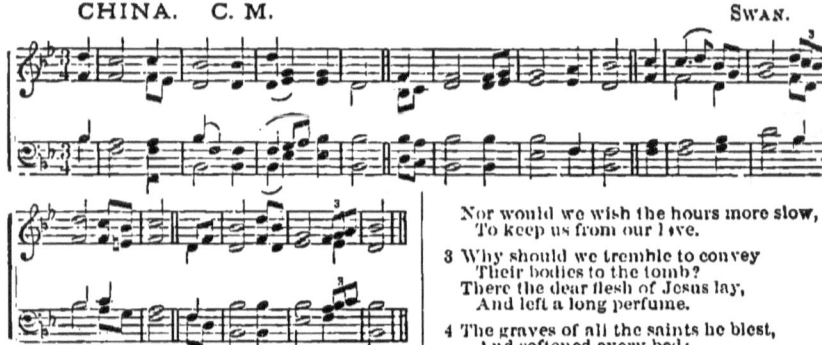

Death of Christian Friends.

1 WHY do we mourn departing friends,
Or shake at death's alarms?
'Tis but the voice that Jesus sends
To call them to his arms.

2 Are we not tending upward, too,
As fast as time can move?
Nor would we wish the hours more slow,
To keep us from our love.

3 Why should we tremble to convey
Their bodies to the tomb?
There the dear flesh of Jesus lay,
And left a long perfume.

4 The graves of all the saints he blest,
And softened every bed;
Where should the dying members rest
But with their dying Head?

5 Thence he arose, ascending high,
And showed our feet the way;
Up to the Lord our flesh shall fly,
At the great rising day.

6 Then let the last loud trumpet sound,
And bid our kindred rise;
Awake, ye nations under ground;
Ye saints, ascend the skies.

REST. L. M. WM. B. BRADBURY.

941 L. M. (322)

Death and Burial of a Christian.

1 UNVEIL thy bosom, faithful tomb;
Take this new treasure to thy trust,
And give these sacred relics room
To slumber in the silent dust.

2 Not pain nor grief nor anxious fear
Invades thy bounds; no mortal woes
Can reach the peaceful sleeper here,
While angels watch the soft repose.

3 So Jesus slept: God's dying Son
Passed through the grave and blest the bed;
Rest here, blest saint, till from his throne
The morning break and pierce the shade.

4 Break from his throne, illustrious morn;
Attend, O earth, his sovereign word;
Restore thy trust; a glorious form
Shall then arise to meet the Lord.

942 S. M. (324)

The Death of an aged Minister.

Tune—BRADEN, next page.

1 "SERVANT of God, well done;
Rest from thy loved employ;
The battle fought, the victory won
Enter thy Master's joy."

2 The voice at midnight came;
He started up to hear
A mortal arrow pierced his frame;
He fell, but felt no fear.

3 Tranquil amid alarms,
It found him on the field,
A veteran slumbering on his arms,
Beneath his red-cross shield.

4 The pains of death are past;
Labor and sorrow cease;
And, life's long warfare closed at last,
His soul is found in peace.

5 Soldier of Christ, well done;
Praise be thy new employ;
And, while eternal ages run,
Rest in thy Saviour's joy.

BRADEN. S. M. WM. B. BRADBURY.

Ritard.

FULTON. 7s. WM. B. BRADBURY.

943 *The Christian Burial.* 7s. (344)

1 BROTHER, though from yonder sky
Cometh neither voice nor cry,
Yet we know for thee to-day
Every pain hath passed away.

2 Not for thee shall tears be given,
Child of God and heir of heaven;
For he gave thee sweet release;
Thine the Christian's death of peace

3 Brother, in that solemn trust
We commend thee, dust to dust;
In that faith we wait, till, risen,
Thou shalt meet us all in heaven

4 While we weep as Jesus wept,
Thou shalt sleep as Jesus slept;
With thy Saviour thou shalt rest,
Crowned and glorified and blest.

KINGSLEY. 11s. GEO. KINGSLEY.

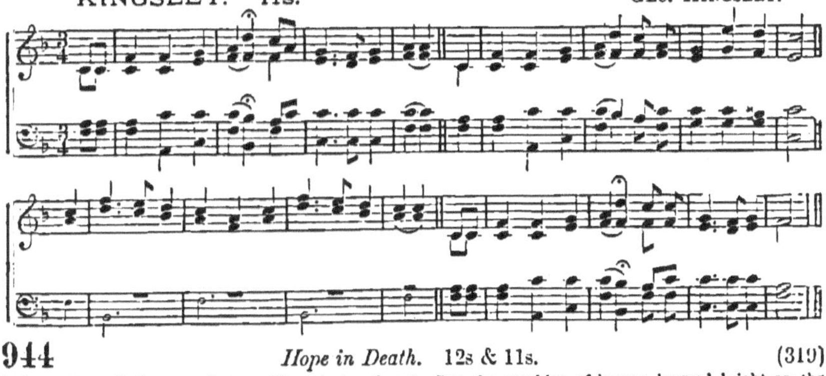

944 *Hope in Death.* 12s & 11s. (319)

1 Thou art gone to the grave; but we will not deplore thee,
Though sorrows and darkness encompass the tomb;
The Saviour has passed through its portals before thee,
And the lamp of his love is thy guide through the gloom.

2 Thou art gone to the grave; we no longer behold thee,
Nor tread the rough paths of the world by thy side;
But the wide arms of mercy are spread to enfold thee,
And sinners may hope, since the Saviour hath died.

3 Thou art gone to the grave; and, its mansion forsaking,
Perchance thy weak spirit in doubt lingered long;
But the sunshine of heaven beamed bright on thy waking,
And the sound thou didst hear was the seraphim's song.

4 Thou art gone to the grave; but we will not deplore thee,
Since God was thy Ransom, thy Guardian, thy Guide;
He gave thee, he took thee, and he will restore thee;
And death has no sting, since the Saviour hath died.

PARRY. 10s. DR. L. MASON.

945

Death in the Prime of Life. 10s. (320)

1 Go to the grave in all thy glorious prime,
In full activity of zeal and power;
A Christian cannot die before his time;
The Lord's appointment is the servant's hour.

2 Go to the grave; at noon from labor cease;
Rest on thy sheaves, thy harvest-task is done;
Come from the heat of battle, and in peace,
Soldier, go home; with thee the fight is won.

3 Go to the grave, for there thy Saviour lay
In death's embraces, ere he rose on high;
And all the ransomed, by that narrow way,
Pass to eternal life beyond the sky.

4 Go to the grave?—no, take thy seat above,
Be thy pure spirit present with the Lord,
Where thou for faith and hope hast perfect love,
And open vision for the written word.

MARSHALL. 7, 6s, & 8. L. MARSHALL.

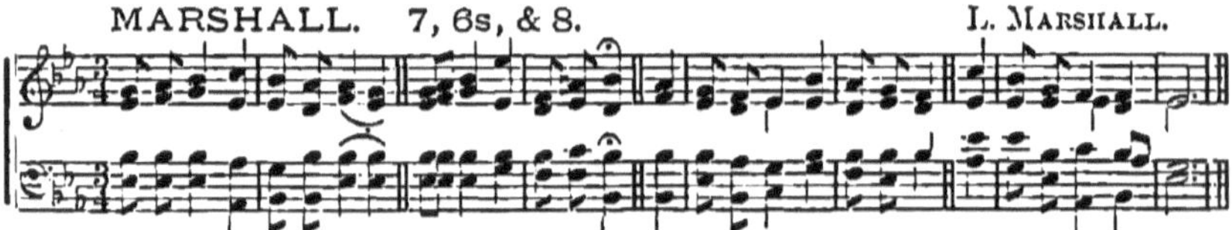

946

Early Death. 7, 6s, & 8. (346)

1 BROTHER, thou art gone to rest;
We will not weep for thee;
For thou art now where oft on earth
Thy spirit longed to be.

2 Brother, thou art gone to rest;
Thine is an early tomb;
But Jesus summoned thee away;
Thy Saviour called thee home.

3 Brother, thou art gone to rest;
Thy toils and cares are o'er;
And sorrow, pain, and suffering, now
Shall ne'er distress thee more.

4 Brother, thou art gone to rest;
And this shall be our prayer,—
That, when we reach our journey's end,
Thy glory we may share.

947

C. M. (329)

Those blessed who die in the Lord.

Tune—NOEL, next page.

1 HEAR what the voice from heaven proclaims
For all the pious dead:
"Sweet is the savor of their names,
And soft their sleeping bed.

2 "They die in Jesus, and are blest;
How kind their slumbers are!
From suffering and from sin released,
They're freed from ev'ry snare.

3 "Far from this world of toil and strife,
They're present with the Lord;
The labors of their mortal life
End in a large reward."

948

Asleep in Jesus. L. M. (323)

Tune—ZEPHYR, next page.

1 ASLEEP in Jesus! blessed sleep,
From which none ever wakes to weep;
A calm and undisturbed repose,
Unbroken by the last of foes.

2 Asleep in Jesus! oh, how sweet
To be for such a slumber meet!
With holy confidence to sing
That Death has lost his venomed sting.

3 Asleep in Jesus! peaceful rest,
Whose waking is supremely blest:
No fear, no woe shall dim that hour
That manifests the Saviour's power.

NOEL. C. M.

949 *Death of an Infant.* L. M. (323)

ZEPHYR.

1 So fades the lovely, blooming flower,
Frail, smiling solace of an hour;
So soon our transient comforts fly
And pleasure only blooms to die.

2 Is there no kind, no healing art
To soothe the anguish of the heart?
Spirit of grace, be ever nigh;
Thy comforts are not made to die.

3 Let gentle patience smile on pain,
Till dying hope revives again;
Hope wipes the tear from sorrow's eye,
And faith points upward to the sky.

ZEPHYR. L. M. — WM. B. BRADBURY.

MOUNT VERNON. 8s & 7s. — DR. L. MASON.

950 8s & 7s. (343)

Comfort in the Death of the Christian.

1 CEASE, ye mourners, cease to languish
O'er the grave of those you love;
Pain and death and night and anguish
Enter not the world above.

2 While our silent steps are straying,
Lonely, through night's deepening shade,
Glory's brightest beams are playing
Round the happy Christian's head.

3 Light and peace at once deriving
From the hand of God most high,
In his glorious presence living,
They shall never, never die.

4 Endless pleasure pain excluding,
Sickness there no more can come;
There, no fear of woe, intruding,
Sheds o'er heaven a moment's gloom.

951 8s & 7s. (342)

Farewell to a Christian Sister.

1 SISTER, thou wast mild and lovely,
Gentle as the summer breeze,
Pleasant as the air of evening,
When it floats among the trees.

2 Peaceful be thy silent slumber,—
Peaceful in the grave so low;
Thou no more wilt join our number;
Thou no more our songs shalt know.

3 Yet again we hope to meet thee,
When the day of life is fled;
Then in heaven with joy to greet thee,
Where no farewell tear is shed.

BLANDNER. S. M. JOHN M. EVANS

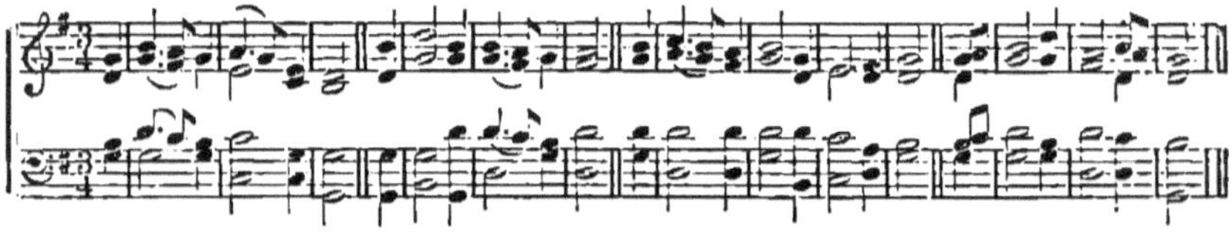

952

This Mortal shall put on Immortality. S. M. (325)

1 AND must this body die?
This mortal frame decay?
And must these active limbs of mine
Lie mouldering in the clay?

2 God, my Redeemer, lives,
And ever from the skies
Looks down and watches all my dust,
Till he shall bid it rise.

3 Arrayed in glorious grace,
Shall these vile bodies shine,
And every shape and every face
Look heavenly and divine.

4 These lively hopes we owe
To Jesus' dying love;
We would adore his grace below
And sing his power above.

INDIANA. 7s. 6 lines. DONIZETTI.

953

Life brought to Light by the Gospel. 7s. 6l. (351)

1 EARTH to earth, and dust to dust,
Lord, we own the sentence just;
Head and tongue, and hand and heart,
All in guilt have borne their part;
Righteous is the common doom,
All must molder in the tomb.

2 Lord, from nature's gloomy night
Turn we to the gospel's light;
Thou didst triumph o'er the grave,
Thou wilt all thy people save;
Ransomed by thy blood, the just
Rise immortal from the dust.

NOEL. C. M.

954 C. M. (329)

The Dead shall live again.

1 THRO' sorrow's night, and danger's path,
Amid the deepening gloom,
We, followers of our suffering Lord,
Are marching to the tomb.

2 Yet not thus hopeless, in the grave,
The vital spark shall lie;
For o'er life's wreck that spark shall rise
To seek its kindred sky.

3 These ashes, too, this little dust,
Our Father's care shall keep,
Till the archangel's trump shall break
The long and dreary sleep.

4 Then love's soft dew o'er every eye
Shall shed its mildest rays,
And the long-silent voice awake
With shouts of endless praise.

955 *The Lord's Coming.* L. M. (335)

Tune—ORWELL, No. 323.

1 THE Lord will come; the earth shall quake;
The hills their ancient seats forsake;
And, withering, from the vault of night,
The stars withdraw their feeble light.

2 The Lord will come; but not the same
As once in lowly form he came,—
A quiet Lamb to slaughter led,—
The bruised, the suffering, and the dead

3 The Lord will come; a dreadful form,
With wreath of flame, and robe of storm,
On cherub wings, and wings of wind,
Anointed Judge of human kind.

4 Can this be he who wont to stray
A pilgrim on the world's highway,
By power oppressed, and mocked by pride?
O God, is this the Crucified?

5 Go, tyrants, to the rocks complain;
Go, seek the mountain's cleft in vain;
But faith, victorious o'er the tomb,
Shall sing for joy, "The Lord is come."

BREST. 8s, 7s, & 4. DR. L. MASON.

956 8s, 7s, & 4. (336)

Saints and Sinners judged.

1 DAY of judgment, day of wonders,—
Hark! the trumpet's awful sound,
Louder than a thousand thunders,
Shakes the vast creation round:
How the summons
Will the sinner's heart confound!

2 See the Judge, our nature wearing,
Clothed in majesty divine;
You, who long for his appearing,
Then shall say, "This God is mine'
Gracious Saviour,
Own me in that day for thine.

3 At his call the dead awaken,
Rise to life from earth and sea;
All the powers of nature, shaken
By his looks, prepare to flee:
Careless sinner,
What will then become of thee?

4 But to those who have confessèd,
Loved, and served the Lord below,
He will say, "Come near, ye blessèd;
See the kingdom I bestow;
You for ever
Shall my love and glory know."

957 C. M. (327)

Because I live, ye shall live also.

Tune—CHINA, No. 940.

1 WHEN downward to the darksome tomb
I thoughtful turn my eyes,
Frail nature trembles at the gloom,
And anxious fears arise.

2 Why shrinks my soul? In death's embrace
Once Jesus captive slept;
And angels, hovering o'er the place,
His lowly pillow kept.

3 Thus shall they guard my sleeping dust,
And, as the Saviour rose,
The grave again shall yield her trust,
And end my deep repose.

4 My Lord, before to glory gone,
Shall bid me come away;
And calm and bright shall break the dawn
Of heaven's eternal day.

958 8s, 7s, & 4. (336)

Christ coming to Judgment.

1 Lo! he comes, with clouds descending,
Once for favored sinners slain;
Thousand thousand saints attending,
Swell the triumph of his train:
Hallelujah!
Jesus shall for ever reign.

2 Every eye shall now behold him,
Robed in dreadful majesty!
Those who set at naught and sold him,
Pierced, and nailed him to the tree
Deeply wailing,
Shall the true Messiah see.

3 Now the Saviour, long expected,
See, in solemn pomp, appear;
All his saints, by man rejected,
Now shall meet him in the air.
Hallelujah!
See the day of God appear.

BREST. 8s, 7s, & 4. DR. L. MASON.

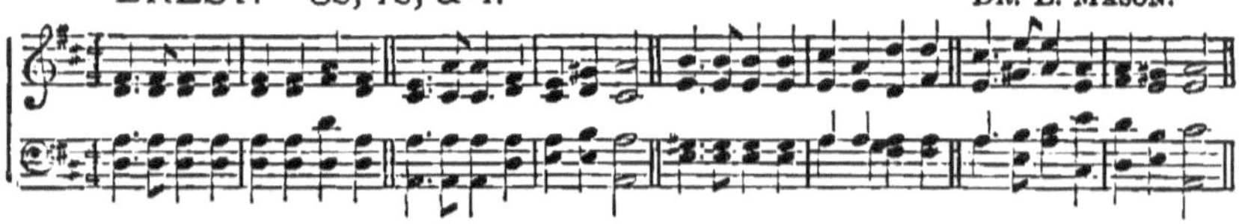

959 L. M. (335)

The Lord Jesus revealed from Heaven.

1 THE day of wrath, that dreadful day,
When heaven and earth shall pass away!
What power shall be the sinner's stay?
How shall he meet that dreadful day?

2 When, shrivelling like a parchèd scroll,
The flaming heavens together roll,
And louder yet, and yet more dread,
Resounds the trump that wakes the dead?

3 Oh, on that day, that wrathful day,
When man to judgment wakes from clay,
Be thou, O Christ, the sinner's stay,
Though heaven and earth shall pass away.

ORWELL. L. M. DR. L. MASON.

960 *Resurrection and Judgment.* S. M. (324)

Tune—BRADEN, No. 314.

1 WAKED by the trumpet's sound,
I from the grave must rise,
And see the Judge with glory crowned,
And see the flaming skies.

2 How shall I leave my tomb?
With triumph or regret?
A fearful or a joyful doom,
A curse or blessing, meet?

(CONTINUED.)

3 I must from God be driven,
 Or with my Saviour dwell;
Must come, at his command, to heaven,
 Or else depart—to hell.

4 O thou that wouldst not have
 One wretched sinner die,
Who diedst thyself, my soul to save
 From endless misery,

5 Show me the way to shun
 Thy dreadful wrath severe,
That, when thou comest on thy throne,
 I may with joy appear.

961 C. M. (311)

Everlasting Absence of God intolerable.

Tune—DUNDEE, No. 811.

1 That awful day will surely come,
 Th' appointed hour makes haste,
When I must stand before my Judge,
 And pass the solemn test.

2 Thou lovely Chief of all my joys,
 Thou Sovereign of my heart,
How could I bear to hear thy voice
 Pronounce the sound, "Depart!"

3 Jesus, I throw my arms around,
 And hang upon thy breast;
Without one gracious smile from thee,
 My spirit cannot rest.

4 Oh, tell me that my worthless name
 Is graven on thy hands;
Show me some promise in thy book,
 Where my salvation stands.

962 *Solemn Questions.* S. M. (345)

1 And will the Judge descend?
 And must the dead arise,
And not a single soul escape
 His all-discerning eyes?

2 How will my heart endure
 The terrors of that day,
When earth and heaven, before his face,
 Astonished, shrink away?

3 But, ere the trumpet shakes
 The mansions of the dead,
Hark! from the gospel's cheering sound
 What joyful tidings spread!

4 Come, sinners, seek his grace,
 Whose wrath ye cannot bear;
Fly to the shelter of his cross,
 And find salvation there.

PILGRIM'S SONG. S. M. Rev. E. W. Dunbar.

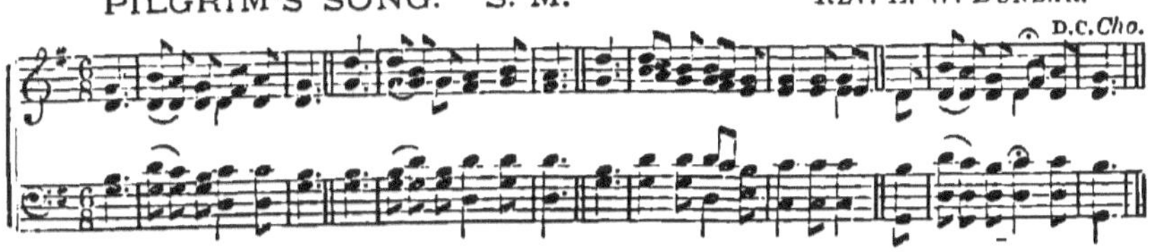
D.C.Cho.

MERIBAH. C. P. M. Dr. L. Mason.

963 C. P. M. (330)

Be thou my Hiding-place.

1 When thou, my righteous Judge, shall come
To take thy ransomed people home,
 Shall I among them stand?
Shall such a worthless worm as I,
Who sometimes am afraid to die,
 Be found at thy right hand?

2 I love to meet among them now,
Before thy gracious feet to bow,
 Though vilest of them all;
But—can I bear the piercing thought?—
What if my name should be left out,
 When thou for them shalt call?

3 Prevent, prevent it by thy grace;
Be thou, dear Lord, my hiding-place,
 In this, th' accepted day;
Thy pardoning voice, oh, let me hear,
To still my unbelieving fear,
 Nor let me fall, I pray.

4 Let me among thy saints be found,
Whene'er the archangel's trump shall sound,
 To see thy smiling face
Then loudest of the throng I'll sing,
While heaven's resounding mansions ring
 With shouts of sovereign grace.

MERIBAH. C. P. M. Dr. L. Mason.

964 *Solemnity of Life.* C. P. M. (330)

1 No room for mirth or trifling here,
For worldly hope, or worldly fear,
If life so soon is gone;
If now the Judge is at the door,
And all mankind must stand before
The inexorable throne.

2 Nothing is worth a thought beneath,
But how I may escape the death
That never, never dies;
How make mine own election sure;
And when I fail on earth, secure
A mansion in the skies.

3 Jesus, vouchsafe a pitying ray;
Be thou my Guide, be thou my Way
To glorious happiness.
Ah! write thy pardon on my heart,
And whensoe'er I hence depart,
Let me depart in peace.

965 C. P. M. (330)

Contemplation of Judgment.

1 O God, my inmost soul convert,
And deeply on my thoughtful heart
Eternal things impress;
Cause me to feel their solemn weight,
And tremble on the brink of fate,
And wake to righteousness.

2 Before me place, in dread array,
The pomp of that tremendous day,
When thou with clouds shalt come
To judge the nations at thy bar;
And tell me, Lord, shall I be there
To meet a joyful doom?

3 Be this my one great business here
With serious industry and fear,
Eternal bliss t' insure,—
Thine utmost counsel to fulfil,
And suffer all thy righteous will
And to the end endure.

4 Then, Father, then my soul receive,
Transported from this vale, to live
And reign with thee above,
Where faith is sweetly lost in sight,
And hope in full, supreme delight,
And everlasting love.

HEAVEN.

BROWN. C. M. Wm. B. Bradbury.

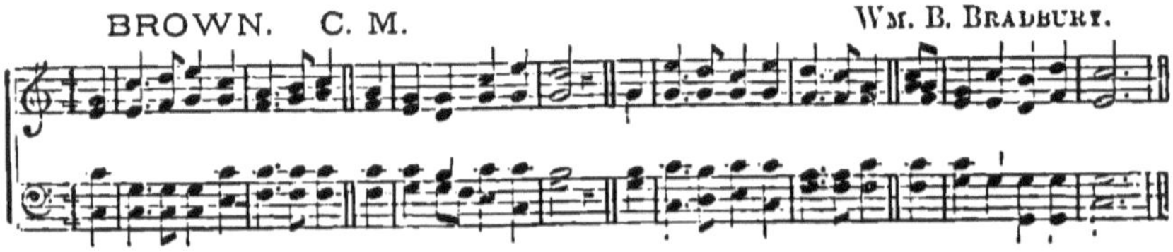

966 *The Attractions of Heaven.* C. M. (333)

1 There is a land of pure delight,
Where saints immortal reign;
Eternal day excludes the night,
And pleasures banish pain.

2 There everlasting spring abides,
And never-fading flowers:
Death, like a narrow sea, divides
That heavenly land from ours.

3 Sweet fields, beyond the swelling flood,
Stand dressed in living green:
So to the Jews old Canaan stood,
While Jordan rolled between.

4 Oh, could we make our doubts remove,—
Those gloomy doubts that rise,—
And see the Canaan that we love
With unbeclouded eyes,—

5 Could we but climb where Moses stood,
And view the landscape o'er,—
Not Jordan's stream, nor death's cold flood
Should fright us from the shore.

JERUSALEM THE GOLDEN. 7s & 6s. ENGLISH.

967

The Paradise eternal. 7s & 6s. (350)

1 O PARADISE eternal,
What bliss to enter thee,
And once within thy portals,
Secure for ever be!

2 In thee no sin nor sorrow,
No pain nor death is known;
But pure glad life, enduring
As heaven's benignant throne.

3 There God shall be our portion,
And we his jewels be;
And gracing his bright mansions
His smile reflect and see

4 O paradise eternal,
What joys in thee are known!
O God of mercy, guide us,
Till all be felt our own.

BEULAH. 7s. E. IVES, JR.

FINE.
D.S.
D.S.

968

The Redeemed in Heaven. 7s. (339)

1 WHO are these in bright array,
This exulting, happy throng,
Round the altar night and day,
Hymning one triumphant song?
"Worthy is the Lamb, once slain,
Blessing, honor, glory, power,
Wisdom, riches, to obtain,
New dominion every hour."

2 These through fiery trials trod;
These from great affliction came;
Now, before the throne of God,
Sealed with his almighty name:
Clad in raiment pure and white,
Victor-palms in every hand,
Through their great Redeemer's might,
More than conquerors they stand.

3 Hunger, thirst, disease, unknown
On immortal fruits they feed;
Them the Lamb, amidst the throne,
Shall to living fountains lead:
Joy and gladness banish sighs;
Perfect love dispels all fears;
And for ever from their eyes
God shall wipe away their tears.

WHITNEY. C. M. Dr. L. Mason.

Dim.

969 C. M. (338)

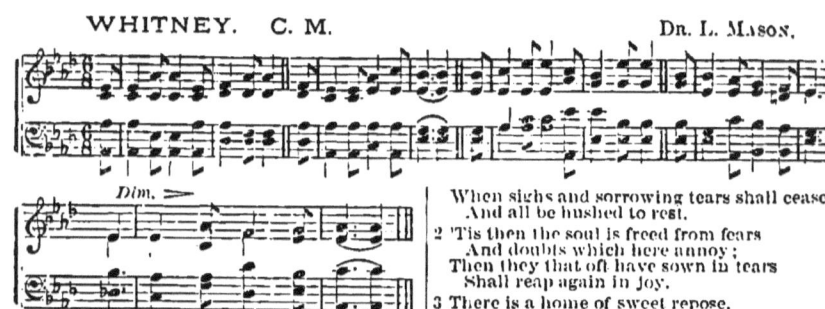

The Peace and Repose of Heaven.

1 There is an hour of hallowed peace
For those with cares oppressed,
When sighs and sorrowing tears shall cease,
And all be hushed to rest.

2 'Tis then the soul is freed from fears
And doubts which here annoy;
Then they that oft have sown in tears
Shall reap again in joy.

3 There is a home of sweet repose,
Where storms assail no more;
The stream of endless pleasure flows
On that celestial shore.

4 There purity with love appears,
And bliss without alloy;
There they that oft had sown in tears
Shall reap again in joy.

NOEL. C. M.

970 C. M. (329)

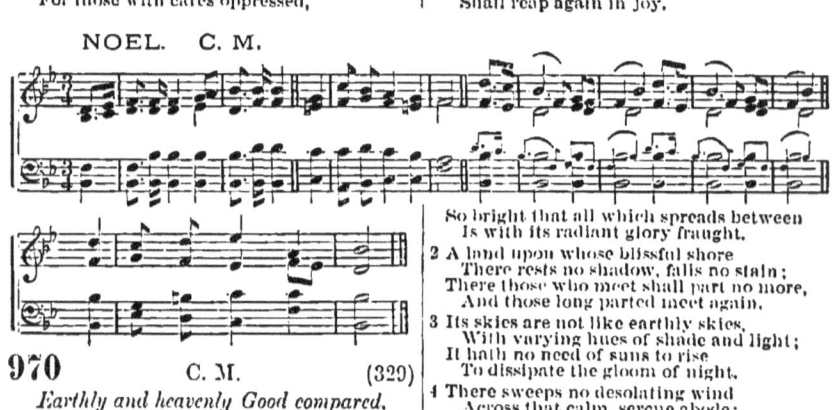

Earthly and heavenly Good compared.

1 These mortal joys, how soon they fade!
How swift they pass away!
The dying flower reclines its head,
The beauty of a day.

2 Soon are those earthly treasures lost
We fondly call our own;
We scarcely can possession boast,
Before we find them gone.

3 But there are joys which cannot die,
With God laid up in store,
Treasures beyond the changing sky,
More bright than golden ore.

4 The seeds which piety and love
Have scattered here below,
In fair and fertile fields above
To ample harvests grow.

971 *The heavenly Land.* L. M. (337)

Tune—Rockingham, next page.

1 There is a land mine eye hath seen,
In visions of enraptured thought,
So bright that all which spreads between
Is with its radiant glory fraught.

2 A land upon whose blissful shore
There rests no shadow, falls no stain;
There those who meet shall part no more,
And those long parted meet again.

3 Its skies are not like earthly skies,
With varying hues of shade and light;
It hath no need of suns to rise
To dissipate the gloom of night.

4 There sweeps no desolating wind
Across that calm, serene abode;
The wanderer there a home may find
Within the paradise of God.

972 *No sin in Heaven.* C. M. (326)

Tune—Gould, next page.

1 Far from these narrow scenes of night,
Unbounded glories rise,
And realms of joy and pure delight,
Unknown to mortal eyes.

2 Fair, distant land!—could mortal eyes
But half its charms explore,
How would our spirits long to rise
And dwell on earth no more!

3 No cloud those blissful regions know,—
Realms ever bright and fair;
For sin, the source of mortal woe,
Can never enter there.

4 Oh, may the heavenly prospect fire
Our hearts with ardent love!
Till wings of faith, and strong desire,
Bear every thought above.

GOULD. C. M.

J. E. GOULD.

Ritard.

ROCKINGHAM. L. M.

DR. L. MASON.

973 10s. (320)

No Night in Heaven.

Tune—PARRY, No. 915.

1 No night shall be in heaven; no gathering gloom
Shall o'er that glorious landscape ever come;
No tears shall fall in sadness o'er those flowers
That breathe their fragrance through celestial bowers.

2 No night shall be in heaven; no dreadful hour
Of mental darkness, of the tempter's power;
Across those skies no envious clouds shall roll,
To dim the sunlight of the raptured soul.

3 No night shall be in heaven; no sorrow's reign;
No secret anguish, no corporeal pain;
No shivering limbs, no burning fever there;
No soul's eclipse, no winter of despair.

4 No night shall be in heaven, but endless noon;
No fast-declining sun, no waning moon;
But there the Lamb shall yield perpetual light,
'Mid pastures green and waters ever bright.

WOODBURY. S. M. Double.

I. B. WOODBURY.

CHORUS.

974 *Dwelling with God.* S. M. (352)

1 "FOR ever with the Lord!"
Amen! so let it be;
Life from the dead is in that word,—
'Tis immortality.

2 Here in the body pent,
Absent from him, I roam,
Yet nightly pitch my moving tent
A day's march nearer home.

3 My Father's house on high,—
Home of my soul,—how near,
At times, to faith's foreseeing eye,
Thy golden gates appear!

4 "For ever with the Lord!"
Father, if 'tis thy will,
The promise of that faithful word
E'en here to me fulfil.

JERUSALEM THE GOLDEN. 7s & 6s. ENGLISH.

975 *Jerusalem the Golden.* 7s & 6s. (350)

1 JERUSALEM the golden,
With milk and honey blest,
Beneath thy contemplation
Sink heart and voice oppress'd:
I know not, oh, I know not
What joys await us there:
What radiancy of glory,
What bliss beyond compare.

2 They stand, those halls of Sion,
Conjubilant with song,
And bright with many an angel,
And all the martyr throng:
The Prince is ever in them,
The daylight is serene;
The pastures of the blessed
Are deck'd in glorious sheen.

3 There is the throne of David,
And there, from care released,
The song of them that triumph,
The shout of them that feast;
And they, who with their Leader
Have conquer'd in the fight,
For ever and for ever
Are clad in robes of white.

PEACE. 8s & 6s. EDGAR REED.

Ritard.

976 *Rest in Heaven.* 8s & 6s. (349)

1 THERE is an hour of peaceful rest
To mourning wanderers given;
There is a joy for souls distressed,
A balm for every wounded breast,
'Tis found alone in heaven.

2 There is a home for weary souls,
By sins and sorrows driven,
When tossed on life's tempestuous shoals,
Where storms arise, and ocean rolls,
And all is drear,—'tis heaven.

3 There faith lifts up the tearless eye,
The heart no longer riven,
And views the tempest passing by,
Sees evening shadows quickly fly,
And all serene in heaven.

4 There fragrant flowers immortal bloom,
And joys supreme are given;
There rays divine disperse the gloom;
Beyond the dark and narrow tomb
Appears the dawn of heaven.

LEBANON. S. M. Double. J. ZUNDEL.

977 *A Mansion not built with Hands.* S. M. Double. (343)

1 I HAVE a home above,
 From sin and sorrow free,
A mansion which eternal love
 Designed and formed for me.
My Father's gracious hand
 Has built this sweet abode;
From everlasting it was planned
 My dwelling-place with God.

2 My Saviour's precious blood
 Has made my title sure;
He pass'd through death's dark raging flood
 To make my rest secure.
The Comforter is come,
 The earnest has been given;
He leads me onward to the home
 Reserved for me in heaven.

3 Loved ones are gone before,
 Whose pilgrim days are done;
I soon shall greet them on that shore
 Where partings are unknown.
But more than all, I long
 His glories to behold,
Whose smile fills all that radiant throng
 With ecstasy untold.

OAK. 6s & 4s. DR. L. MASON.

978 6s & 4s. (340)

My Home is in Heaven.

1 I'M but a stranger here,
 Heaven is my home;
Earth is a desert drear,
 Heaven is my home:
Danger and sorrow stand
Round me on every hand;
 Heaven is my fatherland,—
 Heaven is my home.

2 What though the tempest rage,
 Heaven is my home;
Short is my pilgrimage;
 Heaven is my home:
Time's cold and wint'ry blast
Soon will be overpast;
I shall reach home at last,—
 Heaven is my home.

3 There, at my Saviour's side,—
 Heaven is my home;
I shall be glorified,—
 Heaven is my home:
There are the good and blest,
Those I loved most and best,
And there I, too, shall rest;
 Heaven is my home.

VARINA. C. M. RINK

979 C. M. (331)

The Heavenly Mansion.

1 THERE is a house not made with hands,
Eternal, and on high;
And here my spirit waiting stands
Till God shall bid it fly.

2 Shortly this prison of my clay
Must be dissolved and fall;
Then, O my soul, with joy obey
Thy heavenly Father's call.

3 'Tis he, by his almighty grace,
That forms thee fit for heaven,
And, as an earnest of the place,
Has his own Spirit given.

4 We walk by faith of joys to come;
Faith lives upon his word;
But while the body is our home,
We're absent from the Lord.

5 'Tis pleasant to believe thy grace,
But we had rather see;
We would be absent from the flesh,
And present, Lord, with thee.

980 *Beautiful Zion.* L. M. 6l. (353)

1 BEAUTIFUL Zion, built above,
Beautiful city, that I love,
Beautiful gates of pearly white,
Beautiful temple,—God its light,—
He who was slain on Calvary
Opens those pearly gates to me.

2 Beautiful heaven, where all is light,
Beautiful angels, clothed in white,
Beautiful strains that never tire,
Beautiful harps through all the choir,—
There shall I join the chorus sweet,
Worshipping at the Saviour's feet.

3 Beautiful throne for Christ our King,
Beautiful songs the angels sing,
Beautiful rest, all wanderings cease,
Beautiful home of perfect peace,—
There shall my eyes the Saviour see:
Haste to this heavenly home with me.

BEAUTIFUL CITY. L. M. T. J COOK.

mf
cres.
f
mp

(CONTINUED.)

BEAUTIFUL CITY.—Concluded.

Repeat. pp
Zi - on, Zi - on, love - ly Zi - on! Beau - ti - ful Zi - on, cit - y of our God!

981 L. M. (337)

Going Home to Heaven.

Tune—ROCKINGHAM, No. 295.

1 My heavenly home is bright and fair;
Nor pain nor death can enter there:
Its glittering towers the sun outshine;
That heavenly mansion shall be mine.

2 My Father's house is built on high,
Far, far above the starry sky;
When from this earthly prison free,
That heavenly mansion mine shall be.

3 Let others seek a home below,
Which flames devour, or waves o'erflow;
Be mine the happier lot to own
A heavenly mansion near the throne.

982 C. M. (333)

The New Jerusalem.

Tune—BROWN, No. 966.

1 JERUSALEM, my happy home,
Name ever dear to me!
When shall my labors have an end,
In joy and peace, in thee?

2 Oh, when, thou city of my God,
Shall I thy courts ascend,
Where congregations ne'er break up,
And Sabbaths have no end?

3 There happier bowers than Eden's bloom,
Nor sin nor sorrow know;
Blest seats, through rude and stormy scenes,
I onward press to you.

4 Why should I shrink at pain and woe,
Or feel at death dismay?
I've Canaan's goodly land in view,
And realms of endless day.

5 Jerusalem, my happy home,
My soul still pants for thee;
Then shall my labors have an end,
When I thy joys shall see.

983 S. M. (325)

Aspiration for Heaven.

Tune—BLANDNER, No. 952.

1 FAR from my heavenly home,
Far from my Father's breast,
Fainting, I cry, Blest Saviour, come,
And speed me to my rest.

2 My spirit homeward turns,
And fain would thither flee;
My heart, O Zion, droops and yearns,
When I remember thee.

3 To thee, to thee, I press,
A dark and toilsome road;
When shall I pass the wilderness,
And reach the saints' abode?

4 God of my life, be near;
On thee my hopes I cast;
Oh, guide me through the desert here,
And bring me home at last!

984 7s & 6s. (350)

Longing to be clothed upon.

Tune—JERUSALEM THE GOLDEN, No. 975.

1 OH! for the robes of whiteness;
Oh! for the tearless eyes;
Oh! for the glorious brightness
Of the unclouded skies.

2 Oh! for the "no more weeping"
Within the land of love,—
The endless joy of keeping
The bridal feast above.

3 Oh! for the hour of seeing
My Saviour face to face,—
The joy of ever being
In that sweet meeting-place.

4 Jesus, thou King of glory,
I soon shall dwell with thee,
And sing the wondrous story
Of all thy love to me.

BEYOND THE SMILING. 9s, 4s, & 6s. WM. B. BRADBURY.

CHORUS.

985 9s, 4s, & 6s. (347)

Love, Rest, and Home.

1 BEYOND the smiling and the weeping
I shall be soon;
Beyond the waking and the sleeping,
Beyond the sowing and the reaping,
I shall be soon.
Love, rest, and home,—sweet, sweet home!
Oh, how sweet it will be there to meet
The dear loved ones at home.

2 Beyond the blooming and the fading
I shall be soon;
Beyond the shining and the shading,
Beyond the hoping and the dreading,
I shall be soon.
Love, rest, and home, etc.

3 Beyond the rising and the setting
I shall be soon;
Beyond the calming and the fretting,
Beyond remembering and forgetting,
I shall be soon.
Love, rest, and home, etc.

4 Beyond the parting and the meeting
I shall be soon;
Beyond the farewell and the greeting,
Beyond the pulse's fever beating,
I shall be soon.
Love, rest, and home, etc.

986 *Heaven in Prospect.* C. M. (331)

Tune—VARINA, No. 979.

1 ON Jordan's stormy banks I stand,
And cast a wishful eye
To Canaan's fair and happy land,
Where my possessions lie.

2 Oh, the transporting, rapturous scene
That rises to my sight!
Sweet fields, arrayed in living green,
And rivers of delight.

3 O'er all those wide-extended plains
Shines one eternal day;
There God the Son for ever reigns,
And scatters night away.

4 No chilling winds nor poisonous breath
Can reach that healthful shore;
Sickness and sorrow, pain and death,
Are felt and feared no more.

5 When shall I reach that happy place,
And be for ever blest?
When shall I see my Father's face
And in his bosom rest?

6 Filled with delight, my raptured soul
Would here no longer stay;
Though Jordan's waves should round me roll,
I'd fearless launch away.

PILGRIM'S SONG. S. M. REV. E. W. DUNBAR.

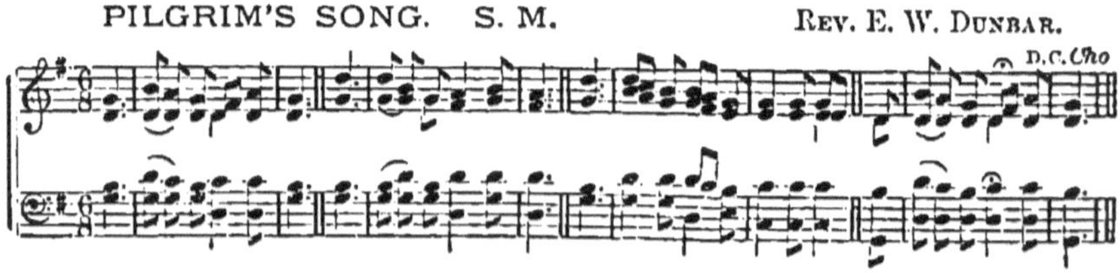
D.C. Cho

987 *The Pilgrim's Song.* S. M. (345)

Tune—PILGRIM'S SONG.

1 A FEW more years shall roll,
A few more seasons come,
And we shall be with those that rest,
Asleep within the tomb.
Then, O my Lord, prepare
My soul for that great day;
Oh, wash me in thy precious blood,
And take my sins away.

2 A few more struggles here,
A few more partings o'er,
A few more toils, a few more tears,
And we shall weep no more.

3 A few more Sabbaths here
Shall cheer us on our way,
And we shall reach the endless rest,
Th' eternal Sabbath-day.

4 'Tis but a little while,
And he shall come again,
Who died that we might live, who lives
That we with him may reign.

988 C. M. (333)

The Hope of Heaven.

Tune—BROWN, No. 966.

1 WHEN I can read my title clear
To mansions in the skies,
I bid farewell to every fear,
And wipe my weeping eyes.

2 Should earth against my soul engage,
And fiery darts be hurled,
Then I can smile at Satan's rage,
And face a frowning world.

3 Let cares, like a wild deluge, come
And storms of sorrow fall!
May I but safely reach my home,
My God, my heaven, my all.

4 There shall I bathe my weary soul
In seas of heavenly rest,
And not a wave of trouble roll
Across my peaceful breast.

PRAYER FOR CHRIST'S COMING.

WATCHMAN. 7s. DR. L. MASON.

SOPRANO.
TENOR.
SOPRANO.
TENOR.
Chorus to 1st and 2d stanzas.
Chorus to 3d stanza.

989 7s. (341)

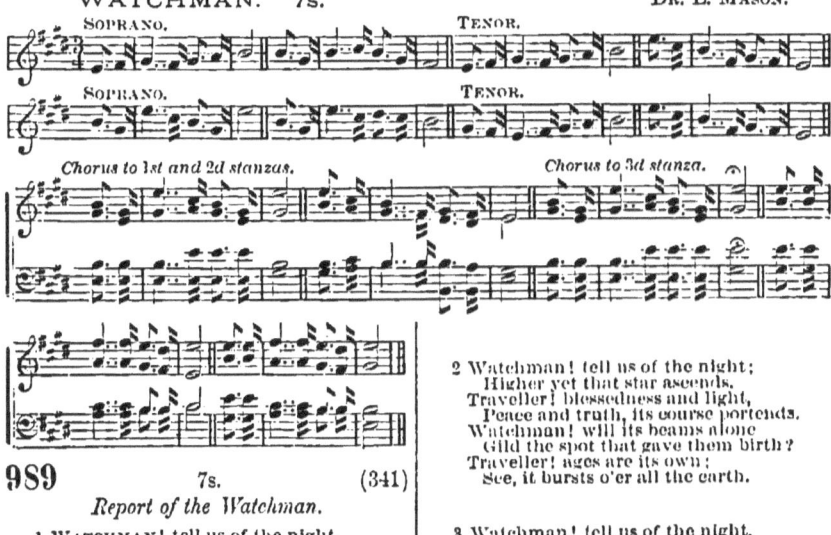

Report of the Watchman.

1 WATCHMAN! tell us of the night,
What its signs of promise are.
Traveller! o'er yon mountain's height,
See that glory-beaming star.
Watchman! does its beauteous ray
Aught of hope or joy foretell?
Traveller! yes; it brings the day,
Promised day of Israel.

2 Watchman! tell us of the night;
Higher yet that star ascends.
Traveller! blessedness and light,
Peace and truth, its course portends.
Watchman! will its beams alone
Gild the spot that gave them birth?
Traveller! ages are its own;
See, it bursts o'er all the earth.

3 Watchman! tell us of the night,
For the morning seems to dawn.
Traveller! darkness takes its flight;
Doubt and terror are withdrawn.
Watchman! let thy wanderings cease;
Hie thee to thy quiet home.
Traveller! lo! the Prince of Peace,
Lo! the Son of God is come.

AMSTERDAM. 7s & 6s. Peculiar.

D.C. Omit.
After Repeat omit.
FINE.

D.C.
D.C.

990 7s & 6s. (342)

Looking unto Jesus.

1 RISE, my soul, and stretch thy wings;
 Thy better portion trace;
Rise from transitory things,
 Toward heaven, thy native place;
Sun and moon and stars decay;
 Time shall soon this earth remove;
Rise, my soul, and haste away
 To seats prepared above.

2 Rivers to the ocean run,
 Nor stay in all their course;
Fire, ascending, seeks the sun;
 Both speed them to their source
So a soul that's born of God
 Pants to view his glorious face,
Upward tends to his abode,
 To rest in his embrace.

3 Cease, ye pilgrims, cease to mourn;
 Press onward to the prize;
Soon our Saviour will return,
 Triumphant in the skies;
Yet a season, and you know
 Happy entrance will be given,
All our sorrows left below,
 And earth exchanged for heaven.

TELEMANS. 7s. C. ZEUNER.

991 7s. (313)

Hasten, Lord, the promised Hour.

1 SEE the ransomed millions stand,
Palms of conquest in their hand;
This before the throne their strain,
"Hell is vanquished, death is slain!

2 "Blessing, honor, glory, might,
Are the Conqueror's native right;
Thrones and powers before him fall,—
Lamb of God, and Lord of all!"

3 Hasten, Lord, the promised hour;
Come in glory and in power;
Still thy foes are unsubdued;
Nature sighs to be renewed.

4 Time has nearly reached its sum;
All things, with the bride, say "Come."
Jesus, whom all worlds adore,
Come, and reign for evermore.

992 L. M. (337)

Christ the Redeemer and Judge.

Tune—ROCKINGHAM, No. 295.

1 Now to the Lord, who makes us know
 The wonders of his dying love,
Be humble honors paid below
 And strains of nobler praise above.

2 To Jesus, our atoning Priest,
 To Jesus, our eternal King,
Be everlasting power confessed,
 Let every tongue his glory sing.

3 Behold, on flying clouds he comes,
 And every eye shall see him move;
Though with our sins we pierced him once
 Now he displays his pardoning love.

4 The unbelieving world shall wail,
 While we rejoice to see the day;
Come, Lord, nor let thy promise fail,
 Nor let thy chariot long delay.

993 *Watch.* 7s & 6s. (321)

Tune—MENDEBAS, No. 918.

1 REJOICE, rejoice, believers,
And let your lights appear;
The shades of eve are thickening,
And darker night is near.

2 The Bridegroom is advancing;
Each hour he draws more nigh;
Up! watch and pray, nor slumber;
At midnight comes the cry.

3 Our hope and expectation,
O Jesus, now appear,
Arise, thou Sun so looked for,
O'er this benighted sphere.

4 With hearts and hands uplifted,
We plead, O Lord, to see
The day of our redemption,
And ever be with thee.

994 S. M. (324)

The Watchful Servant.

Tune—BRADEN, No. 344.

1 YE servants of the Lord,
Each in his office wait;
With joy obey his heavenly word,
And watch before his gate.

2 Let all your lamps be bright,
And trim the golden flame;
Gird up your loins, as in his sight,
For awful is his name.

3 Watch!—'tis your Lord's command;
And while we speak he's near:
Mark every signal of his hand,
And ready all appear.

4 Oh, happy servant he,
In such a posture found!
He shall his Lord with rapture see,
And be with honor crowned.

995 *Come, Lord Jesus.* C. M. (329)

Tune—NOEL, No. 970.

1 LIGHT of the lonely pilgrim's heart,
Star of the coming day,
Arise, and, with thy morning beams,
Chase all our griefs away.

2 Come, blessed Lord, bid every shore
And answering island sing
The praises of thy royal name,
And own thee as their King.

3 Bid the whole earth, responsive now
To the bright world above,
Break forth in rapturous strains of joy,
In memory of thy love.

4 Lord, Lord, thy fair creation groans,—
The earth, the air, the sea,—
In unison with all our hearts,
And calls aloud for thee.

996 C. M. (328)

Kingdom of Christ among Men.

Tune—BEMERTON, No. 919.

1 Lo! what a glorious sight appears
To our believing eyes!
The earth and seas are passed away,
And fled the rolling skies.

2 "The God of glory down to men
Removes his blest abode—
His saints the objects of his grace,
And he their faithful God.

3 "His own soft hand shall wipe the tears
From every weeping eye,
And pains, and groans, and griefs, and fears,
And death itself, shall die."

4 How long, dear Saviour, oh, how long
Shall this bright hour delay?
Fly swifter round, ye wheels of time,
And bring the welcome day.

997 *Come, Lord Jesus.* 7s. (316)

Tune—AINSWORTH, No. 898.

1 COME, Desire of nations, come;
Hasten, Lord, the general doom;
Hear the Spirit and the Bride;
Come, and take us to thy side.

2 Thou who hast our place prepared,
Make us meet for our reward;
Then with all thy saints descend;
Then our earthly trials end.

3 Mindful of thy chosen race,
Shorten these vindictive days;
Hear us now, and save thine own,
Who for full redemption groan.

4 Take to thee thy royal power;
Reign, when sin shall be no more;
Reign, when death no more shall be,
Reign to all eternity!

998 *Longing for Christ.* S. M. (345)

Tune—PILGRIM'S SONG, No. 987.

1 COME, Lord, and tarry not;
Bring the long-looked-for day;
Oh! why these years of waiting here,
These ages of delay?

2 We long to hear thy voice,
To see thee face to face,
To share thy crown and glory then,
As now we share thy grace.

3 Come, and make all things new;
Build up this ruined earth;
Restore our faded paradise—
Creation's second birth.

4 Come, and begin thy reign
Of everlasting peace;
Come, take the kingdom to thyself,
Great King of righteousness.

INDIANA. 7s. 6 lines. DONIZETTI.

999 *Till he come.* 7s. 61. (351)

1 "TILL he come,"—oh, let the words
Linger on the trembling chords;
Let the little while between
In their golden light be seen;
Let us think how heaven and home
Lie beyond that "Till he come."

2 Clouds and conflicts round us press;
Would we have one sorrow less?
All the sharpness of the cross,
All that tells the world is loss,
Death and darkness and the tomb,
Only whisper, "Till he come."

3 See, the feast of love is spread;
Drink the wine, and break the bread:
Sweet memorials,—till the Lord
Calls us round his heavenly board;
Some from earth, from glory some:
Severed only "Till he come."

GRATITUDE. L. M. BOST.

1000 *Praise unceasing.* L. M. (312)

1 To God the Father, God the Son,
And God the Spirit, Three in One,
From all above and all below,
Let joyful praise unceasing flow.
Amen.

Selections for Chanting,

and Miscellaneous Pieces.

CHANT No. 1.—Gloria in Excelsis.

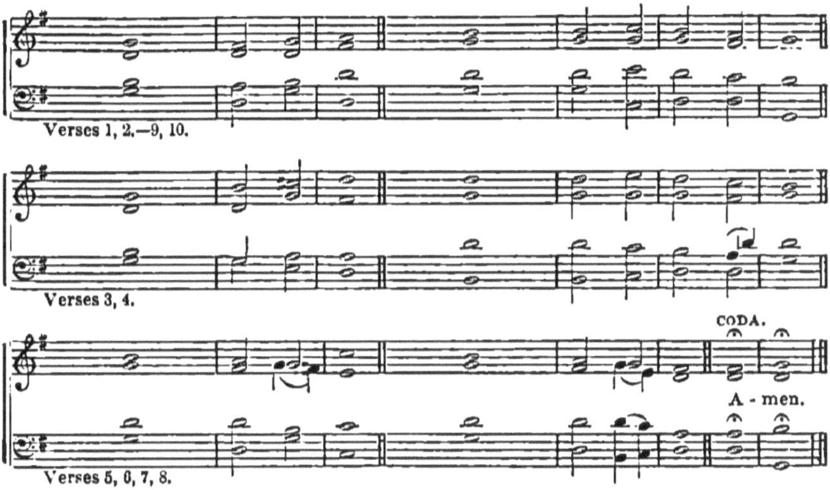
Verses 1, 2.—9, 10.
Verses 3, 4.
CODA.
A - men.
Verses 5, 6, 7, 8.

1. Glory be to | God on | high, ‖ and on earth | peace, good- | will toward | men.
2. We praise thee, we bless thee, we | worship | thee, ‖ we glorify thee, we give thanks to | thee for | thy great | glory.
3. O Lord God, | heavenly | King, ‖ God the | Father | Al- | mighty;
4. O Lord, the only begotten Son | Jesus | Christ; ‖ O Lord God, Lamb of God, | Son— | of the | Father:
5. That takest away the | sins ·· of the | world, ‖ have mercy up- | on— | us.
6. Thou that takest away the | sins ·· of the | world, ‖ have mercy up- | on— | us.
7. Thou that takest away the | sins ·· of the | world, ‖ re- | ceive our | prayer.
8. Thou that sittest at the right hand of | God the | Father, ‖ have mercy up- | on— | us.
9. For thou | only ·· art | holy; ‖ thou | only | art the | Lord.
10. Thou only, O Christ, with the | Holy | Ghost, ‖ art most high in the | glory ·· of | God the | Father. ‖ A- | men.

CHANT No. 2.—Te Deum Laudamus.

JOHN ROBINSON, 1730.

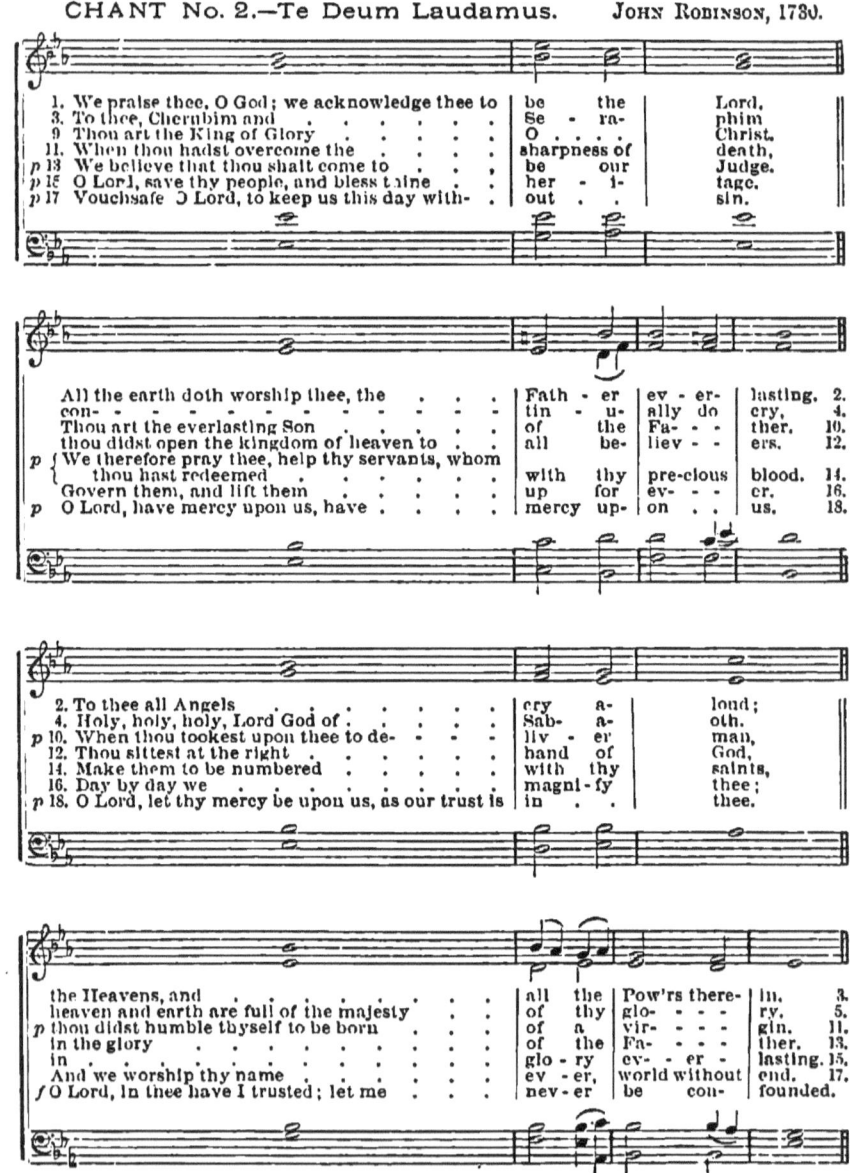

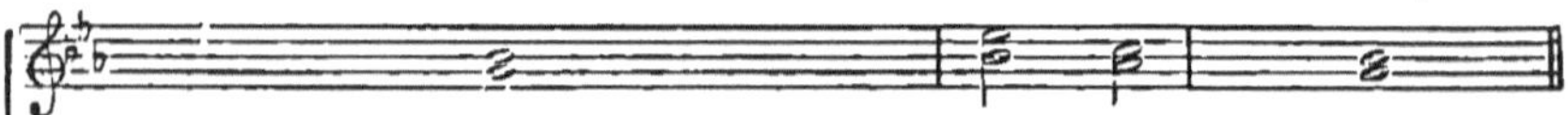

	1. We praise thee, O God; we acknowledge thee to	be	the	Lord.
	3. To thee, Cherubim and	Se -	ra-	phim
	9. Thou art the King of Glory	O		Christ.
	11. When thou hadst overcome the	sharpness	of	death,
p	13. We believe that thou shalt come to . . . ,	be	our	Judge.
p	15. O Lord, save thy people, and bless thine . .	her -	i-	tage.
p	17. Vouchsafe O Lord, to keep us this day with- .	out .	.	sin.

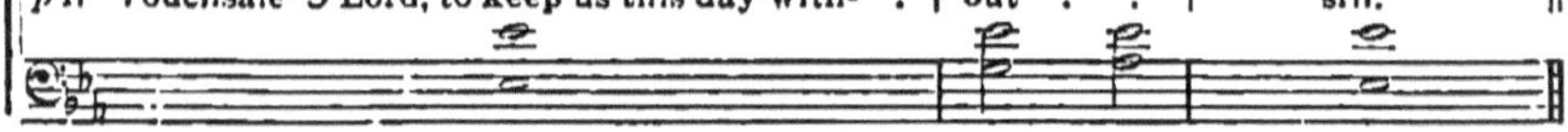

	All the earth doth worship thee, the	Fath -	er	ev -	er-	lasting.	2.
	con- - - - - - - - - - - - - - -	tin -	u-	ally	do	cry,	4.
	Thou art the everlasting Son	of	the	Fa- - -		ther.	10.
	thou didst open the kingdom of heaven to . .	all	be-	liev - -		ers.	12.
p	We therefore pray thee, help thy servants, whom thou hast redeemed	with	thy	pre-cious		blood.	14.
	Govern them, and lift them	up	for	ev- - -		er.	16.
p	O Lord, have mercy upon us, have	mercy	up-	on . .		us.	18.

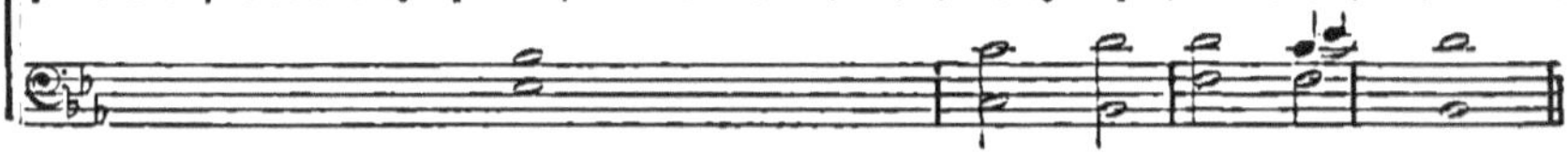

	2. To thee all Angels	cry	a-	loud;
	4. Holy, holy, holy, Lord God of	Sab-	a-	oth.
p	10. When thou tookest upon thee to de- - - - -	liv -	er	man,
	12. Thou sittest at the right	hand	of	God,
	14. Make them to be numbered	with	thy	saints,
	16. Day by day we	magni -	fy	thee;
p	18. O Lord, let thy mercy be upon us, as our trust is	in .	.	thee.

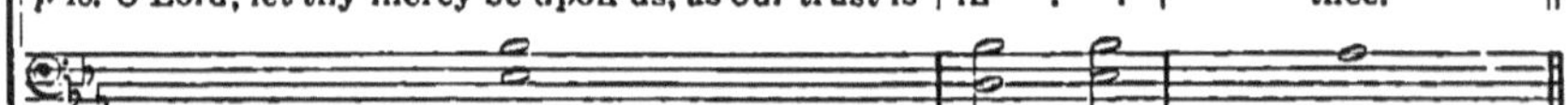

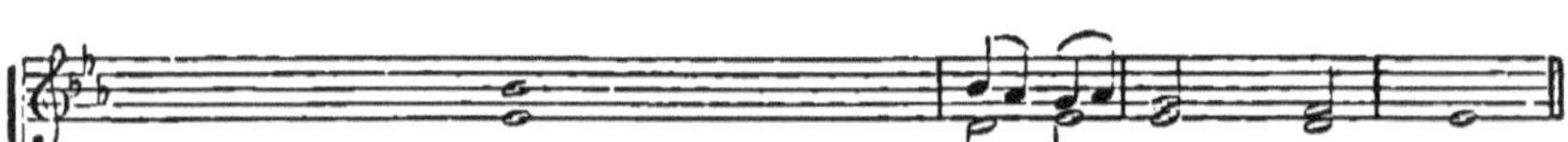

	the Heavens, and	all	the	Pow'rs there-		in.	3.
	heaven and earth are full of the majesty . . .	of	thy	glo- - - -		ry.	5.
p	thou didst humble thyself to be born	of	a	vir- - - -		gin.	11.
	in the glory	of	the	Fa- - - -		ther.	13.
	in	glo -	ry	ev- -	er -	lasting.	15.
	And we worship thy name	ev -	er,	world	without	end.	17.
f	O Lord, in thee have I trusted; let me	nev -	er	be	con-	founded.	

Te Deum Laudamus.—Concluded.

FOUR TIMES.
Solo, alternately 1st Treble and Bass.
Chorus.
5. The glorious company of the Apostles | praise | thee.
6. The goodly fellowship of the Prophets | praise | thee.
7. The noble army of martyrs | praise | thee.
8. Chorus.—The holy Church, throughout all the world, doth ac- | knowledge | thee:
Full Chorus.
The Father, of an | infinite | ma-jes- | ty;
p
ff
Thine adorable, true, and | on - ly | Son; | Also the Holy | Ghost, the | Com-fort- | er. 9.

CHANT No. 3.—"Blest is the hour."

A - men.

1. { BLEST is the hour when cares depart,
   And earthly | scenes are | far,—

   { When tears of woe forget to start,
   And gently dawns upon the heart Devotion's | holy | star.

2. { Blest is the place where angels bend
   To hear our | worship | rise,

   { Where kindred thoughts their musings blend,
   And all the soul's affections tend Beyond the | veiling | skies.

3. { Blest are the hallowed vows that bind
   Man to his | work of | love—

   { Bind him to cheer the humble mind,
   Console the weeping, lead the blind, And guide to | joys a- | bove.

4. { Sweet shall the song of glory swell,
   Spirit di- | vine, to | thee,

   { When they whose work is finished well
   In thy own courts of rest shall dwell, | Blest · · through e—ternity.

CHANT No. 4.—Jubilate.

ROBINSON

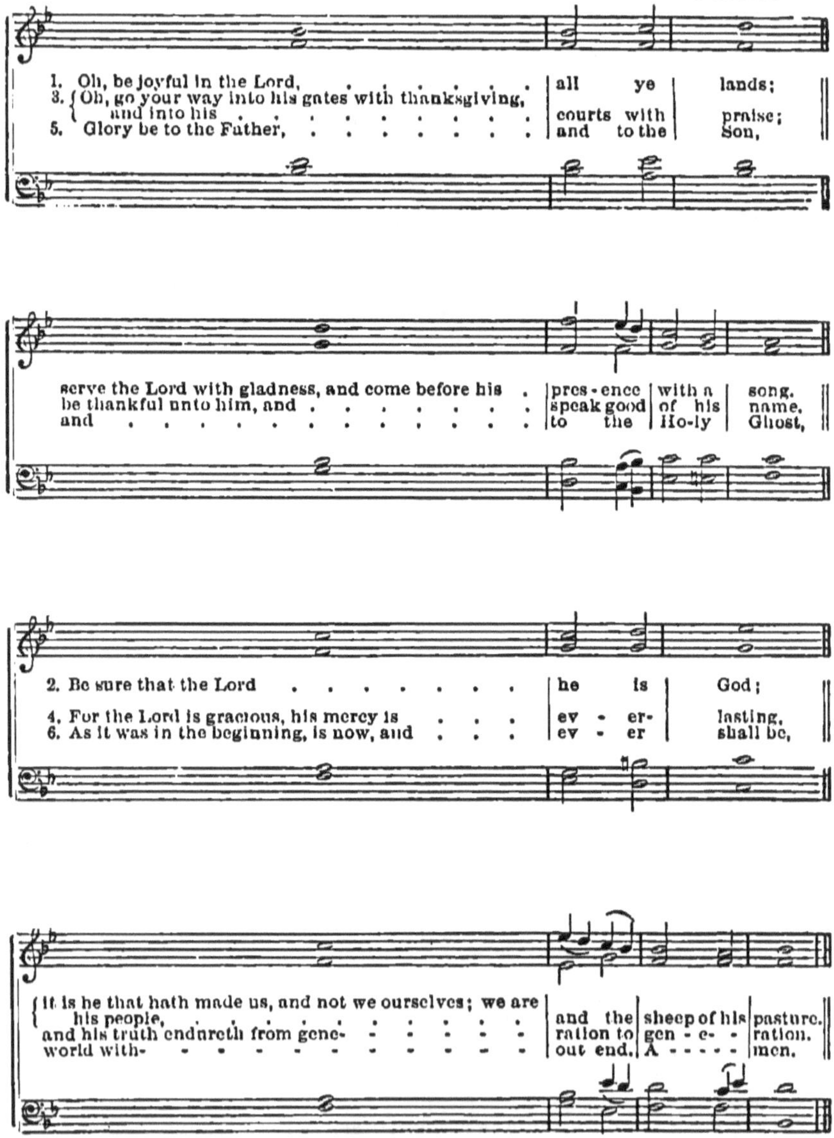
1. Oh, be joyful in the Lord, ... | all ye | lands;
3. Oh, go your way into his gates with thanksgiving, and into his . . . . | courts with | praise;
5. Glory be to the Father, ... | and to the | Son,
serve the Lord with gladness, and come before his . | pres - ence | with a | song.
be thankful unto him, and . . . . | speak good | of his | name.
and . . . . | to the | Ho-ly | Ghost,
2. Be sure that the Lord . . . . | he is | God;
4. For the Lord is gracious, his mercy is . . . | ev - er- | lasting,
6. As it was in the beginning, is now, and . . . | ev - er | shall be,
it is he that hath made us, and not we ourselves; we are his people, ... | and the | sheep of his | pasture.
and his truth endureth from gene- . . . . | ration to | gen - e- - | ration.
world with- . . . . | out end. | A - - - - - | men.

CHANTS.

CHANT No. 5.—Psalm 67.

JOHN M. EVANS.

SOLO.

1. God be merciful unto | us, and | bless us; |
2. That thy way may be known up- | on— | earth, |
3. Let the people | praise thee, O | God; |
4. Oh, let the nations be glad and | sing for | joy: |
5. Let the people praise | thee, O | God; |
6. Then shall the earth | yield her | increase; |
7. God shall | bless | us; |

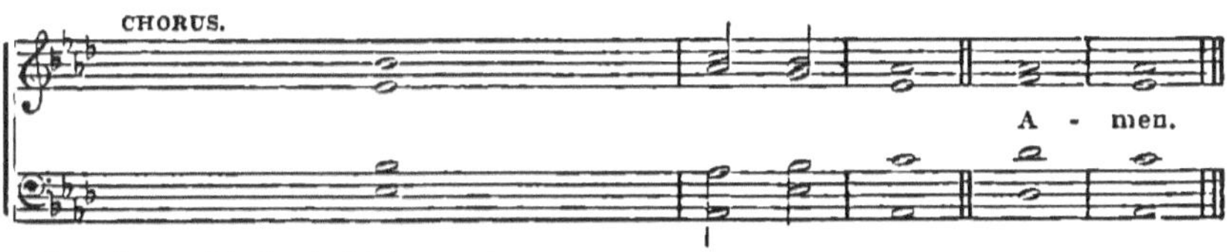
CHORUS.
A - men.

1. and cause his face to | shine up- | on us.
2. thy saving health a- | mong all | nations.
3. let all the people | praise | thee.
4. for thou shalt judge the people righteously: and govern the nations up- | on— | earth.
5. let all the people | praise | thee.
6. and God, even our own | God, shall | bless us.
7. and all the ends of the | earth shall | fear him. | A- | men.

CHANT No. 6.—Psalm 23.

DR. L. MASON.

A - men.

1. The Lord is my shepherd: I | shall not | want.
2. He maketh me to lie down in green pastures; he leadeth me beside the still- | wa- — | ters.
3. He restoreth my soul; he leadeth me in the paths of righteousness for his | name's — | sake.
4. Yea, though I walk through the valley of the shadow of death, I will fear no evil: for thou art with me; thy rod and thy staff they | *p* comfort | me.
5. Thou preparest a table before me in the presence of mine enemies, thou anointest my head with oil; my | cup ·· runneth | over.
6. Surely goodness and mercy shall follow me all the days of my life; and I will dwell in the house of the Lord, for- | ev- — | er. | A- | men.

CHANT No. 7.—Revelation 4:8, 11; 5:12, 13.

A - men.

1. Holy, holy, holy | Lord · · God Al- | mighty, |
Which was, and | is, and | is to | come.

2. Thou art worthy, O Lord, to receive glory and | honor, · · and | power; |
{ For thou hast created all things,
{ And for thy pleasure they | are and | were cre- | ated.

3. Worthy is the Lamb | that was | slain, |
{ To receive power, and riches, and wisdom,
{ And strength, and | honor, · · and | glory, · · and | blessing.

4. Blessing, and honor, and | glory, · · and | power, |
{ Be unto him that sitteth upon the throne,
{ And unto the | Lamb, for- | ever · · and | ever. | Amen.

CHANT No. 8.—Psalm 136.

Solo.
Chorus.
Solo.
Chorus.

Solo. 1. Oh, give thanks unto the Lord, for he is good:
Chorus. For his mercy endureth for ever.

Solo. 2. Oh, give thanks unto the God of gods:
Cho. For his mercy endureth for ever.

Solo. 3. Oh, give thanks unto the Lord of lords:
Cho. For his mercy endureth for ever.

Solo. 4. To him who alone doeth great wonders:
Cho. For his mercy endureth for ever.

Solo. 5. To him that by wisdom made the heavens:
Cho. For his mercy endureth for ever.

Solo. 6. To him that stretched out the earth above the waters:
Cho. For his mercy endureth for ever.

Solo. 7. To him that made great lights:
Cho. For his mercy endureth for ever.

Solo. 8. The sun to rule by day: the moon and stars to rule by night:
Cho. For his mercy endureth for ever.

Solo. 9. To him that smote Egypt in their first-born:
Cho. For his mercy endureth for ever.

Solo. 10. And brought out Israel from among them:
Cho. For his mercy endureth for ever.

Solo. 11. Who remembered us in our low estate:
Cho. For his mercy endureth for ever.

Solo. 12. And hath redeemed us from our enemies:
Cho. For his mercy endureth for ever.

Solo. 13. Who giveth food to all flesh:
Cho. For his mercy endureth for ever.

Solo. 14. Oh, give thanks unto the God of heaven:
Cho. For his mercy endureth for ever. Amen

Treb. 8—8
Alto, 6—5
Ten., 4—3
Bass, 4—1
A - men.

CHANTS.

CHANT No. 9.—Psalm 119.

1. { Thy word is a lamp unto my feet, and a light un- | to my path ; |
{ The entrance of thy word giveth light; it giveth under- | standing ·· un- | to the | simple.

2. { I will delight myself in thy statutes; I will not for- | get thy | word. |
{ So shall I keep thy law continually, for- | ever and | ev | —er.

3. { The law of the Lord is perfect, con- | verting the | soul : |
{ The statutes of the Lord are | right, re- | joicing the— | heart.

4. { Oh, that my ways were directed to | keep thy | statutes ! |
{ Incline thine ear unto me, and write thy | law up- | on my | heart.

CHANT No. 10.—Psalm 105. Conant's Version.

CODA.
Hal - le - lu - jah!

1. Give thanks to Jehovah ; call up- | on his | name, | make known his | deeds a- | mong the | peoples.
2. Sing to him, sing | praise to | him ; | talk of | all his | wondrous | works.
3. Glory in his | holy | name ; | let the heart of them that | seek Je- | hovah ·· re- | joice.
4. Seek after Jehovah | and his | strength ; | seek his | face, seek his | face ever- | more.

CHANT No. 11.—Psalm 130.

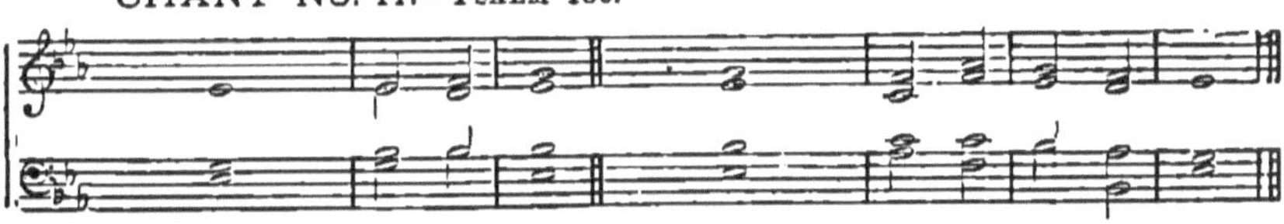

1. Out of the depths have I cried unto | thee, O | Lord.
2. Lord, hear my voice ; let thine ears be attentive to the | voice of ·· my | suppli- | cations.
3. If thou, Lord, shouldst mark iniquities, O Lord, | who shall | stand ?
4. But there is forgiveness with thee, that | thou— | mayest ·· be | feared.
5. I wait for the Lord, my soul doth wait, and in his | word ·· do I | hope.
6. { My soul waiteth for the Lord more than they that watch for the morning, I say, | more than ·· they that | watch ·· for the | morning.
7. { Let Israel hope in the Lord : for with the Lord there is mercy, and with him is | plenteous ·· re | demption.
8. And he shall redeem Israel from | all— | his in- | iquities

CHANT No. 12.—Psalm 29. Conant's Version. Farrant.

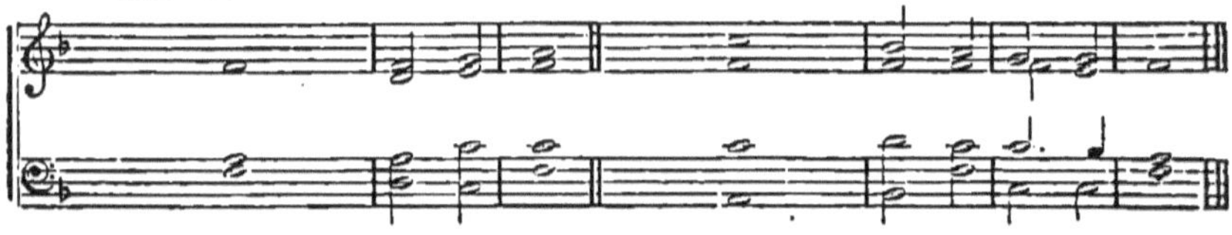

1. Give to Jehovah, ye | sons of | God, ‖ give to Je- | ho - vah | glory and | strength.

2. Give to Jehovah the glory | of his | name; ‖ worship Jehovah in the | beauty of | ho-li- | ness.

3. The voice of Jehovah is on the waters; the God of | glo-ry | thunders. ‖ Jehovah is— | on the | great - - | waters.

4. The voice of Je- | hovah is | mighty; ‖ the voice of Jehovah is | full of | majes- | ty.

5. The voice of Jehovah | breaks the | cedars; ‖ and Jehovah | breaks the | cedars ·· of | Leba-non.

6. The voice of Jehovah | shakes the | wilderness; ‖ Jehovah shakes the | wil-der- | ness of | Kadesh.

7. Jehovah sat in judgment | at the | flood; ‖ and Jehovah | sits ·· a | king ·· for | ever.

8. Jehovah will give strength | to his | people; ‖ Jehovah will | bless his | people with | peace.

CHANT No. 13.—Psalm 24. Conant's Version.

1. The earth is Jehovah's, and the | fulness ·· there- | of; ‖ the world and | they that | dwell there- | in.

2. For he founded it up- | on the | seas, ‖ and established | it up- | on the | floods.

3. Who shall ascend into the | mount ·· of Je- | hovah, ‖ and who shall stand | in his | holy | place?

4. He that has clean hands, and a | pure - - | heart; ‖ who has not lifted up his soul to vanity, and | has not | sworn de- | ceitfully.

5. He shall receive a blessing | from Je- | hovah, ‖ and righteousness from the | God of | his salvation.

6. This is the generation of | them that | seek him, ‖ that seek thy | face, - - | even | Jacob.

7. Lift up your heads, ye gates, and lift yourselves up, ye ever- | lasting | doors, ‖ that the King of | glory | may come | in.

8. Who is this, the | King of | glory? ‖ Jehovah, strong and mighty; Je- | ho - vah, | mighty ·· in | battle.

9. Lift up your heads, ye gates, and lift up, ye ever- | lasting | doors, ‖ that the King of | glory | may come | in.

10. Who then is he, the | King of—glory? ‖ Jehovah of hosts; He | is the | King of | glory.

CHANT No. 14.—Psalm 121.

Conant's Version.

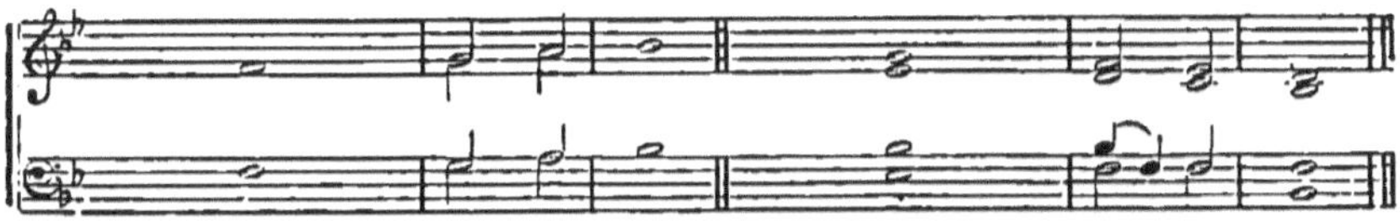

1. {I will lift my eyes unto the mountains; From whence shall | my help | come? ‖ My help is from Jehovah, who made | heaven and | earth.

2. {Let him not suffer thy foot to waver; He that keeps thee, | let him not | slumber. ‖ Behold he will not slumber, and will not sleep, that | keeps - - | Israel.

3. {Jehovah is thy keeper; Jehovah is thy shade on | thy right | hand. ‖ By day the sun shall not smite thee, nor the | moon by | night.

4. {Jehovah will keep thee from all evil; He will | keep thy | soul. ‖ Jehovah will keep thy going out and thy coming in, henceforth and for | ev - er- | more.

CHANT No. 15.—Psalm 46.

1. {God is our | refuge and | strength, ‖ a very present | help in | trouble. ‖ Therefore will not we fear, though the | earth · · be re- | moved, ‖ and though the mountains be carried in- | to the | midst of the | sea;

2. {Though the waters thereof | roar and be | troubled, ‖ though the mountains shake with the | swelling · · there- | of. ‖ There is a river, the streams whereof shall make glad the | city of | God, ‖ the holy place of the tabernacles | of the | Most— | High.

3. {God is in the midst of her; she shall | not be | moved: ‖ God shall help her, and | that right | early. ‖ The Lord of | hosts is | with us; ‖ the God of | Jacob | is our | refuge.

4. {Be still, and know that | I am | God: ‖ I will be exalted among the heathen, I will be exalted | in the | earth. ‖ The Lord of | hosts is | with us; ‖ the God of | Jacob | is our | refuge.

CHANT No. 16.—The Lord's Prayer.

Gregorian.

1. {Our Father who art in heaven; | hallowed | be thy | name: ‖
{Thy kingdom come, thy will be done on | earth · · as it | is in | heaven.

2. {Give us this | day our— | daily | bread; ‖
{And forgive us our trespasses, as we forgive them that | trespass · · a- | gainst— | us.

3. {And lead us not into temptation, but de-liver | us from | evil: ‖
{For thine is the kingdom, and the power, and the glory, for ever. | A— | —men.

PRAYER OF HABAKKUK.

CHANT No. 17.—Recitative. C. F. BLANDNER.

Habakkuk, chap. iii.

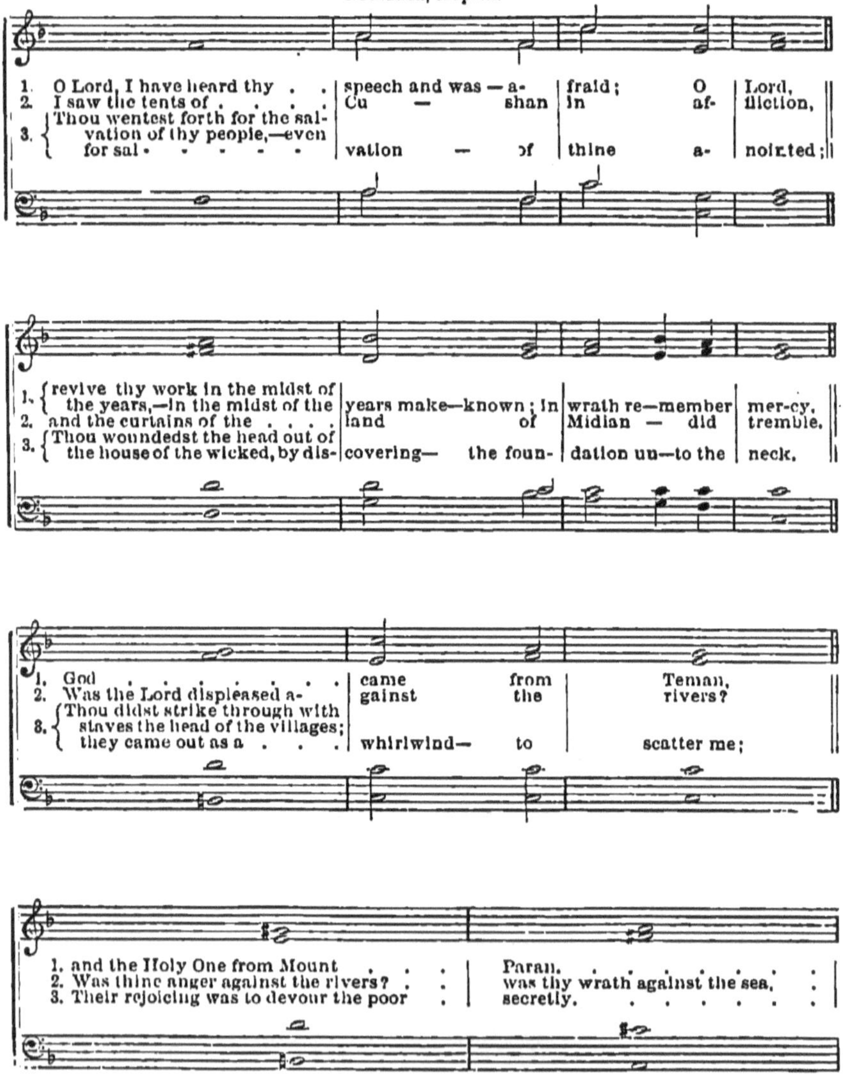
1. O Lord, I have heard thy . . | speech and was — a- | fraid; O | Lord,
2. I saw the tents of . . . . . | Cu — shan | in af- | fliction,
3. Thou wentest forth for the salvation of thy people,—even for sal- . . . . . | vation — of | thine a- | nointed;
1. revive thy work in the midst of the years,—in the midst of the | years make—known; in | wrath re—member | mer-cy.
2. and the curtains of the . . . . | land of | Midian — did | tremble.
3. Thou woundedst the head out of the house of the wicked, by dis- | covering— the foun- | dation un—to the | neck.
1. God . . . . | came from | Teman,
2. Was the Lord displeased a- | gainst the | rivers?
3. Thou didst strike through with staves the head of the villages; they came out as a . . . | whirlwind— to | scatter me;
1. and the Holy One from Mount . . . | Paran. . . . .
2. Was thine anger against the rivers? . . | was thy wrath against the sea, .
3. Their rejoicing was to devour the poor . | secretly. . . . . . .

PRAYER OF HABAKKUK.—Continued.

1. His glory covered the heavens, and the | earth was full of his | praise !
2. that thou didst ride upon thine horses, and thy | cha - riots of sal- - | vation?
3. Thou didst walk through the sea with thine | horses, thro' the heap of great | waters.

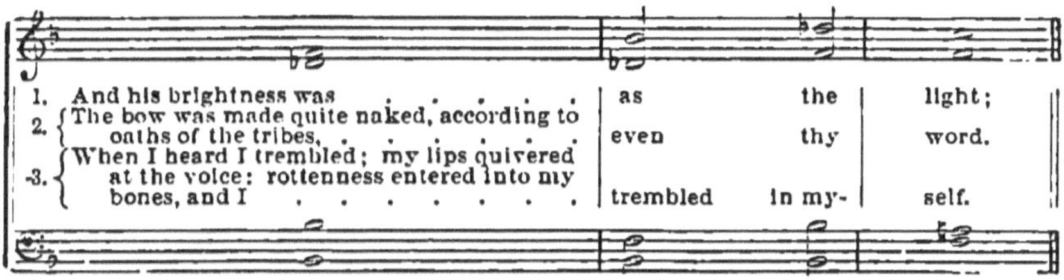
1. And his brightness was . . . . . . | as the | light;
2. The bow was made quite naked, according to oaths of the tribes, ... | even thy | word.
3. When I heard I trembled; my lips quivered at the voice: rottenness entered into my bones, and I . . . . | trembled in my- | self.

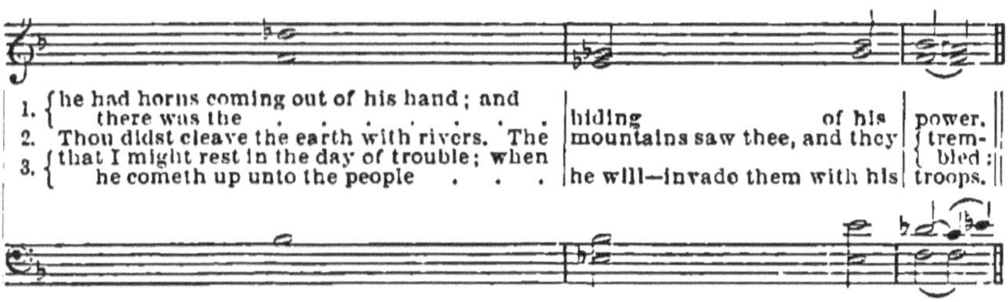
1. he had horns coming out of his hand; and there was the . . . . | hiding of his | power.
2. Thou didst cleave the earth with rivers. The | mountains saw thee, and they | trem- bled:
3. that I might rest in the day of trouble; when he cometh up unto the people . . . | he will—invade them with his | troops.

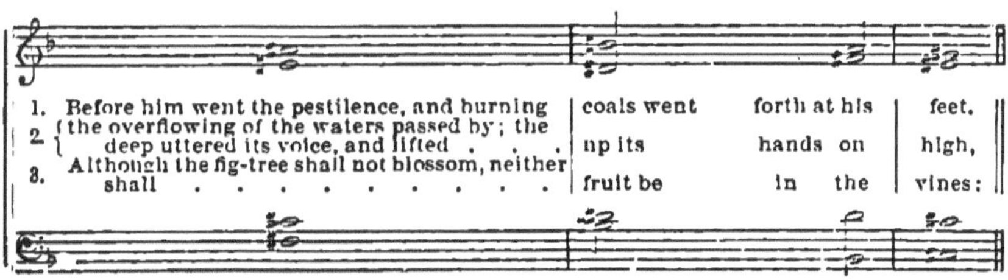
1. Before him went the pestilence, and burning | coals went forth at his | feet.
2. the overflowing of the waters passed by; the deep uttered its voice, and lifted . . . | up its hands on | high,
3. Although the fig-tree shall not blossom, neither shall . . . . | fruit be in the | vines:

PRAYER OF HABAKKUK.—Concluded.

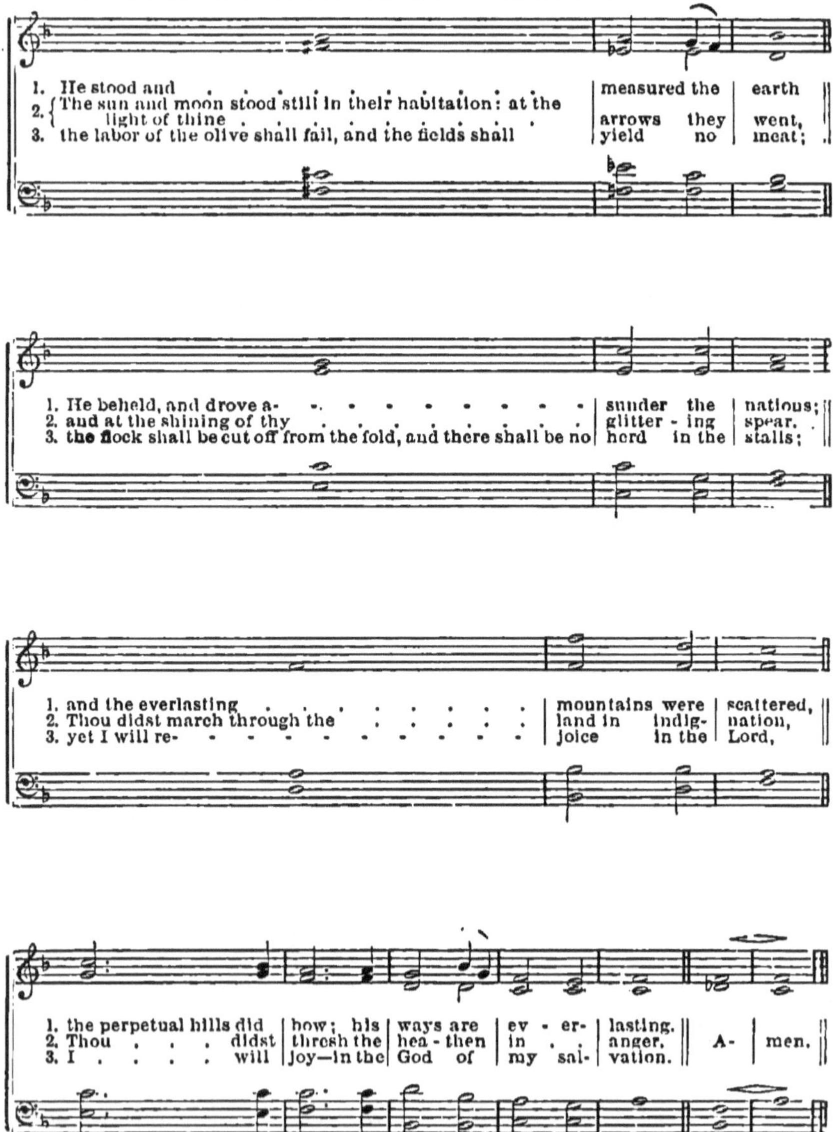
1. He stood and | measured the | earth
2. The sun and moon stood still in their habitation: at the light of thine | arrows they | went,
3. the labor of the olive shall fail, and the fields shall | yield no | meat;
1. He beheld, and drove a- | sunder the | nations;
2. and at the shining of thy | glitter - ing | spear.
3. the flock shall be cut off from the fold, and there shall be no | herd in the | stalls;
1. and the everlasting | mountains were | scattered,
2. Thou didst march through the | land in indig- | nation,
3. yet I will re- | joice in the | Lord,
1. the perpetual hills did | bow; his | ways are | ev - er- | lasting.
2. Thou . . . . didst | thresh the | hea - then | in . . | anger.
3. I . . . . . will | joy—in the | God of | my sal- | vation.
A- | men.

CHANTS.

CHANT No. 18.—Sentence and Chant.

Be - hold the Lamb of God! Be-hold the Lamb of God! who tak-eth a-way the sin of the world.

SOLO.
CHORUS.

1. He is despised and re- | jected ·· of | men, ‖
2. A man of | sorrows ·· and ac- | quainted ·· with | grief.
3. And we hid as it were our | faces | from him. ‖
4. He was despised, and | we es- | teem'd him | not.
5. Surely he hath borne our griefs, and | carried ·· our | sorrows; ‖
6. Yet we did esteem him stricken; | smitten ·· of | God ·· and af- | flicted.
7. But he was wounded for our transgressions, he was bruised for | our in- | iquities: ‖
8. The chastisement of our peace was upon him, and | with his | stripes ·· we are | healed.
9. All we like sheep have gone astray; we have turned every one to | his own | way. ‖
10. And the Lord hath laid on | him ·· the in- | iquity ·· of us | all.

CHANT No. 19.—"Where shall rest be found?"

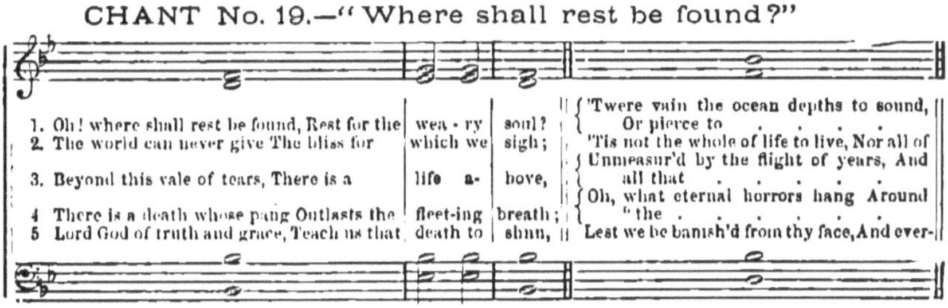
1. Oh! where shall rest be found, Rest for the | wea - ry | soul? | 'Twere vain the ocean depths to sound, Or pierce to . . . . .
2. The world can never give The bliss for | which we | sigh; | 'Tis not the whole of life to live, Nor all of
3. Beyond this vale of tears, There is a | life a- | bove, | Unmeasur'd by the flight of years, And all that . . . . . .
4. There is a death whose pang Outlasts the | fleet-ing | breath; | Oh, what eternal horrors hang Around "the . . . .
5. Lord God of truth and grace, Teach us that | death to | shun, | Lest we be banish'd from thy face, And ever-

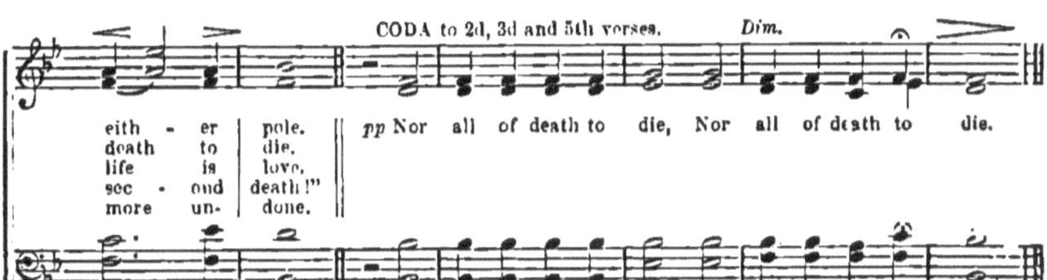
CODA to 2d, 3d and 5th verses.
Dim.
eith - er | pole.
death to | die.
life is | love.
sec - ond | death!"
more un- | done.
pp Nor all of death to die, Nor all of death to die.

CHANT No. 20.—Autumn.

JOHN M. EVANS.

DUETT.

1. THE leaves around me falling, Are preaching | of de - cay: |
The hollow winds are calling, | Come, pilgrim, | come away; |
The day, in night declining, Says I must, | too, de- | cline; |
The year its bloom resigning, Its | lot fore- | shadows | mine.

2. The light my path surrounding, The loves to | which I cling, |
The hopes within me bounding, | The joys that | round me wing,— |
All, all like stars at even, Just gleam and | shoot a- | way, |
Pass on before to heaven, And | chide at | my de- | lay.

3. The friends gone there before me, Are calling | from on high, |
And happy angels o'er me | Tempt sweetly | to the sky; |
Why wait, they say, and wither, 'Mid scenes of | death and | sin; |
Oh, rise to glory, hither, And | find true | life be- | gin.

4. I hear the invitation, And fain would | rise and come, |
A sinner to salvation, | An exile | to his home; |
But while I here must linger, Thus, thus let | all I | see |
Point on, with faithful finger, To | heav'n, O | Lord, and | thee.

CHANT No. 21.—One Sweetly Solemn Thought.

REV. A. TAYLOR.

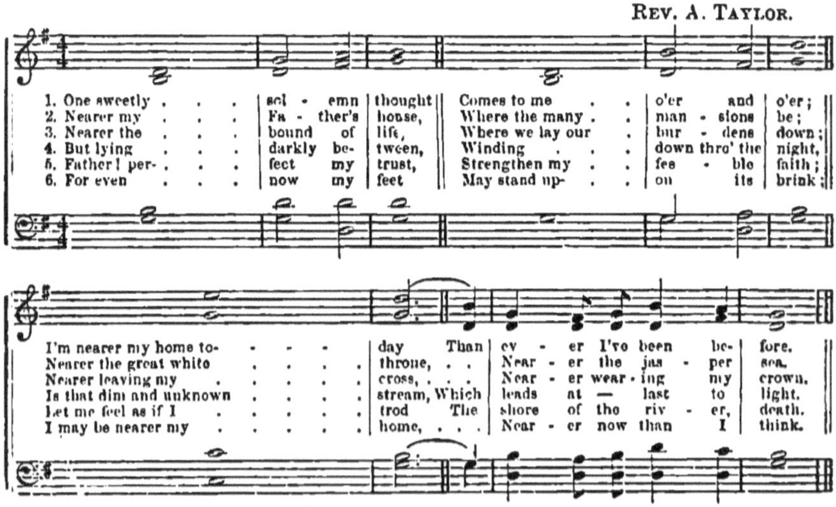
1. One sweetly sol - emn thought Comes to me o'er and o'er;
2. Nearer my Fa - ther's house, Where the many man - sions be;
3. Nearer the bound of life, Where we lay our bur - dens down;
4. But lying darkly be- tween, Winding down thro' the night,
5. Father! per- fect my trust, Strengthen my fee - ble faith;
6. For even now my feet May stand up- on its brink;
I'm nearer my home to- day Than ev - er I've been be- fore.
Nearer the great white throne, Near - er the jas - per sea.
Nearer leaving my cross, Near - er wear - ing my crown.
Is that dim and unknown stream, Which leads at — last to light.
Let me feel as if I trod The shore of the riv - er, death.
I may be nearer my home, Near - er now than I think.

CHANT No. 22.—" Nearer to Thee."

1. Nearer, my God, to thee, | near - er to | thee! || E'en though it be a cross that . . . | rais - eth | me,
2. Though, like a wanderer, the | sun gone | down, || Darkness be over me, my | rest a | stone,
3. There let my way appear | steps un - to | heaven, || All that thou sendest me, In . . . . | mer - cy | given,
4. Then, with my waking thoughts . . . | bright with thy | praise, || Out of my stony griefs | Bethel I'll | raise,
5. Or if on joyful wing, . | cleav - ing the | sky, || Sun, moor, and stars forgot, . . . | Upward I | fly,
Still all my . . | song shall | be, || Near-er, my | God, to | thee! || Near - er to | thee.
Yet in my . . | dreams I'd | be || Near-er, my | God, to | thee! || Near - er to | thee.
Angels to . . | beck - on | me || Near-er, my | God, to | thee! || Near - er to | thee.
So by my . . | woes to | be || Near-er, my | God, to | thee! || Near - er to | thee.
Still all my . . | song shall | be, || Near-er, my | God, to | thee! || Near - er to | thee.

CHANT No. 23.—"As the Hart pants." EDGAR REED.

1. As the o'erwearied hart
Pants for the pure and cooling brooks, that move
And | to the | seas de- | part, ||
So looks my spirit to its Fount above,
And longs to breathe the air which | fans that | scene of | love.

2. Yea! my impatient soul
Thirsts for the mighty and the living God,
Be- | neath whose | good con- | trol ||
My paths through life in glorious hope are trod:
The chastener of my heart, I | bend and | kiss his | rod.

3. And to my soul I say,
Why are thy visions stained with hues of gloom?
Trust | thou in | him whose | way ||
Lay through the cloudy chambers of the tomb,—
Whose smile can gild its depths, and | clothe the | dust in | bloom.

4. Deep calleth unto deep,
The voiceful waves rise heavenward at his will,
And | at his | nod they | sleep; ||
So shall thy Spirit my glad bosom fill,
When I have learned to know and | do thy | holy | will.

5. Why art thou sad, my soul?
Why such disquiet in my thoughtful eye?
As | time's bleak | surges | roll, ||
Soon shall my spirit lift its wings on high,
Where heaven's eternal glow il- | lumes a | fadeless | sky.

CHANTS.

CHANT No. 24.—O Thou for Sinners Slain.

1. Be-hold the Lamb! be-hold the Lamb! O thou, for sinners slain;
2. Be-hold the Lamb! be-hold the Lamb! Archangels—fold your wings—
3. Be-hold the Lamb! be-hold the Lamb! Drop down, ye glorious skies—
4 Be-hold the Lamb! be-hold the Lamb! Saints, wrapt in blissful rest—
5. Be-hold the Lamb! be-hold the Lamb! Worthy is he a-lone
Let it not be in vain That thou hast died: Thee for my Saviour, let me take,
Seraphs—hush all your strings Of mil-lion lyres: The Victim, veiled on earth, in love—
He dies—he dies—he dies For man once lost! Yet lo! he lives—he lives—he lives—
Souls—waiting to be blest—O Lord, how long! Thou church on earth, o'erwhelmed with fears,
To sit upon the throne Of God a-bove! One with the Ancient of all days—
Thee, thee alone my refuge make Thy pier-cèd side.
Unveiled—enthroned—adored above— All heaven ad-mires!
And to his church himself he gives—In-car- - - nate Host!
Still in this vale of woe and tears Swell the full song.
One with the Paraclete in praise— All light—all love!

CHANT No 25.

Arr. by JOHN M. EVANS.

1. On Jordan's stormy banks I stand, And cast a wish-ful eye To Canaan's fair and happy land, Where my pos-ses-sions lie.
2. Oh, the transporting, rapturous scene, That rises to my sight; Sweet fields arrayed in living green, And riv-ers of de-light
3. O'er all those wide-extended plains, Shines one e-ter-nal day; There God the Son for ever reigns, And scat-ters night a-way
4. Filled with delight, my raptured soul Would here no long-er stay; Tho' Jordan's waves around me roll, I'd fearless launch a-way.

CHANT No. 26.—"What is Life?"

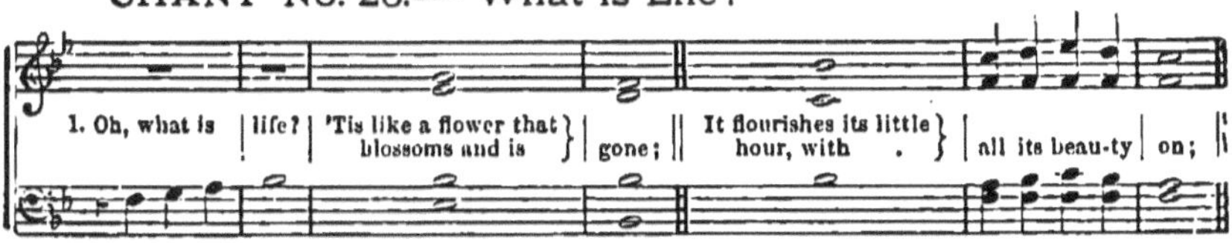
1. Oh, what is | life? | 'Tis like a flower that blossoms and is | gone; || It flourishes its little hour, with . | all its beau-ty | on; ||

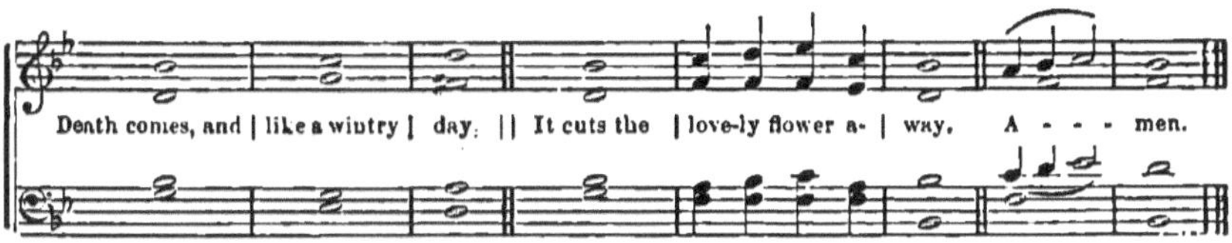
Death comes, and | like a wintry | day; || It cuts the | love-ly flower a- | way. A - - - men.

2 OH, what is life? | 'Tis like the bow
That glistens in the | sky; ||
We love to see its colors glow;
But | while we look they | die; ||
Life fails as | soon; to-day 'tis | here; ||
To-morrow | it may disap- | pear. ||

3 Lord, what is life? | If spent with thee
In humble praise and | prayer, ||
How long or short this life may be,
We | feel no anxious | care; ||
Tho' life de- | part, our joys shall | last ||
When life and | all its joys are | past

CHANT No. 27.—"O thou who dry'st the mourner's tear."

JOHN M. EVANS.

1. O thou who dry'st the mourn-er's tear, How dark this | world would | be, || If, pierced by sin and sor-rows here, we could not | fly to | thee!

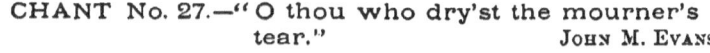

2 THE friends who in our sunshine live,
When winter | comes are flown; ||
And he who has but tears to give,
Must weep those | tears a- | lone. ||

3 When joy no longer soothes or cheers,
And e'en the | hope that | threw ||
A moment's sparkle o'er our tears
Is dimmed and | vanished | too, ||

4 Oh, who could bear life's stormy doom,
Did not thy | wing of | love ||
Come brightly wafting through the gloom,
Our peace-branch | from a- | bove? ||

5 Then sorrow, touched by thee, grows bright
With more than | rapture's | ray; ||
As darkness shows us worlds of light,
We never | saw by | day. ||

CHANTS.

CHANT No. 28.—The Guiding Hand.

S. J. VAIL.

SOLO.
CHORUS.
1. "Is this the way, my Father?" "'Tis, my child; Thou must pass through this tangled, ... drea - ry wild, If thou wouldst reach the city un - de- fil'd, Thy peace - ful home a- bove."
2. "But enemies are around." "Yes, child, I know, Where least expecting thou shalt . . . . . find a foe; But victor thou shalt prove o'er all be- low; On- ly seek strength a- bove."
3. "My Father, it is dark." "Child, take my hand; Cling close to me, I'll lead thee . . . . . . through the land; Trust my all-seeing care; so shalt thou stand Midst glo - ry bright a- bove."
4. "My footsteps seem to slide." "Child, on-ly raise Thine eyes to me, then, in these slipp' - ry ways, I will hold up thy goings; thou shalt praise Me for each step, a- bove."
5. "Oh, Father, I am weary." "Child, lean thy head Upon my breast. It was my love that spread Thy rugged path; hope on till I have said, Rest, rest for aye, a- bove."

CHANT No. 29.—"He knelt, the Saviour Knelt and Prayed."

JOHN M. EVANS.

1. He knelt, the Saviour knelt and prayed, When but his . . . . Fa - ther's eye Look'd through the lonely garden's shade, On that dread ag - o- ny; The Lord of all above, beneath, Was bowed with . . . . sor - row un - to death.
2. The sun went down in fearful hour; The heavens might . . . . . . well grow dim, When this mortality had power To thus o'er- . . . . sha - dow him; That he who gave man's breath might know The very . . . . depths of hu - man woe.
3. He knew them all, the doubt, the strife, The faint, per- . . . . plex - ing dread; The mists that hang o'er parting life All darken'd round his head; And the Deliverer knelt to pray; Yet pass'd it . . . . . . not, that cup, a- way.
4. It pass'd not, though the stormy wave Had sunk be- . . . . neath his tread; It pass'd not, though to him the grave Had yielded . . up its dead; But there was sent him, from on high, A gift of . . . . strength, for man to die.
5. And was his mortal hour beset With anguish and dis- may? How may we meet our conflict yet In the dark, . . nar - row way? How, but through him that path who trod? Save, or we . . . per - ish, Son of God.

CHANT No. 30.—The Land Beyond the Sea.

Words by FABER. Music by D. A. WARDEN.

1. The | land be - yond the | sea! | When will life's | task be | o'er?
2. The | land be - yond the | sea! | How close it | oft- - - en | seems,
3. The | land be - yond the | sea! | Some - times dis- | tinct and | near,
4. The | land be - yond the | sea! | Some - times a- | cross the | strait,
5. The | land be - yond the | sea! | When will our | toil be | done?
6. The | land be - yond the | sea! | Sweet is thine | end- - - less | rest,
Cres.
1. When shall we reach that soft blue shore, | O'er the dark strait whose billows | foam and roar?
2. When flush'd with evening's peaceful gleams, | And the wistful heart looks o'er the | strait and dreams,
3. It grows upon the eye and ear, | And the gulf narrows to a | thread-like mere.
4. Like a drawbridge to a castle-gate, | The slanting sunbeams lie and | seem to wait,
5. Slow-footed years! more swiftly run | Into the gold of that un- | set - ting sun!
6. But sweeter far that Father's breast | Upon thy shores eternal | ly pos - sest;
1. When shall we come to | thee, Calm | land be- | yond the | sea!
2. It longs to fly to | thee, Calm | land be- | yond the | sea!
3. We seem halfway to | thee, Calm | land be- | yond the | sea!
4. For us to pass to | thee, Calm | land be- | yond the | sea!
5. Homesick we are for | thee, Calm | land be- | yond the | sea!
6. For Jesus reigns o'er | thee, Calm | land be- | yond the | sea!
p Dim. Dim.
Be - yond | the sea. . . . || Sweet home, | sweet home, | dear Lord, | I come.
2d ending. 3d ending.

CHANT No. 31.—"Heavenly Rest."

Arranged from Rossini.
By D. A. Warden.

pp
1. There is a calm for . . | those who | weep, || A rest for . | wea - ry pilgrims | found;
2. The storm that sweeps the . | win - try | sky, || No more dis- | turbs their deep re- | pose,
3. Then, traveller in the . . | vale of | tears || To realms of | ev - er - last - ing | light,
4. Though long of winds and . | waves the | sport, || Condemned in | wretch - edness to | roam,
5. Thou soul, renewed by . . | grace di- | vine, || To God's own | im - age, freed from | clay,
1. They softly lie, and . . . . . . | sweet - ly | sleep, | Low | in the | ground.
2. Than summer evening's . . . . . | la - test | sigh, | That | shuts the | rose.
3. Through time's dark wilder- . . . . . | ness of | years | Pur- | sue thy | flight.
4. Thou soon shalt reach a . . . . . | shelt' - ring | port, | A | qui - et | home.
5. In heaven's eternal . . . . . | sphere shalt | shine | A | star of | day.

CHANT No. 32.—"Just as I Am."

D. A. Warden.

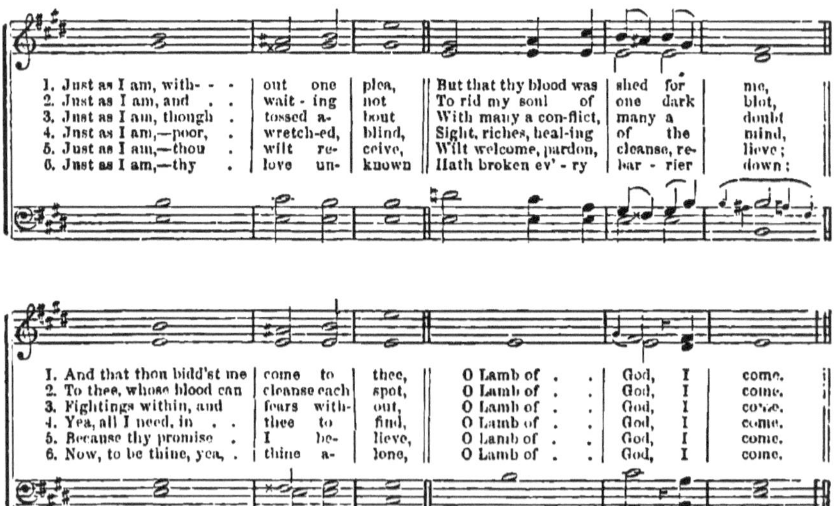
1. Just as I am, with- - - | out one | plea, || But that thy blood was | shed for | me,
2. Just as I am, and . . | wait - ing | not || To rid my soul of | one dark | blot,
3. Just as I am, though . | tossed a- | bout || With many a con-flict, | many a | doubt
4. Just as I am,—poor, . | wretch-ed, | blind, || Sight, riches, heal-ing | of the | mind,
5. Just as I am,—thou . | wilt re- | ceive, || Wilt welcome, pardon, | cleanse, re- | lieve;
6. Just as I am,—thy . | love un- | known || Hath broken ev' - ry | bar - rier | down;
1. And that thou bidd'st me | come to | thee, || O Lamb of . . | God, I | come.
2. To thee, whose blood can | cleanse each | spot, || O Lamb of . . | God, I | come.
3. Fightings within, and | fears with- | out, || O Lamb of . . | God, I | come.
4. Yea, all I need, in . . | thee to | find, || O Lamb of . . | God, I | come.
5. Because thy promise . | I be- | lieve, || O Lamb of . . | God, I | come.
6. Now, to be thine, yea, . | thine a- | lone, || O Lamb of . . | God, I | come.

CHANT No. 33.—Baptismal Chant. LANGDON.

Words by REV. J. W. WILLMARTH.

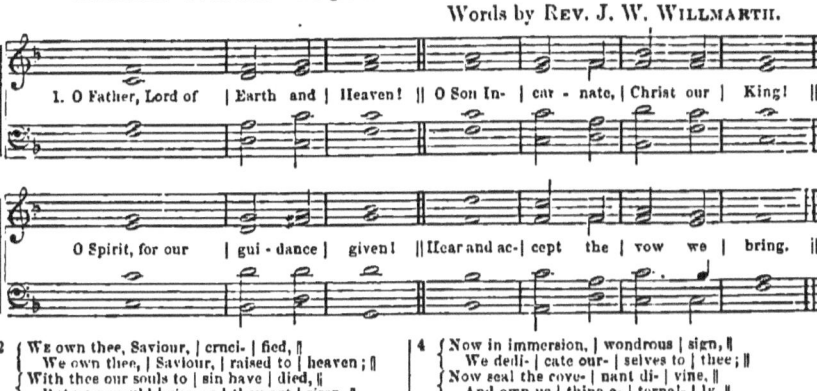

1. O Father, Lord of | Earth and | Heaven! || O Son In- | car - nate, | Christ our | King! ||
O Spirit, for our | gui - dance | given! || Hear and ac- | cept the | vow we | bring. ||

2 { WE own thee, Saviour, | cruci- | fied, ||
We own thee, | Saviour, | raised to | heaven; ||
With thee our souls to | sin have | died, ||
But now would | rise, as | thou art | risen. ||

3 { Thy gospel, Lord, we | would o- | bey, ||
We follow, | and thy | hand shall | guide; ||
We seek through Jordan's | wave the | way ||
That leads thy | loved ones | to thy | side. ||

4 { Now in immersion, | wondrous | sign, ||
We dedi- | cate our- | selves to | thee; ||
Now seal the cove- | nant di- | vine, ||
And own us | thine e- | ternal- | ly. ||

[After the administration.]

5 { We trust the pledge which | thou hast | given, ||
Of grace to | keep us | still thine | own, ||
And, dying, we shall | rise to | heaven, ||
To share thy | glory | and thy | throne. ||

CHANT No. 34.—"Homeward Bound." W. A. TARBUTTON.

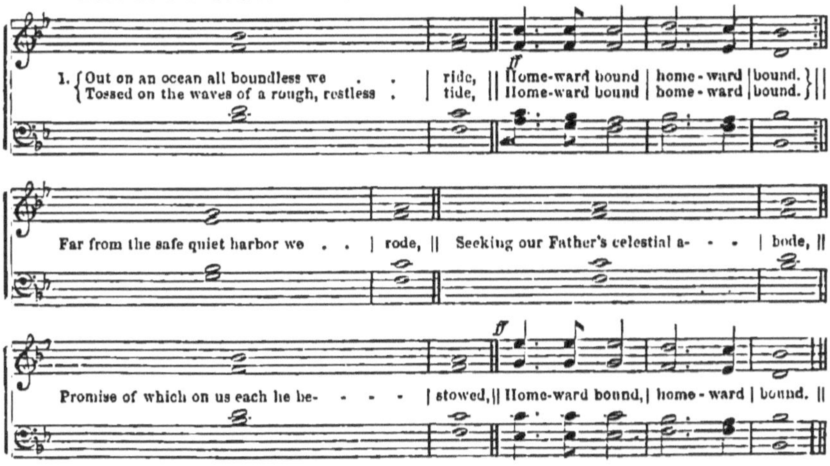
1. { Out on an ocean all boundless we . . | ride, || Home-ward bound | home - ward | bound. }
Tossed on the waves of a rough, restless . | tide, || Home-ward bound | home - ward | bound. }
Far from the safe quiet harbor we . . | rode, || Seeking our Father's celestial a- - - | bode, ||
Promise of which on us each he be- - - - | stowed, || Home-ward bound, | home - ward | bound. ||

2 WILDLY the storm sweeps us on as it | roars, ||
Homeward bound, | homeward bound, ||
Look! yonder lie the bright heavenly | shores, ||
Homeward bound, | homeward bound. ||
Steady, O pilot, stand firm at the wheel, ||
Steady, we soon shall outweather the | gale. ||
Oh, how we fly 'neath the loud creaking | sail. ||
Homeward bound, | homeward bound. ||

3 Into the harbor of heaven we | glide, ||
Home at last, | home at last: ||
Softly we drift on its smooth silver | tide, ||
Home at last, | home at last. ||
Glory to God! all our dangers are | o'er. ||
Standing secure on the glorified | shore, ||
Glory to God! we will shout ever- | more, ||
Home at last, | home at last. ||

CHANTS.

CHANT No. 35.—"Nothing to Do."

J. E. Gould.

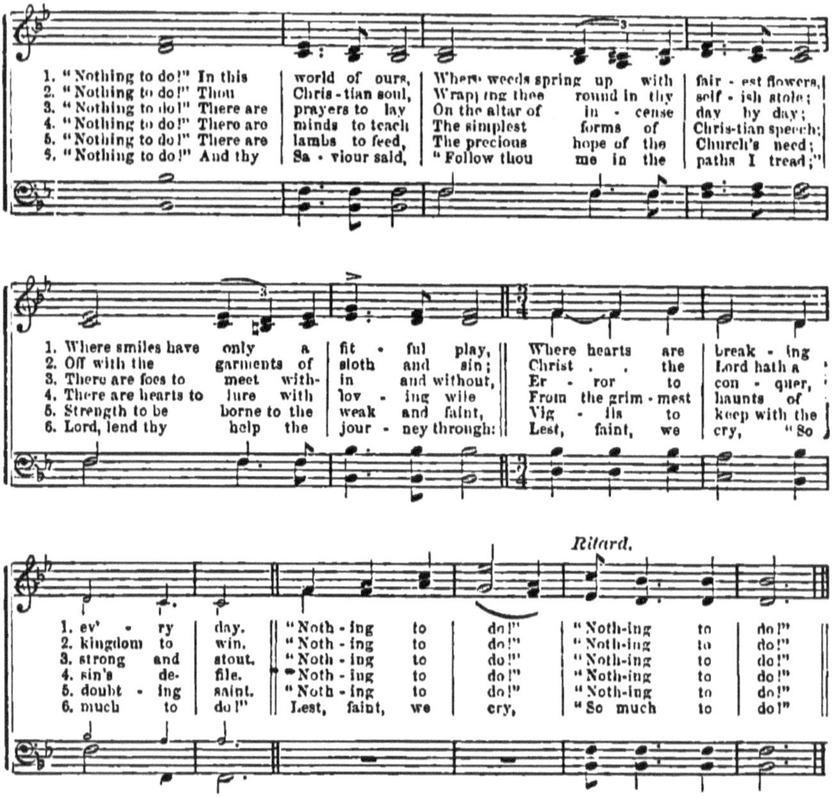
1. "Nothing to do!" In this world of ours, Where weeds spring up with fair - est flowers,
2. "Nothing to do!" Thou Chris - tian soul, Wrapping thee round in thy self - ish stole;
3. "Nothing to do!" There are prayers to lay On the altar of in - cense day by day;
4. "Nothing to do!" There are minds to teach The simplest forms of Chris-tian speech;
5. "Nothing to do!" There are lambs to feed, The precious hope of the Church's need;
6. "Nothing to do!" And thy Sa - viour said, "Follow thou me in the paths I tread;"
1. Where smiles have only a fit - ful play, Where hearts are break - ing
2. Off with the garments of sloth and sin; Christ . . the Lord hath a
3. There are foes to meet with- in and without, Er - ror to con - quer,
4. There are hearts to lure with lov - ing wile From the grim - mest haunts of
5. Strength to be borne to the weak and faint, Vig - ils to keep with the
6. Lord, lend thy help the jour - ney through: Lest, faint, we cry, "So
Ritard.
1. ev' - ry day. "Noth - ing to do!" "Noth-ing to do!"
2. kingdom to win. "Noth - ing to do!" "Noth-ing to do!"
3. strong and stout. "Noth - ing to do!" "Noth-ing to do!"
4. sin's de- file. "Noth - ing to do!" "Noth-ing to do!"
5. doubt - ing saint. "Noth - ing to do!" "Noth-ing to do!"
6. much to do!" Lest, faint, we cry, "So much to do!"

CHANT No. 36.—"Be not Afraid."

John M. Evans.

1. { Brother, on the troubled deep,
When the wild winds . . . . round you sweep, And the waves in madness leap,
2. { When the storm has died away,
And the sun, with . . . . . cheer - ing ray, Now illumes your prosperous way,
3. { Brother, far away from home,
Restless as the . . . . waves' light foam, When temptations round you come,
4. { Brother, when death draweth near,
And your spirit . . . . . shrinks in fear From its portals, damp and drear,

"BE NOT AFRAID."—Concluded.

DUETT.
pp. Dim.
1. Lis - ten, 'tis the voice that | said— It is | I, be not a- | fraid; It is | I, be not a- | fraid.
2. Trust, oh, trust in him who | said— It is | I, be not a | fraid; It is | I, be not a- | fraid.
3. Pray for strength to him who | said— It is | I, be not a- | fraid; It is | I, be not a- | fraid.
4. Trust your soul to him who | said— It is | I, be not a- | fraid; It is | I, be not a- | fraid.
SOLO.

CHANT No. 37.—"No Time to Pray."

J. E. Gould.

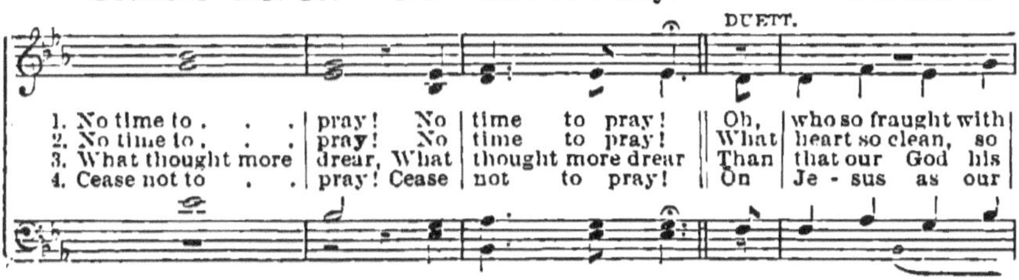
DUETT.
1. No time to . . . | pray! No | time to pray! || Oh, | who so fraught with
2. No time to . . . | pray! No | time to pray! || What | heart so clean, so
3. What thought more | drear, What | thought more drear || Than | that our God his
4. Cease not to . . | pray! Cease | not to pray! || On | Je - sus as our

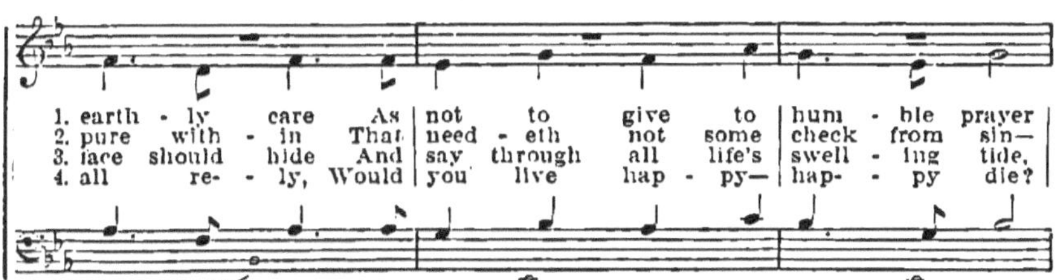
1. earth - ly care As | not to give to | hum - ble prayer
2. pure with - in That | need - eth not some | check from sin—
3. face should hide And | say through all life's | swell - ing tide,
4. all re- - ly, Would | you live hap - py— | hap- - py die?

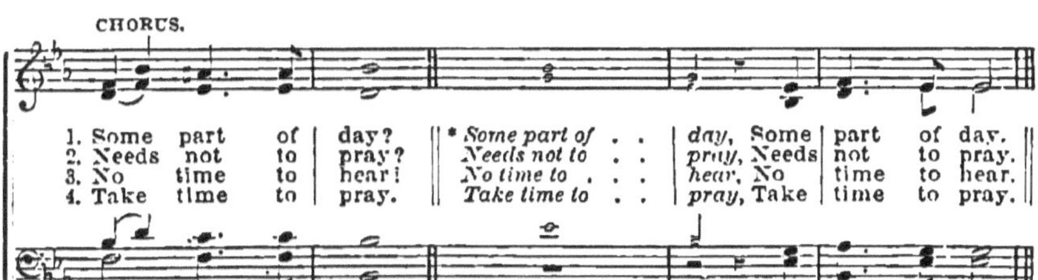
CHORUS.
1. Some part of | day? || * Some part of . . | day, Some | part of day.
2. Needs not to | pray? || Needs not to . . | pray, Needs | not to pray.
3. No time to | hear! || No time to . . . | hear, No | time to hear.
4. Take time to | pray. || Take time to . . | pray, Take | time to pray.

* Voices or instrument, *ad lib.*

CHANT No. 38.—" With Tearful Eyes I look Around."

JOHN M. EVANS.

1. With tearful eyes I look around, Life seems a dark and . . . . | storm - y | sea, ‖

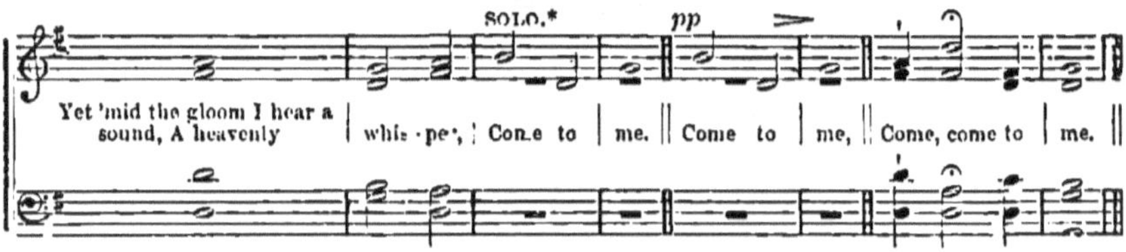
SOLO.*
pp
Yet 'mid the gloom I hear a sound, A heavenly | whis - per, | Come to | me. ‖ Come to | me, ‖ Come, come to | me. ‖

2 It tells me of a place of rest:—
It tells me where my | soul may | flee; ‖
Oh, to the weary, faint, oppressed,
How sweet the | bidding, | Come to me.: ‖:

3 When nature shudders, loth to part
From all I love, en- | joy, and | see,— ‖
When a faint chill steals o'er my heart,
A sweet voice | utters, | Come to me:: ‖:

4 Come, for all else must fail and die:
Earth is no resting- | place for | thee; ‖
Heavenward direct thy weeping eye,
I am thy | portion, | come to | me.: ‖:

5 O voice of mercy, voice of love,
In conflict, grief, and | ago- | ny, ‖
Support me, cheer me from above,
And gently | whisper, | Come to | me.: ‖:

CHANT No. 39.—My Bible.

J. E. GOULD.

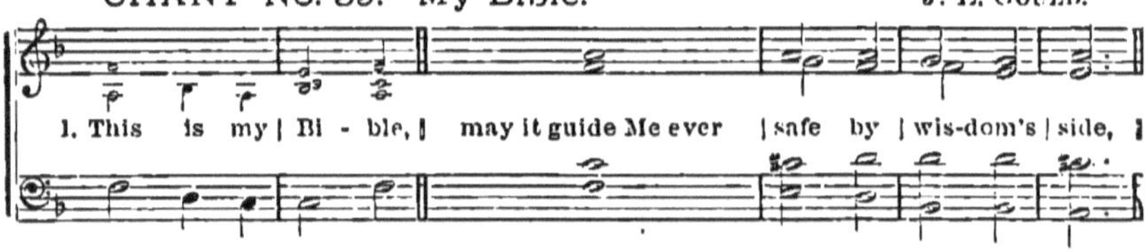
1. This is my | Bi - ble, ‖ may it guide Me ever | safe by | wis-dom's | side, ‖

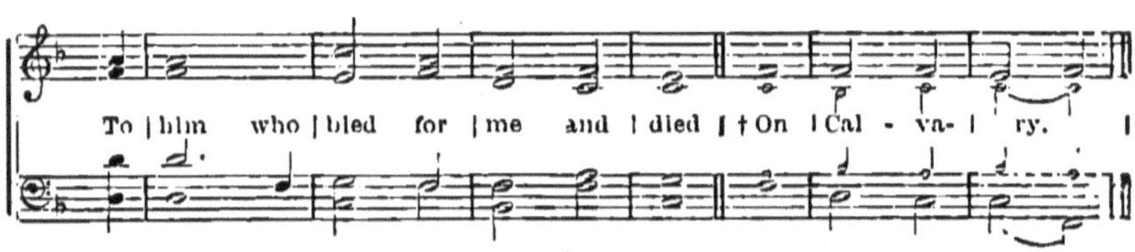
To | him who | bled for | me and | died ‖ † On | Cal - va- | ry. ‖

2 THIS is my Bible ‖ may its light
Illume my | path and | keep me | right, ‖
E'en | through the | shades of | sorrow's | night, ‖
My way to see.

3 This is my Bible, ‖ may it prove
A source of | strength, a | source of | love, ‖
A | fountain | filled from | heaven a- | bove, ‖
Whence I may drink.

4 This is my Bible, ‖ may it feed
Me with the | Bread of | life in- | deed, ‖
And | may my | soul its | precepts | heed, |
In grace to grow.

5 This is my Bible, ‖ may my faith
By it be | strengthened, | and when | death ‖
Shall | call, oh, | may my | fleeting | breath ‖
Its comforts know.

* Without accompaniment.

† Soprano or Bass may sing their parts as Solo, *ad lib.*

CHANT No. 40.—"From the Recesses." J. E. GOULD.

1 { FROM the recesses of a lowly spirit,
Our humble prayer ascends. O | Fa - ther, | hear it; ‖
Borne on the trembling wings of | fear - and | meekness, |
For- | give - its | weakness.

2 { We know we feel, how mean and how unworthy
The lowly sacrifice we | pour - be- | fore thee;— ‖
What can we offer thee,—O | thou - most | holy!— ‖
But | sin - and | folly?

3 { Lord, in thy sight, who every bosom viewest,
Cold are our warmest vows, and | vain our | truest; ‖
Thoughts of a hurrying hour—our | lips re- | peat them— ‖
Our | hearts - for- | get them.

4 { We see thy hand—it leads us, it supports us:—
We hear thy voice—it | counsels - and it | courts us; ‖
And then we turn away!—yet | still - thy | kindness ‖
For- | gives - our | blindness.

5 { Who can resist thy gentle call,—appealing
To every generous thought and | grateful | feeling?— ‖
Oh, who can hear the accents | of - thy | mercy, ‖
And | nev - er | love thee?

6 { Kind Benefactor! plant within this bosom
The | seeds - of | holiness,— | and let them blossom
In fragrance,—and in beauty | bright - and | vernal,— ‖
And | spring - e- | ternal.

7 { Then place them in those everlasting gardens
Where angels walk—and | seraphs - are the | wardens;— ‖
Where every flower, brought safe through | death's - dark | portal, ‖
Be- | comes - im- | mortal.

CHANT No. 41.—"Beyond." W. A. TARBUTTON.

1. Beyond the smiling and the weeping,
I shall be soon;
Beyond the waking and the sleeping,
Beyond the sowing and the reaping,
I shall be soon;

Love, rest, and home,—
sweet home!
sweet home!
Lord, tar - ry not, but come.

1 BEYOND the smiling and the weeping, |
I shall be | soon; ‖
Beyond the waking and the sleeping, |
Beyond the sowing and the reaping, |
I shall be | soon. ‖
Love, rest, and | home, | sweet | home! ‖
Lord, tarry | not, but | come. ‖

2 Beyond the blooming and the fading |
I shall be | soon; ‖
Beyond the shining and the shading, |
Beyond the hoping and the dreading, |
I shall be | soon. ‖
Love, rest, and | home, | sweet | home! ‖
Lord, tarry | not, but | come. ‖

3 Beyond the rising and the setting |
I shall be | soon; ‖
Beyond the calming and the fretting, |
Beyond remembering and forgetting, |
I shall be | soon. ‖
Love, rest, and | home, | sweet | home! ‖
Lord, tarry | not, but | come. ‖

4 Beyond the parting and the meeting |
I shall be | soon; ‖
Beyond the farewell and the greeting, |
Beyond the pulse's fever beating, |
I shall be | soon. ‖
Love, rest, and | home, | sweet | home! ‖
Lord, tarry | not, but | come. ‖

5 Beyond the frost-chain and the fever |
I shall be | soon; ‖
Beyond the rock-waste and the river, |
Beyond the ever and the never, |
I shall be | soon. ‖
Love, rest, and | home, | sweet | home! ‖
Lord, tarry | not, but | come. ‖

CHANT No. 42.—"Shall we meet?" D. A. WARDEN.

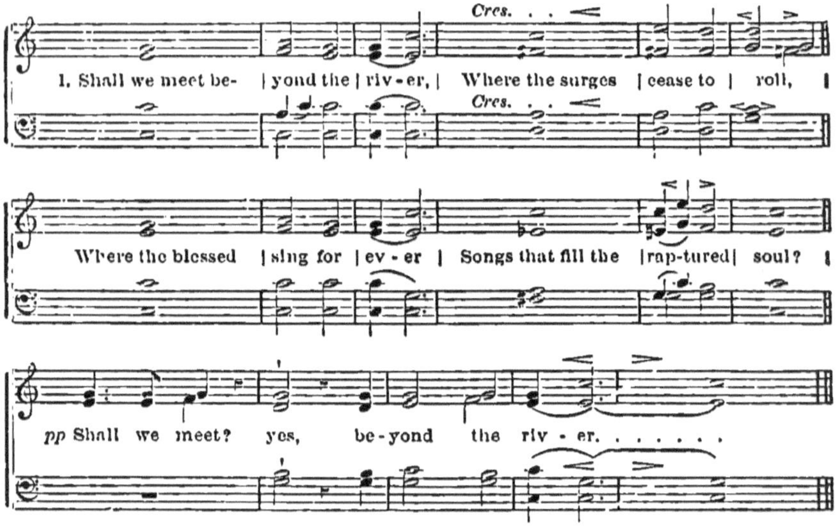
Cres.
1. Shall we meet be- | yond the | riv-er, | Where the surges | cease to | roll, ‖
Where the blessed | sing for | ev-er | Songs that fill the | rap-tured | soul? ‖
pp Shall we meet? yes, beyond the riv-er. . . . . . .

2 SHALL we meet with | all the | loved ones, |
That were torn from | our em- | brace? |
Shall we listen | to their | voices, |
And behold them | face to | face? |
Shall we meet? | yes, be- | yond the | river. ‖

3 Shall we meet with | Christ our | Saviour, |
When he comes to | claim his | own? |
Shall we know his | blessed | favor, |
And behold him | on his | throne? ‖
Shall we meet? | yes, be- | yond the | river. ‖

CHANT No. 43.—"Lowly and solemn be." JOHN M. EVANS.

1. Lowly and solemn be Thy children's cry to thee, | Fath-er di- | vine, ‖
2. O Father, in that hour When earth all helping power | Shall dis-a- | vow, ‖
A hymn of suppliant breath, Owning that life and death | A-like are | thine. ‖
When spear and shield and crown, In faintness are cast down, ... | Sus-tain us, | thou! ‖

3 By him who bowed to take
The death-cup for our sake, |
The thorn, the | rod; ‖
From whom the last dismay
Was not to pass away, |
Aid us, O | God. ‖

4 While trembling o'er the grave,
We call on thee to save,
Father di- | vine: ‖
Hear, hear our suppliant breath,
Keep us, in life and death, |
Thine, only | thine. ‖ A- | men. ‖

No 44.—Worship the Lord.

MOZART.

Allegro.
Oh, wor-ship the Lord in the beau-ty of ho-li-ness, Wor-ship the Lord in the
beau-ty of ho-li-ness, Wor-ship the Lord in the beau-ty of ho- - - -
- - - li-ness, In the beau-ty of ho-li-ness;
Fear be-fore him,
T S
all the earth, Fear be-fore him, all the earth, Fear be-fore him, all the earth;
1st time. 2d time.
in the beau-ty
Wor-ship the Lord in the beau- - - ty of ho-li-ness, Of ho- - - li-ness.
in the beau-ty

No. 45.—SANCTUS.—" Holy Lord God of Sabaoth."

Largo.
Più allegro.
mf. Ho - ly, ho - ly, ho - ly, Lord God of Sab - a-oth! Heav'n and earth are
Unison
full . . . . of thy glo - ry,
Heaven and earth are full of thy glo - ry, Heaven and earth are full of thy
glo - ry, Heav'n and earth are full of thy glo - ry, glo - ry,
glo - ry, glo - ry be to thee; glo - ry, glo - ry,
Rit.
p Adagio.
Cres.
glo - ry be to thee, O Lord, O Lord . . . . . . most high.

No. 46.—"Create in Me a Clean Heart." Wm. B. Bradbury.

Slow.
Cre - ate in me a clean heart, O God, And re - new a right
spir - it with - in me, Cast me not a - way, cast me not a-
Cast me not a-
way . . .
way from thy pres-ence, from thy pres-ence, And take not thy Ho - ly Spir - it, thy Ho - ly
way, cast me not a-way, Take not thy Ho - ly
. from thy pres-ence, from thy pres-ence,
Spir - it from me. Re - store un - to me, ...
Re - store un - to
. . joy of thy sal - va - tion, Re - store un - to me, . .
me the Re-
ff
ff

"Create in Me a Clean Heart."--Concluded.

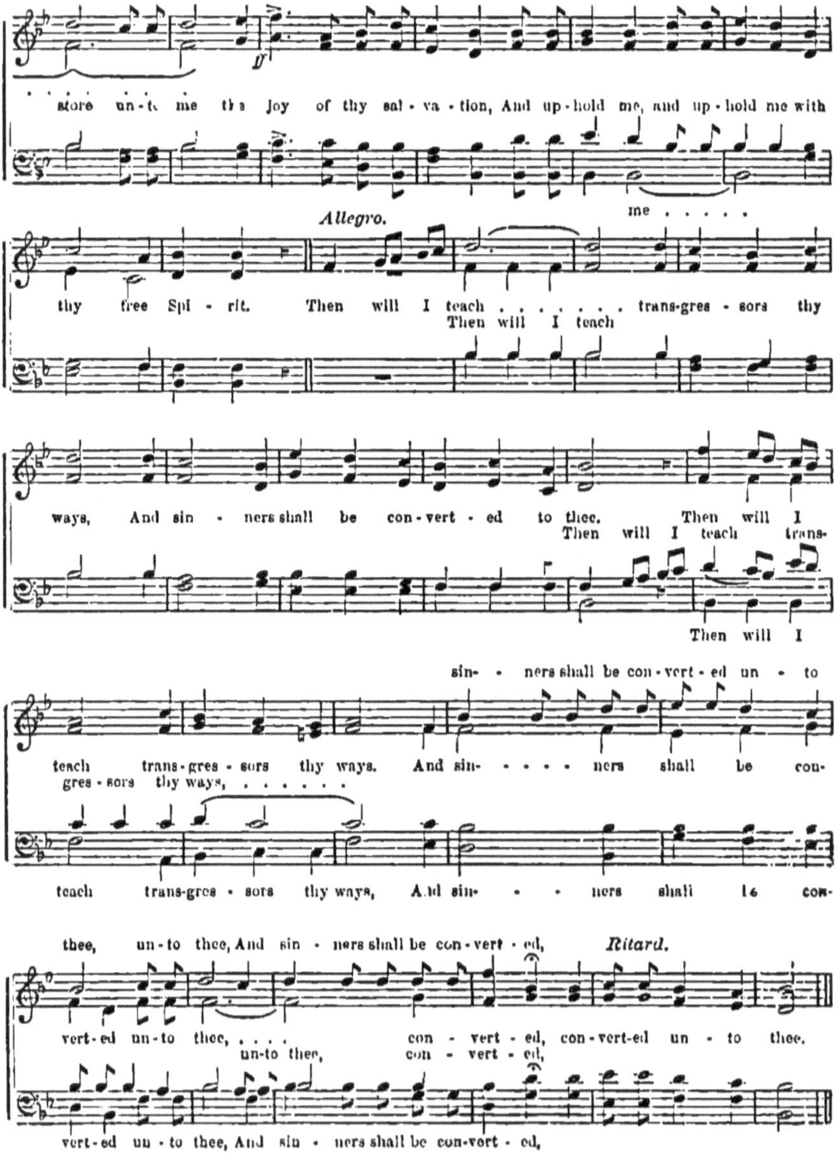

store un-to me the joy of thy sal - va - tion, And up-hold me, and up-hold me with
me . . . . .
Allegro.
thy free Spi - rit. Then will I teach . . . . trans-gres - sors thy
Then will I teach
ways, And sin - ners shall be con - vert - ed to thee. Then will I
Then will I teach trans-
Then will I
sin- - ners shall be con - vert - ed un - to
teach trans - gres - sors thy ways. And sin- - - - - ners shall be con-
gres - sors thy ways, ...
teach trans-gres - sors thy ways, And sin- - - ners shall be con-
thee, un - to thee, And sin - ners shall be con - vert - ed,
Ritard.
vert - ed un - to thee, ... con - vert - ed, con - vert - ed un - to thee.
un-to thee, con - vert - ed,
vert - ed un - to thee, And sin - ners shall be con-vert - ed,

No. 47.—"Come, ye Disconsolate."

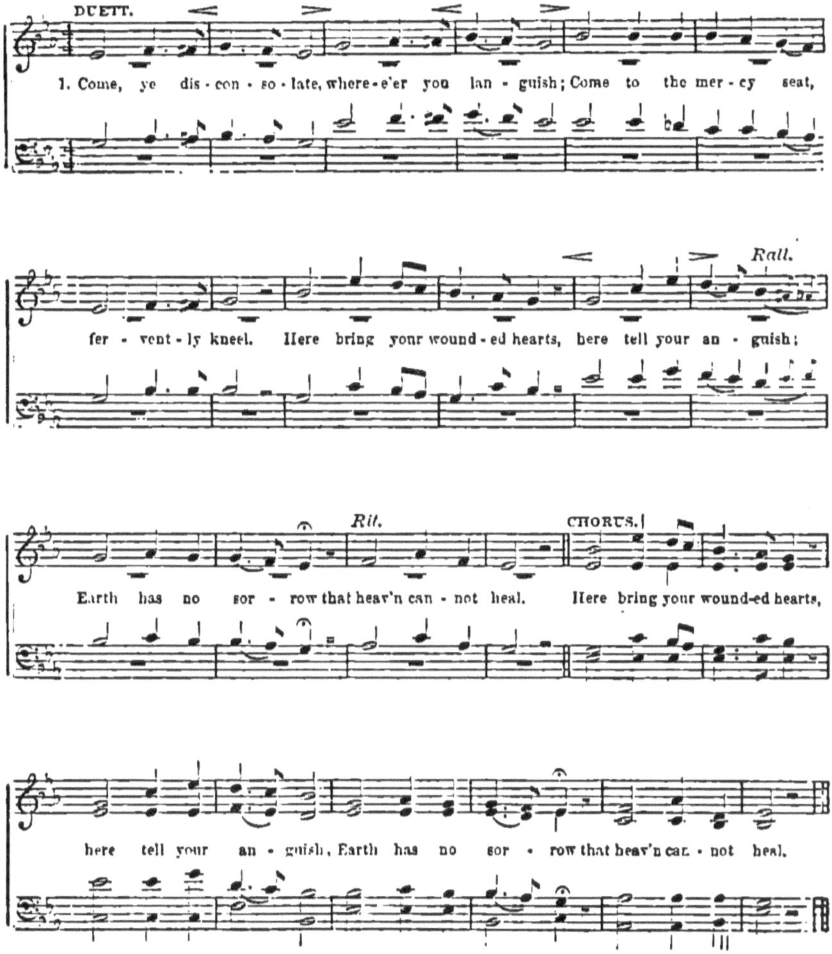
DUETT.
1. Come, ye dis - con - so - late, where - e'er you lan - guish; Come to the mer - cy seat,
fer - vent - ly kneel. Here bring your wound - ed hearts, here tell your an - guish;
Rall.
Earth has no sor - row that heav'n can - not heal.
Rit.
CHORUS.
Here bring your wound-ed hearts,
here tell your an - guish, Earth has no sor - row that heav'n can - not heal.

2 Joy of the desolate, light of the straying,
Hope of the penitent, fadeless and pure,
Here speaks the Comforter, tenderly saying,
Earth has no sorrow that heaven cannot cure.

3 Here see the bread of life; see waters flowing,
Forth from the throne of God, pure from above;
Come to the feast of love; come, ever knowing
Earth has no sorrow but heaven can remove.

No. 48.—EVENING PRAYER.

Arr. from KREUTZER
By C. KUEBLER.

Words by JOHN M. EVANS.

Andante. pp
Fa - ther, from thy throne on high Hear thy chil - dren's plead - ing cry,
mp
Let thy watch - ful eye of love Fol - - low us where-
e'er we rove. Now when ev' - ning shades are clos - ing, Lull-ing earth in sweet re-
pp
pose, Guard us through the si - lent hours; Bid us wake at dawn to praise; Fill our
Cres.
ff
hearts with joy and love, Now when love, our hearts with joy and love.
1st time.
2d time.

No. 49.—"I Love to Tell the Story." W. H. DOANE.

1. I love to tell the sto - ry Of un - seen things a - bove, Of Je - sus and his
glo - ry, Of Je - sus and his love. I love to tell the sto - ry, Be-cause I know it's
true; It sat - is-fies my long-ings As noth - ing else would do.
CHORUS.
I love to tell the
sto - ry, 'Twill be my theme in glo - ry To tell the old, old sto - ry Of Je-sus and his love.

2 I LOVE to tell the story;
  More wonderful it seems
Than all the golden fancies
  Of all our golden dreams.
I love to tell the story,
  It did so much for me;
And that is just the reason
  I tell it now to thee.

3 I love to tell the story;
  'Tis pleasant to repeat
What seems, each time I tell it,
  More wonderfully sweet.
I love to tell the story,
  For some have never heard
The message of salvation
  From God's own holy word.

4 I love to tell the story,
  For those who know it best
Seem hungering and thirsting
  To hear it like the rest.
And when, in scenes of glory,
  I sing the new, new song,
'Twill be the old, old story
  That I have loved so long.

No. 50.—"Safe Within the Veil."

JOHN M. EVANS.

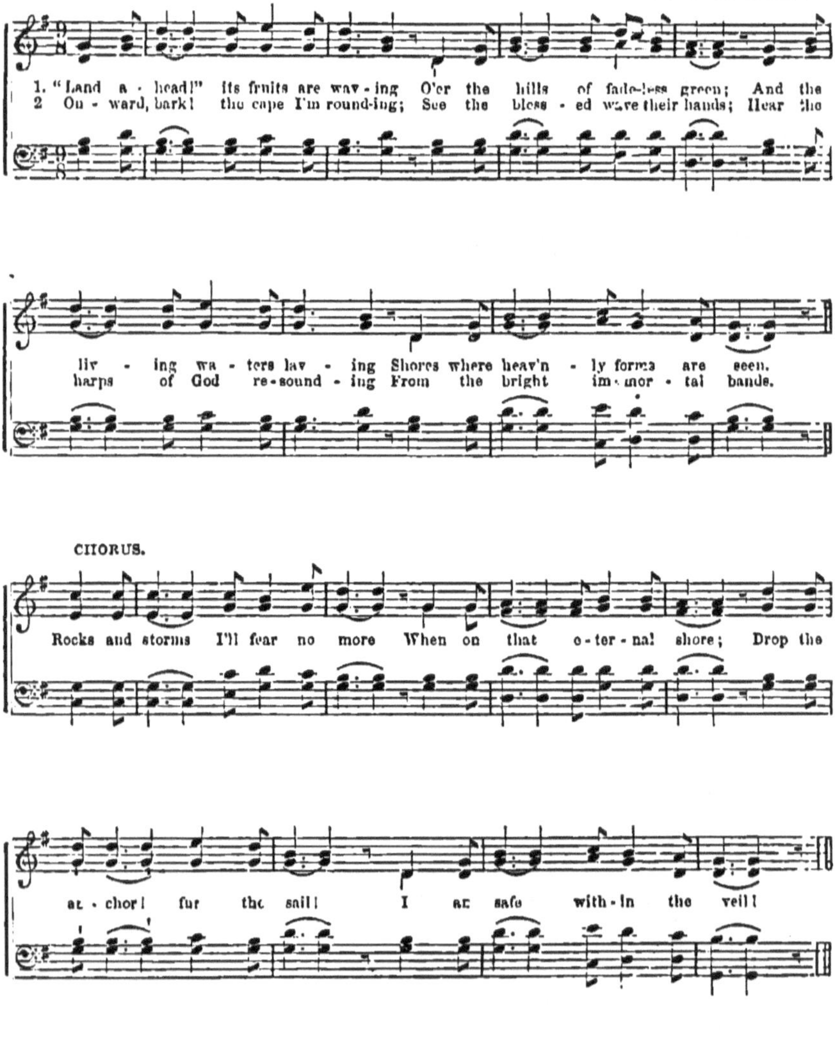
1. "Land a - head!" its fruits are wav - ing O'er the hills of fade-less green; And the
2 On - ward, bark! the cape I'm round-ing; See the bless - ed wave their hands; Hear the
liv - ing wa - ters lav - ing Shores where heav'n - ly forms are seen.
harps of God re - sound - ing From the bright im - mor - tal bands.
CHORUS.
Rocks and storms I'll fear no more When on that e - ter - nal shore; Drop the
an - chor! furl the sail! I am safe with - in the veil!

3 THERE, let go the anchor, riding
On this calm and silv'ry bay;
Seaward fast the tide is gliding,
Shores in sunlight stretch away.—*Cho.*

4 Now we're safe from all temptation,
All the storms of life are past;
Praise the Rock of our salvation,
We are safe at home at last!—*Cho.*

No. 51.—GLORIA.

DR. MADAN.

Glo-ry, hon-or, praise, and pow-er, Be un-to the Lamb for ev-er; Je-sus Christ is
our Re-deem-er, Hal-le-lu-jah, Hal-le-lu-jah, Hal-le-lu-jah, Praise the Lord!

No. 52.—GLORIA PATRI.

TALLIS.

GLORY be to the Father, and | to the | Son: ‖
And | to the | Holy | Ghost; ‖
As it was in the beginning, is now, and | ever"shall | be,
World without | end. A- | men, A- | men. ‖

CHANT No. 53. PSALM 95.

DR. BOYCE.

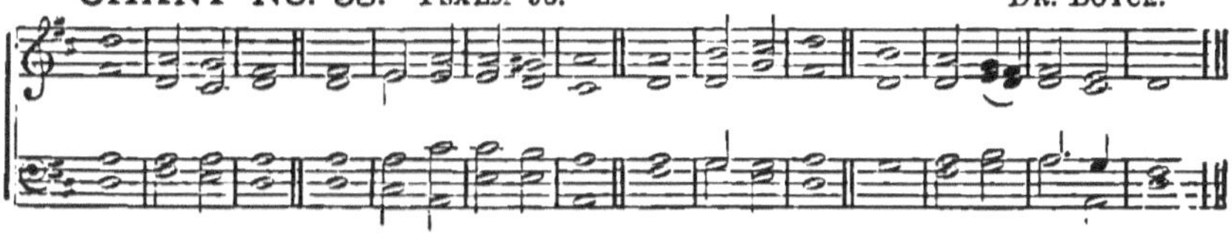

1 Oн, come, let us sing | unto"the | Lord:
Let us heartily rejoice in the | strength of | our sal- | vation.

2 Let us come before his presence | with thanks- | giving,
And show ourselves | glad in | him with | psalms.

3 For the Lord | is a"great | God;
And a great | King a- | bove all | gods.

4 In his hands are all the corners | of the | earth,
And the strength of the | hills is | his— | also.

5 The sea is his, | and he | made it;
And his hands pre- | pared"the | dry— | land.

6 Oh, come, let us worship | and fall | down;
And kneel be- | fore the | Lord our | Maker.

7 For he is the | Lord our | God;
And we are the people of his pasture, and the | sheep of | his— | hand.

8 Oh, worship the Lord in the | beauty"of | holiness;
Let the whole | earth"stand in | awe of | him.

9 Glory be to the Father, and | to the | Son:
And | to the | Holy | Ghost;

10 As it was in the beginning, is now, and | ever"shall | be,
World without | end. A- | men, A- | men.

CHANT No. 54. PSALM 103. DR. BECKWIT .

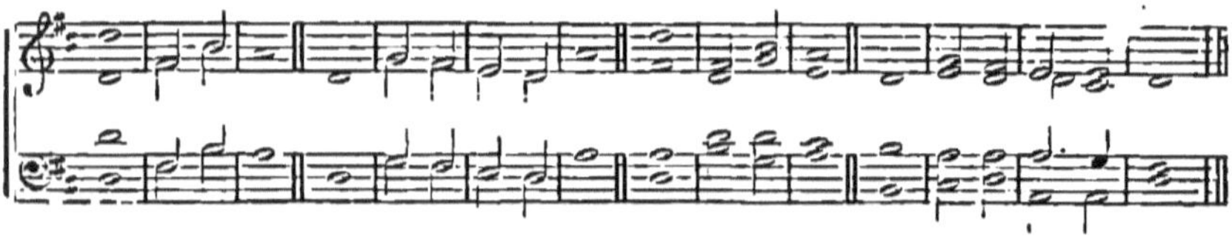

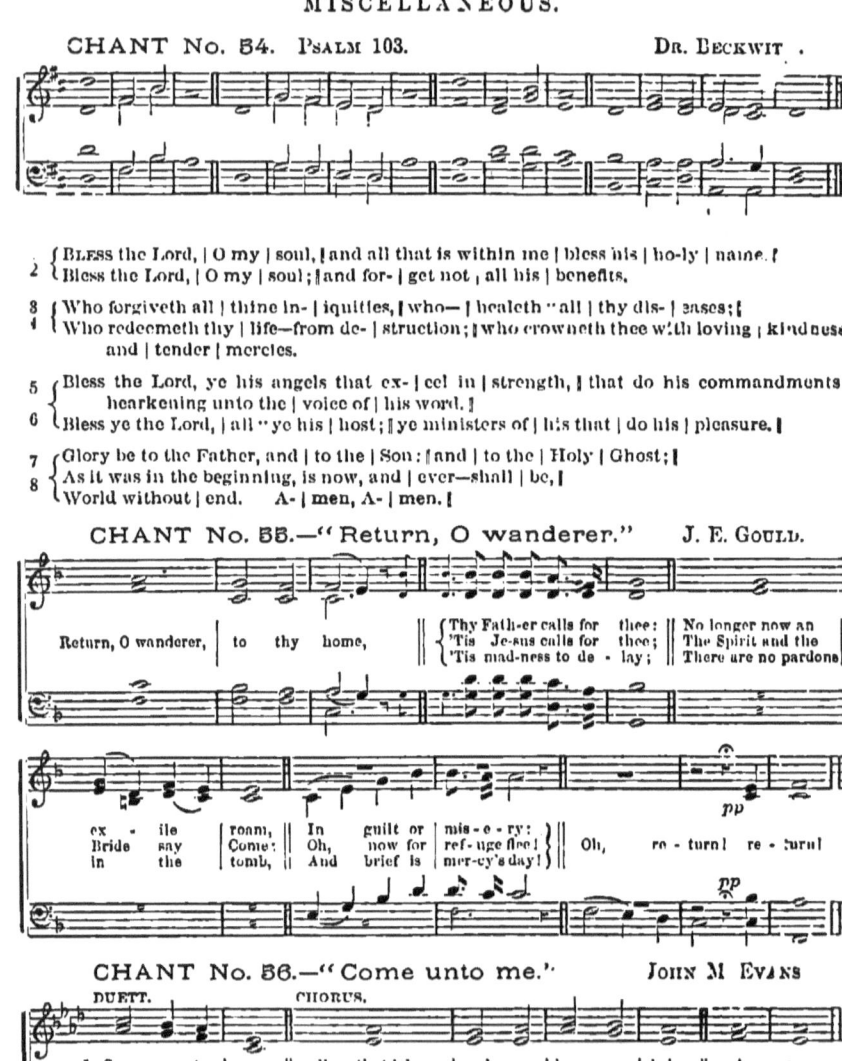

1 { BLESS the Lord, | O my | soul, | and all that is within me | bless his | ho-ly | name. |
2 { Bless the Lord, | O my | soul; | and for- | get not | all his | benefits.

3 { Who forgiveth all | thine in- | iquities, | who— | healeth "all | thy dis- | eases; |
4 { Who redeemeth thy | life—from de- | struction; | who crowneth thee with loving | kindness and | tender | mercies.

5 { Bless the Lord, ye his angels that ex- | cel in | strength, | that do his commandments hearkening unto the | voice of | his word. |
6 { Bless ye the Lord, | all "ye his | host; | ye ministers of | his that | do his | pleasure. |

7 { Glory be to the Father, and | to the | Son: | and | to the | Holy | Ghost; |
8 { As it was in the beginning, is now, and | ever—shall | be, |
World without | end. A- | men, A- | men. |

CHANT No. 55.—"Return, O wanderer." J. E. GOULD.

Return, O wanderer, | to thy home,
Thy Fath-er calls for thee: | No longer now an ex - ile roam, | In guilt or mis-e-ry:
'Tis Je-sus calls for thee; | The Spirit and the Bride say Come: | Oh, now for ref-uge flee!
'Tis mad-ness to de - lay; | There are no pardons in the tomb, | And brief is mer-cy's day!
Oh, re - turn! re - turn!
pp
pp

CHANT No. 56.—"Come unto me." JOHN M EVANS

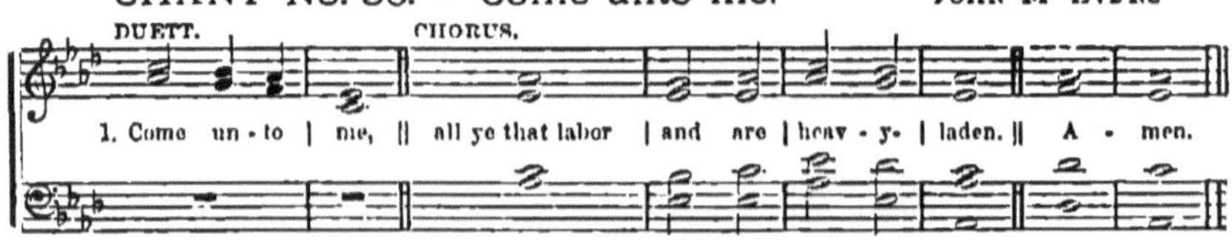
DUETT.
CHORUS.
1. Come un - to | me, || all ye that labor | and are | heav - y- | laden. || A - men.

2. COME unto | me, | come unto me, and | I will | give you | rest.
3. Come unto | me, | take my yoke upon you | and | learn of | me.
4. Come unto | me, | and ye shall find | rest un- | to your | souls.
5. Come unto | me, | for my yoke is easy, | and my | burden | light. | A- | men. |

CHANT No 57. PSALM 51. GREGORIAN.

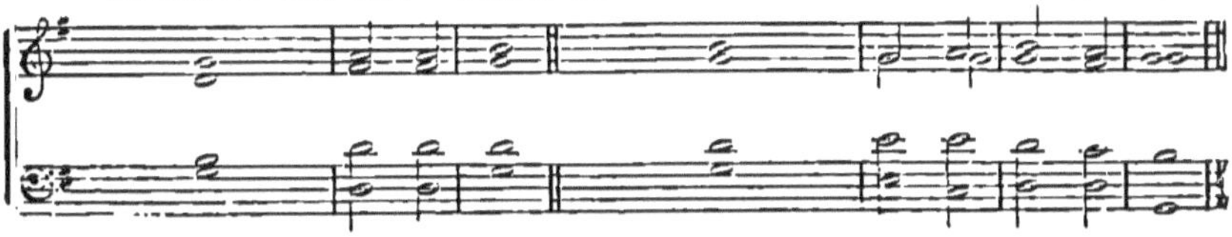

1 {HAVE mercy upon me, O God, according to thy loving-kindness;
According to the multitude of thy tender mercies,
Blot | out '' my trans- | gressions.

2. {Wash me thoroughly from mine iniquities,
And | cleanse me | from my | sin.

3. {For I acknowledge my transgressions,
And my sin is | ever '' be- | fore me.

4. {Against thee, thee only, have I sinned,
And done this | evil | in thy | sight.

5. {Create in me a clean heart, O God;
And renew a right | spirit '' with- | in me.

6. {Cast me not away from thy presence;
And take not thy | Holy | Spirit | from me.

7. {Restore unto me the joy of thy salvation;
And uphold me with | thy free | spirit.

8. {Then will I teach transgressors thy ways,
And sinners shall be con- | verted | unto | thee. Amen.

CHANT No. 58. PSALM 90.

1. {LORD, thou hast been our dwelling-place
In | all '' gene- | rations.

2. {Before the mountains were brought forth,
Or ever thou hadst formed the earth and the world,
Even from everlasting to ever- | lasting | thou art God.

3 {Thou turnest man to destruction;
And sayest, Return, ye | children of men.

4. {For a thousand years in thy sight
Are but as yesterday when it is past,
And | as a | watch '' in the | night.

5. {Thou carriest them away as with a flood,
They are as a sleep;
In the morning they are like grass which | groweth | up.

6. {In the morning it flourisheth, and groweth up;
In the evening it is cut | down, *cut* | *down*, and | withereth.

7. {Who knoweth the power of thine anger?
Even according to thy fear; | so '' is thy | wrath.

8 {So teach us to number our days,
That we may ap- | ply our | hearts '' unto | wisdom.

DOXOLOGIES.

1 L. M.

To God the Father, God the Son,
And God the Spirit, Three in One,
Be honor, praise, and glory given,
By all on earth, and all in heaven!

2 L. M.

Praise God, from whom all blessings flow!
Praise him, all creatures here below!
Praise him above, ye heavenly host!
Praise Father, Son, and Holy Ghost!

3 L. M.

All praise to God the Father be;
All praise, Eternal Son, to thee;
Whom with the Spirit we adore,
For ever and for evermore.

4 L. M.

All praise and glory be to thee,
Whose love hath set thy people free;
Like praise be to the Father done,
And Holy Spirit, Three in One.

5 L. M.

To God the Father, God the Son,
And Holy Spirit, Three in One,
Unceasing praise and glory be,
Now and through all eternity.

6 L. M.

To God the Father let us sing;
To God the Son, and risen King;
And equally with them adore
The Spirit—God for evermore.

7 L. M.

O Lord, the Lord of lords, to thee
Eternal praise and glory be;
Whom with the Father we adore,
And Holy Ghost for evermore.

8 L. M.

To Father, Son, and Holy Ghost,
The God whom earth and heaven adore
Be glory as it was of old,
Is now, and shall be evermore.

9 L. M.

O Holy Father, Holy Son,
And Holy Spirit, Three in One,
Thy grace devoutly we implore,
Thy name be praised for evermore.

10 L. M.

Glory to thee, O God, most high!
Father, we praise thy majesty!
The Son, the Spirit, we adore,
One Godhead, blest for evermore!

11 L. M.

To Father, Son, and Holy Ghost,
The God whom heaven and earth adore
Be glory from the angel host,
And all mankind for evermore.

12 C. M.

To Father, Son, and Holy Ghost,
One God whom we adore,
Be glory as it was, is now,
And shall be evermore.

13 C. M.

Let God the Father, and the Son,
And Spirit be adored,
Where there are works to make him known
Or saints to love the Lord.

14 C. M.

O God the Father, God the Son,
And God the Holy Ghost,
To thee be praise, great Three in One,
From thy created host.

15 C. M.

All glory to the Father be,
All glory to the Son,
All glory, Holy Ghost, to thee,
While endless ages run.

16 C. M.

To Father, Son, and Holy Ghost,
Immortal glory be,
Who was, and is, and shall be still,
To all eternity.

17 S M.

Ye angels round the throne,
And saints that dwell below,
Worship the Father, praise the Son,
And bless the Spirit too.

18 S. M.

Praise Christ, the only Son!
Praise to the Father give!
Praise to the Spirit! One alone,
In whom alone we live.

19 S. M.

The Father and the Son
And Spirit we adore;
We praise, we bless, we worship thee,
Both now and evermore.

20 S. M.

Praise to the Saviour Son
Who came to seek the lost;
And praise be to the Father done,
And to the Holy Ghost.

21 S. M.

To God the Father, Son,
And Spirit glory be,
Now whilst the years of time shall run,
And through eternity.

22 S. M.

Lord Jesus Christ, the Son,
To thee all glory be,
With Father, Spirit, Three in One,
Through all eternity.

23 7s.

Holy Father, Holy Son,
Holy Spirit, Three in One,
Praise and glory be to thee
Now and through eternity.

24 7s.

Hymns of glory and of praise,
Father, unto thee we raise;
Risen Son, all praise to thee,
With the Spirit, ever be

25 7s.

Sing we to our God above
Praise eternal as his love;
Praise him, all ye heavenly host,
Father, Son, and Holy Ghost.

26 7s.

Praise the Father, earth and heaven,
Praise the Son, the Spirit praise,
As it was, and is, be given
Glory through eternal days.

27 7s. 6l.

Praise the name of God most high,
Praise him, all below the sky,
Praise him, all ye heavenly host,
Father, Son, and Holy Ghost;
As through countless ages past,
Evermore his praise shall last

28 7s. 6l.

Blessing, honor, glory, might,
And dominion infinite,
To the Father of our Lord,
To the Spirit, and the Word;
As it was all worlds before,
Is, and shall be evermore.

29 7s & 6s.

Father, Son and Holy Ghost,
One God whom we adore,
Join we with the heavenly host
To praise thee evermore:
Live, by heaven and earth adored,
Three in One, and One in Three,
Holy, holy, holy Lord,
All glory be to thee!

30 7s & 6s.

To thee be praise for ever,
Thou glorious King of kings!
Thy wondrous love and favor
Each ransomed spirit sings;
We'll celebrate thy glory
With all thy saints above,
And shout the joyful story
Of thy redeeming love.

31 10s.

To Father, Son, and Spirit, ever blest,
Eternal praise and worship be addressed;
From age to age, ye saints, his name adore,
And spread his fame, till time shall be no more!

32 8s & 7s.

Praise the God of all creation;
Praise the Father's boundless love;
Praise the Lamb, our expiation,—
Priest and King, enthroned above;
Praise the Fountain of salvation,—
Him by whom our spirits live;
Undivided adoration
To the one Jehovah give.

33 8s & 7s.

Praise the Father, earth and heaven;
Praise the Son, the Spirit praise;
As it was, and is, be given
Glory through eternal days.

34 8s & 7s. 6l.

Glory be to God the Father,
Glory be to God the Son,
Glory be to God the Spirit,
Everlasting Three in One:
Thee let heaven and earth adore,
Now, henceforth, and evermore.

35 8s, 7s, & 4.

Great Jehovah, we adore thee,
God the Father, God the Son,
God the Spirit, joined in glory
On the same eternal throne;
Endless praises
To Jehovah, Three in One.

36 C. P. M.

To Father, Son, and Holy Ghost
Be praise amid the heavenly host,
And in the church below:
From whom all creatures draw their breath,
By whom redemption blessed the earth,
From whom all comforts flow.

37 L. P. M.

Now to the great and sacred Three,
The Father, Son, and Spirit, be
Eternal praise and glory given,
Through all the worlds where God is known,
By all the angels near the throne,
And all the saints in earth and heaven.

38 H. M.

To God the Father, Son,
And Spirit ever blest,
Eternal Three in One,
All worship be addrest;
As heretofore | And shall be so
It was, is now, | For evermore.

39 H. M.

To God the Father's throne
Your highest honors raise;
Glory to God the Son,
To God the Spirit praise;
With all our powers, Eternal King,
Thy name we sing, while faith adores.

40 5s & 6s.

By angels in heaven
Of every degree,
And saints upon earth
All praise be addressed
To God in Three persons—
One God ever blest;
As hath been, and now is
And always shall be.

41 6s & 4s.

To God, the Father, Son,
And Spirit, Three in One,
All praise be given!
Crown him in every song;
To him your hearts belong;
Let all his praise prolong
On earth in heaven!

42 10s & 11s.

Give glory to God, ye children of men,
And publish abroad, again and again,
The Son's glorious merit, the Father's true grace,
The gift of the Spirit, to Adam's lost race.

43 11s.

O Father Almighty, to thee be addressed,
With Christ and the Spirit, one God ever blest,
All glory and worship, from earth and from heaven,
As was, and is now, and shall ever be given!

INDEX OF FIRST LINES.

HYMN

ABBA, Father, we approach thee..J. G. Deck. 792
Abide with me, fast falls the eventide...Lyte. 594
A broken heart, my God, my King.... Watts. 363
A debtor to mercy alone..................Toplady. 556
A few more years shall roll..............Bonar. 987
Again returns the day of holy rest...Mason. 43
Again the Lord of life and...Mrs. Barbauld. 41
Ah, how shall fallen man................. Watts. 317
Ah! wretched, vile, ungrateful..Anne Steele. 830
Alas, and did my Saviour bleed........ Watts. 228
Alas! what hourly dangers.......Anne Steele. 719
All glory, worship, thanks, and....Gerhardt. 195
All hail the power of Jesus' name..Perronet. 271
All praise to thee, eternal Lord........Luther. 194
All that I was, my sin, my guilt.......Bonar. 424
All things are ready—Come..........Midlane. 837
Almighty Father, bless the word.............. 82
Amazing grace! how sweet the.......Newton. 543
Amazing sight! the Saviour stands............ 369
Am I a soldier of the cross...............Watts. 703
Am I called, and can it be.................Gray. 392
A mind at perfect peace with God.C. Paget. 496
A mother may forgetful be.......Anne Steele. 746
And can I yet delay.................C. Wesley. 394
And canst thou, sinner......Mrs. A. B. Hyde. 335
And didst thou, Jesus........."Amelia" 1827. 208
And did the Holy and the Just..Anne Steele. 223
And let this feeble body fail.......C. Wesley. 925
And must I part with all I have...Beddome. 558
And must this body die.................. Watts. 952
And now, my soul, another....Simon Browne. 911
And now the solemn deed is done..S. F. Smith. 808
And will the great, eternal God..Doddridge. 866
And will the Judge descend...... Doddridge. 962
Angels, roll the rock away............T. Scott. 244
Another six days' work is done....J. Stennett. 42
A pilgrim through this lonely world..Bonar. 200
Apostles of the risen Christ, go forth.Bonar. 806
Arise, great God, and let thy......J. Merrick. 889
Arise, my soul, arise.................C. Wesley. 411
Arise, my soul, my joyful powers...... Watts. 169
Arise, my tenderest thoughts......Doddridge. 646
Around the throne of God.....Anne Shepherd. 853
Around thy grave, Lord Jesus....J. G. Deck. 759
Arm of the Lord, awake........ W. Shrubsole. 875
As flows the rapid river...........S. F. Smith. 918

HYMN

Ask ye what great thing I know.....Monsell. 451
Asleep in Jesus! blessed........Mrs. Mackay. 948
As o'er the past my memory.......Middleton. 359
Assembled at thy great command.....Collyer. 886
A throne of grace! then let us go......Cobbin. 580
Awake, and sing the song..........Hammond. 275
Awaked by Sinai's awful sound........ Occum. 322
Awake, my heart; arise, my tongue... Watts. 528
Awake, my soul, and sing..Matthew Bridges. 272
Awake, my soul, and with the sun........Ken. 86
Awake, my soul, lift up.......Mrs. Barbauld. 710
Awake, my soul, stretch every....Doddridge. 711
Awake, my soul, in joyful lays........Medley. 555
Awake, my tongue, thy tribute......Needham. 167
Awake, our souls, away our fears........ Watts. 712
Awake, ye saints, awake.E. Scott & Cotterill. 45

BAPTIZED into the name.................... Davis. 774
Beautiful Zion, built above.G. Gill & Beers. 980
Before Jehovah's awful throne......... Watts. 5
Before the throne of God...Miss C. L. Smith. 441
Begone, unbelief, my Saviour is near.Newton. 669
Begin, my tongue, some heavenly....... Watts. 129
Behold a stranger at the door............Grigg. 379
Behold th' amazing sight..........Doddridge. 224
Behold the glories of the Lamb......... Watts. 273
Behold the grave......S. Stennett & Beddome. 757
Behold the morning sun.................. Watts. 735
Behold the Saviour of...........S. Wesley, Sr. 231
Behold the sin-atoning Lamb.........Fawcett. 220
Behold the sure foundation-stone...... Watts. 738
Behold the throne of grace...............Newton. 577
Behold, what pity touched the heart.. Watts. 234
Behold, what wondrous grace... .... Watts. 521
Be joyful in God, all ye lands...Montgomery. 16
Beneath our feet, and o'er our head...Heber. 922
Be still, my heart, these anxious.......Newton. 657
Be thou exalted, O my God............. Watts. 113
Be thou, O God, exalted........Tate & Brady. 20
Beyond the smiling and the weeping.Bonar. 985
Beyond where Kedron's waters..S. F. Smith. 217
Bless, O my soul, the living God....... Watts. 166
Blessed Saviour, thee I love...........Duffield. 468
Blest are the men whose mercies....... Watts. 649
Blest be the Father and his love. ..... Watts. 311
Blest be the tie that binds................Fawcett. 640

INDEX OF FIRST LINES.

HYMN

Blest hour, when mortal man...........*Raffles.* 68
Blest is the man whose... .....*Mrs. Barbauld.* 645
Blest morning, whose young............. *Watts.* 246
Blow ye the trumpet, blow..........*C. Wesley.* 365
Bread of heaven, on thee we........*J. Conder.* 793
Brethren, while we sojourn here........*Swain.* 720
Brightest and best of the sons...........*Heber.* 193
Bright King of glory! dreadful God.. *Watts.* 174
Bright was the guiding star..*Miss H. Auber.* 192
Broad is the road that leads........... *Watts.* 633
Brother, thou art gone to rest.........*Milman.* 946
Brother, though from yonder sky...*Bancroft.* 943
Brothers, clasp hands, the brief moments.... 913
Builder of mighty worlds on worlds.......... 868
Buried in shadows of the night......... *Watts.* 321
By cool Siloam's shady rill...................*Heber.* 848

Cast thy burden on the Lord. *George Rawson.* 658
Cease, ye mourners, cease to.......... *Collyer.* 950
Chief of sinners though I be.........*McComb.* 431
Children of the heavenly King...... *Cennick.* 550
Chosen not for good in me..........*McCheyne.* 471
Christ and his cross are all our......... *Watts.* 454
Christ is our corner-stone............*Chandler.* 869
Christ, of all my hopes the......*R. Wardlaw.* 571
Christ, the Lord, is risen to-day...*C. Wesley.* 247
Christ, who came my soul........*S. D. Phelps.* 763
Christ, whose glory fills the skies. *C. Wesley.* 598
Come, blessed Spirit, source of.......*Beddome.* 295
Come, desire of nations...............*C. Wesley.* 997
Come, gracious Lord, descend and..... *Watts.* 83
Come, gracious Spirit, heavenly.......*Browne.* 300
Come, happy souls, adore the........*Baldwin.* 755
Come, happy souls, approach your..... *Watts.* 178
Come hither, all ye weary souls......... *Watts.* 374
Come, Holy Spirit, come. Let thy......*Hart.* 303
Come, Holy Spirit, come. With....*Beddome.* 298
Come, Holy Spirit, Dove........*Dr. A. Judson.* 776
Come, Holy Spirit, heavenly dove..... *Watts.* 299
Come in, thou blessed of the Lord......*Kelly.* 840
Come in, thou blessed of the......*Montgomery.* 838
Come, let our voices join to raise...... *Watts.* 23
Come, let us anew.......................*C. Wesley.* 906
Come, let us join our cheerful songs... *Watts.* 280
Come, let us join our friends.......*C. Wesley.* 938
Come, let us lift our joyful eyes......... *Watts.* 2
Come, Lord, and tarry not...............*Bonar.* 998
Come, Lord, in mercy come again..*N. Colver.* 816
Come, my soul, thy suit prepare.......*Newton.* 590
Come, O Creator, Spirit....*Tr. by E. Caswell.* 304
Come, O my soul, in sacred lays...*Blacklock.* 36
Come, sinner, to the gospel feast. *Huntingdon.* 336
Come, sound his praise abroad......... *Watts.* 22
Come, thou almighty King.........*C. Wesley.* 309
Come, thou fount of every...........*Robinson.* 596
Come to the ark, come to the ark............... 385
Come to the blood-stained tree......... 375
Come, weary sinner, in whose.... ...*E. Jones.* 371
Come, weary souls, with sin......*Anne Steele.* 370
Come, we that love the Lord .... *Watts.* 503

Come, ye disconsolate.......*Moore & Hastings.* 587
Come, ye sinners, poor and wretched...*Hart.* 376
Come, thou soul-transforming.....*Jon. Evans.* 81
Come, ye that know and......*George Burder.* 140
Come, ye that love the.............*Anne Steele.* 189
Come, ye who love. *S. Stennett & J. Campbell.* 259
Compared with Christ, in all........ . *Toplady.* 463
Complete in thee, no work of mine..*A. R. W.* 443
Could I recall the buried past.......... 423
Crowns of glory ever bright................*Kelly.* 282

Dark was the night, and cold........*Haweis.* 219
Daughter of Zion, from the......*Montgomery.* 873
Day of judgment, day of wonders...*Newton.* 956
Dear as thou wert, and justly dear.......*Dale.* 939
Dearest of all the names above..... ..... *Watts.* 480
Dear Father, to thy mercy-seat..*Anne Steele.* 672
Dear refuge of my weary soul...*Anne Steele.* 677
Dear Saviour, prostrate at thy....*S. Stennett.* 360
Dear Saviour, we are thine.........*Doddridge.* 608
Death cannot make our souls afraid... *Watts.* 935
Deep are the wounds which......*Anne Steele.* 388
Deep in our hearts let us record......... *Watts.* 227
Delay not, delay not, O sinner...*T. Hastings.* 340
Depth of mercy! can there be.....*C. Wesley.* 357
Descend, celestial Dove..............*J. Fellows.* 778
Did Christ o'er sinners weep.........*Beddome.* 653
Didst thou, dear Saviour........*Jas. Maxwell.* 713
Dismiss us with thy blessing, Lord.....*Hart.* 85
Disowned of heaven, by man.........*J. Joyce.* 884
Done is the work that saves............*Bonar.* 439
Do we not know that solemn word.... *Watts.* 769
Down to the sacred wave.........*S. F. Smith.* 756
Dread Jehovah! God. *C. F. in Ch. Obs.* 1804. 894

Early, my God, without delay......... *Watts.* 60
Earth to earth, and dust to dust...... *Gurney.* 953
Emptied of earth I fain would be...*Toplady.* 613
Ere earth's......*J. G. Hermann tr. Winkworth.* 138
Ere mountains reared their...*Miss H. Auber.* 916
Eternal source of every joy........ *Doddridge.* 899
Eternal Spirit, we confess................. *Watts.* 287
Eternal Wisdom, thee we praise........ *Watts.* 145
Eternity is just at hand............*Anne Steele.* 326
Exalted Jesus, heavenly King............... 845

Faith adds new charms to earthly...*Turner.* 458
Faith is a living power.....*Cath. Winkworth.* 159
Faithful, O Lord, thy mercies...*Montgomery.* 123
Far as thy name is known................ *Watts.* 741
Far down the ages now....................*Bonar.* 745
Far from my heavenly home..............*Lyte.* 983
Far from my thoughts, vain world..... *Watts.* 39
Far from these narrow scenes...*Anne Steele.* 972
Father, for thy promised... ......*A. Midlane.* 820
Father, I know that......*Miss A. L. Waring.* 606
Father, I sing thy wondrous grace.... *Watts.* 481
Father, I stretch my hands to...... *C. Wesley.* 402
Father of all, before thy... ......*J. H. Hinton.* 652
Father of heaven, whose love..........*Cooper.* 312

INDEX OF FIRST LINES.

HYMN

Father of mercies, bow thine. ....Beddome. 802
Father of mercies, God. ....Heginbotham. 117
Father of mercies, in thy.........Doddridge. 804
Father of mercies, in thy ....Anne Steele. 725
Father, whate'er of earthly.......Anne Steele. 620
Fear not, O little. Altenburg tr. C. Winkworth. 747
Firm as the earth, thy gospel stands.. Watts. 430
Follow the paths of Jesus....C. R. Blackall. 701
For a season called to part.............Newton. 912
Forever here my rest shall be......C. Wesley. 421
Forever with the Lord...........Montgomery. 974
For mercies countless as the sands...Newton. 546
Fountain of grace, rich, full.....J. Edmeston. 447
Frequent the day of God returns..S. Browne. 73
Friend after friend departs........Montgomery. 937
From all that dwell below the skies... Watts. 12
From every stormy wind that blows..Stowell. 584
From Greenland's icy mountains.. .....Heber. 881
From the cross uplifted high...........Haweis. 389
From thy dear, pierced side.........Beddome. 239
From whence doth this union........Baldwin. 638

Gently, Lord, oh, gently lead... T. Hastings. 592
Give me the wings of faith to rise..... Watts. 709
Give thanks to God, he reigns above.. Watts. 141
Glorious things of thee are spoken...Newton. 742
Glory be to God the Father.........H. Bonar. 306
Glory to thee, my God, this night........Ken. 99
God bless our native land........J. S. Dwight. 893
God calling yet! shall I not hear. Tersteegen. 391
God in his earthly temple lays......... Watts. 736
God in the gospel of his Son........Beddome. 728
God is love; his mercy.......Sir J. Bowring. 142
God is the refuge of his saints........... Watts. 160
God moves in a mysterious way......Cowper. 153
God, my supporter and my hope....... Watts. 506
God of mercy, God of grace....John Taylor. 358
God of mercy, hear our prayer.. T. Hastings. 650
God of my life, through all my...Doddridge. 932
God of my life, to thee I call...... .....Cowper. 656
God of the morning, at thy voice......... Watts. 87
God of the world, thy glories...S. S. Cutting. 111
God's glory is a wondrous thing........Faber. 697
God's holy law transgressed.........Beddome. 350
God, the Father, high in glory................. 862
God with us, Oh glorious name..Sarah Slinn. 175
Go and tell Jesus, weary, sin-sick soul......... 855
Go preach my gospel, saith the Lord.. Watts. 800
Go preach the blest salvation...Sidney Dyer. 882
Go to dark Gethsemane...........Montgomery. 219
Go to the grave in all thy.. ......Montgomery. 945
Go when the morning shineth. Mrs. Simpson. 579
Go worship at Immanuel's feet......... Watts. 176
Grace! 'tis a charming sound.....Doddridge. 536
Gracious Lord, incline thine ear..Hammond. 399
Gracious Saviour, we adore......S. S. Cutting. 758
Gracious Spirit, Love Divine....John Stocker. 296
Grant the abundance of....Mrs. P. H. Brown. 888
Great God, as seasons disappear. E. Butcher. 902
Great God, attend while Zion sings.... Watts. 65
Great God, how infinite art thou....... Watts. 101
Great God, indulge my humble claim. Watts. 548
Great God, now condescend............Fellows. 856
Great God, the nations of...Thomas Gibbons. 870
Great God, we sing that mighty..Doddridge. 904
Great God, when I approach thy....Bathurst. 427
Great God, with wonder and with...... Watts. 722
Great is the Lord our God.............. Watts. 740
Great is the Lord! what tongue can... Watts. 147
Great King of glory and of grace..... Watts. 315
Great King of saints, enthroned......Conder. 810
Great Shepherd of thy people, hear. Newton. 71
Guide me, O thou great..... ... W. Williams. 694

Had I ten thousand gifts beside.......... 429
Had I the tongues of Greeks and...... Watts. 643
Hail, happy day, thou day of holy...Browne. 49
Hail, my ever blessed Jesus......... Wingrove. 467
Hail, sovereign love, that first..........Brewer. 527
Hail the day that sees him rise....C. Wesley. 262
Hail, thou long expected Jesus....C. Wesley. 191
Hail to the Lord's Anointed......Montgomery. 876
Hail to the Sabbath day...............Bulfinch. 48
Hallelujah! who shall part... Wm. Dickinson. 741
Happy the church, thou sacred place. Watts. 743
Happy the heart where graces reign.. Watts. 644
Happy the souls to Jesus joined...C. Wesley. 749
Hark! my soul! it is the Lord........Cowper. 486
Hark! ten thousand harps and voices. Kelly. 281
Hark! the glad sound, the.........Doddridge. 184
Hark! the herald angels sing......C. Wesley. 188
Hark! the voice of love and......Jon. Evans. 236
Hark! what mean those holy voices. Cawood. 186
Haste, O sinner, now be wise.........T. Scott. 339
Haste, traveller, haste, the night......Collyer. 338
Head of the Church triumphant...C. Wesley. 750
Hear, gracious Sovereign, from...Doddridge. 819
Hear, O sinner; mercy hails you.........Reed. 364
Heart of stone, relent, relent......C. Wesley. 332
Hear what the voice from heaven...... Watts. 947
He dies! the Friend of...... Watts & Wesley. 242
He leadeth me! oh, blessed thought. Gilmore. 693
He lives! he lives! and sits above...... Watts. 263
He lives, the great Redeemer.....Anne Steele. 265
Here at thy cross, incarnate God ..... Watts. 415
Here at thy table, Lord, we meet..S. Stennett. 779
Here, in thy name, eternal God..Montgomery. 861
Here, O ye faithful, see. .....C. H. Spurgeon. 770
High in the heavens, eternal God...... Watts. 110
Holy and reverend is the name.....Needham. 152
Holy Bible! book divine.........John Burton. 731
Holy Father, hear my cry...............Bonar. 314
Holy Ghost, with light divine.............Reed. 302
Holy, holy, holy, Lord! Be....B. Williams. 38
Holy, holy, holy Lord God of..B. Manly, Jr. 133
Holy, holy, holy Lord God of....Montgomery. 134
Holy Spirit, from on high............Bathurst. 305
Holy source of consolation.......B. W. Noel. 292
Hosanna to the Prince of Light........ Watts. 252
How beauteous are their feet........... Watts. 801

INDEX OF FIRST LINES.

HYMN

How beauteous were the marks...*A. C. Coxe.* 202
How blest the man whose cautious..... *Watts.* 517
How blest the righteous.......*Mrs. Barbauld.* 929
How blest the sacred tie that.*Mrs. Barbauld.* 647
How can I sink with such a prop....... *Watts.* 568
How condescending and how kind..... *Watts.* 232
How charming is the place.........*S. Stennett.* 72
How did my heart rejoice to hear....... *Watts.* 64
How firm a foundation, ye saints.*Geo. Keith.* 678
How gentle God's commands.......*Doddridge.* 661
How happy's every child of grace.*C. Wesley.* 489
How happy is the child........*Michael Bruce.* 858
How happy is the Christian's state..*Hudson.* 490
How heavy is the night.................. *Watts.* 318
How helpless guilty nature lies..*Anne Steele.* 291
How honored is the place..................... *Watts.* 737
How oft, alas! this wretched......*Anne Steele.* 829
How oft have sin and Satan strove.... *Watts.* 446
How pleasant, how divinely fair........ *Watts.* 70
How pleased and blest was I............. *Watts.* 66
How precious is the book divine.....*Fawcett.* 729
How sad our state by nature is......... *Watts.* 390
How short and hasty is our life........ *Watts.* 920
How sweet and awful is the place...... *Watts.* 782
How sweet, how heavenly is the........*Swain.* 641
How sweetly flowed the.......*Sir J. Bowring.* 470
How sweet the name of Jesus.........*Newton.* 483
How sweet to bless the Lord....................... 67
How sweet upon this sacred......*Mrs. Follen.* 53
How tedious and tasteless the hours.*Newton.* 519
How vain are all things here below.... *Watts.* 619
Humble souls, who seek............*J. Fawcett.* 753

I BLESS the Christ of God................*Bonar.* 554
If human kindness meets..........*G. T. Noel.* 785
If I must die, oh, let me die.........*Beddome.* 934
If Jesus be my...*Gerhardt tr. C. Winkworth.* 495
If life in sorrow must be......*Madame Guion.* 686
If on a quiet sea.........................*Toplady.* 665
I have a home above...........*Henry Bennett.* 977
I heard the voice of Jesus say.........*Bonar.* 507
I hear the words of love...................*Bonar.* 499
I lay my sins on Jesus....................*Bonar.* 435
I'll bless the Lord, I'll *William Peter*, 1828. 545
I'll praise my Maker with my breath. *Watts.* 33
I love thee, O my God, but not........*Xavier.* 466
I love the Lord; he heard my cries... *Watts.* 462
I love the volume of thy word......... *Watts.* 732
I love thy kingdom, Lord..............*Dwight.* 637
I love to see the Lord below............. *Watts.* 76
I love to steal awhile away.*Mrs. P. H. Brown.* 93
I'm but a stranger here....*Thomas R. Taylor.* 978
Immersed beneath the.........*George Rawson.* 767
I'm not ashamed to own my Lord...... *Watts.* 715
I'm thine, O Lord, and thine alone............ 561
In all my Lord's appointed ways.*J. Ryland.* 762
In all my vast concerns with thee...... *Watts.* 103
In all the impotence of need 444
In duties and in sufferings too......*Beddome.* 206
In evil long I took delight............*Newton.* 539

HYMN

Inscribed upon the cross we see...... *T. Kelly.* 171
In the cross of Christ I........*Sir J. Bowring.* 456
In vain my roving thoughts......*Anne Steele.* 617
I rest my soul on Jesus.. ....*Bonar.* 436
I see the crowd in Pilate's hall........*Bonar.* 226
I send the joys of earth away.......... *Watts.* 612
I sing the almighty power of God..... *Watts.* 46
I stand on Zion's mount...............*J. Swain.* 438
Is this the kind return.................... *Watts.* 321
It is finished: shall we raise...................... 233
I've found the pearl of greatest price.*Mason.* 521
I waited patient for the Lord........... *Watts.* 631
I was a wandering sheep......................*Bonar.* 547
I will love thee, all my.......*Johann Angelus.* 465
I worship thee, sweet will of God......*Faber.* 682
I would love thee, God and..*Madame Guion.* 464
I would not live alway............*Muhlenburg.* 928

JEHOVAH reigns; he dwells in light... *Watts.* 152
Jehovah reigns; his throne is high..... *Watts.* 151
Jerusalem, my.....*J. Mason, D. Burgess*, etc. 982
Jerusalem, the golden.....*John Mason Neale.* 975
Jesus, all-atoning Lamb.... .... *Wesley.* 574
Jesus, and shall it ever be.*Grigg & Francis.* 716
Jesus, delightful, charming name..*Beddome.* 478
Jesus, hail! enthroned in glory.....*Bakewell.* 276
Jesus, I come to thee...............................*Beman.* 397
Jesus, I love thy charming.........*Doddridge.* 485
Jesus. I my cross have taken..............*Lyte.* 564
Jesus, in thy transporting..........*Anne Steele.* 270
Jesus invites his saints....................... *Watts.* 780
Jesus lives, and so shall I...........*C. Gellert.* 266
Jesus lives! henceforth is death...*C. Gellert.* 256
Jesus, lover of my soul...............*C. Wesley.* 413
Jesus, Master, hear me now....................... 795
Jesus, Master, hear my cry....*Anna Shipton.* 406
Jesus, merciful and mild..........*T. Hastings.* 604
Jesus, mighty King in Zion.. ....*Fellows.* 752
Jesus, my all, to heaven is gone......*Cennick.* 412
Jesus, my Lord, my God, my all.*H. Collins.* 475
Jesus, my Lord, my life, my all...*S. Medley.* 400
Jesus, my Lord, 'tis sweet to rest............... 526
Jesus, our Lord, how rich thy....*Doddridge.* 639
Jesus, seek thy wandering sheep..*C. Wesley.* 823
Jesus shall reign where'er the sun..... *Watts.* 872
Jesus, spotless Lamb of God......*J. G. Deck.* 570
Jesus spreads his banner o'er.*Roswell Park.* 783
Jesus, the Lamb of God....................*Bonar.* 531
Jesus, these eyes have never seen....*Palmer.* 473
Jesus, the sinner's friend, to thee..*C. Wesley.* 396
Jesus, the very thought of thee...*E. Caswell.* 509
Jesus, thou art the sinner's friend.*Burnham.* 407
Jesus, thou joy of loving hearts.*Ray Palmer.* 504
Jesus, thou Shepherd of the.........*T. Kelly.* 842
Jesus, thou source of calm repose..*C. Wesley.* 662
Jesus, thy boundless love to me....*J. Wesley.* 472
Jesus, thy name I love............................ 476
Jesus, thy robe of righteousness...*J. Wesley.* 434
Jesus, to thy dear arms I flee. 852
Jesus, we look to thee.. ....*C. Wesley.* 79

INDEX OF FIRST LINES.

HYMN

Jesus, we rest in thee ....J. G. Deck. 510
Jesus, where'er thy people meet......Cowper. 77
Jesus, who knows full well.... ....Newton. 588
Jesus, who upon..J. Angelus tr. C. Winkworth. 559
Jesus, with all thy saints above........ Watts. 542
Join all the glorious names........ ...... Watts. 278
Joyful be the hours to-day............ T. Kelly. 497
Joy to the world! the Lord is come.... Watts. 183
Just as I am, without one.....Miss C. Elliott. 408
Just as thou art, without one trace......Cook. 372

Keep silence, all created things........ Watts. 164
Kindred in Christ, for his dear sake. Newton. 839
Kingdoms and thrones to God belong. Watts. 149
King of kings, and wilt thou....Muhlenburg. 599
Know, my soul, thy full salvation.. .....Lyte. 520

Laborers of Christ, arise...L. H. Sigourney. 695
Lead them, my God, to thee........................ 854
Let all the heathen writers join......... Watts. 734
Let everlasting glories crown............ Watts. 532
Let every creature join......... ...Anne Steele. 11
Let every mortal ear attend............. Watts. 366
Let me but hear my Saviour say....... Watts. 664
Let sinners take their course............ Watts. 31
Let worldly minds the world pursue.Newton. 573
Let Zion's watchmen all awake...Doddridge. 805
Life is the time to serve the Lord....... Watts. 342
Light of the lonely pilgrim's...Sir E. Denny. 995
Like sheep we went astray.............. Watts. 229
Lo! he comes with......C. Wesley & Cennick. 958
Look up, my soul, with cheerful.Anne Steele. 268
Look, ye saints;—the sight is glorious.Kelly. 284
Lord, at thy table we behold......S. Stennett. 786
Lord, dismiss us with thy blessing...Shirley. 84
Lord God, the Holy Ghost.......Montgomery. 822
Lord, how mysterious are thy....Anne Steele. 156
Lord, how secure my conscience was.. Watts. 319
Lord, I am thine, entirely thine....... Davies. 569
Lord, I am vile,—conceived in sin..... Watts. 316
Lord, I approach the mercy-seat......Newton. 409
Lord, I believe, thy power I own... Wreford. 460
Lord, I cannot let thee go................Newton. 593
Lord, I desire to live as.....Charitie L. Smith. 609
Lord, I have made thy word my........ Watts. 730
Lord, I hear of showers of......Eliz. Codner. 825
Lord, I'm oppressed; oh, undertake.Monsell. 404
Lord, in the morning thou shalt hear. Watts. 58
Lord, in the temples of thy.......Anne Steele. 815
Lord, it belongs not to my care...R. Baxter. 685
Lord, I would come to thee.......T. Hastings. 395
Lord Jesus, are we one with........J. G. Deck. 513
Lord Jesus Christ, my life, my light.Behemb. 440
Lord, lead the way the Saviour.. W. Croswel. 648
Lord, let thy goodness lead our land.......... 892
Lord, my times are in thy hand....J. Conder. 684
Lord of Hosts, how bright, how fair.. Turner. 71
Lord of Hosts, to thee we raise.Montgomery. 863
Lord of the harvest, bend thine...... Hastings. 812
Lord of the realms above.................... Lyte. 525

HYMN

Lord of the worlds above.................. Watts. 81
Lord, shed a beam of heavenly.......... Hart. 319
Lord, thou hast scourged our guilty... Watts. 897
Lord, thou hast searched and seen..... Watts. 104
Lord, thou hast won; at length I......Newton. 405
Lord, thou who art enthroned in glory........ 420
Lord, through the desert drear.Mary Bowly. 668
Lord, we adore, thy vast designs....... Watts. 157
Lord, we are thine, bought by.....J. G. Deck. 572
Lord, we come before thee now....Hammond. 73
Lord, we confess our numerous faults. Watts. 170
Lord, when thou didst ascend on high. Watts. 253
Lord, while for all mankind we..... Wreford. 891
Loud hallelujahs to the Lord........... Watts. 19
Love divine, all love excelling......C. Wesley. 603
Lo! what a glorious sight appears..... Watts. 995

Mary to the Saviour's tomb...........Newton. 253
May not the sovereign Lord on high.. Watts. 172
Meekly in Jordan's holy stream.S. F. Smith. 775
Mercy, O thou Son of David............Newton. 211
Mistaken souls that dream of heaven.. Watts. 630
More like Jesus would I be..........F. Crosby. 610
Must Jesus bear the.....T. Shepherd & Allen. 562
My country, 'tis of thee............S. F. Smith. 890
My days are gliding swiftly by........Nelson. 927
My dear Redeemer and my Lord....... Watts. 203
My faith looks up to thee........Ray Palmer. 601
My God, how endless is thy love....... Watts. 94
My God, how wonderful thou art...... Faber. 136
My God, my Father, blissful......Anne Steele. 162
My God, my Father, while I..Miss C. Elliott. 688
My God, my King, thy various praise. Watts. 32
My God, my life, my love................ Watts. 616
My God, my portion and my love...... Watts. 514
My God, permit me not to be............ Watts. 615
My God, the spring of all my joys..... Watts. 516
My God, thy boundless love I......H. Moore. 135
My gracious Lord, I own thy......Doddridge. 563
My heavenly home is bright..... Wm. Hunter. 981
My heart is resting, O...Miss A. L. Waring. 500
My hope is built on nothing less.....E. Mote. 414
My Maker and my King...........Anne Steele. 567
My opening eyes with rapture see.....Hutton. 44
My precious Lord, for thy dear name.......... 484
My rest is in heaven, my rest is not.....Lyte. 679
My Saviour, my almighty Friend...... Watts. 529
My sins, my sins, my Saviour.........Monsell. 222
My soul, be on thy guard...............Heath. 701
My soul complete in Jesus....Mrs. Hinsdale. 789
My soul forsakes her vain delight ..... Watts. 618
My soul, repeat his praise............... Watts. 119
My soul, with joy attend...........Doddridge. 417

Nature with open volume stands...... Watts. 235
Nearer, my God, to thee..Mrs. S. F. Adams. 600
New every morning is the love..........Keble. 90
No change of time shall ever. Tate & Brady. 153
No more, my God, I boast no more..... Watts 425
No night shall be in heaven.... Thos. Raffles. 973

INDEX OF FIRST LINES.

HYMN

No room for mirth or trifling here. *C. Wesley.* 964
Not all the blood of beasts........ *Watts.* 791
Not all the outward forms on earth..... *Watts.* 290
Nothing but leaves—the Spirit.....—*Taylor.* 699
Nothing either great or small......... *Proctor.* 381
Not to condemn the sons of men....... *Watts.* 196
Not to ourselves again.................. *Bonar.* 565
Not to the terrors of the Lord.......... *Watts.* 739
Not what I am, O Lord, but what...... *Bonar.* 549
Not what I feel or do..................... *Bonar.* 426
Now begin the heavenly theme.... *Langford.* 541
Now be my heart inspired to sing...... *Watts.* 181
Now for a tune of lofty praise......... *Watts.* 277
Now from the altar of our hearts...... *Mason.* 97
Now, gracious Lord, thine arm........ *Newton.* 908
Now I have found a Friend...... *Henry Hope.* 498
Now, in parting, Father, bless us...... *Bonar.* 798
Now is th' accepted time................. *Dobell.* 346
Now let my soul, eternal King.. *Heginbotham.* 724
Now let our cheerful eyes survey. *Doddridge.* 267
Now that the sun is beaming bright.. *Ambrose.* 91
Now to the Lord a noble song........... *Watts.* 168
Now to the Lord who makes us know. *Watts.* 992
Now to the power of God supreme...... *Watts.* 530

Object of my first desire............. *Toplady.* 393
O blessed God! to thee I raise..................... 30
O blessed Jesus! Lamb of God... *J. G. Deck.* 279
O Christ our King, Creator, Lord..... *Gregory.* 283
O Christ, our true and....... *Anne Ross Cousin.* 654
O Christ, what burdens bowed thy head........ 442
O Christ! what...... *P. Gerhardt tr. Gambold.* 241
O day of rest and gladness..... *Wordsworth.* 52
O dear and blessed Jesus.......................... 846
O'er the gloomy hills of......... *W. Williams.* 878
O Father, Lord of earth.... *J. W. Willmarth.* 772
O Father, though the anxious. *Mrs. Barbauld.* 55
Oft in danger.. *K. White & Fanny Maitland.* 717
O glorious God of grace............................ 777
O God, my inmost soul convert..... *C. Wesley.* 965
O God, my strength, my hope...... *C. Wesley.* 636
O God of mercy, hear my call.......... *Watts.* 362
O God of our salvation, Lord... *J. Chandler.* 457
O God, our help in ages past............ *Watts.* 120
O God the Father, Christ the Son............... 860
O holy, holy Lord.................................... 313
O holy Lord, our God.................. *J. Young.* 803
Oh, blessed souls are they............... *Watts.* 501
Oh, bless the Lord, my soul...... *Montgomery.* 28
Oh, bless the Lord, my soul, Let all... *Watts.* 125
Oh, bow thine ear, eternal One...... *Pierpont.* 864
Oh, could I find from day to.... *B. Cleaveland.* 622
Oh, could we speak the matchless.... *Medley.* 553
Oh, do not let the word depart... *Eliza Reed.* 348
Oh, for a closer walk with God.. ..... *Cowper.* 626
Oh, for a faith that will not shrink. *Bathurst.* 674
Oh for a heart to praise my God... *C. Wesley.* 623
Oh, for an overcoming faith............ *Watts.* 933
Oh, for a shout of sacred joy.......... *Watts.* 261
Oh, for a thousand tongues to sing. *C. Wesley.* 522

HYMN

Oh for the death of those........ *Montgomery.* 938
Oh! for the robes of......... *Miss C. L. Smith.* 981
Oh, hallowed is the land and blest... *Wieszel.* 4
Oh, happy day that fixed my...... *Doddridge.* 766
Oh, happy day, when first we..... *J. G. Deck.* 505
Oh, how divine, how sweet the joy. *Needham.* 534
Oh, how happy are they............ *C. Wesley.* 491
Oh, how I love thy holy law............ *Watts.* 733
Oh, joyful day! oh, glorious hour... *T. Kelly.* 251
Oh, let him whose *H. S. Oswald tr. F. E. Cox.* 655
Oh, let my trembling soul be. *Sir J. Bowring.* 689
Oh, let thy sacred word impart... *Anne Steele.* 726
Oh, love, beyond the reach of.......... *Conder.* 537
Oh, love divine! oh, matchless..... *E. Turney.* 781
Oh, love, how deep, how broad, how... *Neale.* 285
Oh, mean may seem this house.... *T. H. Gill.* 201
Oh, praise our great and...... *Miss H. Auber.* 511
Oh, praise ye the Lord!........... *Tate, varied.* 6
Oh, speed thee, Christian, *B. T. Onderdonk.* 706
Oh, still in accents sweet and strong............813
Oh, that I knew the secret place....... *Watts.* 595
Oh that my load of sin were....... *C. Wesley.* 354
Oh that the Lord would guide my...... *Watts.* 635
Oh, turn, great Ruler of the....... *J. Merrick.* 625
Oh, turn ye, oh, turn ye, why... *Samson Occum.* 383
Oh, wake our hearts, in gladness..... *Krauth.* 190
Oh, what amazing words of grace.... *Medley.* 373
Oh, where is he that trod the.... *T. T. Lynch.* 210
Oh, where shall rest be found.... *Montgomery.* 328
Oh, wondrous type! oh, vision fair..... *Neale.* 207
Oh, wondrous, vast, surpassing love........... 137
Oh, worship the King, all....... *Sir R. Grant.* 21
O Jesus, in this solemn hour............ *Collyer.* 811
O Jesus, King most wonderful....... *Bernard.* 487
O Jesus, Lord of heavenly grace... *Chandler.* 92
O Jesus! sweet the tears I........ *Ray Palmer.* 240
O Lord, and will thy pardoning....... *Fellows.* 765
O Lord, behold us at thy feet........... *Mrs. T.* 651
O Lord, how full of sweet..... *Madame Guion.* 105
O Lord, how happy should we be. *J. Anstice.* 681
O Lord, our strength and............ *C. Wesley.* 680
O Lord, thou art my Lord........... *Beddome.* 557
O Lord, thy heavenly grace.... *J. F. Oberlin.* 624
O Lord, thy love's unbounded.... *J. G. Deck.* 474
O Lord, thy work revive.. *Mrs. P. H. Brown.* 818
O Lord, when we the path....... ..*J. G. Deck.* 199
O love divine, how sweet thou art. *C. Wesley.* 469
O Love divine, that stooped... *O. W. Holmes.* 675
O love of God, how strong and true.... *Bonar.* 143
Once more, my soul, the rising day.... *Watts.* 89
Once more we meet to pray...... *Matt. Wilks.* 835
One sweetly solemn thought..... *Phœbe Cary.* 924
One there is above all others........... *Newton.* 796
On Jordan's banks, the Baptist's cry.. *Coffin.* 197
On Jordan's stormy banks I....... *S. Stennett.* 986
On thee, O Lord, our God, we. *Saml. Davies.* 895
On the mountain's top appearing....... *Kelly.* 879
O paradise eternal............... *Thomas Davis.* 967
O sacred head, now wounded....... *Gerhardt.* 225
O Saviour, welcome.. *W. Sanders & Bourne.* 566

INDEX OF FIRST LINES.

HYMN

O Saviour, who for man has......*Chas. Coffin.* 260
O sinner, why so................*Watts & Rippon.* 327
O spotless Lamb of God, in.....*Mary J. Deck.* 139
O thou my life, my light, my....*Montgomery.* 159
O thou, my soul, forget no.......*Krishna Pal.* 784
O thou that hearest prayer......*John Burton.* 301
O thou that hear'st the prayer of.....*Toplady.* 401
O thou that hear'st when sinners cry. *Watts.* 361
O thou, the contrite sinner's..*Miss C. Elliott.* 437
O thou, to whom all creatures. *Tate & Brady.* 107
O thou to whose all-searching......*C. Wesley.* 575
O thou who in Jordan didst bow.....*Bethune.* 773
Our country's voice is..*Mrs. G. W. Anderson.* 883
Our Father, God, who art in....*Dr. A. Judson.* 18
Our Father in heaven, we....*Mrs. S. J. Hale.* 17
Our helper, God, we bless thy.....*Doddridge.* 907
Our Saviour bowed beneath...*Dr. A. Judson.* 760
Our souls by love together......*W. E. Miller.* 642
Our times are in thy hand.... *Wm. F. Lloyd.* 659

PASCHAL LAMB, by God appointed. *Bakewell.* 790
Pass me not, O gentle Saviour.................... 831
Peace, troubled soul, whose plaintive. *Shirley.* 384
People of the living God..........*Montgomery.* 841
Pilgrim, rejoice! for the mantle. *F. J. Crosby.* 847
Planted in Christ, the living vine. *S. F. Smith.* 751
Plunged in a gulf of dark despair...... *Watts.* 182
Poor, weak and worthless tho' I am. *Newton.* 418
Praise God, from whom all blessings.....*Ken.* 1
Praise God, ye gladdening.....*Anna Shipton.* 7
Praise, Lord, for thee in Zion waits......*Lyte.* 25
Praise, oh, praise our God and King. *Baker.* 903
Praise the Lord, his glories show.........*Lyte.* 26
Praise the Lord; ye heavens. *J. Kempthorne.* 9
Praise the Redeemer, almighty to......*Groser.* 250
Praise to God, immortal.......*Mrs. Barbauld.* 898
Praise to thee, thou great Creator....*Fawcett.* 34
Praise ye the Lord, let praise....*Anne Steele.* 13
Praise ye the Lord! my heart shall.... *Watts.* 37
Praises to him whose love has given. *Bonar.* 310
Prayer is the breath of God in man. *Beddome.* 581
Prayer is the contrite sinner's...*Montgomery.* 583
Prayer is the soul's sincere.......*Montgomery.* 582
Purer yet, and purer.. 607

RAISE your triumphant songs.......... *Watts.* 551
Rejoice, rejoice, believers.........*L. Laurenti.* 993
Rejoice! ye saints, rejoice....*John H. Evans.* 523
Religion is the chief concern.........*Fawcett.* 859
Remark, my soul, the narrow.....*Doddridge.* 905
Repent! the voice celestial cries. *Doddridge.* 334
Return, my soul, and sweetly rest....*Latrobe.* 128
Return, my wandering soul, return..*Collyer.* 836
Revive thy work, O Lord.........*A. Midlane.* 817
Ride on! ride on in majesty..........*Milman.* 212
Rise, my soul, and stretch thy...*R. Seagrave.* 990
Rise, O my soul, pursue the path...*Needham.* 708
Rocked in the cradle of the...*Mrs. Willard.* 670
Rock of Ages, cleft for me...........*Toplady.* 416

SAFELY through another week.........*Newton.* 57

HYMN

Salvation! oh, the joyful sound......... *Watts.* 538
Saved ourselves by Jesus' blood.........*Kelly.* 814
Saviour, bless thy word to all.............*Kelly.* 63
Saviour, happy should I be......*E. H. Nevin.* 494
Saviour, I think upon that..*M. G. Thomson.* 221
Saviour, I thy word believe........... *Toplady.* 605
Saviour, like a.........*Dorothy A. Thrupp.* (?) 850
Saviour, visit thy plantation...........*Newton.* 824
Saviour, who thy flock art.........*Muhlenburg.* 857
See Israel's gentle Shepherd.......*Doddridge.* 843
See the ransomed millions stand...*J. Conder.* 991
Servant of God, well done........*Montgomery.* 942
Shall hymns of grateful..*James T. Cummins.* 24
Shall we gather at the river.........*R. Lowry.* 914
Shall we go on to sin.......................... *Watts.* 627
Show pity, Lord! O Lord, forgive....... *Watts.* 351
Since all the varying scenes of time..*Hervey.* 154
Sing, O heavens! O earth, rejoice....*Monsell.* 243
Sing to the Lord Jehovah's name....... *Watts.* 35
Sinner, rouse thee from thy sleep. *Onderdonk.* 343
Sinner, what hast thou to show..*Mrs. Tonna.* 331
Sinners, turn; why will ye die.......... *Wesley.* 329
Sinners, will you scorn the message.....*Allen.* 333
Sister, thou wast mild and lovely. *S. F. Smith.* 951
So fades the lovely, blooming....*Anne Steele.* 949
Softly fades the twilight ray......*S. F. Smith.* 54
Softly now the light of day.............*Doane.* 95
Soldiers of Christ, arise............*C. Wesley.* 718
So let our lips and lives express........ *Watts.* 634
Songs of praise the angels sang. *Montgomery.* 27
Son of God, thy blessing grant......... *Wesley.* 591
Soon as I heard my Father say......... *Watts.* 450
Soon may the last glad song 871
Sovereign grace o'er sin abounding......*Kent.* 552
Sovereign of worlds..........*Bap. Mag.* 1816. 874
Sovereign Ruler, Lord of all........... *Raffles.* 355
Sow in the morn thy seed.........*Montgomery.* 698
Spirit divine, attend our prayer......*A. Reed.* 867
Spirit of everlasting grace................*Bonar.* 821
Spirit of holiness, descend........*S. F. Smith.* 297
Stand up, and bless the Lord.....*Montgomery.* 14
Stand up, my soul, shake off thy....... *Watts.* 714
Stand up! stand up for Jesus..........*Duffield.* 707
Stay, thou insulted Spirit, stay....*C. Wesley.* 293
Still, still with thee, when.........*Mrs. Stowe.* 586
Still will we trust, though... *W. H. Burleigh.* 673
Strait is the way, the door is strait.... *Watts.* 631
Stretched on the cross, the.......*Anne Steele.* 230
Sun of my soul! thou Saviour dear....*Keble.* 96
Surely Christ thy griefs hath... ..... *Toplady.* 380
Sweeter sounds than music knows....*Newton.* 535
Sweet feast of love divine....*Edward Denny.* 799
Sweet hour of prayer, sweet hour... *Walford.* 578
Sweet is the memory of thy grace..... *Watts.* 124
Sweet is the work, my God, my King. *Watts.* 59
Sweet is the work, O Lord...................*Lyte.* 69
Sweet land of rest, for thee I sigh.............. 926
Sweet the moments, rich.....*Allen & Shirley.* 488
Sweet was the time, when first I felt. *Newton.* 518
Swell the anthem, raise the...*Nathan Strong.* 900

INDEX OF FIRST LINES.

INDEX OF FIRST LINES.

HYMN

Watchman, tell us of the .....*Sir J. Bowring.* 989
We bid thee welcome in the......*Montgomery.* 807
We come, O Lord, before.*Mrs. P. H. Brown.* 887
We come, we come, with.......*G. W. Bethune.* 844
Weeping saint, no longer mourn.....*Toplady.* 233
We give immortal praise.................. *Watts.* 307
Welcome, delightful morn............*Hayward.* 47
Welcome, sweet day of rest............... *Watts.* 46
Welcome to me the..........*Julia Ann Elliott.* 660
Welcome, welcome, sinner, here...*J. Conder.* 382
We tread the path our..........*Mrs. Barbauld.* 205
What are those soul-reviving... .*Montgomery.* 213
What equal honors shall we bring...... *Watts.* 274
What grace, O Lord, and beauty...*E. Denny.* 198
What glory gilds the sacred page....*Cowper.* 727
What means this eager, anxious throng....... 849
What shall I render to my God......... *Watts.* 102
What shall the dying sinner do......... *Watts.* 387
What sinners value I resign............. *Watts.* 614
What various hindrances we meet...*Cowper.* 585
When all thy mercies, O my God...*Addison.* 115
When as returns this solemn.*Mrs. Barbauld.* 50
When at thy footstool, Lord, I bend....*Lyte.* 403
When downward to the............*Ray Palmer.* 957
When first o'erwhelmed with sin.*J. G. Deck.* 419
When gathering clouds around I...*R. Grant.* 204
When God revealed his gracious....... *Watts.* 502
When I can read my title clear.......... *Watts.* 988
When I survey the wondrous cross.... *Watts.* 787
When languor and disease invade...*Toplady.* 683
When marshalled on the..........*H. K. White.* 544
When overwhelmed with grief.......... *Watts.* 666
When power divine, in.........*Sir J. E. Smith.* 209
When rising from the bed of death.*Addison.* 325
When shall we meet again.*Alaric A. Watts.* 915
When sins and fears prevailing..*Anne Steele.* 452
When streaming from the....... *W. Shrubsole.* 88
When the worn spirit wants.........*Edmeston.* 40
When this passing world is done.*McCheyne.* 533
When thou, my righteous Judge...*C. Wesley.* 963
When thy mortal life is fled.......*S. F. Smith.* 324
When time seems short, and death..*Bethune.* 428
Where can we hide, or whither fly............. 106
While in this sacred rite of thine.*S. F. Smith.* 771
While life prolongs its precious.......*Dwight.* 337

HYMN

While shepherds watched......*Tate & Brady.* 185
While thee I seek......*Miss H. M. Williams.* 29
While, with ceaseless course, the sun..*Newton.* 909
Who are these in bright array...*Montgomery.* 968
Who can forbear to sing..................*Swain.* 833
Who trusts in God, a strong.....*Magdelburg.* 445
Why do we mourn departing friends.. *Watts.* 949
Why, O God, thy people spurn........*Hatfield.* 896
Why should we start and fear to die.. *Watts.* 931
Why sleep we, my brethren? Come.*Hopkins.* 832
Why will ye waste on trifling......*Doddridge.* 323
Wilt thou not visit me...............*Jones Very.* 826
With all my powers of heart and......... *Watts.* 121
With broken heart and contrite......*C. Elven.* 352
With guilt oppressed, bowed down with sin. 353
With joy we hail the sacred day........... *Lyte.* 62
With joy we meditate the grace......... *Watts.* 269
With my substance I will honor.*B. Francis.* 576
With tearful eyes I look......*Miss C. Elliott.* 377
With tears of anguish I lament....*S. Stennett.* 628
With willing hearts we tread.....*S. F. Smith.* 761
Work, for the night is coming..................... 700
Work, for time is flying.............................. 702
Would you win a soul to God......*Hammond.* 455

Ye Christian heralds, go.....*Bap. Mag.* 1816. 877
Ye glittering toys of earth........*Anne Steele.* 621
Ye humble souls, approach your.*Anne Steele.* 109
Ye men and angels, witness now....*Beddome.* 764
Ye nations round the earth, rejoice.... *Watts.* 3
Ye servants of the Lord.............*Doddridge.* 994
Yes, for me, for me, he careth...........*Bonar.* 493
Ye servants of God, your Master..*C. Wesley.* 10
Yes, he is mine! and naught of............*Lyte.* 512
Ye sinners, fear the Lord.................*Dwight.* 341
Yes, my native land, I love thee.*S. F. Smith.* 885
Yes, thou art mine.........................*H. G. G.* 461
Ye trembling souls, dismiss your...*Beddome.* 449
Ye tribes of Adam, join.................... *Watts.* 15
Ye wretched, hungry, starving...*Anne Steele.* 367
Your harps, ye trembling saints.....*Toplady.* 663

Zion stands with hills surrounded.......*Kelly.* 748
Zion, the marvellous story be.....*Muhlenburg.* 187

INDEX OF CHANTS, ETC.

	No.
As the o'erwearied hart	23
Behold the Lamb!	18
Behold the Lamb! Behold the Lamb!	24
Be not afraid, it is I!	36
Beyond the smiling and the weeping	41
Bless the Lord, O my soul. Psalm 103	54
Blest is the hour	3
Come unto me	56
From the recesses	40
Give thanks to Jehovah (Revised Version). Psalm 105	10
Give to Jehovah (Rev. Ver.). Psalm 29	12
Glory be to God (Gloria in Excelsis)	1
Glory be to the Father (Gloria Patri)	52
God be merciful. Psalm 67	5
God is our refuge. Psalm 46	15
Have mercy upon me. Psalm 51	57
He is despised and rejected	18
He knelt, the Saviour knelt	29
Holy, holy, Lord God	7
Is this the way, my Father?	28
I will lift my eyes (Rev. Ver.). Psalm 121	14
Jesus lives! henceforth is death (Hymn)	256
Just as I am	32
Lord, thou hast been our. Psalm 90	58
Lowly and solemn be	43
Nearer, my God, to thee	22
Nothing to do!	35
No time to pray!	37
Oh, come, let us sing. Psalm 95	53
Oh, give thanks unto the Lord. Psalm 136	8
O Lord, I have heard thy speech (Habakkuk's Prayer)	17
Oh, what is life?	26
Oh, be joyful in the Lord (Jubilate)	4
O Father, Lord of earth (Baptismal)	33
Oh, where shall rest be found?	19
One sweetly solemn thought	21
O thou, who dry'st the mourner's tear	27
On Jordan's stormy banks	25
Our Father who art in heaven (Lord's Prayer)	16
Out of the depths. Psalm 130	11
Out on an ocean	34
Return, O wanderer	55
Shall we meet beyond the river?	42
The earth is Jehovah's (Rev. Ver.). Psalm 24.	13
The land beyond the sea	30
The leaves around me falling	20
The Lord is my shepherd. Psalm 23	6
There is a calm for those who weep	31
This is my Bible	39
Thy will be done (Hymn)	690
Thy word is a lamp unto. Psalm 119	9
We praise thee, O God! Te Deum Laudamus.	2
Wilt thou not visit me? (Hymn)	826
With tearful eyes I look around	38

MISCELLANEOUS.

Come, ye disconsolate	47
Create in me a clean heart	46
Father, from thy throne (Evening Prayer)	48
Holy, Lord God of Sabaoth (Sanctus)	45
I love to tell the story	49
Safe within the veil	50
Worship the Lord	44
Glory, honor, praise, and power	51

ALPHABETICAL INDEX OF SUBJECTS.

The figures indicate the NUMBER *of the Hymn.*

A.

ABBA, Father, 411, 521, 792.
Abiding, Christ, with believers, 96, 175, 444, 493, 594, 675.
Abiding in Christ, 424, 442, 513, 571.
with Christ, 974, 975, 977–980, 984.
Absence from Christ, 518, 519, 622, 824, 993, 999.
God, 506, 514, 515, 595, 616, 815, 836, 961, 963, 983.
Acceptance through Christ, 396, 403, 411, 414, 422, 426, 427, 443.
Accepted time, 330, 334, 337, 338, 339, 341, 342, 346–348, 364.
Access to Christ, 175–180, 263–270, 364, 372, 377, 386, 577, 588, 590, 662.
God, 2, 30, 578, 580–587, 589, 595, 672, 677.
Account, the last, 324, 690, 702, 956, 958–962.
Acquiescence in Christ's will, 684–694.
Activity, Christian, 695, 696, 698, 700–702, 813, 913.
Adam, fall in, 315, 316, 390, 467, 537.
Adoption, 162, 450, 521, 548.
Adoration of Christ, 139, 173–176, 181, 191, 194, 195, 203, 206, 208, 214, 221, 225, 239–241.
God, 20, 100, 101, 107, 113, 133, 134.
the Holy Spirit, 287–291.
the Holy Trinity, 306–314.
Advent of Christ, first, 185–195.
design of, 182, 184, 191, 194, 196, 234.
second, 259, 260, 955, 956, 958, 963–965.
Christ desired, 989–999.
Adversity, providential, 29, 153, 154, 156–158, 606, 681, 684, 686, 689, 691–693.
Advocate, Christian, 88, 263–270, 407, 411, 419, 437, 441, 455, 493.
Affection, Christian, 637, 638, 640–644, 647.
Afflicted, sympathy with, 639–641, 645, 649.
Afflictions, blessings of, 154, 655, 692, 698.
Afflictions borne by Christ, 198, 200, 204, 205, 227, 240, 589, 685.
call on God in, 31, 121, 155, 156, 159, 160, 600, 601, 656, 661, 668, 672, 677, 680, 681.
Christ's presence in, 204, 202, 293, 584, 589, 660, 675, 677, 683.
Christ an example in, 198, 202, 205, 206, 218, 219, 221.
coming from God, 29, 153, 154, 159, 490, 659.
deliverance from, 121, 128, 160, 161, 462, 671.
God a support in, 31, 121, 155, 159, 160, 490, 655, 679.
safety in, 29, 153, 154, 160, 672–678.
sanctified, 153, 154, 456, 490, 600, 607, 665.
submission in, 117, 154, 158, 162, 657, 659, 665, 683, 686, 688–693.
tempered with mercy, 153, 159, 659, 663, 678, 679.
trust in, 153, 155, 159, 160, 665, 657, 658, 681.
Agony of Christ, 216–219, 229–230.
Alarm to sinners, 324–326, 337, 343.
All in all, 484, 504, 505, 506, 514, 524, 662, 781.
Almost Christian, 633.
All-sufficiency of Christ, 169, 179, 233, 235, 236, 239, 410, 411, 423, 428, 439, 443, 447, 458, 484, 485, 507, 524, 529, 554, 568, 604, 617.
All things in Christ, 447.
Anchor, hope an, 414, 446.
Angels at the birth of Christ, 186, 188.
joy of, at the sinner's repentance, 534.
know not the joy of forgiveness, 398, 561.
ministering to Christ, 216, 217, 258, 261.
Christians, 127, 150, 645.
praising God, 9, 23, 145, 180.
song of the, 27, 137, 151, 180, 186, 189, 274, 440, 535.
wondering at Christ's love, 137, 168, 653.
Anger of God deprecated, 317–320, 325, 328, 352, 646.
Anointed, Christ the, 186, 876.
Anniversary hymns, 886, 912–915.
Anticipations of heaven, 56, 799, 913–915, 924–928, 966, 967, 974–988.
Apostles commissioned, 800, 806.
Ark, invitation to enter, 385.
Armor, Christian, 704, 706, 707, 710, 714, 717, 718.
Ascension of Christ, 258–262.
Ashamed of Christ, 713, 715, 716.
Asleep in Jesus, 931, 936, 941, 947, 948.
Aspiration after holiness, 91, 92, 99, 106, 132, 133, 230, 240, 241, 298–305, 486, 559, 566, 574, 575, 596–626, 635, 636.
Assistance, God's, implored, 31, 86–88, 121, 402, 404, 406, 409, 437, 450, 452, 591, 593, 666.
Assurance, 296, 417, 430, 431, 438, 441, 444, 445, 461, 468, 489, 493, 499, 512, 516, 520, 549, 554.
Atonement. See CHRIST.
Atonement, commemoration of, 779–799.
completed, 231, 233, 237, 238, 247, 257, 264, 389, 439, 442.
faith in, 233–238, 238–240, 410, 411, 414–417, 419–422, 427–435, 439–448.
glorying in, 229, 231, 235, 424, 425, 434, 451, 454, 456.
God's character shown in, 109, 114, 139, 143, 167, 168, 171, 235, 728.
love to Christ for, 177, 225, 228, 238, 240, 241, 461, 466, 468–470, 474, 476, 477, 480, 482, 486.
praise to God for, 14, 114, 166–171, 228–231, 527, 528, 530, 536–538.
Christ for, 522–526, 531–538, 540–542, 547, 553–555.
sorrow for Christ's sufferings in, 228, 230, 232, 238, 240, 241.
sufficiency of, 233, 240, 245, 370, 381, 410, 411, 413, 414–416, 422–445, 789, 791.
Attributes of God, 100–143.
Awake, called to, 343, 344, 347, 710–712, 831.
Awakened sinner, 351–363.

ALPHABETICAL INDEX OF SUBJECTS.

B.

BACKSLIDER, invitation to, 336.
  returning, 827–832.
Backsliding, mourning over, 815, 818, 824, 827–830, 835.
  recovery from, 163, 165, 825, 826, 831, 834.
Banishment from Christ, 515, 960, 961, 963.
Banner of love, 783.
Baptism, 752–778.
  burial with Christ in, 752, 759, 767–771, 774.
  commemorating Christ's resurrection, 759, 763, 770.
  confessing Christ in, 752–754, 761, 765, 768, 773.
  following Christ in, 752–763.
  joy in, 755, 765, 766, 774–777.
  obeying Christ in, 752–754, 762, 768.
  of Christ, 285.
  prayer after, 772, 774.
  self-consecration in, 754, 758, 759, 762–764, 766.
  Spirit invoked in, 767, 776–778.
  symbolism of, 757, 767, 768, 773.
Barrenness, spiritual, deplored, 199, 719.
Bartimeus, prayer of, 211, 406.
Bearing shame for Christ, 713, 715, 716, 754, 765, 768, 776.
Beatitudes, 202, 649.
Beauty of Christ, 173, 176, 181, 198, 202, 273, 522, 524, 529, 535, 544, 553.
  God's heralds, 801.
  the church, 743, 744.
Believe only, 370, 371, 372, 375, 381, 417, 422, 423, 435, 436, 439.
Believer, security of, 25, 33, 80, 413, 415, 430, 432, 438, 444–446, 448, 449, 452, 461, 493, 495, 506, 511, 523, 526, 568, 693, 737, 740, 741, 747.
Benevolence, 639, 643–645, 648, 649.
Bethlehem, 185, 192, 544.
Bible, 721–735. See SCRIPTURE.
Birth of Christ, 185–192.
  new, 287, 290, 291, 303, 322, 405, 411, 424.
  desired, 353, 361, 396, 397.
Blessedness of afflictions, 153, 154, 600, 607, 655, 692, 968.
  Christians, 25, 28, 33, 37, 61, 64–66, 70, 120, 122, 127, 153, 160, 161, 163, 165, 438, 445–447, 467, 488–521, 523, 524, 526.
  Christian fellowship, 637, 638, 640–642, 647, 739, 749, 751, 838–841.
  divine guidance, 157, 163, 165, 592, 692–694.
  heaven, 966–976, 979–982, 986, 988.
  love, 464–476, 503, 504, 526, 603, 643, 644.
  penitence, 210, 253, 398, 415, 435.
  those who die in Christ, 929–939.
  trust, 33, 37, 121, 410–461, 494, 655–662, 678–681, 684–694.
  worship, 4, 39, 49, 59, 61, 67, 68–70.
Blindness deplored, 318, 321.
  healed, 211.
Blood of Christ, shed for sinners, 228–240, 249, 279, 280, 285, 365, 372, 375, 387–389, 455, 470, 505, 781, 790, 797.
  trust in, 264, 265, 270, 278, 380, 381, 387, 389, 401–404, 406–448, 461, 494–500, 522, 524, 789, 791, 987.
Boasting excluded, 422, 426.
Boldness in prayer, 588, 590, 593.
Bondage to sin, 303, 318, 321, 390, 391, 404, 602.
Book of nature and of Scriptures, 235, 721–724.
  life, 395, 683.
  the divine decrees, 156.
Bosom of Christ a refuge, 392, 413, 436, 507, 526, 602, 746.
  God, 128, 983.
Bought with a price, 569, 570, 572.
Bread of heaven, 382, 504, 694, 717, 779, 780, 793.
Brevity of life, 916–924.
Bride, the church the, 741, 991, 997.
Bridegroom, Christ the, 741, 993.
Broad and narrow way, 631, 633.
Broken heart, 322, 349, 352, 355, 362, 363, 397, 405.
Brother, Christ our, 249, 493, 535, 553.
Brotherly love, 638, 640–642, 647.
Burdens borne by Christ, 201, 202, 204, 222, 227, 240, 442, 589, 685.
  cast on the Lord, 31, 658, 661, 680, 681.
  mutually shared, 640.
  patience under, 154, 158, 162, 664, 682, 684–686, 693.
Burden of sin, 351–354, 356, 362, 427, 440.
Burdened sinner invited to Christ, 372, 374, 376, 380, 384.
  coming to Christ, 400, 404, 409, 419, 422, 426, 435.
Burial of a brother, 940–946.
  child, 949.
  Christian, 940, 941, 944, 945, 947, 948.
  friend, 937, 950.
  pastor, 942.
  sister, 951.

C.

CALL of the gospel, 330, 334, 336, 337, 346, 347, 364–389, 470.
  heard, 390–393.
  unheeded, 323, 333, 335.
Calling, the Christian, 390–393.
Calmness, Christian, 42, 93, 202, 584, 629, 929, 948.
Calvary, 219, 224, 226, 228, 230–234, 236–239, 352, 372, 407, 411, 661, 763.
Canaan, 511, 694, 966, 982.
Captain of our salvation, 714, 747.
Captives set free, 390, 391, 404, 405, 418, 424, 427.
Care of God for his saints, 102, 105, 109, 112, 115, 116, 120–128, 153–165, 449, 450, 493–495.
  cast on God, 31, 121, 154, 157, 655, 657–661, 684–686, 691–693.
Change of heart needed, 290, 291, 316, 322.
  prayed for, 235, 289, 293, 315.
  produced, 228, 289, 318.
Charity, 576, 639, 643, 645, 648, 649.
Chastening, 153, 154, 163, 164, 600.
Chief of sinners, 293, 357, 392, 431.
Children brought to Christ, 843, 857.
  Christ blessing, 843.
  commended to God, 856, 857.
  converted, 852, 853.
  death of, 949, 951.
  hosannas of, 213, 845.
  invited to Christ, 855, 856.
  of God, 117, 126, 128, 162, 444, 450, 464, 521, 548, 720, 792, 798, 977, 981, 983, 986.
  praising Christ, 844–846.
  prayers for the conversion of, 843, 848, 854, 850, 857.
  solicitude for the conversion of, 650–652.
Children's hymns, 844–847, 849–855.
Christ, abiding in, 424, 442, 471, 493, 513, 551, 571, 624.
    with us, 96, 175, 176, 225, 444, 493, 501, 519, 594, 596, 603.
  adored, 173–176, 181, 182, 190, 194, 195, 225, 259, 279, 283, 464–469.
  advent of, 186–190.
    second, 955, 956, 958, 962–964, 989–999.
  advocate, 68, 263–270, 407, 411, 419, 437, 441, 455, 493.
  all in all, 484, 504, 524, 662, 781.
  all-sufficiency of, 233, 235, 236, 239, 410, 411, 423, 428, 439, 443, 447, 458, 484, 485, 507, 524, 529, 554, 568, 604, 617.
  almighty, 477, 529, 681.
  anointed, 411, 876.
  atonement of, 220, 222, 224–275, 365, 368, 370, 372, 380, 381, 389, 408, 410, 411, 414–419, 422, 434–436, 439–443, 451, 453–456, 470, 524.
  ascension of, 242–257.
  baptism of, 285.
  birth of, 27, 185, 188 190, 196.
  blood of, 228, 230, 232, 233, 235, 410, 411, 415, 416, 455, 461, 466, 482, 494–496, 499, 500, 505, 518, 522, 539, 542, 548, 553, 560–572, 623, 637, 638, 680, 741, 757, 779, 787, 790, 791, 797.
  bread of life, 382, 504, 694, 779 780, 793.
  bridegroom, 279, 741, 993.
  brightness of the Father's glory 92, 173, 235.
  captain, 714, 747, 753.
  character of, 173, 176, 179, 180, 181, 198, 200, 202, 206.
  Children's Saviour, 194, 843–857.
  communing with, 39, 47, 54, 77, 95, 204, 225, 239, 240, 241, 283, 442, 577–595, 603, 613, 615.
  compassion of, 177, 182, 199, 204, 228–235, 351, 352, 376, 390, 392, 431, 486, 507, 526.
  condescension of, 198, 202, 203 208.

Christ, conqueror, 231, 237, 239, 245-248, 250, 277, 278, 282, 283, 304, 487, 492.
corner-stone, 420, 869.
coronation, 271, 272, 281, 282, 284, 492.
covenant with, 414, 448, 511, 552, 556.
Creator, 193, 228, 283, 308.
cross of, 171, 224, 228, 230, 231, 235, 237.
crucified, 220, 222, 225, 226, 423, 451, 611, 613.
day-star, 507, 996.
death of, 223-232, 236-238.
deity, 174-177, 181, 191, 197, 306-314, 421, 475, 479, 489.
delight in, 173-181, 233, 235, 440, 447, 451, 456, 463, 469, 472-475, 481, 485, 487.
deliverer, 169, 182, 184, 191, 204, 694.
dependence on, 204, 360, 370, 380, 381, 387, 396, 400, 401, 404, 414, 417, 421-436.
desire of nations, 183, 184, 191, 195.
doing all, 381.
electing love, 172, 392, 471, 540, 652, 782.
entering Jerusalem, 212, 213.
enthroned, 271-286.
equality with God, 174, 178.
exalted, 4, 10, 267, 273, 276, 277, 279.
example, 198-203, 205, 206, 219.
excellence of, 168, 173-177, 179-181, 198, 202.
faith in, 440-461.
faithfulness of, 286, 409, 430, 446, 447, 452, 499, 523.
following, 199, 200, 202, 205, 206. See PATTERN.
foundation, 414, 417, 429, 452, 459, 532, 571, 678.
fount of blessing, 596.
" life, 382, 504.
fountain, 92, 229, 410, 421, 447, 504, 571.
friend, 233, 241, 242, 403, 407, 418, 437, 488, 496, 498, 520, 535, 560, 597, 637, 784, 796.
glory of, 10, 174, 176, 177, 181, 190, 195, 202, 229, 231, 252, 258, 259, 262, 273-278.
gloried in, 417, 425, 434, 451, 456, 468.
guardian, 221, 560.
guide, 221, 285, 560, 592, 601, 666, 750, 758, 763, 764, 849.
happiness in, 233, 488-521.
head of the church, 195, 251, 279, 455, 568, 630, 759, 996.
help of, desired, 92, 349, 353, 354, 356, 357, 361, 390, 396, 398, 399, 400, 403, 406, 407, 420, 440, 444, 447, 591, 593, 594.
hiding-place, 409, 413, 416, 432, 433, 510, 515, 527.
high priest, 264-270, 278, 365, 439, 441, 524.
hope, our, 400, 401, 413, 421, 429, 430, 432, 452.
hosanna to, 184, 187, 190, 212, 213, 415, 760.
Christ, humanity, 201, 285, 480.
imitation of, 199, 202, 203, 205, 206, 558, 562, 564, 609, 610, 648, 653.
Immanuel, 175, 176, 419, 436, 480, 535, 569, 571, 638, 741, 762.
incarnation, 174-177, 201, 285, 312, 370, 390, 422, 480, 537, 549, 778.
indebtedness to, 420, 424-427, 412, 466, 471, 474, 528, 533, 546, 555, 556, 558, 561, 567.
intercession of. See ADVOCATE.
Jehovah, 479, 694.
joy in, 488-513.
Judge, 955, 956, 958-965.
King, 183, 228, 275, 278, 283, 286, 467, 477, 478, 487, 497, 511, 524, 525, 531, 590, 752, 992.
knocking at the door, 369, 379, 391.
Lamb of God, 220, 231, 238, 239, 240, 262, 273, 275, 279, 280, 365, 368, 408, 410, 412, 435, 467, 488, 491, 531, 542, 574, 601, 626, 676, 703, 708, 709, 790, 791.
leader, 550, 575, 701, 714.
life, 214, 215, 440, 478, 505, 560, 583, 781.
light, 91, 92, 440, 465, 478, 487, 504, 505, 507.
Lord of all, 271, 272, 279, 284.
Lord, our righteousness, 390, 401, 404, 414, 425, 429, 434, 439, 528, 529, 533, 553, 556, 680.
love of, 175, 194, 199, 228, 230, 234, 235, 270, 286, 469, 472, 480, 482, 525-527, 540-542, 547, 553-555.
man of sorrows, 177, 200, 233, 284.
mediator, 2, 263-269, 280.
meekness of, 198, 199, 202, 203, 206, 212, 436.
mine, 429-431, 461, 467, 473, 475, 498, 516, 524, 554.
miracles of, 208-211.
name dear, 168, 180, 476-480, 482-485, 621.
not ashamed of, 713, 715, 716, 765, 768.
oath, 414, 446.
offices, 278, 312, 467, 524, 525.
pardon through, 376, 390, 401, 403, 405, 407, 421, 422, 426, 427, 447, 455.
parting with all for, 435, 557-559, 564, 566, 573, 574.
patience of, 198, 202, 572.
peace through, 186, 188, 233, 353, 427, 429, 447, 488, 496, 498, 500, 524.
pearl of price, 524.
physician, 388.
pilot, 669, 676.
praise to, 4, 10, 173, 190, 522-556.
praying, 203, 285.
predicted, 190, 191, 195.
present, 175, 210, 283, 473, 504, 506, 515, 519, 701.
priest, 264-270, 278, 312, 467, 511, 524, 525, 992.
prince, 27, 182, 189, 221, 272, 274, 379, 477, 778, 787, 975, 989.
prophet, 278, 312, 467, 524, 525.
Christ, redeemer, 4, 241, 312, 394, **407**, 458, 461, 467, 952.
refuge, 171, 240, 241, 387, 413, **428**, 523, 597, 666, 667, 678, 680.
remembering. See LORD'S SUPPER.
rest, 478, 479, 500, 507.
resurrection of, 45, 51, 52, 242-257, 758, 759, 763, 767, 776.
rock, 23, 169, 414, 416, 438, 479, 511, 523, 666, 671, 738.
sacrifice, 166, 219, 221, 227, 228-231, 264, 272, 411, 439, 455, 499, 524.
salvation through, 10, 14, 25, 163, 170, 213, 220, 223, 226, 235, 248, 266, 410-435, 440-445, 530, 538.
Saviour, 129, 170, 180, 228, 230-234, 364-389, 410-443.
Shepherd, 221, 229, 547, 843, 849-851, 857.
sinner's friend, 225, 233, 241, 407.
Son of David, 185, 190, 208, 211, 213.
Son of God, 166, 168, 196, 202, 207, 212, 217, 224, 232, 234, 235, 285, 425, 459, 537.
Son of man, 130.
Sovereign, 180, 223, 228, 557, 874.
substitute, 225, 350, 432, 435, 442, 535.
sufferings of, 216-233, 240-242.
sun, 188, 507, 512, 516.
sympathy of, 204, 232, 249, 589.
tempted, 204, 269, 270, 285.
throne of, 176, 181, 184, 194, 273, 274, 277-281, 477, 859, 872, 874.
triumphs of, 183, 212, 213, 258-262, 271-282, 284, 529, 871, 872, 876.
trust in, 25, 204, 233, 235, 238, 410-461.
truth, 214, 215, 413, 430, 438, 441, 452, 530, 554, 560, 583.
unchangeable, 430, 452, 477, 486, 498, 499, 504, 512, 523, 552, 555, 556.
union with, 426, 431, 441, 444, 447, 452, 484, 492, 500, 512, 513, 516, 521, 552, 554, 556, 561, 571, 608, 650.
universal Lord, 181, 183, 184.
way, 214, 215, 412, 560, 583.
weeping, 204, 216, 233, 653.
Christian, abiding in Christ, 424, 442, 493, 513, 571.
absent from Christ, 518, 519, 622, 824, 993, 999.
afflicted, 121, 655-663, 673-675, 678-683.
almost, 633.
anticipating death, 323-325, 473, 923-928.
armor, 704, 706, 707, 710, 714, 717, 718.
aspiring after holiness, 90, 91, 106, 132, 133, 230, 240, 241, 248-305, 486, 559, 566, 574, 575, 596-626, 635, 636.
assurance, 296, 417, 430, 431, 438, 441, 444, 445, 463, 489, 493, 499, 512, 520, 549, 554.
backsliding and returning, 827-832, 836.

ALPHABETICAL INDEX OF SUBJECTS.

Christian, baptized, 752-778.
bearing the cross, 200, 562, 564, 570, 713, 715, 754, 776.
shame for Christ, 570, 713, 715, 716, 765, 768, 776.
benevolence, 639, 643-645, 648, 649.
blessedness. See BLESSEDNESS OF CHRISTIANS.
boldness, 429, 703, 704, 706, 710-719.
breathing after Christ, 518, 519, 553, 558, 569, 575.
breathing after God, 29, 132, 133, 452, 506, 514-516.
brotherhood, 638, 640-642, 647.
burial of, 940, 941, 944, 945, 947, 948.
cared for by God, 30, 121, 127 142, 154-165, 689, 691-694.
casting care on God, 31, 658, 661, 680, 681.
chastened, 490, 673.
choosing Christ, 31, 390, 391, 394, 399.
chosen by Christ, 172, 392, 471, 540, 552, 782.
cheered by God's presence, 506, 508, 514-516, 545.
Christ, the boast of, 417, 419, 425, 456, 546.
joy of, 92, 191, 195, 488-521.
strength of, 396, 408, 412, 414, 415, 418, 423, 438, 440, 444, 445, 447, 523.
communing with God, 29, 105, 577-595, 613.
communion, 637, 638, 640, 642, 647.
compassion, 198, 639, 641, 643, 645, 646, 648, 649, 653, 654.
conduct, 198, 609, 627, 629, 634, 636.
conflict, 349, 352-354, 361, 567, 575, 596, 599, 602, 613, 615, 622, 703-720.
conqueror, 703, 704, 706-709, 711-715, 718.
consecration, 228, 240, 557-576.
courage, 444, 449, 703, 706, 707, 710, 712-716, 720.
dead to sin, 419, 613, 623, 627.
death of, 939-948.
delighting in Christ. See CHRIST.
delivered, 121, 127, 502, 543, 671.
example, 634.
fellowship, 584, 640-642, 751, 838-841.
fidelity, 557-576, 629, 695, 698 701, 704-707, 710-720.
gentleness, 198-200, 202, 206.
graces, 203, 214, 607, 610, 619, 636, 644.
imitating Christ, 202, 203, 205, 206, 562, 609, 610, 648, 653, 709.
importunity, 588, 590, 593, 595.
indebtedness, 20, 23, 462, 466, 527, 528, 533, 536-539, 546-549.
interceding, 650-652, 654.
joy, 488-521, 523, 524, 528, 529, 714.
lamenting absence of Christ, 518, 595, 616, 622, 626.
coldness, 628, 828-830, 832.
Christian, indwelling sin, 349, 353, 356, 360, 361-363, 623, 626, 628, 835.
leaving all for Christ, 558, 564, 566, 573, 612-614, 618-621.
life, 501.
living by faith, 457-460, 665, 667.
looking into Jesus, 412, 423, 440, 444, 445, 452, 457, 460, 461.
love, 637-649.
meekness, 198, 199, 202, 203, 623.
obedience, 390-395, 606, 633-636, 753, 757, 760, 762.
parting with the world, 512, 557, 558, 573, 611-615, 617-620, 626.
pardoned, 398, 488-490, 501, 505, 522, 539, 554.
peace, 400, 422, 496, 498, 499, 522, 524, 714.
perseverance, 523, 526, 531, 532, 536, 543, 549, 552, 556, 741.
pilgrim, 105, 200, 440, 610, 693, 694, 974, 977, 978, 987, 990.
pleading Christ's merits, 396, 401, 403, 404, 416, 419, 422, 425, 427-432, 434, 439, 441-444.
pleading promises, 407-409, 447, 588, 590, 820.
race, 437, 706, 711, 712.
renouncing the world, 557, 558, 563-566, 573, 611, 619, 621.
rest. See REST IN CHRIST.
returning to God, 128, 829, 830, 836.
safety, 25, 31, 109, 127, 411, 413-415, 428, 438, 444-447.
steadfastness, 415, 421, 452, 512, 514, 557-561, 564, 566, 573.
sorrow, 628, 645, 646, 653.
submission, 684-692.
sympathy, 637-642, 645-649.
trust, 410-452, 655-694.
union, 637, 638, 640, 642.
walking with God, 626.
watchfulness, 704-706.
Church, afflicted, 745-748, 750.
beautiful, 736, 742, 744.
beloved, 736, 741, 743, 746.
Christ's abode, 739, 740, 742, 743.
Christ the foundation, 738, 742, 743.
head, 741, 750.
delight in, 736, 739, 740, 741, 744.
deliverance of, 747, 748, 750.
fellowship with, 751.
God in, 736, 742, 743, 748.
glory of, 736, 739, 742.
love to, 637.
members welcomed, 838-840.
one, 739, 745.
officers of, 801-811.
ordinances of, 752, 778, 779, 799.
pilgrim, 745.
safety of, 737, 740, 741, 743, 747.
Cleansing blood, 230, 238, 240, 390, 392, 395, 397, 408, 416, 421, 433, 435, 439, 461, 494, 522, 781, 791, 797.
Close of worship, 81, 85.
Cloud of witnesses, 708, 709, 711.
Coldness lamented, 628, 781, 828-830, 832.
Comfort in trouble, 153, 154, 157, 160, 162, 655-683.
from former mercies, 656, 671.
Comforts lost, lamented, 626, 815, 816, 828-830.
Comforter, the, 287, 292, 294, 300, 302, 364, 587, 605, 662, 798.
Coming of Christ, 184-191, 831.
to Christ, 390-409.
Commission, Christ's 800, 804, 806.
Communion at the Lord's table, 780, 783, 788, 793, 799.
of saints, 637, 638, 640, 642, 647.
with Christ. See CHRIST.
God, 29, 46, 54, 58, 68, 578 580, 584, 585, 595.
Compassion of Christ. See CHRIST.
Christians', 645-648, 653.
God, 109, 125, 126, 178.
Completeness in Christ, 429, 443, 447 521, 789.
Condemnation, justice of, acknowledged, 320, 351-363.
Condescension of Christ. See CHRIST.
of God, 28, 107, 347, 521.
Confession of sin, 349-363, 623-626, 628, 835.
Confidence in Christ, 410-452.
Conflict, Christian, 703-714, 717-720.
Conformity to Christ, 596-636.
desires for, 436, 596, 600, 601, 603, 607, 609, 610, 613, 615, 620, 626, 635, 636.
Conqueror. See CHRIST.
the Christian, 703, 704, 706-712, 714, 715, 718-720.
Conscience unawakened, 319, 539, 547
peace of, 398, 419, 426, 428, 433, 447, 496.
Consecration, entire, 557-561.
prayer for, 569, 575.
grateful, 561, 563, 567, 572.
Contentment. 657-659, 670, 681, 684-686, 693.
Contribution, 576, 643-645, 648.
Convention, 886.
Convert's choice, 762, 841.
prayer for, 842.
welcomed, 838-840.
Conversion, joy of, 491, 502, 505.
joy over, 534, 642, 822, 823.
sovereignty of God in, 172, 289, 290.
Conviction of sin, 303, 305, 319-322, 349-363.
Corner-stone, 868, 869.
Coronation of Christ, 271-286.
Corruption of man's nature, 170, 291, 315, 316, 390, 536, 537.
Country, our, 890, 893.
Courage, 444, 449, 703, 706, 707, 710, 712-716, 720.
Covenant, new, 414, 448, 511, 552, 556, 781.
Created good, unsatisfying, 611, 612, 614, 616.
Creation, praising God, 7, 8, 12, 13, 15, 34, 144, 145.
wonders of, 13, 15, 111, 144, 147.
Cross, attractions of, 111, 171, 228, 230, 235, 240, 421, 451, 455, 539.
bearing the, 200, 562, 564, 570, 713, 715, 754, 776.
Christ on the, 228, 230, 231, 235, 240.
crucifixion to the world by, 415, 419, 425, 431, 451, 456, 468.

Cross, God's character seen in, 139, 143, 167, 168, 171, 235, 728.
glorying in, 228–232, 451, 456.
happiness in, 240, 241, 488.
repentance at the, 240, 405, 539.
subdued by the, 228, 539, 554.
welcome from the, 389.
Crown of glory, 562, 703, 706, 707, 708, 711, 714, 828, 996.
Crucified, only the, 451, 570.
Crucified with Christ, 513, 763.
Crucifixion of Christ, 228–240.
to the world. See Cross.

D.

DAILY bread, 17, 18.
converse with Christ 93, 96.
devotion, 29, 31, 86–99.
mercies, 17, 13, 128.
praise, 14, 86, 93, 94.
providence, 26, 29, 90, 153, 155, 159.
Danger and deliverance, 121, 127, 671, 676.
Darkness of Providence, 153, 156–158, 660 667, 687, 689, 693.
light in, 295, 303, 660, 662, 669.
Day and night, 337, 338, 342, 345, 348, 700, 702.
of grace, 337, 341, 346, 347, 364, 370.
judgment, 324–326, 334, 340, 955, 956, 958–965.
Day-star, 595.
Deacons, choice of, 810.
prayed for, 811.
Dead in Christ, 513.
Deadness to the world, 557, 558, 563–566, 573, 611-619, 621.
Death anticipated, 323–325, 473, 479, 923–928.
approaching, 923, 924, 927.
comfort in, 447, 923.
Christ's presence in, 447, 479, 483, 935.
Christ's victory over, 246, 247, 250.
friends, separated by, 204, 937–939.
hope in, 929–936, 940, 941, 942–951.
of an aged minister, 942.
infant, 949.
Christ, 228–240.
Christians, 939–949.
friends, 937–941.
prayer for support in, 204, 933–936.
victory over, 231, 243, 247, 434, 447, 499 940
Debt paid, 381 422
Debtors to divine mercy, 26, 28, 462, 466, 527, 528, 533 536–539, 546–549
Decision called for, 323, 326, 337, 340, 345, 346, 371.
Decrees of God, 152, 158, 172, 286, 537, 540, 683.
Declension deplored, 815, 818, 824, 826, 831, 834.
Dedication hymns, 860–869.
personal, 228, 240, 557–576.
Defence, God a, 120–124.
Delay dangerous, 326, 330, 335, 337, 348.
Delight in Christ, 173–181, 233, 235, 440, 447, 451, 456, 463, 469, 472–475, 481, 485, 487, 504, 522.
God, 117, 121, 128, 514–516, 520, 629.
Scripture, 722, 724, 727, 729–733.
worship, 2, 3, 5, 16, 29, 31.
Deliverance from affliction, 121, 128, 160, 161, 462, 671.
sin, 233, 238, 239, 290, 291, 410–413, 416–419, 421, 441–444.
Deliverer, Christ our. See Christ.
Departure from God lamented, 626, 628, 827, 829, 830, 836.
Dependence on Christ, 204, 360, 370, 380, 381, 387, 396, 400, 401, 404, 414, 417, 421–436.
God, 35, 120, 155, 159–162, 354.
the Holy Spirit, 287–291, 297–302.
Depravity, 170, 291, 315, 316, 390, 536, 537.
Despondency reproved, 657, 658, 669, 677–679.
Despair checked, 551.
Devotion, daily, 29, 31, 86–99.
enjoyment, in, 36, 67–69, 578, 584, 585.
Diligence, Christian, 705, 706, 709–711, 714.
Direction, providential, 25, 26, 29, 159, 163–165, 634.
Dismission, hymns for, 81–85.
Divinity of Christ. See Christ.
Dominion of Christ, 10, 29, 872, 876.
Door, Christ standing at the, 369, 379, 391.
of mercy, 385.
Drawing nigh to God, 29, 35, 58, 68, 340, 347, 351, 352, 355, 362, 363.
Duties, Christian, 203, 206, 629–631, 633–636.
Dwelling with God, 105, 120, 122, 127.
Dying Christian, 925, 929–935.

E.

EARLY death, 946, 949.
piety, 650–652.
worship, 60, 86, 88, 92.
Earnestness, 695, 696, 698, 700–707, 710, 714, 717–719.
Earth's response to heaven, 24.
Efficacy of the blood of Jesus, 237–240, 340, 360, 362, 365, 368, 370, 389, 410, 411, 414, 416, 419, 431, 443, 481, 474, 499, 505, 518, 522, 524, 542.
Election, 138, 172, 471, 527, 530, 536, 537, 540, 551, 552, 977.
Encouragement, 123, 126, 127, 373, 377.
Enemies, victory over, 121, 127, 495, 707–720.
Entire surrender, 228, 394, 405, 407, 557, 558, 561, 566, 568, 569, 571.
Enjoyment of Christ's love, 469, 472, 478, 487–492.
Eternity contemplated, 115, 326, 328, 960, 964, 965.
of God, 101, 120, 122, 129, 131, 132, 916, 921.
heaven, 967, 970, 973, 974, 982.
Evening hymns, 93–99, 586.
Evening hymns, Lord's Day, 54.
Exaltation of Christ, 4, 10, 267, 273, 276, 277, 279.
saints in heaven, 708, 709, 711 730.
Example, 198, 203, 205, 206, 219, 609, 610, 648, 653.
Excellence of Scripture, 721–725, 727–735.
Experience, testimony of, 127.

F.

FAITH, act of, 390–409, 417, 426, 429 435, 448, 460, 673.
beholds things unseen, 667
effects of, 112, 458, 673.
excellence of, 459.
exercised, 153, 155, 157.
fight of, 706, 707, 709.
gift of God, 402.
in Christ, 394–437, 439–447.
joy of, 458, 667.
living and dead, 630.
prayer for, 402, 457, 460, 674.
shield of, 706, 710.
triumph of, 667.
walking by, 112, 153, 155, 157, 159 667.
work of, 458.
Faithfulness of Christ, 286, 409, 430, 446, 447, 452, 499, 523.
God, 25, 118, 123, 129, 130, 155.
Fall of man, 315, 316, 317, 390.
Falling, kept from, 668.
Family of God, 739, 967, 977.
relation, 650–652, 736.
songs, 90–92, 97–99.
Fasting, 894–897.
Fatherhood of God, 34, 117, 126, 128, 154, 162, 444, 450, 464, 521, 548, 720, 792, 798, 977, 981, 983, 986.
Favor of God preferred, 31, 614, 615.
Fear of death dispelled, 924–935.
God, 22, 35, 103, 104, 106, 108.
Fears banished, 209, 233, 439, 444, 447, 449.
Feast, gospel, 366, 367.
Fellowship, Christian, 584, 640–642, 751, 838–841.
hand of, 838–842.
with Christ, 501, 552, 608, 630.
Fervency desired, 73, 83, 209, 632.
Fight of faith, 706, 707, 709, 710, 717.
Filial confidence, 411, 521.
First love, 491, 505, 513, 626, 766.
Fleeing to Christ for salvation 390, 409.
in sorrow, 204, 584, 655–683.
Following Christ, 199, 202, 203, 206, 206, 558, 562, 564, 609, 610, 648 653, 701.
Forbearance, divine, 122, 125, 129, 501.
Forerunner, Christ's, 197.
Foretaste of heaven, 42, 56, 59, 67, 68, 614.
Forgiveness, divine, 122, 125, 129, 501.
joy of, 398, 467, 488.
Formality lamented, 298, 299, 301, 303, 305, 349.
Forms, outward, vain, 290, 316, 791.
Forsaking all for Christ, 394, 417, 425
Foundation, Christ the, 414, 429, 459 678.

Fountain for sin, 239, 410, 416, 484.
Frailty, human, 101, 126, 916–923.
Freedom from condemnation, 411, 422, 427, 429, 434, 439.
Freedom from sin, 419, 428, 435.
Free grace, 28, 368, 407, 428.
Friend, Christ a. See CHRIST.
Friends in heaven, 937–939, 940, 943, 944, 946, 950, 951.
Fruits of the Spirit, 630, 634–649.
Fulness of Christ. See ALL-SUFFICIENCY.
Funeral hymns, 916–954.
Future, ignorance of, 606, 684, 691.

G.

GAIN to die, 571.
Garden, the spiritual, 823.
Garments of salvation, 390, 434, 528, 529, 680, 739. See CHRIST.
Gate of mercy, 588.
 the strait, 631, 633.
Generosity, 639, 643–645, 648, 649.
Gentleness of Christ, 198–200, 202, 203.
Gethsemane, 216–219.
Gift, the unspeakable, 166, 168.
Glory of Christ. See CHRIST.
 God, 8, 15, 21, 26, 110, 118, 129, 147, 235, 697.
Glorying in the cross, 228, 235, 425, 456.
God, all in all. See ALL IN ALL.
 all-sufficient, 124, 127.
 almighty, 21, 111, 148.
 all things of, 7.
 ancient of days, 21.
 ark of safety, 385.
 author of salvation, 21, 129, 166–170, 229, 235.
 benevolent, 25, 34, 37, 111.
 blessings of, everywhere, 116.
 breathing after, 128, 132, 133, 600.
 cares for saints, 21, 30, 33, 37, 127.
 character of, seen in the gospel, 107, 168, 235, 721, 722, 724, 728.
 communion with, 58, 68, 95, 578, 586, 594.
 compassion of, 28, 166, 170, 232.
 condescension of, 107, 151.
 confidence in, 21, 153–162.
 creator, 12, 15, 23, 34, 36, 37, 111, 122, 144–147, 401.
 decrees of, 156, 158, 172, 286, 540, 683.
 defender, 21, 149, 151, 155, 160.
 delight in, 121, 128, 514–516, 520, 629.
 deliverer, 120, 127, 128, 155, 160, 161, 462, 671.
 dominion of, 8, 12, 148–152.
 dwelling with his people, 120, 127.
 eternity of, 100, 120, 122, 129, 131, 132, 916, 921.
 exalted, 20, 32.
 faithful, 129, 131, 155.
 father, 30, 117, 132, 148, 151, 154, 162.
 friend, 21, 118, 130, 151.
 glorious, 9, 10, 13, 21, 129, 148.
 good, 24, 25, 109, 111, 114, 123, 124, 401.
 governor, 15, 35, 129, 148–152.
God great, 8, 34, 37, 122.
 guardian, 121, 127, 155.
 guide, 156, 161, 506, 657.
 hearer of prayer, 19, 30, 578, 580–585, 595.
 help of his saints, 31, 33, 121, 127, 160.
 hiding himself, 153.
 holy, 14, 38, 132–134, 150.
 hope, 506.
 incomprehensible, 153, 156, 157, 158.
 infinite, 101, 110, 122, 156, 157.
 joy in, 16, 20, 34, 37, 121, 124, 149, 506, 511, 520.
 judge, 150.
 just, 148.
 kind, 102, 125, 154.
 long suffering, 35, 124, 126.
 love, 140, 142, 286.
 love of, 34, 37, 109, 114, 117, 118, 123, 130, 135–139, 143, 167.
 majesty of, 8, 20, 148–152.
 merciful, 12, 28, 113, 114, 117–119, 125, 126, 166, 170.
 most high, 7–9, 148–152.
 omnipotent, 16, 150.
 omnipresent, 12, 105, 106, 108, 116.
 omniscient, 103, 104, 108.
 over all, 5, 15, 35, 116, 151, 152.
 patient, 28, 126.
 perfections of, 26, 110, 118, 122.
 praised, 1–28, 121, 125, 166–169.
 present in the sanctuary, 71, 72.
  with his people, 127, 160.
 promises of, 123, 129.
 providence, 21, 26, 33, 122, 125, 153–159.
 refuge, 109, 127, 128, 160.
 rock, 155.
 safety in, 25, 127, 129, 155, 159, 160.
 searcher of hearts, 104, 108.
 seen in his works, 13, 167.
 shepherd, 16, 163–165.
 shield, 21, 65, 149, 161, 169, 743.
 sovereign, 5, 10, 11, 22, 25, 35, 148–152, 172, 261.
 strength, 14, 120.
 sun, 65, 161, 743.
 support, 31, 112, 127, 508.
 throne of, 22, 120, 132.
 trust in, 25, 109, 120.
 truth of, 113.
 unchangeable, 130.
 unsearchable, 156–158.
 waiting to be gracious, 123, 391, 393.
 wisdom of, 151.
 worship of, 1–39.
Goodness of God, 11, 12, 19, 25, 34, 37, 109, 114, 119, 123, 124, 166–169. See ATONEMENT.
 year crowned in, 898–903.
Gospel armor, 706, 710, 714.
 blessings of, 129, 235, 601.
 diffusion of, 870–889.
 excellence of, 139, 167.
 exemplified in life, 634.
 expostulations, 323–348.
 feast, 366, 367.
 fountain, 239, 410, 416, 484.
 glad tidings, 333.
 hope in only, 350.
Gospel invitations, 364–370, 372–380.
 jubilee, 365.
 not ashamed of, 454, 715.
 order, 741.
 originating in mercy, 129, 166–170.
 praise for, 22, 129.
 precious, 448, 453, 729, 731.
 provisions of, 122, 123, 366–372.
 rejoicing in, 166–169.
 savor of life or death, 454.
 success of, 454, 870–879.
 trumpet, 365, 366.
Governor, God the, 5, 7, 9, 35, 148–152, 172.
Grace, 35, 124, 166, 168, 368, 406, 527, 528, 536, 543, 551, 552.
 abundant, 336–370, 471, 543.
 admired, 14, 19, 124, 167, 229.
 almighty, 178.
 change effected by, 502.
 day of, 22, 35, 330, 337–342, 344–348.
 desired, 230.
 exalted, 14, 124, 169.
 free, 28, 368, 407, 424, 428, 527.
 heirs of, 290.
 immutable, 523, 552, 556.
 miracle of, 467, 488.
 praise for, 19, 35, 124, 166–169, 467, 488, 536, 543, 551.
 preserving, 490, 556.
 quickening, 290, 292, 304, 624.
 reclaiming, 129.
 relying on, 2, 543, 594, 596.
 riches of, 474.
 salvation by, 24, 124, 170, 229, 235, 424, 467, 488, 536.
 sovereign, 35, 129, 172, 536. See ELECTION.
 sufficiency of, 169, 179, 617.
 supporting, 112, 490, 664.
 throne of, 29, 129, 151, 577, 580, 595.
 unfailing, 169, 414.
Gratitude to Christ, 10, 228, 230–234, 406, 522–525, 542, 551.
  God, 7, 9, 11, 20, 25, 28, 34, 37, 102, 115, 124, 125, 166–169, 462.
 sacrifice of, 102, 546, 567, 639.
Greatness of God, 8, 15, 35, 110, 149.
Guidance sought, 161, 693, 694.
Guilt, burden of, 351–354, 356, 364, 427, 440.
 expiated, 228, 229, 232, 233, 435.

H.

HAND of fellowship, 838–842.
Happiness in Christ, 223, 488–521.
  death, 929–936.
  God, 21, 462, 464, 503, 506, 514, 516, 614–616.
 of Christians, 488–491, 550.
  trust, 127
 true, 508.
Happy land, 845, 967, 971, 975, 982, 986.
Harvest hymns, 889–901, 903.
 past, 341.
Headship of the church, 195, 279, 435, 568, 630, 759, 996.
Heart, broken, 322, 349, 352, 353, 362, 363, 397, 405.

Heart, broken, prayer for a, 319, 353, 397.
given to Christ, 228, 234, 363.
hardened, 347.
hardness of, lamented, 349, 353.
new, needed, 320-322.
prayed for, 349 353, 354.
prayer of the, 30.
purity longed for, 519, 603, 617-625, 628.
Hearts, searcher of, 103, 106, 108.
Heathen prayed for, 875, 878, 881.
Heaven, 966-968.
anticipated, 56, 195, 799, 913-915, 924-928, 966, 967, 974, 988.
aspirations for, 168, 926, 966, 974-987
blessedness of, 966-976, 979-982, 986, 988.
children in, 844, 851, 853.
Christ in, 968, 973, 975, 977, 978, 984.
desiring a view of, 966, 975, 988.
end of the Christian's warfare, 968, 975, 987, 988.
God's dwelling-place, 981, 982, 986.
happiness of, 966, 967-988.
heavenly Canaan, 966, 986.
home in, 440, 489, 969, 976-978, 981-983, 985.
longing for, 168, 924-928, 966, 974, 987, 996.
on earth, 412.
peace of, 979, 980, 982, 985.
purity of, 967, 972, 973, 977, 979, 982, 988.
redeemed in, 968.
rest of, 670, 969, 976-978, 985-988.
sight of, 966, 968, 971, 975, 986.
society of, 927, 968, 975, 977, 980, 982.
song of, 968, 975, 979, 980, 984.
Heavenly home, going toward, 440, 847, 923-928, 974, 977, 978, 980, 983, 985, 987.
inheritance, 918, 919.
Jerusalem, 975, 982, 996.
Sabbath, 56, 987.
Heavens display God's glory, 144, 145, 235.
Help in affliction, 121, 127, 155, 157, 160, 600, 601, 656 661, 668, 672, 677, 680, 681.
Helplessness, 291, 349, 388, 390, 396
Hidden life, 441, 554.
Hiding-place, 400, 432, 433, 527, 524.
High Priest, 264, 267, 269, 270.
Holiness of God, 14, 38, 132-134.
partakers of, 132.
prayed for, 132, 133, 231, 240, 241, 298-305, 486, 550, 563, 574, 575, 596, 626, 635, 636.
Holy Scripture. See SCRIPTURE.
Holy Spirit, 277-305.
adored, 1, 287, 306-314, 1000.
anointing of the, 304.
breathings after, 289, 291-293, 295-305, 312, 314.
the comforter, 292, 294, 302, 304, 587, 605, 977.
dependence on, 291.
earnest of, 288, 289, 294, 296.
enlightening, 287, 291, 295, 300, 302, 303, 305.
Holy Spirit entreated, 292, 293, 295-305, 626, 825.
grieved, 293, 626, 699.
guide, 288, 295, 300, 303.
illuminating, 287, 292, 295, 296, 300, 302, 305.
indwelling, 292, 294, 480.
interceding, 583, 997.
invoked, 292, 295-305, 312, 314, 420, 767, 775-778, 798, 821, 822, 860, 862, 867.
love to, 470.
near, 292, 324.
pleading the promise of, 301.
quickening, 289, 290, 299, 312, 625.
regenerating, 287, 290, 291, 298, 303, 312, 315.
sanctifying, 287, 291, 302-305, 314, 471.
sovereign, 289, 290, 291.
witnessing, 296, 741.
Hope, an anchor, 414, 446.
Christ our. See CHRIST.
glorious, 489, 640.
in God, 127, 153, 155.
trouble, 155, 160.
rejoicing in, 489, 490, 493, 497, 500.
Hopes, self-righteous, renounced, 412, 414, 425.
Hosanna, 164, 187, 190, 213, 413, 415, 760.
House of God, 58, 61, 62, 64-68, 70, 71, 74, 75.
Humanity of Christ, 201, 285, 430.
Humiliation, public, 894-897.

I.

I AM his, 461, 561.
Ignorance of the future, 606, 684-691.
Illumination by the Spirit, 287, 292, 295, 296, 300, 302, 305.
word, 721, 723, 725, 727, 731, 732, 735.
Imitation of Christ. See CHRIST.
Immanuel. See CHRIST.
Immortality, 152, 947, 950, 952, 960, 967.
Immutability of Christ. See CHRIST.
God, 110, 129.
Impenitent prayed for, 654, 814.
warned, 323-343.
wept over, 646, 653.
Importunity in prayer, 588, 590, 593, 595.
Incarnation of Christ. See CHRIST.
Incomprehensibleness of God, 153, 156-158.
Inconstancy lamented, 230, 628, 828-830, 832.
Indebtedness acknowledged, 20, 462, 466, 527, 528, 533, 536-539, 546-549.
Indwelling of Christ, 96, 175, 444, 493, 594.
the Spirit, 292, 394, 480, 605.
Ingratitude lamented, 230, 827, 829.
Iniquity, prevalence of, 646.
Inquiry, searching, 486.
Insensibility lamented, 230, 349.
Inspiration of the Scripture, 727-729, 734, 735.
Intercession of Christ, 363, 370. See CHRIST.
Invitations of Christ, 372, 374, 378, 382, 389.
accepted, 390-393.
mercy, 364, 367, 370.
the Spirit, 386.
to sinners, 364-389, 855.
worship, 2, 3, 5, 6, 11, 12, 16, 19, 21-23.
Israel exhorted to praise Christ, 271.
prayer for, 884, 889.

J.

JEHOVAH, 16, 22, 34, 149.
Jerusalem, entry into, 212, 213.
the heavenly, 975, 982.
Jesus, the name of, 168, 180, 436, 441, 444, 476-480, 482-485, 535, 621, 794.
of Nazareth passing by, 819.
John the Baptist, 197.
Joining the people of God, 839-841.
Journeying to heaven, 440, 923-928, 974, 977, 978, 980-983, 985, 987.
Joy in Christ, 234, 236, 448-521.
death, 925, 933, 938.
God, 16, 20, 21, 123, 130, 506, 511, 520.
heaven over penitent, 534.
of conversion, 491, 498, 500-503 505.
forgiveness, 398, 501.
revivals, 814, 815, 823.
none without Christ, 514, 515, 519.
on earth of God's people, 124, 128-503.
Jubilee, 365.
Judgment day, 955, 956, 958-965.
anticipated, 324, 325, 960-965.
fleeing to Christ in prospect of, 963.
hope of mercy in, 955, 956, 961-963.
preparation for, 962-965.
sinners at the, 956, 958, 960.
Justice of God, 148, 151.
Justification by Christ, 245, 360, 365, 370, 381, 389.

K.

KINDNESS, 639, 641, 643-645, 647-649.
King, Christ a, 10, 228, 271-286, 599, 752, 777, 778, 801, 810, 845, 992.
God a, 148-152, 172, 567, 819, 862.
Kingdom of Christ, 637, 806, 870, 996.
Kings and priests, Christians, 797.
Knowledge of Christ blissful, 451, 520, 529, 552, 573, 574, 611.
desired, 549, 598.
vain without love, 643, 644.

L.

LABORERS for Christ, 695-698, 700-702.
increase of, prayed for, 812, 813.
Lamb of God. See CHRIST.
song of Moses and the, 275.
worship of the, 273, 280, 284.

Lamp, Scripture a, 720.
Languor in devotion, 73, 298, 776.
Latter-day glory, 870–876, 878–880.
Law, conviction by the, 317, 319, 420.
  love of the, 629, 635, 733.
  no salvation by, 320.
Life, brevity of, 916–924.
  Christ the, 214, 215, 440, 478, 505, 560, 583, 781.
  the day of grace, 337–342.
Light, Christ the, 91, 92, 440, 465, 478, 487, 504, 505, 507.
Living to Christ, 228, 234, 557–575.
Looking unto Jesus, 412, 423, 701.
Longing to be with Christ, 481, 483, 977, 984, 996.
Long suffering of God, 35, 124, 126, 357, 391.
Lord's Day, 40–56.
  anticipated, 40.
  blessing desired, 47.
  day of rest, 42.
  delight in, 44, 49.
  evening, 54.
  how to spend, 43, 50.
  love of, 53.
  morning, 40–42, 44–47.
  praise for, 41, 45.
  the resurrection day, 45, 51.
  welcomed, 46–48, 52.
  world banished on, 55. See SABBATH.
  prayer, 17, 18.
  supper, 779–799.
  anticipative, 999.
  commemorating Christ's love, 779, 781, 784, 785, 787, 788, 794, 799.
  communing with Christ in, 779, 780, 783, 788, 793, 795, 799.
  declarative of redemption accomplished, 781, 783, 788, 791.
  feast of the soul, 779–783, 793, 795, 799.
  gratitude for a place at, 782, 786.
  self-surrender in the, 781, 784, 789.
  sufferings of Christ shown in, 787, 788, 796.
  table of the Lord, 779, 780, 786, 792.
Lord our righteousness. See CHRIST.
Love essential, 643, 644.
  excellence of, 643, 644.
  of Christ, 173, 177, 199, 206, 228–235, 463, 472.
  celebrated, 779, 788, 793, 794, 797.
  remembered, 781, 784, 795, 799.
  Christians, 637, 638, 640, 642, 647, 785.
  God, 14, 21, 135–138, 142, 167, 169, 171, 178, 460, 537.
  shown in the death of Christ, 139, 143, 537.
  passing knowledge, 549.
  to Christ, 462–487.
  God, 20, 128, 141, 462, 464.
  others for Christ's sake, 637–654.
  the church, 627, 744, 746.
  Scripture, 729–733.
Love to Spirit, 470.
Loving kindness, 555.

M.

MAJESTY of God, 5, 8, 35, 148, 151, 152.
Maker of all things, Christ, 193, 228, 283, 308.
Man fallen, 315–318.
  lost, 318–321.
  mortal, 440, 916–928.
  saved, 410–461.
Manna, heavenly, 483, 511.
Mariner, prayer for, 887, 888.
Mary weeping, 253.
Martyrs glorified, 813.
Mediator, Christ. See CHRIST.
Meditation, 93, 615, 733.
Meekness of Christ. See CHRIST.
  Christians, 198, 199, 202, 203, 623.
Meeting and parting, 912–915.
Memorials of Christ, 799, 999.
Members, reception of, 838–842.
Mercies acknowledged, 5, 20, 21, 32, 34, 115, 125.
Mercy, God's, 12, 35, 114, 119, 128.
  pleaded, 350–363.
  prayed for, 211, 399, 403, 404, 406, 407, 409.
  trusted in, 19, 420, 433, 449.
Mercy-seat, 584, 585, 587, 593, 658, 672.
Merit, human, disclaimed, 420, 422, 424–427, 443.
Messiah, 213.
Millennium, 870–876, 878–880.
Ministers, death of, 942.
  ordained, 806.
  prayed for, 802, 803, 805, 808.
  thanks for, 801, 804, 810.
  welcomed, 807.
Miracle of grace, 467.
Miracles of Christ, 208–211.
  still performed, 210.
Missionary hymns, 870–889.
  meetings, 886.
Missionaries charged, 877, 882.
  commended to God, 870, 877.
  encouraged, 877.
  farewell of, 885.
Missions, 807–883.
  home, 882, 883, 890–893.
Morning hymns, 86–92, 586.
  mercies, 86, 89.
  praise, 86, 90.
  prayer, 87, 88, 91, 92.
  Lord's Day, 40–47.
Mortality of man, 440, 916–928.
Mortification of sin, 623, 627, 630, 631, 633, 634, 636.
Moses, song of, 275, 750.
Mother's prayer, 650–652.
Mourners comforted, 940, 956.
Mourning for sin, 228, 351–354, 356, 362, 427, 440.
Mutual love, 638, 640–642, 647.
Mystery, 687, 689, 691.

N.

NAME of Jesus, 180, 436, 441, 444, 476–479, 482–484, 535, 794.
Narrow way, 631, 633.
National anniversary, 890.
  blessings sought, 891–893.
  fast, 894–897.
  thanksgiving, 900.
Nations blessed by Christ, 4, 16.
Nativity of Christ, 185–195.
Nature and Scripture, 235, 721, 722.
  grace, 168, 723, 724, 735.
  declares God's glory, 9, 13, 15, 144–146, 235.
  of man, 315–317, 390.
Nearness to God desired, 46, 60, 67, 132, 133, 600.
  heaven, 924, 974, 985, 987.
Needful, one thing, 323, 508, 574, 859.
Neglect of religion, 22, 35, 323–327, 333–335, 339, 343.
New birth, 287, 290, 291, 303, 322, 353, 361, 396, 397, 405, 424.
  covenant, 414, 448, 511, 552, 556.
  creation, 603.
  heart, 320–322, 349, 353, 354.
  song, 467, 472, 477, 491, 497, 500, 503, 524, 528, 529, 535, 542, 544, 550, 553, 555.
  year, 906, 908–911.
Now the accepted time, 330, 334–342, 344–348.

O.

OATH of Christ, 414.
  God, 446.
Obedience to Christ, 599, 606, 608, 609, 629, 635, 762.
Object of Christ's coming, 191, 196.
Obligations to Christ, 173, 174, 182, 228.
Officers of the church, 801–811.
Old year, 904, 905.
Old, old story, 453.
Olivet, Mount of, 216–219.
Omnipotence of God, 16, 150.
Omnipresence of God, 12, 105, 106.
Omniscience of God, 103, 104.
One believing look, 423.
One church, 739, 745.
One thing needful, 323, 508, 574, 859.
Only believe, 370, 371, 372, 375, 381, 422, 423, 435, 436, 439.
Only Jesus, 463, 468, 574.
Opening of houses of worship, 860–869.
Ordination of deacons, 810, 811.
  missionaries, 800, 806, 877.
  pastors, 803, 807, 808, 809.
Ordinances, 752, 778, 779, 799, 999.
Outpouring of the Spirit, 822.
Overcoming the world, 611–615, 617–619, 621.

P.

PANTING after God, 60, 70, 132, 133, 600, 612–626.
Pardon abundant, 123, 179, 368, 410, 418.
  free, 123, 370, 372, 375, 381, 390, 396, 408, 411, 413, 423.
  implored, 351–363, 393, 399, 400, 403, 406, 409.
  joy of, 398, 405, 411, 422, 469, 491, 504, 524.

ALPHABETICAL INDEX OF SUBJECTS.

Parental hymns, 650–652.
Parting hymns, 912–915.
Paschal lamb, 231, 790.
Pass me not, 825, 826, 831.
Pastors, charge to, 805, 806.
death of aged, 942.
ordained, 803, 807, 808, 809.
prayer for, 802, 803, 808–810.
thanksgiving for, 804.
welcomed, 807.
work of, 800, 804–806.
Patience of Christ, 198, 202, 572.
Pattern, Christ our, 192, 198–203, 205, 206, 217, 218, 412, 564, 752, 753, 756, 758, 760, 761, 765, 768.
Peace, abiding, 400, 429, 496, 498, 499, 500, 522, 524, 714.
in believing, 384.
death, 929–936.
of conscience, 496.
Pearl of price, 524.
Penitent's inquiry, 357.
prayer of the, 19, 351–363.
Penitence, 35, 349–363.
blessedness of, 240, 253, 398, 415, 435.
Perfections of God, 13, 122, 148, 151.
Perishing, cry of the, 208, 351.
prayer for the, 646, 814.
Perseverance of the saints, 523, 526, 531, 532, 536, 543, 549, 552, 741.
Personal dedication, 228, 405, 412, 417, 557–575.
Physician, Christ a, 388.
Piety, active, 639, 644, 645, 648, 649, 695–702.
early, 858, 869.
Pilgrimage, Christian, 105, 440, 610, 693, 694, 974, 977, 978, 987.
life a, 608.
of the church, 745.
songs, 105, 440, 679, 847, 978, 985, 987, 990, 995.
Pilot, Christ our, 669, 676.
Pisgah, 578, 966.
Plea, the Christian's, 441.
Pleading the name of Christ, 352, 360, 362, 427, 444.
Pleasures of religion, 508.
Poor, pity to the, 639, 645, 649.
Portion, God our, 162, 514, 919, 967.
Praise, adoring, 1, 3–6, 13, 21, 25–28.
to Christ, 2, 173–182, 844–847.
as king, 8, 271–283.
the Lamb, 10, 231, 273–275, 280.
Redeemer, 173, 177, 179–184, 187–191.
Shepherd, 221, 229, 547, 843, 840–851, 857.
from children, 213, 844–846.
God, 30, 32–34, 113, 121.
for creation, 7, 8, 12, 27, 33, 34, 144, 146.
daily mercies, 12, 25, 26, 114, 125, 141.
providence, 21, 26, 111, 116, 122, 141, 163–165.
redemption, 8, 10–12, 27, 28, 32, 114, 119, 129, 135–140, 166–169, 235.
from all nations, 3–5, 11, 12, 15.
angels, 9, 23, 145, 180.
children, 853
Praise to God perpetual, 14, 32, 33, 1000.
resolution to offer, 32, 33.
summons to, 3, 5–12, 16, 35.
universal, 1, 3, 5, 15, 34.
to the Trinity, 306–314.
Prayer, 577–595.
access to God by, 2, 29, 580, 581, 584, 585, 590.
after baptism, 772, 774.
answered, 30, 577, 578, 580, 585, 588, 590, 593, 595.
at the beginning of worship, 29, 39, 57, 62, 63, 78, 79.
baptism, 752, 758, 759, 765, 766, 768, 773, 776–778.
close of worship, 81–85.
dedication services, 860–867.
parting, 912, 913.
the new year, 908–910.
backsliders, 827–829.
boldness in, 588, 590, 593.
children's, 850–852.
delight in, 29, 578, 580, 584, 586, 595.
earnest, 588, 590, 593, 595.
effectual, 30, 581–583, 588.
exhortation to, 579, 580, 588.
evening, 579, 586, 594.
for access to God, 457, 583, 593, 595, 674, 677.
aid, 87, 88, 402, 404, 406, 409, 444, 445, 450, 452, 591, 593, 666.
assurance, 156, 162, 296, 558, 598, 632, 677.
benefit from afflictions, 160, 600, 656, 660, 680, 686.
children, 843, 848, 854, 856, 857.
Christ's coming, 889–909.
cleansing, 132, 239, 390, 395, 397, 408, 415, 416, 421, 433, 435, 791.
closer walk with God, 626.
consecration, 228, 321, 560, 566, 597, 599, 601–613, 622.
contentment, 620, 684, 686, 688, 689.
deacons, 810, 811.
divine indwelling, 44, 83, 86, 294, 302, 303, 605.
evidence of adoption, 162, 521.
faith, 353, 390, 402, 665, 674.
freedom from sin, 390, 392–397, 400, 401, 406–409, 601–613.
grace, 13, 103, 104, 296, 304, 305, 316, 318, 349, 351, 362, 363, 596, 617, 620, 624, 628.
guidance, 120, 161, 303, 326, 668, 676, 691, 693, 694, 849–852.
help, 203, 206, 672, 675–677, 705, 713, 719.
holiness, 287, 292, 294, 297, 300, 302, 596, 598–607, 609–615.
for humility, 634.
likeness to Christ, 596–636.
mariners, 887, 888.
mercy, 351–358, 361, 363, 390–393, 403, 406–409, 420, 421.
ministers, 802, 803, 808, 809.
nation, 890–897.
repentance, 349, 353, 354, 357, 827.
Prayer for resignation to God's will 688, 689, 692.
restoration, 827, 829.
revival, 815–822, 824–826.
spread of the gospel, 870, 871, 874, 875.
steadfastness, 415, 452, 557, 560, 567.
support in death, 931, 932–936.
the church, 62, 637.
Holy Spirit, 291–293, 295–305.
Jews, 884, 889.
Lord's, 17, 18.
morning, 87, 91, 92, 579, 586.
private, 29, 93, 578, 579, 595.
privilege of, 578, 580–585, 589–592, 595.
to the Trinity, 306–314.
without ceasing, 579, 585, 588.
Preaching, blessing implored on, 61, 81, 82.
essential, 454.
successful, 454, 455.
Predestination, 138, 157, 530, 536, 537.
Preparation for death, 326, 328, 337, 338, 342, 930, 931, 933.
heaven, 926, 952.
judgment, 324, 325, 334, 340, 956, 960–965.
Presence of Christ desired, 74–79, 177, 180, 210, 283, 473, 504, 519, 594.
God desired, 105, 106, 116, 508, 515, 516.
the Holy Spirit invoked, 295–305.
realized, 294.
Preservation by Christ, 413–417, 430–418, 495–500, 513, 520.
Priesthood, Christian, 7, 273, 968.
of Christ, 264–269.
Prince of Peace, 27, 189, 221, 272, 975, 989.
Prisoners released, 184, 273, 321, 382.
Privileges, Christian, 2, 4, 16, 584–590, 816.
Prize, the believer's, 711, 714.
Procrastination, warning against, 330, 337–348.
Prodigal reclaimed, 534, 539, 547, 792.
Progress, Christian, 73, 305, 706, 708–720.
Promises, the, 123, 129, 131.
faithful, 123, 129.
pleading, 407–409, 447, 588, 590, 820.
Protection, Divine, 33, 120, 127, 155, 161.
implored, 120, 413, 416.
praise for, 33, 115, 121, 127, 128, 169.
Providence, 17, 18, 21, 29, 111, 115, 122, 153, 156, 606, 681, 684, 686, 689.
gratitude for, 7, 21, 29, 115, 122, 687.
mystery of, 153, 156, 157, 687, 689.
reliance on, 155.
submission to, 29, 154, 158, 684–687, 690–693.
universal, 8, 9, 21, 122, 154.
wise, 154, 689.

ALPHABETICAL INDEX OF SUBJECTS.

Provisions of grace, 110, 119, 123, 124, 167–169.
Public worship, 1–39.
desire for, 64–66, 70, 80.
pleasures of, 3, 5, 59, 65, 67, 69–72, 110.
summons to, 3, 5, 6, 16, 23.
Publican, prayer of, 352.
Purity of heart, 132.

Q.

QUICKENING grace 290, 292, 304, 624.
Spirit, 289, 290, 299, 312, 625.

R.

RACE, the Christian, 706, 711, 712, 930.
Ransom, Christ our, 229, 231, 245, 422, 944.
Ransomed Christians, 14, 251, 257, 418, 569.
Readiness for death, 924–928, 930, 931, 935, 966.
Reasonableness of worship, 11, 15, 22.
Reclaiming grace, 128.
Reconciliation through Christ, 316–318, 320, 321.
Redeemed in heaven, 968.
Redeemer, 4, 10, 21, 228–234, 241.
Redemption, 2, 19, 20, 32, 228–241.
God's character seen in, 109, 114, 139, 143, 166–168, 235, 728.
praise for, 12, 14, 114, 166–169, 228–235, 527, 528, 530, 536–538.
wonders of, 39, 235.
Refuge, God a, 21, 29, 155, 160, 568, 677.
in Christ, 171, 240, 241, 413, 428, 523, 597, 666, 677, 678, 680.
Regeneration by the Spirit, 287, 289, 290, 291, 303, 315.
necessity of, 320–322.
Reign of Christ, 271–286, 872, 874.
Reigning with Christ, 273, 936.
Rejoicing in Christ, 234, 236, 488–521.
God, 3, 16, 20, 160–166, 169.
salvation, 16, 169, 239–241, 520.
Released from guilt, 238, 239.
Religion, its importance, 344, 353, 508, 859.
pleasures, 488–509
urged on the young, 848, 853, 858.
Remembrance of Christ, 781, 784, 785.
Renunciation of sin, 228, 395, 603, 626, 627.
the world, 394, 396, 565, 566, 573, 611–615, 617–619.
Repentance at the cross, 221–226, 228, 230, 539.
call to, 332, 334.
immediate, 341–347.
prayer for, 349, 353, 354, 357, 827.
Repenting sinner, joy over, 534, 833.
Resignation to God's will, 29, 153, 154, 158, 162, 665, 684–694.
Resolutions, godly, 31.
Resolve, the successful, 371, 393.
Resurrection of Christ, 52, 242–257.
Christians, 952–954, 957, 960.
Rest, earthly and heavenly, 56, 987.
in Christ, 412–417, 436, 479, 495, 500, 507, 510, 526, 531, 602, 662, 789.
Rest in God, 128, 160, 161.
heaven, 679, 969, 970–978, 985–988.
wanderer's return to, 128.
Restoration from backsliding, 827–832.
of the Jews, 884, 889.
Retirement, 23, 93, 579.
Retrospect, grateful, 28, 29, 907.
Returning to God, 128, 363, 827–829, 836.
Reunion above, 913–915, 937, 938, 940, 977, 987.
on earth, 912.
Revival, 814–837.
necessity of, 815, 816, 818, 824.
prayed for, 814–822, 824.
rejoiced in, 823, 833.
Reward, the Christian's, 994.
Righteous and wicked, 517.
Righteous, blessedness of. See BLESSEDNESS OF CHRISTIANS.
death of the, 929.
Righteousness by the law impossible, 170, 350, 420, 425, 426.
Christian. See CHRIST.
Rites, vain, 290, 316, 791.
Robe of righteousness, 434, 528, 533, 553, 556.
Rock, Christ a. See CHRIST.
God a, 23, 123, 131, 155, 506.
of ages, 416, 742.
Room for sinners, 336, 366, 367, 393.
Ruler, God a, 10, 15, 22, 35, 124, 148–152.

S.

SABBATH. See LORD'S DAY.
earthly and heavenly, 56, 982, 987.
Sacrifice. See CHRIST.
Safety of Christians, 25, 107, 127, 129, 155, 160, 169, 411, 413–415, 417, 428, 438, 444, 447.
in affliction, 29, 153, 154, 160, 672–678.
in danger, 29, 160.
death, 929, 930, 935, 950.
judgment, 957, 962.
the church, 737, 740, 741, 743, 747, 750.
Saints, blessedness of. See BLESSEDNESS OF CHRISTIANS.
communion of, 637, 638, 640, 642, 647.
one family, 708, 709, 938.
Salvation accomplished, 236–239, 247, 257, 264, 389, 439, 442.
by Christ. See CHRIST.
grace, 24, 229, 235, 424.
complete, 429, 443, 447, 467, 488, 524, 536, 789.
praise for, 10, 14, 20, 24–28, 35, 129, 234, 235, 538.
provided by God, 235.
rejoicing in, 12, 25, 28, 130, 488–521, 538.
Sanctified afflictions, 153, 154, 490, 600, 607, 665.
Sanctification desired, 123, 596, 600, 601, 603, 609, 614, 615, 622, 623, 626, 636.
Sanctuary, blessings sought in, 57, 63, 73, 75, 78.
Christ present in, 64, 77.
Sanctuary, Christ's presence desired in, 74, 79.
joy in, 59, 60, 65, 66, 69, 72, 76.
longed for, 60, 61, 70, 80
praise for, 67, 71.
worship, 58, 68, 81–85.
Satisfaction of Christ, 380, 411, 435, 442.
Saviour, Christ a. See CHRIST.
Scripture, delight in, 722, 725, 726, 730–733.
excellence of, 721, 723, 729, 734, 735.
love to, 724, 729, 731–732.
superiority of, 722, 723, 727, 734.
Seasons, praise for, 898, 899.
Sea, song on, 670.
Seamen, prayer for, 887, 888.
Second coming of Christ, 955, 956, 958, 962–964, 989–999.
Secret prayer, 29, 93, 578, 579, 595.
Secure sinner awakened, 319.
Security in God, 25, 127, 155, 160, 161, 430, 575, 670.
Self-abasement, 170, 222, 226, 315–317, 349, 351, 357, 358, 363, 392, 393, 396, 409.
admonition, 703, 704, 710–712, 714.
consecration, 29, 228, 559, 565, 754, 758, 759, 762–764, 766, 787.
denial, 631, 633, 634.
distrust, 632, 720.
righteousness renounced, 170, 319, 320, 425, 787.
surrender, 31, 228, 394, 405, 407, 412, 557, 558, 561, 566, 568, 569, 571.
Sermon, hymns before, 78, 79, 81.
after, 81–85.
Service of Christ, 228, 557, 562–566, 572.
God, 16, 567, 568.
Sheep wandering, 229, 547, 828.
Shepherd, Christ our, 221, 229, 547, 843, 849–851, 857.
God our, 16, 163–165.
Shepherds at birth of Christ, 186.
Shield of faith, 710, 718.
Shortness of time, 916–924.
Sickness, 29, 78, 125, 471, 494, 680, 683, 688, 691.
Sin borne by Christ. See CHRIST.
confessed, 222, 351, 352, 355–363
defilement of, 395, 399, 403, 404, 407, 408, 410.
deliverance from, 233, 238, 239, 290, 291, 410–413, 416–419, 421, 441–444, 855.
forgiveness of, 28, 160, 171, 312, 360, 361, 368, 376, 403, 407, 408, 410, 411, 419, 421, 433, 435, 439, 447.
indwelling, lamented, 349, 352, 353, 356, 361–363, 623–626, 628, 835.
loathed, 355, 356.
original, 315–317.
renounced, 228, 395, 603, 626, 627.
wounding Christ, 222, 224–227.
Sinai, 258, 322, 527.
and Zion, 527.
Sinners at the bar of God, 324, 325, 956, 959.
awakened, 318, 319, 321, 322.

ALPHABETICAL INDEX OF SUBJECTS.

Sinners entreated, 22, 323, 329, 333, 343, 364.
  expostulated with, 35, 327, 331, 332, 338, 340, 346–348.
  invited to Christ, 364–389, 470.
  joy over penitent, 534, 863.
  resolution of, 371, 393.
  room for, 336, 366, 367, 393.
  sorrowed over, 646, 653, 654.
  warned, 324–326, 337, 338.
Sloth deplored, 832.
Soldiers of Christ, 703–707, 714, 718, 720.
Song of Moses, 275, 750.
  the angels, 27, 132, 137, 151, 186, 188.
Song of the redeemed, 10, 11, 14, 21, 129, 132, 968.
Sons of God, 162, 430, 521, 548.
Sorrow at death of friends, 937, 939, 940, 943–951.
  comfort in, 154, 157, 162, 655–662, 666, 675, 677, 683.
  for sin, 222, 225, 226, 350–363.
Sorrows of Christ, 177, 200, 227, 231–233, 240, 242.
Soul surrender, 653.
Souls, how to win, 394, 455.
Sovereign grace, 129, 172, 552.
Sovereignty of God, 3, 5, 8, 21, 35, 148–152, 172, 286.
Sowing and reaping, 698.
Spirit, Holy. See HOLY SPIRIT.
  of adoption, 401, 521.
Star of Bethlehem, 544.
Stone, hearts of, 332, 347, 349, 827.
Storm, pilot in, 676.
Strait gate, 631, 633, 712.
Stranger, the Christian a, 978.
Strength, according to the day, 25, 28, 664, 678, 682.
  from Christ, 664, 692.
  renewed, 28.
Subdued by the cross, 539.
Submission, Christian, 684–692.
Substitution of Christ, 225, 228–235, 432, 435, 442, 535.
Sufferings of Christ, 228–237, 240–242.
Sufficiency of grace, 28, 129, 169, 411.
Sun of righteousness, 598, 979, 993.
  the soul, 96, 598.
Sunday-school hymns, 843–859.
Support, Divine, 31, 112, 127.
Sympathy, Christian, 637–642, 645–649.
  of Christ, 204, 232, 249, 267, 269, 270, 589.
  with poor and afflicted, 645, 649.

T.

TABLE of the Lord, 779–799.
Taking up the cross, 230, 562, 564, 570, 713, 715, 754, 776.
Teaching, Divine, 214, 215, 725, 728, 729, 733.
Tempest stilled by Christ, 209, 210.
Temple of Christ, 4, 603.
Temptations of Christ, 204, 269, 270, 285.
  hope in, 263–270, 445, 446, 457, 460.
  terminated, 709, 715, 718–720.
Tempted, Christ's sympathy with the, 267–270.
Tenderness, Christ's, 269.
Thanksgiving for harvest, 901, 903.
  for the seasons, 899, 902.
  ministry, 801, 804.
  national, 890–892, 898–903.
Thief, the dying, 410.
Thirsting for God, 60, 70, 182, 183.
Thirsty satisfied by Christ, 366, 378.
Threatenings, 323, 327, 328, 331, 334, 335, 337, 339, 341, 345, 347.
Throne of grace, 29, 129, 181, 419, 577, 580, 595.
Tidings, glad, 333, 364–367, 373, 381, 383.
Time, flight of, 916–921, 923, 924, 927.
  the accepted, 334, 337, 341, 342, 346–348.
  season to prepare for eternity, 337, 341, 342.
  unimproved, 359.
Title to heaven, 988.
Titles of Christ, 186, 188–190, 193, 278, 279, 283, 524, 525.
To-day, call of, 35, 337–348.
Transfiguration, the, 207.
Trials, deliverance from, 153, 155, 655–662, 664, 683.
Trials, ended, 709, 714, 847, 968.
Trinity, praises to the, 306–308, 310, 311.
  prayer to the, 309, 312–314, 860, 862.
Triumphs of Christ, 183, 212, 213, 258–262, 271–282, 284, 529, 710, 714, 859, 872, 874.
Triumphing in Christ, 169, 429, 434, 451, 456, 524, 528.
  over death, 933, 935.
Trouble, help in, 31, 35, 102, 112, 120, 121, 124, 125, 127, 128, 130, 142, 494, 499.
Trumpet, gospel, 365, 366.
  the judgment, 324, 334, 959, 960, 962, 963.
Trust in Christ, 25, 204, 233, 239–241, 410–461.
  God, 28, 31, 33, 112, 155, 161, 445.
Truth, Christ the, 206, 214, 215, 560, 583.
  of God, 110, 113, 118, 121–123, 129–132.
Types of Christ, 511, 790, 791.

U.

UNBELIEF banished, 669.
  deplored, 460.
  deprecated, 452, 673, 674, 689.
Unconverted prayed for, 814, 817, 819.
  sorrowed over, 646, 816.
  warned, 323–331.
Unfaithfulness confessed, 293, 302, 305.
  deprecated, 829.
  lamented, 829, 830, 835, 836.
Unfruitfulness lamented, 73.
Union, Christian, 637, 638, 640, 642.
  with Christ, 426, 431, 441, 444, 447, 452, 484, 492, 500, 512, 513, 516, 524, 552, 554, 556, 561, 571, 608, 670.
Unity of God, 3, 5, 16, 1000.
  the church, 739, 745, 928.
Universal praise, 1, 3, 5, 12, 15, 16, 20, 26, 1000.
Unworthiness confessed, 317, 349–363.

V.

VALUE of life, 337, 342, 345, 316.
Vanity, 916–920.
  of the world, 611–615, 617–619, 621.
Veil, looking within the, 709.
Victory of Christ. See TRIUMPHS.
  over death, 242–257.
Victory of faith, 263, 452.
Vine, the living, 431, 751, 793.
Vows made, 102, 567, 764, 838.

W.

WAITING on God, 29, 158.
Walking by faith, 667, 673, 674, 691, 693.
  with God, 622, 626.
Wanderer exhorted, 836.
  reclaimed, 163, 164.
Wandering lamented, 829, 830.
Warning from the tomb, 922.
Warfare, Christian, 703–720.
Watchfulness, Christian, 704–706.
Watching for souls, 805.
Watchman's report, 989.
Water of life, 366, 378.
Way, Christ the, 214, 215, 412, 560, 583.
  to heaven, strait, 631, 633.
Weak believers encouraged, 269, 430, 432, 444, 446–449, 461, 520, 556, 747.
Weakness of faith deplored, 73, 460.
Weary invited, 371, 374, 376.
Weeping, Christ's, 204, 216, 233, 653.
  for sin, 228, 350, 352, 860, 393.
  over sinners, 616, 816.
Welcome to Christ, 876.
  converts, 838, 842.
  Lord's Day, 46, 48, 52.
  pastors, 807.
  sinners, 352, 383, 389, 541.
Will of God acquiesced in, 29, 154, 156, 158, 162, 655, 688, 692.
  revealed, 721–729.
Winning souls, 455, 805.
Wisdom of God, 103, 104, 106, 108, 110, 118, 122, 145, 146.
Witness of the Spirit, 294, 296, 603, 605.
Word, blessing on the, desired, 63, 76, 81, 82, 84, 85.
Word of God. See SCRIPTURE.
Work, Christian, 695–698, 700, 702, 813, 913.
Work of Christ finished, 231, 237, 233, 439.
Works of God in creation, 7, 9, 12, 15, 27, 144, 147.
  redemption, 10, 14, 28, 166–184, 235.
  providence, 17, 18, 26, 29, 122, 148–165.
Workman, God's true, 697.
World, conversion of, desired. See MISSIONS.
World, end of, 959, 962.
  renounced, 557, 558, 565, 566, 573, 611, 612, 615.
  vanity of, 573, 612, 614, 916–921.
Worship, blessing in, sought, 29, 47, 62, 63, 74–79.
  call to, 2, 4, 5, 8, 12, 21, 22, 23, 26

Worship, close of, 81–85.
evening, 93–99.
joy in, 3, 39, 44, 46, 49, 53, 59, 67–69.
Lord's Day, 53, 54, 57, 59, 62.
morning, 86–92.
public, 5, 6, 11, 16, 22, 23.
universal, 1, 7, 9, 11, 13, 15, 872, 1000.
Worthies, following departed, 708, 709.
Wrestling with God, 593.

Y.

YEAR, close of the, 907, 911.
the new, 904–908.
Yoke of Christ, 374.
Young, accepting Christ, 844, 852.
exhorted, 858.
importance of religion to, 848, 856, 858, 859.
praise of, 213, 844–847.
prayed for, 650–652, 843, 854, 857.
prayer of, 850–852.
Young saved, 853–855.
Youth, mercies of, recalled, 115.

Z.

ZEAL, Christian, 695, 698, 700–707.
want of, lamented, 73.
Zion, beauty, 736–740.
beloved, 637, 744, 746.
God's habitation, 736, 739, 740, 743.
Mount, 439.
prayer for, 751.
prosperity of, 736–738, 743, 744, 750.
safety of, 740, 742, 745–750.
triumphs of, 740, 747, 750.

INDEX OF SCRIPTURES.

The second column of figures indicates the NUMBER *of the Hymn.*

GENESIS.

1 : 2........22, 146
1 : 3........134
1 : 16........144
2 : 3........42, 43, 52
3 : 15........188, 483
3 : 19........922, 952, 953
3 : 24........2
5 : 24........600, 626
6 : 3........340
6 : 9........629
7 : 1........385
8 : 22........899, 902
15 : 8........988
16 : 13........103, 104, 106
16 : 31........104
17 : 18........297, 651
18 : 25........894
18 : 26........891
19 : 17........340, 346, 368
19 : 22........330, 338, 339, 364
22 : 3........86
22 : 5........39
22 : 14........142, 689
22 : 18........271
24 : 31........838, 839
24 : 40........904
24 : 56........715
24 : 63........39, 93, 615
26 : 24........678
28 : 10–22........600
28 : 15........678, 904
28 : 17........68
28 : 19–22........600
31 : 42........127, 495
31 : 45........596
31 : 49........912
32 : 1, 2........25, 127, 545
32 : 24..78, 578, 588, 590, 593
35 : 15........600
44 : 34........646, 650, 652
47 : 9........920, 923, 927, 978
48 : 15, 16........856, 857
49 : 10........190, 191, 870
49 : 18........191, 412
49 : 24........438, 440, 444, 445
50 : 10........937

EXODUS.

3 : 5........58, 59, 133
3 : 12........877
12 : 23........419, 421
13 : 21, 22........691, 693, 694
14 : 15........701, 706
14 : 19, 20........677, 877
15 : 2........151, 666
15 : 11........110, 132, 133
15 : 18........100, 101
15 : 26........115
16 : 4........449, 511
16 : 23........59
17 : 11........585
19 : 4........824
19 : 5........129, 414, 448, 511
19 : 18........258
20 : 6........843
20 : 8........42, 56
20 : 11........40
20 : 24........61, 71
23 : 13........634–636
23 : 27........710
24 : 10–18........586
25 : 17........584, 585, 587, 593
25 : 22........75
25 : 23........576
28 : 9–12........267, 556
28 : 29........264
29 : 38, 43........97, 791
29 : 45........159
31 : 14........40
31 : 17........52
33 : 11........796
33 : 14........500, 681
33 : 18........908
34 : 107, 114
34 : 7........118, 119

LEVITICUS.

3 : 2–8........601, 791
6 : 13........601
10 : 3........684–693
14 : 4–7........316
16 : 21........362
19 : 2........132
23 : 2........55
25 : 9........365
25 : 35........645
26 : 5........120
26 : 6........127
26 : 39–41........351
26 : 40–42........78

NUMBERS.

10 : 29........838
10 : 35, 36........889
14 : 18........117–119
14 : 19........3
14 : 21........870, 871
14 : 24........601, 602
20 : 8–11........511
21 : 8, 9........388, 423
23 : 10........929, 935, 936
23 : 19........113, 129, 130, 609
23 : 23........120
24 : 17........190, 193

DEUTERONOMY.

1 : 33........601
2 : 7........564
3 : 24........8, 107
3 : 25........934, 966
4 : 7........890
4 : 20........748
4 : 23........809, 764
5 : 12–14........55
7 : 6–8........471, 530, 536, 540
7 : 9........123, 131
7 : 10........339
8 : 2........98
8 : 18........21
9 : 56........530, 536, 540
10 : 17, 18........33, 37
10 : 21........161
11 : 18........725
12 : 9........328
18 : 15........278
23 : 14........160
26 : 17........569, 704, 766
28 : 2........125
28 : 66........917
29 : 29........110
31 : 6........555, 877
32 : 3........149
32 : 4........155
32 : 6........827
32 : 10........60
32 : 29..323, 339, 341, 343, 922
32 : 40–52........934, 966
33 : 3........33
33 : 12........556
33 : 25........664, 678, 682, 718
33 : 26........503
33 : 27........100, 160
34 : 1–5........934, 935

JOSHUA.

1 : 5........655
1 : 8........725
1 : 9........677
3 : 14–17........933
18 : 3........906
23 : 8........608
23 : 14, 15........129
24 : 15........346, 347, 505, 766
24 : 27........596

JUDGES.

2 : 4, 5........628
5 : 3........32, 113
8 : 4........611
8 : 23........150
10 : 15........351, 352, 355, 358
11 : 35........766

RUTH.

1 : 8........648, 649
1 : 16........505, 766, 841
1 : 20........659, 686, 691, 693
2 : 12........160, 161, 655, 672

1st SAMUEL.

1 : 17........81, 82, 84, 85
1 : 28........650–652, 843
2 : 2...23, 123, 131, 155, 506
2 : 3........103, 104, 106, 108
2 : 9..127, 155, 160, 161, 169
2 : 10........151, 152
2 : 25........317, 325
3 : 1........725, 729, 733
3 : 9........557, 563
3 : 18..684, 686, 688, 690, 691
4 : 9........707, 714, 718
4 : 18........637
5 : 4........149, 747
6 : 20........317, 325
7 : 12........596, 907
8 : 3........650, 651
12 : 10........353, 356
14 : 6........122, 127
15 : 29........669
16 : 7........104
17 : 45........444, 449
17 : 47........101, 110
20 : 3........917, 919, 922
20 : 17........638, 640
24 : 16, 17........827
25 : 29........658
30 : 6........120, 694

2d SAMUEL.

1 : 26........638
2 : 5, 6........639, 648, 849

8 : 9.......791
7 : 8.......115
7 : 10.......884, 889
7 : 14, 15.......547, 597
7 : 18, 19.......93, 471, 540
7 : 22.......107, 111, 740
7 : 23, 24.......890
7 : 28, 29.......123, 124, 131
9 : 1.......641, 645
12 : 12.......715, 718, 720
14 : 12.......319, 373, 356
12 : 22.......917, 927, 937
14 : 14.......916, 919, 920
15 : 15.......701, 705, 904
15 : 21.......841
15 : 28.......684, 686, 688-692
22 : 2.......23, 123, 131, 155, 606
22 : 3.......149, 161, 169, 743
22 : 3.......100, 127, 160
22 : 4.......11, 14, 20
22 : 7.......462, 544, 545
22 : 17.......478
22 : 31.......21, 118, 734
22 : 32.......155
23 : 5.......414, 448, 511
24 : 14.......686, 688, 690

1st KINGS.

2 : 2.......700, 702, 707, 718
3 : 9.......623, 651, 652
5 : 5.......861, 868
8 : 11.......862, 867
8 : 23.......110, 123, 129
8 : 27.......866
8 : 28.......861
8 : 30.......894, 896
8 : 51.......748
8 : 57.......890, 891
17 : 4.......907
18 : 21.......323, 331, 347
18 : 39.......16, 22
18 : 42.......816, 821, 824
18 : 44.......823, 825
20 : 28.......120, 127
22 : 19.......151, 152

2d KINGS.

2 : 11.......937, 938
4 : 26.......687, 689, 692
5 : 13.......4, 10, 416, 421
5 : 14.......413, 496, 500, 505
6 : 16.......5, 120, 148, 155
6 : 17.......127, 150, 545
7 : 3.......325, 343
7 : 4.......371
7 : 9.......22, 522, 545
19 : 15.......16, 35, 36
19 : 19.......149
20 : 1.......917, 922, 923
20 : 19.......691, 692
23 : 3.......599, 608

1st CHRONICLES.

4 : 10.......606, 635, 636
16 : 8.......6, 10, 14
16 : 9.......11, 13, 16
16 : 10.......16, 23, 27
16 : 11.......29, 31, 37
16 : 12.......22, 100, 115
16 : 15.......414, 448, 511
16 : 23.......3, 5, 7
16 : 25.......13, 16, 29
16 : 26.......144, 145, 146
16 : 29.......2, 4, 5, 8, 12
16 : 31.......5, 10, 148-152
16 : 34.......12, 28, 117-119
17 : 16.......115, 138, 471, 539, 540, 782
17 : 20.......113, 136
21 : 8.......351, 352, 355
21 : 13.......686, 688, 690
28 : 20.......706, 707, 714
29 : 11.......149, 152
29 : 13.......14, 19, 20
29 : 14.......418, 424, 567
29 : 15.......916, 917, 927
29 : 17.......103, 104, 108
29 : 20.......14, 21, 23

2d CHRONICLES.

1 : 7.......590
1 : 10.......596, 606, 623
2 : 4.......861, 863, 865
2 : 5.......147, 740
2 : 6.......866
6 : 14.......110, 113, 125
6 : 18.......866
6 : 14-42.......860-868
7 : 1.......815
7 : 14.......894-897
14 : 11.......402, 404
15 : 2.......330, 335, 347
16 : 9.......103, 104, 108
18 : 18.......36
20 : 6.......148, 149, 151, 153
20 : 12.......155, 160, 161
20 : 17.......707, 710, 718
20 : 21.......125, 126, 166
29 : 10.......505, 608, 766
29 : 23, 24.......410, 419, 421, 791
30 : 6.......836
30 : 9.......373, 376, 388
32 : 7.......712, 714, 719
32 : 8.......109, 112, 120
33 : 12.......121, 600, 656
34 : 31.......597, 599, 608, 613

EZRA.

1 : 6.......576
3 : 3.......88, 97
3 : 11.......119, 121, 125
8 : 22.......152, 160, 161
9 : 6.......315, 355, 357
9 : 7.......894, 895
9 : 13.......827

NEHEMIAH.

1 : 3-11.......818, 827, 835
4 : 6.......14
8 : 10.......488, 497, 500, 503
9 : 5.......14, 16, 22
9 : 6.......144, 146, 147
9 : 12.......694
9 : 15.......504, 717, 793
9 : 17.......119, 125, 126
9 : 20.......483, 511
9 : 33.......320, 350, 351

ESTHER.

4 : 3.......894
4 : 16.......371
6 : 1.......150, 153, 159
8 : 6.......646, 653, 814

JOB.

1 : 11.......685, 688, 689, 690, 692
2 : 10.......153, 154, 156, 157, 158, 684, 686, 687, 691, 693
3 : 17.......946, 947, 969, 976
4 : 17.......158, 317, 320
4 : 19.......916, 917, 919
5 : 6-8.......328, 923, 978
5 : 17-24.......128, 490, 671
5 : 19.......121, 160, 161, 162
5 : 24.......586
5 : 26.......929, 936, 944
7 : 1.......918, 927, 954
7 : 6.......921, 923, 927
7 : 9.......916, 921, 953
7 : 16.......928
7 : 20.......350, 351, 356
8 : 9.......905, 916, 918
8 : 13.......630
9 : 2.......317, 319, 320
9 : 4.......148, 151, 152
9 : 8.......144, 145, 147
9 : 10.......156, 157, 158
9 : 12.......151, 158, 172
9 : 20.......316, 317, 320
9 : 25.......918, 920, 927
9 : 30, 31.......316, 321, 423
10 : 1.......924, 928
10 : 9.......953
10 : 20.......905, 920, 923
11 : 7.......156-158
12 : 7, 8.......141
13 : 15.......655, 659, 665
13 : 23.......316, 318, 349
14 : 1.......916, 917, 919
14 : 2.......918, 920, 923
14 : 3.......317
14 : 4.......315, 316, 318
14 : 5.......919
14 : 14.......952, 953, 954
15 : 14.......315, 316
15 : 15.......132
16 : 21.......595
16 : 22.......920, 924, 927
17 : 14.......922
19 : 25-27.......940, 952, 954
22 : 5.......316
22 : 13.......103, 104, 108
22 : 21.......364-389
23 : 3.......461, 595
23 : 6.......398, 400, 411
23 : 10.......153, 490, 600
23 : 12.......725, 733
23 : 15.......127
24 : 1.......659
25 : 4.......317, 318
25 : 6.......315, 316
26 : 6.......106
26 : 7.......19, 36
26 : 14.......153, 156-158
27 : 8.......630, 631, 633
28 : 28.......838
29 : 2.......590, 626
29 : 11-16.......639, 645, 648, 649
30 : 23.......921, 922, 952
31 : 14.......317
33 : 13.......148, 153, 156, 158
33 : 24.......411, 422, 428
33 : 27, 28.......360, 361, 363
34 : 10.......132-134, 150
34 : 10.......959, 962, 964
34 : 21.......103, 104, 108
34 : 22.......108
34 : 23.......684, 688, 691, 692
34 : 29.......516, 659
35 : 10.......529
36 : 3.......32, 33, 36, 37
36 : 5.......21, 111, 118
36 : 18.......324, 326, 327
36 : 24.......3, 6, 8, 10
36 : 26.......153, 156-158
37 : 11.......25
37 : 23.......153, 156-158
38 : 4.......145, 146
38 : 25.......117
40 : 2.......689
40 : 4.......316, 317
42 : 2.......103, 104, 108
42 : 4.......349, 354
42 : 6.......351, 353, 356, 360

PSALMS.

1 : 1.......489, 490, 517
1 : 2.......729, 730, 732
1 : 3.......25, 33, 122
1 : 5.......324, 955, 956
1 : 6.......58
2 : 1.......152
2 : 4.......148, 151
2 : 6.......281, 284, 876
2 : 7.......187, 190
2 : 8.......271, 279, 281, 871, 872
2 : 12.......417, 419, 430, 440
3 : 3.......21, 65, 119, 161, 169, 743
3 : 4.......121, 462
3 : 5.......86, 89, 90
3 : 6.......127, 209, 441, 447, 449
3 : 8.......23, 245
4 : 1.......362, 419, 428
4 : 3.......448, 577, 578, 580, 581
4 : 4.......88, 96
4 : 5.......31, 112, 155
4 : 6.......88, 91, 92
4 : 7.......488, 496, 500, 524
4 : 8.......96, 98, 99
5 : 1.......577, 588, 589
5 : 3.......58, 86, 89
5 : 4.......58, 517
5 : 5.......21
5 : 7.......57, 62, 64
5 : 11.......21, 33, 37
5 : 12.......65, 149, 169
6 : 4.......825, 826, 828
6 : 9.......462, 529, 545
7 : 1.......413, 415, 421
7 : 9.......646, 816
7 : 17.......30, 32, 33
8 : 1.......110, 111, 116, 144
8 : 2.......844, 845
8 : 3, 4.......107
9 : 1.......14, 32, 33
9 : 4.......150
9 : 7.......100, 120, 130
9 : 8.......874, 875
9 : 9.......655, 656, 662
9 : 10.......25, 109, 120
9 : 14.......25
10 : 1.......595
10 : 16.......148, 150
11 : 1.......112, 155, 161
11 : 4.......61, 64, 65
12 : 6.......727, 730, 733
13 : 5.......415, 417, 418
13 : 6.......28, 125, 462
14 : 1.......315, 316, 318
14 : 7.......873, 875, 884
15.......919
16 : 1.......33, 112, 155
16 : 2, 3.......639, 645, 648
16 : 5.......162, 514, 919
16 : 6.......28, 90, 94

INDEX OF SCRIPTURES.

INDEX OF SCRIPTURES.

91: 15 ... 655, 658, 662
92: 1, 2 ... 59, 69
92: 5 ... 101, 118, 122
93: 1 ... 148–152
93: 2 ... 101, 120, 122
93: 5 ... 132–134
94: 7–10 ... 103, 104, 108
94: 12 ... 153, 154, 163
94: 22 ... 127, 128, 160
95: 1 ... 13, 23, 26
95: 3 ... 35, 110, 149
95: 5 ... 145–147
95: 6–11 ... 22
96: 1 ... 7–12
96: 2 ... 89, 94, 97
96: 4 ... 34, 37, 122
96: 5 ... 144, 146
96: 6 ... 65, 71, 72
96: 9 ... 6, 13, 21
96: 13 ... 955, 956, 958
97: 1 ... 148–152
97: 2 ... 153, 156–158
97: 6 ... 721
98: 1 ... 8, 10, 13
98: 5 ... 26
98: 9 ... 955, 956, 958
99: 1 ... 148, 151, 152
99: 3 ... 132–134
99: 5 ... 23, 35, 36
99: 9 ... 20, 113
100: 1 ... 3, 5, 16
100: 2 ... 6, 13, 22
100: 3 ... 16, 163–165
100: 4 ... 5, 13, 16
100: 5 ... 116, 119, 122
101: 1 ... 121, 124, 127
101: 2 ... 557, 566, 572
102: 2 ... 656, 666
102: 11 ... 101, 917, 918
102: 13 ... 816, 823, 831
102: 23–27 ... 120
103 ... 28, 125, 166
103: 8 ... 119, 123, 124
103: 9–11 ... 118, 119, 123
103: 13, 14 ... 125, 126
103: 15, 16 ... 916, 918, 919
103: 17 ... 118, 119, 124
103: 19 ... 148, 151, 152
103: 20–22 ... 7, 9, 15
104 ... 21
104: 2 ... 145–147
104: 24 ... 144–145
104: 33 ... 12, 24, 32
105: 1 ... 141
106: 1 ... 118, 119, 124
106: 6 ... 315, 316
107: 1 ... 121–128
107: 8 ... 11, 13, 127
107: 23–30 ... 670
108: 1 ... 528, 542, 545
108: 2 ... 26
108: 3 ... 32, 36, 37, 121
108: 4 ... 118, 122, 128
108: 5 ... 20, 113
110: 1 ... 276
110: 3 ... 288, 289, 301
110: 4 ... 264, 267–270
111: 1 ... 128, 524, 528
111: 2 ... 100, 114, 116
111: 4 ... 117, 118, 122
111: 5 ... 25, 146
111: 5, 9 ... 414, 448, 511
111: 10 ... 127
112: 1 ... 489, 491, 500
112: 7 ... 127, 444, 445
112: 9 ... 644, 645
113: 1 ... 7, 9, 10
113: 2 ... 12, 870
113: 3 ... 32, 88
113: 5, 6 ... 101, 107
115: 1 ... 414, 422, 424–426, 530
115: 9–11 ... 127
115: 15 ... 145–147
116: 1 ... 121, 128, 462
116: 2 ... 102
116: 3 ... 351, 353, 356
116: 4 ... 360–363
116: 5 ... 122–125
116: 6 ... 121
116: 7 ... 120
116: 8 ... 128, 531, 543, 547
116: 9 ... 557, 561, 563
116: 12, 13 ... 546
116: 14 ... 102, 128, 545
116: 15 ... 929, 933, 935
116: 16 ... 561, 563, 569
116: 17 ... 528–530, 532
116: 18 ... 102, 128, 545
117: 1 ... 11, 12, 16
118: 1 ... 111, 114, 124
118: 5 ... 121, 128, 462
118: 6 ... 444, 445, 449
118: 8 ... 25, 33, 127
118: 14 ... 14
118: 15 ... 488–491, 500
118: 24 ... 51
118: 25 ... 815, 819, 823
118: 26 ... 212, 213
118: 28 ... 11, 30, 32, 33
118: 29 ... 113, 114, 117
119 ... 722, 730, 733
119: 1 ... 517
119: 5 ... 624, 635
119: 8 ... 629, 635
119: 9 ... 725, 728, 729
119: 10 ... 599, 600, 603
119: 11 ... 731
119: 14, 16 ... 629
119: 18 ... 725
119: 19 ... 978, 983
119: 20 ... 600, 602, 605
119: 24 ... 722, 732
119: 27 ... 722, 728
119: 32 ... 288, 289, 296
119: 33 ... 605
119: 35 ... 613–616
119: 37 ... 615, 618, 619
119: 40 ... 599, 602, 605
119: 41 ... 609, 636
119: 47, 48 ... 629, 635
119: 49 ... 671, 672, 678
119: 50 ... 693, 726
119: 53 ... 646
119: 54 ... 724, 732, 733
119: 57 ... 514, 629, 967
119: 58 ... 566, 569, 573
119: 60 ... 629
119: 67, 71 ... 490, 600, 665
119: 72 ... 722, 724, 730
119: 73 ... 115, 146
119: 75 ... 680, 691, 693
119: 81 ... 575
119: 89 ... 144, 146
119: 90 ... 100
119: 91 ... 145, 147
119: 96 ... 734
119: 97 ... 720, 732, 733
119: 101 ... 629, 635
119: 103 ... 729, 731, 732
119: 105 ... 727, 728, 729
119: 112 ... 629, 635
119: 113 ... 733
119: 114 ... 432, 433, 527
119: 117 ... 438, 444, 447
119: 126 ... 816, 821, 824
119: 127 ... 722, 732, 733
119: 128 ... 612, 618, 730
119: 130 ... 725, 727, 729
119: 133 ... 613, 615, 623
119: 136 ... 646
119: 137 ... 132–134
119: 140 ... 729, 732, 733
119: 158 ... 646
119: 165 ... 496, 500, 524
119: 176 ... 220, 828, 829
120: 1 ... 121, 462, 545
121 ... 161
121: 2 ... 31, 33, 127
121: 3 ... 438, 444, 445
121: 4–8 ... 575, 670
122 ... 62, 65, 66, 70
123 ... 161
124: 8 ... 155
125: 1 ... 160, 161
126: 1 ... 502
126: 2 ... 833
126: 6 ... 698
130: 1 ... 121, 545
130: 3 ... 350, 351
130: 4 ... 118, 122, 325
130: 5 ... 671, 677, 682
130: 7 ... 127, 153, 155
131 ... 684–694
132: 8 ... 861, 866, 867
132: 13 ... 740, 742, 743
132: 14 ... 736
132: 18 ... 747, 748, 750
133 ... 638, 640, 641, 647
134 ... 7
135: 1 ... 7, 9, 13
135: 2 ... 10, 25, 26
135: 4 ... 736, 741
135: 5 ... 35, 110, 149
135: 6 ... 148, 151, 158
135: 7 ... 146
136 ... 109, 113, 114, 117, 118
137: 1 ... 637, 816
137: 2 ... 663
137: 5, 6 ... 637
138: 1, 2 ... 25, 28, 32, 128
138: 3 ... 121, 462, 545
138: 6 ... 107, 126, 136
138: 7 ... 444, 447
138: 8 ... 440, 445, 446
139: 1–12 ... 103, 104, 106, 108
139: 8 ... 88, 90, 586
139: 23, 24 ... 626, 632, 635
140: 6 ... 450, 629
141: 1 ... 591, 593, 595
141: 2 ... 96, 97
141: 3 ... 634, 635
141: 4 ... 517
142: 1 ... 102, 121, 128
142: 5 ... 127, 128, 160
143: 2 ... 317, 350
143: 5 ... 511, 518
143: 6 ... 60, 70, 461, 617
143: 8 ... 86, 88, 92
143: 9 ... 416, 432, 433, 527
143: 10 ... 599, 602, 909
143: 11 ... 290, 295, 298
144: 2 ... 161, 169, 743
144: 3 ... 107
144: 4 ... 917, 920, 921
145 ... 34
145: 2 ... 89, 90
145: 3 ... 110, 147, 149
145: 8 ... 119, 124
145: 9 ... 102, 105, 106
145: 10 ... 113
145: 15, 16 ... 898, 899, 903
145: 18 ... 577, 578, 588
145: 19 ... 589, 595
145: 20 ... 31
146 ... 33, 37
146: 1 ... 28, 125, 163
146: 2 ... 32
146: 5 ... 33, 37, 127
146: 6 ... 144–147
147: 1 ... 4, 24, 28
147: 2 ... 884, 889
147: 5 ... 101, 104, 120
147: 8 ... 898, 903
147: 14 ... 899, 900
148 ... 7, 9, 11, 15
149 ... 3, 5, 6, 13
150 ... 6, 10, 14, 26
150: 6 ... 1, 7, 12, 15, 20

PROVERBS.

1: 8, 9 ... 857–859
1: 23 ... 329, 330, 832
2: 1–6 ... 856–859
3: 5, 6 ... 148–165, 658, 663
3: 9, 10 ... 636, 645, 648, 649
3: 12 ... 153, 154, 163, 165, 600
3: 14–17 ... 509, 858, 859
4: 1–13 ... 856–859
4: 18 ... 92, 440, 465, 478
6: 4–11 ... 831, 832, 898, 899
6: 23 ... 721–735
8: 1, 5 ... 364–369
8: 8, 9, 32–36 ... 629, 730, 732
8: 12 ... 347, 348
9: 1–5 ... 364, 389
10: 4, 5 ... 705, 706, 709–712
10: 7, 25 ... 940, 947, 948, 950
10: 11, 13 ... 517
11: 19, 20 ... 335–337
11: 24, 25 ... 636, 648, 649
11: 30 ... 455, 805, 806
13: 4, 11 ... 705, 706, 709–712
14: 10 ... 655–658
14: 34 ... 890–897
15: 11 ... 103, 104, 106, 108
15: 20 ... 818, 858, 859
15: 31, 32 ... 293, 155
16: 3 ... 100, 161
16: 10, 12, 13 ... 890, 893
17: 1 ... 896
17: 10 ... 152, 155, 161
18: 24 ... 265, 268
19: 17 ... 645, 648, 649
21: 2 ... 104, 106, 108
21: 3 ... 697, 701, 702
21: 21 ... 489, 490, 966–968
22: 6 ... 843, 848, 856–859
24: 11, 12 ... 103, 104, 106, 108
25: 2 ... 156, 157
27: 1 ... 905, 916–920
28: 13 ... 349, 351, 352, 358
29: 1 ... 347, 348
30: 5 ... 727, 731
30: 7–9 ... 684–694

INDEX OF SCRIPTURES.

ECCLESIASTES.

1 : 2, 3, 14..611–615, 617–619
2 : 1–11....611–615, 617–619
3 : 14 101
5 : 1, 2...... .... 64, 66, 78
5 : 4, 5...........102, 557, 764
5 : 10–15..................611–619
7 : 14...29, 153, 154, 156–158
8 : 8...............634, 937, 940
9 : 10...............704, 705, 707
11 : 1, 2...........648, 695, 698
11 : 6...............695, 698, 699
11 : 9...............956, 958, 965
12 : 1........843, 848, 854–859
12 : 13........................158, 162
12 : 14 .....955, 956, 958, 960

CANTICLES.

1 : 4................173, 174, 271
2 : 1..................................877
2 : 4........262, 366–367, 783
5 : 4–6 ....293, 623, 699
7 : 11, 12................ 695, 702

ISAIAH.

1 : 2, 3.................. 323, 327
1 : 18.............239, 373, 376
2 : 2–4..736, 742, 745, 870–872
2 : 4...................................731
2 : 10–12.................955, 956
3 : 10..............489, 490, 496
4 : 6...................737, 740–747
5 : 26.......................875, 878
6 : 6, 7, 8..........800–813, 877
7 : 14–16...175, 176, 185–196
8 : 10.......105, 112, 120, 127
8 : 13, 14......................159–163
8 : 20. ....722, 727, 729
9 : 2, 6 ....189, 193, 245
9 : 7.............................271–286
10 : 3..........................329, 331
11 : 1–9............173, 178, 282
11 : 9............................872, 878
11 : 10..............532, 539, 547
12 : 1–3.. 538–556
12 : 5, 6................................1–39
13 : 6–13..........955, 956, 961
14 : 32..............737, 740, 742
17 : 10, 11...................323, 327
21 : 11, 12 989
25 : 1.. 1–39
25 : 4..................155, 159, 163
25 : 6..................336, 366, 367
25 : 8...............................933, 935
26 : 1, 2..............737, 740, 748
26 : 3..................159, 422, 496
26 : 9...........60, 70, 461, 600
26 : 13..........................626, 628
27 : 5, 6.....118, 400, 496–500
28 : 12...........................412–417
28 : 16..............414, 429, 452
29 : 13–15.......................103–106
30 : 18, 19.........123, 129, 131
30 : 21...........................300, 305
32 : 1, 2..............275. 276, 281
32 : 2..................552, 662, 666
32 : 8 649
32 : 15........... .... 297, 301
32 : 20.......................................698
33 : 6...............451, 452, 573
33 : 15–17.......................511. 520
34 : 1, 2..........................133, 158
35 : 1, 2..............801, 821–823
35 : 8–10....412, 511, 520, 968
35 : 10..........................960–988
40 : 1 658–683
40 : 3–5.............197, 875, 882
40 : 6–8 916–923
40 : 9, 10..............................865
40 : 11........................ .163–165
40 : 31..28
41 : 10...... 678
41 : 17, 18......................677–679
42 : 6, 7......................................189
42 : 16..............156, 161, 506
43 : 2..678
43 : 5, 6......................................873
43 : 25.................. 530
44 : 2, 3...... .... .287, 304
44 : 22............................166–170
45 : 2, 3..........................148–152
45 : 5–7 ....7–9, 148
45 : 19..............372, 374, 391
45 : 22..............412, 423, 701
46 : 3, 4......................................678
48 : 10..............153, 490, 600
49 : 15..........................137, 746
49 : 22..............743, 750, 879
50 : 7–9..............127, 430, 575
51 : 4, 5..........................235, 729
51 : 11 488–521
52 : 1, 2..................45, 710–714
52 : 7..801
53 : 1–3..............177, 200, 233
53 : 4–7..............224, 227–238
53 : 12........................ .263–270
54 : 1, 2..........................710–712
54 : 4, 10, 14, 17.......743–750
55 : 1–3. ....366, 374, 378
55 : 6, 9..........................326, 330
55 : 11..............................722, 735
56 : 2 ....42, 43
57 : 1 ....929, 936
57 : 15..................107, 292, 294
58 : 1–7..........................575, 623
58 : 13, 14...............................43, 50
59 : 1, 2..............222, 225, 305
59 : 19............................151, 247
60 : 1–3..........................878, 880
60 : 11......................................737
60 : 19, 20........966, 971, 980
61 : 1–3......................................184
62 : 2, 3......................................737
62 : 4..............................742, 744
63 : 1–3 284
63 : 15, 16..................................626
64 : 4................................916–923
65 : 17–19................................ 980
65 : 24 .... .581, 582
66 : 1, 2..................................... 132
66 : 22, 23.......................716, 870

JEREMIAH.

1 : 7, 8, 17....................805, 806
2 : 19..829
3 : 4...............................858, 859
3 : 15.............................800, 806
3 : 23......................... 23, 35
4 : 3...............................332, 343
4 : 6...............................737, 747
6 : 26...............................894. 897
8 : 20...............................339, 340
8 : 22..388
10 : 10........................8, 20, 148
11 : 4..748
13 : 16............ 345, 700–702
14 : 7–9..... 293
17 : 7, 8......................................517
17 : 21, 22................... 43, 50
18 : 7–10....................148, 151
22 : 10..939
23 : 3, 4 ....747, 801
23 : 6..321
23 : 28, 29......................721–735
29 : 7..............................804–821
29 : 11–14......................742, 747
30 : 3, 8, 10, 17, 22...736–751
31 : 23.. 744
31 : 33...... 414, 448, 511, 556
32 : 40, 41..................468, 511
33 : 15, 16..................................321
33 : 20, 21..................................123
42 : 5, 6............599, 606, 629
46 : 27, 28.....................444, 445
50 : 4, 5. ....820, 825
51 : 10.. .... 13, 23, 36
51 : 15.... 144–147

LAMENTATIONS.

1 : 12.............................218, 227
3 : 22, 23..........................94, 123
3 : 24................................112, 128
3 : 25................................111, 114
3 : 26..................................29, 158
3 : 27............. 374, 848, 852
3 : 31–33.........109, 125, 126
3 : 40–42..........................128, 836
5 : 19, 20..........................100, 120
5 : 21............. 297, 349, 629

EZEKIEL.

3 : 4–9..............................347, 800
3 : 18..............................805, 807
6 : 10.. 149
8 : 12..............................104, 109
9 : 4..................................297, 301
11 : 19..............................291, 303
14 : 4..290
16 : 8..115
18 : 21–23......................333, 334
18 : 31..............................329, 330
21 : 27..............................871, 874
22 : 14..962
33 : 7..805
33 : 11..............329, 333, 365
33 : 30, 31......................654, 814
34 : 11–17......................229, 547
36 : 17..............................395, 399
36 : 25–27......................291, 298
36 : 21, 32......................425, 530
36 : 36..............................123, 129
36 : 37..............................580, 588
37 : 1–10..........................312, 625
37 : 9..470
37 : 9–14.................................. 290
37 : 26, 27.........................120, 127
47 : 1–12 ....366, 874

DANIEL.

2 : 21..148
2 : 44...............152, 271, 279
2 : 47........................... .103
3 : 17..............................674, 748
4 : 27 337
4 : 34, 35 ....148, 152, 153
5 : 25–28..........................961, 962
6 : 10..............................579, 580
7 : 9..958
7 : 27..872
9 : 5, 8..............................358, 361
9 : 21..581
9 : 24. .... .220, 264
10 : 19.. 664
12 : 2... .... 952, 956
12 : 3..............................702, 967

HOSEA.

4 : 17..............................334, 335
5 : 15..............................829, 830
6 : 3..520
6 : 6..............................290, 791
11 : 8.. 329
13 : 9..835
13 : 14 247
14 : 1, 2 ....832, 836
14 : 4..............................163, 828

JOEL.

1 : 13.. 897
2 : 1..333
2 : 12, 13..........................119, 316
2 : 17.. 894
2 : 27..............................120, 127
2 : 28, 29..........................297, 301
3 : 14.. 956
3 : 18..880

AMOS.

4 : 12..............................326, 962
5 : 4..............................333, 334
5 : 21.. 791
6 : 1....... ....626, 832
7 : 3......... ....123, 391
7 : 8..148
9 : 2, 3..............................104, 106

OBADIAH.

3, 4 347
17............................... 878, 879
21............................... 871, 872

JONAH.

1 : 2..104
1 : 3........................ 106, 108
1 : 6.. 832
2 : 4, 7..............................829, 830
3 : 5..894
3 : 9..............................391, 393
4 : 2 ....123, 125

MICAH.

2 : 7..............................295, 297
2 : 10..............395, 399, 409
2 : 13.. 161
4 : 12..............................876, 878
4 : 7..............................736, 742
4 : 10..............................127, 155
4 : 12..............................153, 155
6 : 3–5..............................124, 141
6 : 6–8............ 50, 102, 374
6 : 10..............................692, 693
7 : 7..413
7 : 18, 19..................... 125, 411

NAHUM.

1 : 2..............................119, 125
1 : 6..............................962, 963
1 : 7..................155, 160, 416
1 : 15.. 801

HABAKKUK.

1 : 13..............132, 133, 134
2 : 4..............................112, 458
2 : 14..............................878, 881
3 : 2........297. 816–819, 824

INDEX OF SCRIPTURES.

3 : 3-6 ....8, 149
3 : 17, 18..............100, 120

ZEPHANIAH.

1 : 12....................104, 148
1 : 14-18...............344, 955
2 : 3...........................416
3 : 9, 10.................874, 875
3 : 14-17...............730, 744

HAGGAI.

2 : 4.....................127, 131
2 : 7..............183, 184, 191
2 : 9......................188, 354
2 : 14.....................403, 410
2 : 23.....................302, 471

ZECHARIAH.

2 : 10, 11...............127, 736
6 : 12.....................189, 190
7 : 13..............................347
8 : 21..............................22, 28
9 : 9.......................212, 213
9 : 12.....................155, 160
13 : 1.....................410, 411
13 : 9.......................21, 506
14 : 9..............................281
14 : 20...................132, 575

MALACHI.

1 : 11..............................875
2 : 7.......................806, 811
3 : 2.......................958, 959
3 : 3................596, 600, 610
3 : 6..............................130
3 : 10.....................824, 827
3 : 16.....................588, 589
4 : 1.......................955, 956
4 : 2.......................166, 181
4 : 6.......................650, 651

MATTHEW.

1 : 21...... 169, 180, 476-480
1 : 23......175, 176, 436, 535
2 : 2..............................191
2 : 6.......................185, 544
2 : 9..............190, 192, 193
2 : 11.....................193, 195
3 : 3..............................197
3 : 9..............................290
3 : 16......285, 759-761, 763, 768, 773, 775-778
4 : 1........204, 269, 270, 285
4 : 4..............25, 694, 717
4 : 16................92, 189, 478
4 : 17.....................333-335
4 : 23, 24.................208, 210
5 : 3........302, 370, 381, 610
5 : 4.......................356, 362
5 : 5...............199, 354, 374
5 : 6...............378, 399, 504
5 : 7.......................198, 645
5 : 8..............................610
5 : 7-9..........................649
5 : 10-12..209, 202, 205, 649
5 : 13-16.........................634
5 : 18.............113, 131, 723
5 : 48.............110, 118, 122
6 : 4...............104, 106, 108
6 : 6...............577, 580, 590
6 : 9-13.........................17, 18
6 : 9........117, 162, 444, 521
6 : 10............806, 871, 872
6 : 11................25, 148, 159
6 : 12..............351, 352, 356
6 : 13..560, 575, 603, 636, 720
6 : 14, 15.........579, 645, 649
6 : 19, 20...611, 612, 613, 617
6 : 21..............................679
6 : 22, 23.........506, 570, 613
6 : 24...............650, 631, 633
6 : 25...............657, 661, 681
6 : 26.....................116, 610
6 : 27..............................686
6 : 28.....................111, 146
6 : 30, 31.........................141
6 : 32.......105, 122, 162, 548
6 : 33..............................127
6 : 34...............657, 659, 684
7 : 7.........577, 588, 590, 593
7 : 8.........580, 581, 588, 595
7 : 11.....................136, 301
7 : 12.....................641, 645
7 : 13..............................633
7 : 14.....................631, 712
7 : 21.....................630, 633
7 : 26, 27.........630, 633, 634
8 : 2.......................349, 356
8 : 16.....................208, 210
8 : 19.....................564, 570
8 : 20..............................200
8 : 26...............209, 669, 676
8 : 27..............................478
9 : 2.........398, 489, 500, 524
9 : 12..............................388
9 : 13.....................102, 124
9 : 15.....................995, 998
9 : 25..............................210
9 : 27...............211, 318, 321
9 : 38.....................812, 813
10 : 26, 28...............441, 449
10 : 31............................610
10 : 32...................715, 956
10 : 37............................558
10 : 38............................564
10 : 42............................648
11 : 5........208, 210, 610, 876
11 : 10............................197
11 : 28.......369-374, 376, 377
11 : 29......417, 419, 421, 500, 510, 526
11 : 30...................374, 510
12 : 6.....................173, 176
12 : 7.....................102, 124
12 : 8.......................51, 52
12 : 19...................198, 202
12 : 29.............184, 390, 602
12 : 50.............493, 535, 639
13 : 8..............................698
13 : 16............................801
13 : 17.............190, 191, 195
13 : 23.......................81, 82
13 : 30...................958, 960
13 : 44...................231, 232
13 : 46............................524
14 : 12............................855
14 : 11...................208, 210
14 : 23...................203, 285
14 : 27.............209, 449, 658
14 : 30.............660, 670, 676
14 : 31...................209, 657
15 : 30...................208, 210
16 : 3...............959, 991, 993
16 : 17...................289, 290
16 : 18.......738, 741, 742, 746
16 : 24..... 200, 562, 564, 570, 713, 715, 754
16 : 25.............328, 335, 369
16 : 27.............955, 958, 962
17 : 2..............................207
17 : 4..........40, 46, 60, 67, 68
17 : 5.....................174, 196
17 : 20............................459
18 : 11.............179, 182, 196
18 : 20.......................77, 79
18 : 22...................641, 645
19 : 13, 14.........843, 850, 857
19 : 21...................558, 564
19 : 27............................564
19 : 29.............192, 565, 572
20 : 15............................172
20 : 28.............177, 182, 184
20 : 30.............208, 210, 211
21 : 8..............................212
21 : 9..............................213
21 : 13.......................61, 64
21 : 16............................845
21 : 19............................699
21 : 22...................588, 590
21 : 42.............738, 868, 869
21 : 43...................742, 748
22 : 9, 10...........336, 366, 367
23 : 37............................464
22 : 42, 43.........190, 208, 213
23 : 37.............340, 341, 653
24 : 22............................997
24 : 30...................958, 992
24 : 35.............113, 131, 723
24 : 42...................705, 994
25 : 6..............................993
25 : 13.............705, 993, 994
25 : 21, 23........................942
25 : 31......955, 962, 965, 992
25 : 34............................956
25 : 40............................648
25 : 41...................960, 961
26 : 22............................632
26 : 26-28.........779, 793, 799
26 : 29............................909
26 : 36-46.........216-219, 222
26 : 41.......................704-706
26 : 42.............688, 690, 692
26 : 64...................958, 992
27 : 23............................226
27 : 26-31........................221
27 : 35...................224, 225
27 : 37............................477
27 : 41-43........................221
27 : 45...................228, 230
27 : 46.............227, 231, 233
27 : 50, 51...............236-238
28 : 1.....41, 45, 46, 246, 250, 253
28 : 2.....................244, 250
28 : 6..............247, 254, 257
28 : 18-20...753, 758, 800, 806, 872, 877

MARK.

1 : 2-4............................197
1 : 9-11...285, 753, 754, 755-763
1 : 13..............................285
1 : 31-34.................208-210
1 : 35..............................203
1 : 40.....................310, 356
2 : 17..............370, 383, 388
2 : 20.....................995, 998
2 : 28.......................51, 52
3 : 27..............184, 390, 602
3 : 34..............493, 535, 639
4 : 8..............................698
4 : 20.......................81, 82
4 : 26-29.........................699
4 : 39, 40...........209, 669, 676
5 : 19.....................180, 462
6 : 30..............................855
6 : 46.....................203, 285
6 : 50..............209, 449, 658
6 : 51..............................478
6 : 56.....................208, 210
8 : 34.....200, 562, 564, 570, 713, 715, 754
8 : 36, 37...........328, 335, 369
8 : 38.....................715, 956
9 : 2..............................207
9 : 5...........40, 46, 60, 67, 68
9 : 7.......................174, 196
9 : 4?..............................648
10 : 14.............843, 850, 857
10 : 21...................558, 564
10 : 28-30...192, 564, 565, 572
10 : 45.............177, 182, 184
10 : 46-52........................211
11 : 9, 10.................212, 213
11 : 13............................699
11 : 17.......................61, 64
11 : 24...................588, 590
12 : 10.............738, 868, 869
12 : 30............................464
12 : 37.............190, 208, 213
13 : 20............................997
13 : 26...................958, 992
13 : 31.............113, 131, 723
13 : 33...................705, 994
14 : 19............................632
14 : 22-24.........779, 793, 799
14 : 25............................909
14 : 32-42.........216-219, 222
14 : 36.............688, 690, 692
14 : 38.......................704-706
14 : 62...................958, 992
14 : 65............................221
15 : 13............................226
15 : 19, 20........................221
15 : 24...................224, 225
15 : 33...................228, 230
15 : 34.............227, 231, 233
15 : 37, 38...............236-238
16 : 2................41, 250, 253
16 : 6..............247, 254, 257
16 : 9..............................253
16 : 15, 16.......753, 759, 800, 806, 872, 877

LUKE.

1 : 6.......................517, 629
1 : 31..............168, 180, 476
1 : 32.....................187, 884
1 : 33.....................872, 875
1 : 35..............191, 196, 591
1 : 42..............190, 194, 195
1 : 68..............166, 168, 169
1 : 78.....................190, 598
1 : 79.....................184, 194
2 : 7................190, 193, 194
2 : 8-14...........185, 186, 193
2 : 10..............................198
2 : 11..............189, 190, 196
2 : 13, 14.................186, 188
2 : 20..............190, 194, 195
2 : 21......168, 180, 476-480
2 : 31, 32.................189, 191
3 : 3-6............................197
3 : 8..............................290
3 : 21, 22.........753, 763, 778

INDEX OF SCRIPTURES.

4:1........204, 269, 270, 285
4:4........25, 694, 717
4:18........196, 208, 232
4:22........198, 202
4:25–27........172
4:40........208, 210
5:12........349, 356
5:16........203
5:31........388
5:32........102, 124
5:34, 35........995, 998
6:5........51, 52
6:12........203
6:20........362, 370, 381, 610
6:21........378, 399, 504
6:22, 23...200, 202, 205, 649
6:31........641, 645
6:35........198, 202
6:40........630, 633, 634
7:15........210
7:22........208, 210, 610, 876
7:27........197
7:42, 43........467, 571, 533
7:47........467, 488
7:50........459, 460, 496
8:8........698
8:15........81, 82
8:21........493, 535, 639
8:22–25........209, 660, 676
8:25........478
8:48........459, 460, 496
9:10........855
9:23........200, 562, 564, 570, 713, 715, 754
9:25........328, 335, 369
9:26........715, 716
9:28–36........207
9:33........40, 46, 60, 67, 68
9:34, 35........174, 196
9:56........196
9:57........564, 570
9:58........200
9:62........557, 560, 570
10:2........812, 813
10:20........489, 490, 495
10:21........172
10:23........801
10:24........190, 191, 195
10:42........323, 463, 508, 574, 859
11:2–4........17, 18
11:2........117, 162, 444, 521, 806, 871, 872
11:3........25, 146, 159
11:4........351, 352, 356, 560, 575, 603, 636, 720
11:9........577, 588, 590, 593
11:10........580, 581, 588, 595
11:13........136, 391
11:22........184, 390, 602
11:28........801
12:4........414, 445, 495
12:6........610
12:8........715, 956
12:15........328
12:22........657, 661, 681
12:24........116, 610
12:27........111, 146
12:28........141
12:30........105, 122, 162, 548
12:31........127
12:32........669, 678, 742, 747, 750
12:34........670
12:35........704–706, 994
12:40........992–994
13:3, 5........334, 341, 347
13:6........699
13:24........326, 337–346
13:28........963
13:34........340, 341, 653
14:15........489, 490, 999
14:16........366, 367
14:22........336, 366, 367, 393
14:27........200, 562, 564, 570, 713, 715, 754
15:2........364, 370, 373
15:4–7........221, 229, 547
15:7........534, 833
15:11–24...534, 539, 547, 792
16:9........576
16:13........630, 631, 633
16:17........723
17:4........198, 202, 645
17:5........73, 600, 601, 605
18:1........577, 588
18:7........581, 588, 593
18:13........351, 352, 356
18:16........843, 850, 857
18:22........558, 564
18:29, 30........192, 565, 572
18:35–43........208, 210, 211
19:10........179, 182, 196
19:17........942
19:37, 38........212, 213
19:40........497
19:41........653
19:42........330, 337, 339
20:17........738, 868, 869
20:41–44........190, 208, 213
21:27........955, 958, 960
21:28........993, 995, 998
21:33........113, 131, 723
21:36........704–706, 994
22:18........999
22:19, 20........779, 793, 799
22:39–46........216–219, 222
22:42........688, 690, 692
22:46........704–706
22:63–65........221, 226
22:69........271–286
23:23........226
23:26........562
23:33........220, 230, 232
23:34........198, 202, 221
23:35........221
23:44........228, 230
23:46........231, 236–238
24:1........253
24:2........244
24:5, 6........247, 254
24:29........504
24:32........75
24:34........257
24:51........258–262

JOHN.

1:1........174–177, 306–311
1:3........193, 228, 283, 308
1:4........91, 92, 138, 214, 215
1:6........197
1:9........410, 465, 478
1:12........521, 518
1:14........174, 175, 181
1:17........178, 179, 181
1:18........139, 140, 143
1:23........197
1:29........220, 231, 239
1:32........763, 775, 778
1:41........524
3:3, 5, 7........320–322
3:6........290, 291
3:8........289, 290
3:14, 15...224, 230, 231, 240
3:16........138, 143, 166, 171
3:17........196
3:18........411, 412, 414
3:36........419, 425, 426
4:14........366, 378, 504
4:15........463
5:17........141, 142
5:18........174
5:24........414, 419, 425
5:29........951, 953, 954
5:39........725, 730
5:15........203
6:16–21........209, 210
6:20........449, 658, 660, 670, 676
6:27........328
6:29........381, 412, 425
6:32........382, 504
6:33........779, 780
6:34........694, 793
6:37........367, 370, 372, 382
6:40........952, 953, 957
6:48........382, 504, 694, 717, 779, 780, 793
7:68........597
7:37........366, 373, 378
7:42........185, 192, 544
7:46........499, 516, 707
8:12........478, 487, 504
8:32........428, 435
8:42........166, 178
8:56........195
8:58........174, 175
9:4........342
9:5........92, 440, 465
9:7........208, 210
10:11........221, 229, 547
10:16........850
10:27........417
10:28........496, 499, 513, 552, 741
11:23........952, 953, 957
11:28........831
12:12, 13........212, 213
12:21........399, 400
12:32........223, 224, 240
12:46........91, 92, 440, 465
12:47........182, 190
13:7........153, 156, 157
13:8, 9........238, 240, 390, 408, 421, 435
13:25........632
13:34........638, 640–642, 617
14:2........262
14:2, 3........974, 977, 978, 981, 998, 999
14:3........259, 264, 500
14:6...214, 215, 412, 560, 583
14:8........168, 174, 175
14:16, 17...287, 292, 294, 300
14:19........430, 441, 442, 493, 496, 499
14:23........444, 493, 594, 675
14:26........287, 292, 295, 300
14:27........429, 496, 498, 499, 500
14:28........993
15:1........431, 751, 793
15:4........424, 513, 571, 591
15:11........488, 493, 498, 500
15:12........638, 640–642, 647
15:16........138, 471, 530, 540
15:26........294, 296, 300, 303
16:8–11........287, 289, 291
16:16........991, 993, 999
16:22........995, 998
17:2........138, 172, 471
17:3........451, 573, 311
17:6........138, 339
17:12........552, 711
18:1........217
18:11........686, 689, 692
18:37........10, 228, 754
19:1–5........221, 225, 226
19:16–18........220, 224, 227
19:19........477
19:30........231, 236, 237, 238
19:34........239, 416, 421
19:37........235, 238, 239
20:11–18........253
21:15........486, 632
21:17........464, 468, 470, 476

ACTS.

1:9........258–262
1:11........955, 958, 993, 997
1:24........103, 104, 106, 168
2:1........832
2:2........289, 290, 297
2:3........301, 303, 304
2:21........381, 382, 401
2:23........226, 227, 230
2:24........242–257
2:33........271–286
2:36........271
2:38........334, 343, 347
2:41........754, 762, 768
3:13........271–286
3:14........242–257
3:19........334, 343, 347
3:21........989, 991, 993
4:11........429, 738
4:12........413, 414, 421
4:20........524
4:24........144–146
5:30........242–257
5:31........271–286
5:41........713, 765, 770
6:3........811
6:6........810
7:33........132–134
7:48........77, 264
7:51........335, 340
7:55........268, 271, 273
8:12........754, 758, 768
8:22........394
8:32........200, 220, 239
8:36........762, 763, 768
8:39........505, 766
9:11........581, 583
9:15........471
9:31........740, 742
10:4........581, 583
10:38........186, 203, 208, 210
10:39........228, 230, 231
10:40........242–257
10:42........955, 956, 958
10:43........410, 411, 419
10:48........753, 774
11:21........833
11:23........557, 560, 561
12:5........550, 588, 589

13 : 1-3............802, 805, 806
13 : 24..........................197
13 : 28............221, 227, 230
13 : 29..........................182
13 : 30..................242-257
13 : 38............361, 365, 370
13 : 39............410-412, 414
13 : 48..........................271
13 : 52......488, 491, 500, 524
14 : 15..................144-145
14 : 17............898, 899, 903
14 : 22..703, 704, 707, 717, 720
15 : 11............530, 536, 538
15 : 18..........................101
15 : 14............287, 288, 290
15 : 25..........................660
16 : 31............350, 387, 411
17 : 11............722, 725, 731
17 : 16..........................646
17 : 21..................144-146
17 : 28..................109, 111
17 : 30..........................334
17 : 31............955, 956, 958
18 : 9..............444, 445, 419
19 : 4............................197
20 : 21............942, 945, 947
21 : 13............561, 565, 571
21 : 14..................668-691
22 : 14..................471, 540
22 : 16..................755, 757
22 : 21......806, 877, 881, 882
23 : 14..................660, 662
24 : 15..................952-965
24 : 16..........................634
24 : 25..................337-348
26 : 5............................319
26 : 7..............190, 191, 195
26 : 28............338, 340, 348
28 : 28..........................271

ROMANS.

1 : 2............................184
1 : 3, 4............190, 194, 252
1 : 5........800, 804, 806, 882
1 : 16..387, 456, 532, 715, 716, 728
1 : 17..................424, 450
1 : 18............317, 325, 959
1 : 19, 20...15, 19, 135, 144-147, 721
1 . 21-32...315, 316, 318, 881
2 : 4.........140, 334, 348, 387
2 : 5-10..................964, 965
2 · 12...........................881
2 . 13..................630, 631
2 : 21-25........................808
2 : 28, 29.......................290
3 : 2.............................724
3 : 4..............129, 130, 133
3 : 9-19...315-322, 349-363, 390
3 : 20........350, 420, 422, 425
3 : 21...........................195
3 : 22..234, 235, 365-370, 381, 398, 401, 435, 441
3 : 23...........................420
3 : 24 ......See under vs. 22.
3 : 25..220, 223, 227-233, 236-240, 380, 410, 416, 419, 439
3 : 26 .... See under vs. 22.
3 : 27..................422-426
3 : 29..............12, 870, 875
3 : 31..203, 607, 609, 610, 627, 634
4 : 5, 23-25...220, 223, 227-233, 236-240, 245, 247, 248, 258, 380, 410, 416, 419, 430
4 : 7, 8..................493, 501
4 : 13...................995-998
4 : 21..............123, 129, 131
5 : 1..384, 380, 414, 441, 458, 499
5 : 2............2, 30, 417, 578
5 : 3, 4....490, 493, 661, 663, 675, 679, 693
5 : 5..135-138, 280, 295, 491, 594, 596
5 : 6..218, 223, 224, 225, 228, 231, 390, 442, 481
5 : 8..............139, 143, 537
5 : 9...531, 536, 548, 552, 556, 720
5 : 10...................440, 441
5 : 12, 15-19...315, 316, 467, 537
5 : 19...................248, 481
5 : 20, 21..166, 527, 536, 552, 555, 556
6 : 1, 2.....611, 627, 630, 631
6 : 3...767, 769, 770, 772, 774
6 : 4...752, 754, 759, 771, 778
6 : 5, 7.....247, 569, 755-759, 763, 768, 772, 773, 776-778
6 : 8............................513
6 : 9, 10...212, 247, 252-257, 263-270
6 : 11............510, 513, 608
6 : 12-22........................627
6 : 13.......561, 563, 569-576
6 : 14......441, 448, 461, 481, 496, 500, 524
6 : 16, 17.......569, 572, 573
6 : 21.......315, 316, 328, 646
6 : 22..............203, 695-702
6 : 23..166-171, 234, 393, 554
7 : 4....................425, 428
7 : 6...431, 448, 565, 569-572
7 : 7-12...318, 319, 320-322, 350
7 : 13-25..291, 315-322, 390, 394, 396, 397, 399, 400, 408, 627, 628
8 : 1.....2, 170, 196, 409, 415, 427, 678, 680, 753, 761, 771, 781
8 : 2-4.....169-171, 177, 178, 184, 228, 781
8 : 5-8.....289-292, 295, 298, 303, 315, 316, 318
8 : 9....................287, 292
8 : 11..291, 304, 520, 757, 763, 767, 773, 775-778
8 : 12, 13...603, 605, 615, 630, 633-636, 710
8 : 14..288, 295, 300, 303, 304
8 : 15.......401, 411, 521, 792
8 : 16..294, 296, 461, 603, 605
8 : 17..417, 418, 441, 452, 492, 512, 552, 556, 594, 608
8 : 18......655, 657, 675, 679, 988, 909
8 : 19-25.................991-999
8 : 19....................520, 521
8 : 23.......745, 979, 996, 997
8 : 24..416, 448, 489, 516, 520
8 : 25....................685, 693
8 : 26, 27................583, 997
8 : 28..23, 127, 154, 490, 493, 498, 594, 659, 665, 673, 681, 689
8 : 28-30..138, 527, 530, 536, 977
8 : 31......130, 495, 498, 556, 714, 715, 720
8 : 32...............34, 143, 171
8 : 33, 34..263-269, 272, 279, 283, 414-417, 434, 439, 441
8 : 35..281, 417, 430, 512, 561, 564, 608, 747, 754, 774
8 : 37......703, 714, 720, 743
8 : 38, 39..430, 446, 552, 556, 663, 741, 772
9 : 1-5.....646, 653, 654, 814, 884, 889
9 : 5...174, 175-177, 181, 185, 187, 190, 191, 479, 480
9 : 11..392, 471, 475, 530, 540
9 : 14-24.........148, 164, 172
9 : 33..............738, 741, 743
10 : 1....................884, 889
10 : 2, 3..........170, 320, 425
10 : 4..390, 401, 425, 429, 434, 439, 481, 529, 536
10 : 5....................320, 322
10 : 9...........................318
10 : 10............713, 715, 716
10 : 11......414, 417, 422, 438, 444-446, 532, 680
10 : 13..........................387
10 : 14-17..801, 870, 877, 879, 882, 883, 885
10 : 21............327, 329, 340
11 : 6...........................530
11 : 11-36.........875, 884, 886
11 : 20............704, 706, 707
11 : 22..........................633
11 : 29..........................130
11 : 33-36.......110, 118, 132, 148-165
11 : 36........5, 12, 19, 23, 134
12 : 1..........4, 561, 563, 574
12 : 2........611, 612-624, 703
12 : 3...........................610
12 : 4-10...612-615, 637-639, 640-644, 647, 648, 695, 696, 700, 805, 810, 832
12 : 14, 17, 19, 21..........221
13 : 1-7..................890-893
13 : 8, 10..........641, 643, 644
13 : 11, 12..626, 628, 635, 636, 827, 832, 924
14 : 4....................623, 636
14 : 8...559-563, 565, 569, 947
14 : 9...242, 247-252, 255-266
14 : 10, 12...............960-965
14 : 11..........................172
14 : 13..........................641
14 : 17..........................289
14 : 19...................638, 640
15 : 1...........................641
15 : 3.......198-200, 202, 203
15 : 5....................202, 208
15 : 6.....14, 25, 62, 65, 77, 83
15 : 29...........................87
15 : 30..........................810
16 : 25-27..166-168, 523, 530, 532, 556
16 : 27......................2, 14, 26

1st CORINTHIANS.

1 : 8..............417, 490, 499
1 : 9................25, 129, 130
1 : 10.............638, 641, 647
1 : 12-23........................454
1 : 30, 31.........321, 480, 522
2 : 2........113, 171, 453, 456
2 : 5............................532
2 : 9............................970
2 : 12...............83, 292, 295
2 : 14.....291, 318, 818, 821
2 : 16...........................470
3 : 4-8.....451, 816, 823, 824
3 : 11..350, 414, 429, 530, 678
3 : 13-15........................699
3 : 16.........4, 294, 304, 603
3 : 19.......122, 145, 151, 152
3 : 21...........................594
3 : 23...................557, 559
4 : 1..............800, 802, 807
4 : 2..............696, 700, 805
4 : 5.....................961-965
4 : 7............................471
4 : 9.....................708, 813
4 : 20.............818, 819, 822
5 : 7..............231, 790, 791
6 : 9..............132, 318, 631
6 : 11.............522, 572, 607
6 : 12....................704-706
6 : 14...........................952
6 : 15.............610, 622-624
6 : 17...................565, 608
6 : 19.........4, 294, 304, 603
6 : 20..559-561, 569-572, 787
7 : 29-31...916, 918-920, 927
8 : 3..393, 486-488, 491-493
8 · 6.....2, 39, 143, 168, 174, 772
9 : 16, 17..805, 807, 809, 810, 812
9 : 22.......616, 652-654, 813, 818, 821
9 : 24-26...706, 708, 711, 712
9 : 27......633, 708, 710, 719
10 : 4.........92, 447, 504, 571
10 : 12............704-706, 719
10 : 16..779-781, 783, 793, 799
10 : 24............641, 645, 647
10 : 26...7, 9, 21, 146, 898-903
10 : 31...8, 563, 696, 697, 700
10 : 33...................202, 203
11 : 23-26.........779-799, 992
12 : 3...................290, 303
12 : 13..................764, 773
12 : 14......739, 838-841, 938
12 : 12-27...606, 696, 701, 702
13 : 1-3.........................643
13 : 2, 8, 13....................641
13 : 5-7..641, 647, 971, 984, 985
13 : 9-12........................642
14 : 15...1, 2, 4-6, 14, 16, 19, 22, 23, 24, 30, 33, 76, 1000
14 : 25..........................818
15 : 1, 2........................728
15 : 3....................216-241
15 : 4....................242-257
15 : 5, 8............253, 254, 257
15 : 10......502, 527, 528, 530, 533, 536

INDEX OF SCRIPTURES.

INDEX OF SCRIPTURES.

INDEX OF SCRIPTURES.

JAMES.

1 : 2..............660, 664, 692
1 : 11....................614, 916
1 : 12..............703, 706, 708
1 : 17..............................130
1 : 22..............625, 630, 631
1 : 25..............501, 517, 563
1 : 27..............611, 645, 619
4 : 14..............916, 918, 919
5 : 7........................900, 992
5 : 9........................131, 964
5 : 11......................126, 128
5 : 13..524, 535, 578, 580, 581
5 : 16..............581, 585, 588

1st PETER.

1 : 3 ....511, 527, 528
1 : 4.........971-973, 977, 981
1 : 5 ....982, 984, 986
1 : 6.........924, 968, 972, 974
1 : 8..........................462-521
1 : 11..........................190, 195
1 : 13..............706, 994, 997
1 : 15, 16...132-134, 607, 609, 611-615
1 : 18, 19..........410-423, 791
1 : 20................129, 166, 169
1 : 21.......242-257, 271-286
1 : 22.......638, 640-642, 647
1 : 23..............295, 300, 723
1 : 24..........................910-923
1 : 25...723
2 : 4...............................738, 742
2 : 5...743
2 : 6.........738, 742, 868, 869
2 : 7..............................462-487
2 : 9.........538, 543, 746, 749
2 : 11..............694, 977, 978
2 : 21-23...198, 199, 202, 206
2 : 24..............220, 224, 229
2 : 25..............229, 467, 547
3 : 8.........638, 640-642, 647
3 : 9...............................198, 202
3 : 12.......490, 499, 501, 508
3 : 14..............447, 449, 495
3 : 18..228, 230, 232, 242-257
3 : 22..............................271-286
4 : 2...............................557-576
4 : 5...............................955-965
4 : 7..................704-706, 994
4 : 8.........638, 640-642, 647
4 : 13..............991, 993, 994
4 : 1-4..............802, 805, 809
4 : 7.........578, 655, 657-661
4 : 8...............................704-706
4 : 10..................3, 4, 12, 13

2d PETER.

1 : 1..................496, 499, 500
1 : 3..................493, 497, 500
1 : 4.........132, 510, 513, 521
1 : 15-18..............................207
1 : 19..............989, 993, 999
2 : 9..................715, 719, 720
3 : 9..................109, 118, 124
3 : 10..................955-962, 992
3 : 13..............991, 995, 998
3 : 18..........................540, 598

1st JOHN.

1 : 3..................552, 608, 630
1 : 4.................................488-521
1 : 5.........106, 122, 133, 136
1 : 7.........238, 240, 408, 416
1 : 9..................373, 376, 380
2 : 1..................263-270, 407
2 : 2..................220, 223, 224
2 : 15 .....557, 558, 565, 573, 611, 612
2 : 28.......424, 442, 513, 571
3 : 1...............................162, 521
3 : 2...998
3 : 3..................598, 601-603
3 : 11.......638, 640-642, 647
3 : 16..............223, 225, 228
3 : 24..............287, 289, 294
4 : 7..........638, 640-642, 647
4 : 8, 9 135-143
4 : 13..............287, 289, 294
4 : 14..........................166, 178
4 : 19..............466, 471, 474
5 : 4..................611, 612, 614
5 : 14..........................581, 583

REVELATION.

1 : 5.........287, 470, 505, 781
1 : 6..................273, 306, 797
1 : 7..................955, 958, 992
1 : 8...............................174, 176
1 : 18..............242, 251, 255
2 : 2.........103, 104, 106, 108
2 : 4..................505, 518, 626
2 : 7...............................967, 971
2 : 8..................242, 251, 255
2 : 10.......703, 711, 714, 828
2 : 23..............103, 106, 108
3 : 4...975
3 : 5...............................711, 715
3 : 20..............369, 379, 391
3 : 21..........................273, 797
4 : 4...273
4 : 8...............................132-134
4 : 11..............145, 147, 149
5 : 6...273
5 : 9.........173, 180, 182, 184
5 : 10..........................273, 797
5 : 12..............173, 180, 182
6 : 9..................708, 709, 968
6 : 11.......................................975
6 : 16, 17..........................955, 959
7 : 9...968
7 : 13, 14..........708, 709, 975
7 : 15.......................................980
7 : 16.......................................968
7 : 17..........................973, 984
11 : 15..........................870-876
11 : 17.......................................997
12 : 12..........................708, 709
13 : 8..........................395, 683
14 : 1-3..............968, 975, 980
14 : 4.........599, 607, 608, 609
14 : 13..........................929-939
15 : 3..........................275, 750
15 : 4..........................874, 875
16 : 5 ....148, 150-152
16 : 15.......................................994
17 : 8..........................395, 683
17 : 14..............271, 284, 599
19 : 5..........................9, 13, 36
19 : 6..........................148-152
19 : 7..............741, 991, 997
19 : 11..............430, 446, 452
19 : 12.......271, 282, 284, 599
19 : 16..............271, 284, 599
20 : 11.......281, 955, 956, 959
20 : 12..............956, 961, 965
20 : 15..........................395, 683
21 : 1...998
21 : 2...975
21 : 4..................968, 969, 971
21 : 5...998
21 : 6..........................366, 378
21 : 9.........279, 741, 991, 997
21 : 23..........................973, 977
21 : 25..............971, 973, 986
21 : 27..........................395, 683
22 : 5..................971, 973, 986
22 : 16..............190, 213, 598
22 : 17..............366, 373, 388
22 : 20..........................989, 999

METRICAL INDEX.

L. M.

HYMN

Alfreton.....113, 121
Ames.....111, 147, 166
Anvern.....37, 65, 743, 871
Attica.....840, 852
Baden.....472, 479, 597
Beautiful City.....980
Belville (*Double*).....165
Bera.....263, 300
Brownel (6 *lines*).....88
Colburn..396, 404, 418, 614, 633, 646
Darien.....617, 634, 664
Darley.....44, 56, 59, 440
Desire.....116, 128, 139
Doane.....105, 157, 171
Duane Street.....412, 434, 527
Duke Street.....150
Elmwood (6 *lines*).....204
Elparan.....32, 70, 82, 86
Ernan.....118, 143, 156
Federal Street.....90, 94, 96, 321, 398, 563, 569, 572, 625, 657, 670
Forest.....403, 415
Germany.....517, 613, 654
Gratitude.....895, 899, 1000
Hamburg.....196, 230, 242, 541
Happy Day.....755, 766
Harmony Grove.....615, 652
Hebron.....85, 98, 772, 802, 808
Hillside.....866, 884, 889
Illa.....104, 106, 138, 721
Jesus of Nazareth.....849
Leyden.....176, 195, 258
Louvan..39, 68, 83, 447, 675, 686
Loving Kindness.....555
Lowry (6 *lines*).....384, 662, 689
Luton.....174, 283, 312
Malvern.....757
Mendon.....784, 872, 886
Meredith.....505, 520, 532
Migdol.....4, 19, 25
Missionary Chant..190, 213, 260, 310, 800, 874
Old Hundred.....1
Olive's Brow.....216
Orwell.....323, 337, 575, 916, 960
Park Street.....110, 167
Rest.....921, 930, 941
Retreat.....377, 585
Rockingham...274, 287, 295, 971
Rolland.....181, 207, 255, 277
Rothwell.....710
Salem.....197, 311
Seasons.....736, 789, 804, 812
Sessions.....327, 338, 348, 484
Solid Rock.....414, 419, 475
Star of Bethlehem.....544, 676
Sweet Hour of Prayer (*Double*) 578
Uxbridge.....141, 212
Vanhall.....523, 624, 643, 647
Ward.....108, 160
Ware...42, 50, 349, 425, 443, 452, 461
Warner.....177, 209, 285
Welton.....203, 235, 265
Willington.....860
Willmarth.....391, 423, 526, 787, 815, 836
Wimborne.....892
Windham.....227, 342
Woodworth.....316, 352, 376, 388
Zephyr.....929, 949

C. M.

Adams....367, 487, 492, 516, 537, 674, 687
Antioch.....178
Arcadia.....385, 621
Arlington.....41, 51
Avon.....109, 164, 170, 905, 911
Avondale.....738, 865
Azmon.....703, 719
Balerma.....218, 622
Barby.....315, 430, 545, 566
Bemerton.....908, 919
Boardman.....644
Brown...7, 64, 366, 478, 522, 538, 966
Byefield...123, 153, 319, 390, 580
Caddo.....199, 234
Chimes.....739, 858
Christmas..182, 252, 267, 706, 711
Clarendon.....480, 514, 534, 573
China.....934, 940
Colchester.....185, 215, 273
Coronation.....254
Cross and Crown...334, 371, 562, 764, 771, 887
Darwin.....107, 115, 159, 442
Darwin (6 *lines*).....606
Downs.....730
Dundee.....811, 891, 897
During.....336, 482, 749, 873
Elizabethtown.....117, 124, 154
Fountain.....407
Geer.....448, 483, 500
Gould.....40, 53, 76, 917, 972
Grigg.....651
Havergal.....360, 421
Heber..18, 60, 198, 246, 289, 320, 359, 457, 518, 609
Helena.....481, 515, 546, 589
Hermon.....449, 458
Henry.....933
Iddo (*Double*).....466, 507, 511
Jazer.....558, 561, 619
Judea.....496, 543, 671
Kedron.....450, 463, 506
La Mira.....192, 269
Logan.....645, 685
Lydia.....129, 145, 169
Manoah..112, 120, 162, 782, 785, 838
Marlow.....132, 136, 290
Melody.....299
Monson.....473, 618, 639
Mount Auburn.....114, 140, 297, 489, 596
Naomi.....462, 595, 672
Newbold.....102, 127, 146
New York.....762, 767
Noel.....947, 954, 970
Ortonville.....173
Peterboro'.....73, 89, 97
Phillips.....226, 232, 291, 424, 539
Romberg.....353, 369, 409
Siloam.....200, 249, 788, 829, 848
St. Martin's.....816, 870
Swanwick.....100
Tamach.....630
Tappan.....432, 460
Van Meter.....568, 635, 705
Varina (*Double*).....979
Wardlaw.....189, 270, 280
Warwick.....35, 58, 62, 722

METRICAL INDEX.

HYMN

Whitney........922, 925, 969
Woodland........779, 797
Woodstock........74, 80, 93

S. M.

Blandner........318, 397, 936, 952
Boyle........817
Boylston........119, 125, 163, 288
Braden....335, 344, 417, 698, 942
Compassion........395, 653
Cranbrook........536, 551
Dennis........224, 294, 298
Evans........350, 426, 616, 696
Ferguson........28, 69, 833, 856
Golden Hill........627, 636, 640
Haydn........499
Kentucky........780, 791, 827
Laban......503, 637, 695, 704, 718
Lebanon (*Double*)........547, 977
Olmutz........317, 659
Olney........386, 554
Ozrem........356, 531, 608
Pilgrim's Song........962, 987
Purves........257, 275, 303, 737
Rialto........248, 272, 286
Shirland........735
Silver Street........14, 22, 72
State Street........557, 565, 756
St. Thomas........801
Thatcher........46, 67, 79
Tioga........495, 521
Woodbury (*Double*)........974

L. P. M.

Nashville........33, 732

C. P. M.

Ariel.......135, 251, 279, 429, 680
Garden........823
Medford........747
Meribah........322, 963

S. P. M.

Dalston........66

S. H. M.

Oberlin........516, 937

H. M.

Bertha........777, 869
Channing........131, 148, 161
Haddam........245, 259, 307
Lenox........365, 411
Lischer........45, 47
Newman........422, 439
Sutherland........11, 15, 24
Zebulon...239, 264, 278, 301, 313

7s.

HYMN

Ainsworth........898, 909
Aletta........355, 486
Amboy........497, 508, 535, 550
Aravesta........233, 296, 302
Beulah........968
Carpenter.......329, 343, 574, 604
Dallas........731
Eltham (6 *lines*)........741, 814
Fulton.....358, 393, 399, 896, 912, 943
Gethsemane (6 *lines*)........210
Hendon........71, 75
Holley........54
Horton........559, 570, 658
Indiana (*Double*)........953, 999
Kozeluck........793
Martyn (*Double*)........413, 763
Messiah........175, 253, 308
Milgrove........26, 63
More like Jesus (*Double*)......610
Nuremburg....560, 593, 632, 650, 682
Peddie (6 *lines*)........392, 494
Rosefield (6 *lines*)...332, 380, 389
Sabbath (6 *lines*)........57
Seymour...238, 305, 314, 455, 571, 717
Solitude........828, 841, 863
Spanish Hymn (*Double*)......133
Telemans......188, 243, 247, 262, 282, 382, 900, 991
Toplady (6 *lines*)...416, 431, 451, 533
Vinton........324, 331, 339
Watchman........989

8s.

De Fleury (*Double*)........219
Foster........130
Union........638

8s & 5s.

Pass Me Not........834

8s & 6s.

Elliott........372, 408, 437
Mustin........217
Peace........976
Thy Will be Done (*Chant*)....690
Welcome Home........851

8s, 6s, & 4s.

Nothing but Leaves........699

8s & 7s.

Autumn........465, 520, 603
Dorrance........191, 211

HYMN

Harwell........186, 276, 292
Mount Vernon........894, 950
Nettleton........467, 488
Ovio........456, 564
Repose........493, 576
Robinson........742, 792
Shall we Gather at the River..914
Shining Shore..445, 477, 754, 927
Stockwell........752
Sutton........9, 34
Thornton........142
Twilight........783, 796, 858

8s, 7s, & 3s.

Even Me........825

8s, 7s, & 4s.

Banes........798
Brest........956
Finney...236, 284, 306, 370, 592, 694
Greenville........81
Invitation........824
Kedesh........850, 885
Putney........758, 768
Unam........333, 364, 552
Zion........748

7s & 6s.

Amsterdam (*Peculiar*)........990
Elmsford........605
Griffith........222
Jerusalem the Golden...967, 975
Jesus Paid it All........381
Mendebas........918
Millennium........759, 876
Missionary Hymn........881
Salvatori........846, 923
The Old, Old Story........453
Webb.......52, 579, 707, 880, 882
Weimar........435, 474

7s, 6s, & 5s.

Work, for the Night is Coming 700

7s, 6s, & 8s.

Rockport........611
Marshall........946

7s, 4s, & 7s.

Diamond........750

7s & 8s.

Jesus Lives (*Chant*)........256

7s, 8s, & 7s.

Kennard........266

METRICAL INDEX.

6s. HYMN

Looking unto Jesus............375
Nearer my Home...............924

6s & 4s.

America....................890, 893
Bethany.........................600
Hemans..........................803
Italian Hymn....................309
Jesus is Mine...................498
Lead Them to Thee...............854
Oak.............................978
Olivet......................476, 601
To-day..........................330

6s & 5s.

Lansingburg.....................655
Unity...........................915

6s & 9s.

Oh how Happy are They......491

6s & 10s.

Wilt Thou not Visit me (*Ch.*).826

5s & 12s. HYMN

Come, let us Anew.............906

9s & 8s.

Castle..........................420

9s, 4s, & 6s.

Beyond the Smiling............985

10s.

Go and Tell Jesus...............855
Lentwood................43, 49, 549
Parry.......................910, 945
Savannah........................512

10s & 4s.

Magoon..........................806

10s & 11s.

Breaking Away...................847
Lyons.....................6, 10, 21

11s.

Eventide....................586, 594

HYMN

Expostulation..340, 383, 679, 831
Goshen..........................773
Kingsley....................928, 944
Portuguese Hymn.........669, 678
Reliance.........................17

11s & 8s.

Hensen............................8
Moreton..........................16

11s & 10s.

Brightest and Best..............193
Come, ye Disconsolate........587
Parting Song....................913

11s, 10s, & 6s.

Henly...........................673

11s, 12s, & 10s.

Hosanna.....................187, 250

12s.

Scotland........................868

www.ingramcontent.com/pod-product-compliance
Lightning Source LLC
Chambersburg PA
CBHW051723300426
44115CB00007B/442
9783337286309